합격을 완성할 단 하나의 선택!
편입수험서 No.1 김앤북

김영편입 **영어** 시리즈

| 어휘시리즈 |

| 1단계 기출 (문법, 독해, 논리) |

| 1단계 워크북 (문법, 독해, 논리) |

| 2단계 기출 (문법, 독해, 논리) |

| 2단계 워크북 (문법, 독해, 논리) |

| 3단계 기출문제 해설집 |

김영편입 **수학** 시리즈

| 1단계 이론서 (미분법, 적분법, 선형대수, 다변수미적분, 공학수학) |

| 2단계 워크북 (미분법, 적분법, 선형대수, 다변수미적분, 공학수학) |

| 3단계 기출문제 해설집 |

축적된 **방대한 자료**와 **노하우**를 바탕으로 **전문 연구진**들의 교재 개발,
실제 시험과 **유사한** 형태의 **문항**들을 개발하고 있습니다.
수험생들의 **합격**을 위한 **맞춤형 콘텐츠**를 제공하고자 합니다.

내일은 시리즈 (자격증/실용 도서)

자격증

정보처리기사 필기, 실기

컴퓨터활용능력 1급, 2급 실기

빅데이터분석기사 필기, 실기

데이터분석 준전문가(ADsP)

GTQ 포토샵 1급

GTQi 일러스트 1급

리눅스마스터 2급

SQL개발자

실용

코딩테스트

파이썬

C언어

플러터

자바

코틀린

SQL

유니티(출간예정)

스프링부트(출간예정)

머신러닝(출간예정)

전기/소방 자격증

2024 전기기사 필기
필수기출 1200제

2025 소방설비기사 필기
공통과목 필수기출 400제

2025 소방설비기사 필기
전기분야 필수기출 400제

2025 소방설비기사 필기
기계분야 필수기출 500제

김앤북의 가치

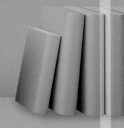

도전 신뢰
끊임없이 개선하며 **창의적인 사고**와 **혁신적인 마인드**를 중요시합니다.
정직함과 **도덕성**을 갖춘 사고를 바탕으로 회사와 고객, 동료에게 **믿음**을 줍니다.

함께 성장
자신과 회사의 **발전**을 위해 **꾸준히 학습**하며, 배움을 나누기 위해 노력합니다.
학생, 선생님 **모두 만족**시킬 수 있는 **최고의 교육 콘텐츠**와 **최선의 서비스**를 위해 노력합니다.

독자 중심
한 명의 독자라도 **즐거움**과 **만족**을 느낄 수 있는 책, 많은 독자들이 함께 **교감**하는 책을 만들기 위해 노력합니다. **분야를 막론**하고 **독자들의 마음속**에 오래도록 깊이 남는 **좋은 콘텐츠**를 만들어가겠습니다.

김앤북은 메가스터디 아이비김영의 다양한 교육 전문 브랜드와 함께 합니다.

김영편입 〽️   김영평생교육원 〽️   미대편입 Changjo

UNISTUDY 〽️   더조은아카데미 〽️   〽️ 메가스터디아카데미

메가스터디교육그룹
아이비원격평생교육원   엔지니어랩

합격을 완성할 단 하나의 선택

김영편입
영어

문법

기출 **2** 단계

김앤북
KIM&BOOK

합격을 완성할 단 하나의 선택

김영편입 영어 문법

기출 **2** 단계

PREFACE

어떤 공부를 하든 간에 단계별 학습은 중요합니다. 기초가 튼튼해야 그 위에 자신의 실력을 계속해서 쌓을 수 있기 때문입니다. 따라서 기초를 쌓은 후 그 이론을 바탕으로 쉬운 문제부터 어려운 문제로 실력을 확장해 나가는 것이 단계별 편입영어 학습법입니다.

이 책은 수험생이 자신의 실력을 확장하기 위해 보는 "기출 2단계" 책입니다. 최신 출제 경향이 반영된 중·고급 난이도 기출문제를 수록해, 실전에 보다 가까이 다가갈 수 있도록 했습니다.

"기출 2단계" 책은 문법, 논리, 독해의 3종으로 구성되어 있습니다. 문법과 논리의 경우, 1단계에서 핵심 문법 이론과 유형별 학습법을 각각 기출문제에 적용하는 훈련을 했다면, 2단계에서는 다양한 유형을 한데 섞어 수록해 실전 응용력을 기를 수 있도록 했습니다. 그리고 독해의 경우, 1단계에서 기출문제를 유형별로 학습하는 데 초점을 맞추었다면, 2단계에서는 기출문제를 분야별로 학습하는 데 중점을 두어 다양한 주제를 학습할 수 있도록 구성했습니다.

이 책을 학습하기 전에 한 가지 주의할 점이 있는데, 그것은 자신의 위치가 어디에 있는지부터 파악하고 공부를 시작하라는 것입니다. "기출 2단계"를 공부하면서 문제에 어려움을 느끼거나 해설을 이해하지 못한 수험생의 경우, 2단계를 잠시 덮고 1단계부터 다시 보시길 권합니다.

자신의 실력은 다른 사람이 만들어 주는 것이 아닙니다. 비록 실력이 향상되는 데 시간이 많이 걸리고 그 속도가 더디더라도, 결국에는 우공이산(愚公移山)이라는 고사성어처럼, 어떤 일이든 끊임없이 노력하면 반드시 이루어지게 될 것입니다.

"기출 2단계"를 통해 실전 문제에 대비하고 실력을 확장하는 계기가 될 수 있기를 기원합니다.

김영편입 컨텐츠평가연구소

HOW TO STUDY

출제자의 관점으로 문제를 바라보자!

○ 한번쯤은 출제자의 입장이 되어 볼 필요가 있습니다. '이 문제에서는 무엇을 물어볼까?', '여기쯤에 함정을 파놓으면 어떨까?' 이렇게 출제자의 관점에서 문제를 바라보면, 모든 문제가 완전히 새롭게 보일 수 있습니다.

문제의 난이도를 몸으로 익혀보자!

○ 강물의 깊이를 알면 더 빠르고 안전하게 건널 수 있듯이, 문제의 난이도가 어느 정도인지 파악하게 되면, 문제를 더 노련하게 접근해 풀 수 있습니다. 그리고 난이도를 몸으로 익힐 수 있는 지름길은 없습니다. 다양한 난이도의 기출문제를 가능한 많이 풀어보는 것이 유일한 방법입니다.

제한시간을 설정하자!

○ 실전에 대비할 수 있는 가장 좋은 방법은 실전과 똑같은 환경에서 훈련하는 것입니다. 문제를 풀 때는 반드시 제한시간을 설정하여 학습하시길 바랍니다. 실전에서와 같은 압박감과 긴장감을 조성하기에 가장 좋은 방법입니다.

오답에서 배우자!

○ 편입시험은 정답만 기억하면 되는 OX 퀴즈가 아닙니다. 문제를 풀고 난 후엔 맞힌 문제보다 틀린 문제에 주목해야 합니다. 어째서 정답을 맞히지 못했는지 일련의 사고 과정을 면밀히 되짚어봐야만 틀린 문제를 다시 틀리지 않을 수 있습니다.

문법, 논리, 독해는 원래 한 몸이다!

○ 본 시리즈는 문법, 논리, 독해라는 세 가지 영역을 나눠서 각각을 한 권의 책으로 구성했지만, 영역 구분에 지나치게 신경 쓰며 학습하는 것은 좋지 않습니다. 오히려 독해문제에서 중요 어휘와 문법구문을 정리하는 방식처럼 서로 영역을 통합해 학습하게 되면 더 큰 시너지를 일으킬 수 있습니다.

실전 문제 TEST

○ 중·고급 난이도의 기출문제를 총 50회분, 1,000문제를 수록하여 실전감각을 익힐 수 있도록 했습니다.

○ 문장의 구조가 복잡하고 어휘가 어려운 최신 기출문제를 가능한 많이 수록하여, 심화 학습이 가능하고 최신 출제 경향을 파악할 수 있습니다.

정답과 해설 ANSWERS & TRANSLATION

○ 각 문제에 출제 포인트를 표시해 문제의 핵심을 쉽게 파악할 수 있도록 했으며, 김영편입 문법 이론서인 『MSG(My Smart Grammar)』에서 관련 문법 사항을 확인해 볼 수 있도록 페이지도 함께 수록했습니다.

○ 특별한 주의가 필요한 오답 선택지에 대해서는 상세히 오답 해설을 실어 다양한 문법 사항을 익힐 수 있으며, 문제에 포함된 중요 어휘의 경우 해설에 함께 수록해 어휘학습을 병행할 수 있도록 했습니다.

CONTENTS

해설편

합격을 완성할 단 하나의 선택

김영편입 영어
문법

기출 **2**단계

TEST

01-50

[01-09] Choose the one that best completes the sentence.

01   What is a mythical princess _____ an extraordinary young woman who extracts a happy ending from a story steeped in adversity, family strife, abuse and other psychosexual horrors?

① yet

② and

③ but

④ so

02   Geologists classify rocks in three groups, according to the major Earth processes that formed them. Anyone who wishes to collect rocks should become familiar with the characteristics of these three rock groups. _____ a geologist classifies rocks is important to transform a random group of specimens into a true collection.

① Know that

② Known as

③ To know how

④ With its knowledge

03   A satellite is composed of 30 modular units, _____ equipped with a set of sensors.

① each of which is

② each of which are

③ some of which is

④ which of them are

04　The carcass of a young mammoth was found frozen and preserved in the northwest part of Russia's Siberia in May of last year. The 6-month-old female mammoth is the most well-preserved example yet found of the beasts. It looked _____ still alive.

① even if it would never be

② unless it has been

③ as if it had not been

④ as though it were

05　Dopamine, _____ to be the brain chemical that signals pleasure, turns out to have more to do with wanting than with liking.

① it has long been reputed

② has long been reputed

③ long been reputed

④ long reputed

06　_____ against him, the alleged spy from France was finally released from the federal prison after a couple of days of confinement.

① Being no evidence there

② To be no evidence there

③ There being no evidence

④ That there was no evidence

07　We must not dismiss _____ people view and approach mental health.

① the role culture plays in how

② how culture plays the role in

③ in how the role culture plays

④ culture in the role plays how

08   In the nineteenth century, when photography was still a relatively new art form, "Pictorialists" were photographers who strove to give their photographs, or "pictures," _____.

① a resemblance to paintings

② resemble paintings

③ or a resemblance to paintings

④ to resemble paintings

09   The _____ the message of the Pakistan Government to close down the channel, ridiculed the decision.

① authorities concerned, while having conveyed

② authorities concerned, while conveying

③ authorities concern, while having conveyed

④ authorities concern, while conveying

[10-19] Choose the one that is NOT correct in standard English.

10   It is ①best ②to set aside ③the multiple-choice questions on a test and ④go them over ⑤at the end.

11   The task of ①advertisements is ②to demonstrate to people ③how few they really know ④about what they want.

12   Many of the plants in the grasslands ①are of direct value as food ②to humans, but the ③kinds are found in different parts of the country vary ④so greatly it is difficult to list them.

13   In the metabolism of the western world the coal-miner is ①second in importance ②only for the man who ploughs the soil. He is a sort of grimy caryatid upon whose shoulders ③nearly all ④that is not grimy is supported.

14 A striking contrast can ①usefully be drawn with the study of Egyptian pottery, which, during ②the last two decades of the twentieth century, moved inexorably — and beneficially — ③the age of subjective description to ④a more rigorous era of objective analysis.

15 Activists in Argentina ①are fighting to improve the living conditions of Arturo, ②the country's last living polar bear. The 29-year-old animal lives at the Mendoza Zoo and has been ③the focus of a heated debate between activists and zoo officials ④regarded his mental and physical health.

16 But, as the pleasure which I hope to give by the Poems ①now presented to the Reader must ②depend entirely on just notions upon this subject, and, ③thus it is in itself of high importance to our taste and moral feelings, I cannot content myself with these detached remarks. ④No error.

17 Among the social movements to have arisen along ①with and since the Industrial Revolution, one that remains somewhat controversial and of which the outcome is still far ②from decided is the animal rights movement. The first attested historical proponent is ancient Greek thinker Pythagoras. Following his belief that humans can reincarnate ③by animal bodies, he argued ④for treating animals the same as humans.

18 One of Six Flags' unique aspects ①was that it wasn't just a random collection of rides; it was developed around a theme: the history of Texas. The park's name was a nod to the six flags that ②are flying over the state at various times — France, Spain, Mexico, the Confederacy, Texas and the United States. The park's rides and attractions were grouped into ③six themed sections that represented the cultures of these governments and enabled visitors ④to experience everything from cowboy culture to Southern belles and pirates.

19 Archaeologists in England have uncovered an Anglo-Saxon cemetery consisting of more than 80 graves ①dating from the 7th to the 9th century CE. The discovery is notable in that it is the first time in Britain that wooden coffins from the Anglo-Saxon period have been found in a well-preserved state; wood usually disintegrates quickly when it ②is buried, but the waterlogged conditions at the site in Great Ryburgh, near Norfolk, kept wooden structures intact. The dead ③are mostly buried in coffins made from the hollowed-out trunks of oak trees; ④other a few graves are lined with wooden planks. The discovery promises to shed new light on the lives of early Christian Anglo-Saxon communities.

[20] Choose the sentence that is NOT grammatically correct.

20 ① The man, whose friends he had abandoned, died a lonely, solitary death.
② In what turned out to be a useless endeavor, the students begged for a higher grade.
③ What matters most at this point is making an effort that can be remembered forever.
④ They were served what it could only be described as garbage for breakfast.

TEST 02

[01-09] Choose the one that best completes the sentence.

01　They are possessed by the impulse to realize an environment, an impulse as deep, arbitrary, and unexplained _____ that "will to live" which lies at the bottom of all explanations.

① in
② as
③ from
④ of

02　Child psychologists have written about the anxiety girls experience due to academic pressures, with many _____ they are not good enough.

① feel
② feeling
③ feelings
④ felt

03　A writer should have a fully formed vision, waiting _____ the page.

① to be empty
② to be emptied onto
③ to be empty onto
④ to being emptied

04 As my mother stood with the broken vase in her hands _____ me for my careless conduct, I stared down at my feet in shame.

① upbraiding
② having upbraided
③ to be upbraided
④ upbraided

05 Culture is like a security blanket, _____ it may appear worn and tattered, outmoded and ridiculous, it has great meaning to its owner.

① to some
② and to some
③ though to some
④ and though to some

06 _____, there is but one safe way for every young person starting a business in life: Be prepared for the rainy day.

① Whatever it comes
② No matter whatever happens
③ Be no matter what
④ Come what may

07 When there is no alternative for a drug, patients and insurance companies have no choice _____ price a drug-maker sets.

① but to pay
② but to pay whatever
③ other than pay whatever
④ other than paying

08 The Romans were startled to see their enemies had battle flags made of an unknown fabric: silk. Within decades, silk was being worn by the wealthy families of Rome. The silk craze grew over the centuries, and _____.

① neither did the price of silk

② neither had the price of silk

③ so had the price of silk

④ so did the price of silk

09 The packaging of living material into discrete vehicles became _____, when biologists arrived on the scene and started asking questions about life, their questions were mostly about vehicles.

① such a salient and dominant feature that

② salient and dominant a feature such that

③ such that salient and dominant a feature

④ such that a salient and dominant feature

⑤ salient and dominant feature such that

[10-19] Choose the one that is NOT correct in standard English.

10 Users of the Internet ①take it for granted ②their ability to ③access all Web sites ④on an equal basis.

11 First jobs may be ①intimidating for everyone, but ②few people have to ③deal with work-related stress at ④so young age as athletes and dancers do.

12 Bold colors and startling patterns ①which are used to ②decorate the theater lobby and ③are repeated both on the walls of the auditorium and in the fabric of the seats. ④No error.

13 If travellers ①go to the trouble and expense of a journey, it is ②not so more from curiosity, ③or because they like ④to see things beautiful and strange, as out of a kind of affectation.

14 More recently, when Slavs found themselves ①ruled by tyrants and saw no hope of escaping, some gloomily concluded that there ②must be something in the character of Slavs which ③dooms them being enslaved. This is ④false reasoning and no free person can believe that.

15 The fleet with which Bonaparte had reached Egypt ①had destroyed by Nelson at Aboukir ②in the first days of August 1798, when 5,000 French were killed and 3,000 ③taken prisoner, the loss of the English ④killed and wounded being only 900.

16 The experimental results which have now ①been given, as well as others, lead to the conclusion that the transparency of different substances, assumed to be ②of equal thickness, is essentially ③conditioning upon their density. ④No error.

17 Oceans ①absorb a significant amount of the solar energy that reaches the Earth's surface because they cover 71 ②percent of the planet. Global warming affects oceans in several ways, one of the most serious ③being to cause icebergs and other sea ice to melt. Ironically, global warming ④has hastened the formation of icebergs, increasing the rate ⑤for which they melt into the sea.

18 An intoxicating ①mix of high rise buildings, neon-saturated streets and pounding commerce all contribute ②to making Seoul one of the world's great 24 hour cities, and a true feast for the senses. ③With its hyper-efficient transport system, a negligible rate of crime and an astonishing wealth of locally produced modern art, it's little wonder that so many tourists from around the world who visit Seoul come away ④hugely impressing.

19   Every generation has its own music. For me, it was the 1980s: Devo, Run-DMC, The Psychadelic Furs, and The Go-Gos. "You don't know about the Go-Gos?" asked one friend. "How can you live?" ①How could I? Of course, I found out about the Go-Gos immediately, ②and, no doubt, saved my life. Now, of course, the 1980s are far gone, and pretty much ③everyone born after 1990 ④finds it perfectly plausible to live without knowing about the Go-Gos. Now it's Beyoncé, BTS, Cardi-B, Twice... ⑤Being the music of today, I can't relate to it myself, but I'm sure young people today will remember it all, even when they become my age. It's the music of their generation.

[20] Choose the sentence that is NOT grammatically correct.

20   ① She married a man seven years her junior.
       ② My uncle in Seoul is owning a lot of buildings.
       ③ There are twelve children on board the ship.
       ④ Not enough is known about what happened in the hotel.

T E S T
03

[01-09] Choose the one that best completes the sentence.

01   _____ player scores the highest number of points will be the winner.

① Any
② Whoever
③ No
④ Whichever

02   _____ the structure of our social networks and our limited attention, it is inevitable that some memes will go viral, irrespective of their quality. Even if individuals tend to share information of higher quality, the network as a whole is not effective at discriminating between reliable and fabricated information. This helps explain all the viral hoaxes we observe in the wild.

① Whether
② Given
③ Unlike
④ Besides

03   In sharp contrast to the present day, ancient Greek and Roman actors rarely wore any make-up at all — despite the fact that they were often required to perform the roles of several different characters in the same play. _____ applying new make-up constantly, actors found it much easier to wear oversized masks in order to signal the many character changes in each play.

① With
② With a view to
③ For the sake of
④ Rather than

04 The ability to control the calendar could have provided a source of power _____ the ancient city.

① who has ruled

② whoever ruled

③ for whom ruled

④ for who has ruled

⑤ for whoever ruled

05 If you are lucky, you may get a chance to see the sun _____ an omega shape, _____ the most beautiful shape for the setting sun.

① make — to consider

② make — considered

③ making — considering

④ making — to consider

06 _____ in his dream of conquering Europe, the map of the continent would look very different today.

① If Napoleon succeeded

② Had Napoleon succeeded

③ Napoleon had succeeded

④ If Napoleon succeeds

⑤ Did Napoleon succeed

07 Why did Shakespeare use plots involving women in male attire? In the era of Queen Elizabeth I, women were not allowed to appear on the stage. Therefore, young boys acted as women, dressing in female clothing. Even if they had been handsome boys, however, it _____ awkward to watch them act the roles of the opposite sex. Therefore, the plot about women disguised as men was indispensable.

① must have been

② must not have been

③ should have been

④ should not have been

08   Those hoping that the regime change in Berlin might give the EU a new pro-market drive
_____.

① as well is likely to disappoint
② are like to disappoint as well
③ are likely to be disappointed as well
④ is like to be disappointed as well

09   Educational theory in the nineteenth century was based on the notion that students
were empty vessels _____.

① and the teacher poured knowledge
② which the teacher poured knowledge
③ into which the teacher poured knowledge
④ which the teacher poured knowledge for

[10-19] Choose the one that is NOT correct in standard English.

10   After months ①spend assembling a formidable roster, the team seems once again ②to
be reaching the caliber ③attained ④in years past.

11   ①The moment you decide what you know is ②more important than what you ③have
taught to believe, you ④will have shifted gears in your quest for success.

12   ①Since the sixteenth century, all the contact the British ②have had with ③peoples
around the world ④have led to thousands of new words being adopted into the
language, from ⑤which Modern English has emerged.

13   ①Now and again I have had horrible dreams, but ②not enough of them to make me lose
my delight in dreams. ③To begin with, I like the idea of dreaming, of going to bed and
lying still and then, by some strange magic, ④wander into another kind of existence.

14 Eryximachus, a doctor, whose fussy officiousness is ①portrayed with admirable humor, then proposes that instead of the usual entertainment by flute-girls the company ②amuses itself with ③talk, and that this shall take the form of a speech from each member of the company ④in praise of love.

15 When France banned Red Bull in 2000, health officials ①cited uncertainties about ②interaction of caffeine, ③the amino acid taurine, and glucuronolactone, a type of sugar that is ④produced by human cells and used in metabolism.

16 Liu Xiaobo, a democracy advocate, impassioned ①literary criticism, and political essayist ②repeatedly jailed by the Chinese government ③for his activism, has won the Nobel Peace Prize ④in recognition of his long struggle for human rights in China.

17 The book is a hand-held gadget too, ①a technology that once transformed the world as the new devices are doing today. At this stage of ②such momentous publishing upheaval, all we can do is ③ask questions and try to make good guesses about the upsides and downsides, the gains and sacrifices, ④moving to a predominately electric publishing.

18 Intelligence is perhaps the most heavily researched construct in all of psychology. Interest in the assessment of intelligence ①began more than 100 years ago. ②Despite the length of time the construct of intelligence ③has assessed, however, there ④remains no singular or standard means to assess it. Furthermore, recent research suggests that intelligence is ⑤even more complex than we have believed.

19 As major industries in the developed world shed jobs through outsourcing and automation, one large corporation ①is bucking the trend: Spain's Mondragon Cooperative. Founded shortly after World War 2, and drawing its name from ②the town of its birth, Mondragon, the cooperative is now Spain's fifth largest company in terms of total assets ③and comprised over 900 individual businesses. Mondragon is totally worker-owned and operated, with worker representatives making decisions about new ventures, new hires, ④and job transfers. So far, Mondragon ⑤has maintained profitability without having to cut its labor force.

[20] Choose the sentence that is NOT grammatically correct.

20
① It is since you are lazy that you lost your job.
② Annoyingly for Jack, his brother was late arriving.
③ Unless you have a valid passport, I cannot book your ticket.
④ Certainly, Mrs McDonald didn't want to have anything to do with them.
⑤ More amusingly than wisely, he kept on insisting on his right to speak.

[01-09] Choose the one that best completes the sentence.

01 In their work, microbiologists contend with living forms so diverse in appearance and habits _____ disguise the common bond presumed to ally them.

① which

② as to

③ much as

④ consequently

02 In the Disney version at least, it is Geppetto's wish, not Pinocchio's, _____ the puppet become real.

① what

② which

③ that

④ as

03 Public transportation in the suburbs and outlying areas is generally not as convenient and reliable _____ in the city.

① as they are

② as it is

③ as those

④ as being around

04 Taking a "do-nothing" and a "comfort first" approach is common for governments near the end of their term. They avoid starting new projects and avoid making any waves. The power of the president is still valid, but officeholders are wary about functioning as spearheads _____ negatively marked by the next administration.

① as

② so as to be

③ for fear of being

④ which have been

05 Newton found that the planets, including the Earth, go around the sun _____ what he called the law of gravitation, and his reward _____ making his great discovery about the Universe was that he was blamed _____ being an atheist.

① by — with — as

② with — of — by

③ with — to — to

④ by — for — for

06 It is foolish to think that a leader's skills can be applied to all occasions, that they can be taught outside a historical context, or _____ as a "secret" of control in every situation.

① he can learn them

② they can learn them

③ they learn

④ that they can be learned

07 The police were overwhelmed with evacuations, but a pair of ex-Marines stepped in, planning everything on the fly, _____ in Iraq. They found a ride, and a boat, and they navigated through the chest-high surf until they found John.

① just as they did

② just as they have done

③ just as they had done

④ just as they would have done

08   Confirming our conversation with our partner in China, I have arranged _____ on Monday.

    ① that the shipment to be ordered

    ② for the shipment to be ordered

    ③ the shipment for being ordered

    ④ with the shipment for being ordered

09   The tiny toddler quickly learned how to stand, walk, _____.

    ① and, to everyone's surprise, run around

    ② and ran around to everyone's surprise

    ③ to everyone's surprise, and was running around

    ④ and, to everyone's surprise, was running around

[10-19] Choose the one that is NOT correct in standard English.

10   His older sister ①suggested Kenneth that he ②come back home to take care of their mother who ③had been seriously ill ④since last July.

11   Although the news ①came as a surprise ②to all in the room, everyone tried to do ③his work ④as though nothing ⑤happened.

12   Evolution always struggles to establish new limits ①and then struggles ②just as hard to break them, to ③transcend over them, and to move beyond them into ④more encompassing and holistic modes.

13   It's ①one thing to have cold hands on a winter's day, but it's ②the other thing to feel cold throughout the year. Many people get cold hands ③year-round due to a number of causes, from genetics ④to chronic illnesses.

14 Just as muscles would become helpless sinews if there ①were no nerves to direct them into action, ②so without communications ③the most advanced industrial equipment and social organizations would become useless. ④No error.

15 Mashenka went into her room, and then, for the first time in her life, it was her lot ①to experience in all ②its acuteness the feeling that is so familiar to persons ③in dependent position, who eat the bread of the rich and powerful and cannot ④speak their minds.

16 Although the controversial issue of bilingual education versus immersion has strong political undercurrents, a number of researchers ①evidence that the ability to speak two languages provides ②significant cognitive benefits ③to speaking only one language. ④No error.

17 After China returned an underwater glider ①it seized from the U.S. Navy off the coast of the Philippines, the Philippine defense secretary said ②his government would put both Washington and Beijing on notice against what ③he called ④its unauthorized presence in the country's ⑤200-mile exclusive economic zone.

18 Many people in the United States do not regard its linguistic diversity as an asset and seem to prefer that English alone ①be used, at least in public. Their reasons ②are many, and there has been a spate of legislation, ballot initiatives, and court rulings on the matter. The "English-only" movement arose in recent decades to push for legislation that ③would outlaw the use of non-English languages and ④are particularly concerned about the use of non-English languages in schools.

19   I'm a writer participating in a journey of chemical self-discovery. Last fall I had myself ①<u>tested</u> for 320 chemicals I might have picked up from food, drink, the air I breathe, and the products that touch my skin — the secret compounds I ②<u>have acquired</u> by merely living. It includes older chemicals that I might have ③<u>exposed to</u> decades ago, such as DDT and PCBs. It also includes pollutants like lead, mercury, and dioxins; newer pesticides and plastic ingredients; plus other compounds that hide beneath the surface of modern life, ④<u>making</u> shampoos fragrant, pans nonstick, and fabrics water-resistant and fire-safe.

[20] Choose the sentence that is NOT grammatically correct.

20   ① I remember closing the gate behind myself.
② Mary worked hard and got herself promoted.
③ Both boys will behave themselves at the game.
④ I believe that Jane and myself have done quite well.
⑤ Tom walked around the park to familiarize himself with it.

T E S T

05

► ► ► ANSWERS P.280

[01-09] Choose the one that best completes the sentence.

01　Fifty European cities introduced tax-supported street lighting by 1700 and made it safe and socially acceptable to move about publicly after dark, a time of day _____ had previously been considered the domain solely of suspicious characters.

　　① when
　　② that
　　③ what
　　④ while

02　For many in the British news media, the engagement of Prince Harry to Meghan Markle, a divorced biracial American, reflected _____ egalitarian Britain had become.

　　① how
　　② when
　　③ where
　　④ whether

03　The megarich don't build pyramids anymore — labor costs and all. But for the past century, the next best thing for them has been to establish art museums with their names _____.

　　① attaching
　　② being attached
　　③ having attached
　　④ attached

04   We have found a cheap and remarkably low-tech disease-control tool that, _____, can reduce transmission by somewhere between 50% and 85%.

    ① when used properly

    ② if using properly

    ③ though using properly

    ④ because used properly

05   When I consider how little of a rarity children are — that every street and blind alley swarms with them — that there are few marriages that are not blest with at least one of these bargains — I cannot for my life tell what cause for pride _____ in having them.

    ① there can possibly be

    ② is there to be

    ③ will not be

    ④ will it be possible

06   You might think scientists _____ every aspect of their home turf by now, but they haven't.

    ① had charted

    ② were being charted

    ③ would have charted

    ④ were charted

07   After the oil embargo, no longer _____ gas-guzzling cars as the cost of gasoline increased.

    ① that people could afford

    ② people could afford

    ③ people to be able to afford

    ④ could people afford

08　During the American Revolution, legend has it that the American patriot Nathan Hale said _____ just before being killed by the British _____ "I only regret that I have but one life to give for my country."

　① , (comma) — , (comma)
　② , (comma) — ; (semi-colon)
　③ ; (semi-colon) — ; (semi-colon)
　④ , (comma) — . (period)
　⑤ ; (semi-colon) — : (colon)

09　The most interesting and important thing is that if the vaccine is successful, which means that if the FDA is convinced about its efficacy and safety, we _____ doses that will be readily available.

　① must have already been manufactured
　② should have already been manufactured
　③ will have already manufactured
　④ shouldn't have already manufactured

[10-19] Choose the one that is NOT correct in standard English.

10　This situation will assist you ①on your path ②toward an exciting new ③life, whatever and ④where that may be.

11　While I wished to obtain ①a sound knowledge of ②all aspects of zoology, I planned ③to devote especially ④to insects.

12　This tendency ①to fill in the holes in our memories of the past ②with material ③from the present is especially powerful when it comes ④to remember our emotions.

13 More ①<u>deadly</u> tsunamis could strike the Indonesian coastline in the ②<u>coming</u> days, authorities ③<u>warn</u>, as the volcano which triggered the weekend's ④<u>devastated</u> wave ⑤<u>continues</u> to erupt.

14 By now, fourteen years ①<u>after</u> the last batch of prisoners was herded ②<u>nakedly</u> into the gas chambers, the story of Auschwitz ③<u>has been</u> told a great many times. Some of the inmates have written of those events ④<u>of which</u> sane men cannot conceive.

15 Although the Declaration of Independence ①<u>may have been</u> the first official political document ②<u>to spell out the goal explicitly</u>, it is probably true that no social system ③<u>has ever survived long if</u> its people had some hope that their government ④<u>would help them achieve</u> happiness.

16 It was only ①<u>the latest</u>, if potentially the most far-reaching, of rap's skirmishes with mainstream culture. As the voice of the young black male, rap ②<u>has become</u> a vivid, contentious cultural symbol. From ③<u>its</u> beginnings in the mid-1970s, rap ④<u>had been</u> met by condescension, rejection and outright fear from ⑤<u>those</u> outside its domain.

17 Plants are experts in survival and can control the direction of their roots to ①<u>maximize</u> the use of resources around them. ②<u>Using specialized cells</u>, they can sense gravity and redistribute hormones, ③<u>called</u> auxins, to stimulate growth and allow vital features of the plant ④<u>develop</u>. However, a big puzzle is ⑤<u>how</u> this transport process occurs at a cellular level.

18 The Swedish *smorgasbord* (①<u>literally</u>, "bread-and-butter table") is not the free-for-all, ②<u>budget-priced</u> buffet that Americans tend to envision when they hear the word. Instead, it's an elegant spread of cold and hot foods inspired by tradition and treated with respect. This is especially ③<u>true of</u> the holiday version — the *julbord*, or Christmas table, ④<u>which</u> families gather together to eat well, drink well, and sing.

19   Imagine that your body temperature soared ①every time you took a hot shower or drank a ②freshly brewed cup of coffee. Managing the state of the internal environment is a major challenge for the animal body. ③Faced with environmental fluctuations, animals manage their internal environment by either regulating or conforming. An animal is said to be a regulator if it uses an internal mechanism to control an internal change ④in the face of external fluctuation. An animal is said to be a conformer if it allows its internal condition to change ⑤in accordance for external changes.

[20] Choose the sentence that is NOT grammatically correct.

20   ① I wish you would not go to the party without me.
② How come wasn't he at the meeting this morning?
③ What would you buy for me if you'd win the lotto?
④ I would be surprised if Becky came home late tonight.
⑤ I wish I didn't have to get up early tomorrow morning.

T E S T

06

►►► ANSWERS P.284

[01-09] Choose the one that best completes the sentence.

01 Recently, there has been a heated global debate about the use of "pro-life" and "pro-choice" in reference to one's position on abortion. Those who are pro-life say the reason why they do not say they are "against abortion" is because the word "abortion" itself is an expression that conceals the criminality of "murdering a fetus." Strictly speaking, they are "against murdering fetuses," but they choose to say they are "pro-life," because to do _____ would make people uncomfortable.

① it

② thus

③ in that way

④ otherwise

02 While there is disagreement about the scale of the problem, most Americans, _____ patients, doctors, or insurance reps, think our health care system faces serious challenges.

① are their

② be they

③ that they are

④ are

03 A book which is worth reading at all is likely to be read more than once, and _____ some idea or some statement makes such an impression that we wish to refer to it again.

① reading as

② each reading

③ as reading

④ at each reading

04   The proper place today, the only place which Massachusetts has provided for her freer and less desponding spirits, is in her prisons, to be put out and locked out of the State. _____ the fugitive slave, and the Mexican prisoner on parole, and the Indian coming to plead the wrongs of his race, should find them.

① Whether or not
② It is there that
③ Now that
④ When it comes to

05   Westerners often consider it impolite not to talk — yet they are at the same time _____ about anything that no one should be caught with an open mouth containing food.

① so ever strict as
② as strict as they are
③ so strict that they are
④ as ever strict as

06   All signs of the market have vanished and in front of the town hall, _____.

① stood there only a platform
② there stood only a platform
③ an only platform stood there
④ an only platform there stood

07   As much of the rest of the world struggled with the coronavirus pandemic, it looked as if many places across Asia and the Pacific _____ the virus.

① had been successfully suppressed
② successfully suppress
③ were successfully suppressed
④ had successfully suppressed

08   The harbor has tripled in size, though _____.

① most of its wharves stand emptiness

② most of its wharves stand empty

③ most of its wharves standing emptiness

④ most of its wharves standing empty

09   It now seems to me that _____ to have reasonably intelligent, hard-working managers who have a sense of pride and loyalty toward their organization.

① what does it matter most in the majority of organizations

② which matters most in the majority of organizations

③ which does it matter most in the majority of organizations

④ what matters most in the majority of organizations is

[10-19] Choose the one that is NOT correct in standard English.

10   ①There is ②no denying that serious empirical research ③has helped make economics the important discipline ④that is today.

11   You ①shouldn't help him; ②ever since you offered him help, he has started ③to depend on others ④for his homework.

12   What better word ①than *serendipity* could define the collectors' triumphs, in which accidentally ②found objects ③discovered to have extraordinary value? ④No error.

13   The sky was clear, ①the cold air, and he ②was wearing a scruffy black coat ③with a white fake-fur collar, sunglasses and ④a grey woollen hat ⑤pulled down over his forehead.

14   Telephones, television sets, and automobiles make life ①both more convenient and more interesting. But ②either of them presents dangers that must be recognized and controlled, unless we ③are willing to let them ④control us.

15   John Dewey, one of the most influential educational reformers of ①the twentieth century, ②campaigned for alternative approaches to ③teach in order to accommodate a pupil's psychological and physical development, as well as ④assist in academic progress.

16   Meanwhile the lighthouse ①had been growing slowly larger. It had now almost assumed color, and appeared like a little gray shadow on the sky. The man at the oars ②could not be prevented ③from being turned his head rather often ④to try for a glimpse of this little gray shadow.

17   It was ironic that the yuppies came to be so reviled ①for their vaunting ambition and outsized expectations, as if they ②invented the habit of more, when in fact they'd only inherited it ③the way a fetus picks up an addiction ④in the womb. The craving was there in the national bloodstream, and the baby boomers found themselves in the melancholy position of wrestling with a two-hundred-year dependency on a drug that was now ⑤in short supply.

18   So ①disgusting was *The New York Times* with the newly published dictionary that it announced it would continue with the 1934 edition, ②prompting Bergen Evans to write: "Anyone who announces that he will be guided by a dictionary published in 1934 is ③talking ignorant and pretentious nonsense." He pointed out that the issue of *Times* ④announcing the decision contained nineteen words condemned by the 1934 edition.

19   Because technology can evolve ①<u>much faster</u> than we can, we will find ourselves in the position of the lower animals — with a mental apparatus that is unequipped to deal thoroughly with the richness of the outside environment. Unlike the animals, ②<u>by which</u> cognitive powers have always been relatively deficient, we have created our own deficiency by constructing a radically more complex world. But the consequence of our new deficiency is the same as ③<u>that</u> of the animals' long-standing one. When ④<u>making</u> a decision, we will less frequently enjoy the luxury of a fully considered analysis of the total situation but will revert increasingly to a focus on a single feature of it.

[20] Choose the sentence that is NOT grammatically correct.

20   ① Martha has two sons she can rely on.
      ② This is the article from which they were quoting.
      ③ She contacted the people whose she's renting house.
      ④ Politicians, who make extravagant promises, aren't trusted.
      ⑤ He set us a problem the answer to which can be found in the textbook.

[01-09] Choose the one that best completes the sentence.

01   A prime example of symbiotic relationship can be seen in lichens. These creatures are composed of a fungal partner and a photosynthetic partner that together form the external and internal portions of a lichen, an organism _____ successful maintenance of a symbiotic relationship between fungi and algae allows it to flourish almost anywhere.

① what
② which
③ whose
④ that

02   _____ half of all the city residents understand the kinds and amounts of the minimum public education necessary for the sustenance of community life.

① There are
② It is
③ Fewer than
④ As much as

03   Fields of knowledge open in the past only to a few _____ open to millions by science.

① throw
② have thrown
③ had thrown
④ have been thrown

04   _____ hired are like Mr. Jackson — well-educated grown-ups who are still childhood inventors in their hearts.

① Much of those

② Much of these

③ Most of these

④ Most of those

05   Understanding superconductivity or knowing why some materials are electric conductors and _____ requires a bit of quantum mechanics.

① others insulators

② others being insulators

③ the other insulators

④ the others be insulators

06   Barbara McLintock was a creative thinker among scientists, one for whom intuition played _____ formal experimentation and analysis.

① as an important role as

② as important a role as

③ as a role important as

④ as important as a role

07   Art mirrors or reflects society, its virtues and vices, but, unlike a mirror, it is active; it affects _____.

① what it is a reflection of

② that it is a reflection

③ what a reflection it is

④ that is a reflection of it

08 It is a truth universally acknowledged that a single man in possession of a good fortune, must be in want of a wife. _____ the feelings or views of such a man may be, this truth is so well fixed in the minds of the surrounding families that he is considered as the rightful property of some one, or other of their daughters.

① However better known
② However little known
③ How little it is known
④ How few known
⑤ How it is known that

09 I believe that all the best faculties of a mature human being exist in the child, and that _____ in youth they will act well and wisely in the adult, but if they are repressed and denied in the child they will stunt and cripple the adult personality.

① if these faculties are encouraged
② unless these faculties were encouraged
③ if these faculties are encouraging
④ unless these faculties are encouraging

[10-19] Choose the one that is NOT correct in standard English.

10 A debate exists in the fine arts and video game cultures ①over ②whether video games can be ③counted on ④as an art form.

11 It has ①long been taken for granted among psychologists that girls tend ②to show ③more empathy than ④are boys.

12 When I met him in the museum ①unexpectedly, he was ②standing up in front of a mesmerizing statue which was not ③known to visitors with his tears ④stream down his face.

13 Hardly ①<u>had</u> she brought one gentleman into the little pantry and helped ②<u>him</u> off with his overcoat, ③<u>then</u> the wheezy hall-door bell ④<u>clanged</u> again and she had to scamper along the hallway to let in another guest.

14 As we are going to see, however, the philosophy of technology is no more ①<u>directly</u> useful for ②<u>defining</u> human and nonhuman connections than epistemology ③<u>has not been</u>, and for the same reason: in the modernist settlement, theory fails ④<u>to capture</u> practice.

15 We clearly need some mechanism ①<u>for discussing</u> economic, trade, and development policies ②<u>so that</u> they can be coordinated to minimize the ③<u>unintending</u> impact upon other countries in the region, and this need is ④<u>all the more</u> imperative in light of our ⑤<u>heightening</u> independence.

16 ①<u>An acquaintance of mine</u> is a journalist who needed to take a trip to a rural area to ②<u>take photographs for</u> a story. He asked me to go along to assist him with carrying equipment, etc. I ③<u>agreed to</u> the amount of money he offered, but now believe that he ④<u>owed</u> me more money.

17 Like animals, plants are eukaryotes — multicellular organisms — that ①<u>split from</u> a common ancestor called Luca ②<u>billions of years ago</u>. To survive, we all sense threats, ③<u>relay messages</u> about them within our bodies or tissues and respond to these challenges. Our actions vary, ④<u>adapted for</u> the lifestyles we maintain in different environments, but ⑤<u>much of our basic cellular machineries</u> is the same.

18 My niece was quite withdrawn in high school but has really blossomed in college. ①Gone are the days of her being a shy teenager; she has found what she loves and is pursuing it. As a matter of fact, although she is ②only in her sophomore year, she is taking two graduate courses. While the family ③always has been proud of her, her recent achievements have made us ④all the more so.

19 ①In characterizing the 1920s as modern, I recognize that the essential transformations began in the late nineteenth century, with rapid industrialization, sprawling urbanization, and massive immigration. Industrial development changed the nature of work and daily life ②and gave rise to an extensive network of corporations that integrated the country into a national economy. The result was to erode the isolation of "island communities" — the towns of antebellum America ③that while part of a market economy ④had nonetheless maintained a degree of local autonomy and order based on "modesty in women, rectitude in men, and ⑤thrifty, sobriety, and hard work in both."

[20] Choose the sentence that is NOT grammatically correct.

20   ① I'd prefer swimming to running.
② I'd prefer to take the bus to the taxi.
③ I'd prefer driving rather than walking.
④ I'd rather he do the work right now.
⑤ I'd rather to take the bus to the taxi.

T E S T
08

▶▶▶ **ANSWERS** P.292

[01-09] Choose the one that best completes the sentence.

01   From that act of civil disobedience _____ spawned the New Power Party, which allied with the DDP and won five legislative seats of its own.

① had

② were

③ has

④ was

02   Opaque and unregulated hedge funds are now involved in as many as 30 percent of the _____ by some big banks.

① deal cutting

② deals cutting

③ deal cut

④ deals cut

03   Several friends and I were excitedly discussing our upcoming vacations when one woman remarked that a neighbor might have to forgo her trip to the West because her dog had just had three puppies and she couldn't leave them unattended. Numerous suggestions were made for the dog's care, only _____. "For goodness' sake!" I finally piped up. "Couldn't the mother's family take them?"

① to be rejected

② to reject

③ of the rejection

④ rejecting

04 You can check out this book _____ it by tomorrow.

① provides you return

② provided you return

③ provided your return

④ provides your return of

05 The mathematical growth model assumes that resources are unlimited, _____ in the real world.

① which rarely is the case

② which is rarely a case

③ which is rarely the case

④ that is rarely a case

⑤ that is rarely the case

06 In many eyewear boutiques, _____ since designers cater to consumer tastes, using a wide variety of unique materials.

① no two pairs are alike

② no two pairs are likely

③ not two pairs are likely

④ not two pairs are alike

07 Sometimes he entertains himself with thoughts of what might have happened _____.

① he had taken up the offer

② the offer he had taken up

③ he had taken the offer up

④ had he taken up the offer

08   _____, the answer to many kinds of pain, from sore joints and back pain to headaches and stomachaches, may be in the kitchen rather than in the medicine cabinet.

    ① As may it sound surprising

    ② Surprising as it may sound

    ③ Sound surprising as it may

    ④ May sound surprising as it

    ⑤ It may sound surprising as

09   A common quip is _____ because politicians pocket money for road surfacing materials.

    ① that new roads are narrower than planned

    ② that new roads are narrower than planning

    ③ which new roads are narrower than planning

    ④ which new roads are narrower than planned

[10-19] Choose the one that is NOT correct in standard English.

10   It is what you eat, not ①how hard you try ②to work off it, ③that matters more ④in losing weight.

11   Across the country, owners of Chinese-American restaurants ①like ②Wang's are ready to retire but have no one to pass ③business ④to.

12   When teachers ①started teaching other foreign languages in the 19th century, they used ②the same translation-based approach as ③has been used for teaching Latin. ④No error.

13 ①Morricone's 1960s compositions for Sergio Leone's westerns, like *The Good, the Bad, and the Ugly*, ②entered the popular culture so deeply that ③most everyone knows their sound, even ④without being aware of it.

14 Comte believed that earlier ①modes of thought, which he called theological and metaphysical, ②were imperfect, ③and that positive knowledge had to be based on natural phenomena ④which properties and relations were verified empirically.

15 It was ①not until they were quite exhausted and ②can no longer maintain the pace ③at which they ④had fled from the race-ground, ⑤that the old man and the child ventured to stop, and sit down to rest upon the borders of a little wood.

16 Modernized farming of the west required relatively ①fewer permanent hands than ②before, though considerable use was made ③of seasonal migrant labor, ④by whom farmers did not have to take responsibility when the working season ended.

17 Luis Chiappe, an expert on early birds at the Natural History Museum of Los Angeles County, suggests that flight ①likely occurred as a by-product of arm flapping ②in ground-dwelled dinosaurs, as the predecessors of birds used their ③feathered arms to increase their running speed or balance themselves ④as they made fast turns.

18 Before the oil spill, more than 60 percent of all oysters ①harvesting in U.S. waters were caught in the Gulf of Mexico. Today that share has dropped to about 40 percent. Many ②threatened and endangered species also live in the Gulf: sea turtles, Florida manatees, whooping cranes, and bald eagles. Dolphins are a frequent sight. Giant squid, jellyfish, and octopuses ③swimming through the Gulf's waters pass some of America's most beautiful but also most ④imperiled coral reefs.

19 The Spanish word for rice, *arroz*, comes from the Arabic word *orez*, giving us a clear signal of the origin of rice growing in Spain. The initial encroachment of the Moors ①into the Iberian Peninsula was made in 711 by a small force ②was led by Tariq ibn Ziyad near Gibraltar. Over the course of the next 60 years, almost all of the territory of ③what is now Spain and Portugal was conquered, becoming al-Andalus, part of the Umayyad Caliphate, the empire ④centered on Damascus that has continued the period of the expansion of Islam that began in the previous century during the lifetime of the prophet Muhammad.

[20] Choose the sentence that is NOT grammatically correct.

20   ① I have some objections to make.
      ② Anybody can make any promises.
      ③ Have you any objections to make?
      ④ She was too taken aback to say anything.
      ⑤ There's scarcely some food left in the kitchen.

TEST

09

▶▶▶ **ANSWERS** P.295

[01-09] Choose the one that best completes the sentence.

01 A solid resumé objective will not only capture the attention of _____ is reading it but encourage him or her to keep reading.

① whoever

② whosever

③ whomever

④ whatever

02 The opinionated egoists tend to have long and narrow whiskers, _____ the refined and scholarly gentlemen are usually close-clipped.

① while for

② while as for

③ while that of

④ while those of

03 The country is changing, and it will change _____ its new government looks like.

① no matter what

② no matter that

③ whoever

④ whichever

04　The snow goose need not bathe to make itself white. _____ do anything but be yourself.

① Neither do you need

② Neither you need

③ Neither need you

④ You either not

⑤ Nor you need

05　I had heard so much about her, but she wasn't _____ I expected.

① quite so clever as

② quite so clever as much

③ just clever as much

④ just much clever as

06　When the earliest modern computers, _____ first-generation computers, were built in the United States in the mid-1950s, they were dramatically different compared to systems of today.

① referring now to as

② referred now as to

③ now referred to as

④ as to referring now

07　He who possesses the divine powers of the soul is a great being, _____. You may clothe him with rags or chain him to slavish tasks. But he is still great.

① may be his place where it is

② his place may be what it is

③ be his place what it may

④ where is his place may be

08   _____ a rich history of Polynesian culture, Hawaii sounds more like a place in a fantasy novel rather than an American travel oasis.

① Formed volcanoes and steeping in

② Formed by volcanoes and steeped in

③ Forming volcanoes and steeping in

④ Forming by volcanoes and steeped in

09   Success in convincing the public to accept deer as part of its diet depends on _____.

① the media distributes information and recipes

② how well information and recipes are distributed by the media

③ information and recipes are distributed by the media

④ how well are information and recipes distributed by the media

[10-19] Choose the one that is NOT correct in standard English.

10   ①Out of suffering ②have emerged the strongest souls; ③the most massive characters ④are searing with scars.

11   ①It is both what you say ②it and how you say ③it that matters when ④it comes to communicating with others.

12   No one ①had expected that D. Warren would take ②being kicked off the team with so ③much resignation; he simply walked sadly out of the locker room. ④No error.

13   The World Conference Against Racism is supposed to put ①on the table such sensitive issues ②that reparation for slavery and the question of ③whether Zionism is racism ④or not.

14　To monkey around and ①monkey business are expressions of the early 1800s, and ②make a monkey out of someone is from 1899, ③all ④being terms based on the increasing number of monkeys seen in circuses and zoos.

15　Indeed, many films and television shows portray the ruling class as generous, eager to share, and ①unattaching to their wealth in their ②interactions with people who are not ③materially privileged. These images contrast with the opportunistic and ④avaricious longings of the poor.

16　Underneath the frenetic action of the *Oldboy* ①lurk ②unanswered questions about guilt, responsibility and morality. The central question of the film, close on the heels of every hairpin plot twist, is ③what an immoral act is still immoral if the sinner is unaware. The question of morality, however, remains ④purely personal.

17　My friend and I went camping this weekend. We put up our tent in a lovely spot beside a ①babbling stream. The birds were ②singing and it felt great to be so far from the noisy traffic of the town. The weather wasn't very good but it was cosy listening to the ③patter of rain on the roof of the tent. When it eventually stopped there was ④an eerie silence all around us. The silence was suddenly ⑤closed when a shot rang out. Someone was shooting rabbits.

18　Created by Jerry Siegel and Joe Shuster in 1932, Superman ①has been seen by many as the quintessential American hero. ②Gifted with superpowers by his origins on the now-destroyed planet Krypton, Superman fights for Earth, his adopted home, ③guarding it against both internal threats and external perils. At the same time, writers for Superman quickly figured out that a character who couldn't be injured or face any appreciable danger was pretty boring, so over the years they ④had kept coming up with weaknesses.

19   Money was a feature of American life that did not become standardized ①until relatively late in the day. Only with the issuing of the first greenback during the Civil War ②the federal government produced any paper money. Unlike coinage, paper money ③was left to banks. Through the first half of the nineteenth century, banks were in the happy position of being able to print their own money. Types of bills proliferated widely. In Zanesville, Ohio, to take one example, ④no fewer than thirty banks churned out money under such colorful appellations as the Owl Creek Bank.

[20] Choose the sentence that is NOT grammatically correct.

20   ① We're getting married next year, but will have no kids.
         ② Have you been knowing John ever since the childhood?
         ③ Fireworks are supposed to have been invented in China.
         ④ We have no idea why Peter was not at work yesterday.
         ⑤ At what age do kids start going to school in your country?

[01-09] Choose the one that best completes the sentence.

01   Pragmatism rejects all absolutistic assumptions about reality, admits the pluralistic nature of reality, and refuses to consider any claims _____ those focused on "fruits, consequences, facts."

① that

② but

③ although

④ then

02   Only now are questions such as how a material was produced, how much energy will be used to take care of it, and what happens to it at the end of its life _____ to echo through the industry.

① begin

② begins

③ beginning

④ has begun

03   On one side of the police barriers _____ of young students, many with their mouths taped shut to symbolize their support for free speech.

① was dozen

② were dozens

③ dozen was

④ dozens were

04   Technically, the spookfish has only two eyes, _____ is divided into two parts.

① each of which

② every of them

③ neither of them

④ all of which

05   The word "Revival" is an unfortunate misnomer. This style was not simply a copy of classic Greek details. More than a revival, it was a unique reimagining. The result was quite original and distinctively American. _____ architecture in America been under less influence from England or France.

① Has it ever

② Given that not

③ Supposing it has

④ Never before had

06   As cell phones have become more prevalent, _____.

① so too does lateness

② so too has lateness

③ lateness has so too

④ lateness does so too

07   The town was just stretched lazily on the plains. It was called Sleepy Town because anyone who passed through it, _____, quite naturally became tired and sleepy.

① strange as it may seem

② whenever it may seem strange

③ because it may seem strange

④ unless it may seem strange

08 Boys _____ wore their hair long and grew beards in a gesture of defiance against society.

① coming to old in the rebellious 1960

② coming to oldness while rebellious 1960s

③ coming of age in rebellious 1960

④ coming of age in the rebellious 1960s

09 Masculinity has tended to be _____ as femininity in the modern world.

① as a construct fissured and complex

② as a fissured and complex construct

③ as fissured and complex construct

④ as fissured and complex a construct

⑤ as fissured and as complex construct

[10-19] Choose the one that is NOT correct in standard English.

10 All of ①companies I ②invested in ③went bankrupt and were ④taken into public ownership.

11 ①To the left of his desk is a very ②orderly bookcase, ③with all the books ④put away ⑤stood upright in the correct place.

12 Let every nation know, ①whether it wishes us good or ill, ②that we shall pay any price, bear any burden, ③meet any hardship, support any friend, ④to oppose any foe to assure the survival and the success of liberty.

13 An example of a law ①declaring English to be the official language of a state ②was passed in 1988 in Arizona; this law required employees of ③the state to act in English and in no ④another language.

14   In Amish communities there is a practice ①called *rumspringa*: at seventeen, their children (until then ②<u>subjected</u> to strict family discipline) are set free, allowed, even encouraged, ③<u>going</u> out and learn and experience the ways ④<u>of</u> the "English" world around them.

15   Although many of the crop circles in the past ①<u>were proven to have</u> hoaxes, crop glyph experts immediately rejected that possibility. ②<u>No footprints had been found</u> in either glyph, and not even one wheat stalk was broken. Instead, all were just bent over, ③<u>woven together</u>, and ④<u>still growing</u>.

16   The competitive nature of democratic societies ①<u>breeds</u> a desire for social distinction, a yearning to rise above the crowd. But ②<u>given</u> the fact that those who do make it to the top in ③<u>socially</u> mobile societies have often ④<u>rising</u> from the lower ranks, they still look like everyone else.

17   For many teachers, this year's ①<u>uprising</u> is decades in the making. The country's roughly 3.2 million full-time public-school teachers are ②<u>experiencing</u> some of the worst wage stagnation of any profession, ③<u>earning</u> less on average, in inflation-adjusted dollars, than they ④<u>doing</u> in 1990, according to Department of Education data.

18   Countless millions of asteroids hug an orbit between Mars and Jupiter, forming a belt that normally poses no harm to life on earth. Occasionally, however, ①<u>lone asteroids are</u> jostled out of the belt, ②<u>some to assume</u> earth-crossing orbits. ③<u>Some 150 asteroids with a diameter</u> of at least one kilometer have been detected so far, with two or three new ones ④<u>which discovered every month</u>.

19 Mavis was waiting at the airport to meet Stephan, her e-mail pal. They ①<u>had written</u> to each other for more than a year now, and ②<u>had finally agreed</u> to meet face to face. Mavis, who ③<u>was going to</u> have her 18th birthday party next week, couldn't wait to see what her email pal looked like, and watched all the passengers coming out of the arrivals gate in a state of excitement. When she saw Stephan approaching, however, she suddenly realized that he ④<u>was</u> an elementary school student.

[20] Choose the sentence that is NOT grammatically correct.

20 ① It's nice to have friends you can relax with.
② It's nice to have friends with that you can relax.
③ It's nice to have friends that you can relax with.
④ It's nice to have friends who you can relax with.
⑤ It's nice to have friends with whom you can relax.

[01-09] Choose the one that best completes the sentence.

01 Employment rates for new college graduates have fallen sharply in the last two years, as _____ starting salaries for those who can find work.

① do

② does

③ has

④ have

02 Because the auditorium will only hold 120 guests, you must _____ March 24 at 5 pm.

① RSVP by

② have RSVP by

③ RSVP until

④ have RSVP until

03 Suggestions run the gamut from parents' signing up young children for organized learning opportunities _____ their instincts and loving their babies.

① to simply trust

② of simple trusting

③ to simply trusting

④ of trusting simple

04 Some have attempted to distinguish dialects from languages by saying that dialects are mutually comprehensible while languages are not. However, this concept may not be as clear-cut _____.

① as when it seems

② as it may at first seem

③ so it seems at first

④ so it may seem

05 I could get nothing into perspective. I was young and ill-educated and I had had to think out my problem in the utter silence that is imposed on every Englishman in the East. I did not even know that the British Empire is dying, _____ that it is a great deal better than the younger empires that are going to supplant it.

① much more I knew

② so as to know

③ still less did I know

④ didn't I know enough

06 Among the aims of university education must be included the acquisition of knowledge, but _____ are the development of intellectual curiosity and the realization that the acquisition of knowledge is pleasurable.

① far greater importance

② far greater importantly

③ of far greater importance

④ of far greater important

07 An acorn, left to itself, becomes an oak, and a geneticist _____ its DNA to make it grow into an elm may justly be said _____ with its natural course.

① have altered — to interfere

② to alter — having interfered

③ altering — to have interfered

④ being altered — interfered

08   If today I lived in a Communist country where certain principles dear to the Christian faith are suppressed, _____ that country's antireligious laws.

① I will openly advocate dissenting

② I would openly advocate disobeying

③ I will openly advocate dispatching

④ I would openly advocate disporting

09   The policy was successful because it instituted regulations that stopped _____ to aggressively push alcohol in ways patrons found hard to resist.

① making it profitable for businesses

② making profitable for businesses for it

③ to make it profitable for businesses

④ to make profitable businesses for it

[10-19] Choose the one that is NOT correct in standard English.

10   He accused me ①of being sneaky, ②which I am not. Actually, I am not ③used to act in ④a deceitful manner.

11   The moment ①for people can ②no longer rely on the news media for facts, is ③when journalism loses its reason ④for being.

12   They need to know ①how to ②dedicate themselves to and sacrifice for the government and society ③so as the next generation ④could have a better life.

13   Environmental pollution ①existed for centuries but only started to be significant following the industrial revolution in the 19th century. The elements involved are not produced ②by nature, and ③the destroying process ④can vary from a few days to ⑤thousands of years.

14 Intensified grazing and browsing pressure by increasing numbers of deer ①<u>are</u> very likely to have caused a reduction in habitat quality and ②<u>contributed to</u> the declines of some woodland birds, but it should not ③<u>be concluded</u> that deer ④<u>are</u> the principal causes of decline in any bird species ⑤<u>on</u> a large scale.

15 It ①<u>has estimated</u> that the US economy was increased from international students. Larry Summers sees the US economy as ②<u>needing</u> the export of higher education in order to grow. As government funding of state schools ③<u>is</u> decreasing, that foreign students' tuition fees are increasing ④<u>is</u> more important.

16 As the finances of the energy-trading firm began ①<u>unraveling</u>, ②<u>what</u> eventually became unmistakable was that the company had been concocting "value" out of thin air, thanks not to the trading strategies ③<u>it</u> promoted as visionary but to financial games that turned a once-solid entity into ④<u>most</u> notorious debacle in an era of corporate scandals.

17 Epistemology deals ①<u>not only</u> with the nature of truth, but also with the ways in which we can know reality. There are a variety of ways ②<u>for which</u> we can know reality, ③<u>each of which</u> has its advocates and detractors. Among the ④<u>ways of knowing</u>, there are: by divine revelation, by authority, through personal intuition, ⑤<u>from our own five senses</u>, and through experimentation.

18 ①<u>Comprised</u> of documents that define the very architecture of legal systems and spell out the rules according to which the exercise of governmental power ②<u>is</u> carried out, constitutions ultimately reflect the political foundations of ③<u>its</u> nations. The Constitution of the United States of America, for example, consists of a single document that was created in a relatively brief interval of time in response to a ④<u>specific</u> politico-historical situation.

19   Since the birth of modern Orthodox Judaism in 19th-century Germany, a central goal of the movement ①<u>has been to</u> normalize the observance of traditional Jewish law — to make it possible to follow all 613 biblical commandments diligently while still ②<u>participating in</u> the reality of the modern world. You must strive to be, as a poet of the time put it, "a Jew in the home and a man in the street." Even as we students of the Maimonides School spent ③<u>half every</u> school day immersed ④<u>in what was</u> a medieval curriculum, our aim was to seem to outsiders — and to — ourselves — like reasonable, mainstream people, not fanatics or cult members.

[20] Choose the sentence that is NOT grammatically correct.

20   ① You must find it exciting working here.
② I owe it to you that the jury acquitted me.
③ We consider it strange that she's not coming.
④ I made to settle the matter my prime objective.
⑤ Something put the idea of her being a spy into his head.

12

▶▶▶ ANSWERS P.306

[01-09] Choose the one that best completes the sentence.

01 It is often impossible to point to a keystone species within functional ecosystems. Only after a keystone species disappears is the role they played _____.

① reveal

② revealing

③ revealed

④ to reveal

02 As scientists peer into the molecular workings of nature, engineers are starting to find information they can apply _____ optics.

① to advanced

② for advance

③ to advancement

④ for advancement

03 Africa is to Europe as the picture is to Dorian Gray — a carrier onto whom the master unloads his physical and moral deformities _____ forward, erect and immaculate. Consequently, Africa is something to be avoided just as the picture has to be hidden away to safeguard the man's jeopardous integrity.

① of his going

② that he has gone

③ so that he may go

④ he might have gone

04   Iraqi citizens who risked their lives _____ U.S. military forces as interpreters were separated from their families.

① when are working with

② while they working at

③ when their work at

④ while working with

05   Consider the effect of the thorough digestion of the books we read. Sam Slick tells us that he has read hundreds of books in his life, but somehow "couldn't keep the parcels sorted" in his mind; and many a mind that hurries through book after book, without waiting to digest anything, gets into that sort of condition, and the unfortunate reader _____ to support the reputation all his friends give him.

① is found to be fit

② finds to be far from fit

③ finds himself far from fit

④ is found to have been fit

06   An individual star may exist for billions or even trillions of years and during the course of its lifetime will undergo a sequence of radical changes that affect its density, mass, and intensity. Referred to as stellar evolution, the process occurs at an infinitesimal rate, _____ directly. Instead, astrophysicists rely on data gleaned from the examination of hundreds of stars, each representing different stages of the stellar evolution.

① not allowing it to observe

② for fear of not being observed

③ making it impossible to observe

④ so that it may be observed

07   It's unclear that the E.U. has the mechanisms for the strong leadership _____.

① needed to drive real change

② needs to driving real change

③ needed to driving real change

④ needs to drive real change

08   _____ that everyone left the auditorium.

① So monotonously did he speak

② He so did speak monotonously

③ Monotonously did he speak so

④ So did he monotonously speak

09   Today's young people have very adult worries about the uncertainty of the future and the lack of jobs in particular, far _____.

① different to what their parents' generation

② from different their parents' generation

③ different what their parents' generation

④ different from their parents' generation

[10-19] Choose the one that is NOT correct in standard English.

10   One way ①for job seekers to get a jump on ②the competition is ③to write to employers directly instead of merely ④wait for ads to appear.

11   The sailors finally ①came to know that the lake was ②the deepest at the spot ③where they were trying ④to anchor the ship.

12 The average rates ①at which people consume resources like oil and metals, and produce wastes like plastics, ②are about ③32 times higher in the developed world than ④they do in the developing world.

13 People cannot learn how their neighbors ①worship to God, why they have ②a particular form of government, where ③their loyalties lie, whether or not they ④accept change readily, or what their ⑤interrelationships are.

14 What is it ①that makes a person ②the very person that she is, ③her alone and not another, an integrity of identity ④that persists over time, undergoing changes and yet still ⑤continuing to be — until she does not continue any longer?

15 Aging is an economic challenge because unless retirement ages are ①drastically increased so that older members of society can continue ②to contribute to the workforce, the working-age population falls at the same time ③as the percentage of dependent elders ④increase.

16 Anyone ①searching for a new theory of human behavior and learning should recall the words of George Santayana: "Those who are ②unable to remember the past are ③doomed to repeat it." Most people have a natural tendency to remain ④locked with existing and ⑤mental models.

17 The next difficulty was to get a contractor who could understand the specifications and ①do the work. Chinese contractors ②could have been found who could read English, but I desired to let the Koreans have an opportunity of ③bidding on the college building. In order to let them know ④what they were bidding, it was necessary to translate the specifications into Korean.

18   Creating your own light setup ①means that you can have plenty of control over the lighting for your indoor shots. You ②don't need to spend a lot on expensive studio lights though, as a simple desk lamp or bright window will still allow you to get great results for your images. ③When used artificial light, considering the position of your light source can have a big effect ④on how your subject looks in your photographs.

19   It is said ①to have taken Leonardo da Vinci over four long years to complete his most famous painting known as the *Mona Lisa* — long enough for his then patron, Francesco del Giocondo, to get impatient. Giocondo ②has commissioned the portrait of his third wife Lisa, but enough was enough. Giocondo eventually refused to pay for the unfinished portrait, and Leonardo ③opted to sell it to the king of France instead. This is the traditional tale — but ④one that is unfortunately based on sparse evidence.

[20] Choose the sentence that is NOT grammatically correct.

20   ① To my regret, she did not accept our offer.
      ② He has nowhere mentioned this idea explicitly.
      ③ Those plastic cups are lighter than those wooden.
      ④ In no circumstances must this door be left open.
      ⑤ No answers have so far been given to them.

[01-09] Choose the one that best completes the sentence.

01 Calvin's wife is quite fastidious about how she appears to other people. Much too nervous _____ she be considered nobody, she is careful to dress way up whenever she goes out.

① if

② lest

③ that

④ when

02 There are people who point out that euphemism or political correctness are other forms of newspeak. They criticize that political correctness restricts the use of discriminative language — on race, sex, age, etc. — _____ it presents a serious infringement on freedom of expression.

① unless

② too little

③ so much that

④ in order that

03 Thinking back on it, it obviously _____ helpful to have you there, but I understand your reason for not making it.

① will have been

② would have been

③ had been

④ would be

04 Most Asian success stories have been ones in which the government forces its people to save, _____ through capital accumulation.

① grows production

② produces growth

③ producing growth

④ growing product

05 This morning I heard Mr. Turner talking to the Spanish lady and the Indian boy, _____ he spoke fluently.

① their languages of both

② both of their languages

③ which languages of both

④ both of whose languages

06 No book is worth anything which is not worth much; _____, until it has been read, and re-read, and loved, and loved again, and marked; so that you can refer to the passages you want in it.

① Nor it is serviceable

② Nor is it serviceable

③ None it be serviceable

④ Neither it be serviceable

⑤ Neither be it serviceable

07 Using this method, men discovered laws of nature that otherwise _____.

① remained unknowing

② remained unknown

③ would have remained unknown

④ would have remained unknowing

08 Albums and CDs _____ several years ago, and this trend shows no sign of reversing.

① are not sold so much were

② are sold not much as they were

③ are not selling as much as they were

④ are selling not so much were they

09 The plastic waste in the ocean breaks down into tiny pieces known as microplastics, _____ or even toxic to sea creatures who ingest it.

① which scientists believe can harm

② which scientists believe can be harmful

③ in which scientists believe can harm

④ in which scientists believe can be harmful

[10-19] Choose the one that is NOT correct in standard English.

10 He ①awaited final instructions ②about ③giving the reward to ④whomever had found the ⑤lost dog.

11 Is biotechnology eroding our definition of ①what ②that means to ③be human and ④changing our sense of identity?

12 ①While it can be argued that ②improving a specific program contributes to the general improvement of the department, I question how ③a gain by one program actually contributes to the welfare of other programs. ④No error.

13 ①Even when a screen image is the best way to convey an idea, a classic writer can keep ②his reader engaged by ③remembering that the idiom literally ④refers to and by playing with the image ⑤to keep it in her mind's eye.

14 There is ①<u>a basic flaw</u> in our thinking about health care. We treat symptoms, not ②<u>the underlying</u> cause of the disease. Yet, ③<u>only way</u> to provide ④<u>long-lasting</u> relief in any degenerative disease, like cancer, ⑤<u>arthritis</u> and heart disease, is to reverse the basic cause of the disease.

15 Mental disorders can often be so ①<u>debilitated</u> they render the sufferer incapable of ②<u>carrying</u> out basic functions of everyday life. On the other hand, many of history's greatest thinkers were ③<u>inflicted</u> with some sort of mental disability. No case is ④<u>as</u> true as John Forbes Nash Jr., who suffers from paranoid schizophrenia.

16 In retrospect, it might seem ①<u>surprising</u> that something as mundane as the desire ②<u>to count</u> sheep was the driving force for an advance as fundamental as written language. But the desire for written records ③<u>has been always accompanied</u> economic activity, ④<u>since</u> transactions are meaningless unless you can clearly keep track of ⑤<u>who</u> owns what.

17 For generations, people have looked at the sky with wonder at ①<u>what lays</u> beyond their reach. Astronomers ②<u>such as</u> Galileo brought the cosmos closer by looking through a telescope. But only relatively recently has the ability to travel into space ③<u>become a reality</u>. One can only guess at what the future may hold ④<u>in terms of</u> our ability to explore the cosmos.

18 It was not until the end of the sixteenth century the pocket as we know it today came into fashion. Before that time, men used ①<u>to carry</u> their keys and money in pieces of cloth attached to their clothing. The first pocket was an open-side seam ②<u>of which</u> men placed their pouch filled with personal carry items. As time passed, the pocket ③<u>was to become</u> a permanent part of the trousers. Variations such as hip and patch pockets were introduced in the ④<u>coming years</u>.

19 The first colonists were largely ①spared the immediate task of giving names to the land, since much of the eastern seaboard ②has been named already by earlier explorers. But as the colonists increased and formed new settlements, some system for labeling unfamiliar landmarks and new communities became necessary. The most convenient device was to adopt names from England. Thus the older states ③abound in names that have counterparts across the sea: Boston, Greenwich, Cambridge, and scores of others. An equally straightforward expedient was to honor members of the royal family, ④as with Charlestown, Jamestown and Carolina.

[20] Choose the sentence that is NOT grammatically correct.

20 ① Where are you planning to stay while the house will be under re-modelling?
② The cathedral could have been destroyed by bombing during the war.
③ The benefit that each employee receives is worth a whole month of salary.
④ Did you see what happened to the money that was right here on my desk?
⑤ I was a little late because the trip took a little longer than I had expected.

[01-09] Choose the one that best completes the sentence.

01 The room contained a great number of students, of whom one-third were boys and _____ girls.

① other

② the other

③ others

④ the others

02 Bigfoot is described as something like a giant gorilla covered with thick fur. According to eyewitness descriptions, it walks upright and has a foul odor, human-like hands and feet, and a terrifying roar. Footprints _____ belong to Bigfoot have been found, but some of the prints appear to be hoaxes.

① saying that

② said to

③ have said

④ to say

03 The zookeeper must make sure the bear is completely off the ground _____.

① as is it weighed

② as to weigh up

③ as it is weighed

④ as it weighs itself

04   The Kodiak is like a brown bear on mega-steroids. This goliath weighed over 737 kilograms and stood 3.85 meters at shoulder height and a mouth-dropping 4.27 meters at the top of his head. That means this Kodiak _____ on you if you had lived on the second floor. Better close those curtains!

① may look in

② could have looked in

③ must look in

④ should have looked in

05   Protecting our privacy demands that we each take ownership of our data and _____ it as well, but uninstalling Facebook and deleting your Instagram account won't keep the data these and other companies have on you _____ bought, sold, analyzed and aggregated.

① protects — was

② protected — were

③ protecting — to be

④ protect — from being

06   Perhaps, then, there is something to his advice that I should cease looking back so much, that I should adopt a more positive outlook and try to make the best of what remains of my day. After all, what can we ever gain in forever looking back and blaming ourselves if our lives have not turned out quite _____?

① as long as we may want

② that they could be

③ as we might have wished

④ so that they might not be

07   In modern digital photography, an image is converted into numbers which are later translated back into various shades of color. In the process, any of these numbers can be easily changed on the computer to produce _____.

① which image is desired
② the image what is desired
③ whatever image is desired
④ whose image is desired

08   John Aikman, one of the best basketball players ever, has been suffering a serious injury, and his fans all wish him _____.

① as speedy a recovery as possible
② as a speedy recovery as possible
③ as a recovery speedy as possible
④ as speedy as possible a recovery

09   Pesticides, _____, travel thousands of miles in the atmosphere to the Arctic.

① are designed to inhibit photosynthesis
② many are designed to inhibit photosynthesis
③ which many are designed to inhibit photosynthesis
④ many of which are designed to inhibit photosynthesis

[10-19] Choose the one that is NOT correct in standard English.

10   You ①will have to read ②much more ③than you now ④in the habit of reading.

11   Symbols ①have become important elements in the language of ②advertising, not so much because they ③carry meanings of their own, ④or because we bring meaning to them.

12 ①<u>A great</u> many things which in times of lesser knowledge we ②<u>imagined</u> to be superstitious or useless prove today on examination ③<u>to be</u> of immense value to people in the past. ④<u>No error</u>.

13 At the very least, ①<u>environmental rights</u> ensure the opportunity to appear and to put important scientific information ②<u>on</u> the record ③<u>so that</u> policymakers must be transparent in their decisions and ④<u>not to ignore</u> the science.

14 ①<u>The most common believed</u> theory argues that accidental genetic mutations changed the inner wiring of the brains of Sapiens, enabling them ②<u>to think</u> in unprecedented ways and to communicate ③<u>using</u> an altogether new type of language. ④<u>No error</u>.

15 ①<u>In a policy brief</u>, research reported ②<u>almost decade</u> ago by the National Council on the Teaching of English (NCTE), ③<u>declared there</u> "are many faces of English Language Learners (ELLs)." Some statistics provide evidence supporting this declaration. ④<u>No error</u>.

16 Because we were ①<u>not running a contest</u> in which we surveyed ②<u>large number of faculty members</u> or a randomly selected ③<u>cross-section to pick winners</u>, we cannot say for certain that ④<u>there are not others</u> who had equal or even superior success.

17 Learn from people at school or work ①<u>who</u> seem to have lots of friends. Observe ②<u>how</u> they make and keep friends. Don't imitate all of the things they do, but try to notice what they do. Then try some of those things ③<u>yourself</u>. Don't be afraid to show people what you're really ④<u>good</u>. Talk about the things you like and do best. Don't hide your strong points. People will be interested in you if there is something ⑤<u>interesting</u> about you.

18   An artistic design made up of overlapping lines carved on a cave wall was discovered buried under sediment, ①which contained Neanderthal artifacts in Gorham's Cave, Gibraltar. Paleolithic art expert Francesco d'Errico of the University of Bordeaux analyzed the engraving and reproduced the process of making it. His analysis shows that a stone tool was used, and ②that each line was carved precisely, indicating ③that it was made by an experienced artist. The design at Gorham's Cave is the clearest evidence yet ④which Neanderthals made artwork, but whatever meaning it carried has been lost in time.

19   Industry demands the ease of movement of ideas and goods: raw materials need to get to the factory, finished merchandise must be distributed, and fuel ①has to be delivered to factories to fire their furnaces. Before the rise of industry, river boats and horse-drawn carriages along muddy roads ②sufficed for local trade. Entrepreneurs and budding industrialists created canals to tame existing rivers ③and channeling new routes for the inland movement of bulk goods. In Britain, canal construction soared, and in turn, created pockets of industry along its path. Canal boats were capable ④of moving more goods quickly and smoothly compared to any previous system that relied on the horse and cart.

[20] Choose the sentence that is NOT grammatically correct.

20   ① This is the person to that you spoke before.
   ② This is the person that you spoke to before.
   ③ This is the person who you spoke to before.
   ④ This is the person whom you spoke to before.
   ⑤ This is the person to whom you spoke before.

[01-09] Choose the one that best completes the sentence.

01 We learn certain things about the other person not so much from what he says as from _____ he says, for whatever we speak we cannot avoid giving our listeners clues about our origins and the sort of person we are.

① that

② where

③ how

④ when

02 With surveillance cameras _____ most urban centers, have we gotten to the point where cameras don't need photographers and photographers don't even need cameras?

① observed

② to observe

③ observes

④ observing

03 Frankly speaking, I did not know what to do with my life in my highschool days. Naturally, so lazy was I in most of subjects those days that I did fail in most of them. Had I only learned English a little more then, my English skill _____ now.

① would have been better

② would be better

③ should have been better

④ must be better

04   The fantasies of children and grown-ups, sometimes Ⓐ_____ daydreams, are always concerned with the future. These 'castle in the air' are the goal of their activity, Ⓑ_____ up in fictional forms as models for real activity.

① calling — built
② calling — building
③ called — build
④ called — built
⑤ called — building

05   The governor of the state of Maryland signed a new law yesterday. The new law makes _____ loud music in your car.

① playing illegally
② it illegal to play
③ illegal playing
④ to play illegal

06   The frequent usage of "the frontier" in the American political program is linked to the image of the American economy as an endlessly fertile continent _____ would never be reached.

① whose boundaries
② its boundaries
③ which boundaries
④ for which boundaries
⑤ boundaries of which

07   When you mistreat someone, even by mistake, it is important to apologize _____.

① for what you have did
② for what you have done
③ what you hurt
④ what you done

08   Those who criticize religion should have an accurate understanding of _____.

① what it is they are criticizing

② what is it they are criticizing

③ what is they are criticizing it

④ what are they criticizing it is

09   Three years after the September 11 attacks, volumes _____ of the earth-shaking events are starting to appear.

① to greatly deepen that we understand

② deepening greatly our understand

③ that greatly deepen our understanding

④ that greatly deepens our understanding

⑤ deepening greatly that we understand

[10-19] Choose the one that is NOT correct in standard English.

10   The temperature ①is expected to plummet, ②in Seoul's morning low on Friday ③dipping ④to minus 8 degrees Celsius.

11   Some studies have ①called into question whether ②high and variable pitch and exaggerated stress ③are the crucial elements in the baby talk ④which infants respond.

12   For a number of ①ancient Greek philosophers, the pursuit of happiness ②was a personal quest, ③albeit, today's modern thinkers tend to see it instead ④as a collective pursuit.

13   While climate change ①might have some people reaching for umbrellas ②more frequently, it could leave ③others praying for more rain ④as warmer weather dries out soil faster and the number of droughts in certain areas ⑤increase.

14 The explosion of concern ①over the condition of the poor nations in the 1950s and 1960s, the increase in assistance and the ②associated political debate, and the explicit imperatives of Vietnam, where a policy intended to forestall or contain Communism ③was under immediate and awful test, all ④pointing, and desperately, to the same need.

15 "People ask me what I want ①to remember for, and I generally say peace and human rights," he says. "I think it's a basic right of a human being ②to have a home that's decent in which ③to raise children, and to have an adequate amount of health care and to have an adequate amount of education ④to take advantage of whatever talent God may have given them."

16 Philip Guston's relationship with the ①work of T. S. Eliot is not only one of shared images; it is ②what the poet referred to as a "unified sensibility." Reflected in the creative act itself, poems, like the painter's canvases, ③are based on the ability of the artist "to show experience ④as both psychological and sensual, while at the same time ⑤infused this portrayal with wit and uniqueness."

17 Rieffenberger thinks the best way to keep bears away from your house is to make sure there is ①no food around. He pointed out the bears aren't coming to make a social call. They are ②looking for something to eat. Rieffenberger recommends ③to put the garbage you throw away in strong metal containers that ④close tightly. He also says not to leave bowls of pet food outside.

18 Ancient Assyrians were inhabitants of one of the world's earliest civilizations, Mesopotamia, ①which began to emerge around 3500 B.C. The Assyrians invented the world's first written language, ②established Hammurabi's code of law, and are credited with many other artistic and architectural achievements. For 300 years Assyrians ③have been controlled the entire Fertile Crescent, from the Persian Gulf to Egypt. In 612 B.C., however, Assyria's capital, Nineveh, was besieged and destroyed by a coalition of Medes, Scythians, and Chaldeans, ④decimating the previously powerful Assyrian Empire.

19   Many wild delphinids regularly interact with birds in a playful manner. For example, after foraging on anchovy schools off the coast of Argentina, some dusky dolphins (*Lagenorhynchus obscurus*) ①<u>have seen</u> carefully grabbing the dangling legs of unsuspecting gulls, quickly surging underwater, and ②<u>then releasing</u> the gulls, effectively dunking the birds. The dolphins are very gentle in their grasp, never causing any harm, and simply appear to ③<u>be having</u> a little fun with their feathered counterparts. As yet unreported elsewhere, this gull-dunking game resembles ④<u>some of</u> the innovative play behavior of captive delphinids.

[20] Choose the sentence that is NOT grammatically correct.

20   ① He is being foolish intentionally.
      ② He is an adult deliberately.
      ③ He purposely didn't write to me about it.
      ④ The chalet was reluctantly destroyed.
      ⑤ The house was resentfully sold last year.

[01-09] Choose the one that best completes the sentence.

01   In film editing, the dissolve is achieved by simultaneously fading out on one shot while fading in on the next _____ the first shot gradually disappears as the second shot gradually becomes visible.

① that   ② so that
③ which   ④ in which

02   Living as a hedonist every now and then has its benefits as well. As long as there are no long-term negative consequences, focusing solely on the present can rejuvenate us. In moderation, the relaxation, the mindlessness, and the fun that come from lying on the beach, eating a fast-food hamburger _____ a hot-fudge sundae or watching television, can make us happier.

① to follow
② having followed
③ follows
④ followed by

03   _____ primarily a government provider has since grown into a huge conglomerate consisting of a catering business and a number of retail stores, which now receive preferential treatment from government agencies.

① Beginning as
② What began as
③ While begun a
④ Did it begin as
⑤ In spite of its beginning as

04   Most students like to read _____ during their spare time.

① these kind of books

② these kind of book

③ this kind of books

④ this kinds of books

⑤ those kind of books

05   Apart from school work, I wrote semi-comic poems which I could turn out _____ astonishing speed — at fourteen I wrote a whole rhyming play, in imitation of Aristophanes, in about a week.

① without somewhat

② by which seemed to be

③ at what now seems to me

④ in that seems to be

06   Viruses and other mobile genes live so closely with cells that we might not realize at first that they are influenced by evolutionary forces _____ influence their hosts.

① independent of those

② independence of those

③ independent of those that

④ independence of those that

07   When you prepare to read, look over the entire reading passage. Look at the photos, illustrations, titles, headings, and anything else that can give you an idea of _____.

① what is the reading about

② about which is the reading

③ what the reading is about

④ about which the reading is

08   _____ new economic vitality, the excessive dependence on energy exports is a problem that must be surmounted.

① A country that badly needed

② For a country that badly needs

③ A country badly needs

④ For a country badly needed

09   Her book is an effort to revive our appreciation of Alexander von Humboldt through _____ of his travels and exploits, reminding us of the lasting influence of his insight.

① her lively account impressively researched

② her impressively researched account lively

③ her lively, impressively researched account

④ her account researched lively, impressively

[10-19] Choose the one that is NOT correct in standard English.

10   The ability to tell a liar ①from a truth-teller is ②one that most people feel ③they need ④it.

11   Taekwondo has helped me ①to build confidence and to channel the anger and frustration I ②had ③as a child ④with a positive outlet.

12   The studio's ①representative design products are match boxes, erasers and pencils — products not ②used ③many these days — ④with modern designs for decorative purposes.

13   Refugees ①posted a tragic dilemma, since they ②fostered so many tensions between member states of the European Union; ③the task was to set an 'ethics of responsibility' ④in order to steer quotas.

14 The farms disappeared because the farmers ①moved to west, to richer lands in ②places like Illinois and Ohio, or migrated to ③the burgeoning industrial cities, ④where earnings were ⑤more reliable and generous.

15 Later, the music ①was wailing beyond the glass, they would watch her through the windows as she ②passed in swift rotation from one pair of black sleeves to the next, her waist ③shaped slender and urgent in the interval, her feet ④filling the rhythmic gap with music.

16 The witness testified that she ①had heard the defendant confess to ②steal a car. She ③was sitting on a park bench, she said, when the defendant, speaking loudly and pointing forcefully toward the parking lot, ④told another man he had just "jacked that silver Toyota."

17 The village can spend money enough on such things as ①farmers and traders value, but it is thought Utopian ②to propose spending money for things which more intelligent men know to be ③far more worth. This town has spent seventeen thousand dollars on a town house, ④thank fortune or politics, but probably it will not spend so much on living wit in a hundred years.

18 Until recently, the electric-powered automobile ①has not received its fair share of attention. No one seemed to care about the possibilities of electric propulsion until a few years ago, when it ②had begun to be considered as an alternative for the polluting, noisy combustion engine. Prior to that, the electric car ③had been dismissed as the hobbyhorse of penniless environmentalists. But when the established automotive industry became interested in the subject and California ④pioneered with a zero-auto-emissions statute, the mood changed. For automotive engineers, a new, exciting time of innovative technical development dawned.

19   Profiling, or criminal investigative analysis, as ①it be called by the FBI, involves the investigation of a crime with the hope of identifying the responsible party, based on crime scene analysis, investigative psychology and behavioral science. Criminal profiling is a cross between law enforcement and forensic psychology. Although it ②has been around for several decades, it is still a relatively new field with few set boundaries or definitions. Moreover, practitioners of criminal profiling do not always agree on methodology or even terminology or definitions. ③Despite their disagreements, however, practitioners of profiling all share a common goal of analyzing evidence gathered at a crime scene and statements ④provided by victims and witnesses in order to develop a description of an unknown offender.

[20] Choose the sentence that is NOT grammatically correct.

20   ① Nigel finished the exam at the same time as George.
　　　② Nigel finished the exam first, then George.
　　　③ Nigel finished the exam before George.
　　　④ Nigel finished the exam when George did.
　　　⑤ Nigel finished the exam when before George did.

[01-09] Choose the one that best completes the sentence.

01   It can be argued that the "all or nothing" choice that is presented to the British voter at election time gives him less control over his government than _____ the American system that allows the voter to elect a Representative, Senators and a President from different parties.

① does
② with
③ for
④ increases

02   The whole conviction of my life now rests upon the belief that loneliness, _____ being a rare and curious phenomenon, peculiar to myself and to a few other solitary men, is the central and inevitable fact of human existence.

① for
② because of
③ far from
④ without

03   This was the beginning of a time of criticism of the theater and its morals which eventually led to the closure of the theaters by the Puritans in 1642. The theater was never again so popular as a medium of entertainment, _____ effective in questioning and analysing the issues and concerns of an age. The Golden Age of English Drama ended in criticism and censorship.

① in order to be
② no matter what
③ nor so
④ as much as

04   Zuckerberg is widely believed to be more comfortable operating behind the scenes, thinking about technology and business, than _____ public discourse, says Standard & Poor's equity analyst Scott Kessler, who follows large Internet companies.

    ① engaged with

    ② engaging in

    ③ was engaged in

    ④ being engaging by

05   A lot of data _____ whether daylight saving time does reduce energy consumption to a significant degree.

    ① remain mixture in

    ② remaining mixture on

    ③ remain mixed on

    ④ remaining mixed in

06   It was not by taking enough readings and then squaring and cubing everything in sight that Copernicus and Kepler thought, or that scientists think today. Copernicus found that the orbits of the planets would look simpler _____ from the sun and not from the earth.

    ① were they looked at

    ② if he had looked at it

    ③ without having looked at them

    ④ if it were not looked at

07   The telescope, though not exactly an item _____, actually was.

    ① we think of it as a weapon

    ② we think of as a weapon

    ③ that thought of as a weapon

    ④ having thought of as a weapon

08   Just as the North American colonies were being founded, a violent and protracted civil war broke out in Britain in 1642, throwing the country into turmoil. This bloody internal conflict was not fully resolved for another two decades. On top of this, the British were also involved in constant competition with other European powers. The task of occupying and defending new territories across the world drained resources _____ on the administration of the colonies.

① what they must have spent
② which might be spent
③ that could otherwise have been spent
④ that they should not have spent

09   _____ so incredible is that these insects successfully migrate to places that they have never even seen.

① That makes the monarch butterflies' migration
② The migration of the monarch butterflies is
③ What makes the monarch butterflies' migration
④ The migration of the monarch butterflies, which is

[10-19] Choose the one that is NOT correct in standard English.

10   ①From downstairs ②came the sound of footsteps, the ③shuffling of feet, television sets, a chair ④was moved, a door being ⑤unlocked.

11   ①For one thing, it is only the last hundred years ②ago ③that higher education has grudgingly ④been opened up to women at all, even to white, middle-class women.

12   Singapore is ①pressing ahead with its search for British judges ②to serve on the court despite ③complaints by local lawyers ④whom it could be a ⑤step backwards to colonial days.

13   Politicians have generated ①such a low degree of trust that they actually ②have to say the phrase "as a matter of principle" ③prior any statement of belief before voters will even ④begin to trust them.

14   If you don't have a dishwasher, you can still save water ①when hand-washed dishes ②by not running the water continuously. Wash dishes in a ③partially filled sink and then rinse them ④using the spray attachment on your tap.

15   Women in the 25 to 44 age group work almost ①as many hours inside the home as outside, and there is only ②a slight difference in the 45 to 64 age group. However, men work ③on average ④three times ⑤long outside the home than inside.

16   The new advertisement is designed around the cliché of the "level playing field," ①by which competitors meet without advantages. To this idea of sportsmanship ②is opposed the new enterpreneurial ruthlessness, ③in which the whole idea is to compete ④unfairly and take advantage of the weaknesses of others.

17   Historically, the criteria used to define the developing world have focused largely ①on economic growth, ②of little concern for questions of equity, sustainability, or empowerment. ③Until the 1990s, for example, the ④most common way of differentiating the developing world from the developed world was ⑤through the use of GDP figures that measured the value of goods and services produced in a country in a given year.

18   When Galileo turned the first telescope toward the heavens, he recorded that the Milky Way, the galaxy in which the Earth ①to spin, is a stretch of innumerable stars grouped together in clusters. Those star clusters are in fact groupings of solar systems, composed of many suns, ②some with planets revolving around them. The Milky Way is 1,000 light-years thick and 100,000 light-years across at ③its widest. There ④are approximately 100 billion solar systems in the Milky Way, comprising 100 billion to 200 billion suns.

19   The film's opening act introduces the Kim family, folding pizza boxes in a squalid basement apartment in Seoul and scrambling from room to room ①<u>in search of</u> free WiFi after the neighboring business locked theirs down with a password. In a single scene the film appears to articulate its title and define its central characters, but the Kims are not ②<u>who you think are</u>. In fact, every time you think you've pinned this film down — ③<u>who's doing what to whom</u>, who is or is not a parasite — you learn it was an impeccably executed sleight of hand. Longtime Bong collaborator Kang-ho Song ④<u>anchors the film with</u> an endearing and slippery performance.

[20] Choose the sentence that is NOT grammatically correct.

20   ① They intended the news to be suppressed.
   ② I regret that she should worry about it.
   ③ I doubt whether they'll accept or not.
   ④ She asked about what he wanted.
   ⑤ They liked the children to visit them.

[01-09] Choose the one that best completes the sentence.

01 Unusual patterns of financial transactions can clue in investigators about a terror suspect. However, there are always exceptions to these patterns, and potential terrorists might do something unusual just to avoid looking suspicious. _____, the profile of your "average" terrorist might not always be accurate. Although the poor and uneducated are considered the most likely to become terrorists, the would-be terrorist on Christmas Day in the U.S was the son of a distinguished Nigerian family.

① Instead
② On the other hand
③ By the way
④ Likewise

02 Above all, we must realize that no arsenal, or no weapon in the arsenals of the world, is so formidable _____ the will and moral courage of free men and women.

① that
② as
③ but
④ what

03 _____ the foots, one young solider, who didn't believe the spirits, demanded that Harvey prove his existence. "Harvey, if you're up there, you got to make me know it."

① On hearing
② It hears
③ As to hear
④ To hear

04 There is a requirement for every applicant that he or she _____ at least 20 years old at the time of application for the subsidy.

① be

② should have been

③ is

④ was

05 The author's typical method of trying to get his readers to look at things in a new way _____ not with a persuasive argument but with a memorable image.

① presenting them

② with them presented

③ that presents them

④ is to present them

06 In this book, Mary Evans explores _____ social theory has engaged with and illuminated the question of relations between genders and the social world.

① the extent to which

② the extent to what

③ the extent which

④ the extent to those

⑤ the extent that it

07 Historians debate exactly why food in China is seasoned with products fermented or pickled in salt, and _____ added directly to food.

① having with no grains of salt

② grains of salt have not

③ with not having grains of salt

④ not with grains of salt

08   Our brethren are already in the field! Why stand we here idle? What is it that gentlemen wish? What would they have? Is life so dear, or peace so sweet, _____ at the price of chains and slavery? Forbid it, Almighty God! I know not what course others may take; but as for me, give me liberty or give me death!

① which is to purchase them
② that was not to be purchased
③ as to be purchased
④ as would have purchased

09   Hoping for the president-elect to conform to the norms of business and politics is like _____.

① a square peg expecting to be fit a round hole in
② fitting a square peg expecting in a round hole
③ a round hole expecting a square peg to fit into
④ expecting a square peg to fit in a round hole

[10-19] Choose the one that is NOT correct in standard English.

10   Cerebral cortex neurons are ①the only ②type of cell ③what ④we can confidently say ⑤is never replaced.

11   Not until the next day ①did she learn that her acting was ②so lackluster that the management had fired her, but other actors had been silent ③out of embarrassment. ④No error.

12   The psychology of Abraham Maslow is one of ①a number of schools of humanistic psychology, ②which take a sanguine view of the human condition, placing more stress on the human being's potential to achieve fulfillment and ③little on sinister forces lurking in ④the recesses of the mind.

13　①With such prices, drug pushers can earn billions of dollars each year ②by pushing their wares ③in even the poorest neighborhoods. Most people agree that so-called drug war is far from ④being won in the United States. Consequently, it has become an obsession for many Americans ⑤finding some solution to the drug problem.

14　The Greeks ①used to distinguish the straight path of reason and scientific knowledge, *episteme*, ②from the clever and crooked path of technical know-how, *metis*. ③Now that we have seen how indirect and mediated are the paths ④took by scientific facts, we may be able to find a different genealogy for technical artifacts as well.

15　Developments in time-keeping technology continued as the ①demanding for clocks increased. Clocks were needed for factories, banking, communications, and transportation. Today, much of modern life happens ②at high speed and ③depends on having the exact time. We must also have international ④agreement on what the exact time is.

16　Warren Buffett is an extraordinary figure. He looks ①not so much like a billionaire as an ordinary guy or perhaps a college lecturer. He ②is immensely quotable: gems such as "It's only when the tide goes out that you realize ③who's been swimming naked" seem to trip off his tongue. He's also extraordinarily modest and self-deprecating and ④has been ascribed much of his fortune to luck.

17　Initially, the rate ①at which minerals were extracted was limited by the high costs associated with mining. However, technological improvements in the industry, ②combined with significant reductions in the expenses associated with transport, ③have made it possible to remove these commodities more efficiently and at a much lower cost, ④resulted in an extraction rate that many experts consider to be unsustainable.

18 North America is a land of immigrants, many of whom left their home countries ①to escape religious persecution. In the early 1700s, a group of Christians from Switzerland came to the United States and Canada. Pious and hard-working, they established farming communities. These people, ②known as the Amish, still live in Ontario, Canada and in several states in the U.S. ③Being avoided the use of modern technology such as computers, their goal has always been ④to maintain the simple farming life that they had in Europe.

19 We also need to increase the utilization of the existing technology — ①many of the current technology are underutilized. The cost of operating IT ②can be reduced by, for example, applying the concept of virtualization to end user computing devices, ③allowing applications to be hosted on centralized servers, making it easier and cheaper for IT to provide new mobile computing services and ④increase the utilization of licenses. The key to dramatically increasing innovation capacity ⑤is to shift IT from low to higher value-added activities so that they can enable the IT capabilities of the rest of the enterprise.

[20] Choose the sentence that is NOT grammatically correct.

20   ① She found in the park the dog I was looking for.
    ② I'm looking forward to the meeting with the singer.
    ③ It is important for Peter to find errors before printing.
    ④ What do you think how long they have been married?
    ⑤ What John did to his wife was to teach her how to drive.

[01-09] Choose the one that best completes the sentence.

01 _____ an abortion is necessary to save the life of the mother is the procedure permitted.

① When
② While
③ That
④ Only if

02 The English major who runs the copying machine is underemployed. _____ the forestry major who can't get a job in his field.

① Also
② It also
③ So is
④ So

03 _____, with an understanding of the target audience's interests, publicity and public relations can effectively promote a company with little expense.

① It is carefully planning
② That carefully planned
③ When carefully planned
④ Carefully planning

04 It seems that few businessmen participated in the charity ball for the street children; otherwise, more money _____.

① would have been raised
② was being raised
③ had been raised
④ might have been raising

05   He predicted that beef eating may peak in 2020, not because people don't like beef anymore, but because there are so many innovative options _____.

① which replacing it

② which to replace it

③ with which replacing it

④ with which to replace it

06   Among all the abilities _____ an individual may be endowed, musical talent appears earliest in life. But its development depends on the environment _____ the child lives.

① with which — on which

② from which — on which

③ to which — in which

④ with which — in which

⑤ from which — in which

07   Descartes was thrilled by the transparent and utterly reliable certainties of mathematics, and he began to wonder whether _____ was something that could be taken over and applied in other areas of knowledge.

① to give mathematics its certainty

② what gave mathematics its certainty

③ mathematics was given its certainty

④ or not mathematics are given its certainty

08   The imagination is a weariable faculty; if we give it too many objects at a time to employ itself upon, it fails under the effort, exactly _____.

① so as the limbs are fatigued

② as the limbs do by bodily fatigue

③ are our limbs employed by fatigue

④ such that our limbs become fatigued

09   The bills of the ruling party _____.

① is as bad or worse than the opposition party

② are as bad or worse than the opposition party

③ are as bad as or worse than the opposition party

④ are as bad as or worse than those of the opposition party

[10-19] Choose the one that is NOT correct in standard English.

10   ①In other words, people with a new heart, liver, or kidney can live ②much longer ③than they ④are used to previously.

11   Anger can mobilize you ①to take action, for example, to set ②limits to the demands others ③make you, to think about why something ④matters to you or to defend yourself if ⑤attacked.

12   ①When the costs of delays and uncertainties ②are added into their calculations, ③both government and private industry often find that it pays ④for canceling projects that would ⑤otherwise be profitable.

13   Thousands of children ①die in car accidents every year. In most cases, the children were not using child safety seats. Even though child safety seats ②are required by law, many parents ③neglect easily. The only solution is to educate parents ④on how the seats can save lives.

14   ①Although retirement is a topic that some people would rather avoid, a lot of people ②had reached that age now, and they are the baby boomers. While ③growing up, these ④sixty seven million baby boomers filled up school classrooms and spiked blue jean sales.

15 I have neither the wish nor the competence ①to embark on the exercise with the tools of the social and biological sciences but more simply in the manner of a novelist ②responding to one famous book of European fiction: Joseph Conrad's *Heart of Darkness*, which better than any other work that I know ③display that Western desire and need which I have just referred ④to.

16 I hate ①being ill. I do not simply mean that I dislike the illness itself (although that is true), but I hate ②that being ill does to my character. ③As soon as I have a headache or a cold or the first signs of flu coming on, I proceed to behave as if I ④were in the grip of some fatal illness, and ⑤to wear an expression of martyrdom which is supposed to indicate that I will bravely face the few days of life that are left to me.

17 Apple's expansion reflects the increasing competition for engineers in Silicon Valley. The ①bidding for programmers is driving salaries higher, which in turn is ②catapulting the average prices of homes in many parts of the San Francisco Bay Area above $1 million. Many high-tech workers are thus ③choosing to live elsewhere, causing major tech employers such as Apple and Google ④looking in new places for the employees they need.

18 Helen Keller lost her sight at a very early age and, so, was very frustrated as a child. First of all, because she could neither hear ①nor speak, she couldn't understand what was happening around her. She felt her mother's lips ②moving as she spoke, but this made no sense to her. She couldn't understand ③what her mother was doing. Secondly, once she learned what words were, she felt she could never communicate with them as quickly as ④sighting people could. As a result of all her frustration, she would often cry and scream until she was ⑤exhausted.

19   Plastic pollution was ①at the center of the sustainability debate in 2018, with governments banning plastic straws and exfoliants with microbeads. The fashion industry has its fair share of responsibility for plastic pollution, considering that 60 percent of the world's garments contain polyester, a material ②derived by polyethylene terephthalate, the most common type of plastic in the world. When washed, polyester garments often release tiny pieces of plastic into the water, ③which end up in the rivers and oceans and can be eaten by animals. A Greenpeace expedition to the Antarctic revealed earlier this year that microplastics ④can be found even in the most remote areas of the planet.

[20] Choose the sentence that is NOT grammatically correct.

20   ① I didn't know that it was such an old house.
          ② This chair isn't strong enough to stand on it.
          ③ Did you meet anyone interesting at the party?
          ④ The more expensive the beef, the better the taste.
          ⑤ The exam was so difficult that hardly anyone passed.

[01-09] Choose the one that best completes the sentence.

01 A business concerned about its efficiency should pay attention to the actions of its staff, because the mistakes of each of its employees often undermine the effectiveness of the organization _____ they are a part.

① that

② of which

③ whereby

④ what

02 Jean-Pierre Raffarin, a former prime minister, wants all French people who hold top jobs in international organizations, where common language is English, _____ on speaking French.

① to insist

② insists

③ insisting

④ insist

03 Cubism is an artistic movement, created by Pablo Picasso and Georges Braque, _____ geometric shapes in depictions of human and other forms.

① who employs

② that employing

③ which employs

④ where it is employed

04 As is a tale, so is life: not how long it is, but how good it is, _____.

① that matters

② matters how

③ how it matters

④ is what matters

⑤ is how it matters

05 Awareness of the harmful effect plastic can have _____ has exploded in recent years.

① the environment

② on the environment

③ in the environment

④ on in the environment

06 Helen worked just so much _____.

① like she was told to

② like what she was told to

③ as she was told to

④ as what she was told to

⑤ as to what she tried to do

07 Measles _____ a large number of people in this city, and now the only means of survival _____ to escape from the city.

① has killed — seems to be

② have killed — seems to be

③ has killed — seem to be

④ have killed — seem to be

08   Until recently, only by a complicated test _____.

① chlamydial infections be detected

② chlamydial infections could be detected

③ could chlamydial infections be detected

④ be chlamydial infections detected

⑤ chlamydial infection detected

09   It was quite embarrassing _____ lost in a small neighborhood.

① of a growing woman's finding her

② for a grown woman to find herself

③ by a growing woman to find herself

④ to a grown woman find her

[10-19] Choose the one that is NOT correct in standard English.

10   ①However strongly the policeman ②demanded them to move from the office, ③only a few agreed ④to do so.

11   ①Since computers started ②to be introduced in education, people have asked ③whether the investment we are making in these technologies ④give us value for money.

12   To our surprise, Erik Dickinson fell ①short of his parents' expectations, ②disappointing them who kept the faith in their son's potential for success, when he ③was proved to be ④a failure as a statesman.

13   ①Much of our perspective on the process of metropolitan settlement dates, ②whether we realize it or not, from a paper ③wrote in 1925 by the sociologist Ernest W. Burgess. It was Burgess ④who defined four urban/suburban zones of settlement.

14 Amazon's recent acquisition of Body Lab's, a software provider of human-aware artificial intelligence that ①understands the 3D body shape and motion of people from photos or videos, ②have many speculating on how ③quickly body imaging technology will improve and ④influence online shopping.

15 As the school year wanes, many eighth graders take note of a fact that ①earlier may not have been obvious: from now on, grades appear on high school records. High school records, not ②to mention test scores, lead to college acceptance letters. The caliber of college one attends ③determines the extent to which one will succeed in life. It sounds kind of ominous, ④isn't it?

16 A number of interesting advances ①have come from the field of nanotechnology recently. For example, computers are getting better as their smaller parts become ②cheaper to make them. In addition, frames for glasses can now ③bend into extraordinary shapes without breaking. Also, silver ④is being incorporated into clothing and food packaging as a natural disinfectant.

17 As the nobleman of cultivated taste surrounds himself with ①whatever conduces to his culture, so let the village do — not stop ②short at a pedagogue, a parson, a parish library. I am confident that, as our circumstances are more flourishing, our means are greater than ③the nobleman. New England can hire all the wise men in the world ④to come and teach her, and not be provincial at all.

18 ①Trekking through the Himalayas, Maggie Doyne met hundreds of orphaned and poverty-stricken Nepalese children. Upon ②returning to her hometown, she asked her community to help her ③build a safe and loving home for these children. To Doyne's surprise, her neighbors supported the idea. With their help, Doyne and the local Nepalese community built the Kopila Valley Children's Home, a home that ④provides young orphans, street children, child laborers, and abused children with an education, health care, and a loving place to grow up. Today, there are 25 children ⑤live in the home, and 60 children are enrolled in school through the Kopila Outreach program.

19   The grimmest examples of germs' role in history come from the European conquest of the Americas that began with Columbus's voyage of 1492. Numerous ①<u>as was</u> the Native American victims of the murderous Spanish conquistadores, they were ②<u>far outnumbered</u> by the victims of murderous Spanish microbes. Why was the exchange of nasty germs between the Americas and Europe so unequal? Why didn't Native American diseases instead decimate the Spanish invaders, spread back to Europe, and wipe out 95 percent of Europe's population? Similar questions arise for the decimation of ③<u>many other native peoples</u> by Eurasian germs, ④<u>as well as for</u> the decimation of would-be European conquistadores in the tropics of Africa and Asia.

[20] Choose the sentence that is NOT grammatically correct.

20   ① How come you are coming out of that building?
   ② My dad will help me to purchase a new apartment.
   ③ What if will you be late for the meeting tomorrow?
   ④ He failed to finish the marathon, but he did his best.
   ⑤ Can you imagine anybody being so stupid like him?

[01-09] Choose the one that best completes the sentence.

01   Every man, in reading, is his own best critic. Whatever the learned say about a book, however unanimous they are in their praise of it, it is no business of yours, _____ it interests you.

① unless

② since

③ when

④ otherwise

02   Regardless of definition, all religions have certain elements in common: rituals to perform, prayers to recite, places to frequent or avoid, holy days to keep, means _____ to predict the future, a body of literature to read and study, truths to affirm, charismatic leaders to follow, and ordinances to obey.

① of that

② by which

③ for what

④ in which

03   About a third of jazz music is in the blues form and _____ over half of the rock 'n' roll pieces.

① are also

② also are

③ so are

④ are so

04　The people detained at the center are _____ today that the abuse must not continue.

① making it known

② making it knowing

③ making it knows

④ making it know

05　All human beings are born with certain inalienable rights. In other words, every person's autonomy should be respected except _____ the exercise of that autonomy conflicts with the public good.

① in cases in which

② for the cases in

③ in a case which

④ for a case in

06　In 1921, a movement started in several parts of the world, _____ was to make table tennis a serious sport.

① which goal

② its goal

③ the goal of which

④ which of the goal

07　Love, although it is said _____, is a vigilant watchman.

① with blindness to afflicted

② to afflict blindness with

③ afflicted blindness to be

④ to be afflicted with blindness

08   He that is of the opinion money will do everything _____ doing everything for money.

① may well suspect

② may well be suspected of

③ may as well be suspected

④ may as well not suspect of

⑤ may as well not be suspected

09   The deepening troubles at the state oil company, _____, threaten to further destabilize a government facing a dire recession.

① the country's economic mainstay is

② it is the country's economic mainstay

③ is the country's economic mainstay

④ the country's economic mainstay

[10-19] Choose the one that is NOT correct in standard English.

10   Because of this ①ranking feature, Google's results are ②more accurate and ③higher quality than ④those of other search engines.

11   Flight speeds of birds ①have clocked many times, but usually at ground speed, and it ②is asserted that migrating birds travel faster ③when migrating than they travel at other times. ④No error.

12   The son ①of Italian immigrants grows up ②poorly in San Francisco and becomes the greatest baseball player ③of his day, marries an American goddess and never ④in word or deed befouls his legend and greatness.

13   A study found that the patients who took six deep breaths in 30 seconds before a reading had a more than three-point ①drop in their systolic blood pressure compared with ②them who rested ③for 30 seconds without deep ④breathing.

14 ①Long ②viewed by many as the stereotypical useless major, philosophy is now being seen by many students ③as in fact a very useful and practical major, ④offers students a host of transferable skills with relevance to the modern workplace.

15 Thailand is ①keenly aware of the effects of tourism. Upwards of 34 million people visit the country from ②abroad every year. With that ③yearly influx of people, ④come a need to ensure that the natural and cultural wonders Thailand is known for are protected.

16 Popular opinion among creatives ①is that art is a process ②which human beings express some idea or emotion, filter it through personal experience and ③set it against a broader cultural context — suggesting then that ④what AI generates at the behest of computer scientists is definitely not art, or at all creative.

17 Peter, who ①had left the summit shortly after I did, soon pulled up behind me. Wanting to conserve whatever oxygen remained in my tank, I asked him to reach inside my backpack and turn off the valve on my regulator, ②which he did. For the next ten minutes I felt surprisingly good. My head ③cleared. I actually seemed less tired than I had with the gas ④turning on.

18 The instinct of curiosity greatly contributes to humans' individual and collective progress. It urges people to seek the ①unknown and to find answers to things not yet ②understood. Thus, in more serious fields, it drives humans to explore and to conquer new frontiers in all dimensions. For example, ③sparkling objects in the night sky have fascinated the human instinct of curiosity to the point ④that humans have found a way to land on the moon and ⑤reached beyond it.

19 Internet distribution of television content changes the fundamental logics ①which television travels, introducing new mobilities into the system, ②<u>adding another layer</u> to the existing broadcast cable and satellite distribution. Internet television does not replace legacy television in a straightforward way; instead it adds new complexity to the existing geography of distribution. The arrival of mature internet-distributed television services such as Netflix is significant in global media debates. Today, one ③<u>no longer needs</u> to travel overseas to access international television, ④<u>for</u> a great deal of it is easily accessible online.

[20] Choose the sentence that is NOT grammatically correct.

20 ① You can use my car so long as you return soon.
② I gave him some cash in case he needed to drink.
③ I will help you despite you didn't help me last time.
④ Provided that the weather is good, we'll go on a trip.
⑤ Having a car is convenient provided you have a garage.

[01-09] Choose the one that best completes the sentence.

01   *The Thinker*, a famous bronze and marble sculpture by August Rodin, depicts a pensive man, that is, one _____ in deep thought.

① captured   ② captures

③ capturing   ④ has been captured

02   It was her view that the country's problems had been exacerbated by foreign technocrats, _____ to ask for their assistance again would be counterproductive.

① not so much   ② so that

③ in so far as   ④ no matter what

03   Out of this contention _____ a set of arguments that has become politically correct wisdom.

① it was born   ② was born

③ born   ④ to be born

04   He, who was a member of the National Assembly before _____ governor in June last year, has been busy attracting domestic and foreign investment to upgrade the province's industries.

① been elected

② electing as

③ having elected as

④ being elected

05　There are a number of steps you can take to determine whether game design is the right field for you and, if it is, _____ for such a career.

① preparing

② preparing yourself

③ to prepare yourself

④ preparation

06　These differences between two photographs _____ with the help of Photoshop.

① should remove

② must have removed

③ could have been removed

④ were able to remove

07　Nearly three hundred musical scrolls have been preserved, _____ for use at royal memorial services.

① of ninety which are

② which of ninety are

③ of which ninety are

④ ninety are of which

08　Many of the former patients remain anonymous, but allege _____ which surgical procedures would be performed on them, not receiving pain medication after surgery, among other allegations.

① to be uninformed by

② to have uninformed

③ being uninformed about

④ being uninformed

09   _____, she had never, in the whole course of their acquaintance, seen anything that betrayed him to be unjust.

① Proud as his manners were

② As his manners were proud

③ Despite being his proud manners

④ On the account of his proud manners

[10-19] Choose the one that is NOT correct in standard English.

10   ①Adjacent to the traditionalists ②were the anti-Communists, many ③of them were ④former Marxists.

11   ①A Catholic diocese in Northern Ireland ②has suspended the "sign of peace" handshake ③on its masses ④due to the risk of infection from a strain of the flu.

12   ①Careful measurements reveal that the reaction rate is ②too slow to account for ③the ozone concentrations observed, i.e. the process predicts higher peak ozone concentrations ④that are observed.

13   It is a bad idea to take a shower during a thunderstorm. If lightning ①hits your house, it can travel through your ②plumbing and shock anyone ③whoever comes into contact with water ④flowing through it.

14   The Government was today ①accused of placing ②much too emphasis on artificial targets after primary school results ③showed that improvements in core subjects are ④failing to keep pace with ⑤rapidly rising expectations.

15   Archaeologist Daniel S. Craig ①from the University of Birmingham ②has been excavating at South Africa's Blombos Cave since 1992, and ③has reported the discovery of a mixture, ④rich in ochre, ⑤storing in two abalone shells.

16   There ①exist today primitive, wingless insects that offer clues to ②whom the earliest insect life may have been ③like; there are the bristletails and silverfish, which probably evolved from arthropods that had many body segments and a pair of stubby legs ④attached to each segment.

17   Shut up ①underground, with only a grating to give a glimpse of garden and sky, Arrietty longs to ②be allowed outside, despite her parents's fear of being seen by their giant, unwitting hosts. Her explorations result in her being spotted by and eventually ③befriends the lonely boy who has come to stay in the house. Soon, the rest of household discovers his secret and Arrietty's family ④must flee.

18   An autistic savant is a person with an unusual ability, skill, or knowledge that is ①much more developed than that of an average person. In fact, many savants have ②highly developed mathematical skills. ③The others are able to retain large amounts of information in their memory. For example, ④some autistic savants can recite entire dictionaries or telephone books word for word. Still others are able to draw detailed maps of an area after ⑤flying over it once in a helicopter.

19   When Google Trends, a tool which tells users how frequently any word has been searched, ①was first released, Google search data didn't seem to be a proper source of information for academic research. Google search data wasn't created as a way to help us understand the human psyche. But it turns out that the trails we leave as we seek knowledge on the internet ②are tremendously revealing. When and where they search for facts, places, or persons can tell us a lot more about what they really think and do than anyone ③might have guessed. This is especially true since people sometimes don't so much query Google ④as confiding in it: "I hate my boss." "I am drunk."

[20] Choose the sentence that is NOT grammatically correct.

20   ① Joan is likely to get married.
      ② It is likely of Joan's getting married.
      ③ I'm hopeless at keeping the garden tidy.
      ④ There's no point telling him anything.
      ⑤ It's not worth while your staying.

[01-09] Choose the one that best completes the sentence.

01 Technology provides instant gratification, whereas science occurs through a slow process. In the hustle and bustle of today's world, we have become increasingly used to the speed afforded by technology, _____ we become angry if our email takes a few seconds to refresh or if our train is delayed by a few minutes.

① lest

② since

③ such that

④ according as

02 _____ to a duel by the officer was just a boy barely reaching the age of fourteen.

① Challenge

② To challenge

③ Challenging

④ Challenged

03 At the close of the Middle Ages, Western man reduced the time of work that man could enjoy hours of leisure _____ his forefathers had hardly dreamed of.

① due to

② to an extent

③ unless

④ according to

04   The party's members were thrilled to win so many seats in the parliament, but _____ the news that they had overturned the majority.

① still was better
② better still was
③ it was still better
④ still better it was

05   No other state received _____ the state of Nevada.

① rainfall as little as
② so few rainfalls as
③ as little rainfall as
④ as few rainfall as

06   Those who favor the new administrative law say that the present law does not set spending limits on lobbyists' gifts to politicians, _____ statewide funds.

① nor it limits
② nor does it limit
③ nor they limit
④ nor do they limit
⑤ nor they are limited

07   Two roads diverged in a wood, and I _____, And that has made all the difference.

① take one by less traveled
② has taken one by less traveled
③ took the one less traveled by
④ had taken one less traveled by
⑤ had taken the one by less traveled

08   _____, there is always a risk that the money will run out if a winner overspends and does not invest wisely.

① However large is the jackpot

② No matter how is the jackpot large

③ However the jackpot is large

④ No matter how large the jackpot is

09   Today, Rwanda's Parliament is set to consider legislation that would for the first time make homosexuality a crime, _____. The bill would also ban any activities that could be construed as "encouraging or sensitizing" same-sex relationships.

① punishable by five to 10 years in prison

② punished by five to 10 years in prison

③ being punished by five to 10 years in prison

④ having been punished by five to 10 years in prison

[10-19] Choose the one that is NOT correct in standard English.

10   ①Gas efficiency, secure, economical, and ②practical, today's cars are better ③than any produced ④before.

11   Animals are happy ①so long as they have health and enough to eat. Human beings, ②one feels, ought to be, but in the modern world ③they are not, at least ④in a great majority of case.

12   ①You are advised to complete the form promptly in full and ②are required to return it to the officers present. ③They will be held responsible for ensuring ④the form processed and ⑤it is then forwarded to the correct department.

13 ①Because it is so expensive to buy a house or just an apartment within a building, buyers usually ②finance their purchase by making a down payment on a percentage of ③the agreed price and ④take out a mortgage on the ⑤remaining balance.

14 Cross-linguistic studies, which compare the abilities of infants ①growing up with different linguistic backgrounds, ②show common categorization by infants, ③even when there are differences in the phonologies of the adult language. ④No error.

15 Warming of 2.6C to 4.8C, ①which climate experts say ②are likely unless stronger action is taken to bring down greenhouse gas emissions, would result ③in as many as 660,000 additional asylum seekers coming to Europe each year ④by 2100.

16 I would like ①to express my thanks to you ②for the truly excellent display for our Trusoft concrete products. ③At our first trade show ④in Munich, many visitors to our booth ⑤remarked the attractiveness of our exhibit space, and we would like to pass on their compliments to you.

17 ①As water from the surface enters the subsurface rock, the pace of its movement is greatly determined by the geological composition of the materials ②it encounters. Sand, gravel, and porous limestone formations tend to allow water to flow relatively ③unimpeded. The ease with which water can move through pore spaces or rock fractures ④are known as hydraulic conductivity.

18 When the necessary amount of an element in an organism is extremely small, it ①is called a trace element. Iodine is a trace element vital to the ②functioning of the thyroid gland, which regulates the rate of the body's chemical activity, or metabolism. A slight iodine deficiency may ③result in a huge swelling on the neck in the region of the gland, a condition ④known as simpler goiter. Complete absence of iodine is fatal. Yet the total amount of iodine in a man's body is only about 1/2,500,000 of the entire body weight. As is the case with all minerals, iodine ⑤must supply to the body in the diet.

19 Use of animals in research is sometimes ①opposing because animal models do not always identically mimic humans. As models, animals may provide additional insights into pathophysiology or disease, but they can also lead research ②astray. Opponents of animal research argue that each species ③has subtle but significant differences that cannot be predicted or fully understood to extrapolate to humans. For example, in a study looking at compounds that reduced ischemic stroke in rodents, none of the compounds were ④efficacious in human trials. The lack of efficacy was potentially due to the difference between natural strokes that develop over time in humans versus the experimentally induced strokes produced in the rodents over a period of weeks.

[20] Choose the sentence that is NOT grammatically correct.

20　① On which month did you say we should get married?
　　② Do you know which bus she is waiting to go home?
　　③ Who do you think we should meet to talk about what?
　　④ Judge her not by how she looks but by what she is!
　　⑤ Why she talks like that is what everyone is curious of!

T E S T

24

[01-09] Choose the one that best completes the sentence.

01 So common are cases of people dying from overwork in Japan _____ the country has a special term for it, *karoshi*.

① and ② which
③ where ④ that

02 Not only were the head of student government, the senior class president, and 96 of the University's 141 honor students _____, but so were two-thirds of the graduates.

① women
② being women
③ were women
④ who were women

03 Saving $1 at the age of 20 is _____ in retirement as saving $1 at the age of 40.

① twice as valuable
② as twice valuable
③ valuable as twice
④ valuable twice as

04 Born in 1935, Christo is one of the best-known living artists. However, the art _____ could never fit inside a museum.

① for that he is famous
② he is famous for
③ he is a fame
④ makes him famous

05 In the car industry, the use of AI robots has made car production a much easier job _____.

① than it once was

② as was it before

③ than it once did

④ as once upon a time was it

06 Water to the building will be _____ repairs between the hours of 4:00 AM and 7:00 PM on Thursday.

① shutting for plumbing

② shut off for plumbing

③ shutting of plumb

④ shut off of plumb

07 As a young dinosaur, *Limusaurus* had sharp teeth, _____ it ate meat.

① which tells scientists that

② that tells scientists which

③ telling that scientists

④ telling which scientists

08 According to a recent poll, owning and living in a freestanding house on its own land is still a goal of a majority of young adults, _____.

① as it was of earlier generations

② as have earlier generations

③ like that of earlier generations

④ just as earlier generations did

⑤ as that of earlier generations

09 In the past, hypnosis was sometimes used as a means of _____.

① helping for people to quit smoking

② help to people to quit to smoke

③ helping people to quit smoking

④ help people to quit to smoke

[10-19] Choose the one that is NOT correct in standard English.

10 The investigator found the ①very car ②that the ③alleged criminal had been witnessed ④use.

11 Who you are, where you are and ①how your family has in the bank have a lot ②to do with whether your child will ③be claimed by obesity or emerge ④unharmed.

12 In his retirement, my grandfather is active ①as he ②had been when he worked ③in business, but now, instead ④holding a full-time job, he does volunteer work.

13 Such a view of ①life's history is highly ②contrary to both conventional deterministic models of Western science and to the deepest social traditions and psychological hopes ③of Western culture. ④No error.

14 Today ①we ornament ourselves with goods and services more to ②impress at other people's minds than to ③enjoy owning a chunk of matter — a fact that ④renders materialism a profoundly misleading term for much of consumption.

15 George Orwell's best work was ①political, but his politics were difficult to ②pin down. Shy in person, ③though vehement on the page, Orwell could fairly describe ④him as simultaneously a left-wing socialist, an anti-communist and a Tory anarchist.

16 Scholars of great Elizabethan and Jacobean literature ①have been happy to find many modern ②matters of state and power, and ③have contented with the ④extraordinary depth of reading and thought ⑤shown by Spenser, Shakespeare, or Jonson.

17 Democrats are now more liberal and Republicans ①more conservative than they were 50 years ago. Some view this phenomenon simply ②as for a reorganization of political tendencies, with little effect on behavior or mass polarization, ③whereas others suggest that this sorting is ④a reflection of a deep polarization emerging in the electorate.

18 When the guns of the Civil War ①finally fell silent, the U.S. Army ②underwent a dramatic drop in manpower. Authorized strength fell from 57,000 in 1867 to half that a decade later and then averaged 26,000 until the war with Spain ③at century's end. Effective strength, however, always ④fell short of authorized strength caused by high rates of sickness and desertion so the Army ⑤was hard-pressing to provide the command and control necessary to maintain order and safety.

19 Over the past decades, ski lifts helped transform ①impoverished and isolated mountain villages into lucrative tourist destinations. Now, their economic dependency on the upscale sport could be their ruin. Billions ②have already been lost since the resorts were closed in March. ③If should Tyrol's entire ski season falter, as much as 3 percent of Austria's Gross Domestic Product could be wiped out. In some ways, the pandemic's impact on ski resorts ④offers a glimpse into the future of a climate 3.6 degrees Fahrenheit warmer. By that time, about a third of the Eastern Alps' resorts will not be able to open ski lifts by the Christmas holidays, ⑤the highest-earning time of the season.

[20] Choose the sentence that is NOT grammatically correct.

20
① We cannot be too careful in choosing our friends.
② I could have helped her only if I hadn't overslept.
③ No one is to be seen on street during the curfew.
④ A lion cannot be tamed unless he is caught young.
⑤ It is unhappy for me to hear that the shop went broke.

[01-09] Choose the one that best completes the sentence.

01 It was due to his lateness _____ such a thing plunged him into the disaster, which eventually changed his whole life.

① when
② that
③ as
④ what

02 On the causes of global warming, skeptics make the argument that most of the greenhouse effect comes from water vapor and only 4% of the carbon dioxide _____ the atmosphere is due to human activity.

① enter
② entered
③ entering
④ enter into

03 An insurance company might send investigators to determine the cause of a mysterious fire. If the investigators sent back a report that the fire was caused by the presence of oxygen in the atmosphere, they would not keep their jobs very long. And yet they would be right. Had there been no oxygen present, there _____ no fire.

① has been
② is
③ will be
④ would be
⑤ would have been

04 A substance that is perfectly all right to a person who has no allergies can cause mild to serious reactions in a person _____.

① has allergies
② who can do allergies
③ with allergies
④ which having allergies

05 This validated registration card or a facsimile copy is to be kept _____ it is issued.

① vehicle of which
② the vehicle with which
③ for the vehicle which
④ with the vehicle for which

06 Inventive as well as thoughtful, she helped people in a way that _____ considered.

① never had been before
② had never before been
③ had been never before
④ never before had been

07 The problem is _____ the singular self does matter.

① that in fiction, let alone in life,
② in fiction, let life alone,
③ that in fiction, let lonely life,
④ in fiction, let alone with life,

08 Nutritionists recommend the juice of barley plants as a means of slowing the aging process and also _____.

① it to cancer patients recommend
② to cancer patients recommend it
③ recommend it cancer patients
④ recommend it to cancer patients

09   Diabetes, together with its serious complications, _____ by heart disease and cancer.

     ① are the nation's third leading cause of death, surpassed only

     ② rank as the nation's third leading cause of death, only surpassed

     ③ ranks as the nation's third leading cause of death, surpassed only

     ④ have been ranked as the nation's third leading causes of death, only surpassed

     ⑤ has the rank of the nation's third leading cause of death, only surpassed

[10-19] Choose the one that is NOT correct in standard English.

10   I have ①no idea how it will turn out, but I'm not worried ②in the slightest because it's so clear ③that she knows exactly ④that is going to look like.

11   ①What sets human beings apart from animals is not the pursuit of happiness, ②which occurs all across the natural world, ③but also the pursuit of meaning, ④which is unique to humans.

12   Throughout the ①developed world, we are at a point ②in our evolution ③at which famine, ④which essentially governed the rise and fall of civilizations throughout history, ⑤are no longer an acute threat.

13   ①Thanks to the natural resources of the country, every American, ②until quite recently, could reasonably ③look forward to making more money than his father, so that, if he made less, the fault must be ④him; he was either lazy or inefficient.

14   A sensible plan, if you ①have been asked to speak ②to an exact limit, is to talk your speech into a mirror and stop at your ③allotted time; then cut the speech accordingly. The more familiar you become with your speech, the more ④confident you can deliver it.

15   ①A survey by the Department of Labor found that ②three fourth of major U.S. firms recorded and reviewed their workers' communications. And about ③half of companies ④polled said they ⑤had fired or disciplined workers for violating the company's computer policies.

16   Theorists and writers ①have recuperated not just stories of slaves and slave owners but also the narrative of European modernity, wealth, and privilege, and have demonstrated how black labor and black intellectual ②work must be understood as ③having created European modernity, and not as if it ④was created by it.

17   Although ①the gathering of fish in schools is a familiar form of animal social behavior, ②how is the school formed and maintained is only beginning to be understood in detail. ③It had been thought that each fish maintains its position chiefly by means of vision. Our work has shown that the lateral line, an organ sensitive to transitory changes in water displacement, ④is as important as vision.

18   In wartime, the British economy became a highly ①specialized machine, ②largely devoting to the armed services and the production of weapons, while the US supplied ③the requirements of the civilian economy. The abrupt withdrawal of Lend-Lease in 1945 did damage to the British economy from which some would say ④it has never recovered. The British population, ⑤well fed throughout the war, now suffered owing to rationing so reduced that in the late 1940s schoolchildren began to display signs of serious malnutrition.

19   One of the modest approaches to institutional reform would build on the idea of strengthening technical support for judges. Frequently discussed options ①including the increased use of court-appointed experts, special masters or technically trained law clerks in complex cases. ②A formal means of moving in this direction is already available under the Federal Rules of Evidence, which grant judges broad powers ③to seek help from court-appointed experts or panels if they believe that such procedures will assist the process of scientific fact-finding. This power, in practice, ④is only rarely used by the federal courts.

[20] Choose the sentence that is NOT grammatically correct.

20

① What I'll do is postpone the meeting.

② What I object to is that he lied about it.

③ Whether we will finish on time ruined the afternoon.

④ While I was working in Boston, I lived with my aunt.

⑤ Whether we will succeed depends primarily on the weather.

[01-09] Choose the one that best completes the sentence.

01   The most important thing to know about prehistoric humans is that they were insignificant animals with _____ impact on their environment than gorillas, fireflies or jellyfish.

① bigger

② no less

③ no more

④ higher

⑤ worse

02   There was a loud laugh, the most startling _____ was the Baronet's.

① of which

② which

③ that

④ it

03   A large department store had an optical department where people could get eye exams and buy glasses. One day the optical department _____ giving free eye exams. So, this was announced over the store's public address system: "The optical department _____ giving a free eye screening today." A lot of people who were shopping at the store heard the announcement and hurried to the optical department, where a long line formed. It turned out, however, that the people weren't waiting for a free eye screening; they were waiting for free ice-cream.

① was — has been

② is — was

③ had been — was

④ was — is

04 _____ is that in digital form, no one's secrets stay secret.

① All are really clear

② What is really clarity

③ All that's really clear

④ What are really clear

05 As early as the 2nd century A.D., the Chinese _____ the three basic elements of printing — paper, ink, and the notion of the woodblock.

① had their command

② had at their command

③ had their command at

④ had at their command of

06 In Japan, _____, advertising influences people to buy more and more. However, the Seikatsu Club is fighting against this.

① as many countries

② as in many other countries

③ as many other countries

④ as in another countries

07 Given its focus on keeping people employed and minimizing strikes and protests, Beijing will not hesitate to invest _____.

① ten of billions more if needed

② ten of billions more if need be

③ tens of billion more if needed

④ tens of billions more if need be

08   Billboards and radio are complementary media, each _____ for certain kinds of advertisements because some messages need to be seen and others need to be heard for them to have their greatest impact.

　　① having advantages over the other

　　② had advantages over the other

　　③ being advantages over the others

　　④ been advantages over the others

09   We have a responsibility toward the other life-forms of our planet _____ the thoughtless behavior of our own human species.

　　① whose continued existence is threatened by

　　② which continued existence is threatening by

　　③ of their continuing existence is threaten by

　　④ of whose continuing existence is threatened by

　　⑤ their continuing existence of which is threatening by

[10-19] Choose the one that is NOT correct in standard English.

10   All ①the students ②in the dormitories were forbidden, ③unless they ④had special passes, ⑤from staying out after 11:45 pm.

11   When we took him ①to a neighborhood restaurant and offered him ②some delicious food, he suddenly cheered up, ③looked us at the eye, and ④treated us friendly, smiling.

12   By the late 1960s, ①the pieces of the puzzle had already ②started to fell into place; but one clue ③was so obvious that nearly everyone ④engaged in the research somehow missed it.

13 English, the native language of ①over 400 million people ②scattering across every ③continent, is used in some way by one ④out of seven human beings around the globe, making it ⑤the most widely spoken language in history.

14 Some of the old worries about AI were ①closely linked to the question of ②whether computers could think. The first massive electronic computers, capable ③of rapid computation and little or no creative activity, were soon ④dubbing "electronic brains."

15 Many species of fish, particularly smaller fish, travel in schools, ①moving in tight formations often with the precision of the most highly disciplined unit on parade. Some move in synchronized hordes, ②as others move in starkly geometric forms. ③In addition to the varieties of shapes of schools of fish, there are ④countless varieties of schooling behaviors.

16 After ①a few thousand years of continuous interchange between the external uses of mathematics and ②its internal structure, these two aspects of the subject have become so ③dense interwoven that picking them apart is almost impossible. The mental attitudes ④involved are more readily distinguishable, though, ⑤leading to a broad classification of mathematics into two kinds: pure and applied.

17 While advances in transplant medicine have made ①it possible to preserve and extend the life of individuals with end-stage organ disease, some scholars note ②what the biomedical view of organ transplantation as a bounded event, ③which ends once a heart, liver or kidney is successfully replaced, ④belies the complex, dynamic, and generative process ⑤embedded in the experience of receiving an organ.

18   Had David posed his question to the scholarly community, they ①would declare that his 'hair eels' were yet another case of pesky parasitic worms and not the fish in an early stage of development. But the factory engineer knew not of peer review. He presented his exceptional findings not to the Royal Society for serious scrutiny, but ②instead to a pair of farmers he bumped into one day, who ③were perplexed by the quantities of silver eel in a ditch on their land. So he explained his theory that this profusion of eels ④had emerged from a beetle's bum and was delighted by their response.

19   In these circumstances, variation in exposure to community violence accounts for slightly less than 10% of the variance in psychological distress among the individuals ①comprising the samples. There is not a one-to-one correspondence between amount of exposure and amount of distress; obviously other variables also ②affect the level of psychological distress. Nevertheless, in a broader context, ③the impact of exposure to community violence on psychological distress is substantial. The effect size for the relationship between exposure to community violence and psychological distress ④is equal or larger than the effect sizes estimated by meta-analyses for other psychosocial stressors ⑤such as the experience of child sexual abuse, natural disasters, and negative life events.

[20] Choose the sentence that is NOT grammatically correct.

20   ① I need a pen, but I haven't got one.
       ② Should I wear the red shirt or the blue?
       ③ Kim had no money, and Pat also had none.
       ④ They sent twenty copies, but several were damaged.
       ⑤ Look through this box of screws and pick out some small.

[01-09] Choose the one that best completes the sentence.

01   Every non-Western society is searching for a path to modernity that it can feel _____ in some way local, authentic and, in that sense, non-Western.

① is

② are

③ being

④ be

02   In most countries faced with the problem of poverty, the single most important fight is the fight to break the cycle of poverty in which a family remains poor for generations because they know no _____ way of life and no means of escape.

① other

② so

③ such

④ another

03   More challenging to attain _____ that nationalists set before themselves, the quest for a united nation.

① the task was

② the task

③ was the task

④ be the task

⑤ being the task

04   Her trip took her thousands of miles over a period of two years, _____ she had to endure treacherous winds and storms as she crossed the Southern Ocean.

① during the time

② time during which

③ during which time

④ which during the time

05   He believes that sharks are eating _____ calories because of the boats and snorkelers.

① less and taking less

② less and taking fewer

③ fewer and taking fewer

④ less and taking in fewer

⑤ fewer and taking in less

06   The only devils in this world are those running around in our own hearts, and that is where _____.

① all our battles should fight

② whole our battles should fight

③ all our battles should be fought

④ whole our battles should be fought

⑤ the whole of our battles should fight

07   Not stirring a muscle, F'lessan watched the exodus. Only when all made their way down the track, spreading out on their separate ways, _____ the opening.

① did the bronze rider approach

② the bronze rider had approached

③ the bronze rider approaches

④ has approached the bronze rider

⑤ approached the bronze rider

08   Bone is one of the hardest materials in the body and, _____, it has a remarkable ability to resist tension and other forces acting on it.

① although relatively light in weight

② having been relatively light in weight

③ that it is relatively light in weight

④ to be relatively light in weight

09   As rainfall began to decrease in the Southwest about the middle of the 12th century, most of the Monument Valley Anasazi abandoned their homes to join other clans _____.

① having less limitations to water access

② with less limitations on water access

③ whose access to water was less limited

④ where they had less limited water access

⑤ where there was access to water that was less limited

[10-19] Choose the one that is NOT correct in standard English.

10   There are many complaints these days ①<u>about gentrification</u> — ②<u>the idea</u> of wealthy people ③<u>revitalize</u> forgotten, ④<u>crime-ridden</u> urban neighborhoods.

11   ①<u>Under the protocols</u> of the blood feud, one act of revenge begot ②<u>another</u>, so that violence ③<u>originating in</u> some forgotten crime ④<u>or slight</u> could reverberate ⑤<u>in generations</u>.

12   Behind the ①<u>acrobats and rawing lions</u>, there can be seen ②<u>a single doleful clown</u>, wandering through the entrance of ③<u>the big-top circus doors</u> without ④<u>once slipping or tripping up</u>.

13   When there are lots of reservations during peak season, these companies can ①charge higher prices and ②still be sure that somebody will ③need their services ④no matter how much it is cost.

14   The ①continued popularity of his novels suggests that the subjects ②which they repeatedly consider and the values ③which they ascribe ④with them are also repeatedly contemplated and ⑤found congenial by their many readers.

15   The accident was a particularly sad one, ①inasmuch as the ②drowned men were quite young and lived with their families in town, and all were intimate friends out on a day of pleasure, ③who had been arranged for some time past. ④No error.

16   Persistent American fears of ①being overshadowed economically by China ②are not entirely ③unfounded since the Asian nation ④whose seemingly boundless energy appears to promise to sustain its growth ⑤hinging upon its ever-expanding domestic market.

17   Indian pashmina, ①better known as cashmere, is a highly prized wool. It's six times thinner than human hair and can cost several thousand dollars on the international market when ②turns into a single scarf. But the nomadic Changpas, ③most of whom are poor and illiterate, don't see much of that money. Middlemen buy the raw pashmina wool for anything from $40 to $80 a kilogram and sell it ④for up to five times more.

18   The birds were soaring round the tree tops until ①it looked as if a vast net with thousands of black knots in it had been cast up into the air; ②which after a few moments sank slowly down upon the trees until every twig seemed to have a knot at the end of ③them. Then, suddenly, the net would be thrown into the air again, as though to be thrown into the air and ④settle slowly down upon the tree tops were a tremendously exciting experience.

19 It is clearer than ever ①before that nationalism and national interests, particularly those of the United States, remain at least as important as ②the interests of particular multinational corporations in shaping conflicts around the globe. The US and the EU have refused to co-operate in the process of ③formulating a UN treaty seeking to prevent human rights abuses by transnational corporations; they did this in spite of ④a majority of UN member-states voted for such a treaty (Inter Press Service 2014). The United States has started to bomb parts of Iraq, in order to ⑤forestall the newly consolidating Islamic State in Syria and Iraq, whose militants are also ranged against Kurdish nationalists seeking to form a national entity of their own.

[20] Choose the sentence that is NOT grammatically correct.

20　　① The hotel was very welcoming.
　　② We much agree with the decision.
　　③ The new by-pass was very much needed.
　　④ I was very much surprised by her news.
　　⑤ I much prefer seeing films at the cinema than on TV.

[01-09] Choose the one that best completes the sentence.

01   Every art causes those to whom the artist's feeling is transmitted to unite in soul with the artist, and also _____ all who receive the same impression.

① with

② about

③ that

④ for

02   In politeness research, the concept of "face" is important with its connotation of the set of rules _____ a person's dignity and group harmony are preserved.

① which

② by which

③ that

④ in that

03   Less measurable _____ profound is a sapping of confidence across our land; a nagging fear that America's decline is inevitable, that the next generation must lower its sights.

① and no more

② and no less

③ but no less

④ but not more

⑤ but no more

04 Football superstardom is most often bestowed _____ least equipped to deal with its temptations and stresses: young men, rich in cash and testosterone, poor in judgment.

① on very people

② by the people

③ on the very people

④ on people by the

05 Now I suppose I land on another person and kill that person. I would not be morally responsible for the unfortunate death, _____ the billiard ball would be morally responsible if it fell from a great height and hit someone on the head.

① any more than

② as much as

③ not so much as

④ so more than

⑤ no more than

06 Everyone charged with a penal offence has the right to _____ until proven guilty according to law in a public trial.

① presume innocent

② be presumed innocence

③ presume innocence

④ be presumed innocent

07 A culture is learned by individuals as the result of belonging to some particular group, and it constitutes that part of learned behavior which is shared with others. It is our social legacy, _____ our organic heredity.

① with as a contrast to

② as to contrasting

③ as contrasted with

④ with contrasting as

08   Not only _____ atoms with their microscopes, but they now can also "feel" them with the aid of a versatile sensing device called the "magic wrist."

① today's scientists are able to see

② are today's scientists able to see

③ being able to see today's scientists

④ are able to see today's scientists

09   Mr. Zimmerman, a well-known meteorologist, told my brother _____ in the island, and advised him to prepare for the worst situation.

① like what the weather conditions would be

② what would be the weather conditions like

③ like what would be the weather conditions

④ what the weather conditions would be like

[10-19] Choose the one that is NOT correct in standard English.

10   Over the past decade, several companies ①devoted ②to develop meat alternatives ③have emerged, and they're now beginning ④to prosper.

11   Whitman wrote *Leaves of Grass* as a tribute to the Civil War soldiers who ①had laid on the battlefields and ②whom he ③had seen ④while serving as an army nurse.

12   My friend offered to ①take up yoga with me but after I ②turned down him he seemed to ③give up on me, and later I realized I had ④thrown away a good chance to change my life.

13   Harris, who left the summit shortly after I did, soon ①pulled up behind me. Wanting to preserve ②what oxygen remained in my tank, I asked him ③to reach inside my backpack and turn off the valve on my regulator, ④which he did.

14 Academic psychology in America ①<u>has been dominated</u> during ②<u>the most of</u> the past half-century by theories of ③<u>learning and memory</u>, and this reflects America's ④<u>practical bent</u> and its concern with how psychology can improve ⑤<u>the way people</u> learn to live.

15 In modern practice, social justice, which asserts that all people should have equal access ①<u>with</u> wealth, health, and opportunity, revolves around ②<u>favoring or punishing</u> different groups of the population, ③<u>regardless of</u> any given individual's choices or actions, ④<u>based on</u> value judgements ⑤<u>regarding</u> historical events, current conditions, and group relations.

16 Laurie Hunter wanted to know what disease was attacking her daughter Amanda, ①<u>who</u> by the age of 2 months was not developing normally. Her muscle tone was low. She wasn't lifting her head. She was ②<u>slowly</u> to talk, and she didn't walk until she was 2. "As a mother, you know that everything that happens to your child is not your fault, ③<u>yet</u> you still feel responsible," says Hunter, 42, a high school English teacher who ④<u>lives</u> in Jackson, New Jersey.

17 Presumably, ①<u>occasional</u> viable crosses between humans and chimpanzees are possible. The natural experiment ②<u>must have been tried</u> very infrequently, at least recently. If such off-spring ③<u>are</u> ever produced, what will their legal status be? The cognitive abilities of chimpanzees compel us to raise searching questions about the boundaries of the community of beings ④<u>which</u> special ethical considerations are due, and can, I hope, help to extend our ethical perspectives.

18 The great challenge of this "Women's Rights" conference is to give voice to women everywhere whose experiences ①<u>go unnoticed</u>, whose words go unheard. Women ②<u>comprise</u> more than half the world's population, 70 percent of the world's poor, and two-thirds of those who ③<u>are not taught</u> to read and write. We are the primary caretakers for most of the world's children and elderly. Yet much of the work we do ④<u>does not value</u> — not by economists, not by historians, not by popular culture, not by government leaders.

19   The growth of interest in digital media over the past two decades has contributed substantively ①to our heightened awareness of medium as a methodological question. The process of theorizing the digital representation of objects of study has also required us to ②attend the meanings of their original medium. But other influences have been crucial as well: the renewed attention to ③textual materiality spurred by Jerome McGann's and D. F. McKenzie's groundbreaking work, accompanied interest in ④the history of the book and ⑤the politics of textual production, all of which have rendered our understanding of authorship and textuality immeasurably more complex.

[20] Choose the sentence that is NOT grammatically correct.

20   ① No sooner did I sleep, I started to snore.
      ② There is not the least snow on the road.
      ③ A whale is no more a fish than a dog is.
      ④ Mt. Everest is tallest among all mountains.
      ⑤ No less than half the students failed the exam.

[01-09] Choose the one that best completes the sentence.

01   The committee meets again on Sunday to vote _____ priority groups should have access to coronavirus vaccines in the next phase of distribution.

    ① that

    ② on which

    ③ which

    ④ whose

02   We can't yet assume Omicron is _____ than previous variants. We must be humble in the face of this virus.

    ① weak

    ② stronger

    ③ less severe

    ④ much serious

    ⑤ seriously

03   In the United States, the emphasis was _____ the Constitution as a symbol or historical object as on the Constitution as a depository of democratic beliefs that were said to be fundamental and unshakable.

    ① not so much as on

    ② so much not on

    ③ not so much on

    ④ on not so much as

04 Carnivorous mammals can endure what would otherwise be lethal level of body heat because they have a heat-exchange network _____ the brain from getting too hot.

① which kept

② which has kept

③ that has been keeping

④ that keeps

⑤ having kept

05 _____ as customers to the luxury group that all sales associates who have worked for Louis Vuitton for more than two weeks from around world are sent to Paris to attend a seminar called "Understanding the Japanese Culture."

① So important are they

② Importantly they are

③ They are important so

④ So important they are

06 Massachusetts Republican Ed Brooke proposed that _____ the White House.

① sends a delegation to

② should be sent a delegation

③ a delegation be sent to

④ a delegation should send

07 Nurturing a sense of empathy, where everyone's progress is valued, _____ a growth mindset in students, enabling them to achieve more in their learning.

① and the course is instilled

② so the course is instilled with

③ the course instills

④ the course instilling of

08   Many suggestions have been made about the origin of the dollar symbol $, _____ it derives from the figure 8, representing the Spanish 'piece of eight'.

　　① that being one of the commonest
　　② being one of the commonest that
　　③ one of the commonest being that
　　④ one being that of the commonest

09   Of all the vast tides of migration that have swept through history, _____ the wave that brought 12 million immigrants onto American shores in little more than three decades.

　　① it may be that none is more concentrated as
　　② perhaps none was more concentrated than
　　③ perhaps it is none that is more concentrated than
　　④ maybe it is none that was more concentrated than
　　⑤ maybe none is more concentrated as

[10-19] Choose the one that is NOT correct in standard English.

10   The ①highly informative book is ②itself a product of — and a ③contribution — this ④cumulative culture.

11   ①In years past, no movie director ②with a shred of pride would think of dabbling ③on commercials. But directing TV ads has become ④downright fashionable even among Hollywood's biggest names.

12   One aspect ①of this hoary problem is the question: "What justification, ②if ever, can be ③given for the claim that one can tell, on the basis ④of someone's behavior, that he is in a certain mental state?"

13   The ①excruciating focus on nuclear weapons and war ②was all the more remarkable because it was irrelevant to the challenges most ③galling to Americans in 1980, the plight of American hostages in Iran and the nation's ④sagged economic position in the world.

14   In trying to discover the truth and ①find the right path, we should exercise our utmost humility and discretion and ②in putting the truth into practice not a shred of selfish interest ③either desire ④should be allowed to intervene, ⑤as the ancient sages teach us.

15   Language, however, is organized in ①such utterly different ways from primate or mammalian ②calls and it conveys such utterly different kinds of meanings, ③that I find ④how impossible to imagine a realistic sequence by which natural or sexual selection could have converted a call system into a language.

16   Never before ①have so many people packed into cities — places such as Los Angeles, Istanbul, Tokyo, and Lima — that are regularly affected by earthquakes. ②Locating near the edge of Earth's huge, shifting plates, these cities face the risk of death and economic disaster from large quakes — and from the tsunamis, fires, and other destruction they often ③cause. We understand earthquakes better than we ④did a century ago. Now, scientists would like to predict them, but is this possible?

17   Although only a small percentage of the electromagnetic radiation that is emitted by the Sun is ultraviolet (UV) radiation, the amount that is emitted would be enough ①to cause severe damage to most forms of life on earth ②were it all to reach the surface of the earth. Fortunately, all of the Sun's ultraviolet radiation does not reach the earth ③because of a layer of oxygen, called the ozone layer, ④encircling the earth in the stratosphere at an altitude of about 15 miles above the earth. The ozone layer absorbs much of the Sun's ultraviolet radiation and prevents it ⑤to reach the earth.

18 ①Having given the assumption that slavery obviously distorts the ideals of America, it is not surprising that the history of the United States is often imagined ②in terms of the progressive revelation of the clear and explicit meaning of this declaration. In his magisterial study of US citizenship, Rogers Smith, for example, has explored ③the extent to which an ascriptive political tradition, one that establishes political identities on the basis of race, gender, and religion, has ④competed with this nation's liberal tradition and worked to block the expression of the Declaration's ideals of freedom and equality.

19 Gates showed his fearful side in ①what became known as the "nightmare memo." In a four-day period, from June 17 to June 20, 1991, Bill Gates's personal fortune dropped more than $300 million as Microsoft stock suddenly ②fell 11 percent when a memo filled with "nightmare" scenarios leaked its way to the *San Jose Mercury News*. Written by Gates himself, the memo listed a series of worries and threats about competitors, technology, intellectual property, legal cases, and Microsoft's customer-support shortcomings and proclaimed that "our nightmare is a reality." Keep in mind that at the time of the memo, Microsoft was rapidly becoming the most powerful player in its industry, with Windows ③in the verge of becoming one of the most dominant software products ever. Anyone who understood Gates would've known that the memo didn't signal a change; he'd always lived in fear, always felt vulnerable, and he ④would continue to do so. "If I really believed this stuff about our invincibility," he said the year after the nightmare memo, "I suppose I would take more vacations."

[20] Choose the sentence that is NOT grammatically correct.

20 ① They regard it as a discourtesy that you didn't notify them earlier.
② I find that he tried to retract his statement hardly surprising.
③ It's not that I don't understand what you're trying to say.
④ It looked as if he was trying to hide his true identity.
⑤ We owe it to you that we got off so lightly.

[01-09] Choose the one that best completes the sentence.

01 It is hard to say which _____ the above-mentioned factors is most responsible for the distortion and misunderstanding of his philosophy.

① by
② with
③ in
④ of

02 The proliferation of regional institutions, their expanding functions _____ both traditional and transitional issues, and the growing incidence of inter-regionalism, may introduce a healthy diversity and leadership into the emerging world order.

① covered
② cover
③ covering
④ are covered

03 Scientists worry that the world's population is expanding at _____ rate than there is enough food to provide for.

① the fast
② the faster
③ a much faster
④ a much more fast

04 _____ exerted by tornadoes that they have been known to lift railroad locomotives off their tracks.

① The great force is

② The force is great

③ Never has the force

④ How great the force is

⑤ So great is the force

05 Drug overdose deaths in the U.S. reached _____ in 2020 at more than 91,000, far exceeding totals for the previous year.

① another record high

② another high recording

③ other record high

④ other high recording

06 The long debate over lowering the voting age in America from 21 to 18 began during World War II and intensified during the Vietnam War, when young men denied the right to vote _____ to fight for their country.

① to be conscripted

② were being conscripted

③ as they were conscripted

④ with being conscripted

07 Republicans are mounting an assault on women's health and freedom that would deny _____ affordable contraception and life-saving cancer screenings.

① millions of women access to

② millions of women to access

③ to access millions of women

④ access to millions of women

08   Underneath the stone _____ where each layer had several items placed on it to serve as offerings to the gods.

① was a multilayered chamber founded

② a multilayered chamber has found

③ were found a multilayered chamber

④ a multilayered chamber has founded

⑤ was found a multilayered chamber

09   _____ the language is the unsettling social syntax in America.

① Puzzling and complicating more than

② Rather puzzled and complicated than

③ More puzzling and complicated than

④ Puzzled and complicating rather than

[10-19] Choose the one that is NOT correct in standard English.

10   There is no ①gainsaying the fact that ②the privileged seldom give up their privileges ③of their own accord without ④coercing into doing so.

11   But ①while the statue still standing, ②amid the entanglements of barbed wire, ③the soldiers took heart and refused to ④completely abandon hope.

12   He sat there, ①lost and lonely in a strange city, ②visualizing the nightmare of ③getting all the paperwork ④organizing again from a distant country while ⑤trying to settle down in a new one.

13   There are no standards for ①how long a hosted data repository will be available, nor ②there are ③agreed-upon procedures for insulating data repository maintenance ④from changes in the host's funding.

14   In the present age, ①in which science has made amazing inventions and discoveries but morality has not developed ②so much, the future of human beings ③would be dark unless the young people ④were not fully trained not only in intelligence ⑤but in morality.

15   Over the years rice ①has become one of the world's most popular foods. It was probably grown first in China ②many thousands of years ago. From there ③it spread to India and other countries. Now rice is grown in ④dozens of countries that have the water and warm temperatures it needs. In fact, rice is the main food for nearly ⑤the half world's people.

16   Numerous facts about cultural diversity ①as well as empirical evidence about universal principles of cognition have contributed to the foundations of many theories ②exploring the links between culture and intelligence. There are several cognitive processes — recognition, categorization, thinking, and memory — ③the analysis of that will perhaps ④shed some light on differences and similarities in intellectual functioning among various ethnic groups.

17   They had driven for more than two hours and had not yet spoken a word. He then heard a strange sound from her, a kind of ①muffled chewing noise, as if something inside her ②were grinding its way out. She looked at him with her ashen face and she burst into tears. He began to cry ③himself, and pulled the car over onto the narrow shoulder of the turnpike, where they stayed for the next half hour or so, the blank-faced cars ④droned by them in the cold, onrushing night.

18   If one looks at living standards in recent years, ①they show that the south east, south, south west, East Anglia and the East Midlands tend to do ②much better than the peripheral areas. Over a century ago, the novelist Mrs. Gaskell wrote a book entitled *North and South*, about a heroine forced to move to the fictitious county of Darkshire, ③who confessed 'a detestation for the north of England'. Mutual prejudice between a complacent population in the south and a proud one in the north ④persist.

19   Radical changes are occurring in ①that democratic societies teach the young, and these changes have not been ②well thought through. Thirsty for national profit, nations, and their systems of education, are heedlessly discarding skills that are needed ③to keep democracies alive. If this trend continues, nations all over the world ④will soon be producing generations of useful machines, rather than complete citizens who can think for themselves, criticize tradition, and understand the significance of another person's sufferings and achievements. The future of the world's democracies ⑤hangs in the balance.

[20] Choose the sentence that is NOT grammatically correct.

20   ① The graft and bribery scandal gave him a black eye.
    ② The same cause does not always give rise the same effect.
    ③ Police wanted all witnesses to give an account of what they saw.
    ④ Even though the chances were slim, he gave it his best shot.

▶▶▶ ANSWERS P.382

[01-09] Choose the one that best completes the sentence.

01   Just as the passengers on a ship see only the one-ninth of an iceberg which is _____ water, so the audience is aware of only a small part of the energy expended in preparing and delivering a speech.

     ① above   ② over

     ③ below   ④ under

02   We're exercising the neural circuits devoted to skimming and multitasking while ignoring _____ used for reading and thinking deeply.

     ① what   ② which

     ③ those   ④ it

03   Scientists say tumors vary from person to person, and so _____.

     ① is their treatment

     ② will they be treated

     ③ should their treatment

     ④ they have been treated

04   When a pack of nine wolves escaped from their enclosure, there were not many people in the zoo, and at no time _____ immediate danger.

     ① was the public under

     ② the public was in

     ③ the public was under

     ④ was the public in

05   He was elected after a campaign _____ expand motorsport participation around the world.

① in that he has promised

② which he has promised

③ that he promised to

④ in which he promised to

06   _____ blessed opportunity and, therefore, such a profound obligation to build "the more perfect Union" of our founders' dreams.

① Since we have before such

② We have never had such before

③ Before we had never a such

④ Never before have we had such a

07   Elizabeth Bishop published relatively few poems in her lifetime, yet most critics considered her _____.

① who as a significant literary figure

② a significant literary figure

③ a literary significant figure

④ as a literary figure she was significant

08   A pack of hyena can catch prey _____ bring down that it pays each selfish individual to hunt in a pack, even though this involves sharing food.

① so larger much than a lone hyena can

② much so larger than can a lone hyena

③ so much larger than can a lone hyena

④ so much larger than a lone hyena can

⑤ much so larger than a lone hyena can

09   _____ Wednesday after the strongest earthquake to hit the poor Caribbean nation in more than 200 years crushed thousands of structures.

① Having gravely injured Haitians pleaded to help

② Gravely injured Haitians pleaded to help

③ Having gravely injured, Haitians are pleaded for help

④ Gravely injured Haitians pleaded for help

[10-19] Choose the one that is NOT correct in standard English.

10   He hastily picked up ①the remains of what ②it looked like a fast food meal, ③sweeping plates from the table and stuffing them ④into a plastic bag.

11   Indeed, doctors — ①especially dermatologists — keep their ②eyes on the skin for all ③manner of clues to ④underlie disease and other conditions ⑤affecting a woman's health.

12   Psychologists in the Freudian mold would ①bring up the concept of a "death wish," a ②deep-seating impulse to flirt ③with personal annihilation and pose several ④more-convincing possibilities.

13   ①Although claims that these food products are based on "sound science," in truth, neither manufacturers nor the government ②has studied the effects of these genetically ③altered organisms or their new proteins ④on people — especially on babies, the elderly, and ⑤the sick.

14   I was sitting at my desk when I ①remembered that this was the day of my chemistry final! I was terrified because I hadn't studied a bit for it. In fact, I had missed ②every lecture all semester. In a panic, I began running across campus desperately searching for the classroom, ③to that I'd never been. It was hopeless; I knew I was going ④to fail and flunk out of college.

15   As soon as I saw the elephant I knew with perfect certainty that I ①should not have shot him. It is a serious matter to shoot a working elephant — it is comparable to destroying a huge and ②costly piece of machinery — and obviously one ought not to do it if it can possibly be avoided. And at that distance, peacefully eating, the elephant looked ③no more dangerous than a cow. Moreover, I did not ④in the least want to shoot him.

16   After wheat, ①the second most important crop to have reached America from the Old World is usually said to be rice. In colonial times, rice made a vital contribution in areas ②where wheat failed. Its introduction in Panama in the late sixteenth century made those areas ③as viable parts of the Spanish empire. It became part of the culinary heritage of much of the Caribbean, especially where Indian labor ④was introduced by the British.

17   While they relieved me of one difficulty, they brought on another even more painful than the one ①which I was relieved of. The more I read, the more I was led to detest my enslavers. I could regard them in no other light ②as a band of successful robbers, who had stolen us from our homes. As I read and contemplated the subject, that very discontentment which Master Hugh had predicted ③would follow my learning to read had already come, ④to torment my soul to unutterable anguish.

18   A president who claims he has an absolute right to declare a national emergency and ①spend government funds that Congress has refused to appropriate for the ends he seeks ②is also assuming the role of a dictator. A president who spouts lies during a prime-time national television address over what he terms an "undeniable crisis" at the southern US border, which is in fact no crisis at all, is using ③whatever means are available to him with a view to ④preserve his base of power.

19 Remaking California's Central Valley wetlands was a complicated project ①that took much of the 20th century. ②Resurrected from degraded farmland and cash-strapped gun clubs, assembled by bulldozer and backhoe, the current patchwork of national wildlife refuges, state wildlife areas, and county preserves ③are much diminished from the four million acres of primeval wetlands that spanned the Central Valley ④before it was farmed. Nevertheless, these habitats are ecologically significant on a hemispheric level, ⑤serving 60 percent of migratory waterfowl on the Pacific Flyway, including three million ducks and two million geese.

[20] Choose the sentence that is NOT grammatically correct.

20   ① Mr. Kang, with whom I worked for many years, is retiring tomorrow.
   ② In my school, I met inspiring peers, some of whom became my friends.
   ③ She asked me a lot of questions, most of which I couldn't answer.
   ④ The building, on the top of which we can see from here, was beautiful.

[01-09] Choose the one that best completes the sentence.

01   Harriet drew up a paper on the subject of liberty. For her liberty was not a question of how far the State ought or ought not to interfere with the activities of citizens. It was a question of tolerance in society itself, of some people being impinged upon by other people. The problem of liberty for her was not one of political liberty _____ social liberty.

① rather

② less than

③ much as

④ so much as

02   A male fruit fly has a single thought — to win the heart of a female fly. On spotting a female, he performs a carefully choreographed dance, orienting toward the female, following her, and tapping on her with his legs. He sings a courtship song by vibrating one wing. _____ his execution is proper and the female is aroused, she accepts his advances and a successful copulation ensues.

① However

② Without

③ If

④ Nor

03   In addition _____, poor sleepers are also at a much higher risk of other serious illnesses and diseases.

① to gain a weight

② gaining weight

③ to weight gain

④ weight gaining

04   _____ our experience that we human beings grow wiser and gain greater control over our lives.

① It is making sense of by

② By making sense of it is

③ By it is making sense of

④ It is by making sense of

05   Regions lying due east or west of one another share the same latitude, and therefore the same day length and seasonality. They are also likely to share similar climates, habitats and diseases, all of which means that crops, livestock and humans can spread east and west more easily, since the conditions _____ are similar.

① that they adapted

② to which they have adapted

③ which were adapted

④ of whichever have been adapted

06   Even today, without Social Security, _____ would be forced into poverty.

① half our nation's elderly

② half of elderly's our nation

③ our nation's elderly of half

④ elderly's our nation half

07   The woolly musk ox, _____ survives on Ellesmere Island.

① once hunted almost to extinction

② hunted almost once to extinction

③ almost hunted once to extinction

④ hunted almost to once extinction

08   In the park _____ lions, monkeys, and flamingos.

① are more than 600 animals including

② more than 600 animals are included

③ more than 600 animals are inclusive

④ are more than 600 animals included

09   The new employee gets along with his colleagues, _____.

① despite he does not speak English

② although he does not speak English

③ for he does not speak English

④ in spite of that he does not speak English

[10-19] Choose the one that is NOT correct in standard English.

10   Just as ①there are no two sets of fingerprints ②alike in the world, ③so that the imprints of animals have ④similar uniqueness.

11   ①Ask a veteran of South Carolina politics ②to name the ugliest chapter in his state's low-down and dirty political history, ③or he may be slow ④to answer.

12   ①At least part of their great secret ②is that ③they both live in the same country. White and black have shared that secret for a long time now, and ④has done an efficient job of keeping ⑤it from each other.

13   In both ①their public and private spheres, the nation is rightly acting to reduce ②many of the risks ③which people have no choice ④but to hazard — on the road, in factories, in the environment, ⑤even in the field of speculative finance.

14 The new e-book, *Globish The World Over*, observes how ①a billion people are in need of a consistent language to do business across the globe, ②describes how the problem is being solved by many non-native English speakers, and discusses the specific outlines of the Globish approach ③that is being note as perhaps the only possibility for true Global talk. ④No error.

15 Post-humanists, aka transhumanists, point to future bio-medical tech like implants as evidence that humans will not evolve in the way we ①have up to now. Google chief engineer, Ray Kurzweil, expounding a theory that is prevalent in Silicon Valley, sees ②known human history ending due to the rapid growth of technological development and a new barely-imagined world ③appeared instead to replace ④it.

16 Most people would like to conserve as ①much of the Earth's resources as possible. Yet such a thing is easier said than ②to do. Whether it is consuming gas to drive to work or using an electricity-powered washing machine, what were once viewed as luxuries or conveniences ③are now considered necessities, and it is a rare person who would actually ④willingly give them up.

17 Sexual selection could be invoked to explain a great deal that ①otherwise seemed inexplicable in terms of natural selection, such as the bright plumage of many male birds that renders them more ②conspicuous to predators. Such structures did not confer any advantage in the struggle for existence, but they were advantageous in the struggle for mates and thus gave ③them possessors a better chance of leaving more offspring than other less ④well-endowed males.

18 No matter how generally motivated you are, all of us have some tasks ①that we don't want to do. Maybe we find them boring, pointless, draining, time consuming, annoying, or anxiety producing. So ②how you get moving in these types of situations? The first step is to recognize that getting motivated doesn't mean that you have to experience a particular feeling, like excitement or anticipation. Instead, motivation is simply one or more reasons you have ③for acting in a certain way. You can decide to do something without ever getting excited about it by finding ④a personally meaningful *why*.

19 Most taxes ①<u>designing to raise revenue</u> have a distorting effect on incentives, especially on people's willingness to work. ②<u>Just as</u> a tax on cigarettes reduces the amount of smoking, an income tax reduces the amount of work people do in the formal sector. My next-door neighbor chose not to work, and instead to stay home and take care of his kids, because his wife's income ③<u>put him in a high income bracket</u>. ④<u>Had he worked and hired</u> a baby-sitter, he would have had to pay taxes on his income and on his baby-sitter's income. By staying at home, he ⑤<u>enjoyed tax-free baby-sitting</u>.

[20] Choose the sentence that is NOT grammatically correct.

20   ① From which store did you say you bought this book?
        ② What do you think which hotel we will be staying at?
        ③ Do you know which group we will be traveling with?
        ④ How come you believe that they will break up soon?
        ⑤ Who did you say will marry whom next week?

[01-09] Choose the one that best completes the sentence.

01 I am not saying that you are not honest, _____ you certainly are; I am only saying that you are not serious about your work.

① which

② though

③ because

④ unless

02 Many of our white brothers, _____ evidenced by their presence here today, have come to realize that their destiny is tied up with our destiny.

① such

② which

③ as

④ being

03 Any prizes for the photography contest that are not claimed within one month will be _____.

① considered forfeit

② forfeit considered

③ forfeited considered

④ considered forfeited

04 Clearly, immigration reform is _____ maintaining our military or managing our money supply.

① as much a federal issue as

② as much as a federal issue

③ as a much federal issue as

④ as a federal issue as much

05 War may sometimes be a necessary evil. But _____, it is always an evil, never a good.

① how necessary it is no matter

② no matter how necessary

③ how it is no matter necessary

④ how no matter necessary

06 Many analysts and investors see the potential of the Chinese electric vehicle _____.

① as too attractive to resist

② so as attractive to resistance

③ so too attractive to resistance

④ as so attractive to resist

07 _____ covered by the sea, which occupies 71 percent of the earth.

① How huge an unknown world is

② A huge unknown world is

③ A huge unknown world

④ So huge is the unknown world

08 It is crucial that paragraphs be visually consistent, so that nothing distracts the eye during reading. For example, if the first paragraph is single-spaced, then the subsequent paragraphs should also be. _____, they really boost the professional appearance of publications.

① Since they seem simple

② So long as they may seem simple

③ Simple as such rules may seem

④ As though such rules may seem simple

09 Just as the prosecutor's role has become familiar, _____ his arrival on the scene.

① are so the epigrams and questions that accompanying

② so are the epigrams and questions accompany

③ are so the epigrams and questions accompanied

④ so are the epigrams and questions that accompany

[10-19] Choose the one that is NOT correct in standard English.

10 America will ①never again have ②as a nation the spirit of adventure ③as it was before the West ④was settled.

11 The company's executives ①are holding meetings to discuss the possibility of offering ②most of employees the opportunity ③to start working ④partly from home.

12 ①Whatever role Pocahontas played, ②that Smith took to be his impending execution ③may have been nothing more than a harmless adoption ceremony ④inducting him into Powhatan's tribe.

13 It is said that under ①no previous historical system did people live as comfortable a material life or have such ②a range of alternative life-experiences ③at their disposal as in this present system. ④No error.

14 ①At issue is whether Treasury Inflation-Protected Securities, commonly ②known as TIPS, are ③too a good deal for investors; Opponents say the government ④has been losing money on them while defenders question ⑤the accounting.

15 The entries for the award for ①the most innovative ad of this year were ②of much high quality than last year's and we were all ③extremely impressed. But in the end, we decided that one entry was ④more innovative, ⑤not to mention funnier than all the others.

16 Liberal analysts ①are more likely to focus on the way that Greenspan's aversion to regulation turned innovative financial products into lethal weapons. In this view, the emergence of an unsupervised market for ②more and more exotic derivatives allowed heedless financial institutions ③put the entire financial system ④at risk.

17 As an example of AI ①pushing the human boundaries of creativity and ②helping us to discover new things, Du Sautoy cites the Continuator, a musical instrument ③training to respond to users. In 2012, French jazz musician Bernard Lubat improvised with the Continuator, which was trained in his style of musicianship, ④leaving audiences unable to distinguish the difference between the machine and the musician.

18 Like people, ants distribute the work to ①be done. Some worker ants get food and feed it to young ants. They are like farmers ②gathering food for people to eat. When the young ants eat the food, they give out ③a liquid that the grown-up ants can eat. In some colonies, the ants feed liquid food to a few special workers. These workers store it in their stomachs, ④which become very large. They spend all their time in the nest giving out liquid ⑤to whomever needs it, just like the person who runs a store.

19 A record 45% of the world's refugees are now in ①"protracted situations" that have lasted five years or more. Syrians are the latest recruits to this ②wretched club, and the welcome ③is wearing thin in the countries to which most have fled. Indeed, dismal prospects in Turkey, Jordan and Lebanon partly explain last year's exodus to Europe. Shocked to learn that they were legally obliged to help the people streaming across their borders, a growing number of European politicians and officials ④are pressing for revisions to the UN's 1951 Refugee Convention and its 1967 protocol, which make up the main framework for international protection of people ⑤fled persecution and provide the basis for the work of the United National High Commissioner for Refugees.

[20] Choose the sentence that is NOT grammatically correct.

20   ① No longer did he charm the audience with his music.
② Never again would they be separated from each other.
③ Not only was he sad but also deeply depressed was he.
④ Only on Sundays did he go to the grocer's to buy food.

[01-09] Choose the one that best completes the sentence.

01 Sisyphus's continuous pushing of the stone up the hill only _____ it roll down again served as the literary model for the third of Zeno's paradoxes.

① having

② having been

③ have

④ to have

02 Beneath the epidermal cells _____ the body-wall muscle, which is relatively thick in some species under certain circumstances.

① exist

② exists

③ exist where

④ where it existed

⑤ where exist

03 For jurors, the believability of a witness often depends _____ the witness presents evidence as on the content or relevance of that evidence.

① on how

② on as how

③ as much how

④ as much on how

04   My experience with kids is probably just as good as, _____, any high school sitter.

① if not better than

② and better than

③ better than

④ not if better than

05   It seems to be related to _____ the people were participating in the program.

① extent to which

② extent which to

③ extent the which to

④ the extent which to

⑤ the extent to which

06   MTV experienced a meteoric rise and expanded way beyond just music videos with live concerts, MTV unplugged, cartoons music awards shows and many other programs. We can also thank MTV for exposing us to non-mainstream music and artists who _____ the spotlight as they did with MTV.

① might have given

② must have been given

③ would have not been given

④ should not have given

07   The Portuguese megalithic structure _____ for religious or ceremonial purposes as well as an astronomical observatory.

① believes to have been used

② is believed to have been used

③ believes to have used

④ is believed to have used

08   Whenever I went shopping with my mother who was an outsider in an English-only world, our task inevitably led to _____ speak up to help my mother.

① so an awkward scene that I had to

② so awkward not a scene for me to

③ too an awkward scene that I had to

④ too awkward a scene for me not to

09   The region is recording a series of extreme droughts that reflect _____ as a result of an increase in greenhouse gases in the world's atmosphere.

① how climate modellers have predicted occurring

② whatever climate modellers have predicted occurring

③ what climate modellers have predicted will occur

④ however climate modellers have predicted will occur

[10-19] Choose the one that is NOT correct in standard English.

10   ①Although how a steam engine works ②are widely known, we still cannot doubt that ③some people have never ④heard of steam engines.

11   The huge blue whale, which ①is the most massive animal that ②has ever lived on Earth, can grow more than 100 feet ③long and weigh as ④many as 130 tons.

12   ①When we are filled with gratitude, we ②are transformed into a higher level of awareness that will change us ③that we live ④with a greater sense of awe and appreciation.

13   Not only is the prose-account ①obsessed with circumstantial detail, but that detail also happens to be extremely apologetic, explaining ②whatever it could happen that a man ③get trapped by the criminal. ④No error.

14 Monocular depth cues are aspects of a scene that ①yield information about depth when ②viewed with only one eye. Even with one eye ③closed, the retinal image of an object you're focused on ④growing smaller as that object moves farther away and larger as it moves closer.

15 Ukraine is vulnerable ①to Russian pressure and subterfuge. Its economy is ②in great straits and remains heavily dependent ③on Russian energy, especially natural gas. Some important reforms ④have introduced, but Ukraine still has a long way ⑤to go in its struggle to establish a stable, independent democratic state.

16 ①With fewer couples marrying in developed nations, many sociologists ②have been fretting over declining birthrates. What is it in our society today that is either keeping people from marrying ③and leading them so easily to divorce? Some argue our everyday workload has increased significantly. ④Couple that with an accompanying rise in communications and electronic devices.

17 Environmental specialists point out that emissions trading, which has been partly regulated since 2005 by the Kyoto Protocol, simply ①exacerbates global warming. They say that the system, which permits countries that have exceeded their limit of greenhouse gas emissions ②buy the right to emit from countries that have not crossed the limit, only ③results in indulging the countries that consume more and emit more, and ④that the effect of gas reduction is meager.

18 Wives in classical Greece were segregated from men other than their husbands, and severely punished ①if caught with a lover. At the least, a woman's husband ②would divorce her and send her back to her family of origin. In one notorious instance, ③an incensed Athenian husband named Euphiletos killed his wife's lover, Eratosthenes, and then won his case in court as justifiable homicide. ④Caught the adulterous pair sleeping together, Euphiletos killed his wife's naked lover on the spot.

19 The human body still stands ①at the center of the debate. Skin color matters a lot. Walking down a New York street with lots of melanin pigment in you skin means that ②whenever you are heading, the police might view you with extra suspicion. But the likes of both President Trump and President Obama will explain the significance of skin color ③in cultural and historical terms. The police view your skin color with suspicion not for any biological reason, ④but rather because of history. Presumably, the Trump camp will explain that black criminality is an unfortunate legacy of historical errors ⑤committed by white liberals and black communities.

[20] Choose the sentence that is NOT grammatically correct.

20 ① We urged Ed to be examined by a specialist.
    ② We urged it to be clear to Ed that he was on probation.
    ③ We wanted there to be an adult present.
    ④ We wanted it to be clear to Ed that he was on probation.
    ⑤ We urged a specialist to examine Ed.

[01-09] Choose the one that best completes the sentence.

01 I think that _____ work is not excessive in amount, even the dullest work is to most people less painful than idleness.

① provided
② unless
③ whatever
④ whereas

02 Empty love is commitment without intimacy or passion, _____ sometimes seen in a 30-year-old marriage that has become stagnant.

① a kind love
② the kind of love
③ kind of loving
④ kind love

03 A number of non-polluting sources of energy, _____ solar energy, wind power, and hydrogen, show great promise for the future.

① and they are
② among which are
③ of which they are
④ some of which there are

04　A new Administration in Washington has a chance to be both supportive of Israel and honest with it. Over the past three years, many Israelis have told me that President George W. Bush was _____.

① a too good friend of theirs
② a good friend of theirs too
③ too good a friend of theirs
④ theirs too good of a friend

05　Space. When most of us think about it, we think of emptiness, of the nowhere _____ we must pass to get somewhere, of sheer distance, or of the starlit reaches of the universe. Time may be money, but space is, well, nothingness, or little more than the empty hollow _____ we find ourselves.

① through which — in which
② from which — of which
③ of which — from which
④ by which — through which

06　Eventually, the technology developed to carry out the Human Genome Project, and _____, will make the whole question redundant.

① the science it has made possible
② the science has made it possible
③ it has made the science possible
④ it has the science made possible

07　Many students have a difficult time _____, especially if they believe the information is general knowledge.

① knowing when to use a citation
② when they know to use citation
③ to know when using citation
④ with knowing when a citation used

08   Stealing someone else's ideas or words and using them in a piece of writing _____ is called plagiarism.

    ① as if they were the writer's original ideas

    ② like it were the original writer's ideas of

    ③ as like the original ideas were the writer

    ④ if the writer's original ideas were like

09   _____, the wolf has been hunted to near-extinction.

    ① Because it is once considering a dangerous predator

    ② Because once considering a dangerous predator

    ③ Once considered a dangerous predator

    ④ Once considering a dangerous predator

    ⑤ Once has been considered a dangerous predator

[10-19] Choose the one that is NOT correct in standard English.

10   A shiver ran through the tree, and the wind ①sent forth a blast that ②would knock me off, had I ③not clung to the branch ④with might and main.

11   ①Surveillance capitalism is an economic system ②centered around the ③commodification of personal data with the core ④purposefully of profit-making.

12   It now ①seems to me that ②it matters most in the majority of organizations is to have reasonably intelligent, hard-working managers ③who have a sense of pride and loyalty ④toward their organization.

13   ①Interested in extra income after ②retiring from a career as a customs broker, Mr. Guippert enrolled in Santa school, ③where the coursework included lessons on ④how to talk with children, ⑤to win over Santa skeptics and building his business.

14   ①What makes parenting in a pandemic so difficult is not, first and ②foremost, the ③increased time commitment. It is not even the close-up view of your children's suffering — watching them become ④withdrawn, struggle to cheer ⑤them up, and lose weight.

15   ①Man is a reasonable being; and as such, receives from science his proper food and nourishment, but so narrow ②is the bounds of human understanding, that ③little satisfaction can be hoped for in this particular, either from the ④extent or security of his acquisitions.

16   Questions typically indicate ①what is unknown. The use of rising intonation in questions is ②coherent with "unknown is up." The use of falling intonation with statements is therefore ③concerned for "known is down." In fact, questions with falling intonation are understood not as real questions but as ④rhetorical questions indicating statements.

17   Mesopotamia and Assyria, if not actually the cradle of mankind, were the theatre ①on which the descendants of Noah performed their first conspicuous part. Events ②that are so various and important must invest the countries ③which they occurred with a deep interest; and that portion of them, in particular, ④which has reference to the early postdiluvian ages, cannot fail to excite the curiosity of those ⑤who delight in marking the moral progress of mankind.

18 Our spacecraft was being strengthened by the insertion of more rivets than were being lost. Only since about ten thousand years ago ①<u>has there been</u> any sign that that process might be more or less permanently reversed. ②<u>That</u> was when a single species, *Homo sapiens*, began ③<u>its</u> meteoric rise to planetary dominance. And only in about the last half-century has it become clear that humanity has been forcing species and populations to extinction at a rate greatly exceeding ④<u>those</u> of natural attrition.

19 The Western was for several decades ①<u>the film genre that was defined masculinity</u>. It was where the silhouettes of John Wayne and Clint Eastwood became inscribed in cultural history, ②<u>framed by legendary directors</u> like John Ford and Sergio Leone. In reality, cowboys were overworked, underfed, and underpaid, but in cinema they could be tough, independent wanderers who chose ③<u>the freedom of the wilderness over the confines of domesticity</u>. And though the Western itself ④<u>has been declared dead</u> many times over, it always picks itself up off the dusty ground, ready for one more showdown. Even now, perhaps only the superhero could threaten the cowboy ⑤<u>as film's ultimate symbol of all-American manhood</u>.

[20] Choose the sentence that is NOT grammatically correct.

20 ① I have no faith to whatever he tells me.
② It was six weeks before I saw him again.
③ What you cannot afford to buy, do without.
④ However rich a man may be, he ought not to be idle.

T E S T

36

▶▶▶ ANSWERS P.402

[01-09] Choose the one that best completes the sentence.

01   The word "Gothic" refers to a style of art and architecture that flourished in Western Europe in the high and late medieval period. The term was initially used contemptuously to disparage these cultural products, which were deemed barbaric. _____ classical architecture had been revived during the Renaissance, the preceding Gothic style came to be seen as ostentatious and lacking in refinement.

① If
② Once
③ Unless
④ Lest

02   A happening was in essence unrepeatable; it came about _____ no one could predict, taking form from vaporous imaginings or sudden impulse.

① in that
② in which
③ where
④ in ways

03   The most effective propaganda is _____, and images tend to be much more shareable than written texts.

① that which will be shared
② which will share that
③ that will be shared
④ which that will be shared

04 It is important to note that cuneiform _____ form of writing.

① was known the earliest

② the earliest was known

③ was the earliest known

④ known the earliest was the

05 Foreign languages are ideally suited to the use of mnemonics. One common mnemonic aid _____ a word in your own language with a word in a foreign language.

① involves using images to link

② involved use images to be linked

③ involving used images is linked

④ being involved using images link

06 Buy now, and split your total _____.

① for four easy free interest payment

② to four easy free-interest payments

③ by four easy, interest free payments

④ into four easy, interest-free payments

07 If a mother shows favouritism, it should be based on differences in expectation of life. The mother, like any individual, is _____ she is to any of her children.

① twice as closely related to herself as

② twice closely as related to herself as

③ closely related twice to herself as

④ closely related to herself as twice as

⑤ closely as twice related to herself as

08   _____, he was still in some most important points a gentleman.

① Unlettered and unpolished as he was

② He was unlettered and unpolished

③ Was he unlettered and unpolished

④ As being he unlettered and unpolished

09   Inaugurated a second time on March 4, 1901, _____ focused on domestic rather than foreign policies.

① William McKinley's new term looked forward to and

② the new term looked forward to William McKinley and

③ looking forward to a new term was William McKinley

④ William McKinley looked forward to a new term

[10-19] Choose the one that is NOT correct in standard English.

10   The languages ①spoken by the Alaskan Eskimos ②and the Inuit of Northern Canada are ③such similar as to be mutually ④intelligible.

11   Back ①then, I assumed that in ②making the selections for this book and writing ③its introduction, I would be ④grappled, like my predecessors, with the questions ⑤implicit in the project.

12   It is not surprising ①that companies try to employ ②those with the right attitude and no experience than others with years of experience who act ③as if they know ④anything.

13   The reader might notice that one of ①the most influential developments explored in this book ②is the rise of the "information state" and its informational apparatus — chanceries, secretaries, surveillance, archives, and ③the like — ④designing to help assert political control over populations.

14 The flesh is not something one has, but, rather the web ①<u>which</u> one lives; it is not simply what I touch of the other, or of ②<u>myself</u>, but the condition of possibility of touch, a tactility that exceeds ③<u>any</u> given touch and that cannot be reducible ④<u>to</u> a unilateral action performed by a subject.

15 ①<u>With</u> a clear view of how interaction ②<u>itself</u> provides sites and processes for the symbolic exploration of social categorization, we can now try to look at formal institutional settings ③<u>where</u> there may not be any canonical genres ④<u>dedicating</u> to the spectacular enunciation of new ethnicities.

16 The dog is the only animal that volunteers ①<u>for duty</u>. If we want other animals — horses, oxen, mules, falcons, bears, or parrots — to ②<u>come to our aid</u>, we must force them or ③<u>bribe them</u>. You might even call horses ④<u>as our slaves.</u> Their spirit must actually be broken before they will agree to ⑤<u>do anything for us</u>.

17 ①<u>Through</u> everyday talk, Uriangateneses are regularly exposed to representations of lives in migration ②<u>organized</u> by the modernist chronotope. Over time, working-class speakers ③<u>learn</u> to use migration discourse as a point of references against ④<u>in which</u> they measure their own lives, regardless of whether they migrate.

18 Anecdotal evidence of a looming crisis in biodiversity is now ①<u>being reinforced</u> by science. In their comprehensive surveys of plants, butterflies and birds over the past 20 to 40 years in Britain, ecologists found significant population ②<u>declines</u> in a third of all native species. The problem would be bad enough if it ③<u>were</u> merely local, but it's not; because Britain's temperate ecology is similar to ④<u>those</u> in so many other parts of the world, it's the best microcosm scientists ⑤<u>have been able to</u> study in detail.

19   Our defense commitments ①<u>remain at the core of</u> the Asia-Pacific security structure, but they will evolve to reflect new circumstances and partnerships ②<u>based on the enhanced capabilities</u> of our allies and friends. Supporting democratic trends and helping to shape a frame-work for economic integration are key policy goals ③<u>which will enhance the sense of Asian-Pacific community</u>. Yet we cannot fully enter the future ④<u>while still burdening from legacies</u> of the Cold War era, particularly the military confrontation on the Korean peninsula. Moving from the Korean armistice to a stable peace and advancing Soviet-Japanese bilateral ties to make possible a peace treaty would be major steps ⑤<u>in transcending those legacies</u>.

[20] Choose the sentence that is NOT grammatically correct.

20   ① He was unkind, not even to me.
    ② He was unkind, and so was Jane.
    ③ He wasn't kind, and neither was Sue.
    ④ He was unkind, wasn't he?
    ⑤ He wasn't kind, not even to her.

[01-09] Choose the one that best completes the sentence.

01 It was the knowledge that, for all her watching, all her patient study, the reason for his humour still eluded her which filled her with foreboding dread. The guarded reserve of his seemed to her unjust, inconsiderate, and alarming. It was _____ he had stepped out beyond her reach into some section, strange and walled, where she could not get at him.

① how
② whether
③ as if
④ why

02 *Gameheaven* has been praised for its business model _____ the global growth of mobile games, earning most of its sales through game sales and partial pay-based games.

① tailor
② to tailor
③ tailoring to
④ tailored to

03 Public goods are those commodities _____ enjoyment nobody can be excluded.

① from whose
② of which
③ by whatever
④ with whom

04   Offering portions of the venture _____ investors through crowdfunding is almost by definition a common enterprise.

① to such great number of
② such to great number to
③ to such a great number of
④ great such a number to
⑤ such to great a number of

05   One thing which made the bond somewhat palatable to me was my high regard for you personally. In retrospect, it seems that the admiration might not have been mutual _____ about me, about my political beliefs and activities.

① you had known a little more
② had known you a little more
③ a more little had known you
④ a little more you had known
⑤ had you known a little more

06   Did you know that your membership _____?

① is due to expire in two months
② due to be expired in two months
③ will expire due to after two months
④ after two months due to expire

07   Competition makes _____ decent jobs without a college degree.

① young adults difficult to obtain
② difficult for young adults to obtain
③ to obtain difficult for young adults
④ it difficult for young adults to obtain

08 The cybernetic revolution has developed more rapidly than _____.

① foresaw several years ago

② foreseen several years ago

③ had foreseen several years ago

④ none have foreseen several years ago

⑤ many could have foreseen several years ago

09 In a group of islands near Florida and north of Cuba _____ known as blue holes.

① an extensive series does lie of unique caves

② do an extensive series of unique caves lie

③ lies an extensive series of unique caves

④ does an extensive series of unique caves lie

⑤ an extensive series lies of unique caves

[10-19] Choose the one that is NOT correct in standard English.

10 The ①various parts of the body require ②so different ③surgical skills that ④many surgical specialities have developed.

11 ①Carved in the limestone of a desert cliff in Egypt is ②a 5,250-year-old tableau of a victorious ruler ③who exploits ④may have been critical to the founding of Egyptian civilization.

12 The central thesis is that ①it is possible and fruitful to theorize ②about the structure and function of discourse independently ③on specific theory about the mechanisms ④that languages use to serve those functions.

13 The ①possibilities of pleasure seemed that morning so enormous and so various that ②have only a moth's part in life, and a day moth's at that, appeared a hard fate, and ③his zest in enjoying meagre opportunities to the full appeared ④pathetic.

14 Pending folder is ①which you put messages ②that you do not need to respond to immediately but ③that you need to keep 'active' for the time being — for example, ④if someone promised to get back to you and you need a reminder to follow up.

15 The issue here is to ①do with whether people are free to ②constructing their identity in ③any way they wish or whether identity construction is constrained by ④forces of various kinds, from the unconscious psyche to ⑤institutionalized power structures.

16 The end of study is ①not to possess knowledge as a man possesses the coins in his purse, ②but to make knowledge ③a part of ourselves, ④that is, to turn knowledge into thought, as the food we eat ⑤turned into the life-giving and nerve-nourishing blood.

17 In 1967, ①accidental weapon detonations on the aircraft carrier USS Forrestal in the Gulf of Tonkin killed 134 crew members, injured 161, and ②required a costly seven-month repair. The disaster was the product of a ③deviation from the rules, made in the interest of flexibility. Many of the aircraft on the carrier ④were fitted with Zuni rocket pods, each ⑤equipping with four unguided rockets.

18 Learning to write is ①in large measure learning to read. To produce something that another person will find ②worth reading, you yourself must read each draft with care, trying to imagine the effect your words are ③likely to have to your reader. An essay may start as a jotting in the margin of a book you are reading or as a brief note in a journal, and it will ④go through several drafts before it is completed.

19   How do we know what we believe we know? What we know is generally considered to be the result of our exploration and understanding of the real world, ①<u>of the way things really are</u>. After all, common sense suggests that this objective reality can be discovered. ②<u>How we know is a far more vexing</u> problem. To solve it, the mind needs to step outside itself, so to speak, and observe itself at work; for at this point we are no longer faced with facts that apparently exist independently of us in the outside world, but ③<u>with mental processes whose nature is not at all self-evident</u>. ④<u>If what we know depends on how we came to know it</u>, then our view of reality is no longer a true image of what is the case outside ourselves, but is inevitably determined also ⑤<u>by the processes which we arrived at this view</u>.

[20] Choose the sentence that is NOT grammatically correct.

20   ① Paul regrets interrupting me.
② Steve keeps interrupting me.
③ I regret being interrupted by Tom.
④ There keep being power black-outs.
⑤ There regret being power black-outs.

[01-09] Choose the one that best completes the sentence.

01   While many applied for the senior researcher's position, only those qualified _____ an interview.

① granted

② were granting

③ were granted

④ have granted

02   Scientists stress that the overall warming trend of the last decade holds much more significance _____ single year's temperatures.

① any do

② than do any

③ than any do

④ do than

03   English monarchs started believing that transforming pirates into privateers was no longer necessary as _____ in the past and instead started feeling that the navy alone should be responsible for fighting England's wars on the oceans.

① they have been

② its being

③ they had been

④ it has been

⑤ their having been

04 _____ passion to succeed they also need to keep trying — the ability not to give up is essential.

① People do not need

② Not only do people need

③ Do not need people

④ Do people not only need

05 Freud finally abandoned hypnosis, merely inviting his patients to lie on a couch in his shaded office and talk _____ their minds.

① of whatever entered

② what entered to

③ about however entering to

④ that entering

06 To lead a genuinely creative life, you must do the things _____.

① cannot you think you do

② you cannot do you think

③ cannot think you do

④ you think you cannot do

07 I suppose everyone has at least one friendship like this in their lives. We were dialectical, she the thesis, I the antithesis. She was direct, trustworthy, kind, and naive; I was manipulative, selfish, and clever. She was my best friend. Hard _____ to figure by the looks of us, she was the good girl, I the bad.

① lest it should be

② if it should have been

③ as it may have been

④ unless it must have been

08 In hindsight, if _____ our company _____ a branch office in Kuala Lumpur, I would have started a class in the Malay language.

① I had known — would be establishing

② I would have known — would have established

③ I had known beforehand — will be establishing

④ I knew — will establish

⑤ I would know — will have established

09 Because mass communication is a fractured interaction, we can identify actual addressees only *post hoc* by reference back to the people _____.

① intending the communicators to address

② the communicators to address intended

③ to address the communicators intending

④ the communicators intended to address

⑤ intended the communicators to address

[10-19] Choose the one that is NOT correct in standard English.

10 The Olympic Games, which take place once every four ①year, are ②considered the most competitive ③of athletic ④competitions.

11 The Egyptian earthquake ①in October 1992 killed 600 residents of Cairo and hospitalized ②thousands of others, ③many of those were expected to die ④as a result of their ⑤injuries.

12 That all men are equal is an assertion ①which, at ordinary times, no sane human being has ever given his assent. A man who ②has to undergo a dangerous operation does not ③act on the supposition that one doctor is ④just as good as another.

13 Minho ①told me that he had attended a presentation on the gender differences that affect memory. He ②mentioned me that Dr. Kim gave the presentation. He also ③reminded me that Dr. Kim wrote several articles on memory and ④informed me of the next presentation.

14 ①Hundreds of millions of devices around the world could ②be exposed to ③a newly revealed software vulnerability, as a senior Biden administration cyber official ④was warned executives from major US industries Monday that they need to take action to address "one of the ⑤most serious" flaws she has seen in her career.

15 Braille characters are constructed ①of a six dot position system. They came from a method of communication created for Napoleon who demanded a silent way for soldiers ②to communicate on the field without light. Although this system was originally rejected because of ③their complexity, ④the blind around the world hail it as a godsend.

16 Yesterday was probably our ①all-time heaviest day of margin calls. But, ②giving the condition of the market, it was not unexpected. When the market makes ③that steep, downward move and there are a lot of stocks affected, you're going to see margin calls. It's almost like a physical law of gravity. Heavy margin debt ④was said to be a big factor in the 1929 stock market crash.

17 Those who distrust science as a guide to conduct, ①whether individual or social, seem to overlook its pragmatic nature. Rightly ②understood, science can point out to us only probabilities of varying degrees of certainty. What science can do for us ③that otherwise we may be too blind or self-willed to recognize ④are to help us to see that what is right for the individual may be wrong for him as a member of a social group.

18   The basis of Golden Lane is an irregular strip of land ①varying in width from four to eight meters between the older, Romanesque walls from the 12th century, and the later walls ②that form the outer north fortification of Prague Castle on the edge of a natural gorge ③known as the Stag Moat. Work on the north fortification of Prague Castle was begun by the architect Benedikt Ried shortly after 1484, ④where King Vladislav Jagiellon decided to leave the Old Town and ⑤settle at the Castle.

19   The Englishman, the gambler and the blond man sat ①jammed together in the forward seat, ②riding backwardly to the course of the stagecoach. The drummer and the cattleman occupied the uncomfortable middle bench; the two women shared the rear seat. The cattleman faced Henriette, his knees almost touching her. He had one arm hooked over the door's window sill to steady himself. A huge nugget slid gently back and forth along the watch chain slung across his wide chest and a chunk of black hair ③lay below his hat. His eyes considered Henriette, reading something in the girl that caused him to show her a deliberate smile. Henriette dropped her glance to the gloved tips of her fingers, ④cheeks unstirred. They were all strangers packed closely together, with nothing ⑤in common save a destination.

[20] Choose the sentence that is NOT grammatically correct.

20   ① Having said that, I disagree that women and men are essentially the same.
    ② Having done these things, she hid them until she was arrested and put in prison.
    ③ Having told that the acoustics were the best behind the balcony, I decided to head there when the doors opened.
    ④ Having covered scores of trials, I am well acquainted with courtroom etiquette.

▶▶▶ ANSWERS P.414

[01-09] Choose the one that best completes the sentence.

01 The comet was first spotted 370 million miles from Earth, by an astronomer who was searching the sky for asteroids, and _____ whom the comet was named.

① to

② for

③ after

④ with

02 When a bacterium becomes too large, it splits in half and forms two new bacteria, _____ its own cell wall and protoplasm.

① each has

② with each

③ has each

④ each with

03 People who live outside of Greencastle give the city higher marks _____ own citizens, according to a survey of Central Indiana residents.

① than it does the

② than do its

③ do than their

④ as they do

04   Engineering is part of STEM education, which aims to engage students with science, technology, engineering, and mathematics yet, as a discipline, _____ for thousands of years. You can see examples of engineering in the Pyramids of Giza, at Stonehenge, the Parthenon, and elsewhere.

① it has been practiced

② had it been practiced

③ has been it practiced

④ has it practiced

⑤ it had practiced

05   When students go into a dictionary to verify or to determine a precise definition, _____ need supervision to make good decisions.

① oftener than they do not

② more often than not they

③ so often as not they

④ as they often not

06   The body produces sweat to keep its temperature from rising too much. However, there is a negative tradeoff in that the more the body sweats, _____.

① the more does it lose fluid

② does it lose the more fluid

③ the more fluid does it lose

④ the more fluid it loses

⑤ it loses fluid the more

07   A new law _____ most fruits and vegetables came into effect in France from New Year's day.

① banned plastic packaging on

② banning plastic packaging on

③ banned plastic packaging into

④ banning plastic packaging into

08   _____, the politician blamed the opposition for his mistake.

    ① Unwilling to admit that he was wrong

    ② He was wrong and unwilling to admit

    ③ Admitting wrong that he was unwilling

    ④ That he was wrong unwillingly admitted

09   The disappearance of buzzing insects doesn't bring about the kind of emotional response that _____.

    ① to polar bears does global warming's threat

    ② global warming's threat does to polar bears

    ③ does global warming's threat to polar bears

    ④ global warming's threat to polar bears does

[10-19] Choose the one that is NOT correct in standard English.

10   ①Certain of the methods developed ②as a result of peace research ③is now being studied at ④institutions of higher learning around the world.

11   Any commentary about Easter Island ①would be incomplete ②without mentioning the theories of ③the Norwegian explorer and the scientist, Thor Heyerdahl, who came to the island in the 1950s. ④No error.

12   The choice is not between peace ①on earth, which is ②beyond man's grasp, ③or mutual destruction, which ④though within his grasp is highly improbable, ⑤but between greater and lesser degrees and frequencies of violence.

13   ①Humanity can only have ②a satisfied sense of direction when it can calculate ③its achievements with the help of an economics which understands that success even in the material world is not obtained ④by the exclusive pursuit of self-interest.

14 What is important is to ①further reflect on the meaning of "conscience." A judge's conscience should be that of a professional, rather than an ②amateur. It is necessary to question whether one's interpretation of statutes is correct and ③what different conclusions another judge might reach. Such careful consideration will help people's trust in the judiciary ④to take root.

15 Clara and Johannes Brahms first crossed orbits in 1853, ①when her beloved husband — the celebrated composer Robert Schumann — encountered in the ②twenty-years-old Brahms a talent so uncommon and promising that he immediately ③set about bringing the music world's ④awed attention to it, writing impassioned letters to all the leading journals and ⑤auguring the young musician's future fame.

16 It is specifically the increase ①in the number of hostile takeovers that is important in our context. ②The question of what the dominant FIGHT metaphor reinforced aggressive business practices or vice versa is a very chicken-and-egg problem, but ③it is safe to say that the socio-economic framework ④sketched above did not exactly discourage conceptual models of aggression ⑤either.

17 They were able to keep the same house and it was still often ①referred to as the parsonage, although it was not really that anymore. The new minister's young wife had ②taken issue with some features of the place, and the church authorities, rather than fix it up, ③had been decided to build a new house so that she could not complain anymore. The old parsonage ④was then sold cheaply to the old minister.

18 Many flops have dream-like stories that are hard to make into films. One example is *Pluto Nash*. This 2002 comedy was about life on the moon in the future. Another famous flop was the 1995 action movie *Waterworld*. The filmmakers tried to create a world with only water, and no land. The movie was ①filmed in the Pacific Ocean, near Hawaii. Not only ②was Hawaii an expensive place to make a movie, but also the ocean cannot be controlled like a regular set. *Waterworld* took twice as ③long to make and cost as ④many as the director had planned.

19 Exactly how and why Stonehenge was constructed remains a mystery. Research suggests that it may have ①designed and built by an ancient religious group who used it for one of two purposes: either as a sacred temple or as an observatory to study the sky. Scientists believe that the enormous stones were ②transported from places around the country to their present site on Salisbury Plain in southern England. Work on the monument is thought to have started around 2000 B.C. and ③continued to 1500 B.C. Today, engineers estimate that approximately 600 people were needed to transport each sarsen stone from its point of origin to Salisbury. Scientists consider this a remarkable feat, ④given that heavy lifting equipment used in modern construction was not available at that time.

[20] Choose the sentence that is NOT grammatically correct.

20
① Now, <u>people being people</u>, all the players acted selfishly.
② <u>All other things being equal</u>, the simplest explanation tends to be the best.
③ <u>Weather permitting</u>, the display will run every night.
④ <u>That being spoken</u>, keeping the current system would be much better than having no system at all.

T E S T

40

▶▶▶ **ANSWERS** P.418

[01-09] Choose the one that best completes the sentence.

01   Seaweed, as a staple item of diet, has been used in Japan and China for a very long time. In the west, seaweed is largely regarded as a health food and _____ there has been an upsurge of interest in seaweed as food in the last 20 years, it is unlikely that seaweed consumption in the west will ever be more than a fraction of that used by Japanese.

① since

② supposing

③ lest

④ although

02   Had I known the carpenter was going to take three days to show up, I _____ the materials and done the work myself. It would have been finished by now.

① will get

② would have got

③ might get

④ will have got

03   Dr. Jensen's daughter is able to switch between English and Chinese, _____ she speaks very fluently.

① both of which

② which of them

③ which of both

④ both which

TEST 40   205

04   The only car available was a red Fiat — _____.

    ① of an Italian car maker

    ② a car of Italian made

    ③ an Italian make of car

    ④ a make of Italian car

05   If you find _____ and would like a similar electronic version, feel free to visit our website.

    ① valuable dictionary

    ② to be a valuable dictionary

    ③ this dictionary valuable

    ④ a dictionary being value

06   Imaginary readers may serve as targets for pious hopes and aspirations, but they are _____ than real readers and critics.

    ① less of practical use

    ② of less use practical

    ③ of less practical use

    ④ less practical of use

    ⑤ of use less practical

07   _____ indeed to live in the most diverse, dynamic and beautiful state in the entire nation.

    ① What a fortunate person are we

    ② What fortunate person we are

    ③ How a fortunate are we

    ④ How fortunate we are

08　Full-time lecturers who want to be reimbursed for travel costs must _____.

① verify their receipts to keep expenses

② verify their expenses to keep receipt

③ keep expenses verifying their receipts

④ keep receipts verifying their expenses

09　Space travel won't just be for billionaires, and commercial companies are lining up _____.

① making a more affordable proposition

② to make more affordable a proposition

③ making it a proposition more affordable

④ to make it a more affordable proposition

[10-19] Choose the one that is NOT correct in standard English.

10　The point ①at which physical decline ②with age ③begins adversely to affect ④a driver's capability ⑤have not yet been studied.

11　Happiness is not, ①except in very rare cases, ②anything that ③drops into the mouth, like a ④ripe fruit, by the ⑤mere operation of fortunate circumstances.

12　Although Galileo was aware ①that accelerations result ②from the actions of forces (e.g., the acceleration of falling ③been produced by the force of ④bodies' weights), he did not concentrate on this part of the topic.

13　The term "dialectic" ①originated in ancient Greece, where it ②was exemplified in Plato's Socratic dialogues, which ③were featured a question-and-answer-based discussion that ④aimed at teasing out the truth about a subject.

14 If one bidder wants to be the winner ①no matter what, he might run a bigger chance of making a mistake. Even if he wins, he may realize that he ②sustained a loss after due consideration. In an auction, the prize goes to ③whoever has the most optimistic view about the value of the object ④having been bid upon.

15 Our activities online are often ①contrasted with real life, as though the things we do online are somehow ②less real. There's a sense of anonymity, so we feel less accountable for our behavior. The Internet also makes it far ③more easily to stumble upon things inadvertently, things that we ④would usually avoid in everyday life.

16 The book exists for us, perchance, which will explain our miracles and reveal new ①ones. The at present unutterable things we may find somewhere ②uttered. These same questions that disturb and puzzle and confound us ③have in their turn occurred to all the wise men; not one has been omitted; and each has answered ④it, according to his ability, by his words and his life.

17 The great debate between rationalism and empiricism is familiar ①to everyone who ②has taken a course in philosophy, psychology or history ③of ideas. It embraces such issues as whether the mind is packed ④by innate structure or is a blank slate ⑤on which the environment writes, and whether knowledge comes from making deductions using theories or gathering data from observation.

18 Some would argue ①that healthcare screening assessments that make race-based scoring adjustments ②are harmful to people of color. As a retired pathologist and medical laboratory director, ③I would certainly not argue that systemic racism does not exist in medicine, ④as it does in almost aspects of American society. But I have heard the opposite argument: that the failure to incorporate racial differences into decision algorithms ⑤also constitutes racism.

19 For many years, Dr. Leuthardt, who ①founded a company called NeuroLutions, had been puzzled by something he often heard from patients who'd lost the use of hand after a stroke. "If you talk to a stroke patient, they can imagine ②moving their hand," he says. "They can try to move their hand. But they just can't actually move it." So Leuthardt had been looking for the source of those thoughts. And he found them in a surprising place: the side of the brain that had not been injured by the stroke. Usually, the brain and body follow what's known as a contralateral model, where the right side of the brain controls the left side of the body. But Leuthardt's team had discovered that control signals were also present on the ipsilateral side — the same side of the brain as the limb being ③controlling. Leuthardt's team built a system that could detect and decode those ipsilateral signals. Then they connected it to a device that would open and close a patient's ④disabled hand for them when they imagined the action. But a mechanical hand wasn't Leuthardt's ultimate goal. He wanted to help his patients regain the ability to move their hand without assistance.

[20] Choose the sentence that is NOT grammatically correct.

20   ① When he will arrive — no one knows for sure.
      ② People are curious to know when he will leave.
      ③ If he will arrive, the band will play the music.
      ④ Take a seat over there and wait, if you will.

[01-09] Choose the one that best completes the sentence.

01 _____ King Arthur chose that particular place to build a capital is a mystery.

① Why

② What

③ Where

④ Whatever

⑤ The ways in which

02 The development of technology should permit a considerable extension of leisure time in which each individual can exercise his preferred activity, _____ it is pottering about the house, gardening, or listening to music.

① where

② when

③ which

④ whether

03 _____ railroads in the U.S. during the 1850's powerfully stimulated the iron industry.

① The building of

② There were built

③ They had built

④ To build

04   It _____ rain tomorrow. That is what the weather forecast predicted.

① supposes to

② is supposed to

③ is supposing to

④ will suppose to

05   We _____ late or we'll miss our connecting flight to New York and be over three hours late arriving at our final destination.

① had better not be

② had be better not

③ had not be better

④ had not better be

06   They found that only when the RNA and DNA match closely _____ the scissors of Cas9.

① the 3D structure of Cas9 activate

② do the 3D structure of Cas9 activate

③ activate the 3D structure of Cas9

④ does the 3D structure of Cas9 activate

⑤ activates the 3D structure of Cas9

07   There is now increasingly a gap between the privacy and security of the rich, who can afford devices that secure their data by default, and of the poor, _____ to protect them by default.

① who does very little to devices

② of what devices do very little

③ whose devices do very little

④ of whose devices do very little

⑤ which does very little to devices

08 I told the grand jury today, and I say to you now, that _____ to lie, to hide or destroy evidence, or to take any other unlawful action.

① did not ask no one at any time

② at any time did I not ask anyone

③ asked no one at no time

④ at no time did I ask anyone

09 Last month's budget also gave tax cuts to companies _____ to companies that shift previously outsourced jobs back to Spain.

① vulnerable to outsourcing as well

② vulnerable with outsourcing so good as

③ vulnerable to outsourcing as well as

④ vulnerable with outsourcing as good as

[10-19] Choose the one that is NOT correct in standard English.

10 It ①was not clear ②whether it was his friend or ③him who had requested the favor. ④No error.

11 According to the recent survey by ①the Seoul Times, the number of citizens who ②are unable to find a book they would like to buy at a bookstore and order it ③at an online bookstore ④are skyrocketing these days.

12 Related research ①conducted in the EU suggests that students who ②learn a second language early on are ③more aware of other cultures and, overall, are stronger in ④its own first language.

13 Services production continued ①to slide by a large margin led by businesses ②relied on interpersonal contact, while manufacturing production ③sank significantly as the production of major export items ④remained stagnant due to the global economic recession.

14   In ancient warfare, an army sometimes would send its mightiest warrior ①to face his counterpart from the ②opposing army in single combat. The outcome would ③embolden one side in the actual battle that ④following, or might preempt it altogether, ⑤sparing unnecessary bloodshed.

15   Conservatives viewed equality ①as another pernicious abstraction that ②was contradicted all historical experience. For conservatives, society was naturally hierarchical, and ③they believed that some men by virtue of their intelligence, education, wealth, and birth ④were best qualified to rule and instruct ⑤the less able.

16   The modest bargain I made with myself was ①that I would live with the name Yousuf, which sounded enough like Joseph to get me ②by, but I would rid myself of the name Mohammad, which I could not fashion into anything that ③pass. And for whatever ④it's worth, I wasn't alone in making these sorts of compromises.

17   The Seven Wonders of the Ancient World ①served a variety of purposes. ②Some were decorative, like the Hanging Gardens of Babylon. ③Others, like the Temple of Artemis at Ephesus, were spiritual. While both beautiful and functional, the Lighthouse of Alexandria ④played a more practical role. Its shining light ⑤guided into the Egyptian harbor ships safely for centuries, placing the port city at the center of Mediterranean trade in the ancient world.

18   Today, many people are quitting for ①different reasons than they did historically, and organizations ②are on high alert. For many employees who are disillusioned, grieving, or burnt out, the prospect of muscling through does not feel sustainable — no matter the increase in compensation. People are taking stock of their lives and ③are more likely than ever to change their career trajectory in notable ways. Another distinctive characteristic of today's attrition is ④the number of people leaving the workforces altogether, fueling a growing labor shortage across industries. Demand is increasing ⑤while supply is decreasing.

19   The use of controls in biological experiments is now universally accepted, but there are many physical, chemical, medical, and industrial investigations ①where a greater use of this technique would be desirable. It is too easy to have a false confidence in one's ability to identify all the important variables and keep them constant. During the Second World War certain absolute experiments on explosives were carried out in a setup which had performed successfully and ②reproducible hundreds of times and which appeared to be well understood. At one point, however, results were obtained which seemed somewhat surprising and which further tests, using controls, showed to have been in error. Elaborate investigations were instituted to find the variable responsible, and it was finally found that after months of shipping the same kind of lumber for the frame of the apparatus, the lumber dealer ③had supplied a different wood just before the experiment went wrong. This was responsible despite earlier tests which had seemed to show that the frame had no influence. The continuous use of controls ④would have prevented the error.

[20] Choose the sentence that is NOT grammatically correct.

20   ① Tell me a reason why you're not extending the same courtesy to me?
　　　② How often have I really told you not to do it that way?
　　　③ What do you think which car I finally decided to buy after all?
　　　④ Do you think you handled the situation the best way you could?
　　　⑤ How come you have to wear such a funny jacket to ride a motorcycle?

[01-09] Choose the one that best completes the sentence.

01   We have not gone ahead and proved that the sun warps spacetime _____ the earth falls along a geodesic whose shadow in three-dimensional space is nearly a circle.

① such that

② such as

③ as is

④ as such

02   _____ Beirut or Bahrain, or even Detroit, you can write a musical prescription for whatever the condition is of the environment that you find yourself in.

① Whether it be

② What be it

③ Whether be it

④ What it be

⑤ Which be it

03   Attempting to prove that photography _____, early photographers at first imitated the paintings of contemporary artists.

① a form of art

② was a form of art

③ as a form of art

④ in a form of art

04   At the center of our solar system _____ the Sun.

① is a star called

② called is a star

③ is called a star

④ called a star is

05   The nature of viruses made _____ to detect for years, even after bacteria had been discovered and studied.

① impossible

② it impossible

③ them impossible

④ impossible for them

06   A 2019 study found that cows _____ 3.3 percent of all greenhouse gas emissions in the US, compared with 50 percent from electricity production and transportation.

① account for

② are accounted for

③ have been accounted for

④ have been accounting for

07   Professional tennis, which got its start in 1926 when the French player Suzanne Lenglen _____ 50,000 US dollars for a tour, only _____ full recognition in 1960.

① had been paid — has received

② was paid — received

③ has been paid — would receive

④ would be paid — had received

08   While it is important for everyone to develop a good relationship with his or her primary care provider, many people who are obese would _____ a doctor who specializes in obesity medicine and a registered dietitian who specializes in obesity and weight management.

① benefit from working with
② be benefited from working
③ benefit to work from
④ be benefit from working with
⑤ benefit with working from

09   _____, there are opportunities to enhance your education.

① Live stream and demand-on classes
② Living stream and demanding-on classes
③ Between live-on stream and demanding classes
④ Between live stream and on-demand classes

[10-19] Choose the one that is NOT correct in standard English.

10   The authors ①acknowledge that women ②tend to say they weigh less than they do, while men ③claim to be taller than ④they do.

11   The experts we spoke ①to disagreed on which ②come first, but all agreed physical ③activity and sleep are the ④two most important components of good health.

12   As soon as working class voters ①were given outlet for their anger, it poured ②out of them. Populism is ③a complex concoction, ④mixing misanthropy and nativism with genuine concerns about economic prospects.

13 In most of our practical activities, we ①rely upon our senses and develop intuitions we can ②trust. When important issues ③raise, regardless of what others may say, our own senses and intuitions are our best ④guides for action.

14 As women in the United States and across the ①industrialized world get fatter, most Japanese women are getting skinnier. Skinnier still are Japanese women younger than 60, who were thin ②by international standards three decades ago and who, ③taking as a group, have since ④been steadily losing weight.

15 Neighborhoods are very clearly ①demarcated according to income level, and there is not much overlap. Poor people live in poor neighborhoods that are characterized by ②dilapidated buildings, broken glass, graffiti, and a general state of disrepair. People are not dedicated to ③create an aesthetically ④pleasing environment.

16 Doctors ①have always seen depression as something that's distinct from ordinary sadness, but what causes it and how best ②to treat it has changed wildly over the years. In the 5th century B.C., Hippocrates ③believed that the body was made up of four humors and that too much "black bile," the humor secreted by the spleen, ④resulting in melancholia.

17 Language comes so naturally to us that it is easy to forget ①what a miraculous gift it is. All over the world members of our species fashion their breath ②into hisses, hums, squeaks and pops and listen to others ③did the same. We do this not only because we like the sounds but ④because details of the sounds contain information ⑤about the intentions of the person making them.

18   Sixty-five million years ago, the age of the dinosaurs suddenly came to an end. The dinosaurs ①all disappeared from the earth. Scientists have always wondered why this ②was happened. A new discovery in Mexico may give them the answer. The discovery is a huge circle ③180 kilometers wide. This circle was probably caused by some very large object ④that hit the earth. When it hit, it ⑤may have caused changes in the earth's climate and sea levels. These changes may have been disastrous for dinosaurs.

19   The remote control device became popular during the 1980's, and it has had a significant impact on the manner ①which people experience television. Industry researchers quickly began ②to observe new viewing patterns that they described as "grazing." Many viewers used the remote control to avoid ③watching commercials, while others learned to scan restlessly through the channels, not watching entire programs, but looking for an arresting image or sound that entices them ④to stop on a particular channel. As one result, many cable networks crafted a signature visual style, using distinctive logos, graphic designs, and other techniques, ⑤that made the network immediately identifiable to the restless, remote-control-enhanced television viewer.

[20] Choose the sentence that is NOT grammatically correct.

20   ① Shouldn't the company do more to increase productivity?
   ② Might we not consider those less fortunate than ourselves?
   ③ I wrote the telephone number down, so as not to forget it.
   ④ I would rather not you said anything about it at all.

▶▶▶ ANSWERS P.430

[01-09] Choose the one that best completes the sentence.

01   A fairly good income is very important; however, it is still more important that a man should follow the vocation for which he is best fitted, _____ it happens to be well paid.

① what

② whether

③ where

④ how

02   Nowhere has the need for mathematical precision _____ more apparent than in the field of computer technology.

① be

② is

③ was

④ been

03   Designed by I. M. Pei, the East Wing of the National Gallery in Washington, D.C. is characterized by the irregular geometric shapes _____ of his work.

① they are typical

② that is typical

③ are typical

④ that are typical

04 A war specialist insisted that all the war horses which took part in that battle _____.

① should have been stallions

② might as well be stallion

③ were a stallions

④ has been stallion

05 There are too many amazing things to experience _____.

① ever to fear holding you back

② to ever fear hold back you

③ ever letting fear holding back you

④ to ever let fear hold you back

06 In the late 1980s, increased trade accounted for well _____ in the United States.

① over half of the new jobs

② over half a new job

③ half over a new jobs

④ the new jobs of over half

07 Designed to be used together, the books cover the four skills while helping students develop the confidence _____ in their education.

① what they need to be excelled

② what they need excel

③ they need to excel

④ they are needed to excelled

08 As darkness fell, the scene grew ever more surreal. A car came racing up the hill, _____ flames.

① snatched and chased by licking

② snatching and chasing by licking

③ snatched and chasing by licked

④ snatching and chased by licked

09 The existence of ice rather than water for the majority of the year means that _____.

① vegetation does not have moisture for growth enough to take place

② vegetation does not have enough moisture for growth to take place

③ vegetation does not have enough moisture for taking place growth

④ vegetation does not have moisture enough for growth to take place

[10-19] Choose the one that is NOT correct in standard English.

10 ①What extent do women ②consciously reject their authentic natures ③to follow male-based expectations ④for how women should appear?

11 The paralyzed man has managed to feed himself ①by his own hand. This ②feat is partly thanks to electrodes, ③implanted in his right arm, which ④stimulates muscles.

12 The artist designed it ①free in charge as a "labor of love." A model was published in 1918 but completion ②was held up ③until after the war when Italian marble for the statue ④became available.

13 ①Looked back now at what I wrote in my middle ②forties, I am struck by the confidence ③with which I pronounced largely on such matters ④as the nature of civilization and the way ⑤in which culture develops.

14 Advertisers have recognized the Net as a ①significant new arena for commercial speech, ②where the gap between promotion and purchase can be progressively ③closed by new forms of electronic commerce ④allowed goods to be ordered ⑤directly from the screen.

15   The new British law makes ①<u>it</u> a criminal offense ②<u>to give</u> or receive money for supplying organs of either a living or dead person. It also prohibits ③<u>acting</u> as a broker in such an arrangement, advertising for organs for payment or ④<u>to transplant</u> an organ from a live donor not closely ⑤<u>related</u> to the patient.

16   We often demand that our occupants fit the structures rather than our structures ①<u>fitting</u> the occupants, and we celebrate slight ②<u>alterations</u> of existing plans as architectural prowess. Although the best builders are able to push the standardized ③<u>components</u> to their structural and aesthetic limits, most of ④<u>structures</u> we are building are destined for the most mundane suburbia.

17   Scientists used to think body fat ①<u>and the cells it was made of</u> ②<u>was pretty much active</u>, just an oily storage compartment. But within that past decade research has shown that ③<u>fat cells act like chemical factories</u> and that body fat is potent stuff: ④<u>a highly active tissue</u> that secretes hormones and other substances with profound and sometimes harmful effects. In recent years, biologists have begun calling fat an "endocrine organ," comparing it to glands like the thyroid and pituitary, which also release hormones ⑤<u>straight into the bloodstream</u>.

18   An example that is often given to illustrate complexity theory is the behaviour of flocks of birds. ①<u>Taking</u> collectively, the behaviour of a flock seems well choreographed and purposeful. It can avoid obstacles, circle over food and prey, and travel halfway around the world while ②<u>performing</u> all sorts of loops and whorls in the sky, yet there is no apparent central controller. Complexity theory offers an explanation of this behaviour based on the assertion ③<u>that</u> the global activity we see exhibited by the flock ④<u>emerges</u> from simple interaction among the individual birds.

19   We are living in the era of cognitive computing. Machines can do much more than ①calculate and organize data — they learn, reason, and interact with people in new ways. During this era, humans and machines will become more interconnected. How can people and computers be connected ②so that collectively they act more intelligently than any person or computer has ever done before? This avenue of thought stretches back to a paper in 1960, "Man-Computer Symbiosis", that predicted that "human brains and computing machines, coupled together, will think in a way ③not approached by the computer we know today." Only with the help of smart machines ④we will be able to deal adequately with the exploding complexity of today's world.

[20] Choose the sentence that is NOT grammatically correct.

20   ① He hardly ever washes the dishes and does rarely cleaning.
          ② Rarely are teenagers completely honest with their parents.
          ③ The student rarely spoke his mind for fear of being ridiculed.
          ④ The school rarely opens on weekends or national holidays.

[01-09] Choose the one that best completes the sentence.

01 Americans, trained _____ they are not to breathe in people's faces, automatically communicate shame in trying to be polite.

① is

② as

③ however

④ since

02 Many described being gripped by an unforgiving fury toward parents who they _____ had deprived them of a home and a family.

① feel

② have felt

③ felt

④ had felt

03 One of Franklin's good ideas was to set up a club where people could share their books. Anyone _____ could stop in and read the books.

① who wanted

② who wanted as

③ who wanted to

④ who wanted for

04 The following tables show the most frequent words that are at least three times as common in newspapers _____.

① as in the other four genres

② of the other four genres

③ than in another four genres

④ as another four genres

05 According to the Food and Drug Administration, a healthy person requires only two grams of creatine per day, _____ is produced in the body by the liver, kidneys, and pancreas.

① the other half

② half of them

③ half the amount

④ half of which

06 I woke up the next morning, thinking about those words — very proud to realize that _____ so much at one time but I'd written words that I never knew were in the world.

① not only I wrote

② only not did I write

③ not only had I written

④ only I had not written

07 Now she must take care of her father _____.

① that she was his parents

② whose was her parents

③ as if she were his parent

④ who were her parent

08   The earliest known document _____ Geoffrey Chaucer is a fragmentary household account book dated between 1356 and 1359.

① bears the name for

② that bears the name of

③ bearing that the name of

④ which bears with the name for

09   _____ it could easily have been my family with our home gone and our lives uprooted.

① Seeing the identical blanket made me realized which

② To see the identical blanket made me to realize that

③ To see the identical blanket made me realize which

④ Seeing the identical blanket made me realize that

[10-19] Choose the one that is NOT correct in standard English.

10   It ①turns out the man was suffering from ②that medical science ③might consider the worst hangover ④in recent history.

11   To support themselves, artists ①must often make a choice between teaching and not ②doing nothing except trying ③to earn money ④by creating art full time.

12   While ①ground-based observatories are usually ②located in highly ③elevated areas with minimal light pollution, they must contend with atmospheric turbulence, ④which limits the sharpness of images ⑤taking from this vantage point.

13   The sudden disruption of the pandemic ①arose fears of panic buying in British supermarkets, as a nation already ②rattled by a mysterious new strain of the virus now had to worry about ③running out of fresh food in the days before Christmas. ④No error.

14 The amount of Earth's surface ①allocated to tropical rain forests has already been reduced to less than ②half of its original area, ③for until recent years the World Bank supported deforestation with loans to finance development schemes ④required clearing forests.

15 If a majority of democratically ①elected representatives vote that a particular law should be created, or a government policy ②puts into practice, then to break the law as a protest against this seems ③to go against the spirit of democracy, particularly if a very small minority of citizens ④are involved in the act of civil disobedience.

16 When Jeff Bezos ①founded Amazon in 1994, it started ②as an online bookstore. But over the last 26 years, the company has not only ③became the largest e-commerce retailer in North America, but also expanded ④into other markets as well. And that diversity ⑤has been one of Amazon's greatest strengths.

17 We know of persons who have generalized ①mistaken about certain companies because of ②a single experience. Stereotypes about people who come ③from certain cultures are widespread and commonly mistaken; hasty generalizations about foreign cultures can be ④downright nasty, and are good illustrations of the fallacious leap to broad generalization ⑤on the basis of little evidence.

18 Both civilian and military leaders face what the authors call "dangerous negotiations," ①in which the traps are many and good advice is scarce. Although the sources of danger are quite different for executives and officers, they ②resort to the ③same kinds of behaviors. Both feel pressure to make quick progress, ④project strength and control, rely on force rather than collaboration, trade resources for cooperation rather than ⑤that they build trust, and make unwanted compromises to minimize potential damage.

19   The Great Plains remained only sparsely populated for many decades, thought of as ①<u>inhospitable</u> desert land, with ②<u>little water</u>, and hostile Indian tribes. By and large, they were not ③<u>opened up</u> to white settlement until after the Civil War of 1861-1865, when the Plains Indians were gradually conquered and eventually deprived of most of their lands by the settlers. With the development of cattle-arming and mining communities also came the growth of towns. Imposing some system of law and order became a major concern in many such places, and another major theme in many westerns, with the figures of the town sheriff, his posse of honest men, and US marshals ④<u>featured</u> prominently. By circa 1870 only a few parts of the Great Plains could be truly described as ⑤<u>unsettled</u>.

[20] Choose the sentence that is NOT grammatically correct.

20   ① The house will be ready for you to inspect in a few days.
      ② The thesis includes a rather difficult argument to refute.
      ③ The report was far too long to read in one evening.
      ④ Her new book is definitely worth looking at it.

[01-09] Choose the one that best completes the sentence.

01　In the U.K., class is nowadays more about celebrity than breeding, the only connection between the famous and the aristocratic _____ that both are comparatively rich.

① is

② to be

③ being

④ will be

02　_____ team wins tonight will go to the championship game that will be held in California.

① Which

② Whose

③ Whoever

④ Whichever

03　Long _____ an outsider's sport, surfing requires intense athleticism and highly technical skills that will be on display for the whole world when it makes its Olympic debut in Tokyo.

① considering

② considered

③ consideration of

④ consider

04   Oysters are mollusks, soft-bodied animals that have no skeletons. Slugs and snails are mollusks. _____.

① So are clams and squid is

② So are clams and squid

③ Clams and squid are so

④ Clams are and squid is so

05   The city is _____ it's easy to get lost.

① such a big place that

② a big such place which

③ such a big place which

④ a big such place that

06   Strength is not a physical measure, because _____ you are, you cannot out-muscle a horse.

① how strong no matter

② no matter what strong

③ no matter how strong

④ strong no matter what

07   Had the laboratory completed their safety study by the scheduled deadline, the company _____ to delay the production of the new line of baby toys.

① would not have had

② does not have

③ would not have been

④ did not have

08 One of the main goals for space exploration has been to find _____, and early unmanned space programs served as steppingstones into space for humans.

① life on other planets
② the life on another planet
③ the life on the other planets
④ a life on the other planet

09 _____ inhabitants have been in the Americas for at least 15,000 years.

① It is a considerable amount of proof which
② There is a considerable amount of proof that
③ It is a considerable amount of proof for
④ There is a considerable amount of proof which

[10-19] Choose the one that is NOT correct in standard English.

10 ①Supporters of bilingual education today ②imply that students like me miss ③great deal by ④not being taught ⑤in their family's language.

11 ①What I did not realize was ②that it is often possible to guess the meaning of rare words from ③their context and ④what they have in any case little impact on the overall intelligibility of ⑤what one is reading.

12 There's no question about the link between Russian wildfires and climate change. The country's ①famed bush — the continents' ②vast, often dry expanse that is ③sparse inhabited but filled with vegetation — has always been ④prone to wildfires.

13 A cell ①which is the basis of a battery must possess high capacity per unit volume in order to show maximum performance ②in a restricted area inside a vehicle and the cell ③needs to have ④much longer lifespan compared to batteries ⑤using in general mobile devices.

14   Schoolmasters agreed that the curriculum ①are already overloaded and requires ②to be lightened, and that the best preparation that the school can give for making a boy likely to be a good soldier when grown up, ③is to develop his intelligence and physique ④as far as the conditions of school life admit.

15   Because people can be impatient ①in their need for information, a successful news outlet relies on ②their reputation of being the first to publish a story. In the time before the Internet, ③when publication required timely printing, the quickest way to get a newspaper on the shelves was to write about an event before ④it happened.

16   Gemstones are minerals ①that occur naturally. The value of a gemstone is measured in various ways. It is measured by the stone's color, clearness, size, and how well the stone ②has been cut. A jeweler cuts a stone to bring out its beauty. A gemstone sparkles because it is cut to have ③angled sides, or facets. The facets reflect the light that ④enter into the stone, ⑤causing it to sparkle.

17   Governments of some countries see ①it as their responsibility to control the amount and kind of risk that their citizens are ②exposing to. They can use legislation to protect personal health, prevent injury in the workplace and help people ③handle financial matters. In other nations, citizens are expected to take care of themselves and carry the responsibility of their own safety and ④that of others.

18   It seems rather improbable that a celestial body ①the size of the Moon could completely block out the tremendously immense Sun, ②as happens during a total eclipse, but this is exactly ③that happens. Although the Moon is considerably smaller in size than the Sun, the Moon is able to cover the Sun because of ④their relative distances from Earth. A total eclipse can last up to 7 minutes, during ⑤which time the Moon's shadow moves across Earth at a rate of about .6 kilometers per second.

19 We always need to ask ourselves, and ①reflect very carefully about, what we want and why we want it. Knowledge appears to be a good thing, but too much knowledge, or perhaps ②pursued that knowledge with too much determination, may very well make our lives pretty miserable. One reason for this is that chasing knowledge beyond certain limits might be ③nothing but a fool's errand. We are somehow assuming that we can know everything, that our minds are powerful enough. But why should we assume that? We are ourselves ④a work of nature, and if nature is powerful enough to create something that is capable of understanding all its workings, then it must also be powerful enough to conceal things from us. There is no guarantee, and in fact it is very unlikely, ⑤that we are actually capable of understanding more than a tiny fraction of the universe.

[20] Choose the sentence that is NOT grammatically correct.

20
① Linguistics is one of the core areas of the humanities.
② Ten years is never a short time to stay home by yourself.
③ In university, not only the faculty but also the students are vital.
④ The number of the infected, unfortunately, are significantly rising.

T E S T

▶▶▶ ANSWERS P.441

[01-09] Choose the one that best completes the sentence.

01   The infant's eagerness to speak and to learn names is a major feature of the development of speech. Children have a mania for naming things. This deserves to be called a "hunter for names" since their learning of names is done neither mechanically nor with reluctance, _____ with enthusiasm.

① but
② as
③ nor
④ if

02   Someone may wonder why I go about in private giving advice and busying _____ with the concerns of others, but do not venture to come forward in public and advise the state.

① me
② myself
③ my
④ mine

03   The lawyer may be found guilty of defrauding his clients, _____ he will face a long-term sentence in jail.

① in which case
② who in case
③ whose case
④ just in case

04 This winter, there are many shades of _____ to be fully vaccinated.

① what it means

② what means it

③ it means what

④ means what it

05 _____ how the banks would respond if their customers had already spent the money.

① Were it not clear

② It was not clear

③ Were it not clearly

④ It was not clearly

06 You _____ the locksmith to open the door for you last night before you broke it yourself.

① must have been called

② ought to have called

③ have had to call

④ had better call

07 Many scientists are saying that it is difficult, _____, to calculate what impact global warming has on the ecosystem.

① not even impossible

② though even impossible

③ if not impossible

④ impossible even though

08 To many men _____ that making the right decision is often difficult, but the best decisions are made from both a cool head and a warm heart.

① comes the realization has

② has come the realization

③ has the realization come

④ have come the realization

09　J. K. Rowling, author of the *Harry Potter* series, deserves praise for enticing children to read books rather than _____.

① play video games or watch television all day

② playing video games or watch television all day

③ all day video games or watch television

④ play video games or watching television all day

[10-19] Choose the one that is NOT correct in standard English.

10　Asia ①certainly has no ②lack of amazing sights, ③sounds and adventures to keep visitors ④awe and on a ⑤lasting high.

11　Surveys in some African cities are finding ①that half of the elderly ②over eighty years old now die in the hospital and ③even higher percentages of those ④less than eighty years old ⑤does.

12　①Should the reports of the company ②dumping toxic waste into the river ③prove to be true, the company ④could not face only enormous fines but also a possible criminal investigation.

13　①Back in 1996 when the summer Olympic Games ②were held in the American city of Atlanta, a local TV station ③reported that all the hotels ④there was fully booked — ⑤with one exception.

14　Concerns ①are mounting over South Korea's fiscal soundness as this year's three supplementary budgets ②are worth a total of 60 trillion won are leading to ③an increase in government debt of ④no less than 111 trillion won in just six months.

15 Just as the inconclusive Byzantine-Persian wars weakened both states and exposed them to the ①Arab invasion and conquest, ②so the inconclusive Ottoman-Persian wars of the sixteenth to eighteenth centuries weakened ③both and exposed them to European commercial penetration, ④led eventually to their helpless manipulation by European Powers in the nineteenth century.

16 In a video of the event that ①has since gone viral, German comedian Florian Schroeder faces the crowd of hundreds ②who question the existence of Covid-19 and suspect face masks to be part of a plot to silence ③his critical opinions, ④telling them he wanted to talk about Hegel's idea of dialectics, a method of argument that ⑤relies on a contradictory process between opposing sides.

17 Last November an opportunity ①arose to travel with a small group to northern Portugal. My grandfather, Costa, was born and ②raised there, and I'd always dreamed of visiting. The itinerary included kayaking, riding, and hiking in the mountains — all things I ③enjoyed. ④Tucking into the agenda was an excursion to Diverlanhose, one of Europe's largest adventure parks. Did I want to go? Of course I did!

18 Using people, or ①transforming others into a means for obtaining an end for oneself, is generally considered ②the very antithesis from ethical behavior. Faced with the violence of colonial, sexual, and even epistemological appropriation, ethical theorists ③have sought to replace domination with respect, ④knowledge with responsibility. But it often seems as though a thought that begins in inter-subjectivity ⑤ends up sounding like a mere defense of the Other against the violence of the Subject.

19 One of the primary reasons Valencia is the home of paella is because it is at the heart of one of the largest rice-growing regions of Spain. Much of the rice ①is grown in paddy fields around La Albufera, a freshwater lagoon to the south of the city. Up until the 17th century, it contained salt water, but it gradually became less brackish. By the 18th century, laborers in these paddy fields and the orange groves that surround them ②had begun to make paella using local ingredients, including chicken, rabbits and ③whatever else was available, or alternatively, from any seafood they had. These two paellas, meat and seafood, are now regarded as being the authentic Valencian ones, whereas others, ④which there are hundreds, are modern interpretation of the classic dish.

[20] Choose the sentence that is NOT grammatically correct.

20   ① He let himself into the room and sat down on the sofa, waiting for her to get home.
    ② Your helping me with my homework will be doing myself no favors.
    ③ Having nothing left to do, he went into the kitchen and made himself some dinner.
    ④ You will drive yourself crazy if you keep thinking about your previous mistakes.

[01-09] Choose the one that best completes the sentence.

01 Refugees are people who are fleeing armed conflict or persecution and _____ denial of asylum has potentially deadly consequences.

① who

② whom

③ whose

④ for whom

02 One of the problems that have made _____ difficult for immigrants to succeed in the United States is the language barrier.

① one

② us

③ them

④ it

03 In those days of paleontology there was one great authority _____ other students of fossil vertebrates might turn for help, namely Baron Georges Cuvier of Paris.

① for whom

② whom

③ from whom

④ to whom

04 I have listened to family members weep as they remember loved ones who would be alive today _____ for social media conspiracy theories.

① it were not

② were it not

③ not it were

④ it not were

05 In the first place photography is no modern discovery, and _____ the idea of one man.

① neither it was

② neither was it

③ nor it was

④ nor was it

06 "Did you criticize him for his mistakes?"

"Yes, but _____ it."

① I'd not rather

② I'd rather not have done

③ I'd rather not doing

④ I'd better not do

07 Elizabeth Taylor was the American motion picture actress _____ the last major star to have come out of the old Hollywood studio system.

① was called by critics

② critics called her

③ critics were called her

④ whom critics called

⑤ whom critics called her

08   Now that _____, the province is advising that people be fully vaccinated before traveling.

    ① have travel rules loosened

    ② travel have loosened rules

    ③ travel have rules loosened

    ④ travel rules have loosened

09   Mother Nature behaved _____, but human nature never fails to surprise.

    ① as everyone warned one day she would

    ② if anyone warn some day it should

    ③ since no one had warned one day he could

    ④ for everyone warn some day may

[10-19] Choose the one that is NOT correct in standard English.

10   ①Of all the written sources from which history ②can be reconstructed, diaries ③are undoubtedly ④the more entertaining.

11   Northern towns are stalling ①even as their neighboring cities ②are doing well partly because dire transport links ③makes the likes of Manchester seem a world ④away from Wigan or Hartlepool.

12   ①Because of the supply-chain crunch, ②what has ramped up demand for hard-to-get products, many retailers are doing less discounting and therefore ③seeing higher profit margins. Is this an opportunity for the industry ④to wean shoppers off their "deals deals deals" mentality?

13   If personality is ①an unbroken series of successful gestures, then there ②was something gorgeous about him, some ③heighten sensitivity to the ④promises of life, as if he ⑤were related to one of those intricate machines that register earthquakes ten thousand miles away.

14   It seems to me that the only fault which we should vigorously attack as soon as they arise and start to develop ①is lying. Those faults grow up with the children. Once let the tongue ②acquired the habit of lying and it is astonishing how impossible it is to make ③it give it up. That is why some otherwise decent men are abject slaves to ④it.

15   For many Americans, homeownership is still viewed ①as a central component of living out the American dream, but the ways ②that many present-day Americans are pushing back ③on modern living arrangements closely ④resembling what ⑤came centuries, even millennia, before in other parts of the world.

16   The ①earlier investigations did not clarify the ②underlying mechanisms or the cells ③involving. Now, by ④studying rats, researchers at the Netherlands Institute for Neuroscience (NIN) in Amsterdam have identified that the ability ⑤to feel the pain of others has to do with "mirror neurons" in the anterior cingulate cortex (ACC).

17   The locations of stars in the sky ①relating to one another do not appear to the naked eye to change, and as a result stars are often considered ②to be fixed in position. Many unaware stargazers falsely assume that each star has ③its own permanent home in the nighttime sky. In reality, though, stars are always ④moving, but because of the tremendous distances between stars themselves and ⑤from stars to Earth, the changes are barely perceptible here.

18 Digital information is ①<u>streaming in</u> from all sorts of sensors, instruments, and simulations, overwhelming our capacity to organize, analyze, and store it. Moore's Law ②<u>has, for decades, accurately predicted</u> that the number of transistors that could be placed on an integrated circuit would double every two years, and until recently, ③<u>they were accompanied</u> by increased microprocessor performance. To increase performance today, we must ④<u>program multiple processors on</u> multicore chips and ⑤<u>exploit</u> parallelism.

19 The sole Native Americans able to resist European conquest for many centuries were those tribes that reduced the military disparity by mastering both horses and guns. To the average white American, the word "Indian" conjures up an image of a ①<u>mounted</u> Plains Indian brandishing a rifle. We easily forget that horses and rifles were originally unknown to Native Americans. They were brought by Europeans and proceeded ②<u>to transform</u> the societies of Indian tribes that acquired them. Thanks to their mastery of horses and rifles, the Plains Indians fought off invading whites longer ③<u>than did any other Native Americans</u>, ④<u>succumbing only massive army operations</u> by white governments in the 1870s.

[20] Choose the sentence that is NOT grammatically correct.

20
① Through the window I saw him run into the building.
② Even from three miles away, the bomb was heard to explode.
③ From the living room window, I could watch him dance in the street.
④ He was observed climb over the tall brick fence in broad daylight.

▶ ▶ ▶ ANSWERS P.448

[01-09] Choose the one that best completes the sentence.

01   This study would have been impossible _____ for the recent availability of wartime German and postwar investigative records.

　① down

　② out

　③ to

　④ but

02   A wind instrument is really just a pipe arranged _____ air can be blown into it at one end.

　① as well

　② due to

　③ so that

　④ therefore

03   Over time, as we get to know one another and spend time together engaged in activities that we care about most, we build a foundation that can weather inevitable storms as well as provide fertile ground for love and happiness _____.

　① of blossoming

　② blossomed

　③ in being blossomed

　④ to blossom

04   According to a 2019 study, Instagram makes body image issues _____ 1 in 3 teenage girls.

① to be worse

② to be good than

③ looking good at

④ better than

⑤ worse for

05   _____ another chance, he would do his best.

① Be given he should

② Given he should be

③ He should be given

④ Should he be given

06   Imagine your grandmother looking like a teenager, playing soccer, and partying at the clubs all night. Or imagine your grandfather teaching you the latest high-tech computer software while listening to loud heavy-metal music. Such a scenario is hard to envision because we _____ aging and the resulting suffering and death as an unavoidable fact of life.

① are taught to accept

② are learned to accept

③ are learning to be accepted

④ are teaching to be accepted

07   My guess is we are going to need _____ our health insurance policy to afford any of these hospitals.

① to every cent we can claim out of

② claiming out of every cent we can

③ claiming we can every cent out of

④ to claim every cent we can out of

08   Literacy is a term whose meaning _____.

    ① fluctuates from one context to another

    ② fluctuating to one from another context

    ③ fluctuate from a context to another

    ④ fluctuated to context from context

09   Although early soap operas _____ when the evening schedule became crowded with comedians and variety shows.

    ① were first aired on evening radio in the 1920s, moving to the daytime hours in the 1930s

    ② were aired first in evening on the 1920s radio, they had moved to the daytime hours of the 1930s

    ③ were first aired on evening radio in the 1920s, they moved to the daytime hours of the 1930s

    ④ aired on evening radio first in the 1920s, they were moved to the 1930s in the daytime hours of the 1930s

    ⑤ were first aired on evening radio in the 1920s, they were moved to the daytime hours in the 1930s

[10-19] Choose the one that is NOT correct in standard English.

10   When I was ①growing up, my friend Bob had a secret stairway in a closet ②leading up to the attic, ③where I thought was ④the classiest thing ⑤ever.

11   Nothing in recent years ①has so widely attracted the interest and ②attention of women ③throughout the world ④for the present popularity of crochet work.

12   No matter how well ①rehearsal a play is, every performance will be ②a little different from every other performance because of variations in the condition and ③spirit of the actors and because of variations in the response of audiences. ④No error.

13 As a result of the significant disruption that ①was being caused by the COVID-19 pandemic, we are ②very aware that many researchers will have difficulty in meeting the timelines ③associated with our peer review process during normal times. ④No error.

14 The world is ①made up with objects. They have properties ②independent of any people or other beings who experience them. For example, ③take a rock. It's a separate object and it's hard. Even if no people or other beings ④existed in the universe, it would still be a separate object and it would still be hard.

15 Societally, we are taught ①to revere and strive for hard work, even as we internalize that ②we're never quite doing it. You might be ③working excessive hours, or you might feel as if ④you are suffocating the weight of demands on your time and body, but that labor ⑤will always lag behind the venerated hard work of someone else.

16 The ①finding by Wolfe-Simon of NASA increases the possibility for finding life in the universe. Nonetheless, she faces some skeptics who wonder if the laboratory procedures ②followed were adequate enough ③to remove all doubt. These scientists argue that proper controls were not in place to ④absolute guarantee the validity of the conclusion drawn.

17 The degree ①to which an adverbial was integrated into clause structure affected its punctuation in two positions: initial position and final position. ②Frequently unpunctuated, adjuncts are closely related to the clauses ③in which they occur. Disjuncts and conjuncts, on the other hand, are sentential adverbs, and their relatively frequent punctuation reflects their loose connection to the clauses ④which they are members.

18   Because traumatic events are unbearable in their horror and intensity, they often exist ①<u>as memories that are</u> not immediately recognizable as truth. Such experiences are best understood not only through the straightforward acquisition of facts but ②<u>a process of discovering</u> ③<u>where and why</u> conscious understanding and memory fail. Literature ④<u>opens a window on</u> traumatic experience because it teaches readers to listen to ⑤<u>what can be told</u> only in indirect and surprising ways.

19   Tinnitus isn't noise. It's something that's going on in your brain. There are no physical vibrations to counteract. It's not sound waves. It's this electrical activity that is impervious to sound suppression technology. The current theory about tinnitus is that it's similar to phantom limb pain. You've heard about when somebody loses a limb — they have an ①<u>amputated</u> arm — they feel that that arm is still there, or they feel pain ②<u>where</u> that arm was but no longer is. Even itching. You can feel itchy fingers on a hand that's no longer there. The idea is that the brain is accustomed to ③<u>receive</u> nerve signals from this part of the body. It's no longer receiving them. So it makes, in effect, its best guess about what should be coming from it. It supplies the last thing it felt from there, or something like it. And the idea is that tinnitus is very often something like that. You lose hearing in some frequency. The brain is used to ④<u>receiving</u> auditory signals at those frequencies; it isn't anymore. So it fills in the gaps with what seems like a sound but is actually just electrical activity in the auditory system in your brain.

[20] Choose the sentence that is NOT grammatically correct.

20   ① It is eager for Tom to please Jerry.
       ② It is hard for Tom to read the book.
       ③ It is important for Tom to find the exit.
       ④ It is dreadful for Tom to go to the place.

[01-09] Choose the one that best completes the sentence.

01 The Industrial Revolution is the name by which the huge social, economic, and technological shift that transformed Europe from an agrarian to an industrial society _____.

① know   ② knows
③ is known   ④ are known

02 The most familiar reason for burnout is exhaustion from working too hard with insufficient rest. Yet that condition alone does not cause burnout, _____ the only route.

① nor is it   ② neither is it
③ nor it is   ④ neither it is

03 I handed over _____ money I had left.

① what little
② which little of
③ what little of
④ what little of it

04 _____ for your advice, I would have made serious mistake.

① If it had been not
② If not had it been
③ It had not been
④ Had it not been

05 Cacao plants are expected to disappear _____ due to warmer temperatures and drier weather conditions.

① as early by as 2050

② as by early as 2050

③ as early as by 2050

④ by as early as 2050

06 The value of credit derivatives _____ 129 percent from last year, to a whopping $12.79 trillion.

① traded globally grown

② traded globally grew

③ trading globally grew

④ trading globally grown

07 _____ and poverty, the region has long been fertile ground for religious extremism.

① Beset by ethnic strive

② Besetting by ethnic strife

③ Beset by ethnic strife

④ Besetting by ethnic strive

08 We see ourselves and our children on postcards and in books. We do not benefit from _____. A foreigner does.

① taken photos of ours

② being taken our photos

③ having our photos taken

④ our photos having taken

09   Nobody knows exactly how many languages there are in the world, partly because of the difficulty of distinguishing between a language _____ about five thousand.

① and the sublanguages or dialects within them, with those who have tried counting typically finding

② and the sublanguages or dialects within it, but those who have tried to count typically have found

③ or the sublanguages or dialects within them, with those who have tried to count typically finding

④ or the sublanguages or dialects within them, but those who tried to count the typically found

⑤ as that of earlier generations

[10-19] Choose the one that is NOT correct in standard English.

10   There are two other bodies ①orbiting near Earth ②that is sometimes ③referred to as moons, though they are not strictly ④worthy of the title.

11   Observation of ①children often shows, as early as in the beginning of ②its second year, a marked ③preference for the parent of the opposite sex and ④other indications of early Oedipal tendencies.

12   This new style of painting did not last ①long and was soon ②followed by an even more drastic transformation ③in Picasso's — and in the rest of the ④world's — understanding of ⑤that painting should be.

13   The United States ①<u>granted</u> asylum to the political dissidents from a foreign country, thus permitting them ②<u>to remain</u> in the United States and ③<u>to not force</u> them ④<u>to return</u> to their native country, where they certainly ⑤<u>would have been</u> imprisoned.

14   The gist of these objections can be developed ①<u>as follows</u>. Relativistic dynamics ②<u>cannot have shown</u> Newtonian dynamics to be ③<u>wrong, for</u> Newtonian dynamics is still used with ④<u>a great success</u> by most engineers and, in selected applications, by many physicists.

15   In our bodies, bacteria ①<u>outnumber</u> human cells by ten to one. All this bacteria ②<u>weighs</u> as much as your brain — nearly three pounds. Most bacteria in our bodies ③<u>are</u> not harmful: in fact, many ④<u>benefits</u> us in important ways. They help us to digest food. They make important vitamins, and they help fight infections.

16   Common sense tells us that it's easier to understand ourselves ①<u>than to understand</u> other people. After all, we tend to think that we have direct access to our own feelings and ideas and ②<u>not to anybody else</u>. Self-understanding ③<u>seems prior to</u> mutual understanding, and in some ways it is. But ④<u>any really deep understanding</u> of why we do what we do, feel what we feel, change as we change, and even believe what we believe, takes us beyond ourselves.

17   In general, which values are ①<u>given priority</u> is partly a matter of the subculture ②<u>one lives in</u> and partly a matter of personal values. The various subcultures of a mainstream culture ③<u>share with</u> basic values but give them different priorities. For example, "bigger is better" may be in conflict with "there will be more in the future" when it comes to the ④<u>question of whether</u> to buy a big car now, with large time payments that will eat up future salary, or whether to buy a smaller, cheaper car.

18 I was just learning the language myself, but I was a quick study, as children ①are with new tongues. I ②had spent kindergarten in almost complete silence, hearing only the high nasality of my teacher and comprehending little but the cranky wails and cries of my classmates. But soon, seemingly mere months later, I ③had already become a terrible ham and mimic, and I ④would crack up my father with impressions of teachers and his friends. My mother scolded me for aping my father's speech, and the one time I attempted to make light of hers I ⑤rate a roundhouse smack on my bottom.

19 Popular participation in conflict in the nineteenth century cannot be understood without examining the role of empire. Individuals had always gone to the colonies for profit or the settle. But individuals also participated in nineteenth-century imperial campaigns for ①a novel reason. Hannah Arendt later dismissively characterized imperialism as "the export of superfluous men and superfluous capital." She was correct ②if colonial functionaries were often from marginal populations — Cecil Rhodes, after all, would advocate imperialism "to settle surplus population" and thus "avoid civil war" — but these marginalized individuals increasingly used their participation in colonial conflicts to make claims to membership in the home nation. Scots, for example, were excluded from membership of the English community, but by participating in the wars against France and the empire in India, they became part of the British nation, ③increasing the war-fighting capacity of ④the latter. Empire was a crucial mechanism in constructing the exchange in the nineteenth century.

[20] Choose the sentence that is NOT grammatically correct.

20   ① BTS ascended to the zenith of stardom in a year defined by struggles to have concerts and meet fans.

② Those funds are already committed, so they are not available for research in developing countries.

③ Children deserve to have their basic needs met and to be surrounded by caring adults.

④ The Dakota tribe is prioritized the distribution of vaccines to those who speak the Dakota language.

[01-09] Choose the one that best completes the sentence.

01 Instead of looking at kids to "prove" that differences in behavior by sex are innate, we can look at the ways we raise kids as an index to _____ tentatively feminist revolution is embraced even by adults who fully expect their daughters to enter previously male-dominated professions and their sons to change diapers.

① as

② what

③ how

④ though

02 _____ is known of the writer Theophilus, but from his writings, we can assume that he was well-educated.

① There

② Little

③ No one

④ Ever

03 _____ about the criticism, he suggested that the president had maintained his silence so as not to interfere with investigations into the incident.

① Asked

② Asking

③ Having asked

④ To be asked

04   If Fleming had not discovered penicillin, there _____ far more fatalities every year than there actually are.

① would have been

② would be

③ are

④ will be

05   Today it emerged that about 500 red-winged blackbirds and starlings _____ in Louisiana. Their tiny corpses littered a short stretch of highway near the city of Labarre after apparently falling dead from the sky.

① have found dead

② found dead

③ had found dead

④ had been found dead

06   As Taiwan approaches elections on Jan. 11, the question for its people is whether they still trust Tsai _____ their democratic way of life.

① to be safeguarded

② to safeguard

③ safeguarded

④ having safeguarding

07   What is most striking about the present moment in the Speaker's career is that at the peak of her power, she _____ her position but rather using it in aggressive, even risky ways.

① is not protecting

② was not protecting

③ had been protecting

④ will have been protecting

08   Paul sold the machine and donated _____ the disabled, as he had a mentally disabled sister.

    ① the money to a charity for

    ② a charity for the money to

    ③ for the money a charity to

    ④ the money for a charity from

09   _____, is finding uses in medicine, archaeology, and criminology.

    ① Originally developed for detecting air pollutants, having the ability to analyze the chemical elements in almost any substance without destroying it, a technique called proton-induced X-ray emission

    ② A technique originally developed for detecting air pollutants, called proton-induced X-ray emission, which has the ability to analyze the chemical elements in almost any substance quickly and without destroying it

    ③ A technique that was originally developed for detecting air pollutants, called proton-induced X-ray emission, which has the ability to analyze the chemical elements in almost any substance quickly and without destroying it

    ④ Originally developed for detecting air pollutants, a technique called proton-induced X-ray emission, which can quickly analyze the chemical elements in almost any substance without destroying it

    ⑤ A technique originally developed for detecting air pollutants, called proton-induced X-ray emission, which can quickly analyze the chemical elements in almost any substance without having to destroy it

[10-19] Choose the one that is NOT correct in standard English.

10   Textbooks ①more than a decade ②old will tell you that you die with the same brain you were born ③of; that growing new ④born cells ⑤is impossible.

11   Every restaurant wants to create ①brand awareness and jump-start business ②with its ③grand open, but you will find many ways how restaurant owners try to make ④a splash.

12   The ①debate over if language is natural, i.e., do we call ②a table a table because that's the way it is?, or conventional, i.e., do we call it a table because that's what we decided to call it?, in Plato's *Cratylus* is ③the very question that everyone ④agrees opens Saussure's teachings and ties them together.

13   Reason is the instrument on which we rightly depend when ①reliable judgements are needed. ②Nonrational instruments — habits and hunches and the like — are commonly employed, we know. But when circumstances are complicated, when our decisions affect our loved ones and ourselves ③gravely, when a great deal is ④on stake in passing judgement, we reason the matter out ⑤as best we can, because that is the most likely course to success.

14   In a game known as Broken Telephone, a child whispers a phrase into the ear of a second child, who whispers it into the ear of a third child, and so on. Distortions ①accumulate, and when the last child announces the phrase, it is comically different ②from the original. The game works ③because of each child does not merely degrade the phrase, which would culminate ④in a mumble, but *reanalyzes* it, ⑤making a best guess about the words the preceding child had in mind.

15   No one has ①ever pretended to ②lie down a set of rules for the invention or discovery of hypotheses. It is ③likely that none could ever be laid down, for that is the creative side of the scientific enterprise. Ability to create is a function of imagination and talent and ④cannot be reduced to a mechanical process. A great scientific hypothesis, with wide explanatory power like those of Newton's or Einstein's, is ⑤as much the product of genius as a great work of art. There is no formula for discovering new hypotheses.

16 The word "cause" is most often used in the sense of necessary condition when the problem ①at hand is the elimination of some undesirable phenomenon. To eliminate it, one needs only to find some condition that is necessary to ②its existence and then eliminate that condition. Thus a physician ③seeks discovering what kind of germs is the "cause" of a certain illness in order to cure the illness by ④prescribing a drug that will destroy those germs. The germs are said to be the cause of the disease in the sense of a necessary condition for it, since ⑤in their absence the disease cannot occur.

17 A U.S. survey reveals that women have been ①getting unhappier over the past 40 years. At the same time, the number of happy men has increased. Surprisingly those women that felt an emotional high in their lives didn't talk much about ②juggling different roles, goals and plans. Instead, they talked about moments that strengthen their lives. The decline in women's happiness applies to all women ③across the board regardless their marital status or job. In particular, ④it's a mystery why women with flexible, family-friendly work hours are even ⑤less happy on a daily basis. It's possible that some people have too many choices, and they are doing more but feeling less.

18 Mummification in Ancient Egypt was developed in response to a gradual change in the burial preferences of its deceased. The artificial preservation of bodies, both human and animal, was practised in Egypt from about 2686 BC ①until the beginning of the Christian era. The earliest Egyptians were buried in the sand, typically in the foetal position to reduce the size of the hole that would need to be dug, and the hot, dry climate would dehydrate the body. The physical features of the body ②would be retained, and this lifelike appearance of the corpse may have supported the belief of an afterlife. As burial practices became more sophisticated, with the construction of elaborate tombs and monuments to ③the dead, the bodies of ④deceased were no longer buried in the desert sand. However, as belief in the afterlife and rebirth was fundamental to Egyptian burial practices, mummification was developed to artificially preserve the body in readiness for the journey to the underworld and to be judged by Osiris.

19   Earlier the same week, a man from the *New York Times* called me and asked if I would ①be willing to write a short story that would appear in the paper on Christmas morning. My first impulse was to say no, but the man was very charming and persistent, and by the end of the conversation I told him I would ②give it a try. The moment I hung up the phone, however, I fell into a deep panic. What did I know about Christmas? I asked myself. What did I know about writing short stories on commission? I spent the next several days in despair, warring with the ghosts of Dickens, O. Henry and other masters of the Yuletide spirit. The very phrase "Christmas story" had unpleasant associations for me, ③and evoking dreadful outpourings of hypocritical mush and treacle. Even ④at their best, Christmas stories were no more than wish-fulfillment dreams, fairy tales for adults, and I'd be damned if I'd ever allowed myself to write something like that. And yet, how could anyone propose to write an unsentimental Christmas story? It was a contradiction in terms, an impossibility, an out-and-out conundrum. One ⑤might just as well try to imagine a racehorse without legs, or a sparrow without wings.

[20] Choose the sentence that is NOT grammatically correct.

20   ① I would rather you came here, tomorrow than today.
  ② It is time you washed away your own ridiculous privilege.
  ③ If only I had a larger budget, this wouldn't be a problem.
  ④ When the test began, I wished I know the answer.

합격을 완성할 단 하나의 선택

김영편입 영어
문법

기출 **2** 단계

해설편

T E S T 01

01 ③	02 ③	03 ①	04 ④	05 ④	06 ③	07 ①	08 ①	09 ②	10 ④
11 ③	12 ③	13 ②	14 ③	15 ④	16 ③	17 ③	18 ②	19 ④	20 ④

01   2022 단국대 ▶▶▶ MSG p.228   ③

전치사 but ▶ What is A but B?(A는 B이외에 무엇이란 말인가?)는 A is nothing other than B(A는 다름 아닌 B이다.)와 같은 의미의 표현이다. 즉 빈칸 이하가 한 덩어리의 명사이므로 '~를 제외하고, ~이외에 (except)'라는 뜻의 전치사 but이 빈칸에 들어가면 의문사 what과 호응하여 이런 표현이 된다.

mythical a. 신화의 extraordinary a. 비범한 extract v. 이끌어내다 steep v. ~에 담그다; 흠뻑 젖게 하다 adversity n. 역경, 불행 psychosexual a. 성심리 (性心理)의

신화 속의 공주는 역경, 가정불화, 학대 그리고 또 다른 성심리적(性心理的) 공포로 가득 찬 이야기에서 행복한 결말을 이끌어내는 비범한 젊은 여성이외에 무엇이란 말인가?

02   2017 가천대 ▶▶▶ MSG p.85   ③

문의 구성 ▶ 빈칸부터 rocks까지가 is important의 주어여야 하는데, 빈칸 다음에 '주어+동사+목적어'의 절이 나와 있으므로, 빈칸에 들어갈 표현은 이 절을 이끄는 접속사적인 요소를 포함하여 문장의 주어가 될 수 있는 것이어야 한다. 따라서 접속사적 요소인 의문사 how절과 이것을 목적어로 취하는 to부정사가 제시돼 있는 ③이 빈칸에 적절하다. ① 원형동사, ② 과거분사, ④ '전치사+명사'는 모두 주어가 될 수 없다.

geologist n. 지질학자 classify v. 분류하다 be familiar with ~에 정통하다 transform v. 바꾸다 specimen n. 견본, 표본

암석을 형성하게 만들었던 지구의 주요 과정에 따라 지질학자들은 암석을 세 가지 집단으로 분류한다. 암석을 수집하기를 원하는 사람이라면 누구나 이 세 가지 암석 집단의 특성을 잘 알고 있어야 한다. 지질학자가 암석을 어떻게 분류하는지를 아는 것은 무작위 표본들을 진짜 소장품으로 바꾸기 위해 중요하다.

03   2013 한국외대 ▶▶▶ MSG p.137, p.174   ①

관계사절에서의 주어와 동사의 수일치 ▶ 30개의 유닛 중 각각의 유닛이 센서를 갖고 있다는 문장을 완성해야 한다. ② 주어의 핵심어인 each는 단수 취급하는데 are가 와서 옳지 않다. ③ 주어의 핵심어인 some은 which가 가산명사 복수인 units를 가리키므로 복수 취급하여 are가 와야 하는데 is여서 옳지 않다. ④ which of them은 which가 관계대명사인 관계절에서는 불가능하고 의문사인 의문문이나 간접의문문에서는 '그것들 중 어느 것'의 의미로 가능하다.

satellite n. 인공위성 be equipped with ~로 갖추다

인공위성은 30개의 모듈러 유닛으로 이루어져 있고, 각각의 유닛은 한 세트의 센서들을 갖추고 있다.

04   2018 가천대 ▶▶▶ MSG p.73   ④

as if[though] 가정법 ▶ as if[though]는 feel, look, seem 등의 동사와 함께 '마치 ~처럼'이라는 뜻으로 쓰인다. 이때 as if[though] 뒤에는 가정법 동사가 오는데, 주절의 시제와 같은 상황의 가정에는 가정법 과거 동사를 쓰고, 주절의 시제보다 앞선 상황에 대한 가정에는 가정법 과거완료 동사를 쓴다. 주어진 문장의 경우는 전자에 해당하므로, 가정법 과거의 형태인 ④가 정답으로 적절하다.

carcass n. (짐승의) 시체 female n. 암컷, 여성 well-preserved a. 잘 보존된

한 새끼 매머드의 시체가 작년 5월에 러시아 시베리아의 북서 지역에서 언 채로 보존돼 있는 것이 발견되었다. 생후 6개월 된 그 암컷 매머드는 지금까지 발견된 동물 중에서 가장 보존 상태가 좋은 표본이다. 그것은 마치 아직 살아있는 것처럼 보였다.

05   2019 한국외대 ▶▶▶ MSG p.141   ④

문의 구성 ▶ 이 문장의 주어는 Dopamine이고, 본동사는 turns out이다. 따라서 빈칸부터 pleasure까지는 주어와 동사 사이에 삽입된 표현이다. which 관계절인 which has long been reputed to be ~ pleasure가 삽입될 수 있는데, 여기서 주격 관계대명사 which와 be동사인 has been이 생략될 수 있으므로, ④가 빈칸에 적절하다.

chemical n. 화학물질 have to do with ~와 관련이 있다

도파민은, 기쁨의 신호를 보내는 뇌 화학물질인 것으로 오랫동안 알려져 있었는데, 좋아하는 것보다는 원하는 것과 더 관련이 있는 것으로 드러나고 있다.

06 2018 가톨릭대 ▶▶▶ MSG p.111 ③

분사구문 ▶ 주절이 완전하므로, 종속절 As there was no evidence를 분사구문으로 고친 ③이 빈칸에 들어가기에 적절하다. ①과 ②는 분사구문과 부정사의 의미상 주어가 주절의 주어인 the alleged spy인 것이 되어 부적절하며, ④는 명사절을 이끄는 that이 종속절의 역할을 할 수 없으므로 정답이 될 수 없다.

alleged a. (근거 없이) 추정[단정]된 release v. 방면(放免)하다, 석방하다 federal a. 연합의, 연방정부의 prison n. 교도소 confinement n. 감금, 억류

자신에게 불리한 증거가 전혀 없었기 때문에, 프랑스의 스파이로 추정된 그 인물은 이틀 동안 감금된 후에 마침내 연방 교도소에서 풀려났다.

07 2017 서울여대 ▶▶▶ MSG p.140 ①

문의 구성 ▶ ②와 ④는 전치사 in이 절을 목적어로 취할 수 없으므로 부적절하며, ③의 경우 타동사 dismiss는 전치사 없이 바로 목적어를 취하므로 역시 정답이 될 수 없다. 따라서 정답은 ①이 되며, 이때 the role과 culture 사이에는 목적격 관계대명사가 생략돼 있으며, how가 이끄는 명사절이 전치사 in의 목적어가 된다.

dismiss v. (고려할 가치가 없다고) 묵살하다 play a role in ~에서 역할을 담당하다

우리는 사람들이 정신건강을 바라보고 접근하는 방식에 있어서 문화가 담당하고 있는 역할을 무시해서는 안 된다.

08 2018 서울여대 ▶▶▶ MSG p.28 ①

문의 구성 ▶ 빈칸 앞의 their photographs, or "pictures"는 give 동사의 간접목적어이므로 빈칸은 give의 직접목적어가 들어갈 자리이며, give의 직접목적어가 될 수 있는 것의 품사는 명사여야 하므로, 빈칸에는 ①이 들어가야 한다.

photography n. 사진술 pictorialist n. 회화주의 사진예술가 strive v. 노력하다, 힘쓰다

사진술이 여전히 비교적 새로운 형태의 예술이었던 19세기에, "회화주의 사진예술가들"은 자신들의 사진, 즉 "그림"을 회화와 닮아 보이게 하려 했던 사진작가들이었다.

09 2010 동국대 ▶▶▶ MSG p.53 ②

시제일치 ▶ authorities concerned가 '관계당국'이라는 뜻으로 적절하고, 메시지를 전달한 시점과 그 결정을 비웃은 시점이 같은 시점이므로 한 시제 앞선 having conveyed가 아니라 conveying이 되어야 한다. ②가 정답이다.

ridicule v. 비웃다, 조롱하다 convey v. 운반하다; 전달하다

관계당국은 그 방송채널을 폐쇄할 것이라는 파키스탄 정부의 메시지를 전달하면서도 그 결정을 비웃었다.

10 2014 상명대 ▶▶▶ MSG p.197 ④

'자동사+전치사'에서 목적어의 위치 ▶ go over는 '자동사+전치사' 형태로 목적어는 반드시 전치사 다음에 위치시켜야 하는데, 목적어로 대명사가 온 경우에도 마찬가지이다. 따라서 ④를 go over them으로 고쳐야 한다. '타동사+부사' 형태의 구동사에서 목적어로 대명사가 왔을 때는 반드시 동사와 부사 사이에 목적어를 써야 하는 것과 다르다. ①, ② it이 가주어, to set 이하가 진주어로 온 형태이다.

set aside 제쳐 놓다 multiple-choice question 객관식 문제 go over ~을 검토하다

시험에서 객관식 문제들은 한 쪽에 제쳐두고 마지막에 검토하는 것이 가장 좋다.

11 2022 한국외대 ▶▶▶ MSG p.152 ③

few와 little의 용법 구분 ▶ few는 셀 수 있는 것에 쓰고 little은 셀 수 없는 것에 쓴다. 얼마나 알고 있는가는 셀 수 있는 것이 아니므로 ③에는 few가 아닌 little을 써야 한다. ③을 how little로 고친다.

task n. 임무; 과업 demonstrate v. 증명하다; 보여주다

광고가 하는 일은 사람들에게 그들이 자신이 원하는 것에 대해 실제로 얼마나 적게 알고 있는지를 보여주는 것이다.

12 2019 한국외대 ▶▶▶ MSG p.105 ③

문의 구성 ▶ but 이하에 두 개의 동사(are found와 vary)가 와서 문법적으로 틀린 문장이 되었다. 문맥상 vary가 but 이하의 본동사이므로, 주어인 kinds를 과거분사 found가 수식할 수 있도록 ③에서 are를 삭제해야 한다. 참고로 ④ so greatly 다음에 접속사 that이 생략되어 있다.

plant n. 식물 grassland n. 초원 of value 귀중한 list v. 목록을 작성하다

초원에 있는 많은 식물들은 인간의 음식으로 직접적인 가치가 있지만, 그 나라의 여러 지역에서 발견되는 식물 종류들이 너무 다양해서 그 식물들의 목록을 작성하기는 어렵다.

13 2018 서강대 ▶▶▶ MSG p.227 ②

전치사의 적절한 사용 ▶ '~다음으로'라는 의미의 표현은 'second to~'이다. 그러므로 ②는 only to로 수정해야 한다. 이때 in importance only는 second와 to 사이에 삽입된 표현으로 이해해야 한다.

metabolism n. 신진대사; 기능, 작용 plough v. 쟁기로 갈다 grimy a. 때묻은, 더러운 caryatid n. 여인상으로 된 기둥

서구 세계가 기능하는 데 있어서 석탄 광부는 땅을 일구는 농부 바로 다음으로 중요한 존재이다. 그는 거의 모든 때 묻지 않은 것들을 밑에서 떠받치고 있는 일종의 때 묻은 기둥이다.

---

14 **2017 서강대** ▶▶▶ MSG p.227　　　　　③

전치사의 적절한 사용 ▶ move from A to B의 구조를 갖추어야 하므로 ③에 from을 추가하여 from the age of~가 되어야 한다.

striking a. 눈에 띄는, 두드러진 pottery n. 도자기 inexorably ad. 멈출 수 없이, 거침없이 subjective a. 주관적인 rigorous a. 철저한, 엄격한 objective a. 객관적인

이집트 도자기 연구에 있어 눈에 띄는 대비가 이뤄지는 시점을 유용하게 나타낼 수 있는데, 이집트 도자기 연구는 20세기의 마지막 20년 동안 주관적인 기술의 시대로부터 엄격한 객관적 분석의 시대로 거침없이, 그리고 이롭게, 넘어갔다.

---

15 **2015 국민대** ▶▶▶ MSG p.117　　　　　④

전치사 regarding ▶ 두 번째 문장의 동사는 lives와 has been이므로, ④처럼 시제를 가진 동사가 접속사 없이 또 다시 와서는 안 된다. ④ 이하가 debate의 내용을 구체적으로 설명하는 역할을 할 수 있도록, ④에서 regarded를 '~에 관하여'라는 의미의 전치사 regarding으로 고치는 것이 적절하다.

activist n. 사회운동가 polar bear 북극곰 zoo n. 동물원

아르헨티나의 사회운동가들은 아르헨티나의 살아 있는 마지막 북극곰인 아르투로(Arturo)의 생활환경을 개선시키기 위해 노력하고 있다. 29살 난 그 동물은 멘도사(Mendoza) 동물원에서 살고 있으며 그의 정신적, 신체적 건강 상태에 관한 사회운동가들과 동물원 관리인들 사이의 열띤 논쟁의 중심에 있어 왔다.

---

16 **2019 중앙대** ▶▶▶ MSG p.218　　　　　③

절의 병치 ▶ 이유를 나타내는 접속사 as가 이끄는 절 2개가 등위접속사 and에 의해 병치된 구조이다. ③의 thus는 결과를 나타내는 접속부사여서 두 번째 절을 이끌 수 없으므로, as로 바꾸어야 한다. 접속사 as를 한 번 쓰고 두 절이 and에 의해 연결된 것으로도 볼 수 있으나 그러려면 콤마(,)가 ③의 thus 앞이 아니라 뒤에 있어야 한다.

poem n. 시 subject n. 주제 content v. 만족시키다 detached a. 초연한

그러나 지금 제시된 시들을 통해 독자에게 주고 싶은 즐거움이 이 주제에 관한 정당한 개념들에 전적으로 의지해야 하므로, 그리고 그것이 그 자체로 우리의 취향과 도덕적 감정에 대단히 중요하므로, 나는 이러한 초연한 진술에 만족할 수 없다.

---

17 **2014 한양대** ▶▶▶ MSG p.227　　　　　③

전치사 into ▶ reincarnate는 '환생하다'라는 의미이며, animal bodies는 환생의 결과 나타난 모습이므로, ③을 상태의 변화, 추이, 결과를 나타내는 전치사 into로 고쳐야 한다. ① along with는 '~와 함께'라는 의미의 표현으로 since와 병치되어 the Industrial Revolution으로 연결된다. ② far from은 '결코 ~이 아니다', '조금도 ~하지 않다'는 의미이며, 뒤에 형용사가 오는 것도 가능하다. ④ 찬성, 동조의 의미를 나타내는 전치사이다.

Industrial Revolution 산업혁명 outcome n. 결과 attest v. 입증하다, 증명하다 proponent n. 제안자; 옹호자 reincarnate v. 환생하다

산업혁명과 함께 그리고 그 이후에 일어난 사회 운동들 가운데, 여전히 다소 논쟁의 여지가 있는 채로 있고 그 결과가 아직 전혀 정해지지 않은 것은 동물 권리 운동이다. 역사상 최초인 것으로 입증된 옹호자는 고대 그리스의 사상가 피타고라스이다. 인간은 동물의 몸으로 환생할 수 있다는 자신의 믿음을 따라, 그는 동물을 인간과 똑같이 대할 것을 주장했다.

---

18 **2013 명지대** ▶▶▶ MSG p.48　　　　　②

과거완료시제 ▶ 주절의 시제가 과거이며 여러 시대에 텍사스 상공에서 휘날렸던 여섯 개의 깃발을 의미하므로 관계사절의 시제는 주절보다 앞선다. 따라서 ②는 과거완료시제인 had flown over가 되어야 한다. ① 주어가 one이므로 동사는 단수가 되어야 한다. 따라서 was는 바르게 쓰였다. ④ enable은 목적어 다음에 목적보어로 to 부정사를 취하는 5형식 동사이다.

nod n. 끄덕임; 승인 belle n. 미인, (특정한 장소의) 최고 미인 pirate n. 해적; 해적선

식스 플래그 매직 마운틴(Six Flags; 식스 플래그사의 테마파크)의 독특한 면 중 하나는 단순히 다양한 놀이기구를 모아놓은 것이 아니라 텍사스 주의 역사라는 하나의 주제로 개발되었다는 것이다. 이 공원의 이름은 여러 시대(프랑스, 스페인, 멕시코, 미국 남부 연방, 텍사스 공화국과 오늘날의 미국)에 텍사스 상공에서 휘날렸던 여섯 개의 깃발을 승인하는 것이었다. 그 공원의 놀이기구들은 여섯 개의 테마를 가진 구역으로 분류되어 있는데, 이 구역들은 각 정부의 문화를 보여주고 관광객들이 카우보이 문화에서부터 남부 미인과 해적에 이르는 모든 것을 경험할 수 있게 해주었다.

---

19 **2017 명지대** ▶▶▶ MSG p.182　　　　　④

형용사의 어순 ▶ other와 a few는 모두 명사를 수식하는 형용사인데, 수량 형용사 a few가 먼저 와야 하므로, ④를 a few other(몇 개의 다른)로 고쳐야 한다.

archaeologist n. 고고학자 cemetery n. 공동묘지 grave n. 무덤 CE n. 서력기원, 서기(=Common Era) in that ~라는 점에서 coffin n. 관(棺) disintegrate v. 분해하다 waterlogged a. 물로 흥건한 intact a. 온전한 hollow out ~의 속을 파내다 trunk n. 나무의 몸통 plank n. 판자, 널빤지 shed new light on ~을 재조명하다

영국의 고고학자들은 서기 7~9세기로 추정되는 80개 이상의 무덤들로 구성된 앵글로 색슨족의 공동묘지를 발굴하였다. 앵글로 색슨 시대의 목관들이 잘 보존된 상태로 발견된 것은 영국에서 처음 있는 일이라는 점에서 이번 발견은 주목할 만하다. 나무는 (땅속에) 묻힐 때 보통 빨리 분해되지만, 노퍽(Norfolk) 근처 Great Ryburgh의 물로 흥건한 공동묘지는 목관들을 온전한 상태로 유지시켜 주었다. 시신들은 대부분 속을 파낸 오크나무 몸통으로 만든 관에 매장되지만, 몇 개의 다른 무덤들은 그 안을 나무판자들로 대어놓았다. 이번 발견으로 초기 기독교 앵글로 색슨 사회의 생활상이 재조명될 전망이다.

---

20   2019 한국외대   ▶▶▶ MSG p.139   ④

정비문 ▶ ④ serve A (with) B는 'A(사람)에게 B(음식물)을 제공하다'는 의미로 쓰이는데, 간접목적어 A가 주어로 가면서 수동태가 되어서 They were served는 맞는 표현이다. 하지만 직접목적어인 what 관계대명사절은 주어(it)와 동사(could be described)를 갖춘 완전한 절이어서 문법적으로 적절하지 않다. 관계대명사 what이 관계절의 주어여야 하므로 what 다음의 it이 삭제되어야 문법적으로 옳은 문장이 된다.

solitary a. 홀로 있는 endeavor n. 노력 beg for ~을 간청하다 matter v. 중요하다 garbage n. 쓰레기

① 자신의 친구들을 버렸던 그 남자는 외롭게 홀로 죽었다.
② 소용없는 것으로 판명된 노력을 기울이며, 학생들이 더 높은 점수를 간청했다.
③ 이 시점에서 가장 중요한 것은 영원히 기억될 수 있는 노력을 하는 것이다.
④ 그들에게는 쓰레기라고 말할 수밖에 없는 음식이 아침식사로 제공되었다.

TEST 02

| 01 ② | 02 ② | 03 ② | 04 ① | 05 ④ | 06 ④ | 07 ② | 08 ④ | 09 ① | 10 ① |
| 11 ④ | 12 ① | 13 ② | 14 ③ | 15 ① | 16 ③ | 17 ⑤ | 18 ④ | 19 ⑤ | 20 ② |

01 2018 단국대 ▶▶▶ MSG p.199 ②

원급비교 ▶ 빈칸 앞에 as deep, arbitrary, and unexplained라는 'as+형용사' 형태가 나왔으므로, 빈칸에는 'as+형용사'와 호응해 원급비교가 되는 as가 들어가야 한다. 따라서 ②가 빈칸에 적절하다. 참고로, 빈칸 다음의 that은 '그'라는 뜻의 한정사(지시형용사)로, will은 '의지'라는 뜻의 명사로 각각 쓰인 것이다.

possess v. (감정 등이 사람을) 사로잡다 impulse n. (갑작스러운) 충동 arbitrary a. 임의적인, 제멋대로인 will n. 의지 lie at the bottom of something ~의 밑바탕에 있다

그들은 어떤 환경을 실현하려는 충동에 사로잡혀 있는데, 그 충동은 모든 설명의 밑바탕에 있는 '삶에 대한 의지'만큼 강렬하고, 임의적이며, 뭐라고 설명할 수 없는 충동이다.

02 2017 서울여대 ▶▶▶ MSG p.116 ②

with 분사구문 ▶ 콤마 앞이 완전한 문장이고, with 뒤에 목적어가 주어져 있으며, 보기에는 동사만 주어져 있는 상황이다. 전치사는 절을 목적어로 취할 수 없으므로, 콤마 이하를 부대상황을 나타내는 'with 분사구문'으로 만들면 옳은 문장이 될 수 있다. 'with 분사구문'에서는 with 다음 명사의 능동적 관계를 나타내면 현재분사, 수동적 관계를 나타내면 과거분사를 쓰는데, 주어진 문장의 경우, with 다음의 many가 feel하는 능동관계이므로 현재분사를 써서 분사구문을 만들어야 한다. ②가 정답이 된다.

academic pressures 학업에 대한 부담

아동심리학자들은 학업에 대한 부담으로 인해 여학생들이 겪는 불안감에 대해 글을 썼는데, 많은 여학생들은 자신들이 공부를 충분히 잘하지 못한다고 생각한다.

03 2015 서울여대 ▶▶▶ MSG p.141 ②

형용사와 동사로 모두 쓰일 수 있는 empty ▶ ① be 다음에 온 empty는 형용사로, the page와 연결될 수 없다. ③ be 다음에 보어로 형용사 empty가 오고, onto the page는 부사구로 문법적으로는 맞게 쓰였으나, '그 페이지 위에 비어 있기 위해 기다리다'는 말이 되어 의미상 어색하다. ④ to는 전치사가 아니라 to부정사로 쓰여서 to 다음에 ~ing형태가 올 수 없다. ② empty가 여기서는 '~에 쏟아 붓다'는 뜻의 타동

로 쓰여 수동태가 된 형태이며, onto the page는 '페이지 위에'라는 뜻의 부사구로 쓰였으므로 ②가 빈칸에 가장 적절하다. 여기서 waiting은 which is waiting에서 which is가 생략된 것이다.

vision n. 상상력; 통찰력 empty a. 텅 빈; v. ~을 쏟아 붓다

작가는 지면에 쏟아 부어지기를 기다리고 있는 완전한 형태의 상상력을 갖추고 있어야 한다.

04 2011 단국대 ▶▶▶ MSG p.105 ①

현재분사와 과거분사의 구분 ▶ 부사절의 주어는 my mother이고 동사는 stood이다. 따라서 '주어와 동사'를 갖춘 완전한 절이 되었으므로 빈칸에는 분사가 올 수 있는데 주어인 my mother가 me를 꾸짖는 주체이므로 능동의 현재분사가 적절하다.

upbraid v. 질책하다, 호되게 나무라다 vase n. 꽃병 stare v. 빤히 쳐다보다, 응시하다

어머니가 나의 부주의한 행동에 대해 질책하며 손에 깨진 꽃병을 들고 서 있었을 때 나는 부끄러워서 내 발에 시선을 고정하였다.

05 2017 서울여대 ▶▶▶ MSG p.119 ④

문의 구성 ▶ '주어+동사'의 구조가 3개(Culture is, it may appear, it has) 있으므로, 이것을 연결해 줄 접속사는 2개가 필요하다. 그러므로 등위접속사 and와 종속접속사 though를 포함하고 있는 ④가 정답이 된다. 나머지 보기들은 접속사의 개수가 충분하지 않으므로 모두 정답이 될 수 없다.

security blanket 안심담요(안도감을 갖기 위해 아이가 갖고 다니는 담요) tattered a. 누덕누덕한 outmoded a. 유행에 뒤떨어진

문화는 안심담요(아이들이 마음의 안정을 찾기 위해 갖고 다니는 담요)와 같으며, 어떤 사람들에게는 그것이 닳아빠진 누더기로, 유행에 뒤떨어지고 우스꽝스러운 것으로 보일지도 모르지만, 그것의 주인에게는 큰 의미가 있다.

06 2022 단국대 ▶▶▶ MSG p.133 ④

양보 구문 ▶ 주절이 완성돼 있으므로, 양보의 부사절을 완성시키는 ④가 빈칸에 들어가기에 적절하다. ① Whatever comes여야 한다. ② No matter what happens여야 한다.

rainy day 만약의 경우, (장래의) 곤궁할 때

무슨 일이 있어도, 인생에서 사업을 시작하는 모든 젊은이들에게 단 하나의 안전한 방법이 있으니, 그것은 바로 장래의 어려울 때를 대비하는 것이다.

07　2017 단국대　▶▶▶ MSG p.85　②

'~하지 않을 수 없다'의 관용표현과 복합관계형용사의 용법 ▶ '~하지 않을 수 없다'는 의미의 표현은 'have no choice but to부정사', 'have no choice other than to부정사' 등으로 할 수 있다. 그러므로 other than 뒤에 원형부정사와 동명사를 쓴 ③과 ④를 먼저 정답에서 제외할 수 있다. ①의 경우에는 명사 price가 관계대명사절의 수식을 받고 있으므로 정관사 the가 price 앞에 있어야 한다. 따라서 정답은 ②가 되며, 이때 whatever는 복합관계형용사로, whatever price a drug-maker sets는 any price that a drug-maker sets의 의미이다.

alternative n. (둘 중, 때로는 셋 이상에서) 하나를 택할 여지; 대안　drug n. 약, 약품

약에 대해 다른 선택의 여지가 없는 경우, 환자와 보험회사는 제약회사에서 정하는 그 어떤 가격도 그대로 지불하는 수밖에 없다.

08　2019 한국산업기술대　▶▶▶ MSG p.224　④

도치구문 ▶ 긍정문 다음에 so가 와서 '~도 역시 마찬가지이다'라는 뜻으로 쓰일 때에는 주어와 동사가 도치된다. 빈칸의 주어는 the price of silk이고 동사는 앞에 나온 일반 동사 grew를 받은 did여야 하므로 ④가 정답이다. 참고로 부정문 다음에는 neither를 쓴다.

startled a. 깜짝 놀란　fabric n. 직물, 천　craze n. (특히 일시적인) 대유행[열풍]

로마 사람들은 그들의 적이 세상에 알려지지 않은 직물인 실크로 만들어진 군기(軍旗)를 들고 있다는 것을 알고 깜짝 놀랐다. (그 후) 몇 십 년 안에, 로마의 부유한 가족들은 실크를 입기 시작했다. 실크 열풍이 수 세기에 걸쳐 고조되었고, 실크의 가격 또한 올라갔다.

09　2022 아주대　▶▶▶ MSG p.130　①

결과를 나타내는 'such+a(n)+형용사+명사+that' 구문 ▶ 'so/such ~ that …(너무나 ~해서 …하다)' 구문의 문장인데 such 다음에는 'a(n)+형용사+명사+that SV'의 어순으로 나열된다. 따라서 빈칸에 적절한 표현은 ①이다.

discrete a. 별개의, 분리된　vehicle n. 수단, 매체　salient a. 가장 중요한; 가장 두드러진　dominant a. 지배적인　feature n. 특징

살아있는 물질을 개별적인 운반체 속에 담는 것이 너무나 두드러지면서도 지배적인 특징이 되어서 생물학자들이 현장에 도착해서 생명체에 관해 묻기 시작했을 때, 그들의 질문은 대부분 운반체에 관한 것이었다.

10　2014 서울여대　▶▶▶ MSG p.35　①

take+목적어+for granted ▶ '~을 당연한 것으로 여기다'는 뜻을 나타낼 때는 'take+목적어+for granted'를 쓰는데, take의 목적어가 it과 their ability to access all Web sites on an equal basis로 2개가 되므로 하나를 제거해야 하는데, 목적어의 길이가 길 경우 문미로 배치가 가능하고 it은 불필요하므로 it을 제거해야 한다. 따라서 ①을 take for granted로 고쳐야 한다. ② their는 Users of the Internet을 받은 대명사이며, ability는 추상명사로 단수로 맞게 쓰였다. ③ access는 타동사로 쓰여 all Web sites를 목적어로 취했다. ④ '동등한 입장에서, 대등하게'라는 뜻의 부사구이다.

access v. ~에 접속하다, 접근하다　on an equal basis 동등하게

인터넷 사용자들은 동등하게 모든 인터넷 사이트에 접속할 수 있다는 것을 당연한 것으로 여긴다.

11　2022 한국외대　▶▶▶ MSG p.163　④

so+형용사+관사+명사 ▶ age가 나이를 의미할 때는 가산명사로 쓰이며, so는 '형용사+부정관사+명사'의 어순을 취한다. 따라서 ④는 so young an age가 되어야 한다.

intimidating a. 겁을 주는[겁나는]　deal with ~을 다루다　athlete n. 운동선수

첫 직업은 누구에게나 겁이 나는 것일 수 있겠지만, 운동선수와 무용수만큼 어린 나이에 일과 관련된 스트레스를 다루어야 하는 사람은 거의 없다.

12　2009 중앙대　▶▶▶ MSG p.135　①

문의 구성 ▶ 관계대명사 which를 삭제해야 Bold ~ patterns 까지가 주어부이고 are used 이하와 are repeated 이하가 and로 병치된 두 술부인 문장이 성립한다. ① which를 삭제한다.

bold a. 대담한　startling a. 놀라운　decorate v. 장식하다　auditorium n. 객석, 관객석

대담한 색들과 놀라운 문양들이 극장 로비를 장식하기 위해 사용되며 관객석의 벽과 의자의 천에서도 되풀이된다.

13　2022 단국대　▶▶▶ MSG p.201　②

not so much A as B 구문 ▶ 'A라기보다는 B이다'라는 의미의 표현은 not so much A as B이므로 ②는 not so much여야 한다. 주어진 문장에서 from curiosity, or because they like to see things beautiful and strange가 A에 해당하고 out of a kind of affectation이 B에 해당한다.

trouble n. 수고　go to the expense of ~에 비용을 들이다　affectation n. 꾸밈; 가식

여행자들이 여행하는 데 수고와 비용을 들인다면, 그것은 호기심 때문이거나 그들이 아름답고 기묘한 것들을 보고 싶어 하기 때문이라기보다는 일종의 가식으로 인한 것이다.

---

14 2021 국민대 ▶▶▶ MSG p.15 ③

동사 doom의 용법 ▶ 타동사 doom은 'doom+목적어+to V(~로 하여금 …하도록 운명 짓다)'로 쓰이므로, ③을 dooms them to be enslaved로 고쳐야 한다. 이때 them은 '슬라브인들'을 지칭한다.

tyrant n. 독재자 doom v. (나쁘게) 운명 짓다 reasoning n. 추론

보다 최근에, 슬라브인들이 독재자의 지배를 받고 그 지배에서 벗어날 희망이 보이지 않았을 때, 일부 사람들은 슬라브인들의 국민성에 그들로 하여금 노예가 되도록 운명 짓는 어떤 것이 있음이 틀림없다고 침울하게 결론 내렸다. 이것은 잘못된 추론이며, 자유인은 어느 누구도 그것을 믿을 리 없다.

---

15 2019 서강대 ▶▶▶ MSG p.44, p.55 ①

능동태와 수동태의 구분 및 과거시제 ▶ ①의 주어인 The fleet은 destroy되는 대상이므로 수동태 문장이 되어야 하며, 명확한 과거를 나타내는 표현 in the first days of August 1798이 있으므로 시제는 과거여야 한다. 따라서 ①을 was destroyed로 고친다.

fleet n. 함대 prisoner n. 죄수; 포로 wounded a. 상처 입은, 부상당한

보나파르트(Bonaparte)가 거느리고 이집트에 도착했던 함대는 1798년 8월 초에 아부키르(Aboukir)에서 넬슨(Nelson)에 의해 파괴되었다. 그때 프랑스인 5,000명이 전사하고 3,000명이 포로가 되었지만, 영국은 손실이 전사자와 부상자를 합쳐 900명에 불과했다.

---

16 2019 중앙대 ▶▶▶ MSG p.105 ③

능동태와 수동태 구분 ▶ that절의 주어인 the transparency(투명도)가 밀도에 따라 정해지는 대상이므로, 수동태가 되도록 ③을 과거분사 conditioned로 고쳐야 한다.

transparency n. 투명도, 투명성 density n. (물질의) 농도, 밀도

다른 실험 결과뿐만 아니라 현재 주어진 실험 결과도, 서로 다른 물질의 투명도와 물질의 두께가 동일한 것으로 가정될 때, 본질적으로 물질의 밀도에 따라 정해진다는 결론을 내리게 한다.

---

17 2018 아주대 ▶▶▶ MSG p.137 ⑤

전치사+관계대명사 ▶ 선행사 the rate와 어울리는 전치사는 at이다. 그러므로 ⑤의 for which를 at which로 수정해야 한다. ③은 and one of the most serious is to cause ~에서 접속사 and를 삭제하고 동사 is를 being으로 바꾼 독립분사구문(종속절의 주어와 주절의 주어가 다른 분사구문) 형태이다.

---

surface n. 표면 the planet 지구 iceberg n. 빙산 melt v. 녹다 hasten v. 재촉하다

바다는 지구의 71퍼센트를 덮고 있기 때문에 지구 표면에 도달하는 태양 에너지의 상당량을 흡수한다. 지구 온난화는 여러 가지 방식으로 바다에 영향을 미치는데, 가장 심각한 방식 중 하나가 빙산과 다른 해빙들을 녹게 만드는 것이다. 아이러니하게도, 지구 온난화는 빙산의 형성을 가속화시키면서, 그 빙산들이 바다에 녹아드는 속도 역시 증가시키고 있다.

---

18 2017 명지대 ▶▶▶ MSG p.10 ④

준보어로서의 분사 ▶ it이 가주어, that 이하가 진주어인 구조에서 that절의 주어가 so many tourists이고, 동사가 come away이며, ④는 주어인 관광객들이 떠날(come away) 때의 상태를 나타내므로 준보어이다. 관광객들이 감명을 주면서 떠나는 것이 아니라 감명을 받고 떠나는 것이므로 hugely 다음의 분사는 수동관계의 과거분사 impressed여야 한다. ④를 hugely impressed로 고친다.

intoxicating a. 들뜨게 하는 high rise building 고층건물 neon-saturated a. 네온사인이 가득한 pound v. (심장이) 두근거리다 feast n. 축제; 귀와 눈을 즐겁게 해주는 것 transport n. 수송; 교통기관 negligible a. 무시해도 될 정도의 astonishing a. 정말 놀라운 it's little wonder that ~은 별로 놀랄 일이 아니다

고층 건물, 네온사인 가득한 거리, 그리고 활기찬 상거래가 기분 좋게 한데 어울려져 있는 모습은 서울을 24시간 잠들지 않는 세계의 거대도시들 중 한 곳이자 오감(五感)을 정말로 즐겁게 해주는 곳으로 만들어 주는 데 모두 기여하고 있다. 서울시의 고도로 효율적인 교통체계, 무시해도 될 정도의 범죄율, 서울에서 자체적으로 생산된 엄청난 양의 현대미술로 인해, 전 세계에서 서울을 방문하는 많은 관광객들이 깊은 감명을 받고 (서울을) 떠나는 것은 별로 놀랄 일이 아니다.

---

19 2019 이화여대 ▶▶▶ MSG p.111 ⑤

현수 분사구문 ▶ 분사구문의 주어가 생략돼 있다는 것은 분사구문의 주어와 주절의 주어가 같다는 것을 의미한다. 그러므로 ⑤에 쓰인 분사구문의 주어는 주절의 주어인 'I'인데, 이럴 경우 'I = the music of today'인 게 되어 옳지 않다. '오늘날의 음악에 대해서는 공감이 가지 않는다.'는 흐름이므로, ⑤를 As for the music of today로 고치면 의미상의 주어 불일치 문제를 해결할 수 있다.

plausible a. 그럴 듯한 relate to ~에 공감하다, 이해하다 as for ~에 관해 말하자면

모든 세대는 그 세대만의 음악을 가지고 있다. 나의 경우에는 1980년대여서, 디보, 런-디엠씨, 사이키델릭 퍼즈, 고고스 같은 음악이었다. "고고스에 대해 모르는구나. 넌 (고고스를 모르고) 어떻게 살 수 있니?" 한 친구가 내게 물었다. 나는 어떻게 살 수 있었는가? 물론, 나는 그 즉시 고고스에 대해 알아보았고, 의심할 여지없이 나를 살려내었다. 물론, 이제 1980년대는 아득하게 지나갔고, 1990년 이후에 태어난 거의 모든 사람들은 고고스에 대해 알지 못하더라도 사는 데 전혀 아무 문제가 없다. 지금은 비욘세, 방탄소년단, 카디-B, 트와이스 등이 그 자리를 차지하게 됐다. 오늘날의 음악에 관해서라면, 나 자신이 그 음악에 공감할 수는 없지만, 나는 오늘날의 젊은이들이 내 나이가 됐을 때도 그 음악을 전부 기억하고 있을 거라고 확신한다. 그것은 그들 세대의 음악이다.

---

20 2021 국민대 ▶▶▶ MSG p.51

정비문 ▶ '소유'를 나타내는 have, own, possess 등의 동사는 원칙적으로 진행형으로 쓰지 않는다. ②에 쓰인 is owning을 owns로 고친다. ③ on board는 그 자체가 전치사적으로 쓰일 수도 있다. ex) On board the ship were several planes. 그 배에는 몇 대의 비행기가 탑재되어 있었다.

junior a. 손아래의, 연하의 on board 승선한, 탑승한

① 그녀는 일곱 살 연하의 남자와 결혼했다.
② 서울에 계신 나의 삼촌은 건물을 많이 가지고 계신다.
③ 그 배에는 12명의 아이들이 타고 있다.
④ 그 호텔에서 일어난 일에 대해서는 충분히 알려져 있지 않다.

| 01 ④ | 02 ② | 03 ④ | 04 ⑤ | 05 ② | 06 ② | 07 ① | 08 ③ | 09 ③ | 10 ① |
| 11 ③ | 12 ④ | 13 ④ | 14 ② | 15 ② | 16 ① | 17 ④ | 18 ③ | 19 ③ | 20 ① |

01 2006 서울여대 ▶▶▶ MSG p.144 ④

복합관계형용사 ▶ 문장의 본동사는 will be이며 그 앞부분은 will be의 주어이다. 그런데 여기에도 시제를 가진 형태의 동사 scores가 있으므로 빈칸에 ①이나 ③이 들어가면 scores 앞에 주격관계대명사 who가 없어 주어를 이루지 못한다. 즉 (의미상 No보다 Any가 적절하므로) Any player who scores~가 되어야 한다. 빈칸 다음에 player가 없다면 복합관계대명사로 ②가 답이 될 수 있다. 그러나 명사 player 앞에는 소유격의 복합관계대명사 whosever나 복합관계형용사만을 쓸 수 있는데 복합관계형용사로는 whichever와 whatever 둘뿐이므로 ④의 Whichever가 적절하다. 다만 'whichever+명사'는 'any+명사 which'와 같으므로 여기서 명사가 player처럼 사람일 때는 which가 부적절한 것 같지만 이런 경우에도 whoever가 아니라 whichever가 원칙이다. 다음의 예문들이 비슷한 예라 할 수 있다. ex.) Whichever player loses his or her headquarters loses the game.(본부를 잃는 선수면 어느 선수나 게임을 진다.) She told the class that whichever student answered the question correctly could have Monday off.(그녀는 질문에 옳게 답하는 학생이면 어느 학생이나 월요일에 쉬어도 좋다고 학급학생들에게 말했다.)

score v. 득점을 올리다

가장 높은 점수를 내는 선수면 어느 선수나 승자가 될 것이다.

02 2017 한국항공대 ▶▶▶ MSG p.117 ②

빈칸에 적절한 전치사 ▶ 가짜 뉴스(날조된 거짓말, hoax)가 우리 사회에서 '바이러스처럼 급속히 퍼져 나가는(go viral)' 이유를 기술하는 글이다. '우리가 가진 사회적 연결망과 제한된 주의력으로는 특정 문화 요소들이 급속히 퍼져나가게 되는 것을 피할 수 없다.'라는 흐름이 되어야 하므로, '~을 고려해 볼 때'를 의미하는 ②가 들어가는 것이 적절하다.

meme n. (비유전적) 문화 요소(유전자가 아니라 모방 등에 의해 다음 세대로 전달됨) viral a. 바이러스처럼 급속히 번져나가는 irrespective of ~와는 관계없이 fabricated a. 날조된, 허구의 hoax n. 거짓말 besides prep. ~외에도

우리의 사회적 연결망과 제한된 주의력을 고려해 볼 때, 어떤 문화 요소들이 그 질적 수준과는 상관없이 급속히 퍼져나가게 되는 것은 불가피한 일이다. 설사 개인들이 높은 질의 정보를 공유한다 할지라도 전반적인 연결망은 신뢰할 만한 정보와 날조된 정보를 구별하는 데 있어서 효과적이지 않다. 이것은 우리가 야생 세계 같은 연결망에서 목격하는 그 모든 거친 가짜 뉴스들이 급속히 전파되는 것을 설명하는 데 도움이 된다.

03 2018 가천대 ▶▶▶ MSG p.227 ④

적절한 전치사구 ▶ 빈칸 뒤의 '화장을 계속 새로 하는 것'과 주절의 '대형 마스크를 쓰는 것'은 화장을 하는 것과 하지 않는 것으로 서로 상반되므로, 대조의 의미를 갖는 표현인 ④ Rather than이 빈칸에 적절하다.

apply makeup 화장을 하다 with a view to ~을 위하여, ~할 목적으로 for the sake of ~때문에, ~을 위해서 rather than ~보다는

오늘날과는 극명하게 대조적으로, 고대 그리스와 로마의 배우들은 그들이 종종 같은 연극에서 몇몇 다른 배역들을 연기해야 했음에도 불구하고 화장을 전혀 하지 않았다. 배우들은 계속 새로운 화장을 하기보다는, 각각의 연극에서 여러 역할의 변화를 보여주기 위해서 대형 마스크를 쓰는 것이 훨씬 더 쉽다는 것을 알았다.

04 2017 아주대 ▶▶▶ MSG p.24, p.143 ⑤

동사 provide의 용법 및 who vs. whoever ▶ 동사 provide는 'provide+사람+with+사물', 'provide+사물+for+사람'의 구문을 취하는데, 문제에서 provided 다음에 사물이 왔으므로, 전치사 for가 없는 ①과 ②는 빈칸에 부적절하다. for 다음에 오는 말은 사람이어야 하며, 동시에 관계사절의 동사 ruled의 주어도 되어야 한다. 따라서 ⑤의 for whoever ruled가 빈칸에 적절한데, ⑤는 원래 for anyone who ruled에서 anyone who를 whoever로 바꿔 쓴 것이다. ④는 for anyone who has ruled가 되어야 빈칸에 적절하다.

calendar n. 역법(曆法); 달력 ancient a. 고대의

역법을 제어할 수 있는 능력이 고대도시를 지배하는 누구에게나 권력의 원천을 제공할 수 있었을 것이다.

05 2017 가톨릭대 ▶▶▶ MSG p.34 ②

지각동사의 목적보어와 과거분사의 용법 ▶ 원형동사와 현재분사는 모두 지각동사 see의 목적보어로 올 수 있으므로 첫 빈칸에는 make와 making이 모두 적절하고, 둘째 빈칸 앞의 '오메가 모양'이 '가장 아름다운 모양으로 여겨지는' 수동의 관계이므로 둘째 빈칸에는 과거분사 considered가 적절하다. 즉 considered 앞에 which is가 생략된 것으로 보면 된다. 따라서 ②가 정답이다.

set v. (해나 달이) 지다

운이 좋으면, 당신은 태양이 오메가(Ω) 모양으로 되는 것을 볼 기회를 가질 지도 모르는데, 이 오메가 모양은 저무는 해의 가장 아름다운 모양으로 여겨지고 있다.

06 2010 아주대 ▶▶▶ MSG p.71 ②

혼합가정법 ▶ 혼합가정법으로 과거에 나폴레옹이 유럽을 정복했다면 현재 지도의 모습이 달라져 있을 것이라는 의미이다. 따라서 빈칸에는 과거 사실에 대한 반대를 나타내는 가정법 과거완료 형태인 'If+S+had+p.p'가 와야 하는데 If가 생략되어 'Had+S+p.p'의 어순으로 도치된 ②가 적절하다.

conquer v. 정복하다 continent n. 대륙

나폴레옹(Napoleon)이 유럽 정복의 꿈을 이뤘다면 오늘날 유럽 대륙의 지도는 아주 달라 보였을 것이다.

07 2018 가천대 ▶▶▶ MSG p.82 ①

과거의 강한 추측 표현 must have p.p. ▶ even if절에 가정법 과거완료 표현인 had been이 있으므로 주절은 과거와 관련된 시제가 되어야 한다. "어린 소년들이 아무리 잘생겼다 하더라도 여성의 역할을 하는 것은 틀림없이 어색했을 것이다."라는 뜻이 되어야 하므로, 과거의 강한 추측을 나타내는 표현인 must have p.p.의 형태가 적절하다. 따라서 ①이 정답이다. 과거의 유감을 나타내는 should have p.p.나 이것의 부정 표현은 의미상 적절하지 않다.

attire n. 옷, 의상 awkward a. 어색한, 서투른 disguise v. 변장하다, 위장하다
indispensable a. 없어서는 안 될, 필수적인

왜 셰익스피어(Shakespeare)는 남장한 여성이 포함된 플롯을 사용했을까? 엘리자베스 1세 시대에, 여성은 무대에 서는 것이 허용되지 않았다. 따라서 어린 소년들이 여장을 하고 여성의 역할을 연기했다. 그러나 그들이 잘생긴 소년이었더라도, 다른 성(여성)의 역할을 연기하는 것을 보는 것은 어색했을 것임에 틀림없다. 따라서 남장여성에 대한 플롯은 필수적이었다.

08 2006 세종대 ▶▶▶ MSG p.46, p.211 ③

주어와 동사의 수일치 & 올바른 수동태 표현 ▶ Those가 문장의 주어이며, 현재분사 hoping은 that ~ a new pro-market drive까지를 목적어로 취하고 있다. 빈칸에는 주어 Those의 동사가 필요하다. 주어 Those는 '~하는 사람들'의 뜻의 복수형이므로 동사 역시 복수형이 되어야 한다. 따라서 우선 ①과 ④는 제외된다. 그런데 disappoint는 '~를 실망시키다'라는 의미의 타동사로만 쓰이므로 ②는 목적어가 없어 부적절하다. 참고로 be like to do 역시 '~할 것 같다'라는 뜻이지만 미국 구어, 방언에서 쓰이는 표현이다. ex.) He is like to succeed.(그는 아마 성공할 거다.) ex.) He was like to have drowned.(하마터면 빠져 죽을 뻔했다.) 따라서 빈칸에 가장 적절한 것은 ③이다.

regime n. 정권 pro-market a. 시장친화적인 as well 또한, 역시

독일의 정권 교체가 유럽연합(EU)에 향후 시장친화적인 활력을 줄 수 있다고 기대하고 있는 사람들은 또한 실망할 수도 있다.

09 2009 세종대 ▶▶▶ MSG p.137 ③

전치사+관계대명사 ▶ The teacher poured knowledge into it이라는 문장을 관계절로 만들면, it이 삭제되고 관계대명사 which가 쓰이며 전치사 into가 그 앞으로 온 ③과 같은 관계절의 형태가 된다.

be based on ~에 바탕을 두다 pour v. 쏟아 붓다

19세기의 교육이론은 학생들이 교사가 지식을 쏟아 부어 넣는 텅 빈 그릇이라는 개념에 근거했다.

10 2022 경기대 ▶▶▶ MSG p.104, p.105 ①

수동을 나타내는 과거분사 ▶ months는 spend하는 행위의 대상이므로 이 둘은 수동관계에 있다. 그러므로 수동을 나타내는 과거분사로 수식해야 한다. ①을 spent로 고친다. ③ caliber는 attain하는 행위의 대상이므로 수동관계를 나타내는 과거분사로 수식했다.

formidable a. 가공할, 무시무시한 roster n. (팀의) 선수 명단 caliber n. 직경; 재능, 역량 attain v. 이루다, 달성하다

어마어마한 선수 명단을 구성하는 데 여러 달을 보낸 후에, 그 팀은 지난 몇 년 동안 달성했던 전력에 다시 한 번 도달하고 있는 것처럼 보인다.

11 2018 한국외대 ▶▶▶ MSG p.59 ③

수동태 ▶ teach는 'teach+목적어+to부정사'의 형태로 쓰는데, ③의 뒤에 목적어가 주어져 있지 않으므로 옳지 않은 표현이다. ③은 문장의 흐름상 "당신이 믿도록 배워왔다"는 의미가 되어야 하므로 수동태가 적절하다. 따라서 ③을 have been taught로 고쳐야 한다. 참고로 decide가 시간의 부사절에서 미래시제(will decide)를 대신한 현재시제이므로, ④에서 미래완료시제를 쓴 것이다.

the moment ~하는 바로 그 순간, ~하자마자 shift v. 바꾸다 quest n. 추구

당신이 알고 있는 것이 당신이 믿도록 배워온 것보다 더 중요하다고 판단하는 순간, 당신은 성공을 추구하는 방법을 바꾸어 놓았을 것이다.

12 2008 성균관대 ▶▶▶ MSG p.211 ④

주어와 동사의 수일치 ▶ 이 문장의 주어는 all the contact로 단수이므로 본동사 have led도 단수 형태 has led여야 한다. ④를 has로 고친다. 주어 all the contact 뒤에 목적격 관계대명사 that이 생략되어 있다.

emerge v. 나타나다, 나오다

16세기 이후로, 영국인들이 전 세계 민족들과 가져왔던 모든 접촉은 수천 개의 새로운 단어들이 영어로 채택되도록 이끌었으며, 그것으로부터 현대 영어가 출현했다.

13 2021 국민대 ▶▶▶ MSG p.218 ④

동명사의 병치 ▶ 두 번째 문장은 등위접속사 and에 의해서 'of 동명사' 셋이 병치되는 구조로 파악해야 한다. 따라서 of dreaming, of going to bed and lying still과 같은 형태가 되도록 ④를 of wandering into 로 고쳐야 한다.

now and again 때때로 to begin with 우선 wander v. 방황하다

때때로 나는 악몽을 꾸었지만 꿈에서의 나의 기쁨을 잃게 할 정도의 악몽은 아니었다. 우선, 나는 꿈을 꾼다는 생각을 좋아하는데, 잠자리에 들어 조용히 누워 있다가 이상한 마법에 의해 또 다른 종류의 존재 속으로 방황하는 생각을 좋아한다.

14 2017 서강대 ▶▶▶ MSG p.75, p.81 ②

주장·제안 등의 동사+that S+'(should)+동사원형' ▶ 동사 propose가 that절을 수반하였고, 그 의미가 '제안하다'이므로 that절의 동사는 '(should) +동사원형'이 되어야 한다. should 대신 shall도 가능하다. 여기서는 두 번째 that절에서 shall을 쓰고 있으므로 ②를 shall amuse 로 고친다.

fussy a. 까다로운 officiousness n. 주제넘음, 거만함 portray v. 묘사하다 amuse v. ~을 즐겁게 해주다 the company 일행

의사인 에릭시마코스(Eryximachus)는 까다로운 거만함이 감탄스러운 유머로 묘사되는 인물로서, 여느 때같이 소녀들의 플루트를 들으며 즐기는 대신에 일행이 대화를 하며 즐기되, 그 대화는 사랑을 찬양하는 그들 각자의 이야기 형식을 띠도록 하자고 그때 제안한다.

15 2019 서강대 ▶▶▶ MSG p.161 ②

정관사의 용법 ▶ 명사가 수식어구로 한정될 때는 명사 앞에 정관사를 붙인다. ②에서 명사 interaction은 of caffeine부터 glucuronolactone 까지의 수식을 받고 있으므로 interaction 앞에는 정관사가 있어야 한다. ②를 the interaction of caffeine으로 고친다.

ban v. 금지하다 Red Bull 레드불(카페인 에너지 음료) cite v. 인용하다, 인증하다 interaction n. 상호작용 metabolism n. 신진대사

프랑스가 2000년에 레드불(Red Bull)을 금지했을 때, 보건 당국자들은 카페인과 아미노산 타우린과 인간의 세포에서 생성되어 신진대사에 사용되는 당(糖)의 한 종류인 글루쿠로놀락톤의 상호작용에 대한 불확실성을 언급했다.

16 2019 서울여대 ▶▶▶ MSG p.217 ①

동격의 병치 ▶ 류샤오보를 꾸며주는 말이 A, B, and C의 형태로 병치 되어 있다. 이 경우 병치된 말은 모두 동일한 성격이어야 한다. A와 C에는 어떤 '사람'인지를 나타내는 말이 온 반면, B에는 사람이 아니라 '문학 비평'이 와서 병치가 되지 않으므로, B 역시 사람을 나타내도록 ①을 'literary critic(문예 비평가)'으로 고쳐야 한다.

democracy advocate 민주주의 지지자 impassioned a. 열정적인 political essayist 정치 평론가 activism n. 행동주의(대중 시위 등의 실력 행사를 중시)

그의 행동주의로 중국정부에 의해 여러 차례 투옥된, 민주주의의 지지자이자 열정적인 문예 비평가이자 정치 평론가인 류샤오보(Liu Xiaobo)는 중국 내에서 오랫동안 인권 투쟁을 벌인 것을 인정받아 노벨평화상을 수상했다.

17 2014 서강대 ▶▶▶ MSG p.97 ④

문의 구성 ▶ ④의 moving이 그 앞의 네 명사와 관련성을 가질 수 없다. 동명사 moving 앞에 of를 넣으면 앞의 네 명사와 공통으로 연결된다. 따라서 ④를 of moving으로 고쳐야 한다. ② such는 명사를 수식하며 'such+a(n)+형용사+명사'의 순서로 쓰이는데, upheaval이 불가산명사이므로 부정관사가 없는 것이 맞다. ③ ask questions는 is의 보어로 쓰여서 to가 생략됐다. 주어로 all we can do가 왔기 때문인데, all/what/the only thing you have to do 등이 주어로 오면 보어로 쓰인 to부정사에서 to를 생략할 수 있다.

gadget n. 도구 momentous a. 중대한 upheaval n. 격변 upside n. 긍정적인 면 downside n. 부정적인 면, 불리한 면 predominately ad. 두드러지게

책은 또한 손에 들 수 있는 도구이며, 오늘날 새로운 기구들이 그러는 것처럼 한때 세상을 변화시켰던 기술이다. 너무나 중대한 출판 변혁의 이 단계에서, 우리가 할 수 있는 일의 전부는 전자출판으로의 현저한 이동의 장단점과 득실에 대해 질문을 던지고 올바른 추측을 하려 노력하는 것이다.

18 2013 이화여대 ▶▶▶ MSG p.57 ③

능동태와 수동태의 구분 ▶ ③의 목적어가 주어져 있지 않으며, 주어인 the construct of intelligence가 assess 당하는 행위의 대상이 되므로, 수동태로 표현해야 한다. ③을 has been assessed로 고친다. ② 전치사이며, 이것의 목적어는 the length of time이다. ④ 주어는 means 이며, 명사 means는 '수단', '방법'이라는 의미로 쓰였을 경우, 단수로도 취급하고 복수로도 취급한다. ⑤ '훨씬'의 뜻으로 비교급을 강조하는 부사이다.

intelligence n. 지능 construct n. 구조물; 구성; 구성개념

아마도 지능이 모든 심리학에서 가장 심도 있는 연구가 이뤄진 개념일 것이다. 지능의 측정에 관심을 갖기 시작한 것은 100년도 더 되었다. 그러나 지능이라는 개념이 평가되어온 오랜 기간에도 불구하고, 그것을 측정하는 단일한 혹은 표준이 되는 수단은 여전히 없는 상태이다. 더욱이, 최근에 이뤄진 연구는 지능이 우리가 생각해 온 것보다 훨씬 더 복잡하다는 사실을 시사하고 있다.

19   2019 이화여대   ▶▶▶ MSG p.53   ③

시제일치 ▶ 두 번째 문장은 몬드라곤의 현재 상황을 언급하고 있는 내용이므로 ③도 현재시제여야 한다. ③을 and comprises over로 고친다.

shed v. 버리다, 포기하다 outsourcing n. 하청, 아웃소싱 automation n. 자동화 corporation n. 주식회사 buck v. 저항하다, 맞서다 cooperative n. 협동조합 asset n. 자산 comprise v. ~으로 이루어져 있다 representative n. 대표 transfer n. 이동

선진국의 주요 산업들이 아웃소싱과 자동화를 통해 일자리를 없애고 있는 가운데, 그러한 추세를 거스르고 있는 한 대기업이 있으니 바로 스페인의 몬드라곤 협동조합(Mondragon Cooperative)이다. 2차 세계대전 직후에 설립되었고 처음 창업했던 마을인 몬드라곤에서 이름을 따온 그 협동조합은 현재 총자산 기준으로 스페인에서 5번째로 큰 회사이며, 900개 이상의 개별 회사들로 이루어져 있다. 몬드라곤은 소유와 운영을 전적으로 노동자들이 하고 있으며, 신규사업, 신규채용, 인사이동에 관한 결정을 노동자 대표들이 내린다. 지금까지 몬드라곤은 인원감축을 해야 할 필요 없이 수익성을 유지해왔다.

20   2022 광운대   ▶▶▶ MSG p.234   ①

정비문 ▶ ② 문장 전체를 수식하는 부사구 annoyingly for Jack이며, be late (in) ~ing(~하는 것이 늦다)의 표현이다. ③ unless는 if ~ not의 뜻이며, '예약하다'는 뜻의 동사 book이 your ticket을 목적어로 받고 있다. ④ 부사 certainly가 문장 전체를 수식하고, 관용구인 have something to do with(~와 뭔가 관련이 있다)에서 부정문이어서 something 대신 anything이 쓰였다. ⑤ 동일인의 두 가지 성질을 비교할 때는 'more ~ than' 형식을 취하므로, more amusingly than wisely가 온 것이며, keep on ~ing는 '계속해서 ~하다'라는 뜻으로, on 다음에 동명사 insisting이 맞게 쓰였다. ① He is late because he met an accident.와 Since we've just had breakfast, we don't feel hungry.에서 because절과 since절 모두 이유를 나타내지만 첫 문장은 늦은 이유를 밝힌 문장이고 둘째 문장은 지금 배고프지 않다는 것을 말하려는 문장이다. 다시 말해, 첫 문장의 focus는 because절에 있는 반면 둘째 문장의 focus는 주절에 있다. 강조구문에는 강한 focus를 갖는 because절이 사용되므로 It is because you are lazy that you lost your job.으로 고쳐야 한다.

valid a. 유효한 passport n. 여권 book v. 예약하다

① 당신이 직장을 잃은 것은 바로 당신이 게으르기 때문이다.
② 잭으로서는 성가시게도, 그의 형은 늦게 도착했다.
③ 유효한 여권이 없을 경우, 티켓 예약을 해드릴 수 없습니다.
④ 확실히, 맥도날드 여사는 그들과 어떤 것도 관계하고 싶어 하지 않았다.
⑤ 현명하게도가 아니라 재미있게도, 그는 계속해서 자신의 말할 권리를 주장했다.

01 ②	02 ③	03 ②	04 ③	05 ④	06 ④	07 ③	08 ②	09 ①	10 ①
11 ⑤	12 ③	13 ②	14 ④	15 ③	16 ③	17 ④	18 ④	19 ③	20 ①

01　2010 홍익대　▶▶▶ MSG p.95　②

so+형용사/부사+as to부정사 ▶ '공통의 관계를 숨길 정도로 다양하다'라는 의미이므로 빈칸에는 'so+형용사+as to ~(~할 정도로[~할 만큼] ~하다)'가 적용되어 ② as to가 적절하다.

microbiologist n. 미생물학자 contend with (문제와) 씨름하다 disguise v. 변장하다

미생물학자들은 그들의 연구에서 외양과 습성이 너무나 다양해서 서로 연관성이 있는 것으로 추정되는 공통의 관계가 잘 드러나 보이지 않는 생물들과 씨름을 하고 있다.

02　2016 홍익대　▶▶▶ MSG p.123　③

'it ~ that …' 가주어 / 진주어 구문 ▶ 빈칸 뒤에 완전한 절이 주어져 있으므로 접속사가 필요하다. 따라서 관계대명사인 ①과 ②를 먼저 정답에서 제외할 수 있으며, 앞에 가주어 it이 있으므로, 이에 대해 진주어가 되는 명사절을 이끄는 역할을 할 수 있는 that이 빈칸에 들어가야 한다.

puppet n. (인형극에 쓰는) 인형, 꼭두각시

적어도 디즈니 버전에서는, 그 꼭두각시 인형이 살아 움직이게 되는 것은 제페토(Geppetto)의 소원이지 피노키오(Pinocchio)의 소원이 아니다.

03　2022 단국대　▶▶▶ MSG p.167　②

대명사의 수일치 ▶ 도시의 대중교통과 교외의 대중교통이 비교되어야 하므로, public transportation을 받는 단수대명사 it을 쓴 ②가 정답으로 적절하다.

public transportation 대중교통 outlying a. 외딴, 외진 reliable a. 신뢰할만한

교외와 외곽 지역에서의 대중교통은 일반적으로 도시에서만큼 편리하거나 신뢰할만하지는 못하다.

04　2016 가천대　▶▶▶ MSG p.191　③

적절한 부사구 ▶ 임기 말의 정부는 새로운 일을 벌이지 않고 무사안일주의를 택한다고 했으므로 공무원들 또한 다음 정부에 부정적으로 낙인찍히지 않도록 조심할 것이다. 따라서 빈칸에는 '~할까 봐 (두려워서)'를 의미하는 부사구 ③ for fear of가 와야 한다. of가 전치사이므로 뒤에 명사나 동명사가 올 수 있는데, 빈칸 뒤에 marked by가 주어져 있으므로, 수동의 동명사 형태가 되어야 한다. 따라서 for fear of being이 적절하다.

make waves 풍파를 일으키다 officeholder n. 공무원 wary a. 경계하는, 조심하는 spearhead n. 창끝; 선봉, 선두

'아무 일도 하지 않고(무사)', '편안을 우선시하는(안일)' 방식을 취하는 것은 임기 말 정부에게는 흔한 일이다. 그들은 새로운 프로젝트를 시작하지 않고, 어떠한 풍파도 일으키는 것을 피한다. 대통령의 권한은 여전히 유효하지만, 공무원들은 다음 정부에게 부정적으로 낙인찍힐까 두려워서 앞장 서는 역할을 하는 것을 경계한다.

05　2017 단국대　▶▶▶ MSG p.227　④

적절한 전치사 ▶ 뉴턴이 중력의 법칙이라고 부른 것에 의해 지구가 공전하는 것이므로 첫 번째 빈칸에는 by가 적절하고, reward는 '~에 대한 보상'이라는 뜻으로 쓰일 때 'for (동)명사'를 취하므로 두 번째 빈칸에는 for가 적절하며, blame은 '~한 행위를 비난하다'라는 뜻으로 쓸 때 전치사 for와 함께 쓰므로 세 번째 빈칸에는 for가 들어가야 한다.

go around the sun 태양 주위를 공전하다 gravitation n. 중력 atheist n. 무신론자

뉴턴은 지구를 포함한 행성들이 이른바 중력의 법칙에 의해 태양 주위를 공전한다는 사실을 발견했는데, 우주에 관한 그의 위대한 발견에 대한 보상은 무신론자라는 비난뿐이었다.

06　2007 서강대　▶▶▶ MSG p.218　④

명사절의 병치 ▶ 올바른 병치구조에 대한 문제이다. think 뒤의 목적어인 that절이 등위접속사에 의해 병치되고 있으므로 빈칸에도 that절이 계속 와야 하고, 문맥상 they가 a leader's skills를 가리키므로 수동태가 되어야 적절한 문장이 된다. 따라서 ④가 정답이다.

occasion n. 경우, 때, 특별한 일 context n. 문맥, 정황, 배경

지도자의 기술이 모든 경우에 적용될 수 있다든가, 그 기술이 역사적 맥락 밖에서 가르쳐질 수 있다거나, 그 기술이 모든 경우에 통제의 '비결'로서 학습될 수 있다고 생각하는 것은 어리석다.

07   2013 경희대   ▶▶▶ MSG p.48   ③

과거완료시제 ▶ just as는 절을 수반하여 '꼭 ~처럼'이라는 의미로 쓰인다. 그들이 개입한 시점은 과거로 나와 있으므로, 이라크에서의 행위는 그 이전인 과거완료로 쓰는 것이 적절하다. 일반 동사(step in)를 대신하는 대동사 do를 사용하여 had done으로 해야 한다. 따라서 ③이 정답이다.

overwhelm v. 당황하게 하다; 압도하다 evacuation n. 피난; 대피 on the fly 신속히

경찰은 주민대피에 엄두를 못 내고 있었지만, 두 명의 전직 해병대원들이 나서서 그들이 이라크에서 했던 것처럼 신속하게 모든 계획을 세워나갔다. 그들은 차량과 배를 찾았고, 가슴높이 차오르는 파도를 뚫고 나아가다가 마침내 존을 발견했다.

08   2010 고려대   ▶▶▶ MSG p.11   ②

자동사와 타동사의 구분 ▶ '조처하다'라는 의미는 arrange for로 표현한다. 따라서 빈칸에 ②가 와야 한다. arrange for가 the shipment를 목적어로 취하고, 이 목적어 the shipment가 to be ordered의 의미상의 주어 역할을 한다.

arrange v. 해결하다, 조정하다 shipment n. 선적, 수송, 발송

중국의 파트너와 나눈 대화를 확인한 후, 나는 월요일에 선적이 이루어지도록 조치를 취했다.

09   2019 한국외대   ▶▶▶ MSG p.89, p.217   ①

등위접속사 and의 병치 ▶ how to 다음에 나온 두 원형동사 stand와 walk가 콤마로 이어져 있으므로, 이 둘과 병치를 이루도록 접속사 and와 그다음에 원형동사 run around가 있는 ①이 정답이다. 참고로 to everyone's surprise는 and와 run around 사이에 삽입된 부사구이다.

toddler n. 걸음마를 배우는 아이, 유아 run around 바쁘게 움직이며 다니다 to one's surprise 놀랍게도

아주 작은 아이는 서고, 걷고, 그리고 모두가 놀랍게도, 여기저기 뛰어다니기를 빨리 배웠다.

10   2021 홍익대   ▶▶▶ MSG p.75   ①

suggest 동사의 용법 ▶ suggest는 3형식동사여서 '~에게'에 해당하는 명사 앞에 전치사 to를 붙여야 한다. 따라서 ①을 suggested to로 고쳐야 한다. ② suggest(제안하다)의 목적어로 쓰인 that절 안에서는 원형동사나 'should 원형동사'를 쓴다. ③ 'since 과거시점'과 현재완료시제가 함께 잘 쓰이지만, 여기서는 suggested가 과거시제이므로 과거완료이다.

take care of ~을 돌보다

케네스의 누나는 지난 7월부터 심하게 앓아 오신 어머니를 돌보기 위해 케네스(Kenneth)에게 집으로 돌아올 것을 제안했다.

11   2004 성균관대   ▶▶▶ MSG p.73   ⑤

as if[though]+가정법 ▶ as if[though] 다음에 가정법 과거 또는 가정법 과거완료 형태가 오며, 그 의미는 각각 '마치 ~인 것처럼', '마치 ~이었던 것처럼'이다. 주어진 문장에서 tried가 과거를 나타내므로 과거사실에 반대되는 가정법 과거완료형이 쓰여야 한다. ⑤ happened를 had happened로 고쳐준다.

come as a surprise 놀라움으로 다가오다

비록 그 소식이 방 안에 있는 모든 사람들을 놀라게 했지만, 그들은 아무 일도 일어나지 않았던 것처럼 자신의 일을 하려고 애썼다.

12   2016 서강대   ▶▶▶ MSG p.15   ③

타동사 transcend ▶ transcend는 주로 타동사로 쓰이므로, ③에서 transcend 뒤의 over를 삭제해야 한다.

evolution n. 진화 transcend v. 초월하다 encompass v. (많은 것을) 포함하다 holistic a. 전체적인

진화는 항상 새로운 한계들을 설정하려고 애쓰고, 그런 다음 그 한계들을 깨고, 그 한계들을 초월하고, 그 한계들을 넘어 좀 더 포괄적이고 전체적인 양식으로 나아가려고 마찬가지로 열심히 애쓴다.

13   2021 국민대   ▶▶▶ MSG p.177   ②

부정대명사 ▶ the other는 둘 중의 다른 하나를 가리킬 때 사용하는데, 문장의 의미상 "겨울철에 손이 찬 것과 일 년 내내 추위를 느끼는 것은 별개다"라는 말이 적절하다. 이는 '~ one thing … another(~와 …는 별개이다)'로 표현하므로 ②는 another thing이 되어야 한다.

have cold hands 손이 차다 year-round ad. 연중 내내, 1년 내내 genetics n. 유전적 특징 chronic illness 만성 질환

겨울에 손이 찬 것과 1년 내내 추위를 느끼는 것은 별개의 문제다. 많은 사람들은 유전적 특징부터 만성 질환에 이르는 다양한 원인들 때문에 연중 내내 손이 차다.

14   2018 중앙대   ▶▶▶ MSG p.70, p.134   ④

문의 구성 ▶ ①에서 가정법 과거로 were가 적절히 사용되었고, ②에서는 Just as ~, so의 상관관계를 잘 이루고 있으며, ③에서는 최상급과 정관사가 나란히 사용되었으므로, 문법적으로 옳은 문장이다.

muscle n. 근육 helpless a. 무기력한 sinew n. 힘줄 nerve n. 신경

만약 근육을 움직이도록 지시하는 신경이 없다면 근육은 무기력한 힘줄이 되어버릴 것이듯이, 만약 통신이 없다면 최첨단의 산업 장비와 사회 조직들도 쓸모없어지고 말 것이다.

15 **2017 서강대** ▶▶▶ MSG p.211 ③

명사의 수일치 ▶ ③은 앞서 나온 명사 persons를 수식하는 형용사구이므로, 그에 맞게 복수명사를 써서 in dependent positions로 바로잡아야 한다. 가산명사 position을 한정사 없이 단수형으로 쓸 수 없기 때문이다. 한편, ①의 목적어는 the feeling이며 ②는 the feeling을 가리키는 대명사이다. ④의 동사 speak는 '언급하다, 기술하다'(mention, describe)의 의미로 사용할 때는 자동사로 활용하여 speak of~, speak about~을 주로 쓰지만 speak the truth, speak the words 등에서와 같이 단순히 '말하다, 진술하다(say, state)'의 의미를 지닐 때는 타동사로 활용된다. 그리고 speak one's mind는 '속마음을 털어놓고 이야기하다'는 의미의 관용적 표현으로 쓰인다.

lot n. 운명 acuteness n. 날카로움, 격렬함 dependent a. 의존적인

마센카(Mashenka)는 자신의 방으로 들어가, 부자와 권력자들이 준 빵으로 살며 자신의 생각은 말할 수 없는 의존적 처지에 있는 사람들에게는 너무나 친숙한 감정을 난생 처음 자신의 운명으로 절절히 맛보았다.

16 **2013 중앙대** ▶▶▶ MSG p.227 ③

적절한 전치사 선택 ▶ 여기서 동사 provide는 'A with/for B' 구문이 아니라 목적어 A만을 취하는 동사로 쓰였다. 주어와 speaking 이하가 비교되는데 significant가 원급으로 되어 있으므로 ③의 to를 than이 아니라 '~에 비해'의 의미를 지니는 over로 바꾸어야 한다. ①의 evidence는 '~을 입증[증명]하다'라는 동사로 쓰였으므로 옳은 표현이다.

bilingual a. 이중 언어를 사용하는 immersion n. 몰입 undercurrent n. (언동의) 속에 품은 진의, 저의

이중언어교육과 언어몰입교육을 둘러싼 논란 많은 쟁점이 정치적 저의를 강하게 가지고 있긴 하지만, 많은 연구자들은 오직 한 언어만 사용하는 것에 비해 두 개의 언어를 말할 수 있는 능력이 상당한 인지적 장점을 제공해준다고 증언한다.

17 **2017 성균관대** ▶▶▶ MSG p.215 ④

대명사의 수일치 ▶ ④는 both Washington and Beijing을 가리키므로, 복수대명사로 받아야 한다. ④를 their로 고친다. ②와 ③은 the Philippine defense secretary를 가리킨다.

glider n. 활주정(艇) defense secretary 국방장관 put ~ on notice ~에게 통보하다 unauthorized a. 공인[승인]되지 않은 exclusive economic zone 배타적 경제 수역(해안선에서 200 해리 안의 경제 수역)

중국이 필리핀 해안에서 미 해군으로부터 포획한 수중 활주정을 돌려준 후에, 필리핀 정부는 자국의 200해리 배타적 경제 수역에 두 나라가 무단 침입한 것에 항의하는 뜻을 미국정부와 중국정부 모두에게 통보했다고 필리핀 국방장관은 말했다.

18 **2016 명지대** ▶▶▶ MSG p.211 ④

주어와 동사의 수일치 ▶ ④에서 are의 주어는 바로 앞에 온 languages가 아니라 The "English-only'' movement이다. 이것은 단수이므로 동사 역시 단수형태가 와야 한다. ④를 is로 고친다.

linguistic a. 언어(학)의 asset n. 자산; 장점 a spate of 봇물처럼 쏟아지는, 잇따른 legislation n. 법률(제정) ballot initiative 국민발의 court ruling 법원판결

미국의 많은 사람들은 미국의 언어적 다양성을 장점으로 여기지 않으며, 최소한 공개석상에서는 영어만 사용하는 것을 선호하는 것처럼 보인다. 그들의 이유는 다양하며, 그 문제에 대해 법률제정, 국민발의, 그리고 법원판결이 봇물처럼 쏟아져 나왔다. 영어가 아닌 언어 사용을 금지하는 법안을 추진하기 위해 최근 수십 년 사이에 '영어만 사용하는' 운동이 일어났으며, 학교에서의 영어가 아닌 언어 사용에 대해 특히나 우려를 표시하고 있다.

19 **2019 한국산업기술대** ▶▶▶ MSG p.67 ③

수동태 ▶ expose는 '~에 노출시키다'라는 뜻의 타동사이며, 목적격 관계대명사 that절의 선행사는 older chemicals이다. 내가 오래된 화학물질에 노출된 것이므로 ③은 수동태로 been exposed to가 되어야 한다. 이때 to는 전치사이다.

lead n. 납 mercury n. 수은 pesticide n. 살충제, 농약 fragrant a. 향기로운 nonstick a. (냄비 따위가) 눌어붙지 않는 water-resistant a. 물이 잘 스며들지 않는, 방수의 fire-safe a. 내화성의, 방화의

나는 화학적 자기발견의 여정에 참여한 작가이다. 지난 가을, 나는 음식과 음료수와 내가 숨을 쉬는 공기와 내 피부에 닿는 제품들로부터 내가 섭취했을지도 모르는 320개의 화학물질에 대한 검사를 받았는데, 그 화학물질들은 그냥 살다가 나도 모르게 얻게 된 비밀 혼합물들이었다. 그것에는 DDT(과거에 쓰이던 살충제)와 PCB(폴리염화비페닐)와 같이 내가 수십 년 전에 노출되었을지도 모르는 오래된 화학물질도 포함되어 있다. 그것에는 또한 납, 수은, 다이옥신과 같은 오염물질도 포함되고, 최신 농약과 플라스틱 재료, 그리고 샴푸를 향기롭게 만들고, 냄비를 눌어붙지 않게 하고, 천을 방수·방화되게 하면서 현대 생활의 표면 아래에 숨어 있는 그 밖의 다른 화합물들도 더 포함되어 있다.

20 **2021 광운대** ▶▶▶ MSG p.24, p.169 ①

정비문 ▶ about, above, behind, beside, in front of, on 등의 위치(공간) 관계를 나타내는 전치사(구)의 경우, 목적어가 주어와 일치하더라도 재귀대명사를 사용하지 않는다. 그러므로 ①은 I remember closing the gate behind me.로 써야 한다. ④ and, but, as, like 등 뒤에서는 선행사 없이 재귀대명사를 단독으로 사용하는 경우가 있다.

behave oneself 예절 있게 행동하다 familiarize oneself with ~에 익숙해지다

① 나는 집을 나오면서 대문을 닫았다고 기억하고 있다.
② 메리(Mary)는 열심히 일해서 승진했다.
③ 두 소년 모두 경기에서 조심해서 행동할 것이다.
④ 나는 제인(Jane)과 내가 꽤 잘해왔다고 생각한다.
⑤ 톰(Tom)은 공원 주위를 걸으면서 그곳과 익숙해졌다.

01 ②	02 ①	03 ④	04 ①	05 ①	06 ③	07 ④	08 ①	09 ③	10 ④
11 ③	12 ④	13 ④	14 ②	15 ③	16 ④	17 ④	18 ④	19 ⑤	20 ②

01   2018 가톨릭대 ▶▶▶ MSG p.137   ②

관계대명사 that ▶ 빈칸 뒤에 주어가 빠진 형태의 절이 주어져 있으므로, 뒤에 완전한 절이 와야 하는 접속사 ①과 ④는 부적절하다. 한편, 빈칸 앞에 선행사인 a time of day가 있으므로 선행사를 포함하고 있는 관계대명사인 what도 빈칸에 들어갈 수 없다. 따라서 정답은 ②가 되며, 이때 that은 a time of day를 선행사로 하는 주격 관계대명사이다.

move about 돌아다니다 domain n. 영역 solely ad. 혼자서, 단독으로 suspicious a. 의심스러운 character n. 특성; 인물

유럽의 50개 도시는 세금으로 지원하는 도로 조명을 1700년 무렵에 도입하였는데, 이로 인해, 날이 어두워진 후에 공개적으로 돌아다니는 것이 안전해졌고 또한 사회적으로도 용인되었다. 하루 중 날이 어두워진 후는 이전에는 범죄 용의자들만이 활동할 수 있는 것으로 여겨진 시간이었다.

02   2019 서울여대 ▶▶▶ MSG p.124   ①

의문사가 있는 간접의문문 ▶ 빈칸 이하는 동사 reflect의 목적어인 간접의문절을 이루게 되며, 빈칸에는 적절한 의문사가 들어가야 한다. '빈칸 + egalitarian'이 become동사의 보어이므로, 형용사 egalitarian을 수식하는 ①의 부사 how(얼마나)가 적절하다.

engagement n. 약혼 divorced a. 이혼한 biracial a. 혼혈의 egalitarian a. 평등주의의

영국의 많은 뉴스 미디어 관계자들에게, 해리(Harry) 왕자가 이혼 경력이 있는 혼혈 미국인 메간 마클(Meghan Markle)과 약혼한 것은 영국이 얼마나 평등해졌는지를 보여주는 것이었다.

03   2012 경희대 ▶▶▶ MSG p.105   ④

현재분사와 과거분사의 구분 ▶ 그들의 이름은 '붙이는 것(능동)'이 아니라 '붙여지는 것(수동)'이므로 과거분사가 적절하고, 진행의 의미가 없으므로 being은 없어야 한다. ④ attached가 정답이 된다.

the next best thing 그 다음으로 가장 좋은 것, 차선책 attach v. 붙이다; 소속시키다

아주 부자인 사람들도 노동비용과 그 밖의 것들 때문에 이제는 더 이상 피라미드를 세우지 않는다. 그러나 지난 세기 동안 그들을 위한 차선책은 그들의 이름들이 붙여진 미술관들을 세우는 것이었다.

04   2021 단국대 ▶▶▶ MSG p.237   ①

삽입절 ▶ 삽입될 부사절의 주어는 it(=tool)인데, 이것은 use하는 행위의 주체가 아닌 대상이므로 수동태가 되어야 한다. 한편, when, as, if, while, though 등의 접속사 뒤에 쓰인 '주어+be동사'는 주절의 주어와 같은 경우에는 생략할 수 있다. 따라서 ①이 정답이 된다. 즉, when it is used properly에서 it is가 생략된 것이다.

disease-control n. 질병통제 transmission n. 전달; 전염

우리는 적절하게 사용되면 전염을 50% 내지 85% 감소시킬 수 있는 비용이 저렴하고 현저히 낮은 기술의 질병 통제 수단을 발견했다.

05   2022 가천대 ▶▶▶ MSG p.125   ①

의문사절(간접의문문)의 어순 ▶ 동사 tell 다음에 목적어가 와야 하는데, 의문사 what이 와서 의문사절이 쓰였음을 알 수 있다. 문맥상 tell 이하는 원래 What cause for pride can there possibly be in having them?이라는 의문문인데, 동사 tell의 목적어인 의문사절이 되어야 하므로, can과 there의 어순이 바뀌어 정치된 형태인 what cause for pride there can possibly be in having them이 된다. 따라서 빈칸에는 ①의 there can possibly be가 적절하다.

blind alley 막다른 골목 swarm with ~이 가득하다 blest a. 복 받은 bargain n. 싸게 산 물건

아이들이 드문 경우가 얼마나 거의 없는지를 — 거리와 막다른 골목마다 아이들로 넘쳐난다는 것을 — 이렇게 거저 얻는 아이들을 한 명도 갖지 않는 결혼생활은 거의 없다는 것을 — 고려할 때, 나는 자식을 낳는 데 어떤 자부심을 가질만한 이유가 있을 수 있는지를 평생 알 수 없다.

06   2013 단국대 ▶▶▶ MSG p.83   ③

조동사 would의 용법 ▶ 문장의 의미가 "당신은 과학자들이 지금이면 이미 ~를 정해놓았을 것이라고 생각할지 모르지만 사실은 당신의 생각과는 달리 그들은 아직 정해놓지 않았다"는 뜻이므로 빈칸에는 과거나 현재완료의 일에 대한 추측을 나타내는 'would + have + 과거분사' 형태인 ③이 적절하다. Someone called you last night.(어젯밤에 누구한테선가 너에게 전화가 왔었어.)라는 말에 That would have been Tom.이라고 말하면 '톰이었을 거야'라는 과거 일에 대한 추측의 말이 된다. 여기서는 by now가 있어서 현재완료의 일을 추측해서 하는 말이

다. If she had gone straight to work, she would have arrived by now.(그녀가 직장으로 곧장 갔더라면 지금이면 이미 도착했을 텐데.)에서처럼 사실과 반대의 가정법에서도 if절에서 과거의 일을 반대로 가정하고 주절에서는 현재완료의 일을 나타낼 수 있다. Because she didn't go straight to work, she has not arrived yet.과 같은 의미이기 때문이다. ① '지금이면 이미'를 의미하는 by now라는 부사구가 있으므로 과거완료 시제로 쓰인 had charted와는 시제가 일치하지 않는다. ②, ④ 빈칸은 every aspect 이하의 목적어를 취하는 타동사가 필요하므로 목적어를 취할 수 없는 수동태 형태는 답이 될 수 없다.

chart v. 계획하다, 정하다 turf n. (거주하여) 잘 아는 지역; (자기의) 전문 영역

당신은 과학자들이 지금이면 이미 자신들의 본령(주된 연구 분야)의 모든 면을 정해놓았을 것이라고 생각할지 모르지만 그들은 아직 정해놓지 않았다.

07 2019 서울여대 ▶▶▶ MSG p.221 ④

부정의 부사어가 문두에 올 때의 도치 ▶ no longer와 같은 부정의 부사어가 문두에(주어 앞에) 올 경우, '의문문 형태의 도치(조동사+주어+동사원형)'가 일어난다. 따라서 빈칸에는 ④의 could people afford가 들어가야 적절하다.

embargo n. 금수(禁輸) 조치, 통상 금지령, 수출입 금지 gas-guzzling a. (자동차가) 연료 소비가 많은, 기름을 많이 먹는 gasoline n. 휘발유

석유 수출금지 조치 이후 휘발유 가격이 상승함에 따라, 사람들은 기름을 많이 먹는 자동차를 더 이상 감당할 수 없었다.

08 2019 이화여대 ▶▶▶ MSG p.233 ①

구두점 ▶ 콤마(,)는 접속사, 부사구, 부사절이 문두에 올 때, 삽입구와 삽입절의 앞뒤에, 동격 명사의 앞에, 계속적 용법의 관계절 앞에, 등위접속사로 연결되는 단어, 구, 절 등을 구분할 때 주로 쓰고, 세미콜론(;)은 두 개의 독립된 절을 등위접속사 없이 연결할 때, 주절 뒤에 접속부사를 수반하는 절이 연결될 때 주로 쓰며, 콜론(:)은 부연설명, 예시, 열거의 내용을 덧붙일 때 쓴다. 주어진 문장에서 just before being killed by the British는 삽입구에 해당하므로, 두 빈칸 모두 콤마가 들어가야 한다.

the American Revolution n. 미국 독립전쟁 legend has it that 전설에 따르면 patriot n. 애국자, 우국지사

전해지는 이야기에 따르면, 미국 독립전쟁 동안 미국의 애국자 네이선 헤일(Nathan Hale)은 영국인들에게 죽기 직전에 "조국을 위해 바칠 목숨이 하나밖에 없는 게 억울할 뿐이다."라고 말했다고 한다.

09 2021 단국대 ▶▶▶ MSG p.50 ③

미래완료 ▶ 백신 개발이 성공할 미래의 때를 기준점으로 그때에는 이미 일어났을 완료의 의미를 나타내는 표현이 필요하며, 빈칸 뒤에 목적어가 있으므로 능동태여야 한다. 따라서 ③이 정답으로 적절하다.

efficacy n. 효능 dose n. (약의) 1회분, (1회의) 복용량; 약 readily ad. 즉시; 쉽사리

가장 흥미롭고 중요한 것은 만약 백신이 성공적으로 개발된다면, 그것은 곧 FDA가 백신의 효능과 안전성에 관해 확신한다면 이라는 말이다 보니, 우리는 곧바로 이용 가능한 용량의 백신을 이미 만들어냈을 것이라는 점이다.

10 2021 세종대 ▶▶▶ MSG p.146, p.218 ④

복합관계사의 병치 ▶ 등위접속사 and에 의해 병치되는 표현들은 그 구조적인 형태나 문법적인 기능이 같아야 한다. 복합관계사 whatever와 병치되고 있는 ④ 역시 복합관계사여야 하므로, 이것은 wherever가 되어야 한다.

path n. (목표에 이르는) 길

이 상황은 당신이 흥미진진한 새로운 삶을 향해 나아가는 길에 도움이 될 것이다. 그것이 무엇이든 또 어디이든 그럴 것이다.

11 2017 한국외대 ▶▶▶ MSG p.101 ③

타동사 devote ▶ devote는 타동사로만 쓰인다. ③ to devote 다음에 목적어 없이 부사어(부사와 '전치사+명사' 구)가 왔으므로, ③을 재귀대명사 myself를 목적어로 취한 to devote myself로 고쳐야 한다.

sound knowledge 정통한 지식 zoology n. 동물학 insect n. 곤충

나는 동물학의 모든 측면에 대해 정통한 지식을 얻기를 희망했지만, 특히 곤충에 대해 전념할 계획을 세웠다.

12 2022 단국대 ▶▶▶ MSG p.101 ④

when it comes to ~ing ▶ when it comes to에서 to는 전치사이므로 그 뒤에 동사가 올 경우에는 반드시 동명사가 와야 한다. ④를 to remembering으로 고친다.

fill in ~을 완전히 메우다 hole n. (메워야 할) 공백[빈자리] present n. 현재

과거의 기억에 존재하는 공백을 현재의 것으로 메우려는 이러한 경향은 우리의 감정을 기억하는 것에 관한 한 특히 강력하다.

13 2019 성균관대 ▶▶▶ MSG p.105 ④

과거분사와 현재분사의 비교 ▶ 의미상 wave는 devastate의 주체이므로 ④는 능동의 의미를 나타내는 현재분사 devastating으로 바꾸어야 한다.

deadly a. 치명적인 coastline n. 해안 devastating a. 대단히 파괴적인 erupt v. 분출하다 volcano n. 화산 trigger v. 일으키다

지난 주말의 파괴적인 파도를 일으켰던 화산이 계속 분출함에 따라, 앞으로 며칠 동안 더욱 치명적인 쓰나미가 인도네시아 해안을 강타할 수 있다고 당국은 경고한다.

14　2017 가천대　▶▶▶ MSG p.10　　　②

준보어 ▶ 죄수들이 벌거벗은 상태로 가스처형실로 넣어지는 것이므로 ②는 준보어이다. 준보어의 역할을 할 수 있는 것은 부사가 아닌 형용사이므로, ②를 형용사 naked로 고쳐야 한다.

batch n. 무리, 집단 herd v. 이동시키다 nakedly ad. 발가벗고 gas chamber 가스 처형실 inmate n. 수감자 conceive v. 상상하다

죄수들 중 마지막 무리가 발가벗은 채 가스처형실로 들어간 지 14년이 지난 지금, 아우슈비츠(Auschwitz) 강제수용소 이야기를 매우 많이 들어 왔다. (아우슈비츠 강제수용소의) 수감자들 중 일부는 제정신인 사람이라면 상상할 수조차 없는 그런 사건들에 대해 글을 썼다.

15　2011 경희대　▶▶▶ MSG p.131　　　③

if와 unless의 구분 ▶ 이 문장에서는 사람들이 희망을 갖고 있지 않으면, 어느 사회 시스템도 존재할 수 없다는 의미가 되어야 논리가 통하므로 ③의 if를 unless로 고쳐야 한다. ①에 쓰인 may have p.p는 '~이었을지도 모른다'라는 뜻으로 과거의 추측을 나타내는 표현이다. ②는 'the first+명사+to부정사' 구문으로 to spell out은 앞의 명사를 수식하는 형용사적 용법으로 쓰인 것이다. ④에서 help는 5형식 동사로 쓰였고, 목적어 다음에 목적보어로 동사원형이 온 형태이다.

declaration n. 선언문 independence n. 독립 spell out 분명히 설명하다 explicitly ad. 분명하게

독립선언문이 그 목표를 분명하게 설명한 최초의 공식적인 정치문서였을지 모르지만, 만일 사람들이 정부가 자신들이 행복을 달성하도록 도울 것이라는 희망을 갖고 있지 않았다면, 어느 사회 시스템도 결코 오래 존재하지 못했다는 것은 아마도 사실일 것이다.

16　2014 이화여대　▶▶▶ MSG p.47　　　④

시제의 구분 ▶ 마지막 문장은 과거시점인 1970년대 중반 이후로 랩이 경험한 것에 대한 내용이므로, 현재완료시제를 써야 한다. ④를 has been으로 고친다. 과거완료는 특정 과거시점을 기준으로 그 이전에 벌어진 일을 표현하는 시제이다.

far-reaching a. 광범위한 skirmish n. 작은 충돌 contentious a. 다투기 좋아하는, 논쟁적인 condescension n. 생색내는 태도 outright a. 솔직한; 명백한

그것은 어쩌면 가장 광범위한 영향을 미치는 것일 수도 있었겠지만, 랩이 주류 문화와 빚은 충돌 가운데 가장 최근의 것에 불과했다. 젊은 흑인 남성의 목소리로서, 랩은 생생하고도 말썽 많은 문화적 상징이 되었다. 그것이 태동한 1970년대 중반부터, 랩은 그 영역 밖의 사람들이 내보이는 생색, 거부, 노골적인 공포에 직면하게 되었다.

17　2017 아주대　▶▶▶ MSG p.31　　　④

동사 allow의 목적격 보어 ▶ 동사 allow는 목적어 다음에 목적격 보어로 to부정사가 오므로, ④를 to develop으로 고쳐야 한다.

maximize v. 극대화하다 specialized a. 전문화된 redistribute v. 재분배하다 vital a. 필수적인 puzzle n. 수수께끼 transport n. 수송 cellular a. 세포의

식물은 생존 전문가여서 뿌리의 방향을 제어하여 주변 자원 활용을 극대화시킬 수 있다. 분화된 세포를 이용하여, 식물은 중력을 감지하고 옥신이라는 호르몬을 재분배하여, 성장을 자극하고 식물의 주요 특징들을 발달시킬 수 있다. 그러나 (여기서) 한 가지 커다란 의문점은 이러한 수송과정이 세포 수준에서 어떻게 일어나는가 하는 것이다.

18　2021 국민대　▶▶▶ MSG p.137　　　④

전치사+관계대명사 ▶ 관계대명사 뒤에는 불완전한 절이 오고 '전치사+관계대명사' 뒤에는 완전한 절이 온다. ④ 뒤에 완전한 절이 왔으므로 이것을 '전치사+관계대명사'로 고쳐야 하겠는데, which의 선행사인 Christmas table의 주위에 사람들이 모여 즐기는 것이므로 which 앞에는 전치사 around가 온다. 따라서 ④를 around which로 고쳐야 한다.

smorgasbord n. 스칸디나비아식 전채(前菜); 그 전채가 낀 식사 literally ad. 글자 뜻 그대로; 사실상 free-for-all a. 입장 자유의, 무료의 budget-priced a. (가계 예산에 부담되지 않는) 적정 가격의 envision v. 상상하다, 마음속에 그리다 spread n. 맛있는 음식, 식탁에 차려진 요리 inspire v. 고무하다; (어떤 결과 등을) 생기게 하다

스웨덴인 '스모가스보드(smorgasbord)'(글자 그대로는 "버터 바른 빵을 둔 식탁")는 미국인들이 그 단어를 들을 때 쉽게 떠올리는 누구나 이용할 수 있는 저렴한 뷔페가 아니다. 오히려 그것은 전통에 따라 정중히 대접하여 차갑고 뜨거운 각종 음식들을 우아하게 차려놓은 것이다. 이것은 가족들이 함께 모여 둘러 앉아 배불리 먹고 마시고 노래 부르는 명절 때의 '율보드(julbord)', 즉 크리스마스 식탁의 경우에 특히 그러하다.

19　2019 아주대　▶▶▶ MSG p.229　　　⑤

in accordance with ▶ '~대로', '~에 따라', '~와 일치하여'라는 의미를 가진 표현은 in accordance with이다. ⑤를 in accordance with로 고친다.

soar v. (온도 따위가) 급상승하다 brew v. (맥주 등을) 양조하다; (차를) 끓이다 internal a. 내부의 be faced with ~에 직면하다 fluctuation n. 변동 conform v. 순응하다

뜨거운 물로 샤워를 하거나 막 끓인 커피를 마실 때마다 체온이 치솟는다고 상상해 보라. 내부 환경의 상태를 관리하는 것은 동물의 몸에게 중요한 문제이다. 환경의 변화에 직면하여, 동물들은 조절이나 순응을 통해 내부의 환경을 관리한다. 어떤 동물이 내부의 메커니즘을 이용하여 내부의 변화를 외부의 변화에 거스르게 제어하는 경우, 그 동물은 조절자라고 한다. 어떤 동물이 내부의 여건을 외부의 변화에 일치되게 변하도록 하는 경우, 그 동물은 순응자라고 한다.

20 2021 광운대 ▶▶▶ MSG p.71, p.233 ②

정비문 ▶ How come 뒤에는 '주어+동사' 어순의 평서문 형태가 와서 '어째서 ~한가'라는 의미를 갖는다. 따라서 ②는 How come he wasn't at the meeting this morning?이 되어야 한다. ①, ⑤ I wish가 이끄는 목적어절에는 가정법 동사가 쓰인다. ③, ④ 가정법 과거의 문장이다.

win v. 얻다, 획득하다 lotto n. 복권, 로또

① 나 없이는 네가 파티에 가지 않겠다면 좋을 텐데.
② 어째서 그는 오늘 아침 회의에 참석하지 않았나요?
③ 만약 로또에 당첨된다면 저에게 무엇을 사주실 건가요?
④ 베키(Becky)가 오늘밤 늦게 집에 돌아온다면 나는 놀랄 거야.
⑤ 내일 아침 일찍 일어날 필요가 없다면 좋을 텐데.

01 ④	**02** ②	**03** ④	**04** ②	**05** ②	**06** ②	**07** ④	**08** ②	**09** ④	**10** ④
11 ①	**12** ③	**13** ①	**14** ②	**15** ③	**16** ②	**17** ②	**18** ①	**19** ②	**20** ③

01　2018 가천대　▶▶▶ MSG p.74, p.122　④

otherwise의 용법 ▶ 문맥상 'to do + 빈칸'은 to say they are against murdering fetuses를 나타내는 것이어야 한다. 이것은 곧 they are pro-life라고 말하는 것과는 다른 방식으로(달리) 하는 것이다. 따라서 빈칸에는 '그와 달리, 그와 다른 방식으로'라는 뜻의 부사 ④ otherwise가 적절하다. otherwise는 '그렇지 않다면'의 뜻의 접속부사로 가정법에 쓰이기도 하지만 여기서는 양태부사로 쓰였다. otherwise와 관계없이, 주어인 to부정사, 즉 to do otherwise가 if절을 대신하여 가정법 문장이 된 것이다.

pro-life a. 낙태에 반대하는 pro-choice a. 낙태에 찬성하는 in reference to ~와 관련하여 abortion n. 낙태 conceal v. 감추다, 숨기다; 비밀로 하다 criminality n. 범죄성, 유죄 murder v. 살해하다 fetus n. 태아

최근, 낙태에 대한 입장과 관련하여 '프로 라이프(pro-life)'와 '프로 초이스 (pro-choice)'라는 용어를 사용하는 것에 대해 전 세계적으로 열띤 논쟁이 있었다. 낙태에 반대하는 사람들은 그들이 '낙태 반대'라고 말하지 않는 이유는 '낙태'란 용어 자체가 '태아 살해'의 범죄성을 은폐하는 표현이기 때문이라고 말한다. 엄밀히 말하면, 그들은 '태아를 살해하는 것을 반대하는' 사람들이지만, 그들은 '프로라이프(pro-life)'라고 말하기로 한다. 달리(태아 살해 반대라고) 말하는 것은 (살해라는 단어 때문에) 사람들을 불쾌하게 할 것이기 때문이다.

02　2022 단국대　▶▶▶ MSG p.121　②

명령문을 이용한 양보 구문 ▶ most Americans가 주어이고 think가 동사여서 빈칸부터 reps까지가 삽입된 표현인데, 술부인 ①과 ④는 삽입될 수 없고 that절인 ③도 삽입될 수 없다. 종속부사절은 삽입될 수 있는데, 양보의 부사절 whether they be patients, doctors, or insurance reps에서 whether가 생략되고 주어와 동사가 도치된 ② be they가 삽입 표현을 이루기에 적절하다.

rep n. 외판원 face v. 직면하다

문제의 규모에 대해서는 의견이 분분하지만, 대부분의 미국인들은 환자이든, 의사이든, 또는 보험사 외판원이든, 우리의 건강관리 시스템이 심각한 문제에 직면해 있다고 생각한다.

03　2012 서울여대　▶▶▶ MSG p.61, p.97　④

전치사+(동)명사 ▶ 빈칸 이하가 완전한 절이므로 빈칸에는 부사어구가 와야 한다. 전치사 at과 명사 each reading이 합하여 부사어구를 이루므로 ④가 적절하다.

at all (부정문) 조금도, 전혀; (긍정문) 여하튼, 어쨌든 간에 refer to ~을 언급하다

조금이라도 읽을 가치가 있는 책은 한 번 이상 읽힐 가능성이 있으며 매번 읽을 때마다 어떤 개념 또는 서술은 너무나 인상 깊어서 다시 언급하고 싶어진다.

04　2022 가천대　▶▶▶ MSG p.234　②

it ~ that 강조구문 ▶ 빈칸 앞에서 매사추세츠 주가 제공해주는 유일한 곳이 바로 '감옥 안'이라고 한 다음 빈칸 이하에 완전한 절이 왔으므로, 빈칸에는 앞의 '감옥 안'을 강조해주는 말이 들어가야 한다. 따라서 it ~ that 강조구문인 ②의 It is there that이 빈칸에 적절하며, 이때 there는 in her prisons를 받은 부사로 쓰였다.

desponding a. 절망적인 lock somebody out ~를 못 들어오게 하다 fugitive a. 도망 다니는 parole n. 가석방 plead v. ~을 변명으로 내놓다; 변호하다

매사추세츠 주가 자유의 몸으로 절망하지 않는 사람들에게 제공해주는 오늘날 유일한 적절한 장소가 바로 매사추세츠 주 밖으로 내쫓고 못 들어오게 하는 감옥이다. 도망 다니는 노예, 가석방된 멕시코 죄수, 그리고 자신의 부족이 저지른 잘못을 변호하러 온 북미 원주민이 그들(자유의 몸으로 절망하지 않는 사람들)을 만날 수 있는 곳이 바로 감옥 안이다.

05　2011 고려대　▶▶▶ MSG p.199　②

원급비교 구문 ▶ 원급비교 구문의 문제이다. as ~ as they are는 '지금 실제로 ~한 만큼'이라는 의미로 'Why should the laws be as strict as they are?(왜 법이 지금만큼 엄격해야 하는가?)'처럼 쓰인다. 따라서 빈칸에는 ②가 적절하다. 결국 문장은 '말하지 않는 것을 무례하게 여기지만 그렇다고 말을 어떻게 해도 되는 것은 아니고 음식을 입안에 가득 넣고 말하는 모습을 보여서는 안 된다는 것에 대해서는 지금처럼 엄격하다'는 뜻이다. ①과 ④의 경우, as ~ as 구문에서 뒤의 as는 부사절을 이끄는 접속사로 뒤에 '주어+동사' 형태의 절이 와야 하므로 옳지 않으며, ③은 '너무 ~해서 …하다'는 의미의 so ~ that 구문으로 의미상 적절하지 않다.

impolite a. 무례한 with an open mouth 입을 벌리고 contain v. 포함하다

서구인들은 말하지 않고 있는 것을 종종 무례하다고 생각한다(즉 말하는 것에 대해서 관대하다). 하지만 동시에 그들은 입에 음식이 들어 있는 상태로 말하는 모습을 보여서는 안 된다는 따위에 대해서는 지금만큼 엄격하기도 하다.

---

06 **2015 한국외대** ▶▶▶ MSG p.222 ②

문의 구성 ▶ '깊은 숲속에 오두막집이 하나 있었다.'라는 의미의 Deep in the forest there was a cottage.에서 알 수 있듯이, Deep in the forest와 같은 장소부사어가 문두에 왔다고 해서 there와 be동사를 또 다시 도치시키지는 않는다. there is 구문에서는 장소부사 there 때문에 주어와 be동사가 이미 도치돼 있는 상황이며, 이는 be동사 대신에 stand를 써도 마찬가지이다. 따라서 ②가 빈칸에 적절하다.

sign n. 표지판, 간판 vanish v. 사라지다 town hall 시청 platform n. 교단, 연단

시장에 있던 모든 간판은 사라져버렸고, 시청 앞에는 연단만이 하나 서 있었다.

---

07 **2021 단국대** ▶▶▶ MSG p.73 ④

as if + 가정법 ▶ as if 뒤에는 가정법 동사가 쓰이며, 기준 시제와 동일 시점을 나타내는 경우에는 가정법 과거가 오고 그보다 앞선 시제를 나타내는 경우에는 가정법 과거완료가 온다. 빈칸 뒤에 목적어가 주어져 있고 다 억제한 완료의 의미가 있으므로, 능동태의 과거완료 시제로 쓴 ④가 정답으로 적절하다.

struggle v. 싸우다 pandemic n. 전국적[세계적]으로 유행하는 병 suppress v. 억제하다

전 세계 다른 많은 지역이 코로나 바이러스 대유행병과 싸웠으므로, 아시아·태평양 지역의 많은 곳은 마치 그 바이러스를 이미 성공적으로 억제한 것처럼 보였다.

---

08 **2018 세종대** ▶▶▶ MSG p.9 ②

문의구성 + 2형식 동사로 쓰인 stand의 용법 ▶ 접속사 though 뒤에 완전한 절이 이어져야 하는데, 분사 단독으로는 정동사 역할을 할 수 없으므로, 현재분사 standing이 정동사로 주어져 있는 ③과 ④를 정답에서 먼저 제외할 수 있다. 한편, stand가 타동사로 쓰이는 경우에는 '참다', '견디다'의 뜻이므로, ①은 문의 의미상 적절하지 않다. 따라서 정답은 ②가 되며, 이때 stand는 '~의 상태[입장]에 있다'는 의미의 2형식 동사로, empty는 stand의 보어이다.

triple v. 3배가 되다 wharf n. 부두, 선창

대부분의 부두가 비어 있음에도 불구하고, 항구의 크기는 3배 늘어났다.

---

09 **2006 경희대** ▶▶▶ MSG p.8, p.139 ④

선행사를 포함한 관계대명사 what ▶ 접속사 that 이하에는 주어와 동사가 갖추어진 절이 와야 한다. ④에서 what은 선행사를 포함한 관계대명사이며, is가 동사이고 그 앞부분이 주어가 되어 that절 안에 주어와 동사가 갖추어지게 된다. ①은 주어 it 앞에 조동사 does가 나온 의문문의 어순이므로 접속사 that이 이끄는 절이 될 수 없으며, ②나 ③의 which는 관계대명사이므로 앞에 선행사가 있어야 한다.

matter v. 중요하다 hard-working a. 근면한 loyalty n. 충성, 충의, 충절

나는 이제 대부분의 조직에서 가장 중요한 것은 조직에 대한 자부심과 충성심을 가진 상당히 총명하고 근면한 관리자를 확보하는 것이라는 생각이 든다.

---

10 **2020 세종대** ▶▶▶ MSG p.102, p.135 ④

주격관계대명사절 ▶ ④에서 that의 선행사는 the important discipline이므로, 그대로 두면 'discipline = today'의 관계를 만들게 되어 옳지 않다. 주격 관계대명사절에 별도로 주어를 표시해 주어야 할 것이므로, economics를 가리키는 대명사 it을 관계절의 주어로 삼는 것이 적절하다. ④를 that it is로 고친다.

there in no ~ing ~하는 것은 불가능하다 empirical a. 경험적인 discipline n. 훈련; 학문

진지한 경험적 연구가 경제학을 오늘날처럼 중요한 학문으로 만드는 데 도움을 주었다는 사실은 부인할 수 없다.

---

11 **2006 중앙대** ▶▶▶ MSG p.82 ①

과거 사실에 대한 유감 should+have+p.p ▶ 세미콜론 뒤에 이어지는 내용으로 보아 예전에 이미 도움을 준 적이 있으며, 그 과거에 일어났던 일에 대해 언급하고 있으므로 ① shouldn't help를 과거의 사실에 대해 유감을 나타내는 표현인 shouldn't have helped로 고쳐야 한다.

depend on ~에 의존하다

너는 그를 도와주지 말았어야 했다. 네가 그에게 도움을 제공한 이후 계속 그는 자신의 숙제를 다른 사람에게 의존하기 시작했다.

---

12 **2017 중앙대** ▶▶▶ MSG p.59 ③

수동태 ▶ in which 이하의 관계사절에서 주어는 objects이므로 ③을 수동태인 are discovered로 바로 잡아야 한다. ① 비교급 better와 짝이 되는 than이다. ② found는 과거분사이며, '발견된'의 의미로 뒤의 명사 objects를 수식한다.

serendipity n. 우연한 발견 triumph n. 승리, 대성공

우연히 발견된 물건들이 엄청난 가치를 가진 것으로 밝혀지는 수집가들의 대성공을 정의하는 단어로 'serendipity'보다 더 나은 단어가 무엇일까?

13 **2019 성균관대** ▶▶▶ MSG p.218 ①

등위접속사에 의한 병치 ▶ 등위접속사 and의 전후에는 단일개념, 같은 역할을 하는 단어·구·절이 연결되어야 한다. ①의 앞·뒤에는 모두 절의 형태가 있으므로, ①을 같은 절의 형태인 the air was cold로 고쳐야 한다.

scruffy a. 꾀죄죄한, 추레한 fake-fur n. 인조 모피 collar n. (와이셔츠) 칼라, (옷의) 깃

하늘은 맑고, 공기는 차가웠으며, 그는 흰색 인조모피 깃이 달린 추레한 검은색 코트를 입고, 선글라스를 쓰고, 회색 모직 모자를 이마 위로 눌러 쓰고 있었다.

14 **2010 고려대** ▶▶▶ MSG p.174 ②

적절한 대명사의 사용 ▶ 주어진 문장에서 주어로 전화, TV, 자동차, 총 3개의 명사가 제시되어 있으므로, 둘인 경우에만 사용하는 either는 사용할 수 없다. 따라서 이어지는 단수동사 presents에 맞게 ②를 each of them이나 any of them으로 고친다.

convenient a. 편리한 present v. 제시하다, 주다

전화, 텔레비전, 그리고 자동차는 삶을 더 편리하고 더 흥미롭게 한다. 그러나 그것들은 어느 것이나 만일 우리가 그것들이 우리를 통제하도록 기꺼이 허용하지 않는 한은 반드시 인식되고 통제되어야 할 위험을 준다.

15 **2021 단국대** ▶▶▶ MSG p.100 ③

전치사+(동)명사 ▶ approaches 뒤에 쓰인 to는 전치사이므로 그 뒤에는 동명사나 명사가 와야 한다. 따라서 ③을 teaching으로 고친다. ④ accommodate와 함께 in order to에 연결되고 있다.

reformer n. 개혁가 accommodate v. 편의를 도모하다; 제공하다 pupil n. 학생; 제자

20세기 가장 영향력 있는 교육개혁자 중 한 명인 존 듀이(John Dewey)는 학업의 진척을 돕기 위해서뿐만 아니라 학생의 심리적, 신체적 발달을 제공하기 위해 교육에 대한 대안적 접근을 추진하는 운동을 펼쳤다.

16 **2013 경희대** ▶▶▶ MSG p.99 ③

능동태와 수동태의 구분 ▶ turn은 이 문장에서 3형식 동사로 쓰였다. 뒤에 목적어 his head가 있으므로 능동태로 고쳐, ③을 from turning으로 써야 한다. ① 2형식 변화 표시 자동사 grow뒤에 보어인 형용사 비교급 larger가 부사 slowly의 수식을 받고 있는 형태이다. ② 동사 prevent의 목적어였던 '노 젓는 남자'가 주어가 되었기 때문에 동사도 수동태로 올바르게 쓰였다. ④ try for는 '~을 얻으려[찾으려] 하다'라는 의미이다.

lighthouse n. 등대 assume v. (특질·양상을) 띠다; (책임을) 떠맡다; (사실로) 추정하다; 가장하다 oar n. (배의) 노 a glimpse of 힐끗, 언뜻

한편 등대가 점차 커지고 있었다. 이제 등대는 거의 색을 띠었고, 하늘에 있는 작은 회색 그림자처럼 보였다. 노를 젓는 남자는 이 작은 회색 그림자를 잠깐씩 보기 위해 종종 고개를 돌리지 않을 수 없었다.

17 **2019 아주대** ▶▶▶ MSG p.73 ②

as if +가정법 동사 ▶ as if 뒤에는 가정법 동사가 쓰이는데, 주절과 같은 시제를 나타내는 경우에는 가정법 과거가 오고 주절보다 하나 앞선 시제를 나타내는 경우에는 가정법 과거완료가 온다. 탐닉하는 습관을 만드는 것은 그 행위로 인해 매도당하게 되는 것보다 앞서 일어난 일이므로, as if 뒤에 가정법 과거완료를 써야 한다. ②를 had invented로 고친다.

yuppy n. 여피족(도시에 사는 젊고 세련된 고소득 전문직 종사자) revile v. 욕하다, 매도하다 vaunting a. 자랑하는, 뽐내는 outsized a. 특대의, 초대형의 inherit v. 상속하다, 물려받다 fetus n. 태아 womb n. 자궁 craving n. 갈망, 열망 bloodstream n. (인체의) 혈류; 활력 melancholy a. 우울한, 울적한 wrestle v. (맞붙어) 싸우다

여피족들이 야망을 자랑스럽게 떠벌리고 지나치게 큰 기대를 품고 있는 것 때문에 마치 탐욕의 기질을 그들이 만들어낸 양 그토록 매도당하게 된 것은 아이러니한 일이었다. 사실 그들은 태아가 자궁 속에서 탐닉하는 습관을 갖게 되는 것처럼 그 기질을 물려받았을 뿐이었다. 탐욕은 그 나라의 기질에 속하는 것이었고, 베이비붐 세대는 이제 공급이 부족한 약에 200년 동안 의존해 온 상황과 씨름해야 하는 우울한 처지에 자신들이 놓여 있음을 알게 되었다.

18 **2022 가천대** ▶▶▶ MSG p.105, p.223 ①

과거분사 ▶ 첫 번째 문장은 강조를 위해 'so+형용사'가 문두로 나가면서 도치가 일어난 형태인데, 새 사전에 대해 『뉴욕타임스』가 넌더리가 난 것이므로, 수동을 나타내는 과거분사를 써야 한다. ①을 disgusted로 고친다. ② 주절에 이어지는 분사구문이다. ④ 선행 명사를 수식하고 있는 현재분사이며, 해당 문장의 정동사는 contained이다.

be disgusted with ~에 넌더리가 나다 edition n. (초판·재판의) 판(版) prompt v. (행동을) 촉구하다, 유발하다 pretentious a. 허세부리는 issue n. 발행물; (특히 출판의) 발행부수, ~호, (제~) 쇄(刷) condemn v. 비난하다

『뉴욕타임스』는 새로 출판된 사전에 너무나도 넌더리가 나서 1934년도 판(版) 사전을 계속 사용할 것이라 발표했는데, 이 발표는 버겐 에반스(Bergen Evans)로 하여금 "1934년에 출판된 사전을 지침으로 삼을 것이라고 발표하는 사람은 누구나 무식하고 허세부리는 헛소리를 하고 있는 것이다."라고 쓰도록 만들었다. 그는 그런 결정을 발표한 호(號)의 『뉴욕타임스』에 1934년도 판 사전이 비난하는 단어 19개가 포함돼 있다고 지적했다.

19   **2016 한양대** ▶▶▶ MSG p.136   ②

관계대명사 ▶ ②의 '전치사+관계대명사'인 by which가 관계절 안에서 부사어로 적절히 쓰여야 하나 쓰이지 못하고 있고, 관계절에서 뒤에 이어진 cognitive powers가 주어 역할을 하고 있으므로 주어를 수식해주는 소유격이 적절하다. 따라서 by which를 whose로 고쳐야 한다.

apparatus n. 장치, 기구 unequipped a. 준비가 안 된 cognitive a. 인지의 deficient a. 부족한 long-standing a. 오래된 revert v. 되돌아가다

기술이 우리 인간보다 훨씬 더 빠르게 진화할 수 있기 때문에, 우리는 외부 환경의 풍요로움을 철저히 다룰 준비가 돼 있지 않은 지적 장치를 지닌 하등 동물의 입장에 처해 있는 우리 자신의 모습을 발견하게 될 것이다. 인지능력이 상대적으로 항상 부족한 동물들과는 달리, 우리는 근본적으로 더욱 복잡한 세상을 만듦으로써 우리 자신의 부족함을 초래해왔다. 그러나 우리의 새로운 부족함은 동물들의 오랫동안 지속되어온 부족함과 그 결과 면에서는 동일하다. 결정을 내릴 때, 우리는 전체상황을 충분히 검토하여 분석하는 호사(풍요)를 빈번히 누리지 못하고 점점 더 전체상황의 한 가지 특징에만 집중하는 쪽으로 되돌아가고 있다.

20   **광운대 2021** ▶▶▶ MSG p.136   ③

정비문 ▶ 소유격 관계대명사 뒤에는 명사가 와야 하므로, ③은 She contacted the people whose house she's renting.이 되어야 한다. ① two sons와 she 사이에는 목적격 관계대명사 whom이 생략돼 있다. ② quote from~(~에서 인용하다)이므로 from which이다. ④ 주어와 동사 사이에 삽입된 계속적 용법의 who 관계절이다. ⑤ set이 '…에게 ~를 정해주다, 과하다, 맡기다'는 뜻의 4형식 동사로 쓰였으며 which의 선행사는 the answer가 아니라 a problem이고 the answer부터 관계절이 시작된다. '~에 대한 해답'은 the answer to ~이다.

quote v. 인용하다 extravagant a. 돈을 함부로 쓰는; 터무니없는

① 마사(Martha)는 의지할 수 있는 아들이 둘 있다.
② 이것이 그들이 인용하고 있던 기사다.
③ 그녀는 자신이 집을 임차하고 있던 사람들에게 연락했다.
④ 정치인들은, 터무니없는 약속을 하는데, 신뢰받지 못한다.
⑤ 그는 우리에게 교과서에서 답을 찾을 수 있는 문제를 정해주었다.

TEST 07

01 ③	**02** ③	**03** ④	**04** ④	**05** ①	**06** ②	**07** ①	**08** ②	**09** ①	**10** ③
11 ④	**12** ④	**13** ③	**14** ③	**15** ③	**16** ④	**17** ⑤	**18** ③	**19** ⑤	**20** ⑤

01 2018 가천대 ▶▶▶ MSG p.136 ③

소유격 관계대명사 ▶ 빈칸 뒤에 완전한 문장이 왔으므로 주격과 목적격으로 쓰이는 관계대명사 which나 that은 올 수 없으며, 앞에 선행사 an organism이 있으므로 선행사를 포함하고 있는 what도 빈칸에 들어갈 수 없다. 따라서 빈칸에는 뒤의 명사 successful maintenance를 수식할 수 있는 소유격 관계대명사 ③ whose가 적절하다.

prime a. 전형적인 symbiotic a. 공생하는 lichen n. 지의류 식물; 이끼 fungal a. 균류[곰팡이]에 의한 photosynthetic a. 광합성의 fungus n. 균류, 곰팡이 (pl. fungi) algae n. 조류(藻類) flourish v. (동·식물이) 잘 자라다

공생관계의 전형적인 예는 지의류 식물에서 볼 수 있다. 이 생물은 지의류의 외부와 내부를 함께 형성하는 곰팡이 파트너(균류)와 광합성 파트너(조류)로 이루어져 있으며, 균류와 조류 사이의 공생관계가 성공적으로 지속되면 거의 모든 곳에서 잘 자랄 수 있는 유기체이다.

02 2012 가톨릭대 ▶▶▶ MSG p.152 ③

fewer than+가산명사 ▶ 동사 understand의 앞부분 전체가 주어이고, 주어부에는 가산명사 half가 있으므로 수에 대하여 쓰이는 대명사 fewer가 있는 ③ Fewer than이 적절하다. ①과 ②는 한 문장 안에 접속사나 관계사 등이 없이 두 개의 동사가 오게 되므로 부적절하다. ④ As much as 다음에는 불가산명사가 와야 한다.

minimum a. 최소의, 최저의 sustenance n. 생계, 생활, 살림

모든 도시 거주자들 중에 사회생활을 지속하기 위해 필수적인 최소한의 공교육의 종류와 양을 이해하고 있는 거주자는 절반이 채 못 된다.

03 2013 단국대 ▶▶▶ MSG p.55 ④

능동태와 수동태의 구분 ▶ 빈칸 앞부분까지가 문장의 주어부분이다. 빈칸에는 알맞은 동사 형태가 들어가야 하는데 지식분야는 사람들에게 '개방되는' 것이므로 수동태로 쓰는 것이 옳다. 정답은 ④ have been thrown이 되며, 이제는 많은 사람들에게 개방되었다는 의미로 현재완료시제가 쓰였다.

throw something open ~을 개방하다, 공개하다

과거에는 단지 소수에게만 개방되었던 지식분야들이 이제는 과학에 의해 수백만의 사람들에게 개방되었다.

04 2019 세종대 ▶▶▶ MSG p.171, p.176 ④

대명사 +수량 수식어 ▶ '~하는 사람들'은 'those who ~'로 하며, 사람은 셀 수 있는 대상이므로 much of로 수식할 수 없다. 그러므로 빈칸에는 ④가 적절하다. 이때, those 뒤에 '관계대명사+be동사', 즉 who are가 생략돼 있는 것으로 파악하는 것도 가능하다.

grown-up n. 성인, 어른 childhood n. 어린 시절 in one's heart 마음속으로는, 몰래

고용된 사람들 대부분은 잭슨(Jackson)씨와 비슷하다. 그들은 교양 있는 성인들이지만 마음속으로는 아직도 어린 시절의 발명가들인 그런 사람들이다.

05 2007 서울여대 ▶▶▶ MSG p.176, p.235 ①

부정대명사 ▶ requires 앞까지 주어부이다. why some materials are electric conductors and others are insulators에서 are가 반복되므로 생략된 것이다. 그리고 앞에 부정형용사 some이 있으므로 빈칸에는 others가 와야 하는데, others는 other materials와 같다.

superconductivity n. 초전도 conductor n. 전도체 insulator n. 절연체 quantum mechanic 양자역학

초전도를 이해하거나, 왜 어떤 물질은 전도체이고 다른 것들은 절연체인지를 아는 것은 약간의 양자역학을 필요로 한다.

06 2012 한국외대 ▶▶▶ MSG p.199 ②

as+형용사+a(n)+명사 ▶ 일반적으로 관사는 'a(n)+부사+형용사+명사'의 어순으로 사용하지만, so, as, too, how 같은 부사가 형용사를 수식할 경우 '부사+형용사+a(n)+명사'의 어순으로 쓴다. 따라서 as important a role as가 올바른 표현이다.

intuition n. 직관, 육감 play a role 역할을 하다 experimentation n. 실험

바바라 맥린톡(Barbara McLintock)은 과학자들 중에서도 창의성이 뛰어난 사상가로, 그에게는 직관적 지식이 형식적인 실험이나 분석만큼 중요한 역할을 하는 그런 사상가였다.

07 **2011 고려대** ▶▶▶ MSG p.139   ①

선행사를 포함한 관계대명사 what ▶ 반영만 하는 거울(mirror)과 달리 예술은 활동적(active)이라고 했으므로, 빈칸에는 ①을 넣어 예술은 예술이 반영하는 것에 영향을 주기까지 한다는 의미가 되도록 하는 것이 적절하다. ②는 동사 affect가 의미상 that절을 목적어로 취하지 않으므로 부적절하다. ③은 감탄문의 형태인데 감탄문도 affect의 목적어가 되기에 부적절하다. ④는 주격의 관계대명사절인데 선행사가 없으므로 부적절하다.

mirror v. 반영하다; n. 거울 **virtue** n. 선, 선행; 미덕 **vice** n. 악, 악덕행위

예술은 사회, 사회의 선과 악을 반영하거나 비춘다. 그러나 거울과 달리 예술은 활동적이다. 예술은 예술이 반영하는 것(사회)에 영향을 끼치기까지 한다.

08 **2019 아주대** ▶▶▶ MSG p.132   ②

양보의 부사절 ▶ 둘째 문장은 this truth부터 주절이 완성돼 있으므로, 빈칸부터 may be까지는 종속절을 이루어야 한다. '의문사ever+피수식어+주어+동사'의 양보의 부사절에서 '주어+동사'가 빈칸 다음에 나와 있으므로 빈칸에는 '의문사ever+피수식어'에 해당하는 ②가 적절하다. ① however 뒤에는 원급의 형용사가 와야 하고 better는 긍정적 의미이므로 적절하지 않다.

fortune n. 재산, 부(富) **be in want of** ~을 필요로 하다 **fixed** a. 고정된, 일정불변한 **property** n. 재산; 소유물; 특성

많은 재산을 가진 독신 남자가 아내를 필요로 함에 틀림없다는 것은 보편적으로 인정된 사실이다. 그런 남자의 감정이나 생각이 아무리 적게 알려져 있어도, 이 사실이 이웃가족 식구들의 마음에 워낙 확고하게 자리하고 있어서 그들은 그를 자신들의 딸들 중 누군가에게 잘 어울리는 남편감으로 생각해 버린다.

09 **2013 경희대** ▶▶▶ MSG p.57   ①

능동태와 수동태의 구분 & 현재시제 ▶ 주어 faculties는 but if 다음의 they are repressed and denied처럼 '고무되는'이라는 수동의 의미이므로 동사는 수동태여야 하고, will act로 보아 가정법 과거가 아니라 현재시제여야 하므로 are encouraged가 적절하다. 따라서 ①이 정답이다. ②, ④의 unless는 if not의 의미로 전후 문맥상 어울리지 않는다.

faculty n. 능력, 재능 **stunt** v. 저해하다, 방해하다 **cripple** v. 불구로 만들다; 무능[무력]하게 하다

나는 성숙한 인간의 최고의 능력들이 모두 아이에게 존재한다고 믿는다. 그리고 이러한 능력들을 어린 시절에 고무시킨다면 이들은 성인이 되어서도 올바르고 현명하게 행동할 것이지만, 만일 이 능력들이 유년기에 억압되고 받아들여지지 않는다면 성인의 인격을 형성하는 것을 저해하고 손상시킬 것이라고 나는 믿는다.

10 **2020 세종대** ▶▶▶ MSG p.30   ③

문맥상 알맞은 동사의 쓰임 ▶ 'count on ~'은 '~에 의지하다'라는 의미이므로 문맥상 적절하지 않다. 글의 흐름상 '~로 간주되다'라는 의미의 'count A as B' 구문이 되어야 하므로, ③에서 on을 삭제해야 한다.

fine arts 미술, 순수예술

미술과 비디오 게임 문화에는 비디오 게임을 하나의 예술 형식으로 간주할 수 있는지에 대한 논쟁이 존재한다.

11 **2013 한국외대** ▶▶▶ MSG p.35, p.123   ④

비교대상의 일치 ▶ 비교급 문장에서 비교의 대상은 같아야 한다. "여자 아이들이 남자 아이들보다 더 많이 공감하고 있다"는 문장에서 접속사 than 이하의 문장은 than boys tend to show이다. 종속절에서 주절의 동사와 술부를 대신할 수 있는 대동사를 사용하여 ④를 do boys나 boys do로 고쳐야 한다. ① 현재완료 구문에서 부사 long은 have/has 다음에 온다. ② 'tend + to V'는 '~하는 경향이 있다'라는 뜻으로 쓰인다. ③ 뒤에 비교급 than이 왔으므로 more empathy는 바르게 쓰였다.

take something for granted ~을 당연한 일로 여기다 **empathy** n. 공감

여자 아이들이 남자 아이들보다 더 많이 공감하는 경향이 있다는 사실을 심리학자들은 오랫동안 당연한 것으로 생각해왔다.

12 **2022 홍익대** ▶▶▶ MSG p.116   ④

부대상황의 분사구문 ▶ 주절인 he was standing ~ visitors 다음에 전치사구가 왔는데, 전치사구는 동사 stream과 함께 쓰일 수 없다. 따라서 부대상황의 분사구문('with+목적어+분사')이 되도록 ④를 streaming으로 고쳐야 한다. with의 목적어인 '눈물'이 '흘러내리는(자동사)' 능동 관계이므로 현재분사로 고치는 것이다.

mesmerize v. 매혹시키다 **statue** n. 동상 **stream** v. (눈물 등이) 흐르다

내가 박물관에서 뜻밖에 그를 만났을 때, 그는 방문객들에게 알려지지 않은 매혹적인 동상 앞에 서 있었으며, 눈물이 그의 얼굴을 타고 흘러내리고 있었다.

13 **2019 홍익대** ▶▶▶ MSG p.50   ③

hardly ~ when … 구문 ▶ 부정의 부사인 hardly가 문두에 오면 도치가 일어나는데, ③의 앞과 뒤에 연결사 없이 두 개의 절이 와서 문장이 어색해졌다. 따라서 hardly가 온 절 다음에 새로운 절을 이끌도록 ③을 접속사 when이나 before로 고쳐야 한다. 'hardly ~ when[before]+주어+동사'는 '~하자마자 …하다'는 뜻의 관용표현이다.

pantry n. 식료품 저장실, 창고 **overcoat** n. 외투 **wheezy** a. (숨쉬기가 힘이 들어서) 쌕쌕거리는 **clang** v. (종이) 울려 퍼지다 **scamper** v. 날쌔게 움직이다 **hallway** n. 복도

그녀가 어떤 남자를 작은 창고로 데려가서 그가 외투를 벗는 것을 도와주자마자, 쌕쌕거리는 현관문의 종이 다시 울렸고 그녀는 재빨리 복도로 나가 다른 손님을 맞이해야 했다.

14 2019 홍익대 ▶▶▶ MSG p.205 ③

A is no more B than C ▶ 비교급 관용 구문 'A is no more B than C'는 'C가 B 아니듯이 A도 B 아니다'라는 뜻인데, 여기서 앞의 주절은 부정이지만 than절의 C는 긍정으로 표현되므로 ③을 not을 삭제한 has been으로 고쳐야 적절하다.

epistemology n. 인식론 settlement n. 개척지, 이주지; 해결

그러나 우리가 알게 되듯이, 인식론이 인간과 비인간의 관련성을 정의 내리는데 직접적으로 유용하지 않듯이, 기술 철학도 또한 인간과 비인간의 관련성을 정의 내리는 데 직접적으로 유용하지 않다. 그리고 똑같은 이유로, 근대주의적 해결에서는 이론은 실제를 손에 넣지 못한다.

15 2008 성균관대 ▶▶▶ MSG p.105 ③

현재분사와 과거분사의 구분 ▶ ③이 impact를 직접 수식하려면 '의도하고 있지 않은(unintending) 영향'이 아니라, '의도되지 않은(unintended) 영향'이 되어야 의미상 적절하다. ③을 unintended로 고친다.

coordinate v. 조율하다, 조정하다 imperative a. 긴급한; 필수적인 in the light of ~에 비추어, ~의 관점에서

의도되지 않은 영향이 그 지역에 있는 다른 국가들에 최소화될 수 있도록 조율하기 위해서, 우리는 분명히 경제, 무역, 개발정책을 논의할 어떠한 체계가 필요한데, 이러한 필요성은 증가하고 있는 우리의 독립성에 비추어볼 때 더욱더 필수적인 것이다.

16 2014 한국항공대 ▶▶▶ MSG p.28, p.43 ④

동사의 의미에 따른 시제 결정 ▶ 마땅한 액수보다 더 적은 액수에 동의한 것은 과거이지만, 그 액수의 차이만큼의 채무(갚아야 할 의무)는 지금 그가 나에게 지고 있는 것이다. 즉 돈을 덜 준 것도 돈을 빌려간 것과 마찬가지로 과거의 행위이지만 그가 나에게 더 주어야 할(갚아야 할) 의무는 지금 있는 것이다. 따라서 ④를 현재시제인 owes로 고쳐야 한다. 그리고 owe는 간접목적어와 직접목적어를 취하는 4형식 동사이다. ① a my acquaintance라고 쓸 수 없으므로 이중 한정을 피하기 위해서 명사 뒤에 'of+소유대명사'가 쓰인 이중소유격이다. ② take a photograph는 '사진을 찍다'라는 뜻으로 쓰이며 photograph는 가산명사이므로 photographs는 맞는 표현이다. ③ agree to는 '~에 동의하다, 승낙하다'라는 뜻으로 to 다음에 '제안, 계획' 등이 오며, agree with는 '~와 의견이 맞다'라는 뜻으로 with 다음에 '사람'이 온다.

acquaintance n. 지인 journalist n. 기자 owe v. 빚지다, 신세지다

나의 한 지인은 기자인데 그는 기사를 위한 사진을 찍기 위해 시골지역으로 여행을 가야 했다. 그는 자기와 함께 가서 장비를 운반하는 등의 일을 도와

달라고 요청했다. 나는 그가 제시한 액수에 동의했지만 지금 나는 그가 나에게 더 많은 돈을 줘야 한다고 생각한다.

17 2019 아주대 ▶▶▶ MSG p.147 ⑤

불가산명사 ▶ machinery는 집합적 물질명사이므로 불가산명사이며, 따라서 복수형으로 쓸 수 없다. 그러므로 ⑤를 much of our basic cellular machinery로 고쳐야 한다. ④에 쓰인 동사 adapt는 '적합하게 하다', '적응시키다'라는 의미의 타동사로 쓰였으며, 수동관계를 나타내기 위해 과거분사로 쓴 것이다.

eukaryote n. 진핵(眞核) 생물 split v. 갈라지다 ancestor n. 선조, 조상 relay v. 연락하다, 중계하다 tissue n. (세포) 조직 cellular a. 세포로 된 machinery n. 기계류; 조직

동물과 마찬가지로 식물도 수십억 년 전에 루카(Luca)로 불리는 공통의 조상으로부터 갈라진 진핵 생물, 즉 다세포 생물이다. 생존을 위해 우리 모두는 위험들을 감지하고, 그 위험들에 대한 메시지를 우리 몸이나 조직 내의 곳곳에 전달하며, 이러한 도전에 대응한다. 우리의 행동은 서로 다른 환경에서 우리가 유지하고 있는 생활방식에 맞게 가지각색이지만, 우리가 가지고 있는 기본적인 세포 조직의 많은 부분은 동일하다.

18 2020 가천대 ▶▶▶ MSG p.193 ③

빈도부사의 위치 ▶ 빈도부사는 조동사와 be동사의 뒤, 일반동사의 앞, 현재완료를 만드는 have와 과거분사의 사이에 위치한다. ③에 쓰인 always는 빈도부사이므로, ③은 has always been proud가 되어야 한다. ①은 보어 Gone이 앞에 나와 주어와 be 동사가 도치된 형태이며, ④의 so는 proud of her를 받고 있다.

niece n. 조카딸 withdrawn a. 내성적인, 내향적인 blossom v. 쾌활해지다, 활기를 띠다 sophomore n. (4년제 대학의) 2학년생 graduate n. 대학 졸업자; 대학원생

내 조카딸은 고등학교 때는 상당히 내성적이었지만 대학에서는 매우 활기찬 성격으로 변했다. 그 아이의 수줍음 많은 10대 시절은 이미 지나갔다. 그녀는 자신이 사랑하는 것을 발견하고 그것을 추구하고 있다. 사실, 그녀는 대학교 2학년생에 불과하지만, 대학원 강의 2개를 수강하고 있다. 가족들은 항상 그녀를 자랑스러워했지만, 그녀의 최근의 학업성취는 우리를 더더욱 그렇게 하도록 만들어 주었다.

19 2018 이화여대 ▶▶▶ MSG p.217 ⑤

명사의 병치 ▶ ⑤에 쓰인 표현은 모두 앞에 있는 based on의 목적어들이다. 전치사의 목적어로는 형용사가 아닌 명사가 쓰여야 하므로, ⑤에 쓰인 형용사 thrifty를 명사 thrift로 고쳐, 밑줄 친 부분을 thrift, sobriety, and hard work로 써야 올바른 병치구조가 완성된다. ③ that은 the towns of antebellum America를 선행사로 하는 주격 관계대명사로, had nonetheless maintained에 이어진다. 이때 접속사 while 뒤에는 '주어+be동사' 즉 they(=the towns of antebellum America) were가 생략돼 있다.

sprawl v. 불규칙하게 퍼지다; 마구 뻗다   urbanization n. 도시화
immigration n. 이주, 이민 corporation n. 법인, 주식회사 integrate v. (각
부분을 전체에) 통합하다 erode v. 좀먹다, 부식하다 antebellum a. 전쟁 이전의,
남북전쟁 전의 autonomy n. 자치, 자치권 rectitude n. 정직, 청렴 sobriety
n. 절주(節酒); 절제

1920년대를 현대로 특징짓는 데 있어서, 나는 급격한 산업화, 무분별한 도
시화, 대규모 이민 등으로 인해 19세기 후반에 근본적인 변화가 시작되었다
는 사실을 인정한다. 산업 발전은 일과 일상생활의 본질을 변화시켰고, 광범
위한 기업 네트워크를 생겨나게 하여 국가를 하나의 국민 경제 기구로 통합
시켰다. 그 결과, 고립돼 있던 "섬 공동체들" ─ 전전(戰前) 미국의 도시들 ─
을 서서히 무너뜨리게 되었는데, 그 도시들은 하나의 시장 경제의 일부였지
만 그럼에도 불구하고 어느 정도의 지방 자치와 "여성의 겸손, 남성의 정직,
그리고 남녀 모두의 검소, 절제, 근면"에 바탕을 둔 질서를 유지하고 있었다.

---

20 **2021 광운대** ▶▶▶ MSG p.81   ⑤

정비문 ▶ would rather 뒤에는 to부정사가 아닌 동사원형이 오며,
prefer가 '~보다'의 뜻으로 전치사 to를 쓰는 데 비해 would rather는
than과 호응한다. ⑤를 I'd rather take the bus than the taxi.로 고친
다. ①, ② prefer 뒤에는 to부정사와 동명사 둘 다 올 수 있다. ③
prefer A rather than B 구문도 가능하다. ④ would rather 다음에 절
이 올 때 가정법 과거(과거시제동사)와 가정법 현재(원형동사) 모두 가
능하다. 즉 I'd rather 다음에 he did여도 좋고 he do여도 좋다.

take v. (교통수단 등을) 타다, 이용하다

① 나는 달리는 것보다 수영하는 게 차라리 낫겠다.
② 나는 택시보다 버스를 타는 게 차라리 낫겠다.
③ 나는 걷는 것보다 운전을 하는 게 차라리 낫겠다.
④ 나는 그가 지금 당장 그 일을 했으면 좋겠다.
⑤ 나는 택시보다 버스를 타는 게 낫겠다.

TEST 08

| 01 ④ | 02 ④ | 03 ① | 04 ② | 05 ③ | 06 ① | 07 ④ | 08 ② | 09 ① | 10 ② |
| 11 ③ | 12 ③ | 13 ③ | 14 ④ | 15 ② | 16 ④ | 17 ① | 18 ① | 19 ② | 20 ⑤ |

01 2017 단국대 ▶▶▶ MSG p.221 ④

문의 구성 ▶ 강조를 위해 부사구가 문두로 와서 주어와 동사가 도치된 형태의 문장으로 파악할 수 있으며, 주어인 the New Power Party가 단수이므로, was가 정답이 된다. ①과 ③이 들어가는 경우에는 the New Power Party가 spawned의 목적어가 되므로, 주어가 없는 문장을 만들게 되어 옳지 않다.

civil disobedience 시민 불복종 spawn v. (어떤 결과 혹은 상황을) 낳다, 야기하다 ally v. 동맹하다, 연합하다 legislative seat (의회의) 의석

그 시민 불복종 행위로부터 시대역량(New Power Party)당(黨)이 생겨났는데, 이 당은 민주진보당(DDP)과 연합하여 5개의 의석을 차지했다.

02 2019 세종대 ▶▶▶ MSG p.105, p.147 ④

명사의 수 + 분사 ▶ as many as로 수식했으므로 가산명사의 복수형인 deals가 적절하다. 또한 deals는 cut하는 행위의 대상이므로 이 둘은 서로 수동관계이며, 따라서 수동을 나타내는 과거분사로 수식해야 한다.

opaque a. 불투명한 unregulated a. 규제받지 않는 cut a deal 계약을 체결하다

현재 규제를 받지 않은 불투명한 헤지펀드가 연루되어 있는 거래는 일부 대형 은행이 체결한 거래들 중 30%나 된다.

03 2016 가천대 ▶▶▶ MSG p.89, p.92 ①

부정사의 수동태 ▶ 많은 제안들이 거절된 것이므로 빈칸에는 부정사의 수동태가 적절하다. 따라서 ①이 정답이 되며, 'only to 부정사'는 부정사의 부사적 용법으로 결과의 의미를 나타낸다.

forgo v. 그만두다 unattended a. 돌보는 사람이 없는 pipe up 불쑥 말하다

몇몇 친구들과 나는 곧 있을 휴가에 대해 이야기를 하느라 매우 들떠있었는데 한 여자가 이웃집 사람이 그녀의 개가 세 마리의 새끼를 얼마 전에 낳아 그들을 내버려둔 채로 떠날 수 없기 때문에 서부로의 여행을 그만두어야 할지도 모른다고 말했다. 개를 돌봐주기 위한 여러 제안이 나왔지만, 번번이 거부되고 말았다. 나는 마침내 "제발! 그 엄마의 가족이 그들을 데려갈 수는 없나요?"라고 불쑥 말했다.

04 2018 세종대 ▶▶▶ MSG p.131 ②

접속사 provided ▶ 빈칸 앞에 완전한 절이 주어져 있으므로, 시제를 가진 동사가 접속사 없이 바로 이어질 수 없다. 그러므로 현재시제 동사 provides로 시작하는 ①과 ④를 먼저 정답에서 제외할 수 있다. 한편, ②와 ③에 쓰인 provided는 '~을 조건으로', '만약 ~라면'이라는 의미의 접속사로 쓰일 수 있는데, 접속사 뒤에는 절의 형태가 와야 하므로, '주어+동사'로 이루어져 있는 ②가 빈칸에 들어가기에 적절하다.

check out (도서를) 대출하다 provided conj. ~을 조건으로, 만약 ~라면

내일까지 반납한다는 조건으로 이 책을 대출하실 수 있습니다.

05 2019 아주대 ▶▶▶ MSG p.138, p.193 ③

절을 선행사로 하는 관계대명사 + 빈도부사의 위치 + be the case ▶ 앞 절 전체를 선행사로 받을 수 있는 관계대명사는 which이고, 빈도부사 rarely는 be동사의 뒤에 위치하며, '사실이다'라는 의미의 표현은 be the case로 한다.

mathematical a. 수학의 assume v. 가정하다 resource n. 자원

수학적 발전 모델에서는 자원이 무한하다고 가정하는데, 이것은 현실세계에서는 거의 사실이 아니다.

06 2019 세종대 ▶▶▶ MSG p.178, p.182 ①

형용사 no + 서술형용사 alike ▶ 명사 pairs는 부사 not이 아닌 형용사 no로 수식해야 하며, be동사의 보어 자리에는 서술형용사 alike가 적절하다. likely가 서술형용사로 쓰이는 경우에는 주로 to부정사를 동반하거나 '가주어-진주어' 구문에서 쓴다.

boutique n. 부티크, 양품점(값비싼 옷이나 선물을 파는 작은 가게) cater to ~에 맞추다

많은 안경점에서는 (안경) 디자이너들이 매우 다양한 독특한 재료를 사용하여 소비자의 취향에 맞추기 때문에 똑같은 안경은 하나도 없다.

07 **2014 한국외대** ▶▶▶ MSG p.70, p.71 ④

가정법 과거완료의 종속절 ▶ what might have happened는 가정법 과거완료의 귀결절의 형태이다. 그러므로 빈칸에는 가정법 과거완료의 조건절인 'if+주어+had p.p.' 형태의 문장이 와야 하겠는데, 여기서 if를 생략하면 'had+주어+p.p' 형태로 도치가 되므로 ④가 정답이다.

entertain v. 즐겁게 하다 take up (제의 등을) 받아들이다

때때로 그는 자신이 그 제안을 받아들였을 경우 일어났을지도 모를 일들을 생각하면서 스스로 즐거워한다.

08 **2017 아주대** ▶▶▶ MSG p.133 ②

as 양보절의 어순 ▶ as 양보절의 어순은 '형용사/부사/무관사 명사+as+주어+동사'이다 따라서 ②가 빈칸에 적절하다.

sore a. 아픈, (욱신욱신) 쑤시는 joint n. 관절 back pain 요통 headache n. 두통, 골칫거리 stomachache n. 복통, 배탈 medicine cabinet (세면대 위의) 약품 수납장

관절통과 요통에서부터 두통과 복통에 이르는 많은 종류의 통증에 대한 해결책은, 놀랍게 들릴지 모르지만, 약품 수납장이 아니라 부엌에 있을지도 모른다.

09 **2018 세종대** ▶▶▶ MSG p.123 ①

명사절을 이끄는 접속사 + 태의 구별 ▶ 빈칸 이하는 is의 보어가 되어야 하는데, 명사절을 이끌 수 있는 것은 which가 아닌 that이므로 ③과 ④를 정답에서 먼저 제외할 수 있다. 한편, than 뒤에는 'they(=new roads) are'가 생략돼 있는데, roads는 plan하는 행위의 주체가 아닌 대상이므로 수동태 문장으로 써야 한다. 따라서 ①이 정답이 된다.

quip n. 경구(警句), 명언; 핑계 pocket v. 챙겨 넣다; 자기 것으로 하다, 착복하다

흔히 하는 핑계는 도로 포장용 자재를 구입하는 데 쓸 돈을 정치인들이 착복하기 때문에 새로 생긴 도로가 계획보다 좁다는 것이다.

10 **2010 고려대** ▶▶▶ MSG p.197 ②

타동사구에서 대명사 목적어의 위치 ▶ '타동사+부사'가 결합해서 하나의 동사 역할을 할 때, 목적어가 대명사일 경우에 그 목적어는 반드시 타동사와 부사 사이에 위치해야 한다. work off는 '타동사+부사'의 관계이고 뒤에 대명사 목적어 it이 있으므로, ②의 to work off it은 to work it off가 되어야 한다.

work off 없애다, 제거하다 lose weight 체중을 줄이다

체중을 줄이는 데 보다 중요한 것은 체중을 줄이려고 얼마나 노력하느냐가 아니라 무엇을 먹는가이다.

11 **2020 세종대** ▶▶▶ MSG p.161 ③

정관사의 용법 ▶ ③이 가리키는 것은 '미국 내 중식당 사업'으로, 이미 언급돼서 서로 알고 있는 대상이다. 이러한 경우에는 해당 명사 앞에 정관사를 두어 한정시키는 것이 원칙이다. ③을 the business로 고친다. owners를 가리키는 their를 사용하여 their business라 해도 좋다.

retire v. 은퇴하다 pass v. 넘겨주다, 건네주다

전국적으로 Wang's(가게 이름)와 같은 미국 중식당의 주인들은 은퇴할 준비가 되어 있지만 사업을 물려줄 사람이 없다.

12 **2017 중앙대** ▶▶▶ MSG p.48 ③

과거완료시제 ▶ 주절의 시제가 used로서 과거시제임을 고려하면, ③은 주절의 시제보다 먼저 있었던 행위를 나타내므로, 과거완료시제인 had been used로 바로잡아야 한다. ① start가 타동사로 사용될 때 목적어의 형태는 ~ing 형태와 to V 형태 어떤 것이든 가능하다. ② the same으로 인해 ③ 앞에 있는 as가 유사관계대명사로 사용되었다.

translation n. 번역

19세기에 교사들이 다른 외국어들을 가르치기 시작했을 때, 그들은 라틴어를 가르치기 위해 사용되었던 것과 똑같은 번역에 기초한 접근법을 사용하였다.

13 **2021 단국대** ▶▶▶ MSG p.176 ③

almost와 most의 용법 구분 ▶ everyone, everything, nothing 등의 부정대명사는 most로는 수식할 수 없고 almost로 수식한다. ③을 almost everyone으로 고친다.

composition n. 작곡; 작품 western n. 서부극, 서부 음악

"석양의 무법자(The Good, the Bad, and the Ugly)"와 같은 세르지오 레오네(Sergio Leone)의 서부영화를 위해 작곡된 모리코네(Morricone)의 1960년대 곡들은 대중문화 속으로 매우 깊이 들어왔고 그 결과 거의 모든 사람들이 의식하지 못하면서도 그 곡들의 음을 알고 있다.

14 **2022 단국대** ▶▶▶ MSG p.136 ④

소유격 관계대명사 ▶ properties부터 empirically까지가 완전한 절이므로 주격과 목적격으로 쓰이는 관계대명사 which는 올 수 없으며, '자연현상들의' 특성과 관계이므로 소유격 관계대명사가 와야 한다. ④를 whose로 고친다.

theological a. 신학적인 metaphysical a. 형이상학의 verify v. 검증하다

콩트(Comte)는 그가 신학적, 형이상학적이라고 불렀던 이전의 사고방식은 불완전하며, 실증적인 지식은 그 특성과 관계가 경험적으로 검증되는 자연현상에 기초해야 한다고 믿었다.

15 **2008 성균관대** ▶▶▶ MSG p.53 ②

시제일치 ▶ It was not until ~ ventured to stop을 보면, 이 문장은 대과거를 포함한 과거 사실의 서술이다. 따라서 ② can no longer를 could no longer로 고쳐야 한다.

race-ground n. 경마장 venture v. 위험을 무릅쓰고 ~하다, 과감히 ~하다

너무 지쳐 더 이상 경마장에서 탈출할 때의 속도를 유지할 수 없게 되어서야 비로소 그 노인과 아이는 겨우 용기를 내어 어느 작은 숲 가장자리에 멈춰 앉아 쉬었다.

16 **2018 국민대** ▶▶▶ MSG p.227 ④

적절한 전치사의 사용 ▶ 'take responsibility for~'의 형태로 쓰므로, ④의 by를 for로 바로잡아야 한다. 한편, make use of~의 형태를 수동태로 전환한 것이므로 ③의 of는 적절한 사용이다.

permanent a. 영구적인, 상근의 considerable a. 상당한 migrant n. 이주자

현대화된 서구식 농업은 농번기가 끝나면 농부들이 책임질 필요가 없는 계절적 이주노동은 상당히 많이 이용했지만, 상근 농장노동자는 예전에 비해 비교적 더 적게 필요로 했다.

17 **2013 서강대** ▶▶▶ MSG p.109 ②

유사분사의 형태 ▶ 유사분사의 형태는 분사로 쓰인 동사와 이것이 수식하는 명사와의 관계를 통해 결정하는데, 만약, 능동관계이면 현재분사 형태를 쓰고, 수동관계이면 과거분사를 쓴다. dwell과 dinosaur는 '공룡이 거주하는' 개념, 즉, 능동의 개념이므로 현재분사 형태를 써야 한다. ②에서 ground-dwelled를 ground-dwelling으로 고친다.

by-product n. 부산물 flap v. 펄럭거리다 dwell v. 거주하다 predecessor n. 선조 feather n. 깃털

로스앤젤레스 카운티의 자연사 박물관의 초기조류 전문가인 루이스 치아페(Luis Chiappe)는, 조류의 조상인 육지에 사는 공룡들이 달리는 속도를 증가시키기 위해 혹은 빠른 방향 전환을 할 때 몸의 균형을 잡기 위해 깃털이 달린 팔을 사용했으며, 비행은 그러한 팔을 젓는 행동의 부산물로 생겨났을 거라고 말하고 있다.

18 **2018 한양대 에리카** ▶▶▶ MSG p.105 ①

과거분사 ▶ ①의 harvesting은 앞에 있는 명사 all oysters를 수식하고 있는데, oysters가 harvest하는 행위의 주체가 아닌 대상이므로 수동 관계에 있다. 따라서 ①을 수동의 의미를 나타내는 과거분사 harvested로 고쳐야 한다. ③ 대왕오징어, 해파리, 문어가 멕시코만 수역을 '헤엄치는' 것이므로, 능동 관계를 나타내는 현재분사 swimming이 적절하다.

oil spill 기름 유출 oyster n. 굴 harvest v. 수확하다, 채취하다 endangered a. (동식물이) 절멸 위기에 처한 imperil v. 위험에 빠뜨리다 coral reef 산호초

기름 유출이 있기 전에 미국 수역에서 채취된 모든 굴의 60퍼센트 이상이 멕시코만에서 잡혔다. 오늘날 그 점유율은 약 40퍼센트로 떨어졌다. 멸종 위기에 처해 있는 많은 종(種)이 또한 멕시코만에서 살고 있는데, 그 종에는 바다거북, 플로리다 매너티, 미국흰두루미, 흰머리독수리 등이 있다. 돌고래는 자주 볼 수 있다. 멕시코만의 수역을 헤엄쳐 다니는 대왕오징어, 해파리, 문어는 미국의 가장 아름답지만 가장 큰 위험에 처해있기도 한 일부 산호초들을 지나간다.

19 **2018 명지대** ▶▶▶ MSG p.105 ②

문의 구성 ▶ ②가 들어 있는 문장의 정동사는 was made인데, 접속사 없이 시제를 가진 동사 was led가 다시 이어지므로 옳지 않은 문장이다. 따라서 ②를 led by로 고쳐서 led by ~ Gibraltar가 a small force를 후치수식을 하도록 해야 한다.

encroachment n. 침입, 침략 peninsula n. 반도 territory n. 영토 conquer v. 정복하다 empire n. 제국 prophet n. 예언자

쌀을 의미하는 스페인어인 'arroz'는 아랍어 'orez'에서 유래하기 때문에, 누가 스페인에 벼농사를 전해주었는가를 우리에게 분명히 알려주고 있다. 무어족이 이베리아 반도(Iberian Peninsula)를 처음 침략한 것은 711년으로, 지브롤터(Gibraltar) 근처에서 타리크 이븐 지야드(Tariq ibn Ziyad)가 이끄는 소규모 병력으로 침략했다. 그 후 60년 동안, 오늘날 스페인과 포르투갈의 거의 대부분의 영토가 정복되어, 우마이야 왕조(Umayyad Caliphate)의 일부인 알 안달루스(al-Andalus)가 되었는데, 이 우마이야 왕조는 예언자 마호메트(Muhammad)가 살았던 시기의 바로 이전 세기에 시작된 이슬람 확장기를 지속시켜간 다마스쿠스(Damascus) 중심의 제국이었다.

20 **2021 광운대** ▶▶▶ MSG p.174 ⑤

정비문 ▶ some은 긍정문에 쓰고 any는 의문문과 부정문에 쓴다. ⑤에 쓰인 scarcely는 부정어에 속하므로 any와 함께 써야 한다. ⑤를 There's scarcely any food left in the kitchen.으로 고친다.

objection n. 반대; 이의, 반론 be taken aback 당황하다, 깜짝 놀라다

① 나는 몇 가지 반대 의견이 있다.
② 누구나 어떤 약속이라도 할 수 있다.
③ 반대 의견 있습니까?
④ 그녀는 너무 당황해서 아무 말도 할 수 없었다.
⑤ 부엌에 음식이 거의 남아 있지 않다.

TEST 09

| 01 ① | 02 ④ | 03 ① | 04 ③ | 05 ① | 06 ③ | 07 ③ | 08 ② | 09 ② | 10 ④ |
| 11 ② | 12 ④ | 13 ② | 14 ② | 15 ① | 16 ③ | 17 ⑤ | 18 ④ | 19 ② | 20 ② |

---

01   2022 단국대   ▶▶▶ MSG p.143   ①

복합관계대명사 ▶ 빈칸부터 it까지가 전치사 of의 목적어가 되는 명사절을 이루어야 하겠는데, 선행사가 없으므로 빈칸에는 복합관계대명사가 적절하다. 뒤에 동사가 있으므로 주격의 복합관계대명사 whoever가 정답이 된다.

capture attention 관심을 사로잡다[끌다]

확고한 목적을 갖고 이력서를 쓰는 것은 그것을 읽고 있는 모든 사람의 관심을 끌뿐만 아니라 계속 읽도록 고무시킬 것이다.

02   2016 가톨릭대   ▶▶▶ MSG p.171   ④

명사의 반복을 피하기 위해 사용하는 지시대명사 those ▶ 독단적인 이기주의자의 구레나룻과 고상하고 학구적인 신사의 구레나룻의 모양을 대조의 접속사 while을 사용하여 비교하고 있는 문장이다. 비교대상이 구레나룻(whiskers)이므로 빈칸에는 while the whiskers of가 들어가야 하겠는데, 반복되는 명사 whiskers를 지시대명사 those를 사용하여 표현한 ④가 빈칸에 적절하다.

opinionated a. 자기 의견을 고집하는, 독선적인 egoist n. 이기주의자 whisker n. 구레나룻 refined a. 세련된, 고상한 scholarly a. 학구적인 clip v. 자르다, 깎다

독선적인 이기주의자는 길고 좁은 구레나룻을 하는 경향이 있는 반면, 고상하고 학구적인 신사의 구레나룻은 대개 짧게 깎은 모양이다.

03   2019 세종대   ▶▶▶ MSG p.132   ①

양보의 부사절을 이끄는 'no matter 의문사' ▶ 마지막에 전치사 like 다음이 비어있는데 what이 like의 목적어가 될 수 있으므로 ①이 적절하다.

country n. 국가, 나라; 지역; 시골

그 나라의 새 정부가 어떠해 보일지라도 그 나라는 변하고 있고 앞으로도 변할 것이다.

04   2019 아주대   ▶▶▶ MSG p.224   ③

문두에 부정어가 쓰인 문장의 도치 ▶ neither나 nor와 같은 부정어가 문두에 오는 경우, 그 뒤에는 '조동사+주어+동사원형'의 형태가 와야 한다. 따라서 Neither 뒤에 조동사 need와 주어 you가 제시돼 있는 ③이 빈칸에 적절하다. ①의 경우, 일반동사로 쓰인 need 뒤에 동사원형 do가 오는 형태가 되어 부적절하다. need가 일반동사로 쓰이는 경우에는 뒤에 to부정사가 와야 한다.

snow goose 흰 기러기 bathe v. 목욕시키다; 담그다, 적시다

흰 기러기는 몸을 하얗게 하기 위해 목욕을 할 필요가 없다. 마찬가지로 당신도 당신 자신의 모습 그대로 있는 것 외에는 아무것도 할 필요가 없다.

05   2013 한국외대   ▶▶▶ MSG p.199   ①

부정의 원급비교 ▶ 부정의 원급비교는 not so ~ as이므로 ①과 ②처럼 clever 앞에 so가 있어야 하고 as는 유사관계대명사이므로 ①처럼 as 다음에 관계절의 주어인 I가 바로 나와야 한다. quite는 '아주'의 의미를 가진 부사로 not과 함께 부분부정을 이루고 있다.

clever a. 영리한, 똑똑한, 재치 있는

나는 그녀에 대해서 굉장히 많이 들어왔지만, 그녀는 내가 예상했던 것만큼 아주 똑똑하지는 않았다.

06   2011 고려대   ▶▶▶ MSG p.30, p.59   ③

refer to A as B ▶ refer to A as B 구문을 수동형으로 하면, A be referred to as B의 형태가 된다. 이 문장은 동사(refer to)의 목적어 the earliest modern computers가 동사(refer to) 앞에 나와 when절의 주어가 되어있으므로, refer to는 수동의 형태가 되고 주어와 동사 (were built) 사이에 삽입될 수 있도록 be동사를 제외한 과거분사의 형태로 되어야 한다. 따라서 빈칸에는 ③이 적절하다. ①은 referring to 다음에 목적어가 나와 있지 않아 답이 될 수 없다. 또 ①과 ④에서 referring은 의미상의 주어가 바로 앞에 나와 있는 컴퓨터가 되어 논리에 맞지 않으므로 정답이 될 수 없다. ②는 ③과 같이 now referred to as로 고쳐야 한다.

first-generation n. (컴퓨터 등의) 제1세대 dramatically ad. 희곡적으로; 극적으로

현재 제1세대 컴퓨터로 언급되고 있는, 가장 초기의 현대식 컴퓨터들이 1950년대 중반에 미국에서 만들어졌을 때, 그것들은 오늘날의 시스템과 비교하면 아주 달랐다.

가장 강인한 영혼들은 고통에서 탄생했으며, 가장 굳센 이들에게는 상처가 새겨져 있다.

---

07 2011 고려대 ▶▶▶ MSG p.133 ③

명령문을 이용한 양보 구문 ▶ 명령문을 이용한 양보 구문(be+S+보어)이다. be his place what it may는 'whatever his place is/may be'로 바꿀 수 있고, '자신의 위치가 어떠할지라도'라는 의미이다.

divine a. 신의; 거룩한 great being 위대한 존재 rag n. 누더기 slavish a. 노예의; 천한

영혼의 신적 능력을 소유하는 자는 자신의 위치가 어떠할지라도 위대한 존재이다. 당신은 그 사람에게 누더기를 입히고, 천한 일에 얽매이게 할 수 있을지 모른다. 그렇지만 그는 여전히 위대하다.

---

08 2015 한국외대 ▶▶▶ MSG p.113 ②

수동 분사구문 ▶ 분사구문에 주어가 명시돼 있지 않다는 것은 분사구문의 주어와 주절의 주어가 같다는 것을 의미한다. 주어진 문장에서 분사구문의 주어는 Hawaii이다. 그런데, Hawaii는 타동사 form과 steep의 대상이며 하와이가 화산에 의해 형성된 것이고 하와이가 폴리네시아 문화의 역사에 의해 깊이 스며들었다는 뜻이 되어야 하므로 수동의 분사구문으로 써야 한다. 따라서 ②가 정답이다.

volcano n. 화산 steep v. ~에 깊이 스며들게 하다 fantasy novel 공상 소설

화산에 의해 형성되어 폴리네시아 문화의 풍부한 역사가 깊이 스며든 하와이는 미국의 휴양지보다는 오히려 공상 소설 속에 나오는 장소인 것 같다.

---

09 2004 세종대 ▶▶▶ MSG p.125 ②

간접의문문의 어순 ▶ (that) 명사절은 전치사의 목적어가 될 수 없으므로 ①과 ③은 정답이 될 수 없다. 간접의문문은 명사절로 전치사의 목적어가 될 수 있으며, 그 어순은 '의문사+주어+동사'이다. 따라서 이와 같은 어순으로 된 ②가 정답이 된다.

distribute v. 분배하다 depend on ~에 달려있다 recipe n. 조리법

대중들에게 사슴을 일상에서 먹는 음식의 일부로 받아들이도록 설득하는 것의 성공여부는 정보와 조리법을 대중 매체가 얼마나 잘 퍼뜨리는가에 있다.

---

10 2016 한국외대 ▶▶▶ MSG p.57 ④

수동태 ▶ sear는 '그슬리다', '~에 낙인을 찍다'라는 뜻의 타동사이다. 이 동사의 목적어가 주어져 있지 않으므로, 수동태 문장으로 바꿔야 한다. ④를 are seared with로 고친다.

massive a. 크고 무거운, 대량의 sear v. 태우다; 낙인을 찍다 scar n. 상처

---

11 2020 서울여대 ▶▶▶ MSG p.139, p.234 ②

관계대명사 what ▶ 관계대명사 what 뒤에는 주어, 목적어, 보어 가운데 하나가 빠져있는 불완전한 절이 수반되어야 하는데, you say it이라는 완전한 형태의 문장이 왔으므로 옳지 않다. 따라서 ②의 목적어 it을 삭제해야 한다.

matter v. 중요하다 communicate v. (서로 마음으로) 소통하다

다른 사람과 대화를 하는 데 있어 중요한 것은 당신이 말하는 것과 당신이 말하는 방식 둘 모두이다.

---

12 2015 중앙대 ▶▶▶ MSG p.97 ④

문의 구성 ▶ ② being kicked off the team은 수동형 동명사로 동사 take의 목적어로 쓰이고 있으며, ③ with so much resignation에서 much는 불가산 명사를 수식할 수 있다. 따라서 문법적으로 틀린 표현은 없다.

be kicked off the team 팀에서 쫓겨나다 resignation n. 사직, 사임; 체념

D. 워런(D. Warren)이 팀에서 퇴출되는 사실을 그렇게도 체념하는 마음으로 받아들이리라고 예측한 사람은 아무도 없었다. 워런은 슬픈 듯이 라커룸에서 걸어 나갔다.

---

13 2017 홍익대 ▶▶▶ MSG p.171 ②

such A as B ▶ 'B와 같은 A'는 such A as B로 나타낸다. 따라서 ②를 as로 고쳐주어야 한다. 한편, put ~ on the table은 '~을 검토하다, 현안으로 다루다'라는 뜻으로, 주어진 문장에서 such sensitive issues 이하가 동사 put의 목적어이다.

racism n. 인종차별 be supposed to ~할 의무가 있다, ~해야 한다 reparation n. 보상, 배상 Zionism n. 시오니즘(유대인들의 국가 건설을 위한 민족주의 운동)

세계 인종차별철폐 회의는 노예제도 배상과 시오니즘이 인종차별인지의 문제와 같은 그런 민감한 문제들을 현안으로 다루어야 한다.

---

14 2009 홍익대 ▶▶▶ MSG p.218 ②

동사의 관용표현 ▶ 동사나 동사 위주의 관용표현을 지칭해서 설명할 때 to monkey around처럼 to부정사로 나타내므로 and 뒤에도 주어가 to부정사가 된다. ② make를 to make로 고친다.

monkey around 빈둥빈둥 놀며 다니다 monkey business 사기; 부정행위 make a monkey out of someone ~을 놀리다

'빈둥빈둥 놀며 다니다'와 '부정행위'는 1800년대 초에 쓰인 표현이며, '놀리다'라는 표현은 1899년부터 쓰이는 표현인데, 이들 표현은 모두 서커스와 동물원에서 보게 되는 원숭이의 수가 늘어난 것에 바탕을 둔 표현들이다.

15 2016 한양대 에리카 ▶▶▶ MSG p.217   ①

형용사 병치 ▶ 'portray 목적어 as 보어' 구문에서 보어에 해당하는 세 형용사(구)가 and에 의해 병치된 구조이다. 그런데 'attach 사람(A) to 대상(B)'는 'A로 하여금 B에 애착을 갖게 하다'는 뜻이며, 수동태인 A is attached to B는 'A는 B에 애착이 있다'는 뜻이다. 따라서 A에 해당하는 목적어 the ruling class가 '자신의 부에 애착이 없다'는 의미관계가 되려면 as 다음의 보어로 세 번째로 나온 ①은 과거분사형인 unattached to여야 한다.

portray v. 묘사하다 unattached a. 매여 있지 않은(to) interaction n. 상호작용 privilege v. 특권을 주다 opportunistic a. 기회주의적인 avaricious a. 탐욕스러운 longing n. 갈망, 열망

사실, 많은 영화와 텔레비전 프로그램은 지배 계층을 물질적으로 혜택 받지 못한 사람들과의 상호작용에 있어서 관대하고, 기꺼이 나누어 가지려하고, 자신들의 부(富)에 애착이 없는 것으로 묘사한다. 이런 이미지들은 가난한 사람들의 기회주의적이고 탐욕스러운 열망과 대조를 이룬다.

16 2022 가천대 ▶▶▶ MSG p.124   ③

접속사 whether ▶ 주어인 명사 question이 '의문'과 관련이 있어서 주격보어절로 의문사 what절이 왔는데, 의문사 what의 경우 가산명사를 수식할 때 감탄문과 달리 관사 없이 what immoral act가 되며 만일 an immoral act만을 주어로 보면 완결된 절 안에서 what의 역할이 없게 되어 부적절하다. 따라서 ③을 의문의 의미도 갖고 완결된 절을 이끄는 접속사 whether로 고쳐야 한다. ① 주어는 unanswered questions 이다.

frenetic a. 열광적인 lurk v. 숨다, 잠복하다 on the heels of ~에 잇따라서 hairpin a. U자 모양의 twist n. (사건·사태의) 예기치 않은 진전, 뜻밖의 전개 sinner n. 죄인

"올드보이"의 광란의 액션 이면에는 죄의식, 책임감, 도덕에 관한 대답 없는 질문들이 숨어 있다. 매번 줄거리가 U턴(급반전)을 할 때마다 바로 뒤이어 제기되는 이 영화의 핵심 질문은 죄를 저지르는 사람이 알지 못하는 경우에도 부도덕한 행위가 여전히 부도덕한가 하는 것이다. 그러나 도덕의 문제는 순전히 개인적인 문제로 남아 있다.

17 2010 숙명여대 ▶▶▶ MSG p.40   ⑤

적절한 동사의 사용 ▶ 일반적으로 '침묵이 깨지다'라는 표현은 silence is broken으로 한다. ⑤ closed를 broken으로 바꿔야 한다.

babbling a. 졸졸 흐르는 cosy a. 아늑한 patter n. 후드득 떨어지는 소리 eerie a. 괴상한, 섬뜩한

친구와 나는 이번 주말에 캠핑을 갔다. 우리는 졸졸 흐르는 개울가의 멋진 장소에 텐트를 쳤다. 새들은 노래하고 있었고 도시의 번잡한 교통에서 멀리 떨어져 있다는 것은 정말 굉장한 기분이었다. 날씨는 그다지 좋지 않았지만 텐트위에 후드득 떨어지는 빗방울소리를 듣는 것이 아늑한 분위기를 자아냈다. 결국 비가 그쳤을 때 우리 주변에는 온통 괴기스러울 정도의 침묵이 흘렀다. 그 침묵은 총성이 울렸을 때 갑자기 깨졌다. 누군가가 토끼들에게 총을 쏜 것이었다.

18 2015 명지대 ▶▶▶ MSG p.105   ④

현재완료와 과거완료의 구별 ▶ 세 번째 문장에서 작가들이 어떤 사실을 알아낸 것은 과거의 일이므로 과거(figured out)로 나타내고 that절의 동사들도 시제일치를 시켰지만, so 다음은 그 결과로 지금까지 해온 일을 나타내므로 현재완료 시제가 적절하다. 그러므로 ④를 have kept coming으로 고쳐야 한다. 만약 과거완료 had kept를 쓰면, figured out한 그때까지 여러 해 동안 해왔었다는 뜻이 되어 인과관계에 어긋난다. ① has been seen by many as는 5형식 수동태인 has been seen as가 쓰였으며, by many가 'as 보어'보다 먼저 온 형태이다. ② 분사구문 Being gifted with에서 Being이 생략된 형태이다. ③ Superman fights for Earth와 이어지는 분사구문으로 guarding it against가 쓰였으며, it은 앞에 언급된 Earth를 받은 대명사이다.

quintessential a. 전형적인 gifted with ~을 타고난, ~한 재능이 있는 figure out 생각해내다 appreciable a. 주목할 만한 come up with ~을 내놓다

1932년 제리 시겔(Jerry Siegel)과 조 슈스터(Joe Shuster)가 만들어낸 슈퍼맨은 많은 사람들에게 전형적인 미국의 영웅으로 인식되어 왔다. 지금은 멸망한 크립톤 행성 태생으로 초능력을 타고난 슈퍼맨은 제2의 고향인 지구를 지키기 위해 싸우며, 내부의 위협과 외부의 위험으로부터 지구를 보호한다. 그와 동시에, 슈퍼맨을 만들어낸 작가들은 다치지 않거나 어떤 큰 위험에도 직면하지 않는 등장인물에 대해 상당히 지루하다는 것을 빠르게 간파했고, 그래서 그들은 여러 해에 걸쳐 계속해서 슈퍼맨의 약점을 내놓았다.

19 2018 명지대 ▶▶▶ MSG p.222   ②

Only가 문두에 나올 때의 도치 ▶ only를 포함한 부사구가 문두에서 강조될 경우, 이 부사구의 다음에 오는 주절에는 의문문 형태의 도치가 일어난다. 따라서 ②를 did the federal government produce로 고쳐야 한다.

issue v. 발행하다 greenback n. 달러 지폐 the Civil War (미국의) 남북 전쟁 coinage n. 화폐 bill n. 지폐 proliferate v. (빠르게) 확산되다 to take one example 한 가지 예를 들면 no fewer than 최소한 ~인 churn out 대량 생산하다 appellation n. 이름

돈은 비교적 최근까지도 해도 표준화되지 않은 미국 생활의 특징이었다. 남북전쟁 중 최초의 달러 지폐 발행을 계기로 해서야 비로소 연방정부는 지폐를 발행하게 되었다. 동전과는 달리, 지폐는 (발행이) 은행에 맡겨졌다. 19세기 전반기 동안에는 은행들이 각자 고유의 지폐를 발행할 수 있는 행복한 입장에 있었다. 여러 유형의 지폐가 널리 확산되었다. 일례로, 오하이오(Ohio) 주 제인즈빌(Zanesville)에서는 30개나 되는 은행들이 올빼미 크리크족 은행(Owl Creek Bank)과 같이 다양한 이름하에 돈을 대량으로 만들어냈다.

정비문 ▶ know는 진행형에 쓰지 않는다. ②를 Have you known John ever since the childhood?로 고친다.

get married 결혼하다 **firework** n. 불꽃놀이 **at work** 일하고 있는

① 우리는 내년에 결혼할 것이지만, 아이는 갖지 않을 것이다.
② 어린 시절부터 줄곧 존을 알고 지내왔나?
③ 불꽃놀이는 중국에서 발명되었던 것으로 추정된다.
④ 피터가 어제 왜 출근하지 않았는지 우리는 알지 못한다.
⑤ 당신의 나라에서는 아이들이 몇 살에 학교에 다니기 시작하는가?

TEST 10

01 ②	02 ③	03 ②	04 ①	05 ④	06 ②	07 ①	08 ④	09 ④	10 ①
11 ⑤	12 ④	13 ④	14 ③	15 ②	16 ④	17 ④	18 ④	19 ④	20 ②

01　2010 숭실대　▶▶▶ MSG p.228　②

전치사 but ▶ claims를 의미하는 지시대명사 those를 목적어로 받는 전치사 역할을 할 수 있는 것은 but이다.

pragmatism n. 실용주의, 실리주의 absolutistic a. 절대론적인 fruit n. (종종 pl.) 소산, 결과

실용주의 철학은 현실에 대한 모든 절대주의적 가정을 배격하고, 현실의 다원성을 수용하면서, 결과와 결말, 그리고 사실에 주안점을 두는 주장이외에 다른 그 어떤 주장도 고려하지 않는다.

02　2011 서울여대　▶▶▶ MSG p.222　③

only가 이끄는 부사어가 문두에 오는 경우의 도치 ▶ Only로 시작되는 부사어 Only now가 문두에 나와서 주어와 동사가 도치된다. 주어는 questions such as 뒤에 명사절 세 개가 이어진 형태로 빈칸 앞까지가 주어 부분이다. 주어 앞에 동사 are가 도치되어 있으므로 빈칸에는 are에 연결될 수 있는 현재분사 ③이 적절하다.

echo v. 울리다, 메아리치다

이제야 어떻게 물질이 생산되며, 얼마나 많은 에너지가 그 물질을 관리하기 위해 사용될 것이며, 결국 그 물질이 사라질 땐 어떤 일이 발생하는지 등의 질문들이 그 산업체에 울려 퍼지기 시작하고 있다.

03　2019 세종대　▶▶▶ MSG p.156, p.222　②

동사의 수일치+막연한 수를 나타내는 표현 ▶ '수백의', '수천의'와 같이 막연히 많은 수를 나타내는 경우, '수사의 복수형+of'를 써서 hundreds of, thousands of처럼 한다. dozen의 경우에도 마찬가지이므로 dozens로 써야 한다. 이때 문장의 주어는 dozens of young students인데, 이것은 복수이므로 동사로는 were가 적절하다.

barrier n. 울타리, 방벽; 장벽 tape v. ~에 테이프를 붙이다 dozen n. 1다스, 12개

경찰 바리케이드의 한쪽에는 수십 명의 어린 학생들이 있었는데, 상당수는 언론의 자유에 대한 지지를 나타내기 위해 입에 테이프를 붙인 채로 있었다.

04　2021 덕성여대　▶▶▶ MSG p.137　①

선행사 + 부분명사 + of which ▶ 빈칸 앞에 완결된 절이 온 다음에 동사가 왔으므로 두 절을 연결하기 위해서는 관계사가 필요하다. 따라서 관계사가 없는 ②와 ③을 먼저 정답에서 제외할 수 있다. '부분명사+of which[whom]'의 구조를 가진 관계절에서 동사는 부분명사에 일치시키는데, 동사가 단수 is이므로 ① each of which가 빈칸에 적절하다.

technically ad. 엄밀히 따지면[말하면] spook n. 유령, 귀신

엄밀히 말하면 스푸크피시(spookfish)는 두 개의 눈만을 가지고 있는데, 각각의 두 눈은 두 부분으로 나뉘어져 있다.

05　2022 가천대　▶▶▶ MSG p.221　④

도치 구문 ▶ 과거분사 been과 호응하는 조동사 has나 had가 포함돼 있지 않은 ②를 가장 먼저 정답에서 제외할 수 있다. ①, ③은 평서문의 어순에 위배되며 주어가 중복된다. 따라서 ④가 정답이 되며, 부정어가 문두로 와서 주어 architecture in America와 조동사 had가 도치된 형태이다.

misnomer n. 부적절한[부정확한] 명칭 distinctively ad. 독특하게

"부흥"이라는 단어는 유감스럽게도 잘못된 이름이다. 이 양식은 단순히 유서 깊은 그리스의 세부적인 요소들을 모방한 것이 아니었다. 그것은 "부흥" 이상의 것으로, 이미지를 다시 독특하게 부여하는 것이었다. 그 결과, 매우 독창적이면서도 유일무이하게 미국적인 것이 태어났다. 미국의 건축이 영국이나 프랑스의 영향을 그렇게 받지 않았던 적은 이전에 없었다.

06　2007 경희대　▶▶▶ MSG p.134　②

as ~, so … ▶ '~와 같이 …도'라는 의미의 'as ~, so …'의 구문이 쓰였다. 빈칸에는 원래 so lateness has become prevalent too가 와야 하는데 반복되는 become prevalent를 생략하고, 주어(lateness)와 조동사(has)를 도치하여 so too has lateness로 사용한 문장이다.

cell phone 휴대전화 prevalent a. 유행하는, 널리 퍼진

휴대전화가 보다 더 유행하게 된 것처럼, 늦음도 그렇게(유행하게) 되었다.

07 **2013 가천대** ▶▶▶ MSG p.133 　　①

양보의 의미를 가진 표현 ▶ '어떤 행동이 이상하게 여겨지는 것'과 '그러한 행동을 자연스럽게 하게 되는 것'은 의미적으로 양보관계에 있다. '형용사/부사/무관사 명사 + as + 주어 + 동사'는 양보의 의미를 갖는 표현이므로, 빈칸에는 ①이 들어가는 것이 적절하다.

stretch v. 뻗치다, 펴다, 늘이다 plain n. 평지, 평야, 평원

그 도시는 평원 위에 한가롭게 펼쳐져 있었다. 이상하게 여겨질지 모르지만, 그곳을 지나가는 사람은 누구나 매우 자연스럽게 피곤해지고 졸렸기 때문에, 그 도시는 '슬리피 타운(Sleepy Town)'이라 불렸다.

---

08 **2008 세종대** ▶▶▶ MSG p.161 　　④

적절한 전치사의 사용 & 올바른 연대 표기법 ▶ 문맥상 '성년이 되다'라는 뜻으로 come of age를 쓰고 연도에 -s가 붙을 경우 앞에는 반드시 the가 수반된다.

wear[grow] a beard 턱수염을 기르고 있다[기르다] defiance n. 도전; 완강한 반항[저항] come of age 성년이 되다 rebellious a. 반항하는, 반체제의

저항하는 1960년대에 성년이 된 남자아이들은 사회에 대한 반항의 몸짓으로 장발에 턱수염을 길렀다.

---

09 **2019 아주대** ▶▶▶ MSG p.163 　　④

관사의 위치 ▶ 부정관사로 시작하는 명사가 too, as, how 등과 함께 쓰이는 경우, 'too[as, how]+형용사+부정관사+명사'의 어순을 취한다.

masculinity n. 남성성, 남자다움 femininity n. 여성성, 여자다움 construct n. 구조물; 구성, 구성 개념 fissured a. 갈라진, 쪼개진

현대 세계에서 남성성은 여성성만큼 분열되고 복잡한 개념인 경향이 있다.

---

10 **2020 서울여대** ▶▶▶ MSG p.175 　　①

부정대명사 all ▶ 부정대명사 all은 'all+(of)+한정사+N'의 구조를 취한다. ①의 경우, companies 앞에 전치사 of만 있고, 한정사가 없으므로 ①을 the companies로 고쳐야 한다.

go bankrupt 파산하다 public ownership 공유(제), 국유(화)

내가 투자한 모든 회사가 파산하여 국유화되었다.

---

11 **2008 성균관대** ▶▶▶ MSG p.116, p.222 　　⑤

with 분사구문 ▶ with 분사구문은 'with+명사(목적어)+분사'의 구조를 가진다. ⑤의 stand는 자동사이므로 수동 의미의 과거분사 stood가

아니라 능동과 진행의 의미를 가지는 현재분사 standing으로 고쳐야 한다. 문장의 주어는 bookcase이며, ④의 put away는 과거분사로 명사 all the books를 후치 수식하고 있다.

orderly a. 정돈된 bookcase n. 책장 put away 보관하다

그의 책상 왼쪽에는 매우 잘 정돈된 책장이 하나 있는데, 거기에 보관된 모든 책들은 적절한 자리에 똑바로 놓여 있다.

---

12 **2021 단국대** ▶▶▶ MSG p. 124 　　④

문의 구성 ▶ whether it wishes us good or ill은 삽입된 부사절이며, know의 목적어로 that절이 온 형태이다. that절의 동사로 pay, bear, meet, support가 왔는데, 3가지 이상을 나열할 경우에는 마지막에 오는 표현 앞에 반드시 and를 붙인다. 따라서 ④를 and oppose로 고쳐야 한다.

pay the price 대가를 치르다 bear the burden 부담을 견디다 hardship n. 곤경 foe n. 적 assure v. 보장하다 liberty n. 자유

모든 나라에게, 그 나라가 우리에게 행운을 빌든 불행을 빌든, 우리는 자유의 생존과 성공을 보장하기 위해 어떠한 대가도 치를 것이고, 어떠한 부담도 견뎌낼 것이며, 어떠한 고난에도 대처할 것이고, 어떠한 친구도 도울 것이며, 어떠한 적에도 대항할 것임을 알려줍시다.

---

13 **2019 세종대** ▶▶▶ MSG p.176 　　④

another와 other의 용법 구분 ▶ no, some, any 등은 부정관사나 정관사 앞에 오지 못한다. another는 'an+other'로 파악할 수 있으며, 자체에 부정관사를 내포하고 있는 것으로 볼 수 있으므로 마찬가지로 no가 앞에 올 수 없다. 따라서 ④를 no와 함께 쓰는 표현인 other로 고쳐야 한다. ① law가 declare하는 행위의 주체이므로 능동관계이며, 따라서 현재분사로 후치 수식했다.

declare v. 선언하다, 발표하다, 포고하다

영어를 주(州)의 공식 언어로 선포한 사례가 되는 법은 1988년 애리조나 주에서 통과되었다. 이 법은 그 주의 직원들이 다른 언어가 아닌 영어로만 업무활동을 하도록 규정했다.

---

14 **2017 홍익대** ▶▶▶ MSG p.59 　　③

'목적어+to부정사'를 취하는 5형식동사의 수동태 ▶ are 다음에 온 과거분사 set, allowed, encouraged 중에 allowed와 encouraged는 'allow /encourage 목적어 + to부정사' 구문에서 목적어를 주어로 만들면서 수동태가 된 과거분사들이며, 그 앞에 being이 생략된 분사구문을 이루고 있다. 따라서 ③을 to부정사인 to go로 고쳐야 한다.

Amish n. 아미쉬파(현대 기술 문명을 거부하고 소박한 농경생활을 하는 미국의 종교 집단) discipline n. 훈육 set ~ free ~을 자유롭게 하다

아미쉬파 교단에서는 '럼스프린가'라 불리는 관습이 있다. 즉 17살에(17살까지는 엄격한 부모의 훈육을 받아야 한다.) 아이들은 (부모로부터) 자유롭게 되어, 밖에 나가서 주변의 '영어권' 세상의 방식들을 배우고 경험하도록 허용되고, 심지어 권장되기까지 한다.

15   2010 동국대 ▶▶▶ MSG p.53   ②

시제일치 ▶ ②와 and 다음의 절은 같은 시점의 상황을 기술한 것이므로 was broken처럼 ②의 had been도 과거시제 was로 고쳐야 한다.

hoax n. 날조, 거짓 footprint n. 발자국 glyph n. 그림 문자, 상형문자 stalk n. 줄기

과거의 많은 미스터리 서클들이 거짓으로 판명되었지만, 미스터리 서클 전문가들은 거짓일 가능성을 바로 부인했다. 두 미스터리 서클 그림 모두에서 발자국이 전혀 발견되지 않았으며 심지어 밀 줄기들이 하나도 부러지지 않았다. 대신에 모두 구부러지고 잘 짜 맞추어져 있었으며 여전히 잘 자라고 있었다.

16   2017 가천대 ▶▶▶ MSG p.105   ④

조동사 have와 함께 쓰이는 과거분사 ▶ 동사 have는 '먹다'는 뜻의 일반 동사, 5형식에 쓰이는 사역동사, 그리고 완료형을 만들어주는 조동사로 쓰인다. 문제에서는 문맥상 '낮은 계급에서 출세하였다'는 사실을 나타내어야 하므로, have를 조동사로 파악해 ④를 risen으로 고쳐야 한다.

breed v. 일으키다, 낳다 distinction n. 명성 yearning n. 욕망, 간절한 생각 rise above the crowd 남들보다 뛰어나다 make it to the top 최고의 자리에 오르다, 성공하다

민주주의 사회의 경쟁적인 성격은 사회적 명성에 대한 욕망을 낳는데, 이 욕망은 남들보다 뛰어나려는 욕망이다. 그러나 사회적으로 계층이동이 가능한 사회에서, 성공한 사람들이 종종 낮은 계급에서 출세하였다는 사실을 고려하면, 그들은 여전히 평범한 사람들처럼 보인다.

17   2019 숭실대 ▶▶▶ MSG p.11   ④

대동사 ▶ 앞 문장의 동사 또는 술부 전체를 대신할 때, 일반 동사의 경우 조동사 do로 대신한다. earn은 일반 동사이므로 대동사로 do가 적절한데, 과거시점 부사구인 in 1990이 왔으므로 시제를 과거로 하여 ④를 did로 고쳐야 한다.

uprising n. 반란, 폭동, 봉기 in the making 만들어지고[형성되고] 있는 full-time a. 전 시간 근무의, 전임(專任)의, 상근의 wage n. 임금, 급료 stagnation n. 정체; 부진, 불경기

많은 교사들에게 올해의 시위는 수십 년 동안 진행되고 있는 것이다. 교육부 자료에 따르면, 이 나라의 약 320만 명의 정규직 공립학교 교사들은 모든 직업 중 최악의 임금 정체를 겪고 있으며, 달러의 인플레이션을 감안했을 때 1990년에 그들이 벌었던 것보다 평균적으로 덜 벌고 있다.

18   2014 한국항공대 ▶▶▶ MSG p.116   ④

with로 시작하는 부대상황의 분사구문 ▶ Some 150 asteroids ~ so far가 완전한 절이고 with 이하는 '명사+which관계절'인데, 매달 두, 세 개의 소행성들이 발견된 것이므로 능동의 discovered는 적절하지 않다. 따라서 'with+명사+과거분사(보어)' 형태의 with로 시작하는 부대상황의 분사구문이 되도록 which를 삭제하여 ④를 discovered every month로 고친다. ① lone은 '한정형용사'로 사용되어 명사를 수식할 수 있다. ② some 다음에 being이 생략된 분사구문으로, 여기서 be to assume의 be to용법은 '예정이나 운명'의 의미이다. ③ 숫자 앞의 some은 '약 ~'의 뜻이다.

asteroid n. 소행성 hug v. ~에 접근해서 지나가다 jostle v. 밀쳐내다, 밀어젖히다 earth-crossing a. 지구와 충돌할 가능성이 있는

셀 수 없이 많은 수백만 개의 소행성들이 화성과 목성 사이에 있는 궤도를 지나가며, 일반적으로 지구에 있는 생명을 위협하지 않는 구름 모양의 띠를 형성한다. 하지만 가끔 혼자 있는 소행성들은 띠 밖으로 밀쳐져, 일부는 지구와 충돌할 가능성이 있는 궤도에 놓이게 된다. 매달 두세 개의 소행성들이 새로 발견되는 가운데, 적어도 1킬로미터의 직경을 가진 약 150여개의 소행성들이 지금까지 발견되었다.

19   2008 서강대 ▶▶▶ MSG p.48   ④

과거완료시제 ▶ 동사의 시제에 대한 문제이다. 문맥상 그녀가 공항에 서서 친구를 기다리다가 스테판을 보면서 그가 초등학생이었다는 사실을 깨닫는다는 점을 알 수 있다. 스테판은 사실 그녀가 그를 초등학생이라고 깨닫기 이전에도 이미 초등학생이었으므로 ④ was는 had been이 되어야 한다.

pal n. 친구, 동료 meet face to face 얼굴을 맞대고 직접 만나다 state n. (정신적인) 상태

메이비스(Mavis)는 공항에서 이메일 친구인 스테판(Stephan)을 만나려고 기다리고 있었다. 그 둘은 벌써 1년 이상 서로 이메일을 주고받아 왔고 마침내 서로 만나기로 동의했었다. 다음 주에 18번째 생일을 맞게 되어 있는 메이비스는 자신의 이메일 친구가 어떻게 생겼는지 보고 싶어 기다릴 수가 없을 지경이 되어 흥분에 찬 상태로 도착 출구에서 나오는 모든 승객들을 지켜보았다. 그러나 스테판이 다가오는 것을 보자 그녀는 돌연 그가 초등학생이라는 것을 알았다.

20   2021 광운대 ▶▶▶ MSG p.138   ②

정비문 ▶ ② 관계대명사 that 앞에 전치사가 올 수 없으므로 옳지 않은 표현이다. ① friends와 you 사이에는 목적격 관계대명사 whom이 생략돼 있다. ④ 목적격 관계대명사 whom 앞에 전치사가 없으면 whom 대신 who를 쓸 수도 있다. ⑤ whom 앞에 전치사가 있으면 who를 쓰지 못하고 whom만 쓴다.

relax v. (즐기는 일을 하면서) 휴식을 취하다, 느긋이 쉬다

함께 편히 쉴 수 있는 친구가 있다는 것은 좋은 일이다.

| 01 ④ | 02 ① | 03 ③ | 04 ② | 05 ③ | 06 ③ | 07 ③ | 08 ② | 09 ① | 10 ③ |
| 11 ① | 12 ③ | 13 ① | 14 ① | 15 ① | 16 ④ | 17 ② | 18 ③ | 19 ③ | 20 ④ |

01 **2015 서울여대** ▶▶▶ MSG p.223   ④

양태의 접속사 as 절에서의 도치 ▶ as는 양태 접속사로 쓰였으며, 원래 as starting salaries for those who can find work have fallen sharply의 문장이다. 앞의 내용과 중복되는 fallen sharply가 생략되어 as starting salaries for those who can find work have가 되는데, 주어가 길어서 as have starting salaries for those who can find work로 도치된 것이다. 따라서 빈칸에는 ④ have가 적절하다.

employment rate 취업률 starting salary 초봉 find work 일자리를 얻다

취직할 수 있는 사람들의 초봉이 급격히 감소했던 것처럼, 대학을 갓 졸업한 사람들의 취업률도 지난 2년 동안 급격히 감소하였다.

02 **2012 한국외대** ▶▶▶ MSG p.225   ①

by와 until의 구분 ▶ 전치사 by는 '늦어도 ~까지'의 뜻으로 행위가 늦어도 어느 시점까지 한 번 일어남을 나타내는 데 반해, until은 '~까지 계속'의 뜻으로 행위가 어느 시점까지 계속되고 있는 것을 나타낸다. 또한 RSVP가 동사로 쓰이므로 ①이 빈칸에 적절하다.

auditorium n. 강당 RSVP v. (파티 등의 초대에) 참석여부를 알리다

그 강당은 120석만 수용할 수 있기에, 귀하께서는 3월 24일 오후 5시까지 반드시 참석여부를 통보해주셔야 합니다.

03 **2019 세종대** ▶▶▶ MSG p.97, p.226   ③

from A to B 와 전치사의 목적어로 쓰이는 동명사 ▶ 'A에서 B에 이르는'은 'from A to B'이며, 이때 to는 전치사이므로 뒤에 동사가 오는 경우에는 동명사의 형태로 와야 한다.

gamut n. (사물의) 전 범위, 전 영역, 전체 run the gamut 망라하다, 모두 포함하다 sign up 등록을 신청하다; 가입하다 instinct n. 본능; 직감; 천성

제안에는 부모가 체계적인 학습 기회를 갖게 하기 위해 아이들을 등록시키는 것에서부터 그냥 아이들의 천성을 믿고 아이들을 아껴주는 것에 이르기까지 온갖 것들이 망라돼 있다.

04 **2020 가천대** ▶▶▶ MSG p.199   ②

'as ~ as …' 구문 ▶ 바로 앞의 as clear-cut과 함께 'as ~ as …' 구문을 이루어야 하므로 ③과 ④를 먼저 정답에서 제외할 수 있으며, 이때 as 뒤에는 주절의 형태가 와야 하므로 ②가 정답으로 적절하다.

distinguish v. 구별하다 dialect n. 방언, 지방 사투리 mutually ad. 서로, 공동으로 comprehensible a. 이해할 수 있는 clear-cut a. 윤곽이 뚜렷한, 명쾌한

어떤 이들은 방언은 서로 이해할 수 있는 반면에 언어는 그렇지 않다고 말함으로써 방언을 언어와 구별하려 해왔다. 그러나 이런 생각은 처음의 겉보기만큼 명확하지는 않을지도 모른다.

05 **2022 가천대** ▶▶▶ MSG p.205   ③

still less 구문 ▶ 빈칸 앞 주절에 쓰인 even에 주목하면 '~는 말할 것도 없고 …조차도 알지 못했다'라는 의미가 되는 것이 적절하다. 그러므로 부정문에 쓰여 '더더욱 ~ 아니다'라는 의미를 갖는 still less가 포함돼 있는 ③이 정답으로 적절하다.

perspective n. 시각 utter a. 완전한 impose v. 부과하다; 강요하다 supplant v. ~에 대신하다

나는 결코 넓은 시각으로 바라볼 수 없었다. 나는 어렸고 교육을 제대로 받지 못했으며 동양의 모든 영국인들에게 강요되는 완전한 침묵 속에서 내 문제를 숙고해서 해결해야 했다. 나는 대영제국이 망해가고 있다는 것을 알지도 못했고, 대영제국이 장차 대영제국을 대체할 새로운 젊은 제국들보다 훨씬 더 좋다는 것은 더더욱 알지 못했다.

06 **2007 한양대** ▶▶▶ MSG p.149   ③

of+추상명사=형용사 ▶ 도치 문장이다. 주어는 'the development~ and the realization~'인데 여기서 ~부분은 수식어구이다. 동사는 are이며, 빈칸에는 are의 보어가 와야 하는데, are 다음에 보어가 오는데 'of+추상명사'가 형용사 역할을 하므로 보어가 될 수 있다. greater는 명사 importance를 꾸미는 형용사의 비교급이며, far는 비교급을 강조하는 부사이다. ④는 of가 없어야 한다.

aim n. 목표 acquisition n. 획득, 습득 intellectual a. 지적인

지식 습득이 대학교육의 목표 중에 포함되어야 하지만, 지적 호기심 개발과 지식 습득이 즐겁다는 깨달음이 훨씬 더욱더 중요하다.

07 **2021 덕성여대** ▶▶▶ MSG p.92, p.105 ③

현재분사 & 완료부정사 ▶ 유전학자가 DNA를 '바꾸는' 능동 관계이므로 첫 번째 빈칸에는 현재분사 형태의 altering이 적절하다. 두 번째 빈칸에는 to부정사가 와야 하는데, 말해지는 시점보다 유전학자가 자연의 섭리를 방해한 행위가 먼저 일어난 것이므로 완료부정사 형태인 to have interfered가 적절하다.

acorn n. 도토리 oak n. 떡갈나무 geneticist n. 유전학자 elm n. 느릅나무

도토리는 혼자 놓아두면 떡갈나무가 되므로, 도토리를 느릅나무로 자라게 하기 위해 도토리의 DNA를 개조하는 유전학자는 당연히 도토리의 자연적인 과정을 방해했다고 할 수 있을 것이다.

08 **2013 경희대** ▶▶▶ MSG p.70 ②

가정법 과거 ▶ 가정법 과거 문장으로 if절에 과거형 동사가 쓰이고, 주절에 ②처럼 '과거형 조동사 + 원형동사'가 수반된다. ④의 disport는 '(장난치며) 놀다'는 의미로 문맥상 적절치 않다.

dear a. 소중한 suppress v. 금하다; 억제하다 dissent v. 의견을 달리하다 dispatch v. 급파하다; (신속히) 처리하다

만일 오늘날 내가 기독교 신앙에 소중한 몇몇 (신앙적) 원칙이 금지된 공산 국가에 살고 있다면, 나는 그 나라의 반종교적 법에 대한 불복종을 공개적으로 옹호할 것이다.

09 **2015 한국외대** ▶▶▶ MSG p.21, p.35 ①

동명사를 목적어로 취하는 stop & 가목적어 구문 ▶ stop은 '~하는 것을 멈추다, 중단하다'는 뜻으로는 동명사를 목적어로 취하고, '~하기 위해 멈추다'는 뜻으로는 to부정사를 취하는데, 주어진 문장에서는 전자의 뜻으로 쓰였으므로 to부정사 ③, ④는 정답이 될 수 없다. 그리고 동명사 making의 목적어는 문맥상 to aggressively push 이하이므로, 이것을 가목적어 it으로 표시하여 5형식 문형을 이루는 ①이 빈칸에 적절하다.

institute v. (제도·습관을) 만들다; 제정하다 regulation n. 규정, 법규

그 정책은 (주류 판매) 업체가 고객들이 저항하기 어려운 방법으로 술을 적극적으로 강요하는 것이 더 이상 이익이 되지 않도록 하는 법규를 제정했기 때문에 성공을 거두었다.

10 **2020 단국대** ▶▶▶ MSG p.100, p.138 ③

be used to (동)명사 ▶ '~에 익숙해져 있다'라는 의미의 be used to에서 to는 전치사이며, 따라서 그 뒤에는 명사나 동명사가 와야 한다. ③을 used to acting으로 고친다. 참고로 '~하곤 했었다'라는 의미의 used to는 일종의 조동사로 뒤에 동사원형이 오며, 과거의 일상적인 습관, 상태를 나타낸다.

accuse A of B A를 B라는 이유로 비난하다 sneaky a. 교활한 deceitful a. 기만적인, 사기의 manner n. 방식

그는 나를 교활하다고 비난했지만, 나는 그렇지 않다. 실제로 나는 기만적으로 행동하는 것에 익숙해 있지 않다.

11 **2017 한국외대** ▶▶▶ MSG p.145 ①

문의 구성 ▶ ① 다음에 조동사 can이 이어지므로 ①은 can의 주어가 되도록 people로 고쳐야 한다. 그럴 경우, people 앞에 관계부사 when이 생략된 관계절이 The moment를 수식하게 되어, The moment ~ for facts가 전체 문장의 주어이며 is가 동사인 구조가 된다.

rely on ~에 의존하다; ~을 믿다, 신뢰하다

사람들이 사실을 알기 위해 뉴스매체를 더 이상 믿을 수 없는 순간이 저널리즘이 그 존재 이유를 상실하는 때이다.

12 **2019 세종대** ▶▶▶ MSG p.95 ③

목적을 나타내는 'so that ~' 구문 ▶ 'so that + 절'은 목적을 나타낸다. ③을 so that으로 고친다. ② to의 목적어는 the government and society이다.

dedicate oneself to ~에 전념하다, 몸을 바치다 sacrifice v. 희생하다

그들은 다음 세대가 더 나은 삶을 살 수 있도록 정부와 사회를 위해 헌신하고 희생하는 법을 알아야 할 필요가 있다.

13 **2019 숙명여대** ▶▶▶ MSG p.47 ①

현재완료시제 ▶ 수세기 동안 환경오염이 존재해왔다는 것을 의미하는 시간 부사구 for centuries가 있으므로 ① existed를 현재완료시제인 has existed로 고친다.

pollution n. 오염 industrial revolution 산업혁명

환경오염은 수세기 동안 존재해왔지만 19세기에 산업혁명이 일어난 후에야 중요한 의미를 갖기 시작했다. 이와 관련된 요소들은 자연적으로 만들어지는 것이 아니며 파괴 과정은 며칠에서 수천 년에 이르기까지 다양할 수 있다.

14 **2021 건국대** ▶▶▶ MSG p.211 ①

주어와 동사의 수일치 ▶ 첫 번째 문장에서 주어의 핵심 명사는 pressure이고 이것은 단수명사다. 따라서 동사의 수도 단수여야 한다. ①을 is로 고친다.

graze v. (가축이) 풀을 뜯어 먹다 browse v. (소·사슴 따위가) 어린잎을 먹다 habitat n. 서식지 contribute to ~의 한 원인이 되다 decline n. 쇠퇴; 하락 principal a. 주요한 decline n. 퇴보; 하락 species n. 종(種), 종류

사슴의 수가 증가함에 따라 잎과 풀을 뜯어먹는 일에 대한 압박이 커진 것이 서식지의 질을 저하시키고 일부 숲속 새들의 수를 감소시킨 원인이 됐을 가능성이 매우 높지만, 사슴이 모든 조류 종(種)을 대규모로 감소시킨 주된 원인이라고 결론 내려서는 안 된다.

---

15 2018 가천대 ▶▶▶ MSG p.55 ①

능동태와 수동태 구분 ▶ '가주어-진주어' 구문으로 It이 가주어, that 이하가 진주어이다. It(=that절)이 estimate하는 행위의 주체가 아닌 그 행위의 대상이므로, 이 문장은 수동태로 써야 한다. 따라서 ①을 has been estimated로 고쳐야 적절하다. ② 'see A as B' 구문으로 as 다음의 B는 A의 보어에 해당하므로 현재분사 needing은 적절하다. ③ 주어가 government funding으로 단수이므로 is는 적절하다. ④ 주어가 앞의 that이 이끄는 명사절이며, 명사절의 경우 단수 취급하므로 is는 적절하다.

estimate v. 추산하다, 추정하다 international student 유학생 tuition fee 수업료

미국 경제는 외국에서 온 유학생들로 인해 증대된 것으로 추정돼 왔다. 래리 서머스(Larry Summers)는 미국 경제가 성장하기 위해서는 고등 교육의 수출이 필요하다고 본다. 공립학교들에 대한 정부의 자금지원이 감소하고 있기 때문에, 외국인 학생들의 수업료가 증가하고 있다는 것은 더욱 중요하다.

---

16 2020 가천대 ▶▶▶ MSG p.161 ④

최상급 앞에 쓰이는 정관사 ▶ 형용사의 최상급 앞에는 정관사가 온다. ④는 notorious와 함께 최상급을 나타내고 있으므로 그 앞에 정관사가 있어야 하며, 따라서 ④를 the most로 고쳐야 한다. ① 자동사 unravel의 동명사이다. ② 주어절을 이끄는 관계대명사이다. ③ the company를 가리키는 대명사이다.

firm n. 회사 unravel v. 풀어지다; 명백해지다 unmistakable a. 틀림없는; 의심의 여지가 없는 concoct v. 조작하다, 꾸미다, 만들어내다 out of thin air 느닷없이, 불쑥, 갑자기 strategy n. 병법, 전략 visionary n. 선지자, 몽상가 notorious a. 악명 높은 debacle n. 와해, 붕괴; (시장의) 폭락, 도산 era n. 시대, 시기 corporate a. 법인의, 단체의

그 에너지 거래 회사의 재정이 밝혀지기 시작함에 따라, 결국 의심의 여지가 없게 된 것은 그 회사가 스스로 선견지명이 있는 전략이라고 선전한 거래 전략에 힘입어서가 아니라 한때 굳건했던 회사를 기업 스캔들 시대에 가장 악명 높은 도산으로 몰아넣은 금융 게임에 힘입어 갑작스럽게 "가치"를 조작하고 있었다는 것이었다.

---

17 019 숙명여대 ▶▶▶ MSG p.137 ②

전치사+관계대명사 ▶ 양태, 방법, 시간 등의 명사가 선행사인 경우, 관계대명사 앞의 전치사는 이 선행사를 목적어로 한다. 이 문장에서 which의 선행사는 a variety of ways인데, ways의 경우 관계대명사 앞의 전치사는 in이나 by를 사용하므로 ②를 in which나 by which로 고쳐야 한다.

epistemology n. 인식론 advocate n. 옹호하는 사람 detractor n. 가치를 깎아내리는[폄하하는] 사람 divine a. 신의 revelation n. 폭로; (신의) 계시

인식론은 진리의 본질뿐만 아니라 우리가 현실을 알 수 있는 여러 방법을 다룬다. 우리가 현실을 알 수 있는 방법에는 다양한 방법이 있는데, 이 방법들 각각에는 그것을 옹호하는 사람들과 그것의 가치를 깎아내리는 사람들이 있다. 현실을 아는 방법에는 신의 계시에 의해, 권위에 의해, 개인적 직관을 통해, 우리 자신의 오감으로부터, 그리고 실험을 통해 등이 있다.

---

18 2020 가천대 ▶▶▶ MSG p.167 ③

대명사의 수일치 ▶ ③이 가리키는 것은 constitutions이므로 복수 대명사 their여야 한다. ① 분사구문을 이루고 있으며 앞에는 Being이 생략돼 있다. be comprised of는 '~로 구성되다'는 뜻이다. ② according to which에서 which의 선행사는 the rules이며 is의 주어는 the exercise이다.

spell out 간결하게 설명하다 constitution n. 헌법 foundation n. 기초, 토대

법률 체계의 구조를 규정하고 정부 권력 행사의 시행 규칙을 설명하는 문서로 구성된 헌법은 궁극적으로 그 헌법을 가진 국가의 정치적 토대를 반영한다. 예를 들어, 미국의 헌법은 특정한 정치-역사적 상황에 대응하여 비교적 짧은 시간에 만들어진 하나의 문서로 이루어져 있다.

---

19 2014 명지대 ▶▶▶ MSG p.183, p.212 ③

전치한정사 뒤에 of가 반드시 쓰이는 경우 ▶ 한정사에는 관사(a/an, the), 지시형용사(this, that, these, those), 소유격 인칭대명사(my/your/his 등), 양화사(any, every, no 등)가 있으나, 양화사의 경우는 전치한정사 all, half, both, double 등이 그 앞에 올 수 없고 반드시 of가 뒤에 와야 한다. 즉 half (of) the book, half (of) this book, half (of) my book은 맞는 표현이지만, half every book은 틀린 표현이고 half of every book이어야 한다. 따라서 ③을 half of every로 고쳐야 한다. ① 주절 앞에 Since가 왔으므로, 주절에는 현재완료시제가 맞게 쓰였다. ② 앞에 while이 와서 원래는 while you are still participating in인데, 주어 you(=to follow의 의미상 주어인 일반인 you)와 be동사 are는 시간의 부사절 while절에서 생략될 수 있어서 생략된 것이며, participate는 타동사로 오인하기 쉬운 자동사로 목적어를 받을 때는 반드시 전치사 in과 함께 쓰인다. ④ what은 the thing which와 같은 말로, in the thing which was가 in what was로 된 것이다.

Orthodox Judaism 정통파 유대교 observance n. (법률 등의) 준수 biblical a. 성서의, 성서에 나오는; 엄청난 commandment n. 계율 man in the street 일반인, 보통사람, 서민 Maimonides n. 마이모니데스(스페인 태생의 유대인 철학자·의사·율법학자) immerse v. 몰입시키다, 열중케 하다 medieval a. 중세의 outsider n. 국외자, 외부인 mainstream a. 주류의 fanatic n. 광신자, 열광적인 애호가 cult member 이단자, 광신교도

19세기 독일에서 현대 정통파 유대교가 탄생한 이후 이 운동의 핵심목표는 전통 유대교 율법 준수를 정상화하는 것, 즉 현대사회라는 현실에 여전히 참여하면서도 성서에 나오는 613개의 계율을 성실히 따르는 것을 가능하도록 하는 것이었다. 당대의 한 시인이 말했듯이, 당신은 "집에서는 유대인, 밖에서는 보통 사람"이 되도록 노력해야 한다. 마이모니데스(Maimonides) 학교의 학생들인 우리는 매 수업일의 절반을 중세 교과 과정에 몰입하면서 보냈지만, 우리의 목표는 외부인과 우리 자신에게 광신자나 이단자가 아니라 분별 있는 주류의 사람들처럼 보이게 하는 것이었다.

---

20 2021 광운대 ▶▶▶ MSG p.35   ④

정비문 ▶ ④ 5형식 구문에서 to부정사나 that절이 목적어로 올 때는 반드시 가목적어 it을 사용하고 to부정사나 that절은 진목적어로 후치해야 한다. 따라서 I made it my prime objective to settle the matter.로 고쳐야 한다. ① 목적어가 동명사일 때는 이 문장처럼 가목적어 it을 두고 후치할 수도 있고, 목적어 자리에 그대로 둘 수도 있다. ⑤ the idea of her being a spy가 타동사 put의 목적어이다.

owe v. 빚지다, 신세지다 jury n. 배심원 acquit v. 무죄를 선고하다

① 당신은 틀림없이 여기서 일하는 것을 흥미롭게 여기게 될 것입니다.
② 배심원들이 나에게 무죄를 선고한 것은 당신 덕분입니다.
③ 우리는 그녀가 오지 않는 것이 이상하다고 생각합니다.
④ 저는 그 문제의 해결을 저의 주된 목표로 삼았습니다.
⑤ 어떤 일을 계기로 그녀가 스파이라는 생각이 그의 머릿속에 심어졌습니다.

TEST 12

01 ③	**02** ①	**03** ③	**04** ④	**05** ③
06 ③	**07** ①	**08** ①	**09** ④	**10** ④
11 ②	**12** ④	**13** ①	**14** ③	**15** ④
16 ④	**17** ④	**18** ③	**19** ②	**20** ③

---

01   2022 가톨릭대 ▶▶▶ MSG p.222   ③

도치구문 ▶ only로 시작되는 부사어가 문두에 올 때 주어와 동사가 도치되는데, 여기서는 Only부터 disappears까지(only+after 절)가 문두에 왔고 the role they played is revealed에서 주어 the role they played와 동사 is가 도치된 것이므로 빈칸에는 과거분사인 ③ revealed가 적절하다. reveal은 '밝히다'라는 의미의 타동사이므로 '밝혀지다'는 수동태 is revealed이다. they는 핵심종을 가리키므로 문법적으로는 it이어야 하지만 핵심종이 여럿이므로 they로 표현한 것이다.

keystone species 핵심종 play a role 역할을 맡다

제대로 기능하고 있는 생태계에서 핵심종을 지목하는 것은 흔히 불가능하다. 핵심종이 사라진 후에야 비로소 이 종들의 역할이 밝혀진다.

---

02   2019 세종대 ▶▶▶ MSG p.140, p.179   ①

apply A to B 와 형용사의 명사수식 기능 ▶ 'A를 B에 적용하다'는 'apply A to B'의 형태로 하며, 명사는 원칙적으로 형용사로 수식한다. 그러므로 전치사 to와 형용사 advanced가 제시돼 있는 ①이 빈칸에 들어가야 한다. 이때 apply의 목적어는 they 앞에 생략돼 있는 목적격 관계대명사 which이다.

peer into 자세히 들여다보다 molecular a. 분자의 optics n. 광학

과학자들이 분자 수준의 자연 활동을 연구함에 따라, 공학자들은 첨단 광학에 적용할 수 있는 정보를 찾기 시작하고 있다.

---

03   2022 가천대 ▶▶▶ MSG p.95, p.139   ③

'so that ~ may …' 구문 ▶ 빈칸 이하는 빈칸 앞에서 언급한 행위의 '목적'에 해당하므로, 목적을 나타내는 ③이 정답으로 적절하다. 참고로 첫 문장에서는 A is to B what[as] C is to D(A와 B의 관계는 C와 D의 관계와 같다) 구문이 쓰였다.

carrier n. (병원균) 매개체, 보균자, 운반체 deformity n. 기형, 불구 erect a. 똑바로 선, 직립(直立)의 immaculate a. 흠 없는, 순결한 safeguard v. 보호하다 jeopardous a. 위험한 integrity n. 성실, 정직; 고결, 본래의 모습

아프리카와 유럽의 관계는 초상화와 도리안 그레이(Dorian Gray)의 관계와 같은데, 초상화는 주인인 도리안 그레이가 꼿꼿이 흠 없이 앞으로 걸어가기 위해 자신의 신체적 도덕적 결함들을 가지고 있게 하는 대상이다. 그 결과, 그 사람의 위험한 본래 모습을 (거짓 없이) 지키기 위해 초상화를 숨겨야 하는 것처럼, (유럽의 본래 모습을 위해서) 아프리카는 회피해야만 하는 것이다.

---

04   2018 세종대 ▶▶▶ MSG p.236   ④

부사절에서 주어+동사 생략 ▶ when, while, if, unless, though 등이 이끄는 때, 조건, 양보의 부사절에서, 부사절의 주어가 주절의 주어와 일치하는 경우 대개 부사절의 '주어+be동사'는 생략이 가능하다. 그러므로 ④가 정답이 되며, 이때 while 뒤에는 they were가 생략돼 있다. ①은 접속사 when 뒤에 주어가 없으므로 정답이 될 수 없고, ②는 현재분사 단독으로는 절의 정동사 역할을 할 수 없으므로 역시 적절하지 않다. ③은 when 다음에 명사 their work이 오고 정동사가 없어 interpreters까지가 절이 아니므로 부적절하다. were는 전체 문장의 동사이다.

risk one's life 목숨을 걸다 interpreter n. 통역사; 해석자

통역사로 미군과 함께 일하면서 목숨을 걸었던 이라크 시민들은 가족들로부터 격리되었다.

---

05   2022 가천대 ▶▶▶ MSG p.30   ③

'find+목적어+목적보어' 구문 ▶ 주어가 unfortunate reader이므로 문장은 부정적인 의미가 되는 것이 적절하다. 따라서 ①, ④는 먼저 제외된다. ②의 경우, finds의 목적어가 주어져 있지 않으므로 부적절하다. 따라서 ③이 정답이 되며, 이때 재귀대명사 himself가 find의 목적어이며 far from fit은 목적격 보어이다.

thorough a. 철저한, 완전한 digestion n. 소화; 이해, 터득 parcel n. 꾸러미, 소포 sort out 정리하다 reputation n. 명성, 신망

우리가 읽는 책들을 철저하게 이해하는 것의 효과를 생각해 보라. 샘 슬릭(Sam Slick)은 자신이 일생 동안 수백 권의 책을 읽었지만 어쩐 일인지 자신의 마음속에 '책의 내용들을 정리할 수 없었다'고 우리에게 말한다. 그리고 무엇이든 이해하기를 기다리지 않고 서둘러 이 책 저 책을 읽어대는 많은 사람들은 그런 종류의 상태에 빠지게 되고, 불행한 독자는 모든 친구들이 자신에게 준 신망을 지탱하기에는 자신이 결코 적절하지 않다고 여기게 된다.

06 **2020 가천대** ▶▶▶ MSG p.111 　　　　③

분사구문 ▶ 별의 진화 과정이 매우 서서히 일어난다면 그 진화 과정을 직접적으로 볼 수는 없을 것이므로, 빈칸에는 ③이 적절하다. ①은 not allowing it to be observed여야 한다. ③은 ①과 달리 making의 목적보어로 난이형용사 impossible이 왔으므로 능동태인 to observe가 맞다. ②와 ④는 구문적으로는 가능하나 의미적으로 부적합하다.

trillion n. 1조(兆) sequence n. 잇달아 일어남; 연속, 연쇄 radical a. 근본적인; 과격한 stellar a. 별의 infinitesimal a. 극소의, 극미의 astrophysicist n. 천체물리학자 glean v. 애써 조금씩 수집하다; 하나씩 조사하다

개개의 별은 수십억 년 혹은 심지어 수조 년 동안 존재할 수 있으며, 살아있는 동안 그것의 밀도, 질량, 강도에 영향을 미치는 일련의 급진적인 변화를 겪게 될 것이다. 별의 진화라고 일컬어지는 이 과정은 극히 미미한 속도로 발생하기 때문에 직접적으로 관찰하는 것은 불가능하다. 대신에, 천체물리학자들은 각각이 서로 다른 진화단계를 보여주는 수백 개의 별들을 조사하여 얻은 데이터에 의존한다.

07 **2018 세종대** ▶▶▶ MSG p.105, p.122 　　　　①

문의 구성 ▶ 빈칸 앞에 the E.U. has the mechanisms for the strong leadership이라는 완전한 절이 주어져 있으므로, ②와 ④처럼 시제를 가진 동사가 접속사 없이 올 수 없다. 한편, ①과 ③의 needed는 leadership을 후치 수식하는 과거분사인데, 'need+목적어+to부정사(~하기 위해(~하는 데) …를 필요로 하다)'에서 목적어를 주어로 한 수동태 'be needed to부정사'에서 be동사 없이 과거분사로 후치 수식하는 것이다. 따라서 뒤에 to부정사가 이어지므로, 빈칸에는 ①이 적절하다.

mechanism n. 기구, 장치, 메커니즘

유럽연합이 진정한 변화를 추구하는 데 필요한 강력한 리더십을 만들어 낼 장치를 가지고 있는지는 불분명하다.

08 **2017 한국외대** ▶▶▶ MSG p.223 　　　　①

도치구문 ▶ so ~ that, such ~that의 용법에서 의미를 강조하고자 so와 such가 문두에 오면, 주어와 동사를 도치한다. He spoke so monotonously that ~의 문장에서 강조를 위해 so monotonously가 문두로 가면, 그 뒷부분은 did he speak that~이 된다.

auditorium n. 관객석; 강당 monotonously ad. 단조롭게; 지루하게

그가 너무 지루하게 연설을 해서 강당에 있던 사람들이 모두 다 나갔다.

09 **2017 한국외대** ▶▶▶ MSG p.112 　　　　④

문의 구성 ▶ far 앞까지가 '주어+동사'를 갖춘 완전한 절이므로 far 이하는 완결된 절 다음에 이어질 수 있는 요소여야 한다. 비교대상이 오늘날의 젊은이들과 부모세대임을 감안하면, and they are far

different from their parents' generation이 이어질 수 있다. 이 부분을 분사구문으로 만들면, and와 they가 삭제되고 are는 being이 되어 생략되므로, ④와 같은 형태가 된다.

uncertainty n. 불확실성 generation n. 세대

오늘날의 젊은이들은, 그들의 부모 세대와 매우 달리, 미래의 불확실성과 특히 일자리 부족에 대해 매우 어른스러운 걱정을 한다.

10 **2020 경기대** ▶▶▶ MSG p.97 　　　　④

전치사의 목적어로 쓰인 동명사 ▶ 전치사 뒤에 동사가 오는 경우에는 그 형태가 동명사여야 한다. ④는 전치사구 instead of의 목적어이므로 동명사 waiting이 되어야 한다. ① for job seekers는 to get의 의미상 주어를 표시하고 있다.

job seeker 구직자 get a jump on (먼저 시작하여) 우위를 점하다, 앞서다

구직자들이 경쟁에서 앞서는 한 가지 방법은 구인광고가 나오기를 그저 기다리는 대신 고용주들에게 직접 이력서를 쓰는 것이다.

11 **2004 단국대** ▶▶▶ MSG p.208 　　　　②

최상급에 정관사를 쓰지 않는 경우 ▶ 최상급 앞에는 일반적으로 정관사를 붙이지만, 같은 사물이나 사람에 있어서 비교를 나타내는 경우 정관사를 붙이지 않는다. ex.) The lake is deepest at this point. cf.) The lake is the deepest in Korea.(한국 내의 여러 호수들과 비교되고 있음) 따라서 ②의 정관사를 삭제해야 한다.

anchor v. 닻으로 고정시키다, 정박시키다

선원들은 자신들이 정박하려는 그 지점이 그 호수에서 가장 깊은 곳이라는 것을 마침내 알게 되었다.

12 **2014 서울여대** ▶▶▶ MSG p.200 　　　　④

배수비교 ▶ 선진국에서의 평균 비율과 개발도상국에서의 평균 비율의 차이가 약 32배라고 했다. 따라서 ④는 they do가 아니라 ②처럼 be동사를 사용해 they are로 써야 하며, 이때 they는 The average rates (at which ~ like plastics)를 받은 대명사이다. ① at which는 뒤에 완전한 절이 왔으므로, '전치사+관계대명사'의 형태로 온 것이며, at은 명사 rates와 잘 호응하는 전치사이다. ② The average rates의 동사로 복수형 are가 올바르게 쓰였으며, about은 '약'이라는 뜻의 부사로 쓰였다. ③ 3배 이상의 배수비교를 나타낼 때는 '배수+비교급+than' 형태를 써서 표현한다.

waste n. 폐기물 developed world 선진국 developing world 개발도상국

사람들이 석유와 금속과 같은 자원을 소비하고 플라스틱과 같은 폐기물을 배출하는 평균적인 비율은 개발도상국보다 선진국에서 무려 약 32배나 더 높다.

---

13 2019 숙명여대 ▶▶▶ MSG p.15

타동사 worship ▶ worship이 '(신 등을) 숭배하다'라는 의미로 쓰일 때는 타동사이므로, 전치사 없이 목적어를 바로 취해야 한다. 따라서 ①을 worship God으로 고쳐야 한다.

loyalty n. 충실, 충성심 readily ad. 손쉽게, 선뜻 interrelationship n. 상호 관계가 있음

사람들은 이웃 사람들이 어떻게 하느님을 숭배하는지, 왜 그들이 특정한 형태의 정부를 가지고 있는지, 그들의 충성심이 어디에 있는지, 그들이 변화를 쉽게 받아들이는지 아니면 그렇지 않은지, 또는 그들의 상호 관계가 무엇인지를 알 수 없다.

---

14 2019 성균관대 ▶▶▶ MSG p.169, p.235 ③

재귀대명사 ▶ ③의 her는 makes의 목적보어인 the very person과 동격인 대명사로, 격은 목적격이 맞으나 여기서는 다른 사람이 아닌 바로 '그녀 자신'이라는 의미가 되어야 하므로 재귀대명사 herself가 적절하다. 따라서 ③을 herself alone으로 고쳐야 한다. 한편, ①의 that은 의문사 What이 강조된 it ~ that 강조구문에서 사용된 that이다. ④의 that은 주격 관계대명사이다.

integrity n. 완전한 본래의 모습, 온전함 persist v. 지속하다 over time 시간이 흐르면서

어떤 사람을 현재의 바로 그 사람, 다른 사람이 아닌 오로지 바로 그 사람 자신으로 만들어주는 것은 무엇인가? 즉 시간이 흘러도 지속되어서, 변화를 겪으면서도 여전히 더 이상 계속되지 않을 때까지 계속되는 자신의 정체성이 온전히 보존된 모습으로 만들어주는 것은 무엇인가?

---

15 2021 동국대 ▶▶▶ MSG p.211 ④

주어와 동사의 수일치 ▶ as가 접속사이므로 ④ increase는 동사이다. 그리고 이 동사의 주어는 the percentage of dependent elders이고 그 핵심 명사는 3인칭 단수인 percentage이다. 따라서 ④ increase를 increases로 고쳐야 한다.

aging n. 고령화 retirement age 정년 drastically ad. 급격하게 workforce n. 노동인구, 총 노동력 working-age population 생산가능 인구, 노동 인구 dependent a. 의존하는, 부양을 받는

고령화는 경제적 난제인데, 그 이유는 정년을 대폭 늘려 고령층이 노동력에 계속 기여할 수 있게 하지 않으면, 부양받는 노인의 비율이 증가함과 동시에 노동연령 인구가 감소하기 때문이다.

---

16 2019 숙명여대 ▶▶▶ MSG p.9

locked in ▶ remain의 보어 locked와 호응하는 전치사는 in이므로 ④를 locked in으로 고쳐야 한다. be locked in은 '~에 갇혀 있다'는 뜻으로 쓰인다.

doom v. 불행한 운명[결말]을 맞게 하다 mental model 심성모형(자기 자신, 다른 사람, 환경, 자신이 상호작용하는 사물에 대해 갖는 인식 모형)

인간 행동과 학습에 대한 새로운 이론을 탐구하는 사람이라면 누구나 조지 산타야나(George Santayana)의 말을 기억해야 한다. "과거를 기억할 수 없는 사람들은 과거를 되풀이하게 되어 있다." 대부분의 사람들은 기존의 심성 모형에 얽매여 있는 타고난 성향을 가지고 있다.

---

17 2017 숭실대 ▶▶▶ MSG p.11

문의 구성 ▶ '~에 입찰하다'는 표현은 'bid on(for)~'이므로 ④를 what they were bidding on(for)으로 바로잡아야 한다.

contractor n. 도급업자 specifications n. 설계 명세서 bid on ~에 입찰하다 translate v. 번역하다

그다음의 어려운 점은 설계 명세서를 이해하고 그 공사를 할 수 있는 도급업자를 구하는 것이었다. 영어를 읽을 줄 아는 중국인 도급업자들은 구할 수 있었겠지만, 나는 한국인들이 대학건물에 입찰할 기회를 갖도록 해주기를 원했다. 그들에게 그들이 무엇에 입찰하는지 알려주기 위해 설계 명세서를 한국어로 번역할 필요가 있었다.

---

18 2017 명지대 ▶▶▶ MSG p.126 ③

문의 구성 ▶ 접속사 When 이하에 주어가 표시돼 있지 않으므로, ③은 틀린 표현이다. 전체 글에서 행위의 주체를 you로 하고 있으므로, When절의 주어를 you로 하여, ③을 When you use 혹은 When you are using으로 고쳐야 한다.

setup n. 배치 shot n. 사진 studio n. 촬영소 artificial a. 인위적인 subject n. 대상; 피사체

당신만의 조명을 배치하는 것은 당신의 실내사진 촬영을 위해 당신이 조명을 충분히 제어할 수 있음을 의미한다. 그렇지만 당신은 비싼 촬영소 조명을 구매하는 데 돈을 많이 쓸 필요는 없다. 왜냐하면 탁상용 전등이나 햇살이 들어오는 창문만으로도 사진을 훌륭한 결과물로 만들어낼 수 있게 해 줄 것이기 때문이다. 인공조명을 사용할 때는, 광원(光源)의 위치를 고려하는 것이 피사체가 사진에서 어떻게 보이느냐에 지대한 영향을 끼칠 수 있다.

---

19 2021 명지대 ▶▶▶ MSG p.48

과거완료시제 ▶ 후원자가 레오나르도 다빈치에게 작품을 의뢰한 시점이 후원자가 레오나르도 다빈치에게 대금지불을 거부한 시점보다 앞서므로, ②를 과거완료시제인 had commissioned로 고쳐야 한다.

patron n. 후원자 commission v. (작품 등을) 의뢰하다 portrait n. 초상화
enough is enough 이젠 참을 수 없다 sparse a. 빈약한

레오나르도 다빈치(Leonardo da Vinci)가 "모나리자"로 알려진 그의 가장
유명한 그림을 완성하는 데는 4년 이상이 걸렸던 것으로 알려져 있는데, 4
년은 당시 그의 후원자였던 프란체스코 델 조콘도(Francesco del
Giocondo)가 참을성을 잃을 정도로 충분히 긴 시간이었다. 조콘도는 그의
세 번째 아내인 리자(Lisa)의 초상화를 의뢰했었지만, 더 이상 참을 수 없었
다. 조콘도는 결국 미완성된 초상화의 대금을 지불할 것을 거부했고, 레오나
르도 다빈치는 대신 프랑스 왕에게 그것을 팔기로 결정했다. 이것이 전해져
내려오는 이야기인데, 안타깝게도 증거가 빈약한 이야기이다.

20 **2022 광운대** ▶▶▶ MSG p.173   ③

정비문 ▶ ① 'to one's+감정명사'는 '~하게도'라는 뜻으로 쓰인다. 따라
서 to my regret은 '유감스럽게도'라는 뜻이다. ② nowhere와 같이 부
정의 부사어가 문두에 올 경우 도치가 일어나지만, 문중에 있을 때는
도치가 일어나지 않는다. ④ in no circumstances는 부정의 부사구이
므로, 의문문형 도치가 맞게 왔다. ⑤ 부정의 의미를 갖는 no가 부사가
아니라 answers와 함께 주어로 쓰일 경우 도치가 일어나지 않으며, so
far(지금까지)는 현재완료시제와 쓰인다. 반면, ③에서 플라스틱으로
만든 '컵'과 나무로 만든 '컵'을 비교하고 있으므로, cups를 대신하는 대
명사 ones를 써서 those wooden ones로 고쳐야 한다.

explicitly ad. 명쾌하게 circumstance n. 환경

① 유감스럽게도, 그녀는 우리의 제안을 받아들이지 않았다.
② 그는 어디에서도 이 생각을 명쾌하게 언급하지 않았다.
③ 저 플라스틱 컵들은 저 나무 컵들보다 더 가볍다.
④ 어떠한 상황에서도 이 문은 열려져 있어서는 안 된다.
⑤ 지금까지 어떠한 대답도 그들에게 주어지지 않았다.

01 ②	**02** ③	**03** ②	**04** ③	**05** ④	**06** ②	**07** ③	**08** ③	**09** ②	**10** ④
11 ②	**12** ④	**13** ③	**14** ③	**15** ①	**16** ③	**17** ①	**18** ②	**19** ②	**20** ①

01 **2020 가천대** ▶▶▶ MSG p.95, p.129 ②

'lest ~ (should) …' 구문 ▶ 몹시 신경이 쓰이는 것은 '하찮은 사람 (nobody)으로 여겨지지 않을까 해서'일 것이다. 그러므로 빈칸에는 lest가 적절하다. 'lest ~ (should) …'는 '~하지 않도록, ~하면 안 되니까, ~하지 않을까 해서'의 의미이며, 주어진 문장의 she와 be 사이에는 should가 생략돼 있다.

fastidious a. 까다로운, 가림이 심한 nobody n. 보잘 것 없는 사람, 하찮은 사람

캘빈(Calvin)의 아내는 자신이 다른 사람들에게 어떻게 보이는지에 대해 상당히 까다롭다. 하찮은 사람으로 여겨지지 않을까 몹시 신경이 쓰이다 보니, 그녀는 외출할 때마다 신중을 다해 옷을 무척 잘 차려입는다.

02 **2016 가천대** ▶▶▶ MSG p.130 ③

결과의 부사절을 이끄는 접속사 ▶ 표현의 자유를 심각하게 침해하게 되는 것은 차별적인 언어의 사용을 제한하는 데 따른 결과에 해당하므로, 빈칸에는 결과의 부사절을 이끄는 표현인 ③ so much that이 적절하다.

point out 지적하다 euphemism n. 완곡 어구[표현] political correctness 정치적 정당성(소수집단을 침해하는 언어나 행동을 피하는 원칙) newspeak n. (특히 정치 선전용의) 모호하고 기만적인 표현, 신언어 infringement n. 침해

완곡 어구 또는 정치적 정당성을 또 다른 형태의 모호하고 기만적인 표현이라고 지적하는 사람들이 있다. 그들은 정치적 정당성이 인종, 성, 나이 등과 관련한 차별적인 언어의 사용을 너무 제한함에 따라 그것이 표현의 자유를 심각하게 침해한다는 것을 보여준다고 비판한다.

03 **2022 덕성여대** ▶▶▶ MSG p.70 ②

가정법 과거완료 ▶ Thinking back on it은 '돌이켜 생각해보면'이라는 뜻이므로 과거를 회상할 때 쓰는 표현이다. 빈칸 다음의 to부정사가 if절을 대신하고 있으므로 주절은 과거 사실의 반대를 가정하는 가정법 과거완료의 귀결절이 되어야 하겠는데, 가정법 과거완료의 귀결절에서 동사의 형태는 '조동사의 과거형+have p.p'이므로 ②가 정답으로 적절하다.

think back on ~을 회상하다 make it (자기 분야에서) 성공하다; (모임에) 가다 [참석하다]

돌이켜 생각해보면, 당신이 그곳에 가있었더라면 분명 도움이 되었을 텐데. 하지만 당신이 가지 못했던 이유를 나는 이해한다.

04 **2018 세종대** ▶▶▶ MSG p.111 ③

분사구문 ▶ 빈칸 앞에 완전한 절이 주어져 있으므로, ①과 ②처럼 접속사 없이 동사가 이어질 수 없다. ③과 ④는 모두 연속동작의 분사구문을 이루고 있긴 하나, ④의 경우, grow가 타동사로 쓰이는 경우에는 '재배하다' 또는 '사육하다'의 뜻이므로, 의미상 적절하지 않다. 따라서 정답은 ③이 되며, 이때 in which 이하는 the government forces its people to save, and it produces growth를 분사구문으로 바꾼 것이다.

capital n. 자본; 수도; 대문자 accumulation n. 집적, 축적

아시아의 성공이야기 대부분은 정부가 국민들에게 강제로 저축을 하도록 하여 자본 축적을 통해 성장을 이뤄내는 성공이야기였다.

05 **2022 가톨릭대** ▶▶▶ MSG p.136 ④

문의 구성 ▶ 빈칸 앞이 완전한 절을 이루고 있으므로, 빈칸 이하에는 두 절을 연결해 줄 수 있는 관계사 또는 접속사가 필요하다. ③과 ④가 이에 해당하는데, 관계대명사의 선행사가 사람인 the Spanish lady와 the Indian boy이고, 빈칸 뒤의 he가 이들의 두 언어 모두를 유창하게 구사한다는 의미가 되어야 하므로 ④가 정답이다.

fluently ad. 유창하게

오늘 아침 나는 터너씨(Mr. Turner)가 스페인 여자와 인도 소년에게 말하는 것을 들었는데, 그는 그들의 두 언어 모두를 유창하게 구사했다.

06 **2016 아주대** ▶▶▶ MSG p.120 ②

nor 도치구문 ▶ "책이란 읽고 또 읽고, 아끼고 또 아끼고, 그리고 그 속에 든 필요한 구절을 찾아볼 수 있도록 표시할 때까지는 쓸모가 없다."라는 의미가 되어야 한다. 앞의 부정문을 받아서 다시 부정문의 연속을 나타내어 '~ 또한 …하지 않다'는 의미를 나타내는 표현은 Nor이며 Nor 뒤에는 도치가 일어나고, 원형동사 be가 아니라 직설법 현재시제 is가 적절하므로, ②가 정답이다.

serviceable a. 쓸모 있는; 실용적인 refer to 언급하다; 찾아보다

그다지 가치 없는 책은 전혀 (읽을) 가치가 없다(아무 책이나 다 (읽을) 가치가 있는 것은 아니다). 책은 또한 읽고 또 읽고, 아끼고 또 아끼고, 그리고 그 속에 든 필요한 구절을 찾아볼 수 있도록 표시할 때에야 비로소 쓸모가 있다.

---

07   2004 경기대   ▶▶▶ MSG p.122   ③

조건절을 대신하는 otherwise ▶ otherwise는 문맥상 '사람들이 이 방법을 쓰지 않았더라면'이라는 의미이다. 즉, 과거사실의 반대를 가정하는 가정법 과거완료시제의 if절을 대신하고 있다. 가정법 과거완료의 문장에서 주절은 '주어+조동사의 과거형+have+p.p'이고, '알려지지 않은 채로 있었을 것이다'라는 의미가 되어야 하므로 ③이 정답이 된다. ④의 unknowing은 '모르는'이라는 의미이므로 사물이 주체가 될 수 없다.

law of nature 자연법칙

이 방법을 사용하여, 사람들은 그렇지 않았다면 알려지지 않은 채로 남아 있었을 자연법칙들을 발견했다.

---

08   2021 세종대   ▶▶▶ MSG p.8, p.199   ③

수동의 의미를 나타내는 동사 + as ~ as 비교 구문 ▶ sell은 능동으로 수동의 의미를 나타낼 수 있는 동사이며, 원급 비교구문은 'as 원급 as ~'의 형태로 나타낸다. 따라서 ③이 적절하다.

reverse v. (정반대로) 뒤바꾸다, 반전[역전]시키다

음반과 CD는 여러 해 전만큼 팔리지 않고 있으며, 이런 추세는 반전될 기미가 전혀 보이지 않는다.

---

09   2017 가톨릭대   ▶▶▶ MSG p.237   ②

문의 구성 ▶ 빈칸 앞까지 완전한 절을 이루고 있다. 이어지는 관계절 안에서 scientists believe는 삽입절이므로, 관계사는 조동사 can의 주어가 될 수 있는 것이어야 한다. 따라서 which가 맞다. 한편, or 다음이 형용사 toxic이므로 병치에 의해 or 앞도 형용사가 있는 can be harmful이 맞다. 따라서 ②가 빈칸에 적절하다.

break down into ~로 분해하다 toxic a. 해로운 ingest v. (음식·약 등을) 삼키다, 먹다

해양의 플라스틱 폐기물은 미세플라스틱(microplastic)이라고 알려진 작은 조각으로 분해되는데, 과학자들은 이 미세플라스틱이 그것을 먹는 바다 생물에게 해로울 수 있으며 심지어 독이 될 수 있다고 생각한다.

---

10   2005 성균관대   ▶▶▶ MSG p.143   ④

복합관계대명사의 격 ▶ 복합관계대명사의 격은 관계절 안에서 결정된다. 복합관계대명사 ④가 관계절 안에서 동사 had found의 주어이므로 ④는 주격관계대명사 whoever여야 한다. 전치사(to) 다음에 있다

고 해서 목적격이라고 생각하면 안 된다. ①은 3형식 동사이므로 다음에 전치사 for 없이 목적어를 바로 취한다. ③은 전치사가 있고 뒤에 명사(the reward)를 목적어로 받아야 하므로 동명사가 쓰였다. ⑤는 '잃어버린'이라는 뜻의 과거분사형 형용사이다.

await v. 기다리다 instruction n. 지시 reward n. 보답

그는 잃어버린 개를 찾아준 사람이면 누구에게나 보답을 해주는 것에 관한 최종 지시를 기다렸다.

---

11   2019 세종대   ▶▶▶ MSG p.184   ②

가주어 it ▶ ②의 자리에는 진주어 to be human에 대한 가주어를 써야 한다. '가주어-진주어' 구문에 쓰이는 대명사는 it이다.

biotechnology n. 생명공학 erode v. 침식시키다; 약화시키다 identity n. 정체성

생명공학기술은 인간이라는 것이 무엇을 의미하는가에 대한 우리의 정의를 무너뜨리고 우리의 정체성을 변화시키고 있는가?

---

12   2019 중앙대   ▶▶▶ MSG p.126, 147   ④

문의 구성 ▶ ① While이 이끄는 양보 부사절에 이어 주절이 배치되어 있다. ②의 동명사 주어는 동사 contributes와 수일치를 이루고 있으며, ③의 gain은 가산명사로서 부정관사 a가 붙은 것은 자연스럽다. 문법적으로 잘못된 곳이 없는 문장이므로 ④가 정답이다.

gain n. 이익, 이득 welfare n. 복지, 안녕

특정한 프로그램 하나를 개선함으로써 부서의 전반적인 향상에 이바지한다고 주장할 수 있겠지만, 나는 어떻게 한 프로그램으로 얻은 이익이 실제로 다른 프로그램들의 안녕에 기여하는지 의문스럽다.

---

13   2019 성균관대   ▶▶▶ MSG p.139   ③

관계대명사 that과 what의 구분 ▶ ③의 that이 접속사라면 그 이하가 완전해야 하는데, 전치사 to의 목적어가 없으므로 불완전한 문장이다. 그러므로 that을 선행사를 포함하는 관계대명사 what으로 바꾸어야 한다.

engage v. (주의나 관심을) 사로잡다 idiom n. 관용구 classic a. 일류의, 최고 수준의

영상 이미지가 어떤 사상을 전달하는 최상의 방법일 때조차도, 일류 작가는 관용표현이 가진 문자 그대로의 의미를 기억함으로써 그리고 이미지를 잘 다루어 독자가 마음의 눈으로 계속 볼 수 있게 해줌으로써, 독자의 관심을 붙들어둘 수 있다.

beyond one's reach ~의 힘이 미치지 못하는, ~의 손이 닿지 않는 astronomer n. 천문학자 cosmos n. 우주; 질서, 조화

여러 세대 동안, 사람들은 그들이 가 닿을 수 없는 곳에 무엇이 있을지를 궁금하게 여기면서 하늘을 봐왔다. 갈릴레오와 같은 천문학자들은 망원경을 통해 봄으로써 우주를 더 가까이 가져왔다. 그러나 우주 속으로 갈 수 있는 능력이 현실이 된 것은 비교적 최근에 와서였다. 우리의 우주탐험 능력이 장차 어떤 모습일지는 오직 추측만 할 수 있을 뿐이다.

---

14 **2019 숙명여대** ▶▶▶ MSG p.161 ③

정관사의 용법 ▶ 서수, 최상급, only, same 등이 있는 명사 앞에는 정관사 the를 사용하므로, ③은 the only way가 되어야 한다.

flaw n. 결함 underlying a. 근본적인 long-lasting a. 오래 지속되는 degenerative a. (병이) 퇴행성의 arthritis n. 관절염

건강관리에 대한 우리의 생각에는 기본적인 결함이 있다. 우리는 병의 근본적인 원인이 아니라, 증상을 치료한다. 그러나 암, 관절염 그리고 심장병과 같은 어떤 퇴행성 질병에 장기간의 완화 효과를 제공하는 유일한 방법은 그 병의 근본적인 원인을 뒤집어 원래로 회복시키는 것이다.

---

18 **2021 명지대** ▶▶▶ MSG p.137 ②

전치사 + 관계대명사 ▶ 처음 등장한 호주머니는 옆이 터진 솔기라고 했는데, 개인 소지품으로 가득한 주머니를 그 솔기 '안에' 넣어두었다고 해야 적절하다. 따라서 ②의 of which를 in which로 고쳐야 한다.

come into fashion 유행하기 시작하다 cloth n. 천, 옷감 seam n. (천의) 솔기, 꿰맨 자국 pouch n. 주머니 trousers n. 바지 hip pocket 뒷주머니 patch pocket (옷의 바깥쪽에 따로 댄) 겉주머니

16세기 말이 돼서야 오늘날 우리가 알고 있는 호주머니가 유행하게 되었다. 그 전에는, 사람들이 옷에 붙어있는 천 조각들 안에 열쇠와 돈을 넣어 다니곤 했다. 처음 등장한 호주머니는 옆이 터진 솔기로, 그 안에 사람들은 개인 소지품으로 가득한 주머니를 넣어두었다. 시간이 지나면서, 호주머니는 영원히 바지의 한 부분이 되었다. 뒷주머니와 겉주머니같이 다양한 호주머니들이 그 후 몇 년 동안 소개되었다.

---

15 **2019 가천대** ▶▶▶ MSG p.105 ①

현재분사와 과거분사의 구분 ▶ 첫째 문장의 주어인 Mental disorders가 '쇠약하게 된'이라는 수동 관계가 아니라 '(사람을) 쇠약하게 만드는'이라는 능동 관계이므로 ①을 debilitating으로 고쳐야 한다.

debilitating a. 쇠약하게 하는 render v. ~로 만들다 inflict v. (고통을) 주다 paranoid a. 편집성의; 피해망상의 schizophrenia n. 조현병

정신질환은 종종 너무나 사람을 쇠약하게 만들 수 있어서 환자들을 일상생활의 기본적인 기능들조차 수행할 수 없게 만든다. 반면, 역사의 위대한 사상가들 중 많은 이들이 이런저런 종류의 정신적 장애로 고통 받았다. 존 포브스 내쉬 주니어(John Forbes Nash Jr.)가 가장 사실인 경우인데, 그는 망상형 조현병을 앓았다.

---

19 **2018 명지대** ▶▶▶ MSG p.48 ②

과거시제와 현재완료시제의 구분 ▶ 이름을 붙이는 일에서 배제된 것보다 이미 명명된 것이 먼저 일어난 일이므로, ②는 were spared와 같은 과거시제나 대과거를 나타내는 과거완료시제가 되어야 한다. 따라서 ②를 was named나 had been named로 고쳐야 하며, 참고로 since는 문제에서 '이유'를 나타내는 접속사로 쓰였다.

colonist n. 식민지 주민 spare v. 겪지 않아도 되게 하다 seaboard n. 해안선, 연안 settlement n. 식민지, 개척지 landmark n. 주요 지형지물, 랜드마크(특정 지역을 상징적으로 대표하는 건조물) device n. (특정한 효과를 낳는) 방법 counterpart n. 대응 관계에 있는 사람[것] expedient n. 방편, 방법, 수단 honor v. 예우하다, 경의를 표하다 as with ~와 마찬가지로

동부해안의 상당부분이 앞서 온 탐험가들에 의해 이미 명명되었기 때문에, 초기의 식민지 주민들은 주로 그 땅에 이름을 붙이는 일을 당장 하지 않아도 됐다. 그러나 식민지 주민들이 늘어나고 새로운 거주지를 형성함에 따라, 익숙하지 않은 랜드마크와 새로운 지역사회에 이름을 붙이는 체계(방식)가 필요하게 되었다. 가장 편리한 방법은 영국에서 이름을 따오는 것이었다. 그래서 오래된 주(州)들에는 바다 건너 영국에도 있는 이름이 많았는데, 대표적으로 보스턴(Boston), 그리니치(Greenwich), 케임브리지(Cambridge) 등이었다. 그리고 이와 똑같이 간단한 방편은 찰스타운(Charlestown)과 제임스타운(Jamestown)과 캐롤라이나(Carolina)의 경우처럼 왕족들에게 경의를 표하기 위한 것이었다.

---

16 **2021 건국대** ▶▶▶ MSG p.15, p.55 ③

수동태와 능동태의 구분 ▶ 타동사 accompanied 다음에 목적어 economic activity가 있으므로 ③은 수동태가 될 수 없다. 따라서 ③을 has always accompanied로 고쳐야 한다.

mundane a. 보통의, 평범한 accompany v. ~을 수반하다 transaction n. 거래 keep track of ~을 계속 파악하고 있다

돌이켜보면, 양(羊)의 수를 세고자하는 욕구만큼 평범한 것이 문자 언어만큼 근본적인 발전을 위한 원동력이었다는 것은 놀라운 일처럼 보일지도 모른다. 그러나 문자 기록에 대한 욕구는 언제나 경제 활동을 수반해서 일어났는데, 누가 무엇을 소유하고 있는지를 계속 명확하게 파악하고 있을 수 없으면 거래는 무의미하기 때문이다.

---

17 **2020 가천대** ▶▶▶ MSG p.36 ①

자동사 lie와 타동사 lay의 용법 구분 ▶ ①에 쓰인 lays는 타동사인데, 그 뒤에 목적어가 주어져 있지 않으므로 옳지 않은 표현이다. 따라서 lays 대신에 자동사 lies를 써야 한다. ①을 what lies로 고친다. ③ the ability to travel into space has become에서 조동사 has가 주어와 도치된 후 이어진 과거분사 become이다.

정비문 ▶ ② 수동태 구문에서 by 다음에 the enemy같은 행위자가 아니라 bombing같은 행위 명사도 올 수 있다. 능동태로 되면 Bombing 이라는 무생물 주어 구문이 될 것이다. ③ worth는 전치사처럼 목적어를 수반하는 형용사로 worth 다음에 a whole month of salary를 목적어로 받았다. ④ 여기서 see는 '알다, 알아채다'의 뜻으로 간접의문절을 목적어로 취할 때 think동사처럼 의문사(what)가 문두로 나가는 것이 아니라 know동사처럼 간접의문절에 그대로 있게 되므로 맞는 문장이다. ⑤ 유사관계대명사 than 절에서 먼저 예상한 것이므로 과거완료로 나타내서 맞는 문장이다. 반면 ①에서 시간이나 조건을 나타내는 접속사가 이끄는 부사절에는 현재시제가 미래시제를 나타내므로, will be 를 is로 고쳐야 한다.

cathedral n. 성당 bombing n. 폭격

① 그 집이 리모델링되는 동안 당신은 어디에 머무를 계획인가?
② 그 성당은 전쟁 기간 동안 폭격으로 파괴될 수도 있었을 것이다.
③ 모든 직원이 받는 혜택은 한 달 급여 정도의 가치가 있다.
④ 너는 내 책상 바로 여기에 있던 돈이 어떻게 되는지 알아챘니?
⑤ 여행이 내가 예상했던 것보다 좀 더 오래 걸려서 조금 늦었다.

| 01 ④ | 02 ② | 03 ③ | 04 ② | 05 ④ | 06 ③ | 07 ③ | 08 ① | 09 ④ | 10 ③ |
| 11 ④ | 12 ③ | 13 ④ | 14 ① | 15 ② | 16 ② | 17 ④ | 18 ④ | 19 ③ | 20 ① |

01   2019 서울여대   ▶▶▶ MSG p.176, p.235   ④

동사의 생략 ▶ 그 방에 있는 학생의 수는 정해져 있는데, 그 중 1/3이 남자라고 했으므로, 나머지 2/3는 여자인 게 된다. 따라서 빈칸에는 '나머지'를 대체할 수 있는 대명사가 필요하다. 일부를 제외한 '특정한 나머지 모두'를 나타낼 때는 the others를 쓰므로, ④가 정답이다. 참고로 the others girls는 원래 the others were girls에서 반복되는 동사인 were가 생략된 형태이다.

contain v. (장소에) 수용하다, ~이 들어있다

그 방에는 매우 많은 학생들이 있었는데, 학생들 중 1/3은 남학생이었고, 나머지는 여학생이었다.

02   2018 가천대   ▶▶▶ MSG p.57   ②

be said to do ▶ 빈칸 다음에 원형동사 belong이 있으므로, 접속사 that이나 과거분사 said나 원형동사 say는 belong으로 연결될 수 없고, to는 원형동사와 함께 to부정사를 이룬다. 따라서 빈칸에는 ②의 said to가 들어가야 한다. be said to do는 '~라는 말이 있다'는 뜻이며, 주어진 문장에서 said to는 which are said to에서 which are가 생략된 형태이다.

Big Foot 빅풋(미국과 캐나다의 태평양 연안 산중에 출몰한다는 원인(猿人)의 별칭) eyewitness n. 목격자 have a foul odor 역한 냄새가 나다 terrifying a. 무시무시한, 섬뜩한 roar n. (사자의) 으르렁거림[포효] footprint n. 발자국 hoax n. 날조, 조작

빅풋은 두꺼운 털로 덮여 있는 거대한 고릴라 같은 존재로 묘사된다. 목격자들의 설명에 따르면, 빅풋은 직립해서 걷고, 몸에서 역한 냄새가 나며, 인간과 비슷하게 생긴 손발을 갖고 있고, 무시무시한 소리를 낸다고 한다. 빅풋의 것이라는 발자국들이 발견된 적 있지만, 그 발자국들 중 일부는 날조된 것으로 보인다.

03   2016 한국외대   ▶▶▶ MSG p.57   ③

적절한 수동태 ▶ 사람이 자신의 체중을 잴 때는 weigh oneself로 표현하지만, 주어진 문장은 사육사가 곰의 체중을 재는 것이므로 곰을 가리키는 it을 주어로 하여 weigh를 수동태로 나타낸 ③이 정답으로 적절하다.

zookeeper n. (동물원의) 사육사; 동물원 근무자 make sure that 확실히 ~하다

동물원 사육사는 곰의 체중을 잴 때 반드시 곰이 지면에서 완전히 떨어져 있도록 해야 한다.

04   2019 가천대   ▶▶▶ MSG p.70   ②

가정법 과거완료 ▶ 빈칸 뒤에 주어져 있는 조건절이 'if+주어+had+과거분사'의 형태이므로 가정법 과거완료이며, 따라서 귀결절의 동사는 '조동사의 과거+have+과거분사'의 형태가 되어야 한다. ②와 ④가 여기에 부합되는데, ④의 경우 과거의 사실에 대한 유감을 나타내는 표현이므로 의미상 빈칸에 적절하지 않다. 그러므로 ②가 정답이 된다.

on mega-steroids 어마어마하게 강력한 goliath n. 골리앗, 거인 weigh v. 무게가 ~이다, ~만큼 무겁다 mouth-dropping a. 입이 떡 벌어질 정도인

알래스카 불곰은 엄청나게 강한 힘을 가진 갈색 곰과 비슷하다. 이 거대한 동물은 몸무게가 737킬로그램이 넘고 어깨 높이가 3.85미터였으며, 머리 꼭대기의 높이는 입이 떡 벌어질 정도인 4.27미터였다. 그것은 만약 당신이 2층에 살았더라면, 이 알래스카 불곰이 당신 집 안을 들여다보고 당신과 눈이 마주칠 수 있었을 거라는 것을 의미한다. 그러므로 저 커튼들은 닫아두는 게 좋을 것이다!

05   2019 가톨릭대   ▶▶▶ MSG p.25, p.75   ④

동사 demand와 keep의 용법 ▶ insist, suggest, demand 등의 주장·제안 동사가 that절을 이끄는 경우, 그 that절 안의 동사는 주어의 수와 시제와 상관없이 '(should) 동사원형'의 형태를 갖는다. 그러므로 첫 번째 빈칸에는 protect가 적절하다. 한편, keep이 '~하지 못하게 하다'는 의미로 쓰이는 경우, 'keep+목적어+from ~ing'의 형태를 취하므로, 두 번째 빈칸에는 from being이 들어가야 한다. keep의 목적어 the data를 these부터 you까지의 관계절이 수식하는 구조이다.

ownership n. 소유권 delete v. 삭제하다 aggregate v. 모으다, 집합시키다

개인정보 보호는 우리들 각자가 우리 자신의 정보에 대한 소유권을 가질 것은 물론 우리들 각자가 그것을 보호할 것을 요구한다. 그러나 페이스북 프로그램을 제거하고 당신의 인스타그램 계정을 삭제한다고 하더라도 이들을 비롯한 다른 회사들이 당신에 관해 가지고 있는 정보들이 판매, 구입, 분석 및 집계되지 못하도록 할 수는 없다.

06　2019 가천대　▶▶▶ MSG p.133　③

양태를 나타내는 as절 ▶ 빈칸 앞의 turn out이 '(사태나 상황이) ~로 되어 가다'라는 의미로 쓰였으므로, 그 사태나 상황을 설명하는 의미를 가진 절이 빈칸에 적절하다. 그러므로 '~대로'의 양태를 나타내는 as절이 제시돼 있는 ③이 정답이 된다.

cease v. 그만두다, 중단하다 look back (과거를) 되돌아보다 outlook n. 전망; 사고방식, 견해 make the best of ~을 최대한 이용하다 blame v. 나무라다, 비난하다

그런데, 아마도 그의 조언에는 내가 과거를 너무 많이 되돌아보는 것을 그만두고, 좀 더 긍정적인 시각을 가지고, 내 하루의 남은 것을 최대한 활용하도록 노력해야 한다는 의미가 있을 것이다. 결국, 우리의 삶이 우리가 바란 대로 되어가지 않았을 경우, 끊임없이 과거를 되돌아보고 스스로를 탓한들 무슨 이득이 있겠는가?

07　2004 명지대　▶▶▶ MSG p.144　③

복합관계형용사 ▶ 디지털 사진에서는 이미지가 숫자로 변환된다고 했다. 따라서 컴퓨터로 이 숫자들을 조작하거나 바꾼다면, 원판과 다른 이미지를 만들어낼 수 있을 것이다. '원하는 그 어떤 이미지도 만들어낼 수 있다'라는 의미가 되어야 하는데, 선행사가 주어져 있지 않으므로 선행사를 포함하고 있는 복합관계형용사를 써서 표현한 ③이 정답이다. ①과 ④는 선행사가 없어서 부적절하며, ②의 경우에는 the image가 선행사이므로, 선행사를 포함한 관계대명사 what을 쓸 수 없다.

convert v. 변환시키다, 전환시키다 translate v. 번역[통역]하다; (다른 형태로) 바꾸다

현대의 디지털 사진에서는, 이미지가 숫자로 변환되는데, 이 숫자는 나중에 다양한 색조로 다시 바뀌게 된다. 그 과정에서, 이들 숫자 중 어떤 것이든 컴퓨터상에서 손쉽게 바꿔 원하는 이미지는 무엇이든지 만들어낼 수 있다.

08　2018 가톨릭대　▶▶▶ MSG p.199　①

as ~ as 구문에서의 올바른 어순 ▶ 'as ~ as' 원급비교 구문에 가산명사가 포함되는 경우에는 'as+형용사+a+단수명사+as' 혹은 'as+형용사+복수명사+as'의 형태로 쓴다. 그러므로 ①이 올바른 어순이다. 참고로 빈칸 앞의 wish는 4형식 수여동사로 쓰였다.

suffer v. (고통·변화 따위를) 경험하다, 입다 injury n. 상해, 상처, 부상; 손상, 손해, 피해

역사상 최고의 농구선수 중의 한 명인 존 에이크먼(John Aikman)은 심각한 부상에 시달려 왔는데, 그의 팬들은 모두 그가 가능한 한 빨리 회복하기를 바라고 있다.

09　2004 세종대　▶▶▶ MSG p.137　④

문의 구성 ▶ 문장의 주어는 Pesticides이고 동사는 travel이다. 이미 완전한 문장이 주어져 있으므로, 콤마와 콤마 사이의 빈칸에는 앞의 주어 Pesticide를 수식하는 절이 들어가는 것이 적절하다. 관계대명사절인 ④가 정답이 된다. ①은 주어가 없으므로 절을 이루지 못하며, ②와 ③은 명사로 쓰인 many가 앞의 주어와 의미 있게 연결되지 못한다.

pesticide n. 농약, 살충제 inhibit v. 억제하다 photosynthesis n. 광합성 the Arctic 북극 지방

광합성을 억제하도록 고안된 많은 농약들은, 대기 속에서 북극 지방까지 수천 마일을 이동한다.

10　2020 수원대　▶▶▶ MSG p.143　③

유사관계대명사절의 구조 ▶ 유사관계대명사절인 than절에서 주어는 you이고 술부는 are now in the habit of reading인데, 술부에서 be동사만 생략할 수는 없다. 따라서 ③을 than you are로 고쳐야 한다. than절의 reading 다음에 목적어 자리가 비어있는 목적격의 유사관계대명사절이다.

be in the habit of ~ing ~하는 버릇이 있다

당신은 지금 늘 습관적으로 읽고 있는 것보다 훨씬 더 많이 읽어야 할 것이다.

11　2004 경희대　▶▶▶ MSG p.201　④

not so much A as B ▶ 의미상 '~하기 때문이 아니라 오히려 …하기 때문이다'라는 표현이 필요하므로 ④ or because를 as because로 고쳐야 한다. not so much A as B는 'A라기보다는 오히려 B이다'라는 의미이다.

element n. 요소, 구성 성분 carry meanings 의미를 가지다

상징은 광고 언어의 중요한 요소가 되었는데, 그것은 상징이 스스로 의미를 가지고 있기 때문이 아니라, 우리가 그것에 의미를 부여하기 때문이다.

12　2018 중앙대　▶▶▶ MSG p.92　③

to 부정사의 시제 ▶ ③은 '과거 사람들(people in the past)에게 엄청난 가치가 있었다'고 표현하고 있으므로 본동사 prove의 현재 시제보다 앞선 시점의 사실을 나타내고 있다. 따라서 이것을 완료형 부정사 to have been으로 고쳐야 한다.

superstitious a. 미신적인 on examination 조사해보니, 검토해보니 immense a. 엄청난

지식이 부족했던 시절에 우리가 미신적이거나 쓸모없는 것이라고 생각했던 많은 것들은 오늘날 검토해 보면 과거 사람들에게 엄청난 가치가 있었던 것으로 드러난다.

13 **2022 덕성여대** ▶▶▶ MSG p.95　　　④

so that ~ can ▶ '~가 …을 하도록'이라는 목적을 나타내는 부사절은 'so that+주어+can/may/must/will+동사원형'의 어순을 취하므로, ④를 cannot ignore로 고쳐야 한다. 앞의 조동사 must 하나만을 사용한다면 뒤에 동사원형으로 이어져야 하므로 not ignore로 고쳐야 한다.

at the (very) least 최소한 policymaker n. 정책입안자 transparent a. 투명한; 명백한

최소한, 환경권은 정책입안자들이 반드시 결정에 있어 투명하고 과학적 지식을 무시할 수 없도록 현장에 나타나 중요한 과학 정보를 기록할 수 있는 기회를 보장해준다.

14 **2019 중앙대** ▶▶▶ MSG p.191　　　①

형용사를 수식하는 부사 ▶ 과거분사 believed를 수식하기 위해서는 부사가 필요하므로 ①에서 common을 commonly로 고쳐야 한다.

accidental a. 우연한 genetic a. 유전의 mutation n. 돌연변이, 변종 unprecedented a. 선례[전례]가 없는

가장 흔히 믿고 있는 그 이론은 우연한 유전자 돌연변이가 현(現) 인류의 뇌 내부구조를 변화시켰으며 이로 인해 현 인류가 전례 없는 방식으로 생각하고 전혀 새로운 형태의 언어를 사용하여 대화할 수 있게 되었다고 주장한다.

15 **2019 중앙대** ▶▶▶ MSG p.159　　　②

가산명사와 쓰는 부정관사 ▶ ②에 쓰인 decade는 가산 명사이므로 부정관사 a를 붙여 almost a decade로 고쳐야 한다.

brief n. (업무) 지침서 council n. 위원회 declare v. 선언하다 statistics n. 통계

한 정책 지침서에 따르면, 국가 영어교육위원회(NCTE)가 거의 10년 전에 보고했던 조사 연구에서 "다양한 영어 학습자(ELLs)들의 얼굴들"이 있다고 선언했다. 일부 통계 수치들은 이러한 선언을 지지하는 증거를 보여준다.

16 **2019 서강대** ▶▶▶ MSG p.151, p.212　　　②

수를 나타내는 올바른 표현 ▶ '다수의', '많은'은 a large number of 혹은 large numbers of로 표현한다. 따라서 ②를 a large number of faculty members 혹은 large numbers of faculty members로 고친다.

survey v. 설문조사하다 faculty members 교수진 randomly ad. 무작위로, 임의로 cross-section n. 횡단면; (여론·사회 따위의) 대표적인 면[사람]

우리가 다수의 교수진이나 무작위로 선정한 대표들에게 설문조사를 실시하여 수상자를 선발하는 콘테스트를 진행하고 있던 것은 아니기 때문에, 동등하거나 심지어 더 나은 성공을 거뒀던 다른 사람들이 없다고 확실히 말할 수 없다.

17 **2021 건국대** ▶▶▶ MSG p.139　　　④

관계대명사 what ▶ 관계대명사 what은 관계절 안에서 주어나 목적어로 쓰여야 하는데, good이라는 형용사의 목적어는 될 수 없다. 따라서 형용사 good 다음에 전치사 at을 넣어서 관계대명사 what이 전치사의 목적어가 될 수 있도록 해야 한다. 참고로 be good at은 '~에 능숙하다'는 의미이다.

observe v. 관찰하다 imitate v. 모방하다, 흉내 내다 strong point 장점

학교나 직장에서 친구가 많아 보이는 사람들에게 배워보세요. 그들이 어떻게 친구를 사귀고 유지하는 지를 지켜보세요. 그들이 하는 모든 것을 모방하지 말고 그들이 하는 행동을 알아차리려 해보세요. 그러고 나서 그런 것(행동)들을 직접 해보세요. 여러분이 정말 잘하는 것을 사람들에게 보여주기를 두려워하지 마세요. 여러분이 좋아하고 가장 잘하는 것들에 대해 말해보세요. 당신의 장점을 숨기지 마세요. 만약 당신에게 흥미로운 점이 있으면 사람들은 당신에게 관심을 가질 것입니다.

18 **2015 명지대** ▶▶▶ MSG p.123　　　④

동격의 that ▶ ④의 관계대명사 which 다음에 완전한 절이 왔으므로 옳지 않은 표현이다. 따라서 이것을 접속사 that으로 고쳐서 evidence와 that 이하가 동격이 되도록 해야 한다. ① which는 sediment를 선행사로 하는 계속적 용법으로 쓰였다. ② show의 목적어 that절을 이끄는 접속사이다. that절이 and에 의해 병치될 경우, and 다음에 온 that은 일반적으로 생략하지 않는다. ③ indicating의 목적절을 이끄는 접속사로 사용되었다.

be made up of ~로 구성되다 overlapping a. 겹치는 carve v. 조각하다 cave n. 동굴 sediment n. 퇴적물 Neanderthal a. 네안데르탈인의 artifact n. 인공유물 paleolithic a. 구석기시대의 engraving n. 판화, 조각 reproduce v. 재현하다 artwork n. 미술품

동굴 벽에 조각된 겹치는 선으로 구성된 예술적인 무늬가 퇴적물에 묻힌 채 발견되었는데, 이 퇴적물에는 지브롤터(Gibraltar)의 고르함(Gorham) 동굴에 살던 네안데르탈인의 유물이 들어있었다. 구석기 시대 미술 전문가인 보르도(Bordeaux) 대학의 프란체스코 데리코(Francesco d'Errico)는 이 조각된 무늬를 분석한 후에 이 무늬를 만드는 과정을 재현했다. 그의 분석에 따르면, 석기가 사용되었고, 각각의 선은 정밀하게 조각되어 있어서, 이것은 이 무늬가 숙련된 예술가에 의해 만들어진 것임을 나타낸다고 한다. 고르함 동굴의 무늬는 네안데르탈인이 미술작품을 만들었다는 가장 분명한 증거이지만, 그 무늬가 전달하는 모든 의미는 세월이 흐르면서 알 수 없게 돼 버렸다.

19 **2021 명지대** ▶▶▶ MSG p.218　　　③

부정사의 병치 ▶ 등위접속사 and를 전후로 to tame과 channeling이 왔다. 사업가들이 운하를 만드는 목적으로 기존의 강을 다듬고 새로운 길을 내기 위해서라고 해야 적절하므로, ③에서 channeling을 to tame과 병치하도록 to channel로 고쳐야 하며, to tame에 이미 to가 있으므로 to channel에서 to는 중복을 피하기 위해 생략할 수도 있다.

furnace n. 용광로 horse-drawn carriage 마차 suffice for ~에 충분하다
entrepreneur n. 사업가 budding a. 갓 진출한, 신진의 canal n. 운하 tame
v. 길들이다 channel v. ~에 수로를 내다 bulk goods 대량으로 운송되는 상품
soar v. 급증하다

산업은 아이디어와 상품의 원활한 이동을 요구한다. 즉 원자재는 공장에 도
착해야 하고, 완제품은 유통되어야 하며, 연료는 공장으로 배달되어 용광로
에 불을 때야 한다. 산업이 출현하기 이전에는, 지역 간 거래를 하는 데 강을
오가는 배와 진흙탕 길을 달리는 마차면 충분했다. 모험적인 사업가들과 신
진 기업가들은 대량의 상품을 내륙으로 이동시키기 위해 기존의 강을 다듬
고 새로운 물길을 내서 운하를 만들었다. 영국에서, 운하의 건설은 급증했으
며, 결과적으로, 운하를 따라 산업지대들이 들어섰다. 운하에 다니는 배들은
말과 수레에 의존했던 이전의 시스템에 비해, 보다 많은 상품을 빠르고 원활
하게 운송할 수 있었다.

---

20 2022 광운대 ▶▶▶ MSG p.138   ①

정비문 ▶ speak 다음에 언어가 와서 '언어를 말하다'는 의미로 쓰일 경
우 타동사로 쓰이지만, '~에게 말을 걸다'는 뜻으로 쓰일 경우 '자동사'
로 쓰이며, 보통 speak to로 쓴다. 따라서 전치사 to의 목적어가 선행
사인 the person이 되므로, 목적격 관계대명사 whom이 쓰인 ④는 맞
는 문장이다. 한편, 전치사 to는 관계대명사 whom 앞으로도 갈 수 있
으므로, ⑤ 역시 맞는 문장이며, ④에서 whom 대신에 who나 that도
사용가능하므로, ③과 ② 역시 맞는 문장이 된다. 그러나 관계대명사
that 앞에는 전치사가 올 수 없으므로, ①은 틀린 문장이다.

speak v. (언어를) 말하다; ~에게 말을 걸다

이분은 당신이 전에 말을 걸었던 사람이다.

01 ③	02 ④	03 ②	04 ④	05 ②	06 ①	07 ②	08 ①	09 ③	10 ②
11 ④	12 ③	13 ⑤	14 ④	15 ①	16 ⑤	17 ③	18 ③	19 ①	20 ②

01 2014 가천대 ▶▶▶ MSG p.201 ③

not so much A as B ▶ not so much는 뒤에 as와 함께 쓰여 'A가 아니라 오히려 B(not so much A as B)'로 쓰이므로, 빈칸에는 what he says와 상대적인 말이 들어가야 한다. for 다음에 우리가 무엇을 말하든 우리의 말을 듣는 사람이 우리가 누구인지에 관해 실마리를 얻게 된다고 했으므로, 우리가 누구인지는 '말하는 내용'과 상관없음을 알 수 있다. 따라서 빈칸에는 우리가 다른 사람에 대해 알게 되는 것이 '그 사람이 말하는 방식'이 되어야 적절하므로 빈칸에는 ③의 how가 정답이다.

clue n. 실마리 origin n. 가문, 혈통, 태생

우리는 타인에 대한 어떤 것을 그가 말하는 내용이 아니라 그가 말하는 방식으로부터 알게 된다. 왜냐하면 무엇을 말하든 간에, 출신이 어떠한지 그리고 어떠한 종류의 사람인지에 대한 단서를 말을 듣는 사람에게 주지 않을 수 없기 때문이다.

02 2019 한국산업기술대 ▶▶▶ MSG p.116 ④

with 부대상황 분사구문 ▶ 전치사 with가 빈칸 앞에 왔으므로 with 부대상황의 분사구문임을 알 수 있다. 목적보어의 자리인 빈칸에는 현재분사, 과거분사, 형용사 등이 올 수 있으며, 따라서 부정사 ② to observe와 시제를 가진 ③ observes는 빈칸에 부적절하다. 목적어가 surveillance cameras이고, 감시카메라가 대부분의 도심지를 관찰하는 주체이므로, 빈칸에는 현재분사 ④ observing이 적절하다.

surveillance n. 감시, 감독 get to the point ~에 중요한 부분에 이르다

감시카메라가 대부분의 도심지를 지켜보고 있어서, 우리는 카메라가 사진사를 필요로 하지 않고 사진사도 카메라를 필요로 하지 않은 지경에 이르렀는가?

03 2020 가천대 ▶▶▶ MSG p.71 ②

혼합가정법 ▶ 마지막 문장에서 Had I only learned English a little more then은 원래 If I had only learned English a little more then이었던 것에서 If가 생략되면서 주어와 조동사가 도치된 것으로, 가정법 과거완료의 조건절의 형태이다. 그런데 귀결절에 현재를 나타내는 now가 있으므로, 귀결절은 가정법 과거의 형태가 되어야 하겠다. 따라서 '조동사의 과거형+동사원형'의 형태인 ②가 정답으로 적절하다. 이

와 같이, 조건절에서 가정하는 내용의 시제와 귀결절에서 상상하는 내용의 시제가 다른 경우의 가정법을 혼합가정법이라 한다.

frankly speaking 솔직하게 말하면 subject n. 주제; 학과, 과목

솔직히 말해, 고등학교 시절에 나는 어떻게 살아야 하는지를 알지 못했다. 당연히, 나는 당시에 대부분의 과목에서 너무나도 게을렀으며 그 결과 대부분의 과목에서 낙제했다. 내가 그때 영어를 좀 더 많이 배우기만 했더라면, 지금 내 영어실력은 보다 나을 것이다.

04 2019 건국대 ▶▶▶ MSG p.105 ④

적절한 분사의 형태 ▶ 공상이 백일몽이라고 '불리는' 것이므로 Ⓐ에는 수동관계를 나타내는 과거분사 called가 적절하다. 두 번째 문장의 주어인 These 'castle in the air'는 허구의 형식으로 '만들어진' 것이므로 Ⓑ에도 수동관계를 나타내는 과거분사 built가 적절하다.

daydream n. 백일몽, 공상 castle in the air 공중누각, 터무니없는 공상 fictional a. 허구적인

때때로 백일몽이라고 불리는 아이들과 성인의 공상은 항상 미래와 관련된다. 이러한 '공중누각'은 허구의 형식으로 실제 활동의 모델로 만들어진, 그들의 활동 목표이다.

05 2019 한국산업기술대 ▶▶▶ MSG p.35 ②

5형식 가목적어 구문 ▶ 5형식 구문에서 to부정사구가 목적보어 뒤로 후치된 경우에는 반드시 가목적어 it을 써야 하므로, 가목적어 it이 쓰인 ②가 정답이다. 주어진 문장은 'make+가목적어(it)+목적보어(illegal)+진목적어(to play loud music in your car)'의 구조를 가진 구문이다.

governor n. 주지사 sign v. 서명하다 illegal a. 불법의

메릴랜드(Maryland)주의 주지사는 어제 새로운 법에 서명했다. 새로운 법은 차안에서 음악을 크게 트는 것을 불법으로 규정한다.

06 2019 아주대 ▶▶▶ MSG p.136 ①

소유격 관계대명사 ▶ 빈칸 전후로 두 개의 절이 나열돼 있으므로 자체에 접속사의 역할이 포함돼 있는 관계대명사가 필요한데, 경계

(boundaries)는 '대륙의' 경계이므로 소유격 관계대명사를 써야 한다. 따라서 ①이 정답이 된다. ⑤는 the boundaries of which여야 한다.

frequent a. 자주 일어나는, 빈번한 usage n. 용법, 사용 frontier n. 국경지방; 변경(邊境), 개척지와 미개척지와의 경계 지방) fertile a. (땅이) 비옥한, 기름진 continent n. 대륙, 육지 boundary n. 경계, 경계선

미국 정치 프로그램에서 "변경(邊境)"이라는 말을 빈번하게 사용하는 것은 경계에 결코 도달할 수 없는 끝없이 비옥한 대륙이라는 미국 경제의 이미지와 결부돼 있다.

07 2019 한국외대 ▶▶▶ MSG p.12 ②

타동사로 혼동하기 쉬운 자동사 apologize ▶ apologize는 타동사로 혼동하기 쉬운 자동사로, 명사(구)를 수반하기 위해서는 뒤에 전치사 for가 와야 한다. 따라서 ③과 ④를 먼저 정답에서 제외할 수 있다. 그런데 have 다음에는 동사의 과거시제가 아니라 과거분사 done이 와야 하므로, 이를 만족시키는 ②가 정답이 된다.

mistreat v. 학대하다, 혹사하다 apologize v. 사과하다

당신이 실수로라도 누군가를 부당하게 대우하면, 당신이 한 일에 대해 사과를 하는 것이 중요하다.

08 2011 서울여대 ▶▶▶ MSG p.125 ①

간접의문문의 순서 ▶ 전치사 of의 목적어로 명사절 중 간접의문절이 '의문사+주어+동사' 순서로 와야 한다. ①은 what it is that they are criticizing이라는 강조구문인 간접의문절에서 that이 생략된 형태로 올바른 어순이다.

religion n. 종교 accurate a. 정확한

종교를 비판하는 사람들은 본인들이 비판하는 것이 무엇인지에 대한 정확한 이해가 있어야 한다.

09 2006 성균관대 ▶▶▶ MSG p.214 ③

관계대명사 that & 선행사와 동사의 수일치 ▶ ③과 ④의 that은 volumes를 선행사로 하는 관계대명사이며, 관계대명사절의 동사는 선행사의 수와 일치하므로 동사도 복수형 deepen으로 써야 한다. 따라서 ③이 답이 된다. ①과 ⑤는 앞에 선행사가 없고 understand의 목적어도 없으므로 that을 쓸 수 없고, ②에서 소유격 our 뒤에 동사를 사용할 수도 없다.

volume n. 책 earth-shaking a. 전 세계를 뒤흔드는

9.11사태가 있고 3년이 지난 지금, 전 세계를 뒤흔드는 사건들에 대한 우리의 이해를 매우 깊게 하는 서적들이 출판되기 시작하고 있다.

10 2019 세종대 ▶▶▶ MSG p.116 ②

with 분사구문 ▶ 전치사 in의 목적어를 Seoul's morning low로 파악하는 경우, dipping 이하의 문법적인 역할을 설명할 수 없다. ② 이하가 '부대상황, 동시동작, 이유 표시' 등에 쓰는 'with 분사구문'이 되도록 하면 이러한 문제점을 해결할 수 있다. ②를 with로 고친다. 이때 ②이하는 'with+목적어(Seoul's morning low on Friday)+현재분사 (dipping)'로 분석할 수 있다. ③ 최저기온(low)이 떨어지는(dip) 행위의 주체이므로 능동관계이며, 따라서 현재분사가 맞다.

temperature n. 기온 plummet v. 급락하다 low n. 최저기온 dip v. 내려가다

기온이 곤두박질칠 것으로 예상되는데, 서울의 금요일 아침 최저기온은 섭씨 영하 8도로 떨어질 것이다.

11 2015 서강대 ▶▶▶ MSG p.137 ④

전치사 + 관계대명사 ▶ 관계대명사 뒤에는 불완전한 문장이 오고, '전치사 + 관계대명사' 뒤에는 완전한 문장이 온다. ④의 경우 관계대명사 which 뒤에 '주어+자동사' 형태의 완전한 문장이 왔으므로 옳지 않다. respond 동사는 '~에 반응하다'의 뜻으로 전치사 to와 함께 쓰므로, ④를 to which infants respond로 고쳐서 which가 전치사 to의 목적어가 되도록 하면 옳은 문장이 된다. ① call ~ into question은 '~에 대해 의문을 제기하다, 의문시하다'는 뜻인데, 주어진 문장은 목적어인 whether절의 길이가 지나치게 길어서 question 뒤로 뺀 형태를 이루고 있다. ③ 주어가 high and variable pitch and exaggerated stress이므로 복수동사로 수일치 되었다.

pitch n. 가락, 음률의 높이, 고저 exaggerate v. 과장하다 infant n. 유아

일부 연구에서는 높고 다양한 음조와 과장된 강세가 유아들이 반응하는 아기들의 말에 있어서 핵심적인 요소인지에 대해 의문을 제기했다.

12 2019 서강대 ▶▶▶ MSG p.131 ③

albeit와 although의 용법 구분 및 의미의 중복 ▶ albeit와 although는 모두 '양보'의 접속사이지만 albeit는 although와 달리 독립된 절을 이끌지 못하고 주어와 동사가 생략된 절의 형태를 갖는다. 따라서 albeit를 although로 고쳐야 하고 그 뒤의 콤마(,)도 없애야 하며 today's와 modern은 의미가 중복되므로 둘 중 하나만 써야 한다. 즉 ③을 although today's thinkers나 although modern thinkers로 고쳐야 한다.

quest n. 추구 albeit conj. 비록 ~이기는 하나 collective a. 집단적인

많은 고대 그리스 철학자들에게 행복의 추구는 개인적인 탐구였지만, 오늘날의 사상가들은 그 대신 행복 추구를 집단적인 추구로 보는 경향이 있다.

13 2019 건국대 ▶▶▶ MSG p.151   ⑤

the number of 복수명사 + 단수동사 ▶ ⑤의 주어는 the number이고
이것은 단수이므로, ⑤increase는 단수동사 increases가 되어야 한다.

dry out ~을 메마르게[건조하게] 하다 soil n. 흙, 토양 drought n. 가뭄, 한발

기후변화는 어떤 사람들로 하여금 우산을 더 자주 가지고 다니게 할지도 모
르지만, 또 다른 사람들로 하여금 더 많은 비가 내리도록 기도하게 할 수도
있는데, 더 따뜻한 날씨가 토양을 더 빨리 건조하게 만들고 특정 지역에서는
가뭄이 발생하는 횟수가 늘어나기 때문이다.

14 2020 가천대 ▶▶▶ MSG p.111   ④

문의 구성 ▶ The explosion부터 1960s까지가 주어를 이루는 첫째 명
사, the increase부터 debate까지가 둘째 명사, the explicit부터
Vietnam까지가 셋째 명사이며, Vietnam을 선행사로 한 where 관계
절이 이어져있어서 ④는 전체 문장의 동사가 와야 하는 자리이므로 시
제를 가진 정동사 형태가 필요하다. ④를 point로 고친다. ① '~에 관하
여'라는 의미의 전치사이다.

explosion n. 폭발; 폭발적인 증가 explicit a. 뚜렷한, 분명한 imperative n.
명령; 의무, 책임 forestall v. 앞지르다; 미연에 방지하다 contain v. 참다, 억제하
다 communism n. 공산주의 awful a. 두려운; 지독한 desperately ad. 필사적
으로; 몹시

1950년대와 1960년대에 가난한 국가들의 상황에 대한 우려가 폭발적으로
증가한 것, 원조와 그와 관련된 정치적 논쟁이 늘어난 것, 그리고 공산주의
를 미연에 방지하거나 억제하기 위한 정책이 즉각적이고 지독한 시련을 겪
고 있던 베트남의 명백한 절대적 필요는 모두 그리고 절실하게 동일한 필요
를 가리킨다.

15 2019 숭실대 ▶▶▶ MSG p.92   ①

부정사의 태 ▶ 부정사의 태는 부정사의 의미상의 주어가 행위의 주체
이면 능동, 행위의 대상이면 수동(to be p.p.)이 되어야 한다. 첫 문장에
서, to부정사에 의해 서술되는 주어인 I는 문맥상 기억하는 주체가 아
니라 기억의 대상이다. 따라서 ①은 to be remembered for가 되어야
한다.

decent a. 괜찮은, 적당한, 알맞은 adequate a. 어울리는, 적당한 take
advantage of ~을 이용하다

"사람들은 저에게 제가 무엇으로 기억되길 원하는지 묻습니다. 그러면 저는
일반적으로 평화와 인권이라고 말합니다. 저는 아이를 키울 버젓한 집을 가
지고, 충분한 건강관리를 받고, 신이 인간에게 준 모든 재능을 이용할 수 있
도록 적절한 교육을 받는 것이 인간의 기본 권리라고 생각합니다."라고 그는
말한다.

16 2021 건국대 ▶▶▶ MSG p.105   ⑤

현재분사 ▶ while 다음에 주어 없이 ⑤ infused가 왔는데, 생략된 주어
인 the artist는 묘사에 재치와 독특함을 불어넣는 주체이므로 ⑤는 현
재분사 infusing이 되어야 한다.

sensual a. 관능적인 infuse v. (특정한 특성을) 불어넣다[스미게 하다]
portrayal n. 묘사

필립 거스턴(Philip Guston)의 T.S. 엘리엇(T.S. Eliot)의 작품과의 관계는
공유된 이미지의 관계일 뿐만 아니라, 그것은 그 시인(엘리엇)이 '통합된 감
수성'이라고 일컬었던 것이다. 창작 행위 자체에 비쳐질 때, 시는 화가의 캔
버스와 마찬가지로 "심리적이고 관능적인 경험을 보여주는 동시에 이 묘사
에 재치와 독특함을 불어넣는" 예술가의 능력에 기초해 있다.

17 2019 한국산업기술대 ▶▶▶ MSG p.21   ③

동명사를 목적어로 취하는 동사 recommend ▶ recommend는 동명
사를 목적어로 취하므로 ③을 putting으로 고쳐야 한다. ④ 여기서는
'닫히다'라는 뜻의 자동사로 쓰였다.

point out 지적[언급]하다 social call 사교성 방문 garbage n. (음식물·휴지
등의) 쓰레기

리펜버거(Rieffenberger)는 당신의 집에 곰이 접근하지 못하게 막는 가장
좋은 방법은 반드시 주변에 음식이 없게 하는 것이라고 생각한다. 그는 곰들
이 사교적 방문을 위해 오는 것이 아니라고 지적했다. 곰은 먹을 것을 찾고
있다. 리펜버거는 당신이 버리는 음식물 쓰레기를 꽉 닫히는 튼튼한 금속 용
기 안에 넣어두라고 권한다. 그는 또한 애완동물의 사료가 담긴 그릇을 밖에
두지 말라고 말한다.

18 2016 명지대 ▶▶▶ MSG p.44, p.55   ③

능동태와 수동태의 구분 ▶ ③의 have been controlled는 수동태인데,
뒤에 목적어가 와서 틀렸다. 따라서 ③을 능동태로 고쳐야 하며, 본문 전
체가 과거시제이므로, 과거시제인 controlled로 바꿔서 시제일치를 시
켜야 한다. ④는 a coalition을 선행사로 한 관계절 which decimated가
현재분사로 바뀐 것이다.

establish v. 제정하다 code of law 법전 be credited with ~한 공로가 있다,
~한 공로를 인정받다 Fertile Crescent 비옥한 초승달지대 besiege v. 포위하
다; 쇄도하다 coalition n. 연합, 동맹 decimate v. 대량으로 살육하다; 심하게
훼손하다 empire n. 제국

고대 아시리아(Assyria) 인들은 세계의 초기 문명들 가운데 하나로 기원전
3,500년경에 출현하기 시작했던 메소포타미아에 살았던 사람들이었다. 아
시리아 인들은 세계 최초로 문자언어를 발명하고, 함무라비 법전을 제정했
으며, 그밖에 많은 예술적 및 건축적 업적을 남긴 것으로 인정받고 있다.
300년 동안 아시리아 인들은 페르시아 만에서부터 이집트에 이르는 비옥한
초승달지대 전역을 지배했다. 그러나 기원전 612년, 아시리아의 수도인 니
느웨(Nineveh)는 메디아(Media), 스키타이(Scythia), 칼데아(Chaldea)의
연합군에 의해 포위되어 파괴되었으며, 이들은 과거 강력했던 아시리아 제
국을 멸망시켰다.

19 **2021 명지대** ▶▶▶ MSG p.55   ①

수동태 ▶ 돌고래가 갈매기 다리를 잡는 것이 '목격되었다'는 의미가 되어야 하므로, 수동태 문장이 되도록 ①을 have been seen으로 고쳐야 한다.

delphinid n. 참돌고래과에 속하는 돌고래 forage v. (식량을) 찾아 돌아다니다 anchovy n. 멸치 school n. (물고기 등의) 떼, 무리 grab v. 붙잡다, 잡아채다 dangling a. 아래로 드리워진, 축 늘어진 gull n. 갈매기 surge v. 물결치는 대로 떠돌다, (재빨리) 밀려들다 dunk v. (장난삼아) ~을 물속에 빠뜨리다 grasp n. 꽉 쥐기, 붙들기 counterpart n. 상대, 대응 관계에 있는 사람[것] captive a. 우리에 갇힌

많은 야생 돌고래(참돌고래과에 속하는 돌고래)들은 장난치는 행동으로 새들과 늘 교류한다. 예를 들어, 아르헨티나 연안 앞바다에서 멸치 무리를 찾아다닌 후 일부 더스키 돌고래(Lagenorhynchus obscurus, 흰배낫돌고래)들은 전혀 의심하지 않는 갈매기들의 내려뜨린 다리를 조심스럽게 잡은 다음 재빨리 물속으로 들어가 물결치는 대로 떠돌다가 갈매기를 놓아주는 방식으로, 효과적으로 새들을 물속에 빠뜨리는 모습이 목격되었다. 이 돌고래들은 갈매기를 잡을 때 매우 조심스럽게 잡아, 어떠한 해도 끼치지 않으며, 그저 깃털달린 상대와 조금 재미있게 놀고 있는 것으로 보인다. 아직 다른 곳에 보도가 되지 않은, 이 갈매기 빠뜨리기 게임은 수족관에 있는 돌고래들의 독창적인 놀이행동과 어느 정도 유사하다.

20 **2022 광운대** ▶▶▶ MSG p.191   ②

정비문 ▶ intentionally, deliberately, purposely는 모두 '의도적으로'의 뜻으로 '자신의 생각대로'를 나타내고 reluctantly(마음 내키지 않게, 마지못해)와 resentfully(싫은 일을 해야 해서 화를 내며 in a way that shows that you feel angry because you have been forced to accept something that you do not like)는 '자신의 생각과는 반대로'를 나타내지만, 다섯 부사 모두 '생각, 의도'와 관련 있는 행위 동사를 수식하기에 적절하다. 따라서 능동태이든 수동태이든 ③, ④, ⑤는 모두 적절하다. 그런데 'be 형용사/명사'는 상태를 나타내지만 'be being 형용사/명사'는 그 시점에서의 일시적인 행동을 나타내므로 ①은 intentionally의 수식을 받기에 적절하지만 ②는 deliberately의 수식을 받기에 부적절하다.

deliberately ad. 의도적으로 resentfully ad. 화가 치미는 가운데

① 그는 의도적으로 어리석은 행동을 하고 있다.
② 그는 의도적으로 어른이다.
③ 그는 의도적으로 그것에 관해 나에게 편지를 써 보내지 않았다.
④ 그 오두막은 마지못해 파괴되었다.
⑤ 그 집은 작년에 화가 치미는 가운데 팔렸다.

TEST 16

01 ②	02 ④	03 ②	04 ③	05 ③	06 ③	07 ③	08 ②	09 ③	10 ④
11 ④	12 ③	13 ①	14 ①	15 ①	16 ②	17 ③	18 ②	19 ①	20 ⑤

01 2021 가톨릭대 ▶▶▶ MSG p.95 ②

문맥상 올바른 접속사 ▶ 빈칸에는 두 절을 연결하는 접속사가 필요한데, 빈칸 다음의 두 절은 빈칸 앞에서 능동적으로 simultaneously fading out ~ on the next하는 목적에 해당하므로 '~하도록'이라는 뜻의 ② so that이 정답이다. 구조적으로는 in which도 가능하지만 빈칸 이하가 선행사인 '그다음 장면(the next (shot))'에서 일어나는 일을 설명한 것이 아니므로 부적절하다.

dissolve n. <영화> 디졸브(한 화면 위에 다른 화면이 겹치면서 먼저 화면이 차차 사라지게 하는 장면 전환) fade out (화면이) 점점 희미해지다 fade in (화면이) 점점 뚜렷해지다[지게하다]

영화 편집에서 디졸브는 두 번째 장면이 점차 보이면서 첫 번째 장면이 점차 사라지도록 한 장면을 점점 희미해지게 하면서 동시에 그다음 장면을 점점 뚜렷해지게 함으로써 성취된다.

02 2020 가천대 ▶▶▶ MSG p.105 ④

후치수식의 과거분사구 ▶ 햄버거는 식사에 해당하고 아이스크림은 후식이나 디저트에 해당하므로, 햄버거를 먹고 난 후에 뒤이어서 아이스크림을 먹는다고 해야 한다. 이와 같은 선후 관계를 나타낼 수 있는 ④가 빈칸에 적절하다. B follows A는 B가 A를 따라가는 것이므로 'A-B'의 순서인데, 이것을 수동태로 하면 A is followed by B가 되며 마찬가지로 'A-B'의 순서를 나타낸다.

hedonist n. 쾌락주의자 rejuvenate v. 활기 띠게 하다 in moderation 적당히

때로는 쾌락주의자로 사는 것도 나름의 좋은 점이 있다. 부정적인 결과가 장기적으로 나타나지 않는 한, 오로지 현재에만 집중하는 것은 우리에게 활기를 되찾게 해줄 수 있다. 적당히만 한다면, 해변에 누워 있는 것, 패스트푸드 햄버거를 먹고 나서 따뜻한 시럽을 얹은 선디 아이스크림을 먹는 것, 혹은 텔레비전을 보는 것에서 오는 쉬는 것, 아무 생각을 하지 않는 것, 그리고 즐거움은 우리를 더 행복하게 만들어 줄 수 있다.

03 2019 한양대 서울 ▶▶▶ MSG p.139 ②

관계대명사 what ▶ 문장의 동사 has grown의 주어가 빈칸에 필요한 상황이므로, 관계대명사 what이 이끄는 명사절이 주어가 되기에 적절하다. ① 동명사 beginning도 주어가 될 수는 있으나, has grown(성장했다)의 주어가 되기에는 의미적으로 부적절하다.

conglomerate n. 대기업 cater v. 음식을 공급하다 preferential a. 우선권의

주로 정부 조달업체로 시작했던 것이 이후에 출장 요리 업체와 수많은 소매 업체들로 구성된 대기업으로 성장했으며, 이 업체들은 지금 정부 기관들의 특혜를 받고 있다.

04 2005 성균관대 ▶▶▶ MSG p.156 ③

this kind[these kinds] of+단수[복수]명사 ▶ 'kind of+명사' 표현은 kind의 수와 명사의 수가 일치되게 this kind of book이나 these kinds of books로 표현하는 것이 원칙이지만 비공식적인 경우나 ③처럼 책은 여러 권이나 종류가 하나인 경우에는 kind의 수와 book의 수가 일치하지 않게 나타내는 것도 허용된다. 그러나 this[these]와 kind[kinds] 사이의 수일치는 반드시 지켜져야 한다. ③을 제외한 다른 선택지는 모두 수일치를 어기고 있다.

spare time 여가 시간, 여유 시간

대부분의 학생들은 여가 시간 동안 이런 종류의 책을 읽기를 좋아한다.

05 2014 가천대 ▶▶▶ MSG p.227 ③

명사 speed와 함께 쓰이는 전치사 at ▶ 명사 speed는 전치사 at을 취하며 what now seems to me astonishing speed(지금 나에게는 놀라운 속도로 여겨지는 것) speed를 의미하므로 ③이 정답이다.

rhyming play 압운 희곡 in imitation of ~을 흉내 내어

학교 숙제 외에 나는 지금 생각해도 아주 놀라운 속도로 희극시 비슷한 시들을 썼다. 열네 살 때 나는 아리스토파네스(Aristophanes)를 흉내 낸 압운 희곡 한 편을 약 일주일 만에 써냈다.

06 2016 가톨릭대 ▶▶▶ MSG p.171 ③

문의 구성 ▶ 명사 evolutionary forces 다음에 또 다른 명사 independence가 올 수 없으므로 ②와 ④를 먼저 제외할 수 있다. independent of(~과 별개의)가 명사 evolutionary forces를 후치 수식해주는 형용사구로, those가 forces를 대신하는 지시대명사로, 그리고 주격관계대명사 that이 빈칸 뒤의 동사 influence와 연결되도록 주어져 있는 ③이 정답이 된다.

gene n. 유전자 host n. 주인; 숙주 independent a. 독립적인; 별개의

바이러스와 또 다른 움직이는 유전자들은 세포와 매우 근접해서 생존하기 때문에 그것들이 숙주에게 영향을 미치는 요인들과는 별개의 진화적 요인들에 의해 지배받을 수 있다는 사실을 처음에는 이해하지 못할 수도 있다.

---

07 **2003 숭실대** ▶▶▶ MSG p.125   ③

간접의문문의 어순 ▶ 전치사 of의 목적어로 명사절이 와야 하므로 ②와 ④는 적절하지 않다. 간접의문문의 어순은 '의문사+주어+동사'이므로 ③이 정답이다.

look over ~을 바라보다; 훑어보다, 조사하다

무언가를 읽으려고 준비할 때 독해지문 전체를 훑어보아라. 사진들과 그림들, 제목들, 표제들과 무엇에 관한 글인지 알 수 있게 해주는 어느 것이든 봐라.

---

08 **2018 세종대** ▶▶▶ MSG p.135   ②

문의 구성 ▶ the excessive부터 주절이 완결되어 있다는 점에 유의하면, ①은 that 관계절의 수식을 받는 명사 A country가 주절 앞에 온 것인데 이것이 주절의 주어와 동격관계가 되지 않으므로 정답이 될 수 없고, ③은 접속사가 없어 뒤의 주절과 연결될 수 없으므로 부적절하다. 한편, ④의 경우에는 전치사 For 뒤에 절이 오는 형태가 되므로 역시 정답이 될 수 없다. 따라서 주절 앞에 '전치사+명사' 구가 온 ②가 정답이 된다.

vitality n. 활력 excessive a. 과도한 surmount v. 극복하다 badly ad. 몹시

새로운 경제적 활력을 몹시 필요로 하는 국가의 경우, 에너지 수출에 대한 과도한 의존은 극복해야 할 문제이다.

---

09 **2016 서울여대** ▶▶▶ MSG p.191   ③

문의 구성 ▶ 빈칸은 전치사 through의 목적어가 되어야 함과 동시에, 빈칸 뒤의 'of 명사'의 수식을 받아야 한다. 따라서 빈칸에 들어갈 표현은 명사로 끝나야 하므로, ③의 her lively, impressively researched account가 정답이 된다.

effort n. (노력의) 결과, 성과 appreciation n. 올바로 평가[이해]하기 exploit n. 영웅적 행위, 위업 lasting a. 영구적인, 오래 가는 insight n. 통찰력 account n. 이야기

그녀의 책은 알렉산더 폰 훔볼트(Alexander von Humboldt)에 대한 우리의 올바른 평가를 그의 여행과 공적에 대한 그녀의 생기 있고 인상적으로 연구된 이야기를 통해 다시 회복시키려는 노력의 결과물이며, 우리에게 그의 통찰력의 지속적인 영향력을 상기시켜준다.

---

10 **2019 서울여대** ▶▶▶ MSG p.167   ④

중복되는 대명사 삭제 ▶ ②의 one을 that 관계절이 후치 수식하고 있는데, 선행사인 one(=an ability)이 관계절 안에서 need의 목적어이므로, need 뒤에 목적어를 두어서는 안 된다. 따라서 ④의 it을 삭제해야 한다. feel 다음에는 접속사 that이 생략되었다.

tell A from B A와 B를 구분하다 liar n. 거짓말쟁이

거짓을 말하는 사람과 진실을 말하는 사람을 구별하는 능력은 대부분의 사람들이 자기들에게 필요하다고 생각하는 능력이다.

---

11 **2019 세종대** ▶▶▶ MSG p.227   ④

channel A into B ▶ channel을 이용하여 'A를 B로 쏟아내다[돌리다]'라는 표현을 하는 경우, B의 앞에는 전치사 into를 쓴다. ④를 into로 고친다. ① help의 목적보어로는 원형부정사와 to부정사, 둘 다 가능하다.

confidence n. 자신감 frustration n. 좌절 outlet n. 배출구, 출구

태권도는 내가 자신감을 쌓고 어렸을 때 가졌던 분노와 좌절감을 긍정적인 배출구로 쏟아내는 데 도움을 주었다.

---

12 **2019 세종대** ▶▶▶ MSG p.195   ③

many와 much의 용법 구분 ▶ ③은 과거분사 used를 수식하는 자리이므로 부사가 와야 하는데, many는 형용사, 명사, 대명사로 쓰이므로 적절하지 않다. 따라서 동사나 과거분사를 수식할 수 있는 much로 고쳐야 한다. ② products를 후치수식하고 있는 과거분사이다.

representative a. 대표적인 match n. 성냥 decorative a. 장식용의, 장식적인

그 스튜디오의 대표적인 디자인 제품은 성냥갑, 지우개, 연필 등 요즘 많이 사용되지 않는 제품들인데, 장식을 위해 현대적인 디자인으로 되어 있다.

---

13 **2021 서강대** ▶▶▶ MSG p.41   ①

적절한 동사 ▶ '어려운 문제를 제기하다'는 pose a dilemma이다. ①의 posted를 posed로 바꾼다.

refugee n. 난민 foster v. 조장하다 ethics n. 윤리학; 윤리, 도덕 steer v. 방향을 조정하다 quota n. 할당, 할당량, 할당액

난민들은 유럽연합 회원국 사이에 많은 갈등을 낳았기 때문에 비극적인 난제였다. 해결해야 할 과제는 (각국의 난민 수용) 할당량을 조정하기 위해 '책임의 윤리'를 세우는 것이었다.

14 **2018 성균관대** ▶▶▶ MSG p.191　　①

전치사 사용 불가 부사 ▶ 운동 방향의 동사 moved 뒤에 장소부사 west(서쪽으로)가 올 경우, west 앞에 전치사 to를 사용할 수 없으므로 ①은 moved west가 되어야 한다.

migrate v. 이주하다 burgeoning a. 급성장하는 earning n. (pl.) 소득, 임금

농장들이 없어진 이유는 농부들이 서쪽으로 이동하여 일리노이와 오하이오 주 같은 곳의 더 비옥한 땅으로 갔거나, 수입이 더 안정적이고 많은 급성장하는 산업도시로 이주했기 때문이었다.

15 **2014 서강대** ▶▶▶ MSG p.114　　①

분사구문 ▶ Later 다음에 두 절이 접속사 없이 연결되어 있으므로 ①을 wailing으로 고쳐 분사구문으로 만들어야 한다. ② 자동사 passed 뒤에 '전치사+명사'의 형태인 in swift rotation이 부사어로 왔다. ③ her waist를 의미상 주어로 봤을 때 능동의 의미를 가진 shaping이 왔으면 목적어가 따라와야 하지만, 수동의 의미인 과거분사 shaped 뒤에 보어인 형용사 slender가 따라 '날씬한 모양으로 된'으로 해석된다. ④ her feet을 의미상 주어로 봤을 때 능동의 의미인 filling 뒤에 목적어 the rhythmic gap이 와서 '리듬의 빈 곳을 채우며'로 해석되므로 문제가 없다.

wail v. 울부짖다; 소리를 내다 swift a. 신속한, 빠른 rotation n. 회전; 교대 slender a. 날씬한 interval n. 간격 gap n. 틈, 간격

잠시 후, 음악이 창 너머로 흘러나오는 가운데, 그들은 그녀가 검은 옷을 입은 사람들의 품에서 품으로 빠르게 옮겨 다니며 춤을 추는 모습을 창문을 통해 지켜보았다. 그녀의 허리는 가늘었고 이따금씩 급히 움직였으며, 그녀의 두 발은 음악과 함께 리듬 사이 간격을 채우고 있었다.

16 **2019 한양대 에리카** ▶▶▶ MSG p.101　　②

confess to+동명사 ▶ '~을 자백하다, 인정하다'라는 의미로 confess to를 쓰는 경우, 이때 to는 전치사이다. 전치사 뒤에 동사가 오는 경우에는 반드시 동명사를 써야 하므로, ②를 stealing으로 고쳐야 한다.

witness n. 증인, 목격자 testify v. 증명하다; 증언하다 defendant n. 피고 confess v. (~을) 고백[자백]하다(to) parking lot 주차장 jack v. 자동차를 털다, 자동차 운전자에게서 금품을 빼앗다

목격자는 피고가 자동차를 훔쳤다고 자백하는 것을 들었다고 증언했다. 그녀는 공원 벤치에 앉아 있었는데, 그때 피고가 큰 소리로 지껄이면서 주차장 방향을 힘차게 가리키면서, 다른 남자에게 자신이 방금 "은색 도요타 자동차를 털었다"라고 말했다고 했다.

17 **2021 가천대** ▶▶▶ MSG p.149　　③

of + 추상명사 = 형용사 ▶ ③은 know의 목적보어 자리이고 목적어는 things를 선행사로 하는 관계대명사 which이다. 목적보어 자리에 명사가 올 수 있긴 하나, 주어진 문장에서 'thing = worth'의 관계가 성립하지 않으므로 ③의 자리에는 형용사가 와야 한다. 'of+추상명사 = 형용사'이므로, ③을 of far more worth로 고쳐야 한다. 물론 형용사 worthy의 비교급 far worthier로 고쳐도 좋다.

Utopian a. 유토피아적인, 공상[몽상]적인; 실현 불가능한 wit n. 기지, 재치, 지혜

마을은 농부와 장사꾼들이 귀하게 여기는 그런 것들에 충분히 돈을 쓸 수 있지만, 좀 더 지적인 사람들이 훨씬 더 가치 있는 것으로 알고 있는 것들에 돈을 쓰자고 제안하는 것은 공상적인 것으로 여겨진다. 이 마을이 도시 주택에 1만 7천 달러를 쓴 것은 행운이나 정치에 감사할 일이지만, 아마도 100년 후에도 살아 있는 지혜에는 그렇게 많은 돈을 쓰지 않을 것이다.

18 **2022 명지대** ▶▶▶ MSG p.44　　②

과거완료시제와 과거시제의 구분 ▶ ② 앞에 온 a few years ago는 특정과거시점을 나타내므로, 과거시제만 뒤에 올 수가 있다. 따라서 과거완료시제가 쓰인 ②를 과거시제인 began으로 고쳐야 한다.

electric propulsion 전기추진 combustion engine 연소기관 dismiss v. 묵살[일축]하다 hobbyhorse n. 좋아하는 화제, 늘 입에 올리는 주제 pioneer v. (새 분야를) 척하다 zero-auto-emission n. 무공해자동차 statute n. 법령 dawn v. (날이) 새다, 밝아지다

최근까지 전기자동차는 온당한 관심을 받지 못했다. 전기추진이 오염과 소음을 일으키는 연소기관에 대한 대안으로 여겨지기 시작한 몇 년 전까지는 아무도 전기추진의 가능성에 대해 관심을 갖지 않는 것 같았다. 그전까지만 해도 전기자동차는 돈 없는 환경운동가들이 늘 들먹이는 주제 정도로 치부되었었다. 그러나 기존의 자동차 업계가 그 주제에 관심을 갖게 되고, 캘리포니아주가 무공해자동차 법을 선구적으로 제정하자, 분위기가 바뀌었다. 자동차 엔지니어 입장에서, 혁신적인 기술 개발의 새롭고 흥미진진한 시대가 밝아왔다.

19 **2021 명지대** ▶▶▶ MSG p.31, p.59　　①

5형식 수동태 및 생략 ▶ ①에서 it은 profiling을 받은 대명사로, 직설법의 as it is called criminal investigative analysis by the FBI라는 5형식 수동태에서 반복되는 criminal investigative analysis가 생략된 형태이므로, ①을 it is called로 고쳐야 한다.

party n. 당사자 cross n. (두 가지 다른 것의) 혼합, 이종 교배 law enforcement 법집행 forensic psychology 법심리학 set a. 정해진, 고정된 practitioner n. 변호사 등 전문직 종사자; (특정 분야의) 현역 terminology n. 전문용어, 술어 statement n. 진술, 진술서 description n. 기술, 묘사; (경찰 등의) 인상서(범죄자나 가출자 등을 체포하거나 찾기 위하여 외모의 특징을 적어서 돌리는 글) offender n. 범죄자

美 FBI(연방수사국)에서 그렇게 불리는 바 프로파일링, 즉 범죄 수사 분석은 범죄현장분석, 수사심리학, 그리고 행동과학에 기초하여, 범죄의 책임이 있는 당자자의 신원을 알아내기를 기대하며 범죄를 수사하는 것과 관련된 것이다. 범죄자 프로파일링은 법집행과 법심리학의 교차점이다. 범죄자 프로파일링이 나온 지는 수십 년이 되었지만, 그것은 여전히 정해진 경계나 정의가 거의 없는 상대적으로 새로운 분야이다. 게다가 범죄자 프로파일링을 전문으로 하는 프로파일러들은 방법론이나 심지어 전문용어나 정의에 있어서도 항상 의견이 일치하지는 않는다. 그러나 이러한 의견의 불일치에도 불구하고, 프로파일러들은 신원미상의 범죄자에 대한 인상서(人相書)를 만들어 나가기 위해 범죄현장에서 수집된 증거와 피해자들과 증인들이 제공한 진술을 분석한다는 공통된 목표를 모두 공유하고 있다.

---

20 **2022 광운대** ▶▶▶ MSG p.126   ⑤

정비문 ▶ 주절의 의미와 부사절의 의미가 중복될 경우 부사절의 술부를 생략하거나 축소할 수 있다. ①, ②, ③은 모두 George 다음에 반복되는 finished the exam이 생략되었으며, ④와 ⑤의 did는 finished the exam 대신에 대동사로 쓰인 것이다. 그러나 ⑤의 경우 접속사 when과 접속사 before가 하나의 절을 이끌 수 없으므로, when이나 before 둘 중에 하나를 삭제해야 한다. ②의 then은 접속사로 쓰인 것이다.

exam n. 시험(=examination)

① 나이젤(Nigel)은 조지(George)와 동시에 시험을 끝냈다.
② 나이젤(Nigel)이 시험을 먼저 끝낸 다음, 조지(George)가 시험을 끝냈다.
③ 나이젤(Nigel)은 조지(George)가 시험을 끝내기 전에 시험을 끝냈다.
④ 나이젤(Nigel)은 조지(George)가 시험을 끝냈을 때 시험을 끝냈다.
⑤ 나이젤(Nigel)은 조지(George)가 시험을 끝냈을 때/끝내기 전에 시험을 끝냈다.

TEST 17

| 01 ① | 02 ③ | 03 ③ | 04 ② | 05 ③ | 06 ① | 07 ② | 08 ③ | 09 ③ | 10 ④ |
| 11 ② | 12 ④ | 13 ③ | 14 ① | 15 ⑤ | 16 ① | 17 ② | 18 ① | 19 ② | 20 ③ |

01   2015 가천대 ▶▶▶ MSG p.11   ①

대동사 do ▶ 앞 문장의 동사 또는 술부 전체를 대동사 do로 대신할 수 있는데 the American system이 단수이므로 빈칸에는 ① does가 적절하다. 여기서는 gives him control over his government를 대신한 것이다.

all or nothing 양자택일의, 전부 아니면 아무것도 아닌 present v. 제시하다 voter n. 유권자 Representative n. (미국의) 하원의원 Senator n. (미국의) 상원의원

선거에서 영국 유권자에게 부여되는 "양자택일"의 선택은 미국의 선거제도보다 유권자에게 정부에 대한 통제권을 덜 준다고 주장될 수 있다. 미국의 선거제도는 유권자에게 서로 다른 당 출신의 하원의원, 상원의원, 대통령을 선출할 수 있도록 한다.

02   2014 가천대 ▶▶▶ MSG p.103   ③

문맥상 적절한 전치사 far from ▶ 빈칸에서부터 solitary men까지는 삽입구로, that절의 주어인 loneliness에 대한 동사가 is이다. that절에서 고독함이 인간의 존재에 있어 핵심적이고 필연적이라고 하였으므로, 빈칸에는 드물고 유별난 현상이 결코 아니라는 말이 들어가야 문맥상 적절하다. 따라서 ③의 far from(결코 ~가 아닌)이 정답이다.

conviction n. 확신 rest upon ~에 달려 있다; ~에 기초하다 loneliness n. 고독함 phenomenon n. 현상 solitary a. 고독한 inevitable a. 필연적인

내 인생의 완전한 확신은 고독함이 내 자신과 소수의 다른 고독한 사람들에게만 특별한, 드물고 이상한 현상이 아니라 (바로) 인간 존재의 핵심적이고 필연적인 사실이라는 믿음에 기초한다.

03   2020 가천대 ▶▶▶ MSG p.224   ③

부정의 의미를 포함하는 연결사 ▶ 빈칸 앞에 완전한 문장이 주어져 있으므로 연결사의 역할을 할 수 있는 표현이 필요하다. 한편, 전후 문장의 흐름상 빈칸을 포함한 문장도 '극장이 몰락한 것에 따른 여파'와 관련된 의미여야 하므로, 빈칸 앞 문장처럼 부정어가 있어야만 부정적인 의미를 나타낼 수 있다. 그러므로 앞의 부정문을 받아 '…도 ~하지 않다'는 의미를 가지는 접속사 nor가 제시되어 있는 ③이 빈칸에 적절하다.

closure n. 폐쇄 Puritan n. 청교도 medium n. 매체 censorship n. 검열, 검열제도

이것이 연극과 연극의 도덕성에 대한 비판의 시발점이었으며, 이는 결국 1642년에 청교도들에 의해 극장이 폐쇄되는 결과로 이어졌다. 연극은 다시는 오락 매체로서 인기를 끌지 못했고, 한 시대의 이슈와 관심사를 탐구하고 분석하는 데도 효과적이지 못했다. 영국 연극의 황금기는 비판과 검열로 막을 내렸다.

04   2011 경희대 ▶▶▶ MSG p.111   ②

비교대상의 일치 ▶ 비교대상은 항상 같아야 하는 것이 원칙이다. 앞의 operating behind the scenes와 비교될 수 있는 것은 동명사로 되어 있는 ②와 ④중에 하나인데, engage in이 '종사하다'라는 의미이므로 정답은 능동태로 쓰인 ②가 된다.

behind the scene 막후에서 discourse n. 강연

주커버그(Zuckerberg)는 대중 강연을 할 때보다는 기술과 사업에 관해 생각하면서, 막후에서 더 마음 편하게 (사업을) 운영한다고 사람들은 널리 믿고 있다고 큰 인터넷 회사들을 주시하고 있는 스탠더드 앤드 푸어스사의 자산 평가사인 스캇 케슬러(Scott Kessler)는 말한다.

05   2018 세종대 ▶▶▶ MSG p.9   ③

문의 구성 ▶ 현재분사 단독으로는 문장의 정동사 역할을 할 수 없으므로 ②와 ④를 정답에서 먼저 제외시킬 수 있다. 한편, It remains a problem.(그것은 여전히 문제이다.)에서처럼 remain의 보어로 명사가 불가능한 것은 아니나, 여기서는 명사 mixture를 보어로 취하면 '자료가 혼합이다'라는 부적절한 의미가 되는 반면, 과거분사 형태의 형용사 mixed를 보어로 취하면 '자료가 혼합되어(엇갈리고) 있다'는 적절한 의미가 된다. 따라서 ③이 빈칸에 적절하다.

daylight saving time 일광절약시간제, 서머타임 mixed a. 뒤섞인, (의견 등이) 엇갈리는

일광절약시간제가 에너지 소비를 상당한 정도로 줄이는지의 여부에 대해 많은 자료들이 서로 엇갈리고 있다.

06   2021 가천대 ▶▶▶ MSG p.71   ①

가정법 과거 및 if 생략 ▶ 빈칸이 들어있는 that절 안의 주절에 가정법 과거 형태인 '주어+would+동사원형'이 왔으므로, if절에도 가정법 과

거에 해당하는 'if+주어+과거동사'가 와야 한다. 그런데, that절 안의 주절의 주어가 the orbits of the planets로 복수이며, 행성은 관찰하는 주체가 아니라 '관찰되는 객체'이므로, 빈칸에는 if they were looked at이 와야 한다. 이때 if를 생략하면 도치가 일어난다. 따라서 ①의 were they looked at이 빈칸에 적절하다.

square v. ~을 제곱하다 cube v. ~을 세제곱하다 orbit n. 궤도

코페르니쿠스(Copernicus)와 케플러(Kepler)가 생각했거나 오늘날 과학자들이 생각하는 것은 자료를 충분히 읽고 나서 보이는 모든 것을 제곱하고 세제곱해서가 아니었다. 코페르니쿠스는 행성들의 궤도가 지구에서가 아니라 태양에서 관찰된다면 보다 단순하게 보일 것이라는 것을 발견했다.

07 2016 서울여대 ▶▶▶ MSG p.30 ②

think of A as B와 목적격 관계대명사의 생략 ▶ 모든 보기에 think of A as B(A를 B로 간주하다)가 쓰였는데, item 다음에 목적격 관계대명사 which가 생략되었음을 감안하면, an item이 we think of의 목적어가 되고, as a weapon이 목적격 보어가 되는 ②의 we think of as a weapon이 빈칸에 적절하다. 참고로 주어진 문장은 원래 The telescope, though (it is) not exactly an item (which) we think of as a weapon, actually was (a weapon)에서 괄호안의 것들이 생략된 형태이며, though not ~ as a weapon은 부사절이 주어와 동사 사이에 삽입된 형태이다.

telescope n. 망원경

망원경은 엄밀히 말해 우리가 무기로 간주하는 물건은 아니지만, 과거에는 실제로 무기였다.

08 2018 가천대 ▶▶▶ MSG p.74 ③

직설법 + otherwise + 가정법 ▶ 영국이 전 세계에 걸쳐 새로운 영토를 차지하고 지키느라 역량이 고갈되었다고 했으므로, 빈칸에는 식민지를 운영하는 데 역량을 집중하지 '못했다'는 내용이 와야 한다. 따라서 '그렇지 않았다면 ~에 쓸 수도 있었을'이라는 뜻인 ③이 답인데, 이때 otherwise 앞에는 직설법이, otherwise 뒤에는 가정법이 온다. 주어진 문장의 경우, otherwise 앞에 직설법 과거시제인 drained가 왔으므로, 빈칸에는 과거사실의 반대를 가정하는 표현인 가정법 과거완료의 귀결절이 와야 한다.

colony n. 식민지 protracted a. 장기화된 civil war 내전 break out 발생하다, 발발하다 throw into ~에 빠뜨리다 turmoil n. 혼란, 불안 resolve v. 해결하다 on top of ~에 더하여, 게다가 occupy v. 차지하다 territory n. 영토 drain v. (자원 등을) 고갈시키다 administration n. 관리, 운영

북아메리카 식민지가 건설되고 있었던 바로 그때, 격렬하고 장기간에 걸친 내전이 1642년에 영국에서 발발하여, 영국을 혼란에 빠뜨렸다. 유혈이 낭자했던 이 내전은 그 후 20년이 지난 뒤에도 완전히 해결되지 않았다. 게다가 영국은 유럽 다른 열강과의 끊임없는 (영토) 경쟁에 빠져 있었다. 전 세계에 걸쳐 새로운 영토를 차지하고 지키는 일은 그렇지 않았다면 식민지 운영에 (제대로) 쓸 수 있었을 역량을 고갈시켜 버렸다.

09 2003 세종대 ▶▶▶ MSG p.139 ③

선행사를 포함한 관계대명사 what ▶ 전체 문장의 동사는 is이고 보어로 접속사 that이 이끄는 명사절이 왔다. 주어진 선택지로 보아 빈칸에는 주어 역할을 할 수 있는 명사절이 와야 한다. what은 선행사를 포함한 관계대명사로 명사절을 이끌어 주어 역할을 할 수 있다.

monarch butterfly 제주왕나비과 나비 migration n. 이주 incredible a. 놀라운

제주왕나비과 나비들의 이동에서 놀라운 점은 이 곤충들이 이전에 본 적도 없는 장소로 성공적으로 이주해 간다는 사실이다.

10 2019 성균관대 ▶▶▶ MSG p.105 ④

분사의 한정용법 ▶ the sound를 수식하는 명사들이 of 이하에서 열거되고 있는데, ④와 같이 동사가 개입해 있으면 하나의 독립적인 절이 되어버리므로 병치가 깨진다. ④를 a chair를 후치 수식하는 분사 being으로 고쳐야 한다.

footstep n. 발소리, 발자국 shuffle v. 발을 끌며 걷다 unlock v. ~을 열다

아래층으로부터 발걸음 소리, 발을 끄는 소리, TV 소리, 의자 움직이는 소리, 문 열리는 소리가 났다.

11 2007 경기대 ▶▶▶ MSG p.234 ②

It ~ that 강조구문 & 부사 ago ▶ It ~ that 강조구문의 that절이 지금까지 계속되어온 일을 나타내는 현재완료시제이므로 강조되는 요소는 과거시점인 ago가 아니라 지금까지의 기간을 나타내는 표현이어야 한다. 따라서 ② ago를 삭제해야 한다.

for one thing 한 가지 이유는 grudgingly ad. 마지못해서

한 가지 이유는, 고등교육이 여성들에게, 심지어 백인 중산층 여성들에게조차도 미흡하게나마 개방되어온 것이 불과 지난 100년밖에 되지 않는다는 것이다.

12 2008 성균관대 ▶▶▶ MSG p.123 ④

동격의 명사절을 이끄는 접속사 that ▶ whom it could be a step backwards to colonial days는 whom을 제외하고도 주요소가 다 갖춰진 완전한 절이다. 따라서 목적격 관계대명사 ④ whom의 역할을 설명할 수 없으므로 whom은 잘못 쓰였다. 절 전체가 complaints의 내용이므로 동격절을 이끄는 접속사 that으로 고쳐야 한다.

press ahead with ~을 밀어붙이다, 강행하다 court n. 법정 colonial a. 식민지의

싱가포르는 그렇게 하는 것이 식민지 시대로의 퇴행이 될 수 있다는 자국 변호사들의 불평에도 불구하고 법정에서 일할 영국인 판사들을 다급하게 앞장서 찾고 있다.

13 **2019 경기대** ▶▶▶ MSG p.204 ③

형용사 prior와 전치사 prior to의 구분 ▶ ③에 쓰인 prior는 '사전의'라는 뜻의 형용사이므로 그 뒤에 any statement라는 목적어를 취할 수 없다. ③을 prior의 의미를 가지고 있으면서 전치사로 쓰이는 prior to나 before로 고친다.

generate v. 발생시키다[초래]하다 phrase n. 관용구, 구절 as a matter of principle 원칙에 따라 statement n. 성명서; 진술 voter n. 선거인, 유권자

정치인들은 너무나 낮은 신뢰도를 쌓아온 까닭에, 믿음을 주는 말을 하려면 그 앞에 "원칙에 따라"라는 말을 먼저 해야 할 지경이 되었으며, 그래야 유권자들이 그들을 신뢰하기를 시작이라도 할 것이다.

14 **2017 국민대** ▶▶▶ MSG p.113 ①

문의 구성 ▶ ①에서 접속사 when 뒤에 주어 없이 동사만 주어진 점이 옳지 않으며, 분사구문으로 파악하더라도 주어인 you와 hand-wash는 능동관계이므로 과거분사를 쓴 것은 옳지 않다. 따라서 ①을 when hand-washing으로 고칠 수 있으며, 이것은 분사구문에서 접속사를 생략하지 않고 남겨둔 형태 혹은 when you are hand-washing에서 '주어+be동사'를 생략한 것으로 설명할 수 있다. ② running은 전치사 by의 목적어로 쓰인 동명사이며, 준동사를 부정하는 경우 부정어를 준동사 앞에 둬야 하므로 not이 running 앞에 왔다. ④ 동시동작을 나타내는 분사구문이다.

dishwasher n. 식기세척기 rinse v. 헹구다, 씻어내다 spray attachment 분무장치 tap n. (통에 달린) 주둥이, (수도 등의) 꼭지, 급수전(汲水栓)

식기세척기가 없더라도, 손으로 그릇을 씻을 때 물을 계속해서 틀어놓지 않음으로써 여전히 물을 절약할 수 있다. 물을 일부 채운 싱크대에서 그릇을 세척하고, 그런 다음 수도꼭지와 연결된 호스 분무기를 사용하여 헹구어라.

15 **2018 상명대** ▶▶▶ MSG p.200 ⑤

비교급과 원급비교의 구분 ▶ ⑤의 뒤에 비교급 표현과 호응하는 than이 주어져 있으므로, ⑤를 long의 비교급인 longer로 고쳐야 한다.

slight a. 약간의, 적은, 근소한 on average 평균하여, 대체적으로

25~44세의 연령대에 속한 여성들은 집안에서도 집 밖에서도 거의 같은 시간을 일하고 있는데, 45~64세의 연령대에서도 별반 다르지 않다. 그러나 남성들은 집안에서보다 집 밖에서 평균 3배 더 오래 일한다.

16 **2019 가천대** ▶▶▶ MSG p.137 ①

전치사+관계대명사 ▶ '공평한 경쟁의 장(場)'은 경쟁자들이 서로 만나는 장소이므로, 장소의 개념을 가진 전치사와 함께 써야 한다. 따라서 ①을 in which로 고쳐야 한다.

level playing field 공평한 경쟁의 장 entrepreneurial a. 기업가의, 실업가의 ruthlessness n. 무자비함

그 새로운 광고는 경쟁자들이 아무 유리한 점 없이 만나는 "공평한 경쟁의 장(場)"이라는 상투적인 문구를 중심으로 만들어졌다. 이러한 스포츠맨십의 개념과 반대되는 것이 새롭게 나타난 기업가들의 무자비함인데, 거기서는 온통 불공정하게 경쟁하고 다른 사람들의 약점을 이용하려는 생각뿐이다.

17 **2022 건국대** ▶▶▶ MSG p.227 ②

전치사 ▶ '관심을 가지고, 관심 있게'라는 뜻의 부사어는 with concern이다. 따라서 ②를 with로 고친다. ⑤ 'by 명사[동명사]'나 'through 명사[동명사]'는 방법을 나타내는 부사어이므로 the way가 주어일 때 보어로 적절하다.

criterion n. 표준, 기준(pl. criteria) equity n. 공평, 공정 sustainability n. 지속 가능성 empowerment n. 권한 분산 differentiate v. 구별 짓다, 구별하다

역사적으로, 개발도상국을 정의하는 데 사용된 기준은 주로 경제성장에 초점을 두어 왔고 공정성, 지속가능성, 또는 권한 분산의 문제에 대해서는 거의 관심을 갖지 않았다. 예를 들어, 1990년대까지 개발도상국과 선진국을 구별하는 가장 일반적인 방법은 특정한 해에 한 국가에서 생산된 재화와 용역의 가치를 측정한 국내총생산(GDP) 수치의 사용을 통해서였다.

18 **2019 명지대** ▶▶▶ MSG p.85 ①

부정사와 동사의 구분 ▶ 첫 번째 문장에 쓰인 in which와 같은 '전치사+관계대명사'의 형태 뒤에는 완전한 절이 와야 한다. 따라서 주어인 the Earth에 대한 동사가 되도록 ①의 to spin을 3인칭 단수인 the Earth에 맞게 spins로 고쳐야 한다. 관계구는 주어 없이 '전치사+관계대명사+to부정사'로만 가능하다.

the Milky Way 은하수 galaxy n. 은하 spin v. 회전하다 innumerable a. 셀 수 없이 많은 star n. 별; 항성(恒星) cluster n. 무리; 성단(星團) solar system 태양계 revolve around ~을 공전하다 comprise v. ~을 구성하다

갈릴레오(Galileo)가 첫 번째 망원경을 하늘을 향해 돌렸을 때, 그는 지구가 자전하는 은하인 은하수는 성단(星團)을 이루면서 모여 있는 일련의 수많은 항성들이라고 기록했다. 그런 성단들은 사실 태양계들이 집단으로 모여 있는 것으로, 이것은 많은 항성들로 구성되어 있으며, 일부 항성들에는 항성들을 공전하는 행성들이 딸려 있다. 은하수는 두께가 1,000 광년이고, 직경은 가장 넓은 곳이 10만 광년이다. 은하수에는 대략 1,000억 개의 태양계가 존재하며, 1,000~2,000억 개의 항성들로 구성되어 있다.

19 **2020 명지대** ▶▶▶ MSG p.136 ②

관계대명사와 삽입절 ▶ 관계대명사 뒤에 '주어와 think 등의 동사'가 올 경우 삽입절로 볼 수 있다. 삽입절을 제거하고 나서도 관계대명사와 호응하는 말이 왔는지를 보면 문법적 적합성을 확인할 수 있다. ②에서 삽입절인 you think를 제거하고 보면, who are가 남는다. 이때 who가 주격관계대명사가 되려면, are 다음에 보어가 와야 하는데 보어가 없다. 따라서 who are를 who they are로 고쳐야 하는데, 이때 they는 who the Kims are에서 the Kims(김씨 가족) 대신 대명사 they가 쓰인 것이다. ②를 who you think they are로 고친다.

fold v. (종이 등을) 접다 squalid a. 지저분한 scramble v. 바삐 서둘러 하다
articulate v. (감정을) 분명히 표현하다 pin down ~을 정확히 이해하다
parasite n. 기생충 impeccably ad. 완벽하게 sleight of hand 교묘한 속임수
anchor v. 고정시키다 endearing a. 사람의 마음을 끄는

영화의 첫 장면은 김씨 가족을 소개하는데, 김씨 가족은 서울의 어느 지저분
한 반지하 공동주택에서 피자 상자들을 접고 있으며, 이웃집에서 와이파이
를 암호로 잠근 후에는 이 방 저 방 다니며 무료 와이파이를 분주하게 찾고
있다. 이 한 장면으로 영화는 영화의 제목과 중심인물들 각자의 특징을 분명
하게 보여주고 있는 것처럼 보이지만, 김씨 가족은 당신이 생각하는 그런 가
족이 아니다. 사실, 당신이 이 영화를 정확히 파악했다고 생각할 때마다, 즉
누가 무엇을 누구에게 하고 있는지, 누가 기생충이며 누가 기생충이 아닌지
를 파악했다고 생각할 때마다, 당신은 그것이 완벽하게 처리된 교묘한 속임
수였다는 것을 알게 된다. 오랫동안 봉준호 감독과 함께 일 해온 송강호는
관객을 사로잡는 매끈한 연기로 영화에 안정감을 준다.

20 **2022 광운대** ▶▶▶ MSG p.124   ③

정비문 ▶ ① 동사 intend는 'intend+목적어+to부정사'의 구문을 취하
며, 뉴스가 금지하는 대상이므로, 수동의 to부정사여서 맞는 문장이다.
② 감정동사 regret 다음에 온 that절의 동사는 '직설법 시제'나
'should+동사원형'이 올 수 있으므로 맞는 문장이다. ④ 전치사 about
이 관계사 what이 이끄는 절을 목적어로 받을 수 있어서 맞는 문장이
다. ⑤ 동사 like는 동사 want와 같이 '동사+목적어+to부정사'라는 5형
식 구문을 취하므로 맞는 문장이다. 반면, ③에서 동사 doubt는 목적어
로 if절이나 whether절을 받을 수 있지만, '~일지 의심하다'는 '~이지
않을 것으로 생각하다'는 뜻이므로 or not이 없어야 한다. 그리고
accept은 타동사이므로 목적어가 있어야 한다. 따라서 ③은 I doubt
whether they'll accept it.으로 고쳐야 한다.

suppress v. 억압하다, 억누르다

① 그들은 그 뉴스를 보도되지 않게 할 작정이었다.
② 그녀가 그것에 대해 걱정하다니 유감이다.
③ 나는 그들이 받아들일지 말지 의심스럽다.
④ 그녀는 그가 원하는 것에 대해 물었다.
⑤ 그들은 아이들이 그들을 방문해주기를 원했다.

01 ④	02 ②	03 ①	04 ①	05 ④	06 ①	07 ④	08 ③	09 ④	10 ③
11 ④	12 ③	13 ⑤	14 ④	15 ①	16 ④	17 ④	18 ③	19 ①	20 ④

01   2018 가천대   ▶▶▶ MSG p.122   ④

적절한 접속부사 ▶ 빈칸 앞에서 테러용의자들의 특이한 행동이 수사관들에게 단서를 줄 수 있지만, 수사에 혼선을 주기 위해 일부러 특이한 행동을 테러용의자들이 하기도 한다고 언급한 다음, 빈칸 다음에서 당신이 생각하는 테러리스트같이 여겨지는 사람들이 실제로는 아닐 수도 있다고 했다. 빈칸을 전후한 내용이 모두 '테러용의자들에 대한 예상이나 편견이 실제와는 다를 수 있다'는 것이므로, 빈칸에는 ④의 Likewise(마찬가지로)가 가장 적절하다. ① 대신 ② 반면 ③ 그런데

transaction n. 거래 clue in ~에게 단서를 주다 suspect n. 용의자 profile n. 인물소개란, 프로필 would-be a. 장차 ~이 되려고 하는 distinguished a. 유명한, 저명한

특이한 유형의 금융거래는 수사관들에게 테러 용의자에 관한 단서를 줄 수 있다. 그러나 이런 유형에는 항상 예외가 있으며, 잠재적인 테러리스트들은 단지 수상쩍어 보이는 것을 피하기 위해 특이한 행동을 할지도 모른다. 마찬가지로, 당신이 '일반적으로' 테러리스트라고 생각하는 프로필이 항상 정확한 것은 아닐지도 모른다. 가난하고 교육을 받지 못한 사람들이 테러리스트가 될 가능성이 가장 높다고 여겨지지만, (실제로) 미국에서 크리스마스에 테러를 감행하려다 미수에 그쳤던 사람은 저명한 나이지리아 가문의 아들이었다.

02   2012 명지대   ▶▶▶ MSG p.209   ②

원급을 이용한 최상급 표현 ▶ 'no+명사+is+so+원급+as ~'는 '~만큼 …하는 것은 없다'라는 뜻으로 원급을 이용해 최상급의 뜻을 나타내는 표현이다. 따라서 빈칸에는 ② as가 들어가야 한다.

arsenal n. 무기; 무기고 formidable a. 무서운, 위협적인 will n. 의지

전 세계의 그 어떤 무기나 무기고에 있는 무기도 자주적인 사람들의 의지와 정신적 용기만큼 가공할 위력을 갖고 있지는 않다는 것을 우리는 특히 깨달아야 한다.

03   2019 단국대   ▶▶▶ MSG p.103   ①

동명사의 관용표현 on ~ing ▶ one young soldier가 주어, demanded가 동사, that 이하가 목적어로 온 완전한 주절이 빈칸 다음에 왔으므로, '_____ the foots'는 주절을 수식해 주어야 한다. on ~ing는 '~하자마자'라는 뜻의 관용구로, 주절을 꾸며줄 수 있으므로, ①의 On hearing이 정답이다. ② 연결사 없이 두 개의 절이 왔으므로 부적절하다. ③ as to는 '~에

관하여'라는 뜻의 전치사로 hear는 전치사의 목적어 형태인 동명사 hearing이 되어야 한다. ④ To hear는 부정사로 빈칸에 들어갈 수는 있지만, '~하기 위해(목적)'나 '~한다면(조건)'의 의미로 부적절한 의미가 된다.

spirit n. 영혼, 정령 be up there 그 곳에 있다

발자국 소리를 듣자마자, 정령을 믿지 않던 한 젊은 군인은 하비(Harvey)에게 자신의 존재를 확실히 드러내 보일 것을 요구했다. "하비, 만약 네가 거기 그 위에 있다면, 네가 거기 있다는 것을 내게 알려줘야 해."

04   2019 단국대   ▶▶▶ MSG p.76   ①

'당위'의 뜻을 가진 명사의 동격절의 형태 ▶ requirement(요구)와 같이 '당위'의 뜻을 가진 명사 다음에 온 that절에는 반드시 주어 다음에 'should 동사원형'이나 '동사원형'이 와야 하므로, 빈칸에는 동사원형인 ①의 be가 적절하다.

requirement n. 자격 요건 applicant n. 지원자, 신청자 subsidy n. 보조금, 장려금

모든 신청자는 보조금을 신청할 당시 최소 스무 살은 돼야 한다는 자격요건이 있다.

05   2020 가톨릭대   ▶▶▶ MSG p.86, p.121   ④

문의 구성 ▶ 처음부터 빈칸 앞까지가 주어이므로 빈칸에는 시제를 가진 동사로 시작되는 ④가 적절하다. 주어는 'method of 동명사', 'try to부정사', 'get 목적어 to부정사' 구문이 이어진 것이다. 그리고 술부는 is가 동사, to present 이하가 보어이며, present 이하는 present A with B(A에게 B를 제시하다)와 not A but B(A가 아니라 B) 구문이 각각 쓰였다.

typical a. 전형적인, 일반적인 persuasive a. 설득력 있는 memorable a. 기억에 남을만한

저자가 독자들로 하여금 새로운 방식으로 세상을 바라보게 하는 전형적인 방법은 독자들에게 설득력 있는 주장을 제시하는 것이 아니라 기억에 남을 만한 이미지를 제시하는 것이다.

06 **2011 아주대** ▶▶▶ MSG p.137 ①

문의 구성 ▶ explores의 목적어와 이 목적어를 선행사로 하는 관계대명사가 필요하다. 빈칸 뒤에 완전한 문장이 왔으므로 '명사+전치사+관계대명사'의 형태가 와야 하므로 ①이 적절하다. ②는 선행사가 the extent로 앞에 있으므로 선행사를 포함한 관계대명사 what이 쓰였기 때문에 정답이 될 수 없고, ③은 빈칸 뒤에 완전한 문장이 왔으므로 관계대명사절에서 which의 역할이 없기 때문에 오답이다. which는 전치사의 목적어가 되어야 한다. ④의 경우 전치사 to 다음에는 명사나 동명사의 형태가 와야 하는데 절이 와서 적절하지 않다. ⑤에서는 that절에 이미 주어가 있으므로 it은 불필요하다.

illuminate v. 설명하다, 해명하다 engage with ~와 관여하다 illuminate v. 설명하다

이 책에서 메리 에번스(Mary Evans)는 얼마만큼 사회이론이 성과 사회 세계의 관계에 대하여 관여해왔고 그 문제를 설명해왔는가 하는 그 정도를 분석한다.

07 **2016 서울여대** ▶▶▶ MSG p.121 ④

문의 구성 ▶ not A but B(A가 아니라 B)는 B, and not A로 나타낼 수 있다. 주어진 문장에서는 B에 해당하는 것이 'with 명사(products ~ salt)'의 형태로 and 앞에 나와 있으므로, 빈칸에는 not A에 해당하는 'not with 명사'로 된 ④의 not with grains of salt가 적절하다.

seasoned with ~로 맛을 낸 fermented a. 발효된 pickled a. ~에 절인 grain n. 알갱이

중국음식은 음식에 직접 첨가되는 소금 알갱이로가 아니라 발효되거나 소금에 절인 재료로 맛을 내는지에 대한 정확한 이유를 사학자들이 논쟁한다.

08 **가천대 2021** ▶▶▶ MSG p.95 ③

so + 형용사 + as to V ▶ 속박과 노예제도는 구입하는 행위의 대상이므로 수동으로 나타내야 한다. 따라서 능동태가 온 ①과 ④는 빈칸에 부적절하다. ②는 not이 와서 구입되는 것과 반대의 의미가 되어 역시 부적절하다. 따라서 ③의 as to be purchased가 정답인데, as to는 'so+형용사'와 함께 쓰여서 'so+형용사+as to V(~할 만큼 형용사하다)'라는 뜻으로 쓰인다.

brethren n. 형제, (종교상의) 교우(敎友), 동포 stand idle 손 놓고 있다 gentleman n. (미국 상하원의) 의원 dear a. 소중한 slavery n. 노예제도 almighty a. 전지전능한

우리 동포들은 이미 싸움터에 나가 있는데 왜 우리는 여기서 손을 놓고 있는 것입니까? 의원들이 바라는 것은 대체 무엇입니까? 그들은 무엇을 갖게 될까요? 속박과 노예제도라는 대가를 지불하고 구입할 정도로 인생이 그렇게 소중하고 평화가 그렇게 달콤합니까? 전능하신 하나님, 그것을 금하소서! 저는 다른 사람들이 어떤 길을 걸을지는 알지 못합니다. 하지만 저의 경우는, 자유가 아니면 죽음을 달라는 것입니다!

09 **2017 한국외대** ▶▶▶ MSG p.31 ④

expect+목적어+to부정사 ▶ 5형식 동사로 쓰인 expect는 'expect+목적어+to부정사'의 형식을 취한다. 따라서 동명사 expecting의 술부로 목적어 a square peg과 목적보어 to fit in이 제시돼 있는 ④가 정답이다.

a square peg in a round hole 부적임자, 기대할 수 없는 것

대통령 당선자가 기업과 정치의 규범에 순응하길 희망하는 것은 둥근 구멍에 사각형 못이 들어맞기를 기대하는 것과 같다(전혀 기대할 수 없다).

10 **2022 한양대** ▶▶▶ MSG p.136, p.138 ③

관계대명사 ▶ 선행사 the only type of cell이 있으므로 선행사를 포함하는 관계대명사 what은 옳지 않다. ③ what을 주격 관계대명사 that으로 고쳐야 한다. 이때 we can confidently say는 관계절 속의 삽입절이다.

cerebral cortex 대뇌피질 confidently ad. 자신 있게

대뇌피질 뉴런은 우리가 결코 대체되지 않는다고 자신 있게 말할 수 있는 유일한 종류의 세포이다.

11 **2021 중앙대** ▶▶▶ MSG p.130, p.221 ④

문의 구성 ▶ ① 'not until 명사'라는 부정의 부사어구가 문두에 와서 주어와 동사가 도치되었다. ② lackluster는 '활기 없는'이라는 뜻의 형용사로 'so 형용사 that절'의 구문을 이루고 있다. ③ out of joy(기뻐서)처럼 'out of 감정명사'의 한 예로, 이런 관용표현의 경우 감정명사는 무관사가 원칙이다. 밑줄 친 세 부분이 모두 문법적으로 옳으므로 ④가 정답이다.

lackluster a. 활기 없는 the management 경영진 fire v. 해고하다

그녀는 자신의 연기가 너무나도 밋밋해서 경영진이 자신을 해고했다는 사실을 다음날이 되어서야 알게 됐지만, 다른 배우들은 난처해서 아무 말도 하지 않고 있었다.

12 **2021 서강대** ▶▶▶ MSG p.219 ③

비교급 병치 ▶ placing 다음은 '목적어+on 명사'가 병치된 구조이다. 앞에서 more stress로 비교급을 썼으므로, 뒷 부분도 동일한 형태가 되도록 ③의 little을 비교급인 less로 고쳐야 한다.

sanguine a. 낙관적인 place stress on ~을 강조하다 potential n. 잠재력 sinister a. 불길한; 사악한 lurk v. 잠복하다 recess of the mind 마음속 깊은 곳

에이브러햄 매슬로우(Abraham Maslow)의 심리학은 많은 인본주의 심리학파들 중 하나이다. 인본주의 심리학자들은 인간이 처한 상황을 낙관적으로 보며, 인간의 성취 잠재력은 더 많이 강조하고, 마음속 깊은 곳에 숨어 있는 사악한 힘은 덜 강조한다.

13　**2022 건국대**　▶▶▶ MSG p.85　　　　　　　　⑤

가주어-진주어 구문 ▶ 마지막 문장은 '가주어-진주어' 구문이며, 가주어로 it이 사용되었다. 따라서 ⑤는 진주어로 to부정사여야 할 것이므로 to find로 고쳐야 한다.

drug pusher 마약 밀매인 push v. (마약 따위를) 밀매하다 ware n. 상품, 판매품 neighborhood n. 지구, 지역 obsession n. 강박관념, 망상

그러한 가격들로 인해, 마약 밀매상들은 심지어 가장 가난한 지역에서도 그들의 상품을 팔아서 매년 수십억 달러를 벌 수 있다. 대부분의 사람들은 소위 마약과의 전쟁이 미국에서는 결코 승리할 수 없다는 것에 의견이 일치한다. 그 결과, 마약 문제의 해결책을 찾는다는 것이 많은 미국인들에게는 망상이 되었다.

14　**2019 홍익대**　▶▶▶ MSG p.105　　　　　　　　④

동사와 과거분사의 구분 ▶ now that은 이유를 나타내는 because와 같은 접속사로, Now that ~ facts가 부사절이 되는데, 부사절 안에 have seen의 목적어인 how로 시작하는 간접의문절에서 are와 took이라는 두 개의 동사가 별도의 연결사 없이 존재하므로 어색해졌다. 따라서 밑줄 친 ④에서 paths를 후치수식 하도록 took을 과거분사 taken으로 고쳐야 한다.

reason n. 이성 clever a. (성실성이 없고) 약삭빠른 crooked a. (길 등이) 구부러진 mediate v. 중재하다 take a path 길을 걷다 genealogy n. 계보(系譜); 자손, 혈통 artifact n. 인공물, 가공품 as well 또한, 역시

그리스인들은 이성과 과학 지식의 곧은 길, '에피스테메(episteme)'를 기술 노하우의 약삭빠르고 구부러진 길, '메티스(metis)'와 구분하곤 했다. 과학적 사실이 걷는 길이 얼마나 간접적이고 중재된 것인지를 알게 되었으므로, 우리는 기술적 인공물의 다른 계보를 또한 발견할 수 있을지도 모른다.

15　**2019 한양대 에리카**　▶▶▶ MSG p.147　　　　　　　①

문맥상 적절한 명사 ▶ '수요'라는 의미의 명사는 demanding이 아닌 demand이다. ①을 demand for로 고친다.

time-keeping n. 계시(計時), 시간 계측 transportation n. 운송, 수송; 운송기관

시계에 대한 수요가 늘어남에 따라 시간 계측 기술도 계속해서 발전했다. 공장, 은행, 통신, 수송 분야에서 시계가 필요했다. 오늘날, 현대 생활의 많은 부분은 빠른 속도로 일어나며 시간을 정확하게 아는 것에 의존해 있다. 우리는 또한 정확한 시간에 대해 국제적인 합의를 해야 한다.

16　**2019 명지대**　▶▶▶ MSG p.55　　　　　　　　④

능동태와 수동태의 구분 ▶ 마지막 문장의 ascribe 다음에 목적어 much of his fortune이 왔으므로, 해당 문장은 능동태가 되어야 한다. 따라서 ④를 has ascribed로 고쳐야 하며, 이때 ascribe A to B(A를 B 탓[덕]으로 돌리다)라는 표현이 쓰였다.

extraordinary a. 비범한, 뛰어난 figure n. (세간의 이목을 끄는) 인물 not so much A as B A라기 보다는 오히려 B billionaire n. 억만장자 immensely ad. 엄청나게 gem n. 보석처럼 아름다운 것, 주옥 tide n. 밀물, 바닷물 trip off the tongue (말이) 술술 잘 나오다 modest a. 겸손한 self-deprecating a. 자기를 낮추는

워런 버핏(Warren Buffett)은 비범한 인물이다. 워런 버핏은 억만장자같이 생겼다기보다 평범한 인물이나 대학 강사처럼 생겼다. 그가 한 말은 엄청나게 인용되고 있다. "썰물이 되고 나서야 비로소 누가 발가벗고 헤엄치고 있는지 알 수 있다."와 같은 주옥같은 말이 그의 입에서 술술 나오는 것 같다. 그는 또한 대단히 겸손하고 자기를 낮추며, 그가 모은 재산 대부분을 운이 좋았던 탓으로 돌려왔다.

17　**2021 가천대**　▶▶▶ MSG p.111　　　　　　　　④

분사구문 ▶ However로 시작하는 두 번째 문장에서 주어는 technological improvements, 동사는 have made이다. cost까지 완전한 절이 온 다음에 연결사 없이 정동사 resulted가 다시 와서 틀린 문장이다. 따라서 ④ 이하가 분사구문이 되도록 resulted를 resulting으로 고쳐야 한다.

mineral n. 광물 extract v. (광석을) 채취하다 associated with ~와 관련된 mining n. 채굴 commodity n. 원자재 unsustainable a. 지속 불가능한

처음에는, 광물이 채취되는 속도가 채굴과 관련된 고비용으로 인해 제한을 받았다. 그러나 수송과 관련된 상당한 비용 감소와 함께 업계의 기술적 발전이 이러한 상품(광물)을 보다 효율적이고 훨씬 더 저렴한 비용으로 캐낼 수 있게 했으며, 전문가들이 지속 불가능하다고 여기는 채취 속도에 도달하게 되었다.

18　**2019 한양대 에리카**　▶▶▶ MSG p.113　　　　　　　③

분사구문의 태 ▶ 타동사 avoid의 수동태 다음에 목적어인 명사가 나와 있으므로 ③을 능동태인 Avoiding으로 고쳐야 한다. Avoiding의 의미상 주어는 정확히 말하면 they이지만 they와 관련된 their goal이 주절의 주어로 왔으므로 허용된다.

immigrant n. 이민자, 이민 persecution n. (종교상의) 박해 pious a. 신앙심이 깊은

북아메리카는 이민자들의 땅으로, 그 이민자들 중에는 종교적 박해를 피해 고국을 떠나온 사람들이 많았다. 1700년대 초에, 한 무리의 기독교인들이 스위스에서 미국과 캐나다로 건너왔다. 독실하고 부지런했던 그들은 농업 공동체를 만들었다. 아미시파(派)로 알려져 있는 이 사람들은 캐나다의 온타리오 주(州)와 미국의 여러 주(州)에서 여전히 살고 있다. 컴퓨터와 같은 현대 기술의 사용을 거부한 그들의 목표는 항상 자신들이 유럽에서 했던 그 소박한 농경 생활을 그대로 유지하는 것이었다.

19 **2020 이화여대** ▶▶▶ MSG p.212 ①

부분표시어의 수일치 ▶ 주어에 부분표시어가 포함돼 있는 경우, 동사는 부분 표시어 뒤에 온 명사에 수를 일치시키고, 가산명사 복수형 앞에는 many of를, 불가산 단수명사 앞에는 much of를 각각 쓴다. 따라서 ①을 many of the current technologies are나 much of the current technology is로 고쳐야 한다.

utilization n. 이용, 활용 virtualization n. (컴퓨터에 의한) 가상현실화 centralize v. 중심에 모으다; 집중시키다 capacity n. 수용량; 용량; 재능, 능력 enterprise n. 기업; 기획

우리는 또한 현존하는 기술의 활용도를 높여야 한다. 현재의 기술 중 많은 것이 활용도가 매우 낮다. IT를 운용하는 비용은 가령, 가상현실화의 개념을 최종 사용자의 컴퓨터 장치에 적용하고, 애플리케이션이 중앙 집중 서버에서 호스팅 될 수 있게 하며, IT가 보다 쉽고 적은 비용으로 새로운 모바일 컴퓨터 서비스를 제공하고 라이선스의 활용도를 높임으로써 줄일 수 있다. 혁신 역량을 획기적으로 높이는 비결은 IT를 저부가가치 활동에서 고부가가치 활동으로 전환하여, 나머지 사업 분야의 IT 역량이 발휘될 수 있도록 하는 것이다.

20 **2022 광운대** ▶▶▶ MSG p.125 ④

정비문 ▶ ④ Do you think?와 How long have they been married?를 합쳐서 의문문을 만들 때, think, guess, suppose, believe, imagine 등의 동사가 쓰인 경우 의문사가 문두로 가므로, How long do you think they have been married?가 되어야 한다.

look forward to ~을 기대하다, ~을 즐거운 마음으로 기다리다

① 그녀는 내가 찾고 있던 개를 공원에서 발견했다.
② 나는 그 가수와의 만남을 기대하고 있다.
③ 피터는 인쇄하기 전에 오류를 찾는 것이 중요하다.
④ 당신은 그들이 결혼한 지 얼마나 됐다고 생각합니까?
⑤ 존이 아내에게 한 일은 운전하는 법을 가르쳐주는 것이었다.

01 ④	**02** ③	**03** ③	**04** ①	**05** ④	**06** ④	**07** ②	**08** ②	**09** ④	**10** ④
11 ③	**12** ④	**13** ③	**14** ②	**15** ③	**16** ②	**17** ④	**18** ④	**19** ②	**20** ②

01 **2010 서울여대** ▶▶▶ MSG p.222　　④

적절한 접속사의 사용 ▶ 동사가 두 개이므로 앞은 부사절이 되어야 하는데, 주절의 주어(the procedure)와 동사(is permitted)가 이미 도치되어 있으므로 문장이 부정어구로 시작됨을 알 수 있다. Only if만이 가능하다.

abortion n. 유산, 낙태 procedure n. 순서, 차례; 절차; 처리

산모의 생명을 살리기 위해서 낙태가 필요한 경우에만 그 수술은 용납된다.

02 **2005 경희대** ▶▶▶ MSG p.224　　③

so+(조)동사+주어 ▶ '~도 또한 마찬가지이다'라는 표현은 'so+(조)동사+주어'의 형태로 쓴다. 정답은 ③이다.

underemployed a. 능력 이하의 일을 하는 forestry n. 임학, 산림학

복사기를 운영하는 그 영어전공자는 능력이하의 일을 하고 있으며, 자기 전공분야에서 일자리를 구할 수 없는 임학전공자도 마찬가지이다.

03 **2006 동국대** ▶▶▶ MSG p.113　　③

분사구문 ▶ publicity and public relations 이하가 주절이므로 빈칸에는 수식어인 부사(구/절)가 와야 한다. ①은 접속사가 없는 절이 되어서 부적절하고, ②는 불필요한 that을 제거하고 that을 부사절을 유도하는 종속접속사 when이나 if로 대체하면 된다. ④의 경우 분사구문의 주어는 주절의 주어와 동일할 때 생략되는데 광고와 홍보는 주의 깊게 계획된 것이므로 현재분사가 아니라 과거분사 planned가 되어야 한다. 원래의 절 when they are carefully planned를 분사구문으로 하면 carefully planned가 되어야 한다. ③은 이 절에서 주어와 be동사를 생략한 것으로 적절하다.

publicity n. 광고, 선전 public relations 홍보 (활동)

광고 타깃의 관심을 이해하여, 주의 깊게 계획된 광고와 홍보는, 거의 비용을 들이지 않고도 회사의 판매촉진을 효과적으로 행할 수 있다.

04 **2011 단국대** ▶▶▶ MSG p.74　　①

직설법과거+otherwise+가정법 과거완료 & 수동태 ▶ otherwise는 '그렇지 않으면, 그렇지 않았더라면'이라는 의미로 앞의 직설법 구문을 이용하여, 조건절로 바꾸어 쓸 수 있다. 이 문장에서는 직설법 과거의 동사 participated가 앞에 왔으므로 빈칸에는 가정법 과거완료가 필요하다. 그리고 돈은 모금되는 것이므로 수동형인 ①이 빈칸에 적절하다.

charity ball 자선 무도회 raise money 돈을 모금하다

거리의 아이들을 위한 자선 파티에 참석한 사업가가 거의 없었던 것 같다. 그렇지 않았다면 더 많은 돈을 모금했을 것이다.

05 **2021 서울여대** ▶▶▶ MSG p.138　　④

전치사 + 관계대명사 + to부정사 ▶ replace는 전치사 with와 함께 replace A with B(A를 B로 대체하다)의 형태로 쓰이므로, 빈칸에는 with which(= so many innovative options) they can replace it(= beef)이 들어갈 수 있다. 그런데, 이때 관계절을 to부정사구로 축약하면 with which to replace it라는 관계구가 된다.

predict v. 예언하다, 예보하다 peak v. 최고점[한도]에 달하다, 절정이 되다

그는 사람들이 쇠고기를 더 이상 좋아하지 않아서가 아니라 그것을 대체할 수 있는 획기적인 선택사항들이 매우 많기 때문에 2020년에 쇠고기 소비가 정점에 이를 수도 있다고 예측했다.

06 **2018 광운대** ▶▶▶ MSG p.137　　④

전치사 + 관계대명사 ▶ '전치사+관계대명사'의 구조에서 어떤 전치사를 써야 하는가는 관계사절 내의 동사 혹은 형용사가 해당 문맥에서 어떤 전치사와 호응하여 쓰이는가를 판단해서 결정해야 한다. 첫 번째 빈칸의 경우, '~을 타고나다'는 표현은 'be endowed with~'이므로 with가 적절하고, 두 번째 빈칸의 경우, 아이가 환경 '안에서' 사는(the child lives in the environment) 것이므로, 전치사 in이 적절하다.

endow A with B A에게 B를 주다 be endowed with ~을 타고나다

개인이 타고날 수 있는 모든 재능들 중에 음악적 재능이 인생에서 가장 일찍 나타난다. 그러나 그 재능의 발전은 아이가 살고 있는 환경에 달려 있다.

07 2020 가톨릭대 ▶▶▶ MSG p.124 ②

문의 구성 ▶ whether절에서 빈칸 다음에 동사 was가 왔으므로 빈칸에는 주어로 명사에 해당하는 표현이 적절한데, ③과 ④는 절이므로 부적절하다. ①의 to부정사는 수학에 확실성을 부여하는 행위를 나타내고 ②의 what 관계절은 수학에 확실성을 부여하는 어떤 것을 나타낸다. 그런데, be동사 was는 '등호(=)'와 같은 것이므로 주어와 같은 것인 something은 that 관계절의 내용으로 볼 때 '차용되고 적용되는 행위'가 아니라 '차용되고 적용되는 어떤 것'이다. 따라서 빈칸에는 what 관계인 ②가 적절하다. 예를 들어, To succeed in academia was something that I wanted to do.(학계에서 성공하는 것이 내가 하기를 원하는 것이었다.)의 경우는 something, 즉 to succeed in academia가 내가 행하는 행위이므로 맞는 문장이 되는 것이다.

thrilled a. (너무 좋아서) 황홀한 transparent a. 투명한 mathematics n. 수학

데카르트(Descartes)는 수학의 투명하고 완전히 믿을 수 있는 확실성에 매료되었으며, 수학에 확실성을 부여하는 것이 다른 지식 분야에도 차용되어 적용될 수 있는 것인지를 궁금해 하기 시작했다.

08 2016 한국외대 ▶▶▶ MSG p.133 ②

종속절의 접속사 as와 대동사 do ▶ 비슷한 경우를 견주어 말할 때 as는 '~와 마찬가지로'의 뜻으로 쓰인다. 이때 as는 접속사이므로, 그 뒤에는 ②와 같이 주어와 동사를 포함하는 절이 이어진다.

weariable a. 피로해질 수 있는 faculty n. 능력; 학부 at a time 따로따로, 한 번에 limb n. 팔다리, 의족; 가지 fatigued a. 피로해진, 지친

상상력은 피로해질 수 있는 능력이다. 즉, 우리가 상상할 대상을 상상력에 한 번에 너무 많이 부여하면, 팔다리가 몸의 피로로 인해 그렇게 되듯이 상상력도 그러한 노력으로 인해 잘 작동되지 않는다.

09 2005 홍익대 ▶▶▶ MSG p.199, p.203 ④

비교대상의 일치 ▶ 비교문에서 비교되는 대상은 반드시 병치를 이루어야 한다. 앞에 제시된 '집권당의 법안들'에 맞춰 '야당의 법안들'이 비교 대상으로 와야 하는데, 같은 '법안들'이라는 말의 반복을 피하기 위해서 대명사 those로 바꿔야 한다.

bill n. 법안 ruling party 집권당 opposition party 야당

집권당의 법안들은 야당의 법안들만큼 나쁘거나 혹은 더 나쁘다.

10 2022 세종대 ▶▶▶ MSG p.79 ④

조동사 used to ▶ ④에 쓰인 be used to (동사원형)는 '~하는 데 사용되다'라는 의미이므로 글의 흐름상 적절하지 않다. 이것을 과거의 습관이나 상태를 나타내는 조동사 used to로 고쳐야 한다.

heart n. 심장 liver n. 간(肝) kidney n. 신장

다시 말해, 새로운 심장, 간, 신장을 가진 사람들은 그들이 이전에 그랬던 것보다 훨씬 더 오래 살 수 있다.

11 2020 건국대 ▶▶▶ MSG p.140, p.218 ③

문의 구성 ▶ 주어는 Anger, 본동사는 mobilize, 목적어는 you, 목적격보어는 세 개의 to 부정사(to take, to think, to defend)가 병치된 문장이다. 그런데 'take action to 부정사(~하기 위해 조치를 취하다)' 구문의 to 부정사인 to set limits to the demands 다음에 others make you가 the demands를 수식하는 관계절로 왔다. make를 4형식동사나 5형식동사로 보아서는 의미상 적절하지 않은 문장이 되고 3형식동사로 보아 'make a demand of~(~에게 요구하다)'의 구문이 되어야 한다. 따라서 ③을 make of you로 고쳐야 한다. to set, to think, to defend가 병치되어 to take action에 이어지는 것으로도 볼 수 있으나 그러면 두 번째 '~에 대해 생각하기 위해 조치를 취하다'가 의미적으로 어색해 부적절하다.

take action 조치를 취하다 set limits to ~을 제한하다

분노는 당신으로 하여금, 예를 들면, 다른 사람들이 당신에게 하는 요구를 제한하기 위해 조치를 취하거나, 어떤 것이 당신에게 왜 중요한지에 대해 생각하거나, 공격을 받는 경우에 자신을 보호하게끔 해줄 수 있다.

12 2009 한국외대 ▶▶▶ MSG p.85 ④

가주어(it)-진주어(to부정사) 구문 ▶ pays 앞의 it이 가주어이고 pays가 1형식 동사이므로 ④는 진주어로 to부정사 형태인 to cancel이 되어야 한다. ②는 비용이 계산에 더해지는 것이므로 수동태로 쓰였으며, ⑤ otherwise는 가정법 표현 would be와 함께 쓰인 부사이다.

calculation n. 계산(함), 셈 profitable a. 이익이 되는

지연과 불확실성의 비용이 계산에 더해질 때, 정부기관과 사설기관 둘 모두는 그런 비용이 아니라면 수익성이 있을 그런 사업들도 취소하는 것이 득이 된다는 것을 종종 알게 된다.

13 2020 가천대 ▶▶▶ MSG p.15 ③

타동사의 목적어 ▶ neglect는 타동사이므로 반드시 뒤에 목적어를 수반해야 한다. 따라서 ③에 쓰인 neglect 뒤에는 종속절 속의 child safety seats를 받는 대명사가 있어야 한다. ③을 neglect them easily로 고친다.

neglect v. (의무·일 따위를) 게을리 하다; 무시하다

매년 수천 명의 아이들이 자동차 사고로 죽는다. 대부분의 경우, 그 아이들은 어린이 안전 좌석을 사용하지 않고 있었다. 어린이 안전 좌석은 법으로 규정돼 있지만 많은 부모들은 쉽게 그것을 무시한다. 유일한 해결책은 어린이 안전 좌석이 생명을 구할 수 있다는 점을 부모들에게 교육하는 것이다.

14 **2019 홍익대** ▶▶▶ MSG p.53

시제일치 ▶ ②의 had reached는 과거완료시제로, 현재시제 부사인 now와 함께 쓰일 수 없다. 따라서 ②를 현재완료시제인 have reached 로 고쳐주어야 하는데, 현재완료시제는 과거부터 현재까지의 시제를 포함하므로, now와 함께 쓰일 수 있다.

retirement n. 은퇴 baby boomer (특히 2차 세계대전 후의) 베이비 붐 세대인 사람 fill up ~을 가득 채우다 spike v. 급상승시키다

은퇴는 일부 사람들이 회피하는 주제이지만, 많은 사람들은 지금 은퇴 연령에 도달했다. 바로 그들이 베이비붐 세대이다. 6700만 명에 달하는 이들 베이비붐 세대들은 어른으로 성장하는 동안 학교 교실을 가득 메웠으며, 청바지 매출을 급격히 끌어올렸다.

15 **2021 가천대** ▶▶▶ MSG p.141, p.214 ③

관계대명사의 선행사와 동사의 수일치 ▶ ③ display는 주어인 주격 관계대명사 which의 선행사가 단수인 Heart of Darkness이므로 displays로 고쳐야 한다. better부터 know까지는 부사어로 주어인 which와 동사 사이에 삽입되어 있고 관계절 that I know가 any other work을 수식한다.

competence n. 능력 embark on ~에 착수하다 novelist n. 소설가 fiction n. 소설

나는 사회학이나 생물학의 도구를 가지고 그 일에 착수하고자 하는 바람도 능력도, 또 단순하게 조셉 콘래드의 『암흑의 핵심(Heart of Darkness)』이라는 영국의 유명한 소설에 응답하는 한 소설가의 방식으로 하고자 하는데, 이 『암흑의 핵심』이라는 책은 내가 방금 언급한 그 서양의 욕망과 욕구를 내가 아는 다른 어떤 작품보다 더 잘 드러낸다.

16 **2022 건국대** ▶▶▶ MSG p.139

관계대명사 what ▶ ②는 hate의 목적어가 되는 명사절을 이끄는 역할과 자신이 이끄는 절 안에서 타동사 do의 목적어가 되는 역할 모두를 수행해야 하므로, 선행사를 포함한 관계대명사 what으로 고쳐야 한다. ① hate의 목적어로 쓰인 동명사이다. ④ as if 뒤에는 가정법 동사가 온다.

flu n. 독감, 인플루엔자 proceed v. 계속하다 in the grip of ~에게 잡혀; (병에) 걸려 fatal a. 치명적인 martyrdom n. 순교; 수난; 순교자적 고통

나는 아픈 것이 싫다. 단순히 질병 자체를 싫어한다는 것만 말하려는 것이 아니라 (그것이 사실이지만), 아픈 것이 내 성격에 미치는 바를 싫어한다. 두통이나 감기에 걸리거나 독감 증세가 나타나자마자, 나는 마치 무슨 치명적인 병에 걸린 것처럼 행동하고, 순교의 고통을 느끼는 듯한 표정을 지으면서 내게 남은 며칠 동안의 삶을 용감하게 마주할 것임을 보여주려 한다.

17 **2019 덕성여대** ▶▶▶ MSG p.31 ④

cause+목적어+to부정사 ▶ cause가 5형식 동사로 쓰이는 경우, 목적보어 자리에는 to부정사가 온다. 그러므로 ④를 to look으로 고쳐야 한다.

bidding n. 입찰; (경매의) 가격 제시, 호가 catapult v. ~로 쏘다, 발사하다, 발진시키다

애플(Apple)의 사업 확장은 실리콘밸리에서 증가하고 있는 엔지니어 영입 경쟁을 반영하는 것이다. 프로그래머 영입을 위한 경쟁적 노력이 급료를 끌어올리고 있으며, 이것은 또한 샌프란시스코 베이 지역 여러 곳의 주택 평균 가격을 100만 달러 이상으로 치솟게 하고 있다. 그래서 많은 첨단 기술자들이 다른 곳에서 살기로 결정하고 있으며, 이로 인해 애플과 구글 같은 주요 첨단기술 기업의 고용주들은 그들이 필요로 하는 직원들을 새로운 곳에서 찾고 있다.

18 **2020 건국대** ▶▶▶ MSG p.179

명사를 수식하는 형용사 ▶ 다섯 번째 문장의 주절은 앞을 보지 못하는 헬렌 켈러와 앞을 볼 수 있는 사람들을 비교한 동등 비교 구문이다. '앞을 볼 수 있는', '시력이 정상인'이라는 뜻의 형용사는 sighted이므로 ④를 sighted로 고쳐야 한다. 참고로 sighting은 '목격', '관측'의 뜻으로 쓰이는 명사이다.

lose one's sight 시력을 잃다 frustrated a. 좌절감을 느끼는 exhausted a. 기진맥진한

헬렌 켈러(Helen Keller)는 아주 어린 나이에 시력을 잃어서 어렸을 때 매우 좌절감을 느꼈다. 무엇보다도, 그녀는 말을 들을 수도 말을 할 수도 없었기 때문에 그녀 주위에 어떤 일이 일어나는지 이해할 수 없었다. 그녀는 자신의 어머니가 말을 할 때, 입술을 움직인다는 것을 알고 있었지만, 이것이 그녀에게는 무의미한 것이었다. 그녀는 어머니가 무엇을 하고 있는지 이해할 수 없었다. 다음으로, 그녀가 단어들이 무엇인지 알게 되자, 자신은 결코 그 단어들로 시력이 정상인 사람들만큼 빨리 의사소통할 수 없을 거라 그녀는 생각했다. 이런 모든 좌절감으로 인해 그녀는 지칠 때까지 자주 울고 비명을 지르곤 했다.

19 **2020 명지대** ▶▶▶ MSG p.55

derive A from B의 수동태 ▶ derive는 'derive A from B(A를 B에서 파생시키다)'라는 용법으로 쓰이는 동사이다. 이를 수동태로 고칠 경우, A is derived from B가 되므로, ②를 derived from으로 고쳐야 한다. ③ which의 선행사는 the water가 아니라 tiny pieces of plastic인데 pieces가 복수여서 which 다음의 복수동사 end는 수 일치하여 맞다.

straw n. 빨대 exfoliant n. 각질제거제 microbead n. 미세입자 garment n. 의류, 옷 end up in 결국 ~로 끝나다 expedition n. 원정대 the Antarctic 남극

각국 정부들이 미세입자가 들어있는 플라스틱 빨대와 각질제거제를 금지함에 따라, 플라스틱 오염은 2018년에 지속가능성 논쟁의 중심에 있었다. 전 세계 의류의 60%에 폴리에스테르가 들어있다는 것을 감안하면, 플라스틱 오염에 대한 상당한 책임이 패션업계에 있는데, 이 폴리에스테르는 세계에

서 가장 흔한 형태의 플라스틱인 폴리에틸렌 테레프탈레이트(PET)에서 파생된 물질이다. 세탁하면, 폴리에스테르 의류는 종종 극미세 플라스틱 조각들을 물속으로 배출하게 되는데, 이 극미세 플라스틱 조각들은 결국 강과 바다로 흘러가며, (물속의) 동물들이 극미세 플라스틱 조각들을 먹게 된다. 그린피스(Greenpeace) 남극 원정대는 미세 플라스틱 조각들이 심지어 지구의 가장 외딴 지역에서도 발견될 수 있다는 것을 올해 초 밝혀주었다.

---

20 2020 광운대 ▶▶▶ MSG p.95

정비문 ▶ ① 동사 know의 목적어로 명사절 that절이 왔으며, such는 'such+a[an]+형용사+명사'의 어순을 올바르게 취하고 있다. ③ 부정대명사 anyone을 interesting이 후치수식해주고 있다. ④ 'the 비교급, the 비교급'이 쓰인 경우로, 보통 'the+비교급+주어+동사, the+비교급+주어+동사'의 어순을 취하는데, 이때 be동사는 생략가능하다. ⑤ 'so ~ that' 구문이 쓰였는데, 이때 hardly anyone은 'almost no one'과 같은 의미의 주어로, 주어의 경우 hardly가 있어도 도치가 일어나지 않는다. 따라서 ⑤는 맞는 문장이다. 반면, ②에서 enough가 to부정사와 함께 쓰여 '형용사+enough+to 동사원형'의 어순을 맞게 취하고 있지만, 주어인 This chair가 to stand on it의 it이 가리키는 것이므로, 중복되는 it을 삭제해야 한다. 마찬가지로 The chair is light enough to lift.(그 의자는 들어올리기에 충분히 가볍다.)는 맞지만 The chair is light enough to lift it.(그 의자는 그것을 들어올리기에 충분히 가볍다.)는 틀린 문장이다.

beef n. 소고기 pass the exam 시험에 합격하다

① 나는 그 집이 그렇게 오래된 집이라는 것을 알지 못했다.
② 이 의자는 위에 (올라가) 서있기에 충분히 튼튼하지 않다.
③ 그 파티에서 관심을 끄는 누군가를 만났니?
④ 소고기는 가격이 더 비쌀수록, 맛이 더 좋다.
⑤ 그 시험은 너무 어려워서, 거의 어느 누구도 합격하지 못했다.

01 ②	**02** ①	**03** ③	**04** ④	**05** ②	**06** ③	**07** ①	**08** ③	**09** ②	**10** ②
11 ④	**12** ③	**13** ③	**14** ②	**15** ④	**16** ②	**17** ③	**18** ⑤	**19** ①	**20** ③

01   2014 단국대 ▶▶▶ MSG p.137   ②

전치사+관계대명사 ▶ 빈칸 이하는 the organization을 수식할 수 있는 관계대명사절이어야 하는데, 빈칸 뒤에 완전한 절이 왔으므로 '전치사+관계대명사'가 들어가야 한다. they are a part of the organization이므로 전치사는 of여서 ②의 of which가 적절하다. ① that이 관계대명사인 경우 뒤에 불완전한 절이 와야 하는데 완전한 절이 왔다. 또한 동격의 명사절로 볼 수도 있지만 의미상 적절하지 않다. ③ whereby는 by which와 같은 표현이다. ④ 빈칸 앞에 명사 organization이 있으므로 선행사를 포함한 관계대명사 what은 올 수 없다.

pay attention to ~에 주의를 기울이다 undermine v. 서서히 손상시키다

효율성을 걱정하는 기업은 직원의 행동에 주의를 기울여야 하는데, 직원들 각자가 저지르는 실수가 종종 그들이 그 일부를 이루는 전체 조직의 효율성을 서서히 손상시키기 때문이다.

02   2012 서울여대 ▶▶▶ MSG p.27, p.33   ①

want+목적어+to부정사(목적보어) ▶ a former prime minister는 주어인 Jean-Pierre Raffarin과 동격이며, where common language is English는 international organizations를 수식하는 관계부사절이다. 주어와 동사 사이에 삽입된 문장이 길어서 복잡해 보이지만 주어는 Jean-Pierre Raffarin이고, 동사는 wants이며, 목적어는 all French people이다. want가 5형식 동사로 쓰일 때 목적보어로는 to부정사가 와야 하므로 ① to insist가 정답이다.

prime minister 국무총리, 수상 common language 공용어

전 프랑스 수상인 장 피에르 라파랭(Jean-Pierre Raffarin)은 영어가 공용어로 사용되는 국제기구에서 고위직에서 일하는 모든 프랑스 사람들이 불어로 말하는 것을 주장하길 원한다.

03   2020 가톨릭대 ▶▶▶ MSG p.138   ③

문의 구성 ▶ ②는 that 이하에 시제를 가진 동사가 없어 관계절이 되지 않고 ④는 3형식동사 employ의 수동태 다음에 목적어 명사가 오게 만들므로 부적절하다. ①은 선행사를 '피카소와 브라크'로 본 것이므로 수일치에 의해 employ여야 한다. ③은 created부터 Braque까지는 삽입된 것이고, 선행사는 an artistic movement여서 관계대명사 which와 단수동사 employs 모두 적절하다.

cubism n. 입체파, 큐비즘(20세기 초의 미술 운동) geometric a. 기하학적인

큐비즘은 파블로 피카소(Pablo Picasso)와 조르주 브라크(Georges Braque)가 창시한 것으로, 인간과 사물의 형태를 묘사하는 데 있어 기하학적인 모양을 사용하는 예술 운동이다.

04   2018 아주대 ▶▶▶ MSG p.234   ④

문의 구성 ▶ 주어로 의문사가 이끄는 간접의문절이 주어져 있으므로, 빈칸에는 먼저 동사인 is가 오고, '중요한 것'에 해당하는 표현으로 '선행사를 포함하는 관계대명사 what과 동사 matters로 이루어진 관계절 what matters'가 이어지면 된다. 따라서 ④가 적절하다. 여기서 matter는 '중요하다'는 의미의 완전자동사이다.

tale n. 이야기 matter v. 중요하다

인생은 이야기와 같다. 얼마나 기냐가 아니라, 얼마나 좋으냐가 중요한 것이다.

05   2021 서울여대 ▶▶▶ MSG p.37   ②

have an effect on ▶ 전체 문장의 주어는 Awareness of the harmful effect이고 동사는 has exploded이므로, plastic부터 빈칸까지는 앞의 명사를 수식하는 역할을 해야 한다. 그런데 명사 effect는 have an effect on의 형태로 '~에 영향을 미치다'라는 의미로 쓰인다. 따라서 ②가 정답이 되며, effect 뒤에는 목적격 관계대명사 which가 생략돼 있다.

awareness n. 인식 explode v. 폭발하다; (인구 등이) 폭발적으로 불어나다

플라스틱이 환경에 미칠 수 있는 해로운 영향에 대한 인식이 최근 들어 폭발적으로 커졌다.

06   2007 동아대 ▶▶▶ MSG p.142   ③

유사관계대명사 as ▶ as much나 so much의 짝으로는 원급비교를 이루도록 as가 오는데 as가 유사관계대명사이므로 as 다음은 또 관계대명사인 what절이 아니라 그냥 '주어+동사'로 이루어진 절이 이어진다. 맨 끝의 to는 to work을 대신한 대부정사이다.

be told to do ~하라는 말을 듣다

헬렌(Helen)은 지시받은 것만큼만 일했다.

07 **2018 가톨릭대** ▶▶▶ MSG p.211 ①

주어와 동사의 수일치 ▶ 질병의 명칭인 measles는 형태는 복수지만 단수로 취급하며, '방법'의 의미로 쓰인 means는 단수와 복수로 모두 쓰이긴 하나, 도시에서 탈출하는 것이 유일한 생존 방법이라고 했으므로 두 번째 빈칸에는 단수동사가 적절하다. 따라서 ①이 정답이다.

measles n. 홍역 means n. 수단, 방법 escape v. 탈출하다

이 도시에서 많은 사람들이 홍역으로 목숨을 잃었으며, 이제 유일한 생존 방법은 그 도시에서 탈출하는 것인 것 같다.

08 **2015 상명대** ▶▶▶ MSG p.222 ③

only 부사구에 의한 도치 ▶ only를 포함한 부사구가 문두에 나와 강조될 때에는 부정 부사어가 문두에 올 때와 마찬가지로 도치가 일어난다. 따라서 'only 부사어+조동사+주어+본동사'의 형태로 쓰인 ③ could chlamydial infections be detected가 빈칸에 들어가야 한다.

chlamydial a. 클라미디어(성병 등의 병원체)의 infection n. 감염 detect v. 발견하다

최근까지는, 오직 복잡한 검사에 의해서만 클라미디어 감염이 발견될 수 있었다.

09 **2021 세종대** ▶▶▶ MSG p.90 ②

부정사와 의미상 주어 ▶ 가주어 it에 호응하는 진주어 to부정사가 필요하며, to부정사의 의미상 주어는 'for+(대)명사'로 나타낸다. 따라서 ②가 적절하다.

embarrassing a. 난처한, 쑥스러운; 창피한

성인 여성이 작은 동네에서 길을 잃은 것은 꽤나 난처한 일이었다.

10 **2022 서울여대** ▶▶▶ MSG p.33, p.75 ②

동사 demand의 용법 ▶ 동사 demand는 사람을 목적어로 삼지 않으며, 'demand+목적어+to do'의 형태로는 쓰지 않는다. demand는 that절을 목적어로 받으며 that절의 동사는 '(should)+동사원형'이어야 한다. 따라서 ②를 demanded that they나 demanded that they should로 고쳐야 한다.

move v. 이사하다, 이동하다

경찰이 그들에게 사무실에서 이사해갈 것을 아무리 강력히 요구해도 소수만이 그렇게 하기로 동의했다.

11 **2019 한국외대** ▶▶▶ MSG p.211 ④

주어와 동사의 수일치 ▶ whether 절의 주어는 the investment이고, we are making in these technologies는 the investment를 수식하는 관계대명사절이며, 본동사는 give이다. 주어인 the investment가 단수이므로 동사를 수 일치시켜서 ④는 단수동사 gives가 되어야 한다.

make an investment in ~에 투자하다 value for money 돈[가격]에 합당한 가치

컴퓨터가 교육에 도입되기 시작한 이후, 사람들은 이 기술에 우리가 하고 있는 투자가 투자한 돈에 합당한 가치를 우리에게 주고 있는지를 물어왔다.

12 **2017 한양대** ▶▶▶ MSG p.10 ③

동사 prove의 용법 ▶ prove 동사는 분명한 행위자에 의해 증명 과정을 통해 증명된다는 의미일 때는 5형식동사의 수동태로 be proved to be ~로 쓰이지만, 문제에서처럼 증명하는 분명한 행위자 없이 시간이 지나면서 드러나고 판명된다는 의미일 때는 2형식동사 구문 prove to be ~로 쓰이는 것이 일반적이다. 따라서 ③을 proved로 고쳐야 한다.

fall short of ~에 미치지 못하다 faith n. 믿음, 신뢰 statesman n. 정치가

우리로서는 놀랍게도, 에릭 디킨슨(Erick Dickinson)은 정치가로서 실패자인 것으로 드러났을 때, 그의 부모님의 기대에 못 미치게 되어, 아들의 성공 잠재력을 계속 믿었던 부모님을 실망시켰다.

13 **2019 단국대** ▶▶▶ MSG p.105 ③

동사와 과거분사의 구분 ▶ whether we realize it or not은 삽입절로, 이를 제거하고 보면, dates는 from과 연결되는데, 이때 dates는 문맥상 명사가 아니라 '시작되다'라는 뜻의 동사로 쓰였다. 한 문장에 dates와 wrote라는 두 개의 동사가 주어져 있는 상황이므로, ③의 wrote를 a paper를 후치수식해주는 과거분사인 written으로 고쳐야 한다. 참고로 a paper written은 원래 a paper which was written에서 '관계대명사+be동사'인 which was가 생략된 형태이다.

perspective n. 견해 metropolitan a. 대도시의 settlement n. 거주 date from ~때부터 시작되다 define v. ~의 경계를 정하다 suburban a. 교외의 zone n. 지대, 지역

우리가 그것을 알든 모르든, 대도시의 정착 과정에 관해 우리가 가지고 있는 견해의 많은 부분은 사회학자 어니스트 버지스(Ernest W. Burgess)가 1925년에 저술한 한 논문에서 시작된다. 네 개의 도시/교외 정착 지대를 정의한 사람이 바로 버지스였다.

14 2019 단국대 ▶▶▶ MSG p.211 ②

주어와 동사의 수일치 ▶ ②에 쓰인 동사 have의 주어는 photos or videos가 아니라, Amazon's recent acquisition of Body Lab's이다. 따라서 단수 주어에 맞게 동사도 단수가 되어야 하므로 ②를 has로 고쳐야 한다.

acquisition n. 인수 artificial intelligence 인공 지능 3D a. 3차원의, 입체의 speculate on ~을 생각하다

사진이나 동영상으로부터 사람들의 입체화된 체형 및 동작을 파악하는 인간인지 인공 지능 소프트웨어 제공업체인 바디 랩스(Body Lab's)를 아마존이 최근에 인수한 것은 많은 사람들로 하여금 신체 이미지화 기술이 얼마나 빠르게 향상되어 온라인 쇼핑에 영향을 미칠지를 생각해 보게 한다.

15 2020 가천대 ▶▶▶ MSG p.233 ④

부가의문문 ▶ 부가의문문은 주절이 긍정문이면 부정으로, 부정문이면 긍정으로 하고, 주절에 be동사나 조동사가 있으면 사용한 be동사나 조동사를 그대로 쓰며, 주절의 동사가 일반 동사이면 do동사를 써서 나타낸다. 마지막 문장의 경우, 주절의 동사가 일반 동사인 sounds이므로 적절한 부가의문문은 doesn't it이다. 따라서 ④를 doesn't로 고친다. ① 부사로 쓰인 early의 비교급이다. ② not to mention은 '~은 말할 것도 없고'라는 의미의 관용표현이다.

wane v. 작아지다; 끝이 가까워지다 take note of 주목하다 acceptance letter 합격 통지서 caliber n. 직경; 재간; 등급, 품질 extent n. 크기, 길이; 정도, 범위 ominous a. 불길한, 나쁜 징조의

8학년이 끝나가면서, 많은 8학년 학생들은 이전에는 분명하지 않았을지도 모를 한 가지 사실에 주목한다. 그것은 지금부터는 성적이 고등학교 내신 성적에 나타난다는 점이다. 시험 점수는 말할 것도 없고, 고등학교 내신 성적은 대학 합격 통지서로 이어진다. 다니는 대학의 등급이 인생에서 거두게 될 성공의 정도를 결정한다. 좀 불길하게 들린다. 그렇지 않은가?

16 2020 가천대 ▶▶▶ MSG p.126 ②

문의 구성 ▶ 두 번째 문장의 as절에서, to make의 목적어는 주어인 their smaller parts이며, 따라서 make 뒤에 다시 목적어를 표시해서는 안 된다. make 뒤의 목적어 them을 삭제하여 ②를 cheaper to make로 고쳐야 한다. ③ bend가 자동사로 쓰였다.

bend v. 휘어지다 incorporate v. 통합하다, 합병하다 disinfectant n. 소독제, 살균제

최근 들어 나노기술 분야에서 흥미로운 발전이 매우 많이 있었다. 예를 들어, 컴퓨터는 작은 부품을 만드는 것이 더 저렴해짐에 따라 점점 성능이 좋아지고 있다. 뿐만 아니라, 안경테는 이제 부러지지 않으면서 특이한 모양으로 휘어질 수 있다. 또한 은(銀)은 천연 소독제로 의복과 식품 포장재 속에 함유되고 있다.

17 2021 가천대 ▶▶▶ MSG p.168 ③

비교대상의 일치 ▶ 비교구문에서는 비교대상이 일치해야 하는데, greater than 전후로 our means와 the nobleman이 와서 비교대상이 일치하지 않는다. 따라서 ③의 the nobleman을 the nobleman's means로 고치거나 means를 생략한 the nobleman's로 고쳐야 한다. ②는 '도중에, 갑자기'라는 뜻의 부사로 동사 stop을 수식한다.

nobleman n. 귀족 cultivated a. 교양이 있는, 세련된 conduce to ~에 도움이 되다 pedagogue n. 교사 parson n. 교구 주임 목사 parish n. (교회·성당의) 교구 flourish v. 번창하다 provincial a. 지방의; 편협한

취미가 세련된 귀족이 자신의 교양에 도움이 되는 것이면 무엇이든 자기 주변에 두는 것처럼, 마찬가지로 그 마을도 그렇게 하게(교양에 도움 되는 무엇이든 주변에 두게) 하고, 도중에 (교양에 도움 되는 것으로서) 교육자, 교구목사, 교구도서관 정도에서 멈추게 하지 마라. 나는 우리의 주변 환경이 (교양에 도움 되는 것으로) 더욱 풍성함에 따라, 우리의 자산이 귀족의 자산보다 더 크다고 확신한다. 뉴잉글랜드는 세상의 모든 현인들을 고용하여 데려와서 그녀(뉴잉글랜드)를 가르치게 할 수 있고 그러면 전혀 편협할 수가 없다.

18 2022 건국대 ▶▶▶ MSG p.105 ⑤

현재분사 ▶ ⑤를 포함하고 있는 문장의 정동사는 be동사 are이다. 그러므로 ⑤를 앞의 명사를 수식하는 분사 형태로 고쳐야 옳은 문장이 될 수 있다. children이 live하는 행위의 주체이므로 능동을 나타내는 현재분사가 적절하다. ⑤를 living으로 고친다. ① 주절의 주어가 trek하는 행위의 주체이므로 능동의 분사구문이 되었다. ② upon[on] ~ing는 '~하자마자'라는 의미의 관용표현이다. ③ help의 목적보어로는 to부정사와 원형부정사가 모두 가능하다. ④ 관계대명사의 수는 선행사에 일치시킨다.

trek v. 여행하다, 걸어서 가다 orphan v. 고아로 만들다 poverty-stricken a. 가난에 시달리는 outreach n. (지역 주민에 대한 기관의 적극적인) 봉사[원조] 활동

매기 도인(Maggie Doyne)은 히말라야 산맥을 여행하면서 가난에 시달리고 있던 네팔의 고아 수백 명을 만났다. 고향으로 돌아오자마자, 그녀는 지역 사회에 이 아이들을 위한 안전하고 사랑스러운 집을 지을 수 있도록 자신을 도와달라고 부탁했다. 놀랍게도, 그녀의 이웃들은 그 생각을 지지해주었다. 그들의 도움을 받아, 도인과 네팔 지역 사회는 코필라 벨리(Kopila Valley) 어린이집을 지었는데, 이것은 어린 고아들, 거리의 어린이들, 어린이 노동자들, 그리고 학대받는 아이들에게 교육과 건강관리와 자라날 사랑스러운 장소를 제공하는 집이다. 오늘날, 25명의 아이들이 그 집에 살고 있으며, 60명의 아이들이 코필라 원조 프로그램을 통해 학교에 등록되어 있다.

19 2020 명지대 ▶▶▶ MSG p.133 ①

as 양보절 ▶ as 양보절은 '형용사+as+S + V'의 어순을 취하는데, 이때 주어가 매우 길 경우, 주어와 동사의 자리가 바뀔 수 있다. 두 번째 문장에 as 양보절이 쓰였는데, 주어가 복수이므로 ①의 was를 were로 고쳐야 한다.

Native American 아메리카 원주민 conquistador n. 정복자 outnumber v. ~보다 수적으로 우세하다 nasty a. 끔찍한 decimate v. 떼죽음 당하게 하다 wipe out ~을 완전히 없애버리다 the tropics 열대 지방

역사에서 병원균이 행한 역할의 가장 암울한 사례는 1492년 콜럼버스(Columbus)의 항해로 시작된 유럽인들의 아메리카 대륙 정복에 있다. 스페인 정복자들에게 목숨을 잃었던 아메리카 원주민들의 희생자 수가 매우 많긴 했지만, 이 희생자 수는 스페인 병원균에게 목숨을 잃었던 아메리카 원주민들의 희생자 수에 비하면 압도적으로 적었다. 왜 아메리카 대륙과 유럽 대륙 사이를 오가는 끔찍한 병원균의 숫자가 그렇게 달랐을까? 왜 (유럽 대륙) 대신 아메리카 대륙에 있던 질병들이 스페인 침략자들을 떼죽음 당하게 하고 유럽으로 건너가서 유럽 인구의 95%를 궤멸시키지는 못했던 것일까? 아프리카와 아시아의 열대지방에서 유럽의 예비 정복자들의 (원주민) 대학살뿐 아니라, 유라시아 병원균이 초래한 많은 다른 원주민들의 대학살에 대해서도 유사한 의문이 생긴다.

20   2022 광운대 ▶▶▶ MSG p.75   ③

정비문 ▶ ③ what if ~는 '~하면 어떡하지?'라는 의미로, 그 뒤에는 '주어+동사'가 온다. What if you will be late for the meeting tomorrow?가 되어야 한다. ① how come 뒤에는 '주어+동사'가 오며, why의 의미를 가진다. ② help의 목적격 보어로는 to부정사와 원형부정사가 모두 가능하다. ⑤ imagine은 동명사를 목적어로 취하며, anybody는 동명사의 의미상 주어이다.

how come 어째서

① 어째서 그 건물에서 나오시는 건가요?
② 아빠는 내가 새 아파트를 구입하도록 도와줄 것이다.
③ 만약 당신이 내일 회의에 늦으면 어떡하죠?
④ 그는 마라톤 완주에 실패했지만, 최선을 다했다.
⑤ 그 사람처럼 멍청한 사람을 상상할 수 있겠어요?

TEST 21

01 ①	**02** ②	**03** ③	**04** ①	**05** ①	**06** ③	**07** ④	**08** ②	**09** ④	**10** ③
11 ①	**12** ②	**13** ②	**14** ④	**15** ④	**16** ②	**17** ④	**18** ⑤	**19** ①	**20** ③

01 **2007 한양대** ▶▶▶ MSG p.131 ①

적절한 접속사의 사용 ▶ ④ otherwise는 부사이므로 빈칸 앞뒤의 두 절을 연결할 수 없고 ② since와 ③ when은 접속사여서 두 절을 연결할 수 있지만 의미상 부적절하다. '~이 아닌 한, 만약 ~이 아니면'이라는 의미의 ① unless가 정답이다.

critic n. 비평가 unanimous a. 만장일치의

독서할 때 모든 사람은 그 자신의 최고의 비평가이다. 박식한 사람들이 책에 대해 무엇을 말하든 간에, 그들이 책에 대해 아무리 만장일치로 격찬하든 간에, 만약 책이 여러분의 관심을 끌 수 없다면 그것은 여러분과 상관없는 책이다.

02 **2015 가천대** ▶▶▶ MSG p.138 ②

관계구(전치사+관계대명사+to부정사) ▶ 앞뒤로 열거된 다른 것들과 마찬가지로 빈칸에서 future까지도 선행명사 means를 수식하는데, 명사를 수식하는 관계절이 '전치사+관계대명사'로 시작될 때 관계절의 동사를 to부정사로 바꾸어 '전치사+관계대명사+to부정사'의 관계구로 나타낼 수 있다. 관계절의 경우와 마찬가지로 관계대명사 앞의 전치사는 선행명사에 의해 결정되는데 by means of(~에 의해서)에서 알 수 있듯이 means는 by와 함께 쓰이므로 빈칸에는 ②가 적절하다.

ritual n. (종교적) 의식 recite v. 암송하다 holy day (종교적) 축제일, (특히 일요일 이외의) 성일(聖日) ordinance n. 의식

정의에 상관없이, 모든 종교는 공통적으로 특정한 요소들이 있다. 예를 들면, 행해야 할 의식행사, 암송해야 할 기도문, 자주 방문해야 할 곳이나 피해야 할 곳, 지켜야 할 성일(聖日), 미래를 예측할 방법, 읽고 공부할 다수의 서적, 단언해야 할 진리, 따라야 할 카리스마 넘치는 지도자들과 준수해야 할 의식 등이 그것이다.

03 **2021 서울여대** ▶▶▶ MSG p.224 ③

'so + (조)동사 + 주어' 구문 ▶ 앞의 긍정적 진술에 덧붙여 '~도 역시[또한] 그러하다'는 의미를 갖는 표현은 so가 먼저 오고 주어와 (조)동사가 도치된 'so+(조)동사+주어'이다. 따라서 빈칸에는 ③이 적절하다.

a third 1/3

재즈 음악의 약 3분의 1은 블루스 형태이고 로큰롤의 절반 이상도 또한 그러하다.

04 **2021 한국외대** ▶▶▶ MSG p.168 ①

가목적어 구문 ▶ '~을 알리다'는 뜻의 make ~ known 구문이 쓰였는데, make의 목적어가 명사가 아니라 that절일 경우, 가목적어 it을 내세우고 진목적어인 that절은 문미에 배치할 수 있다. 따라서 가목적어 it과 목적격 보어인 known이 쓰인 ①의 making it known이 빈칸에 적절하다.

detain v. 감금하다, 억류하다 abuse n. 학대

그 센터에 감금된 사람들은 학대가 계속되어서는 안 된다는 것을 오늘 알리고 있다.

05 **2011 고려대** ▶▶▶ MSG p.137 ①

전치사+관계대명사 ▶ ②와 ④를 넣으면 ②의 the cases와 ④의 a case가 주어 역할을 하게 되어 뒤에 오는 동사 conflicts와 절을 형성하게 되는데, except for 다음에는 절이 올 수 없으므로 ②와 ④는 정답이 될 수 없다. 관계대명사 which 다음에 완전한 절이 오려면 관계대명사 앞에 전치사가 위치해서 '전치사+which'의 형태가 되어야 한다. 따라서 ①이 정답이 된다.

inalienable a. 양도할 수 없는, 빼앗을 수 없는 autonomy n. 자율, 자치, 자주

모든 인간은 어떤 양도할 수 없는 권리를 갖고 태어난다. 다시 말해, 그 자율의 행사가 공공의 이익과 충돌되는 경우를 제외하고는 모든 사람의 자율은 존중되어야 한다.

06 **2013 서울여대** ▶▶▶ MSG p.136 ③

소유격 관계대명사절 ▶ 한 문장 안에 두 개의 본동사 started와 was가 있는 문장이므로, 접속사가 필요하며 그 역할을 관계대명사 which가 맡고 있다. 여기서 which를 달리 표현하면 and it이 되는데, it은 앞에 언급된 a movement를 지칭한다. 해석상, '운동'이 탁구를 중요한 스포츠로 만드는 것이 아니라, '운동의 목표'가 탁구를 중요한 스포츠로 만드는 것이므로 관계대명사로 표현하면 whose goal이나 the goal of which로 된다. 따라서 정답은 ③ the goal of which이다. ① 관계대명사 which

뒤에는 불완전해야 하는데 which goal은 which이하의 구조가 완전하므로 답이 될 수 없다. ④ which of the goal은 어순이 잘못 됐다.

table tennis 탁구

1921년에 세계 여러 지역에서 하나의 운동이 시작됐는데, 그 운동의 목표는 탁구를 중요한 스포츠로 만드는 것이었다.

07 2022 한국외대 ▶▶▶ MSG p.57   ④

to 부정사의 수동태 ▶ say 동사는 '주어+be said+ to부정사'의 형태로 쓰여 '~라고 전해지다, ~라는 말이 있다'라는 의미로 쓰인다. it은 love를 가리키고 눈이 멀어 고통을 당한다는 의미가 되기 위해서는 부정사의 수동태가 쓰여야 하므로 ④가 정답이다.

vigilant a. 방심하지 않는 watchman n. 경비원, 파수꾼 blindness n. 맹목, 무분별(無分別) afflict v. 괴롭히다, 피해를 입히다

사랑은, 비록 눈먼 사랑이 고통 받는다는 말이 있지만, 방심하지 않는 파수꾼이다.

08 2018 아주대 ▶▶▶ MSG p.83   ②

may well과 may as well의 구별 ▶ may well은 '~하는 것도 당연하다'는 의미인 반면, may as well은 '차라리 ~하는 편이 낫다'라는 의미이다. 그리고 '~로 의심받다'는 의미가 되어야 하므로, 수동태인 be suspected of로 나타내야 한다. the opinion (that) money will do everything에서 동격의 절을 이끄는 접속사 that이 생략된 것이다.

suspect v. A(사람) of B(범죄, 혐의 등) A가 B한 것이라고 의심하다

돈이면 무엇이든 다 된다고 생각하는 사람은 돈을 위해 무엇이든 한다고 의심받는 것이 당연하다.

09 2018 세종대 ▶▶▶ MSG p.236   ④

삽입 가능한 동격 표현 ▶ 빈칸 앞은 주어이고 빈칸 뒤는 술부여서 둘을 그대로 이으면 완전한 문장이 되므로 빈칸에는 삽입 표현이 적절하다. 절이 주어와 동사 사이에 삽입되려면 반드시 접속사가 필요하다. 그러므로 접속사 없이 주어와 동사가 이어진 ①과 ②는 부적절하고, ③ 술부도 삽입될 수 없다. 따라서 명사구인 ④가 정답이 되며, 이것은 바로 앞의 the state oil company와 동격을 이룬다.

deepening a. 악화되는 threaten v. 협박하다; (나쁜 일이) 일어날 것 같다, (위험 따위가) 임박하다 destabilize v. 불안정하게 하다, 동요시키다 dire a. 무서운; 비참한 recession n. 퇴거, 경기후퇴 mainstay n. 큰 돛대의 버팀줄, 대들보

그 나라 경제의 대들보인 국영 석유 회사의 악화되는 문제가 심각한 경기침체에 직면해 있는 정부를 더욱 불안정하게 할 우려가 있다.

10 2022 서울여대 ▶▶▶ MSG p.149   ③

of+추상명사 ▶ be동사 are 이하에는 results의 성질을 나타내도록 형용사가 보어로 와야 하겠는데, ③에는 명사가 보어로 주어져 있으므로 옳지 않다. 'of+추상명사'는 형용사의 역할을 할 수 있으므로, ③을 of higher quality로 고치면 옳은 문장이 될 수 있다. ④ those는 results를 대신하고 있다.

rank v. 등급을 짓다, 평가하다 feature n. 특징, 특색

이 순위 지정 기능 때문에 구글의 검색 결과는 다른 검색 엔진의 그것보다 더 정확하고 질적으로도 더 뛰어나다.

11 2018 중앙대 ▶▶▶ MSG p.57   ①

수동태 ▶ 새들의 비행 속도는 '측정되는' 것이므로 수동태로 표현해야 한다. 따라서 ①을 have been clocked로 바꾸어야 한다.

clock v. (속도 등을) 기록하다 assert v. 주장하다 migrate v. 이동하다, 이주하다

새들의 비행 속도는 여러 차례 측정되었지만 대개는 지상 속도로 측정된 것이고, 이주하는 새들은 다른 때보다 이주하는 동안에 더 빨리 이동한다고 주장된다.

12 2010 명지대 ▶▶▶ MSG p.10   ②

완전자동사의 유사보어 ▶ grows up 뒤에 올 수 있는 유사보어의 올바른 형태는 형용사이므로 ②의 부사 poorly를 형용사 poor로 바꿔 주어야 한다. 원래 보어를 필요로 하지 않는 완전자동사가 보어를 취할 경우 그러한 보어를 유사보어(준보어)라 말한다.

goddess n. (애정의 대상으로서) 여신 같은 존재, 절세미녀 befoul v. 더럽히다, 헐뜯다

그 이탈리아 이민자들의 아들은 샌프란시스코에서 가난하게 자라 당대의 가장 뛰어난 야구 선수가 되어 미국의 한 절세미녀와 결혼하고 말이나 행동에 있어서 그가 쌓아온 업적과 위대함을 결코 더럽히지 않는다.

13 2019 국민대 ▶▶▶ MSG p.171   ②

them과 those의 구분 ▶ 인칭대명사 them 뒤에는 수식어구가 올 수 없으므로, 수식어구가 올 수 있는 those로 ②를 고쳐야 한다. ①과 ④는 명사이다.

take a deep breath 심호흡을 하다 systolic blood pressure 수축기 혈압

혈압을 재기 전에 30초 동안 여섯 번의 심호흡을 한 환자는 30초 동안 심호흡 없이 쉬고 있었던 환자들과 비교했을 때 수축기 혈압이 3포인트 이상 떨어졌다는 것을 한 연구가 발견했다.

summit n. (산의) 정상, 꼭대기; 절정 pull up 멈춰 서다 conserve v. 절약하다; 보존하다 turn something off (전기·가스 등을) 끄다 clear v. (머리나 정신이) 맑아지다

내가 정상을 떠난 직후 정상을 떠났던 피터는 곧 내 뒤에 멈춰 섰다. 나의 산소탱크의 산소가 얼마나 남았든 간에 그 산소를 절약하기 위해, 나는 그에게 내 배낭 안에 손을 넣어서 조절장치의 밸브를 잠가달라고 부탁을 했고, 피터는 내 부탁을 들어주었다. 그 이후 10분 동안, 나는 놀라울 정도로 기분이 좋았다. 내 머리가 맑아진 것이다. 실제로 나는 산소가 켜져 있을 때보다 덜 피곤한 것 같았다.

---

14   2019 단국대   ▶▶▶ MSG p.111   ④

동사와 분사구문의 구분 ▶ Long viewed by ~ major가 philosophy를 수식해 주고 있으며, philosophy ~ practical major가 완전한 주절이 되므로, offers 이하가 완전한 주절에 연결될 수 있도록 ④를 and offers나 분사구문인 offering으로 고쳐주어야 한다.

stereotypical a. 진부한; 정형화된 a host of 수많은 transferable a. 전이 가능한, 다른 일에서도 쓸 수 있는 with relevance to ~에 관한

오랫동안 많은 사람들에 의해 진부하고 쓸모없는 전공으로 간주되어온 철학이 지금은 많은 학생들에 의해 사실상 매우 유용하고 실용적인 전공으로 여겨지고 있으며, 현대의 직장과 관련된 수많은 이전 가능한 기술들을 학생들에게 제공해주고 있다.

---

18   2022 건국대   ▶▶▶ MSG p.218   ⑤

to 부정사의 병치 ▶ 마지막 문장에서 that절의 reached는 have found의 found와 병치된 것이 아니라 to land와 병치된 것이므로 ⑤를 to reach 또는 reach로 고쳐야 한다. 참고로 to 부정사가 병치될 때는 뒤의 to는 생략할 수 있다.

frontier n. 변경(邊境); (특정 지식·활동 영역의) 한계 dimension n. 차원, 관점 sparkling a. 반짝거리는; (음료가) 거품이 이는, 탄산이 든 fascinate v. 마음을 사로잡다, 매혹하다

호기심이라는 본능은 인간의 개인적 그리고 집단적 진보에 크게 기여한다. 그것은 사람들로 하여금 미지의 것을 찾고 아직 이해되지 않는 것들에 대한 답을 찾게 한다. 따라서 보다 중대한 분야에서, 호기심은 인간으로 하여금 새로운 변경(邊境)을 모든 차원에서 조사하고 정복하게 한다. 예를 들면, 밤하늘의 반짝이는 천체는 인간이 달에 착륙하고 그 너머에 도달하는 방법을 발견했을 정도로 인간이 가진 호기심이라는 본능을 매료시켰다.

---

15   2020 국민대   ▶▶▶ MSG p.211   ④

주어와 동사의 수일치 ▶ 두 번째 문장은 부사구의 의미를 강조하기 위해 With that yearly influx of people이 문두에 왔고 본동사 come과 주어 a need가 도치된 문장이다. 주어는 단수인 a need이므로 동사도 단수 동사여야 한다. ④를 comes로 고친다.

keenly ad. 날카롭게; 열심히 upwards of ~이상 influx n. 흘러듦, 유입

태국은 관광의 효과를 확실하게 인식하고 있다. 3,400만 명 이상의 사람들이 매년 외국에서 그 나라를 방문한다. 매년 사람들이 유입되면서 태국의 유명한 자연과 문화의 경이들이 보호되게 해야 할 필요성도 함께 대두되고 있다.

---

19   2022 명지대   ▶▶▶ MSG p.137   ①

완전한 절과 함께 쓰이는 '전치사+관계대명사' ▶ 불완전한 절과 함께 쓰이는 관계대명사 다음에 완전한 절이 와서 틀렸다. 완전한 절과 쓰이기 위해서는 '전치사+관계대명사' 형태가 되어야 하므로, ①을 through which로 고쳐야 한다.

distribution n. 배급, 유통 mobility n. 유동성 straightforward a. 간단한 geography n. 지형, 지형도

TV 콘텐츠의 인터넷 유통이 TV 방송의 기본 논리(원칙)를 변화시켜서, 새로운 유동성을 시스템에 도입시켜, 기존의 케이블 방송과 위성 방송에 더해 새로운 방송 포맷을 추가한다. 인터넷 TV가 기존 TV를 간단히 대체하지는 않는다. 대신 인터넷 TV는 기존의 유통 지형에 새로운 복잡성을 추가한다. 넷플릭스 같이 인터넷으로 유통되는 성숙한 TV 서비스의 도래는 세계 미디어 논쟁에서 중요하다. 오늘날 우리는 해외 TV를 보기 위해 해외로 더 이상 나갈 필요가 없다. 왜냐하면 엄청난 양의 해외 TV프로그램을 인터넷으로 쉽게 접할 수 있기 때문이다.

---

16   2020 국민대   ▶▶▶ MSG p.137   ②

관계대명사 앞의 전치사 ▶ a process는 선행사이며 ② 이하에 완전한 문장이 주어져 있으므로 관계대명사 which는 적절하지 않다. 관계대명사 앞에 전치사가 있어야 하겠는데, 선행사가 a process이므로 by가 오는 것이 적절하다. 따라서 ②는 by which로 고쳐야 한다.

creative a. 창조적인; n. 창의적인 사람 behest n. 명령, 요청

창작자들 사이에서의 통설은 예술은 인간이 어떤 생각이나 감정을 표현하고, 그것을 개인적 경험을 통해 걸러내어 더 넓은 문화적 맥락의 배경에 맞도록 설정하는 과정이라는 것인데, 그렇다면 이는 컴퓨터 과학자들의 명령에 따라 인공지능이 생성하는 것은 예술도 아니고 전혀 창의적이지도 않다는 것을 시사한다.

---

17   2021 가천대   ▶▶▶ MSG p.116   ④

부대상황의 분사구문 ▶ 부대상황의 분사구문을 나타낼 때는 'with+목적어+분사'의 형태가 와야 하는데, 이때 목적어와 분사의 관계가 능동이면 현재분사, 수동이면 과거분사를 취한다. 주어진 문장의 경우, 산소는 '켜지는' 대상이므로 수동관계를 나타내는 과거분사가 와야 한다. 따라서 ④를 turned on으로 고쳐야 한다.

20　**2022 광운대** ▶▶▶ MSG p.131, p.228　　　③

정비문 ▶ ③ despite는 전치사이므로 그 뒤에 절이 올 수 없다. despite를 양보의 접속사 though 혹은 although로 고친다. ④, ⑤ provided 혹은 provided that은 접속사 if의 대용어구로 쓰인다.

so long as ~하기만 하면 **garage** n. 차고

① 빨리 돌아오기만 한다면 내 차를 써도 좋다.
② 그가 술을 마셔야 할 경우에 대비해 나는 그에게 약간의 현금을 주었다.
③ 당신은 지난번에 나를 도와주지 않았지만 나는 당신을 돕겠다.
④ 날씨가 좋으면 우리는 여행을 갈 것이다.
⑤ 차고가 있다면 차가 있는 것이 편리하다.

01 ①	**02** ②	**03** ②	**04** ④	**05** ③	**06** ③	**07** ③	**08** ③	**09** ①	**10** ③
11 ③	**12** ④	**13** ③	**14** ②	**15** ⑤	**16** ②	**17** ③	**18** ③	**19** ④	**20** ②

01 　2017 단국대　▶▶▶ MSG p.105　　　　　①

과거분사 ▶ 빈칸 앞의 one은 man을 대신하는 역할을 하는 대명사로 쓰였으며, that is가 삽입 표현이므로 one 앞부분은 이미 완전한 형태의 절을 이루고 있는 것으로 파악할 수 있다. 따라서 빈칸에는 one을 수식할 수 있는 표현이 들어가야 한다. 시제를 가진 동사인 ②와 ④의 경우, 술부는 one을 수식할 수 없으므로 정답에서 먼저 제외할 수 있다. 한편, capture는 '사로잡다', '붙잡다'는 의미의 타동사로, one(=a man)이 생각에 사로잡힌 대상이므로, one과 capture는 수동 관계에 있다. 따라서 빈칸에는 수동의 의미를 가진 과거분사 ① captured가 들어가야 한다. 이때 captured 앞에 '관계대명사+be동사', 즉 who is 가 생략된 것으로 파악하는 것도 가능하다.

bronze n. 청동 marble n. 대리석 sculpture n. 조각, 조각 작품 depict v. (그림·조각으로) 그리다; (말로) 묘사[서술]하다 pensive a. 생각에 잠긴, 시름에 잠긴 듯한; 구슬픈

오귀스트 로댕(August Rodin)의 청동과 대리석으로 만든 유명한 조각상인 '생각하는 사람'은 생각에 잠겨 있는 사람, 다시 말해 깊은 생각에 빠져 있는 사람을 묘사하고 있다.

02 　2014 단국대　▶▶▶ MSG p.112　　　　　②

적절한 접속사 ▶ 'It ~ that절(가주어-진주어)' 구문인데 진주어인 that절 안에서 두 개의 절을 연결하는 접속사가 필요하다. 의미상 결과를 나타내어야 하므로 ②의 so that이 적절하다. ① not so much는 'not so much A as B(A라기 보다는 오히려 B이다)'의 원급 관용 표현으로 주로 쓰인다. 접속사가 아니어서 뒤에 절이 올 수 없다. ③ in so/as far as는 접속사이지만, '~하는 한에 있어서는'의 의미이다. ④ no matter what는 '비록 무엇이 ~일지라도'의 의미로 양보의 부사절을 이끈다.

exacerbate v. 악화시키다 technocrat n. 기술 관료 counterproductive a. 역효과를 낳는

국가의 문제들이 외국의 기술 관료들에 의해 악화되었으므로 다시 그들의 지원을 요청하는 것은 역효과를 낳게 될 것이라는 것이 그녀의 견해였다.

03 　2019 단국대　▶▶▶ MSG p.221　　　　　②

부사구가 문두에 나간 도치 ▶ 부사구 Out of this contention이 문두에 나와 주어와 동사가 도치된 문장이며, that이하는 a set of arguments를 선행사로 하는 주격 관계대명사절이다. 따라서 빈칸에는 본동사가 필요한데, ①은 주어가 중복되므로 적절하지 않고, ③ born은 과거분사로 본동사가 될 수 없으며, ④ to부정사 또한 본동사가 될 수 없다. 따라서 ② was born이 빈칸에 적절하다.

contention n. 논쟁, 언쟁

이 논쟁에서 정치적으로 올바른 지식이 된 일련의 주장이 탄생했다.

04 　2020 단국대　▶▶▶ MSG p.100　　　　　④

수동태 동명사 ▶ 주어는 He이고, 본동사는 has been이며, who부터 last year까지는 삽입된 관계대명사절이다. before가 전치사로 쓰였으므로 뒤에 동명사가 와야 하며, 그는 주지사로 당선되는 객체이므로 수동태가 되어야 한다. 따라서 수동태 동명사 ④가 빈칸에 적절하다.

National Assembly n. 국회 province n. 지방, 지역

지난해 6월 주지사로 당선되기 전에 국회의원이었던 그는 그 지역의 산업을 성장시키기 위해 국내외 투자를 유치하느라 바빴다.

05 　2019 단국대　▶▶▶ MSG p.218　　　　　③

to부정사의 병치 ▶ 빈칸 앞의 if it is는 삽입돼 있는 문장이므로 구문에 영향을 주지 않는다. There are a number of steps 다음에 목적격 관계대명사 which가 생략되어 있으며, 'take+목적어+to부정사'의 구문으로 쓰여, to determine이 왔으므로, 등위접속사 and 다음도 to부정사가 와야 한다. 따라서 ③ to prepare yourself가 빈칸에 적절하며, prepare oneself for는 '~의 준비를 하다'는 뜻으로 쓰인다.

take a step 조치를 취하다 field n. 분야

게임 디자인이 당신에게 적합한 분야인지 판단하기 위해, 그리고 만약 그렇다면, 그 직업에 대비하기 위해, 당신이 취할 수 있는 몇 가지 조치가 있다.

06 **2020 덕성여대** ▶▶▶ MSG p.76, p.83 ③

수동태 ▶ 주어인 differences는 동사 remove의 주체가 아니라 대상 (객체)이어서 '제거하는' 것이 아니라 '제거되는' 것이므로 수동태로 써야 한다. 여기서 could have pp는 가정법으로 보아 '포토샵의 도움이 있었더라면 제거될 수 있었을 텐데'로 해석할 수도 있고, 직설법으로 현재에서 본 과거의 추측으로 '포토샵의 도움으로 제거될 수 있었을 것이다'로 해석할 수도 있다.

photograph n. 사진

두 사진 사이의 이러한 차이는 포토샵의 도움으로 제거될 수 있었을 것이다.

07 **2022 한국외대** ▶▶▶ MSG p.137 ③

관계대명사 ▶ 관계대명사 which의 선행사는 nearly three hundred musical scrolls이며, 이것 중 90개가 사용된다는 의미가 되어야 한다. 따라서 빈칸에는 ninety of which are나 of which ninety are가 적절하므로 ③이 정답이다.

scroll n. (종이·가죽의) 두루마리, 족자 preserve v. 보존하다

약 300여개의 음악 족자(악보)가 보존되어 있으며, 그 중 90개가 왕실 추모식에 사용된다.

08 **2021 한국외대** ▶▶▶ MSG p.20, 125 ③

동명사의 병치와 전치사 ▶ 빈칸 뒤에 온 which surgical procedures ~ after surgery는 간접의문절로, 이 간접의문절을 받기 위해서는 원칙적으로 전치사가 필요하다. 따라서 전치사가 없는 ②와 ④는 빈칸에 부적절하고, allege 다음에는 동명사가 목적어로 와서 뒤에 나온 부정의 동명사 not receiving과 병치를 이루게 된다. 따라서 ③의 being uninformed about이 적절하다.

anonymous a. 익명의 surgical a. 수술의 pain medication 진통제

이전에 환자였던 사람들 중 상당수가 여전히 익명으로 있지만, 그들에게 어떤 수술절차가 행해질 것인지에 대해 아무 통지를 받지 못했음을 주장하는데, 다른 주장들보다 특히 수술 후 진통제를 받지 못했음을 주장한다.

09 **2017 가천대** ▶▶▶ MSG p.133 ①

양보의 '보어+접속사 as' 구문 ▶ 주절의 내용이 "그녀로서는 그에게서 불의한 점을 발견하지 못했다."라는 것이므로 빈칸에는 '그의 거만한 태도에도 불구하고'라는 양보의 의미가 적절하다. 따라서 '보어+as+주어 +동사'의 구문인 ①이 적절하다. ② As절로 되면 양보가 아니라 이유의 뜻이다. ③ being을 삭제해야 한다. ④ the가 없는 on account of는 '~ 때문에'의 뜻이지만 이것도 양보의 뜻이 아니다.

proud a. 거만한 manners n. 예의범절, 태도 acquaintance n. 지식, 앎 betray v. 드러내다 unjust a. 불의한, 부당한 account n. 이야기

비록 그의 태도는 거만했지만, 그녀는 알게 된 모든 과정에서 그가 불의한 사람이라는 것을 보여주는 점은 전혀 발견하지 못했다.

10 **2022 서울여대** ▶▶▶ MSG p.135 ③

관계대명사 ▶ 콤마 전후로 완전한 두 절이 접속사 없이 나열돼 있는 점이 옳지 않다. 따라서 ③의 대명사 자리에는 '접속사+대명사'의 역할을 하는 관계대명사를 써야 하므로, ③을 of whom으로 고친다.

adjacent a. 인접한, 부근의 anti-Communist n. 반(反)공산주의자

전통주의자들과 가까운 곳에 반(反)공산주의자들이 있었는데, 그들 중 상당수는 이전의 마르크스주의자들이었다.

11 **2018 서강대** ▶▶▶ MSG p.227 ③

전치사의 적절한 사용 ▶ ③에서 '미사 중에'라고 표현할 때 전치사는 on이 아니라 in이어야 한다. its는 diocese를 가리킨다.

diocese n. (가톨릭) 교구 suspend v. (공식적으로) 중단하다 Mass n. (종종 m-) (특히 로마 가톨릭 교회에서) 미사 strain n. 변종

북아일랜드의 한 가톨릭 교구에서는 변종 독감 감염의 위험으로 인해 미사 도중에 "평화의 인사"를 나누면서 하는 악수를 중단하였다.

12 **2016 한양대 에리카** ▶▶▶ MSG p.143 ④

유사관계대명사 than ▶ ④는 주격관계대명사의 자리이다. 그런데, 선행사 앞에 비교급 표현이 쓰였으므로, 이것을 유사관계대명사 than으로 고쳐야 옳은 문장이 된다.

account for 설명하다 concentration n. 농도 i.e. 즉 peak n. 절정

면밀한 측정에 따르면, 반응 속도가 너무나도 느려서 관찰된 오존 농도를 설명할 수 없다. 다시 말해, 그 과정은 관찰되는 것보다 더 높은 최대 오존 농도를 예상한다는 것이다.

13 **2020 국민대** ▶▶▶ MSG p.135, p.143 ③

복합관계대명사와 관계대명사의 용법 구분 ▶ 복합관계대명사에는 선행사가 이미 포함되어 있는데, ③의 앞에는 선행사인 anyone이 나와 있으므로 복합관계대명사를 사용할 수 없다. 그러므로 ③을 관계대명사 who로 바꾸어야 한다.

thunderstorm n. 뇌우 lightning n. 번개 plumbing n. 배관 come into contact with ~와 접촉하다

뇌우가 칠 때 샤워하는 것은 좋은 생각이 아니다. 만약 번개가 당신의 집에 내리치면, 번개는 집의 배관을 타고 흘러, 배관 속을 흐르는 물과 접촉하는 사람은 누구든지 감전시킬 수 있다.

---

14 2007 한국외대 ▶▶▶ MSG p.196 ②

명사를 수식하는 형용사 ▶ ②의 too는 부사이므로 명사 emphasis를 수식하지 못하고, much는 형용사여서 수식할 수 있다. 따라서 ②를 too much로 고친다.

core n. 핵심 subject n. 과목 keep pace with ~와 보조를 맞추다, ~에 따라가다

초등학교의 시험결과가 핵심 과목에서의 학력향상이 빠르게 증가하는 기대에 미치지 못하고 있다는 것을 보여준 후에, 정부는 오늘 인위적인 목표를 지나치게 많이 강조했다고 비난받았다.

---

15 2020 상명대 ▶▶▶ MSG p.105 ⑤

과거분사 ▶ ⑤는 a mixture를 수식하고 있는데, a mixture는 store하는 행위의 주체가 아닌 대상이며, 따라서 수동관계에 있다. 수동 관계는 과거분사를 통해 나타내므로, ⑤를 stored로 고쳐야 한다. ② 현재완료 진행시제는 '계속적' 의미를 보다 명확하게 나타내는 역할을 한다.

archaeologist n. 고고학자 excavate v. 발굴하다 ochre n. 황토(黃土) abalone n. 전복

버밍엄 대학의 고고학자 다니엘 S. 크레이그(Daniel S. Craig)는 1992년부터 남아프리카공화국의 블롬보스(Blombos) 동굴에서 발굴 작업을 해오고 있으며, 두 개의 전복조개에 저장돼 있는 황토가 풍부한 혼합물의 발견을 보고했다.

---

16 2019 국민대 ▶▶▶ MSG p.139 ②

의문사 what의 용법 ▶ ②는 전치사 to의 목적어가 되는 의문사절을 이끌고 있다. 그런데 주체(the earliest insect life)가 사물이므로, 사람을 나타내는 의문사 whom이 아닌 what을 써야 한다. 따라서 ②를 what으로 고쳐야 하며, 'what X is like'는 'X는 어떠한지'라는 의미의 간접 의문절이다. ① 주어는 복수명사 insects이다. ④ stubby legs가 attach하는 행위의 대상이므로 서로 수동관계이며, 그래서 과거분사를 쓴 것이다. 바로 앞에 which were가 생략된 것으로도 봐도 가능하다.

primitive a. 원시적인 wingless a. 날지 못하는 clue n. 단서, 실마리 bristletail n. 좀 silverfish n. 좀벌레 arthropod n. 절지동물 segment n. 단편, 조각; 체절(體節) stubby a. 뭉툭한, 짧막한 attach v. 붙이다; 첨부하다

오늘날에도 날지 못하는 원시적인 곤충들이 존재하고 있어서 초기 곤충들의 생활이 어떠했을지에 대한 단서를 제공해주고 있는데, 바로 좀과 좀벌레이다. 이들은 아마도 많은 체절을 갖고 있었고 각 체절에 한 쌍의 뭉툭한 다리가 붙어 있었던 절지동물로부터 진화했을 것이다.

---

17 2021 가천대 ▶▶▶ MSG p.218 ③

동명사의 병치 ▶ ③의 befriends의 주어를 Her explorations로 볼 경우, 주어와 동사의 수일치가 되지 않고 부적절한 의미가 된다. 따라서 ③을 동명사 being과 함께 전치사 in의 목적어로 파악하여 ③ 역시 동명사인 befriending으로 써야 한다. the lonely boy는 전치사 by의 목적어기도 하고 동사 befriend의 목적어기도 하다.

grating n. 쇠창살 give a glimpse of ~을 힐끗[얼핏] 보다 long v. 애타게 바라다 unwitting a. 알아차리지 못하는 spot v. 발견하다 befriend v. 친구가 되다 flee v. 달아나다

지하에 갇혀 있어서 창살을 통해 정원과 하늘이 어렴풋이 보일 뿐인 까닭에, 비록 부모님은 주인집의 아무것도 모르는 거구의 식구들 눈에 띌까 두려워하시지만, 아리에티(Arrietty)는 바깥으로 나갈 수 있기를 간절히 바라고 있다. 그녀의 모험으로 인해 그녀는 그 집에 머물러 온 외로운 소년의 눈에 띄게 되고 결국 그 소년과 친구가 된다. 얼마 안 있어, 그 집의 나머지 식구들이 그 소년의 비밀을 알게 되고, 아리에티의 가족은 달아나야만 한다.

---

18 2020 건국대 ▶▶▶ MSG p.176 ③

부정대명사 ▶ '일부/많은 사람들은 ~하고, 다른 사람들은 ~하고, 또 다른 사람들은 ~한다'라고 설명할 때 'Some/Many people ~, others ~, and still others ~'라고 표현한다. 그런데 ③ The others는 셋 이상에서 일부를 제외한 나머지 모두를 가리키므로, 마지막 문장에서 Still others로 설명할 수 없게 된다. 따라서 ③은 Others로 고쳐야 한다.

autistic a. 자폐성의, 자폐증의; n. 자폐증 환자 savant n. 학자, 석학; 서번트(특정 분야에 뛰어난 재능을 가진 정신 장애인) retain v. (계속) 유지[보유]하다 recite v. 암송하다; (열거하듯) 죽 말하다, 나열하다 word for word 정확히 말한[글자] 그대로

자폐적 서번트(천재장애인)는 평범한 사람보다 훨씬 더 발달된 특별한 능력, 기술 또는 지식을 가지고 있는 사람이다. 사실, 많은 서번트들은 고도로 발달된 수학 능력을 가지고 있다. 다른 서번트들은 그들의 기억 속에 많은 양의 정보를 간직할 수 있다. 예를 들면, 일부 자폐적 서번트들은 사전 또는 전화번호부 전체를 그대로 외워서 말할 수 있다. 또 다른 서번트들은 헬리콥터로 한번 비행한 후에 어떤 지역의 상세 지도를 그릴 수 있다.

---

19 2022 명지대 ▶▶▶ MSG p.201 ④

not so much A as B ▶ as가 들어있는 ④ 앞에 not so much가 왔으므로, 관용구문인 not so much A as B(A라기 보다는 B인)가 쓰였음을 알 수 있으며, 이때 A와 B의 문법적 구조는 같아야 한다. 주어진 문장에서 A의 자리에 동사원형 query가 쓰였으므로, B의 자리에도 동사원형이 쓰여야 한다. ④를 as confide로 고친다.

trail n. 흔적 query v. 질문하다 confide v. (비밀을) 털어놓다 drunk a. 술이 취한

어떤 단어가 얼마나 자주 검색되는지를 이용자들에게 알려주는 구글 트렌드가 처음 공개되었을 때, 구글 검색 데이터는 학술 연구를 위한 적절한 정보 공급원인 것 같지 않았다. 구글 검색 데이터는 인간의 마음을 우리가 이해하

도록 도움을 주기 위한 하나의 방법으로 만든 것은 아니었다. 그러나 인터넷에서 지식을 검색하면서 우리가 남기는 흔적들은 매우 많은 것을 보여주는 것으로 드러난다. 사실들, 장소들, 인물들을 언제, 어디서 검색하느냐가 검색하는 사람이 실제로 무엇을 생각하고 무엇을 하는지에 관해 생각보다 훨씬 더 많은 것을 우리에게 알려줄 수 있다. 이것이 특히 사실인 이유는 사람들이 때때로 구글에 질문하기보다는 "직장 상사가 나는 너무 싫어." "내가 술이 취했나 봐"라고 하면서 구글에 솔직히 털어놓기 때문이다.

---

20 **2022 광운대** ▶▶▶ MSG p.185　　　　②

정비문 ▶ ② be likely 다음에는 to부정사 혹은 that절이 온다. 가주어 It을 사용할 때는 주로 that절이 진주어로 오므로 of Joan's getting married를 that Joan gets married로 고쳐야 한다.

get married 결혼하다 tidy a. 단정한; 정돈된 there's no point ~ing ~해봐야 소용없다

① 조안(Joan)이 결혼할 것 같다.
② 조안(Joan)이 결혼할 것 같다.
③ 나는 정원을 정돈하는 일에는 형편없다.
④ 그에게 무슨 말을 해도 아무 의미가 없다.
⑤ 당신이 머물만한 가치가 없다.

01 ③	02 ④	03 ②	04 ②	05 ③	06 ②	07 ③	08 ④	09 ①	10 ①
11 ④	12 ④	13 ④	14 ④	15 ②	16 ⑤	17 ④	18 ⑤	19 ①	20 ②

01 **2017 가천대** ▶▶▶ MSG p.172 ③

종속부사절을 이끄는 such that ▶ 빈칸 앞에서 "우리는 기술이 가져다주는 속도에 점점 익숙해졌다."라고 했고 빈칸 뒤에는 "이메일을 새로 고치는 것이 느려지거나 기차가 연착하면 화를 내게 된다."라고 했으므로 빈칸에는 '~할 정도로'나 '그래서'의 의미로 해석되는 ③의 such that이 적절하다. 즉, '이메일을 새로 고치는 것이 느려지거나 기차가 연착하면 화를 내게 될 정도로 속도에 익숙해졌다'거나 '속도에 익숙해져서 이메일을 새로 고치는 것이 느려지거나 기차가 연착하면 화를 내게 된다'는 뜻이다. 이 such that은 앞의 명사와 결부되어 쓰이기도 하고 문제의 경우처럼 주절에 이은 종속부사절로 쓰이기도 한다. 예를 들어, His math skill is such that he can solve all the problems given to him.(그의 수학 능력은 주어진 문제를 모두 풀 수 있을 정도의 능력이다.)처럼 is의 보어로 쓰이기도 하고 His math skill has reached a level such that he can solve all the problems given to him.(그의 수학 능력은 주어진 문제를 모두 풀 수 있는 정도의 수준에 이르렀다.)처럼 명사를 수식하기도 한다. 이 경우 such a level that ~으로 나타낼 수도 있다. 그런데 다음 두 문장은 such that이 특정 명사와 결부되었다기보다 문제의 문장처럼 종속부사절을 이끄는 경우이다. If an atom could be enlarged such that we could see it with our naked eye, what would it look like?(원자가 육안으로 볼 수 있을 정도로 확대될 수 있다면/확대되어서 그래서 육안으로 볼 수 있다면, 그것은 어떤 모습일까?) All of reality is interwined, such that we cannot pass judgment on one aspect of reality without passing judgment on all of reality.(현실 전체가 서로 얽혀있어서, 그래서 우리는 현실 전체에 대한 판단을 내리지 않고는 현실의 한 측면에 대한 판단을 내릴 수 없다.)

instant a. 즉각적인 gratification n. 만족 hustle and bustle 번잡함 afford v. 가져오다, 가져다주다 refresh v. 생기를 되찾게 하다; 가장 최신 정보로 리프레시하다

기술은 즉각적인 만족을 주는 반면, 과학은 느린 과정으로 일어난다. 오늘날 세상의 번잡함 속에서, 우리는 기술이 가져다주는 속도에 점점 익숙해져서, 이메일 페이지를 가장 최근의 것으로 새로 고치는 데 몇 초가 걸리거나 우리가 탈 기차가 몇 분이라도 지연되면 우리는 화를 내게 된다.

02 **2019 단국대** ▶▶▶ MSG p.223 ④

문두의 보어 뒤 도치 ▶ 주어가 문미로 후치되어 보어가 문두에 오면 주어와 동사가 도치된다. 이 문장의 주어는 just a boy barely reaching the age of fourteen이고 동사는 was인데, 14살 소년이 장교에게 결

투 신청을 받은 것이므로, 빈칸에는 과거분사 ④ Challenged가 적절하다. 'challenge 사람 to a duel(아무에게 결투를 신청하다)' 구문이 수동태로 된 문장이다.

duel n. 결투; (양자간의) 싸움 officer n. 장교

그 장교의 결투 신청을 받은 것은 14살에 불과한 소년이었다.

03 **2014 가천대** ▶▶▶ MSG p.140 ②

목적격 관계대명사의 생략 ▶ ①과 ④는 전치사로 그 다음에 명사가 와야 하는데 절이 와서 부적절하고, 마지막의 of 다음에 목적어가 비어있는 불완전한 절이므로 접속사 ③도 부적절하다. 명사 extent가 of 다음에 들어갈 명사에 해당하여 관계절의 수식을 받는 선행사로 된 ②가 빈칸에 적절하며, 목적격 관계대명사는 생략되었다.

forefather n. 조상, 선조 leisure n. 여가

중세 말에 서양 사람은 자신의 선조들이 거의 꿈꾸지 못했을 정도로 여가 시간을 즐길 수 있게 노동시간을 줄였다.

04 **2022 한국공학대** ▶▶▶ MSG p.223 ②

도치구문 ▶ but 이하의 주어는 the news로, 빈칸에는 동사와 보어가 필요한데, 보어가 앞으로 가게 되면 주어와 동사가 도치가 되므로 good의 비교급인 better가 앞으로 가고 동사 was가 와야 한다. 이때 still은 비교급을 수식하는 부사로 비교급 앞이나 뒤에 올 수 있다. 따라서 ②가 정답이다.

thrilled a. 아주 기쁜, 아주 신이 난 parliament n. 의회, 국회 overturn v. (판결 등을) 뒤집다, 전복시키다

당원들은 국회에서 그렇게 많은 의석을 얻어서 기뻐했지만, 그들이 다수당을 뒤집었다는 소식이 훨씬 더 좋았다.

05 **2019 덕성여대** ▶▶▶ MSG p.209 ③

비교구문+불가산명사 ▶ 네바다 주의 적은 강수량과 다른 주의 적은 강수량을 비교하는 의미가 되어야 하며, rainfall은 불가산명사이므로 few가 아닌 little로 수식해야 한다.

state n. (미국의) 주 rainfall n. 강수량

네바다 주(州)만큼 강수량이 적은 주는 없었다.

06 2015 아주대 ▶▶▶ MSG p.224   ②

도치가 일어나는 nor ▶ nor 다음에는 주어가 대명사일지라도 도치가 되므로 ①, ③, ⑤는 빈칸에 들어갈 수 없으며, 제한하는 주체가 the present law로 단수이므로, it이 쓰인 ②의 nor does it limit가 빈칸에 적절하다.

favor v. 찬성하다 administrative law 행정법 statewide a. 주(州) 전체의

새로운 행정법을 찬성하는 사람들은 현행법이 로비스트들이 정치인들에게 주는 선물에 대해 지출 한도를 정해 놓고 있지 않으며, 주(州) 전체 기금에도 제한을 가하지 않는다고 주장한다.

07 2018 아주대 ▶▶▶ MSG p.53, p.173   ③

시제 & 과거분사의 후치수식 ▶ 두 길 중의 하나이지만, 후치 수식을 받으므로 one앞에 the를 쓴다. '~(길)로 다니다'가 travel by이므로 목적어에 해당하는 the one(=the road)을 수식하는 것은 과거분사 traveled by이다. 빈칸 앞 절의 상황에서 빈칸에 들어갈 내용의 행동을 한 것이므로, 빈칸에 들어갈 동사의 시제는 과거가 적절하다. 따라서 ③이 정답이다. And that has made에서 시제가 현재완료인 것에서도 ④의 과거완료 시제(had taken)는 잘못된 것임을 알 수 있다.

diverge v. 갈라지다, 분기하다 make all the difference 중요한 영향을 미치다

숲속에 두 길이 갈라져 있었다. 나는 사람들이 덜 다닌 길을 택했고, 그것으로 모든 것이 달라졌다.

08 2007 단국대 ▶▶▶ MSG p.132   ④

no matter 구문의 어순 ▶ 'no matter+의문사(how)+형용사/부사(large)+주어(the jackpot)+동사(is)'의 어순을 따라야 하므로 ④가 정답이다.

jackpot n. 당첨금, 상금, 횡재 run out 바닥나다, 다 쓰다

당첨금이 얼마나 많은 지와는 상관없이, 만약 우승자가 낭비를 하고 현명하게 투자하지 않는다면 언제든지 돈이 바닥날 위험이 있다.

09 2010 동국대 ▶▶▶ MSG p.179   ①

적절한 형용사의 사용 ▶ 뒤에 '징역 5년에서 10년까지'라는 말이 가능한 형량을 나타내므로 과거분사인 ②의 punished(처벌된, 처벌되는)나 ③의 being punished(처벌되고 있는)보다 ①의 punishable(처벌할 수 있는)이 빈칸에 더 적절하다.

parliament n. 의회, 국회 legislation n. 법률 제정 homosexuality n. 동성애 construe v. 해석하다; 추론하다

오늘 르완다 의회는 처음으로 동성애를 징역 5년에서 10년까지의 실형으로 처벌할 수 있는 범죄로 만드는 법 제정을 고려하고 있다. 그 법안은 또한 동성관계를 '자극하거나 독려한다'라고 생각될 수 있는 어떠한 행동들도 금지할 것이다.

10 2022 서울여대 ▶▶▶ MSG p.217   ①

병치 ▶ today's cars 이하는 주절이고 그 앞은 Being이 생략된 분사구문이다. ①의 뒤에 be동사의 보어로 secure, economical, practical과 같은 형용사가 주어져 있으므로, ①도 형용사의 형태여야 한다. ①을 Gas efficient로 고친다.

gas efficient 연료효율이 좋은 secure a. 안전한 economical a. 경제적인

연비가 뛰어나고, 안전하고, 경제적이며, 또한 실용적이기 때문에, 오늘날의 자동차들은 이전에 생산된 그 어떤 자동차보다 더 좋다.

11 2019 국민대 ▶▶▶ MSG p.131, p.212   ④

'부분 표시어 + of' 뒤에 쓰인 명사의 수 ▶ 'half, most, majority+of'와 같이 부분 표시어가 쓰인 표현 뒤에 명사가 오는 경우, 그 명사가 가산명사인 경우 복수명사로 쓰고 불가산명사인 경우 단수명사를 쓴다. ④에서 a great majority of 다음에 쓰인 case는 가산명사이므로 복수 형태로 써야 한다. ④를 in a great majority of cases로 고친다. ② one feels는 삽입절이며, ③의 뒤에는 앞 문장에 쓰인 happy가 생략돼 있다.

a great majority of 대다수의

동물들은 건강하고 먹을 것만 충분하면 행복하다. 우리는 인간도 당연히 그래야 한다고 생각하지만, 현대 세계에서 인간은 적어도 대다수의 경우 그렇지 못하다.

12 2020 상명대 ▶▶▶ MSG p.33   ④

ensure의 용법 ▶ ensure는 5형식 문형으로 쓰지 않으며, that절을 목적어로 하는 형태로 주로 쓴다. 따라서 ④는 이어지는 and 이하와 마찬가지로 절의 형태여야 한다. ④를 the form is processed로 고친다. 접속사 that은 생략할 수 있다.

promptly ad. 신속히; 즉시 in full 전부 ensure v. ~을 책임지다, 보장[보증]하다, (성공 등을) 확실하게 하다 forward v. (편지 따위를) 회송하다, 전송하다

양식을 신속하게 모두 채워 넣을 것을 권합니다. 그런 다음 그것을 참석한 직원들에게 되돌려주셔야 합니다. 그 직원들은 양식이 처리되고 올바른 부서로 전달되도록 하는 책임을 질 것입니다.

13 **2020 상명대** ▶▶▶ MSG p.218 ④

동명사의 병치 ▶ '주택 대금의 일부는 계약금으로 내고 나머지는 대출을 받아 조달한다'는 흐름이 되어야 하므로, ④는 making a down payment와 병치를 이루어 전치사 by의 목적어가 되어야 하고 전치사 뒤에 동명사가 오므로, ④를 taking out a mortgage로 고쳐야 한다.

down payment (할부금의) 계약금 mortgage n. (담보) 대출, (주택) 융자 balance n. 차액, 차감잔액; (은행계좌의) 잔고

주택 한 채 혹은 건물 안의 아파트 한 채를 사는 데 매우 많은 돈이 들기 때문에, 매수인들은 대개 합의된 가격의 일정 비율은 계약금으로 내고 나머지 액수에 대해서는 담보대출을 받음으로써 구입 자금을 조달한다.

---

14 **2022 중앙대** ▶▶▶ MSG p.105, p.211 ④

문의 구성 ▶ ① infants를 수식하는 현재분사 growing이고, ② 주어가 Cross-linguistic studies로 복수이므로 주어와 수일치하여 show이고, ③ 부사절을 이끄는 접속사 when 앞에 부사 even이 사용되어 틀린 곳이 없는 문장이다.

cross-linguistic a. 언어 간의 phonology n. 음운 체계

언어 간 연구는 상이한 언어 배경에서 자라는 영아들의 능력을 비교하는 연구로서, 성인 언어의 음운 체계에 차이가 있을 때에도 영아에 의한 일반적인 범주화를 보여준다.

---

15 **2018 경기대** ▶▶▶ MSG p.136 ②

관계사절의 주어와 동사의 수일치 ▶ 관계대명사의 수는 선행사에 일치시킨다. Warming of 2.6C to 4.8C는 단수이므로, 이것을 선행사로 하는 관계대명사절의 동사도 단수동사여야 한다. 따라서 ②를 is로 고쳐야 한다.

bring down ~을 줄이다, 낮추다 emission n. (빛·열 따위의) 방사, 발산; 배기가스, 배출물질 asylum seeker 난민, 망명 신청자

기후 전문가들은 온실 가스 배출량을 줄이기 위해 보다 강력한 조치가 취해지지 않으면 섭씨 2.6도 내지 4.8도의 온난화가 일어날 것으로 이야기하고 있는데, 이렇게 되는 경우 매년 추가적으로 유럽으로 들어올 난민들이 2100년이면 이미 660,000명에 이를 것이다.

---

16 **2020 상명대** ▶▶▶ MSG p.11 ⑤

remark의 용법 ▶ remark는 '주목하다'라는 의미일 때는 타동사로 쓰이고, '의견을 말하다'라는 의미일 때는 자동사로 쓰여 전치사 on[upon]과 함께 쓴다. 문맥상 ⑤는 '(우리의 전시공간이) 매력적이라고 이야기했다'라는 의미로 보아야 한다. 이 부분을 다음 문장에서 compliments로 받고 있기 때문이다. 따라서 ⑤에서 remark는 자동사로 쓰인 것이므로, 뒤에 전치사 on[upon]이 있어야 한다. ⑤를 remarked on[upon] the attractiveness로 고친다.

---

display n. 전시; 전시회 booth n. (칸막이를 한) 작은 공간, 부스 compliment n. 칭찬, 찬사

우리의 트루소프트(Trusoft) 콘크리트 제품들을 매우 훌륭하게 전시해주신 데 대해 당신께 감사하다는 인사를 드리고 싶습니다. 뮌헨에서 열린 우리의 첫 상품전시회에서, 부스를 찾은 많은 방문객들이 우리 전시 공간이 매력적이라고 이야기하셨는데, 우리는 그분들이 해주셨던 칭찬의 말을 당신께 전하고 싶습니다.

---

17 **2021 가천대** ▶▶▶ MSG p.211 ④

주어와 동사의 수일치 ▶ ④가 들어있는 문장에서 ④ are의 주어는 rock fractures가 아니라 The ease이다. 이것은 단수이므로, 동사 역시 단수형이 되어야 한다. 따라서 ④의 are를 is로 고쳐야 한다. with which ~ rock fractures는 The ease를 수식하는 관계절이다.

surface n. 지표면 pace n. (일의) 속도 composition n. 성분 encounter v. 마주치다 gravel n. 자갈 porous a. (구멍이 많은) 다공성의 limestone n. 석회암 unimpeded a. 방해받지 않는 fracture n. 갈라진 틈 hydraulic conductivity 수리전도도(水理傳導度)

지표면의 물이 지표면 아래의 암석으로 흘러들어감에 따라, 물의 운동 속도는 물이 이동하면서 만나는 물질의 지질학적 성분에 의해 크게 좌우된다. 모래, 자갈, 그리고 다공성 석회암층은 물이 비교적 방해받지 않고 흐를 수 있게 해주는 경향이 있다. 물이 토양입자 사이의 틈이나 암석의 갈라진 틈을 통해 이동할 수 있는 용이함은 수리전도도(水理傳導度)로 알려져 있다.

---

18 **2022 건국대** ▶▶▶ MSG p.57 ⑤

수동태 ▶ 마지막 문장에서 타동사 supply의 목적어가 없고, 주어인 iodine(요오드)는 식단을 통해 신체에 공급되는 대상이므로 ⑤는 수동태가 되어야 한다. 따라서 ⑤를 must be supplied로 고쳐야 한다.

organism n. 유기체, 생물 trace element 미량 원소 iodine n. 요오드 vital a. (생명유지에) 필수적인 thyroid gland 갑상선 gland n. (분비)선(腺), 샘 swelling n. 융기, 팽창 simple goiter 단순갑상샘종 fatal a. 치명적인, 죽음을 초래하는

유기체 내에서 어떤 원소의 필요량이 극미할 때 그것을 미량 원소라고 한다. 요오드는 신체의 화학 작용, 즉 신진대사의 속도를 조절하는 갑상선의 기능에 필수적인 미량원소이다. 약간의 요오드 결핍은 갑상선이 있는 목 부위가 크게 부어오르게 할지도 모르는데, 이것이 단순갑상샘종으로 알려진 질환이다. 요오드가 완전히 없는 것은 치명적이다. 그러나 몸 안에 있는 요오드의 총량은 전체 몸무게의 약 1/2,500,000에 불과하다. 모든 미네랄의 경우와 마찬가지로, 요오드도 식단을 통해 몸에 공급되어야 한다.

---

19 **2022 한국항공대** ▶▶▶ MSG p.67 ①

수동태 ▶ 주어인 Use of animals in research는 oppose하는 행위를 할 수 없으며, 그러므로 행위의 주체가 아닌 대상으로 파악해야 한다. 따라서 첫 문장은 수동태가 되어야 한다. 따라서 ①은 과거분사 opposed가 되어야 한다.

mimic v. 모방하다 insight n. 식견, 통찰력 pathophysiology n. 병리 생리학 lead ~ astray ~을 잘못된 방향으로 이끌다 extrapolate v. 추론하다 compound n. 화합물 ischemic stroke 뇌경색, 허혈성, 뇌졸중 rodent n. 설치류 (동물) efficacious a. 효과적인 induced a. 유도된, 유발된

연구에 동물을 사용하는 것은 동물 모델이 항상 인간을 완전히 똑같이 모방하는 것은 아니기 때문에 때때로 반대에 부딪힌다. 모델로서의 동물이 병리 생리학이나 질병에 추가적인 통찰력을 제공할지도 모르지만, 동물은 또한 연구를 잘못된 방향으로 이끌 수도 있다. 동물 연구에 반대하는 사람들은 각각의 종(種)이 인간에게로 확대하여 추론하기에는 예측될 수 없거나 완전히 이해될 수 없는 미묘하지만 중요한 차이를 가지고 있다고 주장한다. 예를 들면, 설치류에서 허혈성 뇌졸중을 줄였던 화합물을 조사하는 연구에서, 그 화합물 중 어느 것도 인간을 대상으로 시험했을 때에는 효과적이지 않았다. 효과가 없었던 것은 인간에게서 오랜 시간에 걸쳐 발병하는 자연적인 뇌졸중과 실험을 통해 유발시켜 몇 주에 걸쳐 생기게 한 설치류의 뇌졸중 사이에 차이가 있었기 때문이었는지도 모른다.

20 **2019 광운대** ▶▶▶ MSG p.12, p.125 ②

정비문 ▶ ①, ②, ③과 관련하여, 간접의문문에서 주절 동사가 say나 think인 경우에는 의문사가 문두에 오고 know인 경우에는 의문사가 know의 목적어 절에 있게 된다. 두 경우 모두 목적어 절은 '주어+동사' 어순이다. ① 주절 동사가 say인 의문문으로 의문사인 On which month가 문두에 왔다. ③ 주절 동사가 think여서 의문사 who(m)가 think의 목적어 절을 이끄는 의문사로 think 다음에 있지 않고 문두에 왔으며 또 하나의 의문사 what은 원래의 자리에 그대로 있어서 옳은 표현이다. When do you think Hans studied at which university? (너는 한스가 언제 어느 대학에서 공부했다고 생각하니?)의 at which university도 원래 자리에 그대로 있는 의문사이다. ④ not A but B(A가 아니라 B) 구문이 쓰였으며, how she looks는 '그녀의 외모'를, what she is는 '그녀의 인격'을 각각 의미하는 관용표현이다. ⑤ Why she talks like that(그녀가 그렇게 말하는 이유)이 주어, what은 is의 보어이자, 전치사 of의 목적어로 각각 맞게 쓰였다. ② 주절 동사가 know인 의문문이므로 의문사 which bus가 문두에 오지 않고 know의 목적어 절 맨 앞자리에 온 것은 맞지만, she is waiting for the bus to go home이므로 waiting 다음에 for를 넣어 waiting for to go home이 되어야 한다.

get married 결혼하다 curious a. 호기심이 강한, 알고 싶어 하는

① 너는 우리가 어느 달에 결혼해야 한다고 말했니?
② 너는 그녀가 집에 가기 위해 어느 버스를 기다리고 있는지 아니?
③ 너는 우리가 누구를 만나서 무엇에 대해 이야기를 해야 한다고 생각하니?
④ 그녀를 외모로 판단하지 말고 인격으로 판단해라!
⑤ 그녀가 그렇게 말하는 이유는 모두가 궁금히 여기는 것이다!

T E S T **24**

| 01 ④ | 02 ① | 03 ① | 04 ② | 05 ① | 06 ② | 07 ① | 08 ① | 09 ③ | 10 ④ |
| 11 ① | 12 ④ | 13 ② | 14 ② | 15 ④ | 16 ③ | 17 ② | 18 ⑤ | 19 ③ | 20 ⑤ |

01 **2020 서울여대** ▶▶▶ MSG p.223   ④

문두의 보어 도치 & so ~ that 구문 ▶ so ~ that 구문에서 형용사 보어가 강조되어 주어와 동사가 도치된 구문이다. 'so+보어(common)+동사(are)+주어(cases of ~ in Japan)+that'으로 이루어지므로 빈칸에는 접속사 ④ that이 필요하다.

die from overwork 과로로 사망하다

일본에서 과로로 사망하는 사람들의 사례가 너무 흔해서 그 나라에는 그것을 지칭하는 'karoshi(과로사)'라 부르는 특별한 용어가 있다.

02 **2014 서울여대** ▶▶▶ MSG p.121   ①

상관접속사 not only A but (also) B ▶ 상관접속사 'not only A but (also) B' 구문에서 not only가 문두에 쓰이면 주어와 동사가 도치가 된다. 따라서 the head of student government ~ honor students가 주어, were가 동사가 되며, 이 동사에 대한 보어가 없으므로 빈칸에는 보어 역할을 할 수 있는 어구가 들어가야 한다. 따라서 ①의 women이 적절하다.

student government 학생회 senior a. 4학년의 honor student 우등생

학생회 회장, 4학년 회장, 그리고 그 대학의 우등생 141명 중 96명이 여성이었을 뿐 아니라, 졸업생의 3분의 2도 여성이었다.

03 **2020 서울여대** ▶▶▶ MSG p.200   ①

배수 원급비교 ▶ 배수의 표현 뒤에는 '배수+as ~ as'를 쓰므로, '배수(twice)+as+보어(valuable)'의 어순으로 쓰인 ①이 빈칸에 적절하다.

save v. 저축하다 retirement n. 은퇴, 퇴직, 정년(停年)

20세에 1달러를 저축하는 것은 40세에 1달러를 저축하는 것보다 은퇴할 때 두 배나 가치가 있다.

04 **2018 한국산업기술대** ▶▶▶ MSG p.140   ②

관계절 ▶ 이미 완전한 형태의 문장이 주어져 있으므로, 빈칸에는 앞의 명사 the art를 수식하는 표현이 들어가야 한다. 따라서 목적격 관계대명사가 생략된 he is famous for가 빈칸에 적절하며, 이것은 형용사절

로서 앞의 명사를 수식하는 역할을 한다.

best-known a. 가장 잘 알려진 fit v. ~에 적합하다

1935년에 태어난 크리스토(Christo)는 가장 잘 알려져 있는 현존 예술가들 중 한 사람이다. 그러나 그를 유명하게 만든 예술작품은 미술관 안에 들여놓기에 결코 적합할 수 없을 것이다.

05 **2019 덕성여대** ▶▶▶ MSG p.203   ①

비교구문과 대동사 ▶ 비교급 easier가 있으므로 than이 와야 하고, than절의 주어 it이 car production을 가리키고 than절은 than it once was an easy job이므로 여기서 술부를 was로 대신한 ①이 빈칸에 적절하다.

AI n. 인공지능(=artificial intelligence)

자동차 산업에서, 인공지능 로봇의 사용은 자동차 생산을 예전보다 훨씬 더 편한 일이 되게 했다.

06 **2020 세종대** ▶▶▶ MSG p.55, p.227   ②

수동태 + '목적'을 나타내는 전치사 for ▶ 주어인 물(Water)이 차단(shut)하는 행위의 주체가 아니라 차단되는 대상이므로 수동태가 되어야 하며, 배관 수리(plumbing repairs)는 단수 조치의 목적에 해당하므로 목적의 전치사 for가 필요하다.

plumbing n. (수도·가스의) 배관 수리(공사) repair n. 수리

목요일 오전 4시에서 오후 7시 사이에 배관 수리를 위해 그 건물로 들어가는 물이 차단될 것이다.

07 **2020 세종대** ▶▶▶ MSG p.28, p.138   ①

관계대명사의 계속적용법 + 4형식 동사 tell ▶ 앞의 절 전체를 선행사로 하는 관계대명사는 which이며, tell은 4형식동사로 쓰일 때 'tell+목적어+that절'의 형태를 취할 수 있다.

dinosaur n. 공룡

어린 공룡이었을 때 '리무사우루스(Limusaurus)'는 날카로운 이빨을 갖고 있었는데, 이는 과학자들에게 리무사우르스가 육식을 했다는 것을 말해준다.

08 **2022 숙명여대** ▶▶▶ MSG p.133, p.235 ①

문의 구성 ▶ 빈칸 앞까지 완결된 절이므로 빈칸에는 접속사가 필요하다. 그리고 it은 "owning and living in a freestanding house on its own land"를 가리키는 대명사이며, 젊은이들과 이전 세대를 비교하고 있으므로 동사 was 다음에는 of earlier generations가 필요하다. of 앞에는 a goal이 생략되었다. 따라서 ①이 정답이다.

poll n. 여론조사 freestanding a. (조각·담 등이) 독립해 있는, 버팀 없이 서 있는

최근 여론 조사에 따르면, 자신의 땅에 단독 주택을 소유하고 사는 것은 그것이 이전 세대의 목표였던 것처럼 지금도 여전히 대다수 젊은이들의 목표이다.

09 **2019 덕성여대** ▶▶▶ MSG p.34, p.97 ③

동명사와 동사 help의 용법 ▶ 전치사 of의 목적어로 동명사 helping이 와야 하고, help 동사는 5형식으로 쓰일 때 'help+목적어+to부정사' 혹은 'help+목적어+원형부정사'로 쓰이며, quit은 동명사를 목적어로 취한다. 앞서 언급한 세 가지 조건을 모두 만족시키는 ③이 정답으로 적절하다.

hypnosis n. 최면, 최면술 quit smoking 담배를 끊다

과거에는, 사람들이 담배를 끊도록 도와주는 수단으로 최면술이 때때로 사용되었다.

10 **2020 수원대** ▶▶▶ MSG p.59 ④

지각동사의 수동태 ▶ 지각동사 witness가 5형식으로 쓰일 경우, '주어+witness+목적어+동사원형'의 형태를 취하는데, 이를 수동태로 고칠 경우, 'be witnessed to부정사 (by 주어)' 형태가 되며, 이때 주어가 일반인을 가리킬 경우, 'by 주어'는 생략 가능하다. 따라서 ④를 to use로 고쳐야 한다.

alleged criminal 범죄용의자 witness v. 목격하다

그 수사관은 범죄용의자가 이용하는 것이 목격된 바로 그 차를 발견했다.

11 **2021 서울여대** ▶▶▶ MSG p.125 ①

의문사 ▶ ①이 이끄는 의문사절에 타동사 has의 목적어가 없으므로 옳지 않다. 따라서 의문부사 how를 명사 역할을 하는 how much나 의문대명사 what으로 고쳐야 한다. ④ 완전자동사 emerge 뒤에 쓰인 준보어이다.

have a lot to do with ~와 많은 관련이 있다 obesity n. 비만

당신이 어떤 사람인지, 당신이 어디에 사는지, 당신의 가족이 은행에 얼마를 가지고 있는지는 당신의 아이가 비만에 희생될 것인지 혹은 아무 탈 없이 태어날 것인지와 많은 관련이 있다.

12 **2021 단국대** ▶▶▶ MSG p.229 ④

부사 instead와 전치사 instead of의 구분 ▶ instead는 '그 대신'이라는 뜻의 부사로, instead를 그대로 둘 경우, "지금은 그 대신 정규직을 하며, 자원봉사를 한다"는 말이 되어 은퇴했다는 의미와 맞지 않는다. 문맥상 "지금은 정규직으로 일을 하는 대신, 자원봉사를 한다"는 말이 되어야 하므로, ④를 of holding으로 고쳐야 한다.

full-time job 정규직 do volunteer work 자원봉사를 하다

은퇴하신 나의 할아버지는 직장에서 일하셨을 때처럼 활동적이시지만, 지금은 정규직으로 일하시는 대신, 자원봉사를 하신다.

13 **2013 중앙대** ▶▶▶ MSG p.218 ②

병치 ▶ both A and B 구문에서, A와 B에 오는 표현은 그 문법적 역할과 구조가 같아야 한다. 따라서 both가 들어갈 위치는 형용사 contrary와 전치사 to 사이가 적절하다. and 다음의 'to 명사'인 to the deepest ~ Western culture와 병치를 이루기 위해서이다. ②를 contrary both to로 바로 잡아야 한다.

conventional a. 전통적인 deterministic a. 결정론적인

생명의 역사에 대한 그러한 견해는 서구과학의 전통적인 결정론적인 모델 및 서구문화의 가장 깊은 사회적 전통과 심리적 기대와는 매우 상반된다.

14 **2016 서강대** ▶▶▶ MSG p.40 ②

동사 impress의 용법 ▶ ②에 쓰인 impress는 주로 타동사로 쓰이면서, 'impress+목적어+ 전치사(on, with)+명사'의 형태를 수반한다. 또한 명사 impression을 make나 have의 목적어로 하여 '~에게 인상[감명]을 주다'는 뜻을 나타낼 수도 있다. 따라서 ②를 impress ourselves on이나 make an impression on으로 바로잡는 것이 적절하다.

ornament v. 장식하다 chunk n. 상당히 많은 양

오늘날 우리는 많은 물질을 소유하는 것을 즐기기보다는 타인의 마음에 깊은 인상을 주기 위해 상품과 서비스들로 우리 자신을 장식하는데, 이는 '물질주의'라는 용어를 우리가 하는 소비 중의 많은 부분을 크게 잘못 이해시키는 용어로 만들어버리는 사실이다.(이런 사실에 비추어보면 우리는 물질주의라는 용어를 사용함으로써 우리가 하는 소비 중의 많은 부분을 크게 오해하고 있는 것이다.)

15 **2005 한양대** ▶▶▶ MSG p.169 ④

재귀대명사의 쓰임 ▶ 대명사는 앞에 나온 어떤 것을 다시 가리키는 데 쓴다. 본문의 경우 ④ him은 오웰(Orwell) 외에 어떤 사람이 있어야 하는데, 없으므로 적절치 못한 표현이다. 의미상 오웰이 묘사하고 있는 대상은 '자기 자신'이기 때문에 ④ him 대신에 재귀대명사 himself를 써야 올바른 표현이 된다.

pin down 파악하다 vehement a. 열심인, 열정적인; 격렬한 anarchist n. 무정부주의자

조지 오웰(George Orwell)의 최고 작품은 정치적이지만, 그의 정치학은 파악하기 어렵다. 비록 작품 속에서는 열정적이지만 개인적으로는 수줍음이 많았던 오웰은 자기 자신을 좌익 사회주의자이자 반공주의자인 동시에 토리당 무정부주의자로 적절하게 묘사했다.

16   2005 한국외대 ▶▶▶ MSG p.63   ③

수동태와 능동태의 구분 ▶ ①은 Scholars가 복수 주어이므로 동사도 have로 수일치가 되어 있고 현재완료시제 또한 문제가 없다. ②에서 matter는 본래 자동사로 '중요하다, 문제가 되다'라는 뜻 외에도 명사로 '문제'라는 뜻으로 사용되므로 matters라는 표현에 문제가 없다. ④의 extraordinary는 형용사로서 depth라는 명사를 꾸며주고 있다. ⑤의 shown by는 앞의 reading and thought를 수식하는 과거분사구이다. Spencer, Shakespeare, or Jonson 세 사람에 의하여 보여진 학식과 사상이라 해석되므로 전혀 오류가 없다. ③은 and를 사이에 두고 Scholars라는 동일한 주어로 2개의 동사가 병치되고 있으므로 'have+p.p'로 수일치시켜야 한다. 그런데 수는 일치되어 있지만 수동태로 사용해야 하는 표현이 능동형으로 쓰였으므로 잘못되었다. ③을 have been contented with로 고쳐야 한다. 참고로, '제 분수에 만족하고 있다'라고 표현하려면 He is contented(content) with his lot이라고 써야 한다.

scholar n. 학자 Jacobean a. (영국의 왕) 제임스 1세 시대의 literature n. 문학 extraordinary a. 놀라운; 비범한

엘리자베스와 제임스 1세 시대의 뛰어난 문학을 연구하는 학자들은 국가와 권력에 관련되는 수많은 현대 문제들을 발견하여 기뻐했고, 스펜서(Spenser), 셰익스피어(Shakespeare) 또는 존슨(Jonson)에 의해 보여진 놀라울 정도의 깊이 있는 학식과 사상에 대하여 만족스러워했다.

17   2020 홍익대 ▶▶▶ MSG p.30   ②

view A as B 구문 ▶ view A as B 구문은 'A를 B로 보다[여기다]'라는 의미로, B의 자리에는 A를 설명하는 보어가 온다. 주어진 문장의 경우, a reorganization of political tendencies가 B의 자리에 온 보어에 해당하므로, 그 앞에 전치사 for는 필요하지 않다. ②에서 for를 삭제해야 한다.

Democrat n. 민주주의자; 민주당원 liberal a. 진보적인 Republican n. 공화주의자; 공화당원 conservative a. 보수적인; 신중한 phenomenon n. 현상 reorganization n. 재편, 재조직 polarization n. 대립, 양극화 sorting n. 분류, 구분 electorate n. 선거민, (전체) 유권자

50년 전에 비해 현재의 민주당원은 더 진보적이고 공화당원은 더 보수적이다. 어떤 사람들은 이러한 현상을 행동이나 대중 양극화에 거의 영향을 미치지 않는 정치적 성향의 재편에 불과한 것으로 보는 반면, 다른 사람들은 이러한 구분이 유권자들에게서 나타나고 있는 깊은 양극화를 반영하는 것이라 여긴다.

18   2022 이화여대 ▶▶▶ MSG p.109   ⑤

수동의 과거분사 ▶ 군대가 명령을 내리는 데 어려움을 겪었다는 뜻이 되려면 ⑤의 hard-pressing을 hard-pressed(돈/시간에 쫓기는, 곤경에 처해진)라는 수동의 과거분사로 고쳐야 한다.

hard-pressed a. ~하는 데 애를 먹는, 쪼들리는 drop n. 감소, 하락 manpower n. 인력 authorized strength 인가 병력 desertion n. 탈영

남북전쟁의 포화가 마침내 잦아들었을 때 미 육군은 인력의 급격한 감소를 겪었다. 인가된 병력은 1867년 5만 7,000명에서 10년 후 절반으로 줄어들었다가 19세기 말 스페인과 전쟁을 할 때까지 평균 2만 6,000명 수준을 유지했다. 그러나 효과적인 병력은 높아진 질병율과 탈영 비율로 인해 늘 인가 병력에 못 미쳤고, 그래서 미 육군은 질서와 안전을 유지하는 데 필요한 명령과 통제를 제공하는 데 어려움을 겪었다.

19   2021 아주대 ▶▶▶ MSG p.69, p.71   ③

가정법 미래에서 if 생략과 조동사 should의 도치 ▶ 가정법 미래 조건절 If Tyrol's entire ski season should falter에서 접속사 If가 생략되면 주어와 조동사 should가 도치된다. 따라서 ③에서 If를 생략하고 Should로 시작하거나, If는 그대로 두고 should를 falter 바로 앞으로 옮겨야 한다.

ski lift (스키 타는 사람들을 실어 나르는) 리프트 impoverish v. 빈곤하게 하다 lucrative a. 수익성이 좋은 upscale a. 부자의, 상류 계급의 ruin n. 붕괴, 몰락, 파산 falter v. 불안정해지다, 흔들리다 wipe out ~을 완전히 파괴하다[없애 버리다] pandemic n. 전국적인 유행병 glimpse n. (완전히는 못 보고) 잠깐[언뜻] 봄, 일별 Fahrenheit n. 화씨

지난 수십 년간 스키 리프트들은 궁핍하고 소외된 산간마을들을 돈 잘 버는 관광명소로 탈바꿈시키는 데 일조했다. 이제는 그 부유한 스포츠에 대한 경제적 의존이 그 마을들을 파산에 이르게 할 수도 있다. 3월에 리조트들이 폐쇄된 이후 지금까지 이미 수십억 달러의 손실이 발생했다. 티롤(Tyrol) 지방의 전체 스키 시즌이 좌절된다면, 오스트리아 국내 총생산의 3%가 사라지게 될 것이다. 어떤 점에서는, 세계적 역병이 스키 리조트들에 미치는 영향을 통해 기후가 화씨 3.6도 더 더워질 미래를 언뜻 들여다볼 수 있다. 그때가 되면 이미 동부 알프스 리조트들의 1/3이 시즌 최고 성수기인 크리스마스 휴일 때까지도 스키 리프트를 개장할 수 없을 것이다.

20   2019 광운대 ▶▶▶ MSG p.83, p.179   ⑤

정비문 ▶ ① cannot 다음에 too가 나오면, '아무리 ~해도 지나치지 않다'로 해석하며, 전치사 in의 목적어로 동명사 choosing이 온 것이다. ② if절에는 'if+주어+had p.p.'가, 주절에는 '주어+could have p.p.'가 각각 와서 가정법 과거완료의 동사들이 올바르게 쓰였다. ③ is to be seen은 '가능'을 뜻하는 be to 용법으로 쓰였다. ④ unless는 '만약 ~이 아니면'을 뜻하는 접속사로, unless 앞이 주절, unless 이하가 조건절로 쓰였으며, is caught young은 '어린 상태로 잡히다'는 뜻으로, young이 주어의 상태를 나타내는 준보어로 쓰였다. ⑤ unhappy는 사람을 주어로 하는 형용사이므로, ⑤를 I am unhappy to hear that the shop went broke.로 고쳐야 한다.

curfew n. 통행금지시간 tame v. 길들이다 go broke 파산하다

① 친구를 고르는 데 있어서는 아무리 신중해도 지나치지 않다.
② 내가 늦잠을 자지만 않았어도, 그녀를 도와줄 수 있었을 텐데.
③ 통행금지시간 동안, 거리에 사람이라곤 보이지 않는다.
④ 사자는 어릴 때 잡히지 않으면 길들일 수 없다.
⑤ 나는 그 가게가 파산했다는 소식을 들어 기분이 좋지 않다.

TEST 25

01 ②	02 ③	03 ⑤	04 ③	05 ④	06 ②	07 ①	08 ④	09 ③	10 ④
11 ③	12 ⑤	13 ④	14 ④	15 ②	16 ④	17 ②	18 ②	19 ①	20 ③

---

01 2013 가천대 ▶▶▶ MSG p.234   ②

It ~ that … 강조구문 ▶ 2개의 절이 연속적으로 나열된 상태이므로, 빈칸에 들어가기에 적절한 접속사를 찾는 문제라 할 수 있다. that이 들어가면 문두의 It was와 함께 함께 강조구문을 이루게 되므로 옳은 문장이 된다.

plunge v. 던져서 넣다; (어떤 상태에) 몰아넣다 disaster n. 재해, 재난, 참사; 큰 불행

그따위 것이 결국 자신의 삶 전체를 바꿔 놓은 큰 불행으로 그를 내던지게 만든 것은 다름 아닌 그의 지각 때문이었다.

---

02 2008 단국대 ▶▶▶ MSG p.105   ③

현재분사와 과거분사의 구분 ▶ 빈칸 뒤에 atmosphere를 목적어로 받고 앞에 있는 the carbon dioxide를 수식하기 위해서는 타동사의 현재분사인 ③ entering만이 가능하다.

skeptic n. 회의론자 greenhouse effect 온실 효과 water vapor 수증기 atmosphere n. 대기; 분위기

지구 온난화의 원인들에 대해서, 회의론자들은 대부분의 온실 효과가 수증기로부터 발생되고 대기 중으로 들어오는 이산화탄소 중 단 4퍼센트만이 인간의 활동 때문이라고 주장하고 있다.

---

03 2012 숙명여대 ▶▶▶ MSG p.71   ⑤

가정법 과거완료 구문의 도치 ▶ 콤마 앞에 위치한 Had there been no oxygen present는 If there had been no oxygen present에서 If를 생략하면서 도치가 이루어진 형태이다. 이것은 가정법 과거완료의 조건절의 형태이므로, 귀결절의 동사 형태는 '조동사의 과거형+have p.p'여야 한다. ⑤가 정답이다.

insurance company 보험회사 presence n. (특정한 곳에) 있음, 존재함 oxygen n. 산소

보험회사는 원인불명의 화재의 원인을 판정하도록 조사관들을 보낼 것이다. 만약 조사관들이 대기 중에 산소가 있어서 화재가 발생했다는 보고서를 보내면, 그들은 직장을 곧 잃게 될 것이다. 그러나 조사관들은 옳을 것이다. 만약 그곳에 산소가 없었더라면, 화재는 발생하지 않았을 것이다.

---

04 2019 덕성여대 ▶▶▶ MSG p.227   ③

명사를 수식하는 전치사구 ▶ 빈칸 앞에 완전한 문장이 주어져 있으므로 앞의 명사 a person을 수식하는 전치사구 ③이 빈칸에 적절하다. ① 완전한 절 뒤에 접속사 없이 새로운 술부가 이어질 수 없다. 앞에 관계대명사 who가 있어야 한다. ④ 알레르기를 가지는 주체는 사람이므로 관계대명사 who를 써야 하며, 분사 단독으로는 문장의 동사 역할을 할 수 없으므로 시제를 가진 정동사를 써야 한다.

substance n. 물질, 물체 allergy n. 알레르기 reaction n. 반응, 반작용

알레르기가 없는 사람에게 완벽하게 좋은 물질이 알레르기가 있는 사람에게는 가벼운 반응 내지 심각한 반응을 일으킬 수 있다.

---

05 2020 세종대 ▶▶▶ MSG p.137   ④

관계대명사절 ▶ 빈칸 앞에 3형식동사 keep의 수동태인 be kept가 주어져 있으므로, 그 뒤에 ①, ②와 같이 명사구가 이어질 수는 없다. ③의 경우, 관계대명사 which 뒤에 it is issued라는 완전한 절이 오게 되어 적절하지 않다. '전치사+관계대명사(for which)'인 ④가 정답이다.

validate v. 승인하다, 인정하다 registration n. 기입, 등록 facsimile copy 복사본 issue v. 발행하다, 출판하다

이 승인된 등록카드나 복사본은 등록카드가 발행된 해당 차량에 보관되어야 한다.

---

06 2012 서울여대 ▶▶▶ MSG p.193   ②

부사의 위치 ▶ 완료시제에 많이 쓰이는 never는 have 다음에 오는 것이 일반적이고, before는 never 다음이나 맨 끝에 오는 것이 일반적이다. 따라서 빈칸에는 ②가 적절하며 that had never been considered before도 가능하다.

inventive a. 발명에 재능이 있는, 독창적인 thoughtful a. 사려 깊은, 인정 있는

생각이 깊을 뿐만 아니라 창의적인 그녀는 전에 결코 생각되지 않았던 방식으로 사람들을 도왔다.

07 **2007 세종대** ▶▶▶ MSG p.94, p.123

문의 구성 ▶ 문두에 '주어(The problem)+동사(is)'가 주어져 있는데 문미에 다시금 주어와 동사가 있는 것으로 보아, 명사절이 동사 is의 보어가 됨을 알 수 있다. 따라서 명사절을 이끄는 접속사 that이 들어가야 한다. that이 쓰인 ①과 ③ 중 '~은 말할 것도 없고, ~은 물론이고'라는 의미의 let alone이 쓰인 ①이 정답이다.

singular a. 남다른, 특이한; 둘도 없는 self n. 자아 matter v. 중요하다

문제는 삶에서는 말할 것도 없고 소설에서도 단일한 자아가 중요하다는 것 이다.

08 **2019 덕성여대** ▶▶▶ MSG p.28 ④

recommend A to B ▶ recommend는 give처럼 간접목적어를 뒤로 보낼 때 전치사 to를 쓰는 동사이다. 즉 recommend A B = recommend B to A(A에게 B를 추천하다)이다. 따라서 ④가 적절하다.

nutritionist n. 영양전문가, 영양학자 recommend v. 추천하다 barley n. 보리

영양학자들은 보리 주스를 노화과정의 속도를 늦추는 수단으로 추천하고 있으며 그것을 암 환자들에게도 권하고 있다.

09 **2022 숙명여대** ▶▶▶ MSG p.154 ③

문의 구성 ▶ 질병의 이름인 diabetes(당뇨병)는 형태는 복수이지만 단수로 취급한다. 동사도 단수형이 되어야 할 것이므로 복수동사인 ①, ②, ④는 빈칸에 적절하지 않다. 그리고 심장병과 암에 이어 당뇨병이 3대 사망 원인이라는 의미가 되기 위해서는 by heart disease and cancer 앞에 only가 위치해 only가 두 질환을 한정하도록 해야 한다. 따라서 ③이 빈칸에 적절하다.

diabetes n. 당뇨병 complication n. 합병증

심각한 합병증과 함께 당뇨병은 심장병과 암에 이어 국내 세 번째로 주된 사망 원인으로 꼽는다.

10 **2021 한국외대** ▶▶▶ MSG p.125 ④

간접의문절 ▶ 명사절을 이끄는 접속사 that 이하에는 완전한 절이 온다. 그러나 ④의 명사절에서는 that 다음에 주어가 없고 전치사 like 다음도 비어있다. 따라서 how it will turn out의 it을 가리키는 it을 주어로 삼고 like의 목적어에 해당하는 의문사 what을 사용하여 ④를 what it is로 고쳐야 한다.

not ~ in the slightest 조금도 ~ 않다

그것이 어떻게 판명될지는 모르지만, 그것이 어떠할지를 그녀가 정확히 아는 것이 명백하기 때문에 나는 조금도 걱정하지 않는다.

11 **2021 서울여대** ▶▶▶ MSG p.121 ③

not A but B 구문 ▶ ③에 쓰인 but also는 not only와 호응해서 쓰는 표현인데 반해, 주어진 문장에는 not만 주어져 있으므로 not only A but also B 구문이 아닌 not A but B 구문이 되어야 한다. ③에서 also를 삭제한다.

pursuit n. 추적; 추구 unique a. 유일무이한; 독특한

인간을 동물과 구분 짓는 것은 자연계 모든 곳에서 일어나는 행복의 추구가 아니라 인간만의 특징인 의미의 추구다.

12 **2013 성균관대** ▶▶▶ MSG p.141 ⑤

관계사절에서의 주어와 동사의 수일치 ▶ ③ at which가 이끄는 관계사절 안에 다시 ④ which가 이끄는 관계절이 삽입된 형태이다. ⑤ are의 주어는 famine이므로 주어와 동사의 수일치가 되지 않은 상태이다. ⑤를 is로 고쳐야 한다. 전치사 throughout의 경우, 장소(world), 시간(history)의 명사를 목적어로 취할 수 있다.

evolution n. 전개, 발전; 진화 famine n. 기근; 굶주림 civilization n. 문명 acute a. 날카로운; 심각한

역사적으로 문명의 흥망성쇠를 본질적으로 지배해왔던 굶주림이 선진 세계 전역에 걸쳐 더 이상 심각한 위협이 되지 않는 수준으로 우리는 발전했다.

13 **2016 가천대** ▶▶▶ MSG p.167 ④

소유대명사 ▶ 소유대명사는 명사의 중복을 피하려 하는 경우에 사용한다. 원래는 "the fault must be his fault"인데 명사의 반복을 피하기 위해서는 소유대명사를 써야 하므로, ④는 his가 되어야 한다.

natural resource 천연자원 look forward to ~를 고대[기대]하다 lazy a. 게으른, 나태한

미국의 천연자원 덕분에 모든 미국인들은 매우 최근까지 그들의 아버지보다 더 많은 돈을 벌 것이라고 이치에 맞게 고대했었다. 그래서 미국인이 돈을 (아버지보다) 더 적게 벌면, 그 잘못은 필경 그 자신의 잘못이었다. 그가 게으르거나 무능해서였다.

14 **2014 가천대** ▶▶▶ MSG p.204 ④

"the 비교급, the 비교급" 구문의 어순 ▶ the 비교급~, the 비교급…은 '~하면 할수록, 더욱 더 …하다'라는 뜻으로 쓰이며, 이때 the 비교급은 뒤에 오는 절의 동사 뒤에 있던 보어, 목적어, 부사구 등이 문두로 온 것이다. 주어진 문장에서, the more confident는 절 맨 끝에서 동사 deliver를 수식하는 부사인 것이 문두로 온 것이므로 the more confidently여야 한다. 따라서 ④의 confident는 confidently로 고쳐야 한다. ① 첫 문장에 삽입된 if절은 가정법 절이 아닌 직설법으로 조건의 부사절이며 부탁을 '받은' 완료된 의미를 나타내므로 시제는 맞다.

② speak는 자동사로 쓰였으며, 전치사 to(까지)는 명사 limit 앞에 쓰여 '어떤 한계까지'의 뜻이 된다. ③ allotted는 '할당된'이란 뜻의 과거분사이다.

allotted a. 할당된 deliver v. (의견을) 말하다, (연설을) 하다

만약 당신이 정확한 시간 내에 연설해달라고 부탁받았다면 현명한 방법은 거울을 보며 연설을 하여 할당된 시간에 연설을 멈추고 그런 다음 이에 따라 연설을 줄여나가는 것이다. 당신이 연설에 숙달될수록, 더 자신 있게 연설할 수 있다.

15 2019 상명대 ▶▶▶ MSG p.184   ②

올바른 분수 표현 ▶ 분수 표현은 분자에 기수, 분모에 서수를 쓰며, 분자가 2이상일 경우 분모에 -s를 붙여 복수형으로 쓴다. 따라서 4분의 3은 three fourths로 써야 하므로, ②를 three fourths of로 고친다. ③ '~중에 절반'은 (a) half of ~이다. ④ polled는 companies를 후치 수식하는 과거분사이다. ⑤ 회사가 여론 조사에 참여한 시점보다 근로자들을 해고한 시점이 앞서므로 과거완료시제를 썼다.

fire v. 해고하다 discipline v. 훈련하다; 징계하다 violate v. 위반하다

노동부의 조사에 따르면, 미국의 주요 회사들 중 4분의 3이 근로자들의 통신내역을 기록하고 검토했다고 한다. 그리고 조사에 참여한 회사들 중 약 절반 정도가 회사의 컴퓨터 정책을 위반한 근로자들을 해고하거나 징계했다고 밝혔다.

16 2022 홍익대 ▶▶▶ MSG p.73   ④

as if 가정법 ▶ as if 다음에는 가정법 과거와 가정법 과거완료만 올 수 있으므로, 직설법 시제인 ④의 was는 부적절하다. ③에서 완료형 분사가 온 다음, 등위접속사 and로 이어져 있으므로, ④를 기준시제보다 한 시제 앞선 시제를 가정하는 가정법 과거완료 동사 had been으로 고쳐야 한다.

recuperate v. 회복시키다, 되찾다 narrative n. 이야기 privilege n. 특권 demonstrate v. 보여주다

이론가들과 작가들은 노예와 노예 소유주의 이야기뿐 아니라, 유럽의 근대성, 재산, 그리고 특권에 대한 이야기까지 되살려 냈으며, 어떻게 해서 흑인의 노동과 흑인의 지적 작품이 마치 유럽의 근대성에 의해 만들어진 것처럼 이해되어서는 안 되며, 그것이 유럽의 근대성을 만들어낸 것으로 이해되어야 하는지를 보여주었다.

17 2020 한양대 에리카 ▶▶▶ MSG p.125   ②

의문사가 이끄는 간접의문문의 어순 ▶ 접속사 although가 이끄는 부사절이 왔으므로, 콤마 다음에는 주절이 이어지는데, 의문사 how가 왔으므로 의문사가 이끄는 간접의문절이 주절의 주어이다. 이때 의문사가 이끄는 간접의문절의 어순은 의문사가 주어인 경우, '의문사+동사', 그리고 의문사가 주어가 아닌 경우, '의문사+주어+동사'의 어순을 취한

다. 의문사 다음에 the school이라는 주어가 왔으므로, ②를 '의문사+주어+동사' 형태인 how the school is로 고쳐야 한다.

school n. (물고기 등의) 떼[무리] vision n. 시각 lateral line <어류> 옆줄, 측선(몸의 측면에 있는 감각기관) transitory a. 일시적인, 덧없는, 무상한 displacement n. 이동

물고기가 무리지어 모이는 것이 동물이 보여주는 사회적 행동의 친숙한 형태이긴 하지만, 그 무리가 어떻게 형성되고 유지되는가는 이제야 자세히 이해되기 시작한다. 지금까지는 각각의 물고기가 주로 시각이라는 수단으로 자신의 위치를 유지한다고 여겨졌었다. (그러나) 우리가 실시한 연구는 물의 이동에 있어서의 일시적인 변화를 감지하는 기관인 측선이 시각만큼 중요하다는 것을 보여주었다.

18 2019 이화여대 ▶▶▶ MSG p.113   ②

수동 분사구문 ▶ ②에 쓰인 타동사 devote 뒤에 목적어가 주어져 있지 않으므로, 능동의 분사구문은 옳지 않다. the British economy가 devote하는 행위의 '대상'이므로 수동 분사구문이 되어야 하며, 따라서 ②를 largely devoted to로 고쳐야 한다. 이때 ②의 앞에는 being이 생략되었다.

specialized a. 전문화된, 분화된 devote v. (돈·시간 따위를) 바치다; 쏟다 civilian a. 일반인의, 민간의 abrupt a. 느닷없는, 갑작스러운 withdrawal n. 철수; 철회 Lend-Lease n. 무기대여법(미국이 연합국에게 무기와 물자를 지원한 제도) rationing n. 배급제도 malnutrition n. 영양실조

전시(戰時)에 영국 경제는 고도로 전문화된 기계가 되어, 주로 군대와 무기 생산에 전념했던 반면, 미국은 민간 경제에서 필요로 하는 것들을 공급해 주었다. 1945년에 갑작스럽게 렌드리스(Lend-Lease, 무기대여법)가 철회되자 영국 경제는 큰 피해를 입었으며, 아직도 그 피해로부터 회복하지 못했다고 말하는 이들도 있다. 전쟁 기간 내내 음식을 풍족하게 먹었던 영국인들은 크게 줄어든 배급으로 고통을 겪었으며, 그 결과 1940년대 후반부터 어린 학생들에게 심각한 영양실조의 징후가 나타나기 시작했다.

19 2019 명지대 ▶▶▶ MSG p.117   ①

동사와 현재분사의 구분 ▶ 분사 단독으로는 문장의 정동사 역할을 할 수 없다. 그러므로 ①에 쓰인 including을 시제를 가진 정동사로 고쳐야 한다. ①을 include the increased로 고친다.

modest a. 적절한, 온당한 technically trained 전문교육을 받은 law clerk 변호사·판사 등의 서기 grant v. 부여하다, 주다 fact-finding n. 진상조사

제도 개혁에 대한 적절한 접근방식들 중 하나는 재판관에 대한 전문적인 지원을 강화하자는 생각에 기초할 것이다. (이와 관련하여) 자주 논의되는 옵션에는 법원이 임명한 전문가나 특별 집행관이나 전문교육을 받은 서기를 복잡한 재판에서 더 많이 이용하는 것이 포함된다. 이런 방향으로 진행하는 데 필요한 공식적인 수단은 연방증거법(FRE)에 의거하여 이미 이용 가능하다. 연방증거법은 법원이 임명한 전문가나 배심원단에게 도움을 요청할 수 있는 광범위한 권한을, 재판관이 그런 절차가 과학적인 진상조사 과정에 도움이 된다고 판단할 경우, 재판관에게 부여하고 있다. (그러나) 이러한 권한은 연방법원에서는 실제로 거의 이용되지 않는다.

정비문 ▶ ① 주어가 what 관계절이고 to부정사가 보어가 될 경우, to
는 생략될 수 있다. ② object to의 목적어가 what이 되며, is 다음에
온 that절이 보어로 맞게 쓰였다. ④ While이 이끄는 부사절 다음에 주
절이 온 것으로, 과거진행형 시제와 과거시제는 같이 쓰일 수 있다. ③,
⑤ Whether we will finish on time과 Whether we will succeed는
모두 주어가 되지만, Whether절은 '~인지 여부'라는 뜻이므로,
depend on(~에 달려있다)과는 잘 어울리지만 ruin(망치다)과는 어울
리지 않는다. 따라서 ③이 정답이다.

on time 시간을 어기지 않고, 정각에 object to ~에 반대하다 ruin v. 망치다

① 내가 앞으로 할 일은 그 회의를 연기하는 것이다.
② 내가 반대하는 것은 그가 그것에 대해 거짓말을 했다는 점이다.
③ 우리가 시간을 어기지 않고 마칠 것인지 여부가 그날 오후를 망쳤다.
④ 내가 보스턴에서 일하고 있는 동안, 나는 고모와 같이 살았다.
⑤ 우리가 성공할지 여부는 주로 날씨에 달려있다.

01 ③	**02** ①	**03** ④	**04** ③	**05** ②	**06** ②	**07** ④	**08** ①	**09** ①	**10** ⑤
11 ③	**12** ②	**13** ②	**14** ④	**15** ②	**16** ③	**17** ②	**18** ①	**19** ④	**20** ⑤

---

01 2022 숙명여대 ▶▶▶ MSG p.205 ③

no more ~ than ▶ that절의 주어인 they는 선사시대 인간을 가리키는데, 고릴라, 반딧불이, 해파리가 환경에 영향을 미치지 않는 하찮은 동물이므로 선사시대 인간도 이들과 '마찬가지로 영향을 미치지 않는' 하찮은 동물이 되려면 빈칸에는 이들보다 '더 많은 영향을 미치는 것이 전혀 아닌'의 뜻으로 ③ no more가 적절하다. A … no more ~ than B 는 'A는 B와 마찬가지로 ~아니다'라는 뜻이다.

prehistoric a. 선사시대의 firefly n. 반딧불이 jellyfish n. 해파리

선사시대 인간에 대해 알아야 할 가장 중요한 점은 그들이 고릴라, 반딧불이 또는 해파리와 마찬가지로 환경에 영향을 미치지 않는 하찮은 동물이었다는 것이다.

---

02 2020 수원대 ▶▶▶ MSG p.137 ①

'선행사, 최상급 + of which + 동사' 구문 ▶ 접속사 없이 두 개의 절이 와서 어색하다. 따라서 빈칸에는 접속사나 접속사 역할을 하는 말이 와야 하겠는데, ②와 ③의 주격관계대명사는 관계절이 the most startling을 수식하여 앞 절과 연결되지 않는다. 그러므로 ①의 of which가 빈칸에 적절한데, the most startling of which는 원래 and the most startling of the loud laugh에서 반복되는 the loud laugh와 접속사 and 대신 관계대명사 which가 쓰여 the most startling of which가 된 것이다.

startling a. 깜짝 놀라게 하는 baronet n. 준(准)남작

큰 웃음이 있었는데, 그중에서 가장 깜짝 놀라게 하는 웃음은 준남작의 웃음이었다.

---

03 2010 경희대 ▶▶▶ MSG p.53 ④

시제일치 ▶ one day는 과거의 어느 날을 의미하므로 첫 번째 빈칸에는 과거를 나타내는 표현이 와야 한다. 따라서 ②와 ③은 제외한다. 두 번째 빈칸 다음에 today가 나와 있으므로 빈칸에는 현재시제가 와야 한다. 따라서 정답은 ④이다.

optical a. 눈의 public address system 확성 장치 screening n. 검사; 선발

한 대형 백화점에 사람들이 시력검사를 받고 안경을 살 수 있는 안경점이 있었다. 어느 날, 그 안경점은 무료 시력검사를 하고 있었다. 그래서 확성기를 통해 이러한 사실을 알렸다. "안경점에서 오늘 무료 시력검사를 합니다." 백화점에서 물건을 사고 있던 많은 사람들이 그 방송을 듣고 서둘러서 안경점으로 갔는데 거기에는 긴 줄이 있었다. 그러나 사람들이 무료 시력검사를 위해 기다리고 있는 줄이 아님이 밝혀졌다. 그들은 공짜 아이스크림을 기다리고 있었다.

---

04 2018 세종대 ▶▶▶ MSG p.138 ③

문의 구성 ▶ 빈칸은 주어를 이루어야 하므로, 대명사 All과 이것을 선행사로 하는 관계대명사절로 이루어져 있는 ③이 빈칸에 적절하다. ①은 절인데 명사절을 이끄는 접속사가 없어 주어가 될 수 없으므로 빈칸에 부적절하며, ②는 clarity 대신 형용사 clear가 되어야 한다. ④의 경우, 관계대명사 what이 이끄는 명사절이 주어가 될 수 있으나, are가 아니라 is여야 한다.

clarity n. 투명; 명쾌함 clear a. 분명한

정말로 분명한 전부는 디지털 형태로는 그 누구의 비밀도 비밀로 지속되지 않는다는 것이다.

---

05 2013 서울여대 ▶▶▶ MSG p.197 ②

have ~ at one's command ▶ 빈칸에는 빈칸 뒤의 명사를 목적어로 가질 수 있는 ②의 '타동사 + 부사구'가 문법적으로 알맞다. had의 목적어가 길어서 뒤로 후치한 것이다. ③도 '타동사 + 명사 + 전치사'로 뒤의 목적어를 가질 수 있는 구조이기는 하나 의미상으로 맞지 않다. had a (good) command of여야 한다.

have ~ at one's command ~을 마음대로 쓸[구사할 수] 있다 woodblock n. 목판

일찍이 2세기에, 중국인들은 세 가지 인쇄의 기본 요소들, 즉 종이, 잉크, 그리고 목판으로 만든 제품을 마음대로 사용할 수 있었다.

---

06 2003 숭실대 ▶▶▶ MSG p.176 ②

other와 another의 구분 ▶ 빈칸은 일본을 제외한 다른 나라들을 일컬으므로 many other가 적절하며 뒤의 countries가 복수이므로 another는 쓸 수 없다. 일본과 다른 나라들의 비교이므로 앞에서 국가 앞에 in을 썼듯이 as 다음에도 in이 필요하다. 따라서 ②가 정답으로 가장 적절하다.

advertising n. 광고 country n. 국가, 나라

많은 다른 나라들에서처럼 일본에서도 광고가 사람들에게 좀 더 많이 사도록 영향력을 끼친다. 하지만 세이카츠(Seikatsu) 클럽에서는 이것에 대항하여 싸우고 있다.

07 2010 동국대 ▶▶▶ MSG p.156 ④

명사의 수량표시 ▶ 막연한 수를 표시할 때는 dozen, score, hundred, thousand 등의 수의 단위에 '-s'를 붙이고, 'of+복수명사'를 취한다. '필요한 경우에'라는 의미를 나타낼 때, if needed나 if necessary 외에도, 관용적으로 if need be를 쓴다. 따라서 이 둘을 모두 만족시키는 ④가 정답이다.

minimize v. 최소화하다 strike n. 파업 hesitate v. 주저하다

직원들의 고용을 유지하고, 파업과 시위를 최소화시키는 데 중국정부가 초점을 맞추는 것을 고려할 때, 중국정부는 필요하다면 수백억 달러를 추가적으로 투자하는 것에도 주저하지 않을 것이다.

08 2021 한국산업기술대 ▶▶▶ MSG p.111 ①

분사구문 ▶ 처음부터 media까지가 완결된 절이며, 그다음에 each를 의미상 주어로 하여 올바른 분사구문으로 된 것은 ①이다. each has advantages over the other를 분사구문으로 바꾸어 has가 having으로 된 것이다. 두 개의 매체를 언급하는 것이므로 둘 중 나머지 하나는 the other이지 ③과 ④의 the others가 아니다.

billboard n. 광고판 complementary a. 상호보완적인

광고판과 라디오는 상호보완적인 매체로서 각각이 특정한 종류의 광고에는 다른 것에 비해 장점이 있는데, 이는 광고가 가장 큰 영향을 미치기 위해서는 어떤 메시지는 보게 해야 하고, 또 어떤 메시지는 듣게 해야 하기 때문이다.

09 2016 아주대 ▶▶▶ MSG p.136 ①

적절한 관계대명사절 ▶ 빈칸에 보기를 넣으면 두 개의 동사 즉, have와 is가 있게 되므로, 빈칸에는 접속사를 자체에 포함하고 있는 관계사가 반드시 필요하다. 그러므로 관계사가 없는 ③을 먼저 정답에서 제외할 수 있다. ①의 경우, 의미상 the other life-forms of our planet's continued existence의 관계가 성립하고, 소유격 관계대명사 whose 뒤에 관사 없는 명사가 올바르게 왔으므로 빈칸에 적절한 표현이다. 현재분사 continuing과 과거분사 continued 모두 가능하다. ② 주격 관계대명사 which인 점과 수동태에 현재분사 threatening을 쓴 점이 옳지 않다. ④ of 때문에 is의 주어가 없다. ⑤ 수동태에 현재분사 threatening이 와서 옳지 않다.

thoughtless a. 분별없는; 경솔한 species n. 종류; 종(種)

우리는 그들의 존속이 인간이라는 종(種)의 분별없는 행동에 의해 위협받고 있는 지구상의 다른 생명체들에 대해서도 책임을 지고 있다.

10 2021 숙명여대 ▶▶▶ MSG p.25 ⑤

forbid + 목적어 + to 부정사 ▶ 금지동사 forbid는 'forbid+목적어+from ~ing'의 형태로 쓰이지 못하고 'forbid+목적어+to 부정사'의 형태로 쓰인다. 목적어가 주어로 나가 수동태가 된 구조이므로, 동사 다음에 남은 to 부정사가 와야 한다. ⑤를 to stay로 고친다.

dormitory n. 기숙사 pass n. 출입증, 통행증 stay out (밤에) 집에 안 들어오다, 외박하다

기숙사에 있는 모든 학생들은 특별한 출입증이 없다면 오후 11시 45분 이후 밖에 있는 것이 금지되었다(11시 45분 이전에 들어와 있어야 했다).

11 2008 단국대 ▶▶▶ MSG p.162 ③

look ~ in the eye ▶ look을 타동사로 써서 '~를 똑바로 쳐다보다'라는 의미를 나타낼 때, look ~ at the eye가 아니라 look ~ in the eye로 써야 한다. ③을 look us in the eye로 고친다. ④의 friendly는 부사로 쓰인 것이다.

delicious a. 맛있는 cheer up 격려하다, 기운이 나다 friendly ad. 친절하게, 다정하게

우리가 그를 근처 레스토랑에 데려가서 그에게 몇 가지 맛있는 음식을 대접했을 때, 그는 갑자기 기운을 냈고 우리를 쳐다보고 웃으면서 다정하게 대했다.

12 2019 서강대 ▶▶▶ MSG p.38 ②

동사 fell과 fall의 구분 ▶ fall(떨어지다, 넘어지다)은 자동사이고 fell(넘어뜨리다)은 목적어를 취하는 타동사이다. 뒤에 목적어가 없으므로 ②에 쓰인 타동사 fell 대신 자동사 fall을 써야 한다. ②를 started to fall into place로 고친다.

fall into place (복잡하거나 이해하기 어려운 것이) 딱 맞아떨어지다[분명히 이해가 되다] engage v. 종사하다, 바쁘다

1960년대 후반에는 이미, 퍼즐의 조각들이 맞아 떨어지기 시작했었다. 그러나 하나의 실마리는 너무나도 분명한 것이어서 그 연구에 참여한 거의 모든 사람들이 웬일인지 그것을 놓치고 말았다.

13 2021 성균관대 ▶▶▶ MSG p.105 ②

상태를 나타내는 과거분사 ▶ 주어는 English이고 동사는 is used이다. 대륙에 흩어져 사는 사람들이라는 의미이므로, 상태를 나타내는 과거분사를 써서 400 million people (who are) scattered …로 써야 한다. '관계대명사 + be동사'는 흔히 생략한다. ②를 scattered로 고친다.

native language 모국어 scatter v. 분산시키다; 흩어지다 continent n. 대륙

모든 대륙에 흩어져 있는 4억 명이 넘는 사람들의 모국어인 영어는 전 세계적으로 일곱 명 중 한 명이 어떤 식으로든 사용하고 있으며, 역사상 가장 널리 사용되고 있는 언어이다.

14 2022 홍익대 ▶▶▶ MSG p.55   ④

능동태와 수동태의 구분 ▶ ④의 앞에 온 were의 주어는 the first massive electronic computers로, 컴퓨터는 부르는 주체가 아니라, '불려지는' 객체이므로, ④를 dubbed로 고쳐야 하며, 이때 dub A B(A를 B라는 별명으로 부르다)의 수동태인 A is dubbed B(A는 B라는 별명이 붙다)라는 형태가 쓰였다.

massive a. 엄청나게 큰 computation n. 연산

인공지능에 관한 해묵은 우려들 중 일부는 컴퓨터가 생각할 수 있느냐의 문제와 밀접하게 연관되어 있었다. 빠른 연산을 할 수 있고, 창조적인 활동을 거의 또는 전혀 할 수 없는 엄청나게 큰 최초의 전자컴퓨터는 곧 '전자두뇌'라는 별명이 붙었다.

15 2008 가천대 ▶▶▶ MSG p.132   ②

적절한 접속사의 사용 ▶ 주절의 synchronized와 as절의 geometric의 관계로 보아 상반되는 내용이 연결되고 있음을 알 수 있다. 따라서 접속사 ② as를 양보의 접속사 while로 바꾸는 것이 적당하다.

school n. (물고기의) 떼[무리] horde n. 무리, 떼 disciplined a. 훈련된 starkly ad. 아주, 완전히 geometric a. 기하학적인

많은 종의 물고기, 특히 작은 물고기들은 훈련을 아주 잘 받은 부대가 가두행진 하듯이 정확하게 빈틈없는 형태로 무리를 지어 이동한다. 어떤 것들은 동시에 떼를 지어 움직이는 반면, 다른 것들은 완전히 기하학적인 형태로 이동한다. 물고기 무리들의 다양한 형태 외에도, 무수히 많은 집단행동 양식들이 있다.

16 2020 건국대 ▶▶▶ MSG p.191   ③

형용사를 수식하는 부사 ▶ 첫 번째 문장의 주절의 'so ~ that …' 구문에서 형용사 interwoven을 수식할 수 있는 것은 부사이므로 ③ dense를 densely로 고쳐야 한다.

interchange n. 교환, 교체 densely ad. 밀집하여, 빽빽이 interweave v. 복잡하게 서로 얽히다 pick apart 떼어놓다 distinguishable a. 구별할 수 있는, 식별할 수 있는

수천 년 동안 수학의 외적인 사용과 내적인 구조 사이에 교환이 계속된 후, 이제는 그 학문(수학)의 이 두 가지 측면이 너무나 복잡하게 얽히게 되어서 그것들을 서로 떼어놓기가 거의 불가능하다. 하지만 연관된 정신적 태도는 쉽게 구별할 수 있어서, 두 종류의 수학 즉, 순수 수학과 응용 수학으로 광범위하게 분류된다.

17 2020 한양대 서울 ▶▶▶ MSG p.123   ②

명사절을 이끄는 접속사 that ▶ 관계대명사 what 뒤에는 불완전한 절이 오는 반면, 명사절을 이끄는 접속사 that 이하에는 완전한 절이 온다. 주어진 문장에서 ②의 what 이하를 보면, the biomedical view가 주어, belies가 타동사, process가 목적어로 와서 완전한 절이므로, ②는 what이 아닌 that이 되어야 한다.

transplant n. 이식 end-stage a. 말기의 bounded a. 한계가 있는 liver n. 간 kidney n. 신장 belie v. ~을 착각하게 만들다 embed v. 끼워 넣다, 내장시키다

이식 의학의 발달로 말기 단계의 장기 질환 환자들의 생명을 보존하고 연장할 수 있게 된 반면, 어떤 학자들은 장기 이식을 심장, 간 또는 신장이 성공적으로 교체되는 것으로 끝나는 하나의 경계 지어진 사건으로 이해하는 생체 의학적 관점은 장기를 받아들이는 체험에 내재된 복잡하고 역동적이며 발생적인 과정을 오해하게 만든다는 것에 주목한다.

18 2019 한국항공대 ▶▶▶ MSG p.71   ①

if가 생략된 가정법 과거완료 ▶ 조건절은 If David had posed his question ~ 에서 접속사 If가 생략됨으로써 도치가 일어났다. 조건절의 동사가 'had+p.p'이므로 가정법 과거완료 구문이며, 따라서 주절의 동사 형태는 '조동사 과거형+have+p.p.'여야 한다. ①을 would have declared로 고친다.

scholarly a. 학자의 eel n. 장어 pesky a. 성가신 parasitic a. 기생하는 peer review 동료평가(같은 분야의 전문가들이 하는 심사평가) exceptional a. 이례적인 scrutiny n. (면밀한) 조사 bump into ~를 우연히 만나다 ditch n. 도랑, 개천 bum n. 엉덩이, 항문

데이비드(David)가 자신의 질문을 학계에 제기하였더라면, 그들은 그의 '실뱀장어들'이 성가신 기생충의 또 다른 예일 뿐 발달 초기 단계의 어류는 아니라고 발표했을 것이다. 그러나 이 공장 기술자는 동료(전문가)평가에 대해서는 전혀 모르고 있었다. 그는 자신의 이례적인 발견을 영국 학술원(Royal Society)에 제출하지 않았고, 그 대신 어느 날 그가 우연히 만난 두 명의 농부들에게 보여주었는데, 그들은 자신들 농토의 한 도랑에 그토록 많은 은(銀) 뱀장어가 있다는 것에 당혹스러워하였다. 그래서 그는 그토록 많은 뱀장어들이 한 딱정벌레의 항문에서 나왔다는 자신의 이론을 설명했고 농부들의 반응에 매우 기뻐했다.

19 2022 아주대 ▶▶▶ MSG p.217   ④

등위접속사에 의한 병치 ▶ 등위접속사 or의 전후에는 같은 역할을 하는 단어·구·절이 연결되어야 한다. or 전후의 말은 모두 the effect sizes를 공통관계 목적어로 삼기 때문에 ④의 is equal에 전치사 to가 더해져야 the effect sizes를 목적어로 가질 수 있다. 즉, is equal to or larger than이 되어야 한다.

account for ~만큼 차지하다; ~의 원인이다 distress n. 고통, 고충 correspondence n. 대응 variable n. 변수 substantial a. (정도가) 상당한 sexual abuse 성폭행

이러한 상황에서, 지역사회 폭력에 대한 노출의 변화는 표본을 구성하는 개인들의 심리적 고통의 변화 중에서 10% 약간 미만의 원인이다. 노출의 양과 고통의 양 사이에 일대일 대응은 없다. 분명히 다른 변수들도 심리적 고통의 수준에 영향을 미친다. 그럼에도 불구하고, 더 넓은 맥락에서는, 지역사회 폭력에 대한 노출이 심리적 고통에 미치는 영향은 상당하다. 지역사회 폭력에 대한 노출과 심리적 고통 사이의 관계의 효과 크기는 아동 성폭행, 자연재해 및 부정적인 인생사들을 경험하는 것과 같은 여타 심리적 스트레스 요인들에 대한 메타 분석에 의해 추정되는 효과 크기와 같거나 더 크다.

---

20 **2019 광운대** ▶▶▶ MSG p.173 ⑤

정비문 ▶ ① a pen(어떤 펜)과 같이 불특정대상을 받는 대명사는 one 이고, the pen과 같이 특정대상을 받는 대명사는 it이다. ② 원래 Should I wear the red shirt or the blue one?인데, 한정사인 the가 있어서 one이 가리키는 대상이 shirt인 게 명확하게 드러나므로, one 을 생략하고 the blue가 된 것이다. ③ none은 '아무 것도 ~아니다'는 뜻으로, 'no 가산명사'를 대신할 수도 있고 'no 불가산명사'를 대신할 수도 있다. 여기서는 no money를 대신한 none이다. ④ several은 '몇몇, 몇 개'를 의미하는 수사로 several of the twenty copies의 의미로 쓰였고, several이 복수이므로, 동사 were가 맞게 왔다. ⑤ 원래 Look through this box of screws and pick out some small ones.인데, 한정사 the가 쓰인 ②와 달리, ' ones를 생략할 수 없고 small 다음에 ones 를 써야 한다. 따라서 ⑤가 정답이다. 다만 small이 없으면 some ones 라 하지 않고 some이라 한다.

copy n. 복사본, 사본 screw n. 나사못

① 나는 펜이 하나 필요한데, 펜을 갖고 있지 않다.
② 나는 빨간색 셔츠를 입어야 하나 아니면 파란색 셔츠를 입어야 하나?
③ 김(Kim)은 돈이 하나도 없었으며, 팻(Pat) 역시 돈이 하나도 없었다.
④ 그들은 복사본 20부를 보냈는데, 몇 부가 손상되었다.
⑤ 나사못이 들어있는 이 상자를 들여다보고 작은 나사못 몇 개를 골라라.

TEST 27

01 ①	02 ①	03 ③	04 ③	05 ④	06 ③	07 ①	08 ①	09 ①	10 ③
11 ⑤	12 ①	13 ④	14 ④	15 ③	16 ⑤	17 ②	18 ①	19 ④	20 ②

01 2013 서울여대 ▶▶▶ MSG p.136, p.141 ①

관계대명사절 안의 동사의 수일치 ▶ 명사 modernity 뒤에 나온 that은 주격관계대명사이며 그 다음의 it can feel은 '관계대명사 다음의 삽입절' 형태이므로 빈칸에는 주격관계대명사 that의 동사가 시제를 가진 형태로 나와야 한다. 그리고 선행사는 단수명사인 a path이므로 ①의 is가 정답이다. 한편 in some way는 is와 보어인 local, authentic and non-Western 사이에 삽입된 것이며 in that sense는 'local하고 authentic하다는 의미에서'라는 뜻으로 삽입되었다. 위의 문장을 관계대명사를 이용하지 않은 두 개의 문장으로 풀어 쓰면 다음과 같다. Every non-Western society is searching for a path to modernity.+It(Every non-Western society) can feel the path to modernity is in some way local, authentic and, in that sense, non-Western. (뒤 문장의 밑줄 부분이 관계대명사 that으로 되어 앞 문장의 밑줄 부분 뒤로 감)

path n. (사람·사물이 나아가는) 길[방향] modernity n. 현대성 authentic a. 진정한

모든 비(非)서구 사회는 그 사회가 어떤 면에서 그 사회에 특유하고 진정한 길이라고, 또 그런 의미에서, 비(非)서구적인 길이라고 생각할 수 있는 현대성에 이르는 길을 모색하고 있다.

02 2013 가천대 ▶▶▶ MSG p.177, p.209 ①

other와 another의 구분 ▶ 명사 way를 수식하기 위해서는 형용사가 필요한데 ② so는 부사이므로 답이 될 수 없고 ③ such는 '앞에 이미 언급한, 그와 같은'을 뜻하는 형용사이므로 문맥상 맞지 않다. 따라서 빈칸에는 '다른'을 뜻하는 other나 another가 들어가 way를 수식해야 문맥이 통하는데, 빈칸 앞의 no가 한정사이므로 한정사를 포함한 another는 들어갈 수 없고 형용사인 other만 들어갈 수 있다.

poverty n. 빈곤 generation n. 세대 escape n. 탈출, 도피, 모면

빈곤 문제에 직면하고 있는 대부분의 나라들에서 가장 중요한 단 한 가지 싸움은 가족이 삶의 다른 방식과 (가난을) 모면하는 방법을 전혀 모르기 때문에 수 세기 동안 가난한 채로 있는 빈곤의 순환을 끊는 싸움이다.

03 2015 상명대 ▶▶▶ MSG p.223 ③

도치(보어+be동사+주어) ▶ 빈칸에는 동사 set의 목적어로 선행사로

간 형태가 들어가야 하므로 ①은 들어갈 수 없으며, ②, ④, ⑤는 문장에 시제를 가진 동사가 없는 결과가 되어 정답으로 적절하지 않다. ③이 들어가는 경우, "More challenging to attain was the task that nationalists set before themselves, the quest for a united nation."은 "The task that nationalists set before themselves, the quest for a united nation, was more challenging to attain."에서 보어인 More challenging to attain이 문두로 나가서 주어와 동사가 도치되었고 the quest for a united nation은 주어와 동격인 명사로 뒤에 이어진 형태로 파악할 수 있다.

challenging a. 사람의 능력을 시험하는 attain v. 달성하다, ~에 이르다 nationalist n. 민족주의자 quest n. 추구 united a. 통합된, 통일된

민족주의자들이 스스로 설정한 과업인 통일된 국가의 추구가 더 달성하기 힘들었다.

04 2012 서울여대 ▶▶▶ MSG p.139 ③

관계형용사 which ▶ 관계형용사란 명사 앞에 쓰여 '접속사+형용사'의 역할을 하는 관계사를 뜻한다. 관계형용사 which가 빈칸 앞의 a period of two years를 선행사로 가리키고 명사 time을 수식할 수 있다. 그리고 빈칸 뒤의 절이 완결되었으므로 앞에 전치사 during이 오면 앞의 절과 뒤의 절이 이어질 수 있다. 따라서 ③ during which time이 적절한 구조이다.

treacherous a. 배반하는; 불안정한; 위험한 cross v. 건너다 Southern Ocean 남빙양

그녀의 여행은 2년에 걸쳐 수천 마일이 걸렸는데, 그 시간 동안 그녀는 남빙양을 건너면서 위험한 바람과 폭풍우를 견뎌야만 했다.

05 2017 아주대 ▶▶▶ MSG p.147 ④

가산명사와 불가산명사의 구분 ▶ 먹는 양은 셀 수 없으므로, eating 다음에 fewer 대신 less를 써야 한다. 따라서 eating 다음에 fewer가 온 ③과 ⑤는 빈칸에 들어갈 수 없다. 빈칸 뒤의 calories(열량)는 가산명사의 복수형태이므로, 이것에 대한 수식은 less가 아닌 fewer로 해야 한다. 여기서 ①을 제외시킬 수 있다. 한편, 열량을 '섭취한다'고 해야 하므로, ②와 ④ 중에서는 '섭취하다'는 뜻의 take in이 쓰인 ④를 정답으로 선택할 수 있다.

shark n. 상어 snorkeler n. 스노클 잠수부

그는 보트들과 스노클 잠수부들 때문에 상어들이 덜 먹고 칼로리를 덜 섭취한다고 믿고 있다.

06 **2018 아주대** ▶▶▶ MSG p.182 ③

한정사의 어순 ▶ 전치한정사 all은 한정사인 소유격 our 앞에서 사용되어야 하며, 주어인 battles는 fight하는 대상이므로, 수동태로 나타내야 한다. 따라서 ③이 정답이다. 전치한정사가 아닌 형용사 whole은 한정사인 our 뒤에 와야 하므로 ④는 our whole battles~로 바뀌어야 한다.

devil n. 악마 run around 날뛰다

이 세상의 유일한 악마는 우리 마음속에서 날뛰는 악마들이며, 그곳이야말로 우리의 모든 전투가 벌어져야 하는 곳이다.

07 **2022 아주대** ▶▶▶ MSG p.222 ①

only가 포함된 부사어가 문두에 오는 경우의 도치 ▶ only가 포함된 부사어가 문두에 오는 경우에 도치가 일어나는데, only when절이 둘째 문장의 문두에 왔으므로 주어 the bronze rider가 조동사 did와 도치되고 원형동사 approach가 이어진 ①이 정답이다.

stir v. 꿈쩍하다, 약간 움직이다 exodus n. (많은 사람들이 동시에 하는) 탈출[이동] make one's way 나아가다 bronze a. 청동의

플레산은 꿈쩍도 하지 않고 탈출을 지켜보았다. 모두가 트랙을 따라 내려가 각자의 길로 퍼져 나갔을 때에야 비로소 그 청동 기수(騎手)는 출입구에 다가갔다.

08 **2012 가톨릭대** ▶▶▶ MSG p.236 ①

부사절에서 '주어+be동사'의 생략 ▶ 문맥상 빈칸에는 주어 Bone에 대한 부연설명으로 '접속사+주어+동사(although it is relatively light in weight)'의 부사절이 올 수 있다. 그런데 시간, 조건, 양보의 부사절에서는 주절의 주어와 같은 주어 it과 be동사인 is를 생략할 수 있으므로 ①이 가장 적절한 표현이다. 일반적 사실에 대한 내용이므로 문장 안의 모든 동사는 동일하게 현재시제를 사용한다. 따라서 ②와 같이 완료분사 구문이 오면 한 시제가 앞서게 되므로 부적절하다.

light a. 가벼운 weight n. 무게 tension n. 긴장; 팽팽함; 장력

뼈는 신체에서 가장 단단한 물질들 중 하나이며, 비록 무게가 비교적 가볍지만, 뼈에 작용하는 장력과 그 외의 다른 힘들에 저항할 수 있는 굉장한 능력을 갖고 있다.

09 **2022 숙명여대** ▶▶▶ MSG p.136 ③

관계대명사절 ▶ limitations는 little로 수식할 수 없으며, clans는 '사람의 무리'를 나타내므로 장소의 관계부사절이 아니라 관계대명사절로 수식하는 것이 적절하다. 즉 '씨족들의' 물 접근이지 '씨족들에서' 물 접근을 가졌다는 것이 아니다. 그러므로 ③이 정답이 된다.

rainfall n. 강우량 abandon v. 포기하다, 버리다 clan n. 씨족; 당파

12세기 중엽 무렵에 남서부에서 강우량이 감소하기 시작하자, 모뉴먼트 계곡의 아나사지(Anasazi)족(族) 대부분은 자신들이 살던 집을 버리고 물에 대한 접근이 덜 제한된 다른 씨족들과 합류했다.

10 **2021 서울여대** ▶▶▶ MSG p.97 ③

문의 구성 ▶ 전치사 of 뒤에 정동사 revitalize가 올 수 없다. 전치사 뒤에 동사가 오는 경우에는 동명사의 형태로 와야 하므로 ③은 revitalizing이 되어야 한다. 이때 wealthy people은 동명사 revitalizing의 의미상 주어이다.

complaint n. 불평; 불평거리, 고충 gentrification n. (슬럼화한 주택가의) 고급주택화, 젠트리피케이션 revitalize v. 소생시키다, 부흥시키다 crime-ridden a. 범죄에 시달리는

오늘날 젠트리피케이션에 대해 많은 불평이 있는데, 젠트리피케이션은 잊혀지고, 범죄에 시달리고 있는 도시 지역들을 부유한 사람들이 되살린다는 개념이다.

11 **2007 성균관대** ▶▶▶ MSG p.225 ⑤

올바른 전치사 표현 ▶ ⑤ in generations는 '여러 세대가 지나고 나서'라는 뜻이므로 문맥에 맞지 않다. ⑤를 '여러 세대 동안'이라는 뜻의 for generations로 고친다.

protocol n. 규칙, 의전; 의정서 feud n. 오랜 불화, 원한 beget v. 잉태시키다, 낳다 slight n. 경멸, 모욕 reverberate v. 울려 퍼지다; 반사하다; 반향하다

피의 원한이라는 규칙 하에서는, 하나의 복수 행위가 또 다른 복수를 낳기 때문에 어떤 잊혀진 범죄나 모욕에서 비롯되는 폭력은 여러 세대 동안 되풀이될 수도 있다.

12 **서강대 2019** ▶▶▶ MSG p. ①

문의 구성 ▶ raw는 동사로 쓰지 않으므로 ①에서처럼 현재분사 형태로 쓸 수 없다. 따라서 ①에서 rawing을 lion과 의미적으로 호응하는 roaring으로 고쳐야 한다.

acrobat n. 곡예사 raw a. 익히지 않은, 날것의 roaring a. 으르렁대는 doleful a. 슬픈, 쓸쓸한, 음울한 clown n. 어릿광대 wander v. 돌아다니다, 어슬렁거리다 big top (서커스의) 대형 천막 slip v. 미끄러져 넘어지다 trip up 헛디디다, 발이 걸려 넘어지다

곡예사와 으르렁대는 사자들 뒤에 한 번도 미끄러져 넘어지거나 걸려 넘어지는 일 없이 대형천막으로 된 서커스장 입구를 돌아다니는 단 한 명의 슬픈 어릿광대를 볼 수 있다.

13   2019 서강대 ▶▶▶ MSG p.56   ④

수동태 불가동사 cost ▶ 동사 cost는 수동태 문장에 쓰지 않는다. 따라서 ④를 능동태인 no matter how much it costs로 고쳐야 한다.

reservation n. 예약 peak season 성수기 charge v. (요금 등을) 부담시키다, 청구하다

예약이 많은 성수기 동안, 이 회사들은 더 높은 가격을 매기면서도 아무리 많은 비용이 들더라도 누군가는 그들의 서비스를 필요로 할 거라고 여전히 확신할 수 있다.

14   2021 성균관대 ▶▶▶ MSG p.26   ④

ascribe A to B ▶ ascribe는 'ascribe A to B(A를 B의 것으로 여기다)'의 형식을 취한다. 따라서 ④를 to로 고친다.

ascribe v. (원인 등을) ~에 돌리다, ~에 기인하는 것으로 하다 contemplate v. 숙고하다 congenial a. 마음에 맞는

그의 소설들의 지속적인 인기는 그 소설들이 반복적으로 고려하는 주제와 그 소설들이 자신의 것으로 여기고 있는 가치들을 많은 독자들도 반복해서 숙고하고 마음에 맞는다고 생각하고 있다는 것을 암시한다.

15   2021 중앙대 ▶▶▶ MSG p.135   ③

관계대명사 ▶ 관계사 who 절의 내용이 a day of pleasure를 선행사로 해야 하므로 ③의 관계사를 who에서 which로 바꾸어야 한다.

inasmuch as ~이므로 intimate a. 친밀한 arrange v. 마련하다, 준비하다, 주선하다 for some time past 지난 얼마동안

그 사고는 익사한 사람들이 아주 젊은 사람들이었고, 가족들과 도시에 나와 살고 있었고, 그리고 모두가 아주 가까운 친구들로, 지난 얼마 동안 준비해 온 즐거운 날을 맞아 밖으로 나온 참이었으므로 특히 슬픈 사고였다.

16   2020 한양대 ▶▶▶ MSG p.105   ⑤

문의 구성 ▶ 접속사 since가 이끄는 절의 주어인 the Asian nation에 연결되는 동사가 필요한데, 그 동사는 시제를 가진 정동사여야 하므로 ⑤를 hinges로 바꾸어야 한다.

persistent a. 지속적인 overshadow v. 빛을 잃게 만들다 unfounded a. 근거가 없는 boundless a. 무한한 hinge upon ~에 달려 있다

경제적으로 중국에 압도될 것이라는 지속적인 미국인들의 두려움이 완전히 근거가 없는 것은 아닌데, 그것은 무한해 보이는 에너지가 성장을 견인할 것 같은 그 아시아 국가가 계속 팽창하는 내수 시장에 의존하고 있기 때문이다.

17   2015 명지대 ▶▶▶ MSG p.236   ②

문의 구성 ▶ 두 번째 문장의 It은 인도산 파시미나를 지칭하며, 이것으로 수천 달러를 받을 수 있다고 했으므로, when 이하는 '어떤 상황일 때' 수천 달러를 받을 수 있는지를 설명하는 내용이어야 한다. '그 파시미나가 하나의 스카프가 될 때'라는 말이 되어야 문맥상 자연스러우므로 when it is turned into a single scarf로 고칠 수 있는데, 이때 it is는 주절의 주어와 같은 주어와 be동사여서 생략할 수 있다. 따라서 ②를 turned into로 고쳐야 한다. ① better known 앞에는 '주격관계대명사+be동사'인 which is가 생략돼 있다. ③ most of whom은 and most of them에서 접속사 and와 대명사 them을 관계대명사로 바꿔 쓴 형태이다. ④ '~을 …의 가격에 팔다'는 뜻의 sell A for B가 쓰였으며, up to는 수사 앞에 쓰여 '최대 ~까지'라는 의미로 쓰인다.

prized a. 소중한, 귀중한, 중요한; 가치 있는 pashmina n. 파시미나(히말라야 고산 지대에 사는 산양 복부의 털로 짠 고급 직물, 부드럽고 실크와 같은 윤기가 있어 숄이나 고급 스카프의 재료로 쓰임) cashmere n. 캐시미어(고급 옷을 만드는 데 쓰이는 부드러운 모직) nomadic a. 유목의, 방랑의 illiterate a. 글일 읽거나 쓸 줄 모르는

캐시미어라는 이름으로 더 잘 알려진 인도산 파시미나는 아주 귀한 양모이다. 파시미나는 사람의 머리카락보다 6배 가늘며, 하나의 스카프로 만들어질 경우 국제시장에서 수천 달러를 받을 수 있다. 그러나 창파(Changpa)족의 유목민들은 대부분 가난하고 글을 읽거나 쓸 줄 모르며, 그 돈의 상당 부분은 다른 사람들이 챙기고 있다. 중간상인들은 가공하지 않은 파시미나 양모를 1킬로그램 당 대략 40~80달러에 사서 최대 5배가 넘는 가격에 판다.

18   2022 가천대 ▶▶▶ MSG p.167   ③

대명사의 수일치 ▶ ③의 them은 every twig를 받고 있으므로, 이것을 it으로 고쳐야 한다.

soar v. 날아오르다 knot n. 매듭 cast v. 던지다 sink v. 가라앉다 twig n. (나무의) 잔가지 tremendously ad. 엄청나게

새들이 나무 꼭대기 주변으로 날아오르고 있었다. 마침내 마치 수천 개의 검은 매듭으로 이루어진 거대한 그물이 공중에 던져진 것처럼 보였다. 얼마 후 새들은 천천히 나무 위로 내려앉아서 마침내 가지마다 끝에 매듭이 있는 것 같았다. 그러다가 갑자기 그물이 다시 공중으로 던져졌다. 마치 그물이 공중으로 던져지고 천천히 나무 꼭대기 위로 내려앉는 것이 엄청나게 신나는 경험이기라도 한 것처럼 말이다.

19　2021 이화여대　▸▸▸ MSG p.228　④

전치사 뒤의 동명사 ▶ in spite of 뒤에서 a majority of UN member-states가 뒤의 vote의 의미상의 주어이며 전치사 in spite of 다음에는 동명사가 와야 하므로 ④를 a majority of UN member-states voting for로 고쳐야 한다.

nationalism n. 민족주의　national interest n. 국익　multinational corporation n. 다국적 기업　formulate v. 공식화하다　treaty n. 조약, 협약　consolidate v. 공고히 하다, 강화하다　ranged against a. 대립하는, 적대하는　entity n. 독립체, 실체

과거 어느 때보다 더 분명해진 것은, 민족주의와 국익, 특히 미국의 민족주의와 국익이 전 세계에서 갈등을 형성하는 데 있어 여전히 최소한 특정 다국적 기업들의 이익만큼 중요하다는 것이다. 미국과 EU는 다국적 기업들에 의한 인권 유린을 방지하려는 UN 협약을 공식화하는 과정에서 협조하지 않으려 했다. 이들은 UN 회원국 대다수가 이러한 협약에 찬성표를 던졌는데도 불구하고 협력을 거부한 것이다(Inter Press Service 2014). 미국은 이라크 내 지역들을 폭격하기 시작했다. 시리아와 이라크 내에서 새로이 세력을 공고히 하고 있는 이슬람국가(급진 수니파 무장 단체)를 미리 막기 위해서이다. 이슬람국가의 전투원들은 고유한 자신들만의 민족국가를 형성하려는 쿠르드 민족주의자들과도 대립하고 있다.

20　2019 광운대　▸▸▸ MSG p.195　②

정비문 ▶ ① very는 현재분사를 수식할 수 있으므로 very welcoming은 옳은 표현이다. ③, ④ 부사 much는 과거분사 needed와 surprised를 수식하며 부사 very는 부사 much를 수식하므로 맞다. ②, ⑤ 동사 prefer, admire, appreciate, enjoy, regret 앞에는 much와 very much가 모두 올 수 있으나 동사 agree, like, want, hope, doubt, fear 앞에는 much는 올 수 없고 very much만이 올 수 있다. 따라서 ②는 We very much agree with the decision.으로 고쳐야 한다.

welcoming a. 따뜻이 맞이하는, 우호적인　by-pass n. (자동차의) 우회도로

① 그 호텔은 매우 우호적이었다.
② 우리는 그 결정에 아주 동의한다.
③ 그 새로운 우회도로는 매우 필요했다.
④ 나는 그녀의 소식에 매우 놀랐다.
⑤ 나는 TV보다는 영화관에서 영화를 보는 것을 훨씬 선호한다.

| 01 ① | 02 ② | 03 ③ | 04 ③ | 05 ① | 06 ④ | 07 ③ | 08 ② | 09 ④ | 10 ② |
| 11 ① | 12 ② | 13 ② | 14 ② | 15 ① | 16 ② | 17 ④ | 18 ④ | 19 ② | 20 ① |

01 **2013 가천대** ▶▶▶ MSG p.217   ①

병치에 알맞은 전치사 선택 ▶ 문맥의 의미상 같은 인상을 받는 모든 사람들과도 마음 안에서 하나가 되도록 한다는 것이 적절하다. 등위접속사 and 앞의 the artist가 전치사 with와 같이 쓰였고 빈칸 앞의 '또한'을 의미하는 also로 보아 빈칸에도 같거나 비슷한 의미의 전치사가 필요하다. 따라서 ① with가 적절하다.

transmit v. 전염시키다; 전달하다 impression n. 인상

모든 예술은 예술가의 감정을 전달받는 사람들로 하여금 그 예술가와, 그리고 또한 같은 인상을 받는 모든 사람들과도, 마음 안에서 하나가 되도록 한다.

02 **2014 가톨릭대** ▶▶▶ MSG p.137   ②

전치사+관계대명사 ▶ 빈칸 이하가 완전한 절이므로 관계대명사 which나 that은 들어갈 수가 없고 부사절 접속사인 in that(=since)은 의미상 부적절하다. 관계사절의 동사가 수동태를 형성하고 있는 것으로 미루어 'by+관계대명사' 형태의 by which가 옳은 표현이다.

politeness n. 정중함, 예의 connotation n. 내포, 암시 dignity n. 존엄, 체면 preserve v. 보존하다, 지키다

예의에 관한 연구에서 "체면"의 개념은 그것에 개인의 존엄과 집단의 조화를 보존하는 일련의 규칙들이 내포되어 있어서 중요하다.

03 **2011 아주대** ▶▶▶ MSG p.223   ③

도치 구문 ▶ 빈칸 앞뒤가 반대되는 내용이 되어야 한다. 따라서 역접의 접속사 but 다음에 '(수량, 정도가) 같은 정도로, 마찬가지로'라는 뜻인 no less가 와야 반대의 의미가 된다. 참고로 이 문장은 '보어+be동사+주어'의 어순으로 도치된 것으로 보어를 강조하기 위해 문두에 위치시킨 것이다.

sap v. 약화시키다, 차츰 무너뜨리다 nagging a. (통증·의심 등이) 계속되는; 잔소리하는 inevitable a. 피할 수 없는 lower one's sight 자신의 목표를 낮추다

측정하기는 힘들지만 그래도 마찬가지로 심각한 것은 온 나라에 퍼져 있는 자신감의 약화이다. 이는 미국의 쇠퇴는 피할 수 없고 다음 세대는 자신의 목표를 낮춰야 한다는 계속되는 두려움을 말하는 것이다.

04 **2013 경희대** ▶▶▶ MSG p.27   ③

bestow A on B의 수동태 표현 ▶ bestow A(자질, 지위) on B(사람)가 'B에게 A를 부여하다'는 뜻의 표현이다. 이 문장은 A에 해당하는 Football superstardom이 주어로 나가 수동태로 된 것이므로 빈칸에는 on people이 와야 하며 people 앞에는 '바로 그'라는 뜻으로 명사를 강조하는 표현인 the very가 올 수 있다.

superstardom n. 슈퍼스타의 지위 bestow v. 부여하다 testosterone n. 테스토스테론(남성호르몬)

축구 슈퍼스타의 지위가 그 지위의 유혹과 스트레스에 대처하는데 가장 덜 준비된 바로 그런 사람들에게 주어지는 일이 자주 있는데, 그들은 돈과 테스토스테론은 많지만 판단력은 약한 젊은이들이다.

05 **2012 성균관대** ▶▶▶ MSG p.205   ①

not A any more than B ▶ 구문적 이해와 지식을 묻는 문제이다. 'B가 아닌 것처럼 A도 아니다'라는 의미의 not A any more than B(=no more A than B) 구문이 쓰인 문장이다. would 다음의 not과 연결되어 ①이 들어가는 것이 옳다.

land on ~에 뛰어내리다; ~에 떨어지다 billiard n. 당구

이제 나는 내가 다른 사람 위에 떨어져 그 사람을 죽인다고 가정해본다. 당구공이 높은 데서 떨어져 누군가의 머리를 맞힌다고 해도 당구공에 도덕적인 책임이 없을 것인 것처럼 그럴 경우 나에게도 그 불행한 죽음에 대한 도덕적인 책임이 없을 것이다.

06 **2018 세종대** ▶▶▶ MSG p.31   ④

부정사의 올바른 태와 형용사 보어 ▶ 빈칸에 쓰일 to부정사의 의미상 주어는 문장의 주어인 Everyone이다. 이것은 presume하는 행위의 주체가 아니라 대상이므로 수동태로 나타내야 한다. 그러므로 능동의 to부정사를 쓴 ①과 ③을 먼저 정답에서 제외할 수 있다. 한편, presume은 'presume+목적어+(to be) 보어'의 형태로 쓰이는데, '결백'이라고 추정되는 것이 아니라 '결백하다'고 추정되는 것이므로 보어로 형용사를 쓴 ④가 빈칸에 들어가야 한다.

charge v. 비난하다; 고발하다, 고소하다 penal offence 형사범죄 guilty a. 유죄의 trial n. 공판, 재판 presume v. 추정하다, 상상하다 innocent a. 결백한, 무죄의

형사 범죄로 고발된 모든 사람들은 공개 재판에서 법에 따라 유죄로 입증될 때까지는 무죄로 추정될 권리를 가진다.

07 2011 고려대 ▶▶▶ MSG p.236 ③

접속사+과거분사 ▶ our organic heredity를 our social legacy와 대조되도록 '~한 바와 같은 그런'이라는 의미의 접속사 as절로 나타낸 것이다. 원래 as it(=our social legacy) is contrasted with our organic heredity에서 주어와 be동사가 생략되어 ③처럼 'as+과거분사'의 형태가 된다.

constitute v. 구성하다 legacy n. 유산, 유증, 물려받은 것 heredity n. 유전(적 특징), 유전형질

개인들은 특정한 집단에 속해서 문화를 배우며, 그리고 문화는 타인들과 공유하는 학습된 행동의 일부를 구성한다. 문화는 유기적인 유전형질과 대조되는 그런 우리의 사회적 유산이다.

08 2008 가톨릭대 ▶▶▶ MSG p.121, p.221 ②

부정의 부사어가 문두에 오는 경우의 도치 ▶ 부정의 부사어인 not only가 문두에 나오면 주어와 동사가 도치된다. 따라서 are today's scientists able to see로 쓰는 것이 옳다.

atom n. 원자 microscope n. 현미경 versatile a. 다용도의 wrist n. 손목

오늘날의 과학자들은 그들의 현미경으로 원자들을 볼 수 있을 뿐만 아니라, 그들은 이제 '마법의 손목'이라고 불리는 다기능 감지 장치의 도움으로 원자들을 '느낄' 수도 있다.

09 2015 가톨릭대 ▶▶▶ MSG p.125 ④

간접의문문의 어순 ▶ 타동사 tell이 4형식으로 쓰인 것으로 직접목적어가 필요한 상황인데, 전치사구는 목적어가 될 수 없으므로, ①, ③을 정답에서 먼저 제외할 수 있다. 간접의문문은 목적어로 쓰일 수 있는데, 이것의 어순은 '의문사+주어+동사'이므로, ④가 정답이 된다.

well-known a. 유명한 meteorologist n. 기상학자

유명한 기상학자인 짐머만(Zimmerman)씨는 내 동생에게 그 섬의 날씨가 어떤지 얘기했으며, 그에게 최악의 상황에 대비할 것을 권했다.

10 2021 서울여대 ▶▶▶ MSG p.65 ②

be devoted to + 동명사 ▶ be devoted to는 '~에 전념하다'라는 의미인데, 이 표현에 쓰인 to는 전치사이므로 그 뒤에 동사가 오는 경우에는 동명사가 와야 한다. ②를 to developing으로 고친다. 이때 ① 앞에는 '관계대명사+be동사', 즉 which are가 생략돼 있는 것으로 볼 수 있다. ③ 주어는 several companies이다. ④ begin은 to부정사와 동명사를 모두 목적어로 취할 수 있다.

devote v. (돈·시간 따위를) 바치다; (전적으로); 헌신하다 prosper v. 번영하다, 성공하다

지난 10년 동안, 육류 대체품 개발에 전념한 몇몇 기업이 등장했으며, 그 기업들은 지금 번창하기 시작하고 있다.

11 2004 세종대 ▶▶▶ MSG p.36 ①

lie와 lay의 구분 ▶ 자동사 lie는 lie-lay-lain, 타동사 lay는 lay-laid-laid의 형태로 불규칙 변화한다. 동사 다음에 목적어에 해당하는 말이 없으므로 ①의 자리에는 자동사가 와야 한다. 그런데, 휘트먼이 『풀잎』을 쓴 시기보다 군인들이 전쟁터에 누워 있던 일이 더 먼저 일어난 일이므로 과거완료시제를 사용해야 한다. 따라서 ① had laid를 had lain으로 고쳐주어야 한다.

tribute n. 찬사 또는 칭찬을 나타내는 말 battlefield n. 싸움터, 전장

휘트먼(Whitman)은 자신이 군 간호사로 복무하는 동안 목격했던, 전장에서 쓰러진 남북전쟁의 군인들에 대한 헌사로 『풀잎(Leaves of Grass)』을 썼다.

12 2019 경기대 ▶▶▶ MSG p.197 ②

'타동사+부사' 형태의 구동사의 목적어로 쓰인 대명사의 위치 ▶ give up, turn down, put off 등과 같이 '타동사+부사'의 형태로 된 구동사에 명사 목적어가 오는 경우에는 그 목적어가 타동사와 부사의 사이에 올 수도 있고 부사 뒤에 올 수도 있지만, 목적어가 대명사인 경우에는 반드시 타동사와 부사 사이에 위치해야 한다. 그러므로 ②를 turned him down으로 고쳐야 한다.

take up (특히 재미로) ~을 배우다; (직장 등을) 시작하다 turn down (제안 등을) 거절하다 give up on (~에 대해 기대 등을 갖기를) 포기하다 realize v. 실감하다, (생생하게) 깨닫다

내 친구는 나와 함께 요가를 해보겠다고 제안했지만, 내가 거절한 후에 나에 대해서는 포기하는 것 같았다. 그리고 나중에 나는 내 인생을 바꿀 좋은 기회를 날려버렸다는 것을 깨달았다.

13 2014 가천대 ▶▶▶ MSG p.144 ②

복합관계형용사 ▶ 관계형용사절 what oxygen remained in my tank는 all the oxygen that remained in my tank의 뜻으로 그 자체로는 문법적으로 맞지만 all의 의미가 있다 보니 preserve의 목적어가 되기에 부적절하고 '다 써버리다'는 뜻이 되는 consume이나 use up의 목적어로는 적절하다. 이와 달리 복합관계형용사절 whatever oxygen remained in my tank는 any oxygen(=any of the oxygen) that remained in my tank와 같은데 any에는 I wish I had any of his courage.(그의 용기가 조금이라도 내게 있다면 좋으련만.)에서처럼 '조금이라도'의 뜻이 있어서 의미적으로 preserve의 목적어가 되기에 적절하다. 따라서 ② what을 whatever로 고쳐야 한다. ① 주어가 Harris이며 본동사는 pulled이고 그 사이에 관계대명사 절이 삽입된 구조이

다. pulled up이 여기서는 '자동사+부사'로 쓰였고 과거의 사건을 말하므로 과거시제이다. ③ 'ask+목적어+to V'는 '~에게 …을 부탁하다'라는 뜻으로 쓰인다. ④ 선행사가 절의 일부인 to reach부터 regulator까지이므로 관계대명사 which는 바르게 쓰였다.

summit n. 정상, 꼭대기 shortly after 금세, 곧 pull up 멈추다 regulator n. 조절기

내가 떠난 직후에 정상을 떠난 해리스(Harris)는 금세 내 뒤에 멈춰 섰다. 내 탱크에 남아있는 산소를 조금이라도 보존하기 위해 그에게 내 배낭 안에 손을 뻗어 조절기의 밸브를 잠가달라고 부탁했는데 그는 그렇게 했다.

14 　2008 한국외대 ▶▶▶ MSG p.176 　②

부정대명사 most of ▶ ②의 most는 형용사의 최상급에 쓰인 것이 아니라 부정대명사로 쓰인 것으로, 이때는 앞에 관사를 붙이지 않는다. ②를 most of로 고쳐야 한다.

dominate v. 지배하다 bent n. 기호, 경향, 성향

미국에서 학문으로서의 심리학은 지난 반세기 대부분 동안 학습 및 기억 이론에 의해 지배되어 왔다. 그리고 이는 미국의 실용적 경향과 심리학이 어떻게 사람들이 살아가는 법을 배우는 방식을 개선시켜줄 수 있는가 하는 점에 대한 미국의 관심을 반영하는 것이다.

15 　2021 성균관대 ▶▶▶ MSG p.227 　①

access to ▶ 명사 access 다음에는 관용적으로 전치사 to를 쓴다. 따라서 ①을 to로 고쳐야 한다.

assert v. 단언하다; 강력히 주장하다 access n. 접근, 출입 punish v. 벌하다, 응징하다 revolve around ~을 중심으로 하다

모든 사람이 부, 건강, 그리고 기회에 평등하게 접근할 수 있어야 한다고 주장하는 사회 정의는, 현대의 관행에서 어떤 주어진 개인의 선택이나 행위와는 상관없이, 역사적 사건, 현재의 조건, 집단 관계에 관한 가치 판단에 근거하여, 서로 다른 인구 집단을 선호하거나 처벌하는 것을 중심으로 하고 있다.

16 　2013 명지대 ▶▶▶ MSG p.9 　②

be 동사의 보어 ▶ be 동사의 보어로 부사는 쓰일 수 없으므로 ②는 slow가 되어야 한다. 참고로 be slow to do는 '~하는 것이 느리다'라는 뜻으로 쓰인다. ① who의 선행사는 Amanda로 적절하게 사용되었으며, by the age of 2 months는 부사구로 삽입되었고 관계사절의 동사는 was이다. ③ 역접의 접속사 yet이 적절하게 사용됐다. ④ 마지막 문장의 시제가 현재이며 주격관계대명사 who의 선행사는 a high school English teacher이므로 동사의 수는 단수가 적절하다. 따라서 lives는 적절하게 사용됐다.

muscle tone 근긴장도 lift one's head 고개를 들다 fault n. 과실, 잘못

로리 헌터(Laurie Hunter)는 그녀의 딸 아만다(Amanda)가 생후 2개월이 되었을 때 이미 정상적으로 자라지 못하고 있는 것에 대하여 그녀를 아프게 하는 질병이 무엇인지 알기 원했다. 아만다의 근긴장도는 약했으며 고개를 들지 못했다. 그녀는 말하는 것이 느렸으며, 두 살이 될 때까지 걷지 못했다. "엄마로서 아이에게 일어나는 모든 것이 엄마의 잘못은 아니라는 것을 알지만, 여전히 책임감을 느낍니다"라고 뉴저지주 잭슨시에 살고 있는 고등학교 영어 선생님인 42세의 헌터는 말한다.

17 　2022 가천대 ▶▶▶ MSG p.137 　④

전치사+관계대명사 ▶ 불완전한 절과 함께 쓰이는 관계대명사 which 다음에 완전한 절이 와서 틀렸다. ④ 다음에 온 due는 전치사 to와 호응해서 due to가 '~이 주어져야 하는'이라는 의미로 쓰이므로, ④의 which를 to which로 고쳐야 한다.

presumably ad. 아마도 cross n. 이종 교배 infrequently ad. 드물게 off-spring n. 자식, 새끼 compel v. ~을 하게 만들다 searching question 날카로운 질문

아마도, 인간과 침팬지 간의 이종교배가 가끔은 실행 가능할지도 모른다. 적어도 최근에는 자연적인 실험이 매우 드물게 행해졌음이 틀림없다. 만일 그런 자손들이 태어난다면, 그들의 법적 지위는 어떻게 될까? 침팬지의 인지 능력은 특별한 윤리적 고려가 되어야 하는 생물집단의 경계에 관해 날카로운 질문을 제기하게 만들며, 나는 우리의 윤리적 시각을 넓히는 데도 도움을 줄 수 있기를 희망한다.

18 　2021 국민대 ▶▶▶ MSG p.57 　④

동사의 태 ▶ much of the work는 value하는 행위의 주체가 아닌 대상이므로 수동태 문장이 되어야 한다. ④를 is not valued로 고친다.

unnoticed a. 남의 눈에 띄지 않는 population n. 인구 caretaker n. 돌보미

이 "여성 권리" 회의가 가진 큰 과제는 자신들의 경험이 주목받지 못하고, 자신들의 말이 경청되지 못하고 있는 도처의 여성들에게 발언권을 주는 것이다. 세계 인구의 절반 이상이, 세계 빈곤층의 70퍼센트가, 그리고 읽고 쓰는 법을 배우지 못하는 사람들의 3분의 2가 여성이다. 우리는 전 세계 대부분의 어린이들과 노인들을 위한 주된 돌보미들이다. 그러나 우리가 하고 있는 일의 많은 부분은 경제학자들에 의해서도, 역사가들에 의해서도, 대중문화에 의해서도, 정부 지도자들에 의해서도 인정받지 못하고 있다.

19 　2021 이화여대 ▶▶▶ MSG p.15 　②

자동사와 전치사 ▶ 문맥상 '~에 주의를 기울인다'는 표현이어야 하므로, ②의 attend를 attend to로 고쳐야 한다.

substantively ad. 사실상 methodological a. 방법론적인 representation n. 재현 attend to ~에 주의를 기울이다 authorship n. 저자, 원저자; 저술업 immeasurably ad. 헤아릴 수 없을 만큼, 측정 불가능할 만큼

디지털 미디어에 대한 지난 20여 년 동안의 관심의 증가는 미디어를 방법론적 문제로 보는 우리의 인식을 더욱 높여 놓는 데 상당한 기여를 했다. 연구 대상의 디지털 재현을 이론화하는 과정 때문에 우리는 연구 대상의 원래 매체의 의미에도 주의를 기울여야 하게 되었다. 그러나 다른 영향들도 중요했다. 즉 제롬 맥건(Jerome McGann)과 D. F. 맥켄지(D. F. McKenzie)의 혁신적인 연구로 촉발된 텍스트의 물질성에 대한 새로운 주의, 그에 수반된 책의 역사에 대한 관심, 그리고 텍스트 생산의 정치 등이었는데, 이것들이 모두 저자 문제와 텍스트성에 대한 우리의 이해를 헤아릴 수 없을 만큼 더 복잡하게 만들었다.

---

20 **2019 광운대** ▶▶▶ MSG p.50   ①

정비문 ▶ ② not the least는 '조금도 ~않다', '전혀 ~이 아니다'라는 뜻의 최상급 관용표현으로 맞게 쓰였다. ③ A is no more B than C is D(A가 B가 아닌 것은 C가 D가 아닌 것과 같다)라는 관용표현이 쓰였으며, 이때 D가 B와 동일한 대상일 경우에 D는 생략할 수 있다. ④ 형용사 최상급이 'among/of all 복수명사' 앞에 올 때 정관사 the가 있는 것이 원칙이나, 바로 뒤에 명사가 없고 be동사 다음이면 the 없이도 가능하다. the가 있으면 명사성이 강하고 the가 없으면 형용사의 서술적 의미가 강하다. ⑤ no less than은 '~만큼이나 많은'이라는 뜻으로, as much[many] as와 같은 의미로 쓰이며, half는 'half+the+명사'의 어순으로 쓰여 맞는 문장이다. ① no sooner는 than과 함께 쓰여 '~하자마자 …하다'라는 뜻으로 쓰이며, 이때 no sooner 다음에는 과거완료시제가 오고, than 다음에는 과거시제가 온다. 따라서 ①을 No sooner had I slept than I started to snore.로 고쳐야 한다.

snore v. 코를 골다 whale n. 고래

① 나는 잠들자마자, 코를 골기 시작했다.
② 길에는 눈이 전혀 없다.
③ 고래와 개는 모두 물고기가 아니다.
④ 에베레스트 산은 모든 산 중에서 가장 높다.
⑤ 무려 그 학생들 중 절반이나 그 시험에 떨어졌다.

01 ②	02 ③	03 ③	04 ④	05 ①	06 ③	07 ③	08 ③	09 ②	10 ③
11 ③	12 ②	13 ④	14 ③	15 ④	16 ③	17 ⑤	18 ①	19 ③	20 ②

01 2021 수원대 ▶▶▶ MSG p.126   ②

의문형용사가 이끄는 명사절 ▶ '~에 대해 투표하다'는 'vote on something'의 구문을 취하는데, 주어진 문장에서 의문형용사 which가 이끄는 명사절이 전치사 on의 목적어가 될 수 있으므로 ②가 빈칸에 적절하다.

committee n. 위원회 priority n. 우선순위 have access to ~에 접근할 수 있다, ~를 이용할 수 있다 phase n. 단계 distribution n. 배포

위원회는 일요일에 다시 만나 다음 배포 단계에서 어느 우선 집단이 코로나바이러스 백신을 이용할 수 있어야 하는지에 대해 투표할 것이다.

02 2022 숙명여대 ▶▶▶ MSG p.203   ③

비교급 ▶ 빈칸 다음에 than이 왔으므로 빈칸에는 비교급이 와야 한다. 비교급이 사용된 보기는 ②와 ③인데, 두 번째 문장에서 우리가 오미크론 바이러스에 직면하여 겸손해야 한다고 했다. 이것은 이전 바이러스보다 '덜 심각하다'고 섣불리 추정하는 교만한 태도를 보이지 말아야 한다는 말이므로 ③ less severe가 빈칸에 적절하다.

assume v. ~이라 가정하다, 간주하다 variant n. 변이체, 이형(異形) humble a. 겸손한

우리는 아직 오미크론이 이전 변이보다 덜 심각하다고 추정할 수 없다. 우리는 이 바이러스에 직면하여 겸손해야 한다.

03 2010 고려대 ▶▶▶ MSG p.201   ③

not so much A as B 구문 ▶ not so much A as B 구문은 'A가 아니라 B'라는 의미로, A와 B는 문법적으로나 구조적으로도 그 형태가 같아야 한다. 주어진 문장에서 A에 해당하는 것은 on the Constitution as a symbol or historical object이고 B에 해당하는 것은 on the Constitution as a depository ~ unshakable이다. 따라서 빈칸에는 not so much와 on이 나온 ③이 적절하다.

constitution n. 헌법 depository n. 창고, 보고, 저장소 unshakable a. 흔들 수 없는

미국에서 헌법은 상징이나 역사적인 대상으로서 강조된 것이 아니라, 근본적이고 흔들 수 없는 것이라고 언급되는 민주적인 신념의 보고로서 강조되었다.

04 2022 숙명여대 ▶▶▶ MSG p.43   ④

시제 ▶ 일반적인 사실에 대한 진술이므로 현재 시제를 써야 한다.

carnivorous a. 육식성의 mammal n. 포유류 동물 lethal a. 치명적인

육식 포유류는 뇌가 너무 뜨거워지지 않게 하는 열 교환 네트워크를 가지고 있기 때문에, 만약 그렇지 않으면 치명적인 수준일 체열을 견딜 수 있다.

05 2003 아주대 ▶▶▶ MSG p.223   ①

so ~ that … 구문의 도치 ▶ 'so ~ that …' 구문이 되어야 의미상 적절하다. 보어를 강조하기 위해 문두에 둘 때, 주어와 동사는 도치된다.

sales associate 영업사원

그들은 명품 그룹에 아주 중요한 고객이기 때문에, 세계 각처에서 2주 이상 루이비통(Louis Vuitton)을 위해 일해온 모든 영업사원들은 '일본 문화 이해하기'를 주제로 하는 세미나에 참석하기 위해 파리로 파견되고 있다.

06 2021 세종대 ▶▶▶ MSG p.75   ③

제안의 동사 + that+주어 + (should) 동사원형 ▶ insist, propose, suggest, demand 등의 주장, 제안, 요구의 동사가 that절을 목적어로 취하는 경우, that절 안의 동사는 '(should) 동사원형'이어야 한다. 따라서 ③이 정답이 된다. ④ 타동사 send의 목적어를 명시하거나 수동태 문장으로 써야 한다.

Republican n. 공화당원, 공화당 지지자 delegation n. 대표단 the White House 백악관

매사추세츠 주의 공화당원인 에드 브룩(Ed Brooke)은 대표단을 백악관으로 파견할 것을 제안했다.

07 2021 세종대 ▶▶▶ MSG p.111   ③

문의 구성 ▶ Nurturing a sense of empathy는 분사구문이고 where everyone's progress is valued는 종속 부사절로 분사구문에 이어져 있으므로, 빈칸 이하는 주절을 이루어야 한다. 따라서 주어와 정동사가 제시돼 있는 ③이 정답이 된다.

nurture v. 양육하다; 가르쳐 길들이다 empathy n. 공감, 감정이입 mindset n. 사고방식 instill v. (사상 따위를) 스며들게 하다, 주입시키다, 조금씩 가르치다

모든 사람의 발전을 가치 있게 여기는 곳에서, 공감 의식을 길러줌으로써, 그 과정은 학생들에게 성장 지향적 사고방식을 심어주어, 학습에서 더 많은 것을 이룰 수 있게 해준다.

08 2016 서울여대 ▶▶▶ MSG p.114 ③

독립분사구문 ▶ 빈칸 이하는 $의 기원에 관한 많은 의견들 중 하나에 관한 내용이어야 하므로, 빈칸에는 ③이 들어가는 것이 적절하다. ③은 and one of the commonest is that에서 접속사 and를 삭제하고 동사 is를 being으로 바꾼 독립분사구문(종속절의 주어와 주절의 주어가 다른 분사구문) 형태이다.

derive from ~에서 유래하다 figure n. 숫자 piece of eight (옛날 스페인의) 페소 은화

달러의 상징인 $의 기원에 관한 많은 의견들이 제시되어왔는데, 가장 널리 알려진 의견들 중 하나는 $가 스페인의 '페소 은화'를 나타내는 숫자 8에서 유래했다는 것이다.

09 2022 숙명여대 ▶▶▶ MSG p.209 ②

비교급을 이용한 최상급 표현 ▶ 빈칸 앞에 '~중에'라는 표현이 있으므로, 비교급으로 최상급 의미를 나타내는 ②가 정답으로 적절하다. ③과 ④는 장황한 표현(wordy expression)으로 부적절하다.

migration n. 이주 sweep through 일소하다, 휩쓸다 decade n. 10년간

역사상 밀려온 모든 거대한 이주의 물결 가운데, 30여 년 만에 1,200만 명의 이민자들을 미국 해안으로 들어오게 한 그 물결만큼 집중적이었던 것은 아마도 없을 것이다.

10 2021 세종대 ▶▶▶ MSG p.227 ③

contribution to ▶ 대시 속의 and a contribution은 a product of와 함께 this cumulative culture에 이어지고 있는데, 명사 contribution은 전치사 of가 아닌 to와 함께 쓰므로 to를 반드시 명시해야 한다. ③을 contribution to로 고친다.

informative a. 유익한 contribution n. 기부, 기부금; 기여 cumulative a. 누적되는

매우 유익한 그 책은 그 자체가 이 누적된 문화의 산물이며 또한 그에 대한 기여이다.

11 2014 한국항공대 ▶▶▶ MSG p.11 ③

적절한 전치사(dabble in) ▶ '~에 잠깐 손을 대다'라는 뜻의 dabble은 전치사 in을 취하는 동사이다. 따라서 ③은 in commercials가 되어야 한다. ① in years past는 '과거에'의 뜻으로 쓰이며, in past years라고 쓸 수도 있다. ② a shred of는 '아주 조금, 티끌'이라는 뜻이다. ④ downright는 부사, 형용사로 모두 쓰일 수 있으며 이 문장에서는 형용사 fashionable을 수식하는 부사로 쓰였다.

downright ad. 철저히, 완전히 big name 명사, 유명인; 일류 연기자

과거에는 조금이라도 자존심이 있는 영화감독이라면 상업광고에 손을 댈 생각을 하려 하지 않았다. 하지만 이제는 TV광고를 연출하는 것이 할리우드의 유명한 감독들 사이에서도 완전히 유행이 되었다.

12 2015 서강대 ▶▶▶ MSG p.237 ②

if any와 if ever의 용법 구별 ▶ if ever는 주로 빈도부사 rarely, seldom, scarcely 다음에서 '혹 그런 일이 있다 하더라도'라는 뜻으로 쓰인다. 예를 들면 He seldom, if ever, speaks ill of others.(그는 다른 사람을 험담하는 일이 혹 있다 하더라도 거의 없는 편이다.)이다. if any는 There are few mistakes, if any.(만약 있다 하더라도 틀린 곳이 거의 없다.)에서처럼 few나 little 같은 부정의 수량사 다음에서 '~이 혹 있다 하더라도'의 뜻으로 쓰이거나, Correct errors, if any.(틀린 곳이 있으면 고쳐라.) 같은 명령문, 혹은 주어진 문장에서처럼 의문사 다음에서 '만일 혹 있다면'의 뜻으로 쓰인다. 따라서 ②를 if any로 고쳐야 한다.

hoary a. 백발의; 낡은, 진부한 justification n. 타당한 이유, 정당화; 변명

이러한 진부한 문제의 한 가지 측면은 "사람이 어떤 심적 상태에 있다는 것을 그 사람의 행동을 근거로 알 수 있다는 주장에 만일 그 어떤 정당성이라도 혹 부여할 수 있다면 어떤 정당성을 부여할 수 있는가?"라는 질문이다.

13 2011 이화여대 ▶▶▶ MSG p.105 ④

현재분사와 과거분사의 구분 ▶ 동사 sag는 일반적으로 자동사로 사용되므로 ④를 능동, 진행 의미의 현재분사 sagging으로 고쳐야 한다. 그러면 sagging economic position이 '낮아지는 경제위상'이라는 뜻의 표현이 된다. ① excruciating은 뒤의 명사 focus를 수식하는 형용사이다. ② was는 주어가 the excruciating focus로 단수이므로 단수동사를 쓴 것이다. ③은 앞의 명사 the challenges를 수식하는 것으로, 난제들이 괴롭히는 것이므로 능동, 진행 의미의 현재분사 galling이 왔고 앞에 most가 있으므로 최상급의 의미가 된다.

excruciating a. 몹시 고통스러운; 몹시 괴롭히는; (종종 원뜻을 벗어나서) 대단한, 이만저만이 아닌 galling a. 짜증나게 하는, 괴롭히는 plight n. 곤경, 어려움 sag v. 내려앉다, 기울다; (시세·물가 등이) 떨어지다

핵무기와 핵전쟁에 대한 엄청난 집중은 그러한 집중이 이란에서의 미국인 인질사태와 세계에서 점차 낮아지는 미국의 경제 위상과 같은 1980년에 미국사람들을 가장 괴롭혔던 난제들과는 관련이 없었기 때문에 더더욱 눈에 띄었다.

---

14 2021 성균관대 ▶▶▶ MSG p.119 ③

접속사 ▶ interest와 desire를 연결하는 ③의 either는 접속사가 아니므로 연결할 수 없다. 따라서 ③의 자리에는 등위접속사가 들어가야 하며, 문맥상 or가 적절하다.

exercise v. (능력 등을) 발휘하다 utmost a. 최대한도의, 극도의 humility n. 겸손, 겸양 discretion n. 신중, 분별, 사려 shred n. 조각, 파편; 약간, 소량 intervene v. 개입하다, 간섭하다; 중재하다 sage n. 현인, 현자

고대의 현자들이 우리에게 가르쳐 주듯이, 진리를 발견하고 올바른 길을 찾으려 할 때는 우리가 최대한의 겸손과 신중함을 발휘해야 하며, 그 진리를 실행에 옮길 때는 일말의 이기적인 관심이나 욕망도 개입되어서는 안 된다.

---

15 2016 홍익대 ▶▶▶ MSG p.35 ④

가목적어 it ▶ I find 이하에서 타동사 find의 진목적어는 impossible 뒤의 to부정사구이며 impossible은 목적보어이다. 따라서 ④는 진목적어인 to부정사구를 대신하는 가목적어 it이 되어야 한다.

utterly ad. 아주, 전혀, 완전히 primate n. 영장류 (동물) mammalian n. 포유류 (동물)

그러나 언어는 영장류나 포유류의 부르는 소리와는 완전히 다른 방식으로 이루어져 있고 완전히 다른 종류의 의미를 전달하기 때문에, 나는 자연선택 혹은 성(性) 선택이 영장류나 포유류의 부르는 소리 체계를 언어로 바꿔놓을 수 있었던 현실적인 일련의 연속된 사건들을 상상하는 것이 불가능하다고 생각한다.

---

16 2021 한국산업기술대 ▶▶▶ MSG p.113 ②

분사구문 ▶ locate는 '위치시키다'라는 뜻의 타동사이므로 '~에 위치해 있다'는 be located at[in]이라는 수동태로 나타낸다. '이 도시들이 가장자리 가까이 위치해 있어서'라는 의미의 As they are located near the edge를 분사구문으로 바꾸고 being을 생략하면 과거분사로 시작하는 분사구문이 되므로 ②를 Located로 고쳐야한다.

pack v. 채우다 earthquake n. 지진 quake n. 지진 predict v. 예측하다

전에는 로스앤젤레스, 이스탄불, 도쿄, 리마와 같이 정기적으로 지진의 영향을 받는 도시에 이렇게 많은 사람들이 밀집해 있던 적이 결코 없었다. 지구의 거대한 움직임은 지각 판의 가장자리 가까이에 있어서, 이 도시들은 대규모 지진으로 인한, 그리고 지진이 종종 일으키는 쓰나미, 화재, 그 밖의 다른 파괴로 인한, 죽음과 경제적 재난의 위험에 직면해 있다. 우리는 한 세기 전보다 지진에 대해 더 잘 알고 있다. 이제 과학자들은 지진을 예측하길 원한다. 하지만 가능할까?

---

17 2018 건국대 ▶▶▶ MSG p.25 ⑤

prevent + 목적어 + from ~ing ▶ 타동사 prevent는 목적어 다음에 'from 동명사'를 취하는 3형식 동사로, '~이 …하지 못하도록 막다'는 뜻으로 쓰인다. 그런데 마지막 문장에서는 'prevent+목적어' 다음에 to부정사가 왔으므로, ⑤를 from reaching으로 고쳐야 옳은 문장이 될 수 있다. ②는 가정법 과거의 조건절 If it all were to reach에서 if가 생략되고 주어와 동사가 도치된 형태다.

electromagnetic radiation 전자기 방사선 emit v. (빛·열·향기 등을) 방사하다, 내뿜다 ultraviolet radiation 자외선 stratosphere n. 성층권(成層圈: 지상 약 10~50km 사이의 지구 대기층) altitude n. (해발) 고도

태양에 의해 방출되는 전자기 방사선 중에서 자외선은 극히 일부지만, 만약 그 전부가 지구 표면에 닿게 된다면, 방출되는 그 양만으로도 지구에 사는 대부분의 생명체에 심각한 피해를 입히기에 충분할 것이다. 다행스럽게도 태양의 자외선 전체가 지구에 도달하지는 못하는데, 지구 표면 위 15마일 정도 높이의 성층권에서 지구를 감싸고 있는 대기의 오존층이라 불리는 산소층이 있기 때문이다. 오존층은 태양 자외선의 많은 양을 흡수하며 자외선이 지구에 도달하지 못하도록 막는다.

---

18 2012 서강대 ▶▶▶ MSG p.117 ①

전치사 given ▶ given은 전치사로 뒤에 명사나 that절과 결합하여 '주어진다고 하면, 가정하면, 생각하면'이라는 뜻으로 쓰인다. 따라서 ①을 Given으로 고쳐야 뒤에 the assumption을 목적어로 받으면서 의미가 자연스러운 문장이 된다.

distort v. 왜곡하다 revelation n. 폭로; 계시 explicit a. 명백한, 명시적인 declaration n. 선언

노예제도가 미국의 이상을 명백히 왜곡하고 있다고 가정하면, 사람들이 미국역사를 이러한 선언의 명백하고도 명시적인 의미의 점진적인 계시의 관점에서 종종 생각하는 것은 놀라운 일이 아니다. 예를 들면, 로저스 스미스(Rogers Smith)는 미국 시민권에 대한 권위 있는 연구에서 어떤 귀속적인 정치전통, 즉 인종, 성, 그리고 종교에 근거하여 정치적 정체성을 확정짓는 전통이 미국의 자유주의적 전통과 어느 정도로 경쟁을 해왔고 자유와 평등이라는 독립선언문의 이상을 표현하는 것을 막는 작용을 어느 정도로 해왔는지를 연구했다.

---

19 2020 한국항공대 ▶▶▶ MSG p.227 ③

올바른 전치사 ▶ on the verge of ~는 '막 ~하려고 하다', '바야흐로 ~하기 직전이다'는 의미를 갖는다. 그러므로 ③의 in을 on으로 바꾸어야 한다.

stock n. 주식 leak v. 새어 나가다 intellectual property 지적 재산권 shortcoming n. 약점, 단점 proclaim v. 선언하다 keep in mind 명심하다 on the verge of ~ 금방 ~하려고 하는 invincibility n. 무적, 불패

빌 게이츠(Bill Gates)는 "악몽의 비망록"이라 알려진 것에서 자신의 두려움에 가득 찬 면을 드러냈다. "악몽"의 시나리오로 가득 찬 그의 비망록이 『산호세 머큐리 뉴스』 신문사로 유출되었던, 1991년 6월 17일부터 6월 20일

까지 4일 동안 마이크로소프트의 주식이 11% 급락하면서 그의 개인 자산은 3억 달러 이상 감소했다. 게이츠 자신이 작성한 이 비망록은 경쟁사, 기술, 지적 재산권, 법률 소송사건 및 마이크로소프트의 고객 지원 약점에 대한 일련의 걱정과 위협을 나열하고, "우리의 악몽은 현실이다."라고 선언했다. 이 비망록이 세상에 알려졌던 당시, 윈도우즈가 바야흐로 가장 지배적인 소프트웨어가 되면서 마이크로소프트는 빠르게 업계의 가장 강력한 선도자가 되어가고 있었음을 기억할 필요가 있다. 게이츠를 이해하는 사람이라면 누구나 그의 비망록이 어떤 변화의 신호를 보내는 것은 아니라는 것을 알았을 것이다. 그는 항상 두려움 속에서 살았고 항상 취약하다고 느꼈으며 앞으로도 계속 그럴 것이었다. 악몽의 비망록 사건 이듬해 그는 "우리는 천하무적이라는 이런 말이 정말로 믿어진다면, 나는 지금보다 더 많은 휴가를 가겠지요."라고 말했다.

20 **2014 광운대** ▶▶▶ MSG p.168

정비문 ▶ ②에서 동사 find는 5형식으로 쓰였는데, 목적어로 that절이 주어져 있다. find의 목적어로 to부정사나 that절이 쓰인 경우 가목적어 it을 쓰고 진목적어는 문장 뒤로 위치시키는 것이 일반적이다. 따라서 I find it hardly surprising that he tried to retract his statement.로 고쳐야 적절하다. ① regard A as B는 'A를 B로 여기다[간주하다]'라는 의미로, 목적어로 that절이 쓰였기 때문에 가목적어 it을 쓰고 that절은 문미에 위치시켰다. ③ that은 명사절을 이끄는 접속사이다. It을 비인칭 주어로, that절을 is의 보어절로 봐도 좋고, It을 가주어로 that절을 진주어로 보고 is not 다음에 true가 생략된 것으로 봐도 좋다. It may be that절(~일지도 모른다)이나 It seems that절(~인 것 같다)의 경우도 마찬가지이다. ④ as if는 '마치 ~인 것처럼, ~와도 같이'라는 의미의 접속사이다. 여기서는 as if가 가정법이 아니라 직설법으로 쓰였다. ⑤ owe A to B는 'A를 B의 덕택으로 돌리다'라는 의미로, 목적어인 A에 that절이 왔기 때문에 이것을 문미로 위치시키고 대신 가목적어 it을 써준 형태의 문장이다.

discourtesy n. 무례 notify v. 통보하다 retract v. 취소하다 owe v. ~에 돌리다, ~의 덕택으로 알다 get off lightly (벌·피해 등을) 잘 피하다, 가볍게 넘어가다

① 그들은 당신이 그들에게 더 일찍 알리지 않은 것을 무례하다고 여긴다.
② 그가 그의 말을 취소하려고 한 것이 나에게는 그리 놀라운 일은 아니다.
③ 네가 말하려고 하는 것을 내가 이해하지 못하는 것은 아니다.
④ 그는 자신의 정체를 숨기려고 하는 것 같았다.
⑤ 우리가 그렇게 잘 넘어간 것은 당신 덕택이다.

01 ④	**02** ③	**03** ③	**04** ⑤	**05** ①	**06** ②	**07** ①	**08** ⑤	**09** ③	**10** ④
11 ①	**12** ④	**13** ②	**14** ④	**15** ⑤	**16** ③	**17** ④	**18** ④	**19** ①	**20** ②

01　2015 단국대　▶▶▶ MSG p.227　④

문맥상 알맞은 전치사 ▶ say의 목적절에서 주어로 쓰인 which는 의문대명사이다. which에는 한정된 대상에서 일부를 선택한다는 의미(~중에 어느 것)가 내포돼 있는데, 주어진 문장에서 빈칸 뒤의 the above-mentioned factors가 그 대상에 해당하므로, 빈칸에는 '부분', '일부'의 관계를 나타내는 전치사 of(~중에)가 들어가야 한다.

above-mentioned a. 위에서 언급한　factor n. 요인　distortion n. (사실 등에 대한) 왜곡

위에서 언급한 요인들 중에 어느 것으로 인해 그의 철학에 대해 왜곡과 오해가 생겨나고 있는지를 말하기는 어렵다.

02　2022 단국대　▶▶▶ MSG p.217　③

문의 구성 ▶ 등위접속사 and에 의해 세 개의 명사구가 병치되는 구조로, 빈칸에는 앞의 명사를 수식하는 분사 형태가 들어가야 한다. 빈칸 뒤에 목적어 both traditional and transitional issues가 있으므로 현재분사 covering이 적절하다.

proliferation n. 확산　transitional a. 변천하는, 과도적인　incidence n. (사건·영향 따위의) 범위, 발생률　diversity n. 다양성　emerging a. 신흥의, 신생의

지역 기관의 확산, 전통적이고 과도기적인 문제를 다루는 그들의 기능의 확장, 그리고 지역 상호간 사건 발생의 증가는 신흥 세계 질서에 건강한 다양성과 지도력을 창출할 수 있다.

03　2021 덕성여대　▶▶▶ MSG p.195　③

비교급 ▶ 비교급과 함께 쓰는 than이 뒤에 있으므로 빈칸에는 fast의 비교급 표현인 faster가 와야 하며, 여기서 속도(rate)는 특정한 것의 특정한 속도가 아니라 여러 속도 중 하나의 속도이므로 rate에 대한 관사도 the가 아니라 a가 적절하다. 따라서 빈칸에는 ③ a much faster가 적절하다. 이때 much는 비교급을 강조하는 역할을 한다.

population n. 인구

과학자들은 세계 인구가 충분한 식량으로 부양할 수 있는 것보다 훨씬 더 빠른 속도로 팽창하고 있다고 우려하고 있다.

04　2008 숙명여대　▶▶▶ MSG p.223　⑤

문의 구성 ▶ 우선 ②의 경우 is exerted 사이에 형용사 great는 적절치 못하다. ④도 How에 의해 great가 도치된 형태인데, 형용사 great가 is exerted 사이에 있으므로 적절치 못한 표현이다. ③은 부정어 Never에 의해 도치된 형태로 목적어가 없어 옳지 못한 표현이다. ①이 쓰이면 접속사 that이 어떤 역할을 하는지 모호하다. 따라서 강조부사 so에 의해 도치된 형태이며, 원인과 결과를 나타내는 so ~ that 구문이 되는 ⑤가 적절한 표현이다.

exert v. (힘 따위를) 발휘하다; 노력하다(for); (압력 등을) 장기에 걸쳐 지속적으로 행사하다　locomotive n. 기관차

토네이도에 의해 가해지는 힘은 너무나 커서 토네이도는 기관차를 탈선시킬 수도 있다고 알려져 있다.

05　2022 세종대　▶▶▶ MSG p.176　①

another + 단수명사 ▶ other 뒤에는 복수명사가 오고 another 뒤에는 단수명사가 온다. 그러므로 ③과 ④를 정답에서 먼저 제외할 수 있다. 그런데 ②의 recording은 '기록하는 행위'를 의미하는 명사이므로 문맥상 적절하지 않다. 따라서 정답은 ①이 되며, 이때 record는 '기록적인'이라는 의미로 쓰였고 high는 '최고수준', '최고수치'라는 의미의 명사로 쓰였다.

overdose n. (약의) 과다 복용　exceed v. (한도·범위를) 넘다

미국의 약물 과다복용 사망자는 2020년에 91,000명을 넘어서 다시 한 번 최고 기록을 세웠는데, 이는 전년도 총 사망자수를 크게 웃도는 것이었다.

06　2019 가톨릭대　▶▶▶ MSG p.105　②

부사절의 올바른 동사 ▶ when절의 주어 young men에 이어지는 정동사가 필요한 상황이므로, be동사가 주어져 있는 ②가 빈칸에 적절하다. 빈칸 앞의 denied가 young men의 정동사가 아니라 young men을 후치 수식하는 과거분사임에 유의한다. 이때 deny는 '(남이 원하는 것을) 거부하다[허락하지 않다]'는 의미이며, 'deny+사람+사물' 혹은 'deny+사물+to 사람'의 형태로 쓴다. denied 앞에 who were가 생략돼 있는 것으로 이해하면 된다.

voting age 선거 연령 intensify v. (정도나 강도가) 심해지다; 격렬해지다 conscript v. 징집하다, 징병하다

미국에서 선거 연령을 21세에서 18세로 낮추는 것을 둘러싼 오랜 논쟁은 2차 세계대전 동안 시작됐으며, 투표권이 인정되지 않는 젊은이들이 나라를 위해 싸우도록 징집되고 있던 베트남전 동안에 더욱 격화됐다.

07 2012 서울여대 ▶▶▶ MSG p.28 ①

수여동사 deny ▶ deny는 4형식 수여동사이므로 간접목적어 'millions of women'과 직접목적어 'access to 명사'가 나란히 이어지는 ①이 정답이다. 'access to ~'는 '~를 이용[입수]할 수 있는 방법(수단, 권리, 자유)'의 뜻이다.

mount an assault 공격을 개시하다 contraception n. 피임(법); 산아 제한 cancer screening 암검진(癌檢診)

공화당원들은 여성의 건강과 자유에 대한 공격을 시작하고 있는데, 이것은 수백만 명의 여성들에게 적당한 피임을 하고 생명을 구하는 암 검진을 받을 권리를 부인하게 될 것이다.

08 2021 아주대 ▶▶▶ MSG p.222 ⑤

장소 부사어가 문두에 오는 경우의 도치 ▶ 장소 부사어가 문두에 오면 On the hill stands a castle.처럼 1형식 자동사와 주어가 도치되는데, 동사가 진행시제인 'be동사+현재분사'나 수동태인 'be동사+과거분사'일 경우 이 전체가 주어와 도치된다. 전자의 예는 Off the coast was floating a cargo ship.이고 후자의 예는 본 문제의 문장이다. 따라서 ⑤가 빈칸에 적절하다. '발견되었다'이므로 was founded가 아니라 was found이며, 이렇게 도치됨으로써 선행사인 chamber와 관계사 where가 자연스럽게 이어진다.

multilayered a. 여러 층으로 이루어진, 다층의 chamber n. 방, 실 found v. 세우다, 설립하다 offering n. (신께 바치는) 공물[제물]

그 돌 밑에서 여러 층으로 이루어진 내실(內室)이 발견되었는데, 각각의 층에 신들에게 바치는 제물들이 놓여있었다.

09 2021 세종대 ▶▶▶ MSG p.223 ③

적절한 형용사의 형태 ▶ 도치가 이루어진 문장이며, 주어는 the unsettling social syntax이다. 주어가 사물이므로, 감정타동사 puzzle의 현재분사 형태인 puzzling이 적절하고 '복잡한'이라는 의미의 형용사 complicated가 올바르다.

unsettling a. 심란하게 하는, 동요시키는 syntax n. 구문론, 통사론; 체계, 구성 puzzling a. 당황하게 하는, 곤란하게 하는, 종잡을 수 없는

미국에서 불안정한 사회 체계는 언어보다 더 혼란스럽고 복잡하다.

10 2008 한양대 ▶▶▶ MSG p.97, p.102 ④

올바른 동명사의 형태 ▶ without 다음의 동명사의 의미상 주어는 '특권을 가진 자들'이므로 ④는 능동태가 아닌 수동태 being coerced가 되어야 한다.

gainsay v. 부정하다 privilege n. 특권 of one's own accord 자발적으로 coerce v. 강요하다

특권을 가진 자들이 강요받지 않고서는 자발적으로 자기의 특권을 포기하는 경우는 드물다는 사실을 부정할 수 없다.

11 2021 서강대 ▶▶▶ MSG p.116 ①

접속사 구문 / 분사구문 ▶ 접속사 while이 있는 분사구문에서는 while driving to work(차를 몰고 출근을 하다가)처럼 의미상의 주어가 주절의 주어와 일치해서 없는 것이 원칙이다. 주절의 주어와 다른 의미상의 주어가 있다면 차라리 be동사를 사용하여 절로 표현해야 한다. 즉 ①은 while the statue was still standing이 되어야 한다. 분사구문으로 쓰려면 ①을 전치사 with를 사용하여 with the statue still standing으로 고쳐야 한다.

statue n. 동상, 조각상 entanglement n. (pl.) 철조망; 장애물 barbed wire 가시철사 take heart 힘내다

그러나 동상이 아직도 서있는 가운데, 가시철조망에 둘러싸인 가운데서 병사들은 힘을 내었고, 희망을 완전히 버리기를 거부했다.

12 2011 성균관대 ▶▶▶ MSG p.35 ④

get+목적어+목적보어(과거분사) ▶ 5형식 불완전타동사는 목적어와 목적보어를 취하고, 이때 목적어와 목적보어는 주어와 동사의 주술관계를 형성한다. 주어진 문장에서 전치사의 목적어로 사용되고 있는 동명사 getting은 all the paperwork를 목적어로, 그리고 organizing을 목적보어로 취하고 있다. '서류업무가 정리되는' 수동의 관계이므로 목적보어 ④ organizing을 organized로 고쳐야 한다. ①은 형용사 lonely가 등위접속사 and에 의해 병치되어 형용사 lost가 쓰인 것이며, ②는 분사구문으로 뒤에 목적어 the nightmare가 있으므로 현재분사 visualizing이 쓰였다. 주절의 주어와 종속절의 주어가 he로 같으므로 ⑤ trying 앞에 주어는 생략되었다.

visualize v. 눈에 보이게 하다, 시각화하다; 상상하다 settle down 정착하다

그는 낯선 도시에서 혼자 외로이 어찌할 바 모른 채, 그곳에 앉아서 새 도시에 정착하려 노력하면서 시골에서 온 모든 서류 업무를 다시 정리하는 악몽과 같은 일을 떠올렸다.

13 **2022 홍익대** ▶▶▶ MSG p.224 　　　　　　②

도치 ▶ ② 앞에 부정의 부사 nor가 있으므로 그 뒤에는 도치가 일어나야 한다. ②를 are there로 고친다.

repository n. 용기(容器); 저장소; (지식 등의) 보고(寶庫) insulate v. 격리하다, 고립시키다; 차단하다 maintenance n. 유지, 보수

호스팅된 데이터 저장소를 얼마나 오래 사용할 수 있는지에 대한 기준은 없으며, 데이터 저장소 관리를 호스트의 자금조달 변화로부터 차단하기 위한 합의된 절차도 없다.

---

14 **2021 성균관대** ▶▶▶ MSG p.131 　　　　　　④

부정적인 의미의 접속사 unless ▶ unless는 '~하지 않으면(if not)'이라는 부정적인 의미의 접속사이므로 그 절에 not이 사용될 수 없다. 따라서 ④를 were로 고쳐야 한다. would be와 were는 가정법 표현이다.

amazing a. 굉장한 morality n. 도덕성, 윤리

과학이 놀라운 발명과 발견을 했지만 도덕은 그만큼 발전하지 못한 현 시대에, 만약 젊은이들이 지능뿐만 아니라 도덕에 있어서도 충분한 훈련을 받지 않으면 인간의 미래는 암울할 것이다.

---

15 **2019 건국대** ▶▶▶ MSG p.183 　　　　　　⑤

전치한정사 half의 용법 ▶ 전치한정사 half는 한정사인 소유격 the world's 앞에 와야 하므로 ⑤는 half the world's가 되어야 한다. 혹은 half를 명사로 사용하여 half of the world's로 고쳐도 된다. '명사(half)+전치사(of)+한정사(the world's)+명사(people)'의 구조이다.

rice n. 쌀 temperature n. 기온, 온도

지난 몇 년간 쌀은 전 세계에서 가장 대중적인 식량 중 하나가 되었다. 쌀은 아마도 수 천 년 전에 중국에서 처음 재배됐다. 중국에서부터 쌀은 인도와 다른 나라들에 퍼져나갔다. 현재 쌀은 쌀이 자라는 데 필요로 하는 물이 있고 기온이 따뜻한 수십 개의 나라에서 재배된다. 실제로 쌀은 전 세계 인구 중 거의 절반의 주식(主食)이다.

---

16 **2014 명지대** ▶▶▶ MSG p.138 　　　　　　③

관계대명사 that과 which의 구분 ▶ There are several cognitive processes와 the analysis of that will perhaps shed some light ~를 연결하기 위해 several cognitive processes를 선행사로 한 관계대명사로 that 대신에 which를 사용하여 ③을 the analysis of which로 고쳐야 한다. 전치사의 목적어로 관계대명사 that을 쓸 수 없기 때문이다. ① Numerous facts about cultural diversity와 empirical evidence about universal principles of cognition을 연결하는 등위상관접속사로 as well as가 쓰였다. ② 현재분사 exploring 이하가 many theories를 수식해 주고 있다. ④ shed light on은 '~을 조명하다'는 뜻

으로, light 앞에 형용사인 some이 쓰여 light를 수식하고 있다. some은 a little과 같다.

empirical a. 경험적인 cognition n. 인식, 인지, 지각 categorization n. 분류, 범주화 shed light on ~을 비추다; 밝히다, 해명하다 ethnic group 인종 집단

보편적인 인지 원리에 관한 경험적 증거뿐 아니라 문화적 다양성에 대한 수많은 사실들은 문화와 지능 사이의 연관성을 탐구하는 많은 이론들의 토대에 기여해 왔다. 인지 과정에는 여러 가지가 있는데, 인식, 범주화, 사고, 그리고 기억으로, 이것들을 분석하면 다양한 민족 집단들 사이의 지적 기능의 차이점들과 유사점들에 관해 어쩌면 밝힐 수 있게 될 것이다.

---

17 **2022 가천대** ▶▶▶ MSG p.105 　　　　　　④

현재분사 ▶ 마지막 문장에서 He began to cry ~ the turnpike는 주절이고 where ~ or so는 관계부사절이다. 따라서 the blank-faced cars 이하는 주절에 이어진 분사구문인데, 주어인 the blank-faced cars가 drone하는 행위의 주체이므로 능동 관계를 나타내는 현재분사를 써야 한다. ④를 droning으로 고친다. 이때 ④ 뒤의 by는 수동태에서 행위자를 나타내는 표현 앞에 쓰는 전치사 by가 아니라 '~의 옆에서'라는 의미로 쓰인 전치사임에 유의한다. ② as if 뒤에는 가정법 동사가 오며, 주절과 같은 시제를 나타내는 경우 가정법과거 동사를 쓴다.

muffle v. (소리를) 지우다, 둔탁하게 하다 chew v. 씹다 ashen a. 잿빛의, 창백한 burst into tears 갑자기 울음을 터뜨리다 pull over (차를) 길 한쪽으로 대다 turnpike n. 유료 고속도로; 통행료 징수소 drone v. 윙윙거리다 onrushing a. 돌진하는, 무턱대고 달리는

그들은 두 시간 넘게 운전했고 아직 한 마디도 하지 않았다. 그때 그는 그녀로부터 이상한 소리를 들었는데, 그것은 마치 그녀 안의 무언가가 꿈틀거리며 밖으로 빠져 나가고 있는 것처럼, 소리 죽여 씹고 있는 듯한 소리였다. 그녀는 창백한 얼굴로 그를 바라보더니 갑자기 울음을 터뜨렸다. 그 자신도 울기 시작했고, 고속도로의 좁은 갓길에 차를 세웠다. 그곳에서 그들은 30분 정도 더 머물렀으며, 깊어가는 추운 밤에 무표정한 자동차들이 그들 옆을 윙윙거리며 지나가고 있었다.

---

18 **2022 가천대** ▶▶▶ MSG p.211 　　　　　　④

주어와 동사의 수일치 ▶ 마지막 문장에서 between a complacent ~ in the north가 Mutual prejudice를 꾸며주는 형태로, Mutual prejudice가 문장의 주어이다. 주어가 3인칭 단수이므로 ④의 persist를 persists로 고쳐야 한다.

peripheral a. 주변적인 heroine n. (소설 등의) 여자 주인공 fictitious a. 허구의, 가상의 detestation n. 혐오 complacent a. 현실에 안주하는

최근 생활수준을 살펴보면, 남동부, 남부, 남서부, 이스트 앵글리아(East Anglia), 그리고 이스트 미들랜즈(East Midlands)가 주변 지역보다 더 잘사는 경향이 있음을 보여준다. 100년 이상 전에, 소설가 개스캘(Gaskell) 부인은 『North and South』라는 제목의 책을 썼는데, 이 책은 다크셔(Darkshire)라는 가상의 카운티로 강제 이주해야 하는 여주인공에 관한 이야기로, 그녀는 '잉글랜드 북부에 대한 혐오'를 고백했다. 현실에 안주하는 남부지역 사람들과 자부심 강한 북부지역 사람들 간의 상호간의 편견은 없어지지 않고 지속되고 있다.

19 2018 이화여대 ▶▶▶ MSG p.139 ①

선행사를 포함한 관계대명사 what ▶ Radical changes are occurring in 뒤에는 전치사 in의 목적어가 되는 명사절을 이끄는 역할과 자신이 이끄는 절 안에서 teach의 직접목적어가 되는 역할을 동시에 할 수 있는 표현이 필요하다. 관계대명사 what은 자체에 선행사를 포함하고 있으면서 명사절을 이끌 수 있으므로, 앞서 언급한 역할을 모두 할 수 있다. 따라서 ①을 what democratic societies teach로 고쳐야 한다. ③ keep이 5형식 동사로 쓰였으며, democracies가 목적어이고 alive가 목적보어이다. ⑤ 주어는 democracies가 아니라 The future이다.

radical a. 근본적인; 급진적인, 과격한 thirsty a. 목마른; 갈망하는 heedlessly ad. 부주의하게, 무분별하게 discard v. (쓸데없는 것 따위를) 버리다 hang in the balance 몹시 불안정한 상태에 있다, 미해결 상태에 있다, 불확실하다

민주적인 사회가 젊은이들에게 가르치는 것에 근본적인 변화가 일어나고 있으며, 우리들은 이러한 변화들을 주의 깊게 생각하지 않아 왔다. 국가의 이익에 목이 말라 있는 까닭에, 국가와 교육제도는 민주주의를 유지하기 위해 필요한 기술들을 무분별하게 버리고 있다. 이러한 추세가 계속된다면, 전 세계의 국가들은 머지않아 스스로 생각하고 인습을 비판하고 다른 사람의 고통과 업적의 의미를 이해할 수 있는 완전한 시민의 세대들이 아니라, 유용한 기계의 세대들을 생산하고 있을 것이다. 세계 민주주의 국가들의 미래는 불확실하다.

20 2020 한국외대 ▶▶▶ MSG p.227 ②

정비문 ▶ give rise to는 '낳다', '일으키다' 등의 의미로 쓰인다. ②에서 give rise 다음에 전치사 to 없이 목적어 the same effect가 왔으므로, rise 다음에 전치사 to를 넣어야 한다.

graft n. 독직, 부정이득 bribery n. 뇌물수수 give someone a black eye 남의 눈을 멍들게 하다; ~의 성격이나 평판을 손상시키다 witness n. 목격자; 증인 give an account of ~에 대한 이야기[보고]를 하다, 설명[해명]하다 slim a. (가능성 등이) 희박한 give it one's best shot 최선을 다하다

① 부정이득과 뇌물수수 스캔들은 그의 평판을 손상시켰다.
② 같은 원인이 항상 같은 결과를 생기게 하는 것은 아니다.
③ 경찰은 모든 목격자들이 그들이 본 것에 대해 설명해주기를 원했다.
④ 가능성이 희박했음에도 불구하고 그는 최선의 노력을 다했다.

TEST 31

| 01 ① | 02 ③ | 03 ③ | 04 ④ | 05 ④ | 06 ④ | 07 ② | 08 ④ | 09 ④ | 10 ② |
| 11 ④ | 12 ② | 13 ① | 14 ③ | 15 ① | 16 ③ | 17 ② | 18 ④ | 19 ③ | 20 ④ |

tumor n. 종양, 종기 **treatment** n. 치료, 치료법

과학자들은 종양이 사람마다 다르기 때문에 치료법도 사람마다 달라야 한다고 말한다.

01　2014 가천대　▶▶▶ MSG p.134, p.226　①

적절한 의미의 전치사 ▶ just as ~, so …는 '~하는 것과 마찬가지로, …하다'라는 뜻으로 쓰인다. so 이하에서 청중은 연설을 준비하고 행하는 데 소비한 에너지의 작은 부분밖에 인식하지 못한다고 했으므로, 배에 탄 승객 또한 물위에 있는 빙산의 일부밖에 보지 못할 것이다. 따라서 물위에 있는 빙산이라는 의미가 되게 빈칸에는 ①의 above가 적절하다. above는 '기준점[수면]에서 그 이상[위]에'를 가리키며 over는 '기준점[수면]에서 일정 공간을 두고 떨어져서 위에'를 가리킨다. 예를 들어, 강물 위의 다리는 a bridge over the water이다.

iceberg n. 빙산 **expend** v. (돈·에너지를) 쏟다[들이다] **deliver a speech** 연설하다

배에 탄 승객들이 물위에 나온 빙산의 9분의 1밖에 볼 수 없는 것과 마찬가지로, 청중은 연설을 준비하고 행하는 데 소비한 에너지의 작은 부분밖에 인식하지 못한다.

02　2019 단국대　▶▶▶ MSG p.171, p.219　③

반복되는 명사 대신 쓰이는 those ▶ while ignoring은 원래 while we're ignoring에서 we're가 생략된 형태이다. while을 기준으로 두 개의 절이 대구를 이루고 있으므로, ignoring 다음에도 주절에 쓰인 동사의 목적어인 the neural circuits가 오거나 the neural circuits를 대신할 대명사가 와야 한다. 복수명사를 받는 지시대명사는 those이므로 ③이 정답이다.

exercise v. 훈련하다 **neural circuit** 신경회로 **devoted to** ~에 전념하는; ~을 전문으로 하는 **skim** v. 대충 읽다 **multitask** v. 한꺼번에 여러 일을 처리하다

우리가 자세히 읽고 깊이 생각하는 데 쓰이는 신경 회로들은 무시하는 동안에는 대충 읽기와 다중작업을 전담하는 신경 회로들을 가동하고 있는 것이다.

03　2019 가톨릭대　▶▶▶ MSG p.224　③

so+조동사+주어 ▶ '종양이 사람마다 다르므로 치료법도 사람마다 달라야 한다'는 의미가 돼야 하겠는데, 긍정문 뒤에서 앞 문장과 다른 주어가 이어지면서 '~도 또한 그러하다'는 의미를 나타내는 경우, 'so+조동사+주어'의 형태로 쓰므로, ③이 빈칸에 적절하다. 즉, 주어 뒤의 vary from person to person은 생략되었다.

04　2022 세종대　▶▶▶ MSG p.221　④

도치 / in danger ▶ 부정어가 포함된 부사구 at no time이 문두에 왔으므로 주어와 be동사가 도치되어야 하며, '위험한 상태에 처해 있다'라는 표현에서 danger 앞에는 전치사 in을 쓴다.

pack n. (사냥개·이리·비행기·군함 등의) 한 떼[무리]; (악당 따위의) 일당 **enclosure** n. 울타리를 친 장소; 울타리를 두름 **at no time** 결코 ~하지 않다

아홉 마리의 늑대 무리가 우리에서 탈출했을 때, 동물원에는 사람들이 많지 않았기 때문에, 일반인들은 결코 직접적인 위험에 처하지 않았다.

05　2022 세종대　▶▶▶ MSG p.137　④

전치사+관계대명사 ▶ 관계대명사 뒤에는 불완전한 절이 오고 '전치사+관계대명사' 뒤에는 완전한 절이 온다. 모든 보기에서 관계사 뒤에 완전한 절이 있으므로, 전치사+관계대명사, in which가 제시돼 있는 ④가 정답으로 적절하다. ① in that은 '~라는 점에서'라는 의미여서 부적절하고 주절과 시제도 어울리지 않는다.

elect v. 선거하다, 선출하다 **campaign** n. 군사행동; 선거운동, 유세

그는 모터스포츠 참여를 전 세계로 확대하겠다고 약속한 선거운동 이후에 당선되었다.

06　2021 세종대　▶▶▶ MSG p.221　④

도치구문 ▶ 문장의 주어와 동사가 필요한 상황인데, 접속사 since나 before가 문두에 온 ①과 ③은 빈칸 이하 전체를 부사절로 만들게 되므로 적절하지 않다. ②의 경우 뒤의 명사 blessed opportunity와 수식하는 such 사이에 부사 before가 끼어들어 부적절하다. 따라서 ④가 정답이 되며, 부정어를 동반한 부사 never before가 문두에 와서 주어(we)와 조동사(have)가 도치된 형태이다.

blessed a. 축복받은, 행복한 **profound** a. (지식·이해 등이) 깊은[심오한] **obligation** n. 의무 **founder** n. 창립자, 설립자, 시조

우리는 이렇게 축복받은 기회를, 따라서 우리 건국주체들이 가졌던 꿈의 "보다 완벽한 국가"를 건설해야 한다는 깊은 의무감을, 예전에는 결코 가져본 적이 없다.

가난한 카리브 해 국가를 강타한 200년 만에 가장 강한 지진이 수천 개의 건물을 파괴한 후 수요일에 심하게 상처를 입은 아이티 인들이 도움을 요청했다.

07 **2022 서강대** ▶▶▶ MSG p.30 ②

5형식 구문 & 형용사의 어순 ▶ consider는 3형식 동사이거나 5형식 동사인데, 이미 목적어 her가 주어져 있으므로 목적보어만 찾으면 된다. 따라서 ① 수식하는 who관계절은 목적보어가 될 수 없고, ④ she를 who로 고치면 figure를 후치 수식하여 구조적으로는 가능하지만 이보다는 관계절을 없애고 형용사 significant를 앞으로 보내어 전치 수식하게 하는 것이 더 좋다. ②와 ③은 형용사 어순의 문제인데, 명사와 의미적 관련성이 강한 형용사일수록 명사와 가까운 자리에, 즉 다른 형용사보다 뒤에 온다. literary(문학의)는 figure(인물)가 문학과 관련된 일을 한다는 기능(function)을 나타내는 형용사로 coffee table의 coffee나 fishing boat의 fishing 같은 사물의 용도(purpose)를 나타내는 형용사와 유사하여, 주관적 판단(opinion)을 나타내는 형용사 significant보다 뒤에 오게 된다. 따라서 ②가 적절한 어순으로 정답이다.

poem n. 시 lifetime n. 평생, 일생 literary figure 문인

엘리자베스 비숍(Elizabeth Bishop)은 살아 있는 동안 비교적 소수의 시를 발표했지만, 평론가 대부분은 그녀를 중요한 문인으로 간주했다.

08 **2021 아주대** ▶▶▶ MSG p.130 ④

올바른 비교 표현 ▶ prey 다음에 which is가 생략된 수식어구가 이어진 것으로 볼 수 있다. much는 비교급 형용사 larger를 수식하는 부사이며, so는 much를 수식하는 또 다른 부사이다. 여기서 so와 빈칸 다음에 나오는 that은 상관적으로 사용되어 so ~ that 구문을 형성한다. 비교 구문의 than절에서 '주어+동사' 어순이 원칙이므로 ④가 빈칸에 적절하다.

pack n. (함께 사냥을 하거나 하기 위해 모인 동물들) 무리[떼] prey n. 사냥감 pay v. (일·물건이) ~에게 수지맞다, ~에게 이익을 주다

한 무리의 하이에나들은 하이에나 한 마리가 쓰러뜨릴 수 있는 사냥감보다 너무나도 더 큰 사냥감을 잡을 수 있어서, 비록 먹이를 나눈다고 하더라도, 무리를 지어 사냥하는 것이 이기적인 각각의 개체에게 이익이 된다.

09 **2010 동국대** ▶▶▶ MSG p.191 ④

문의 구성 ▶ 빈칸 뒤가 부사절이므로 빈칸에는 주어와 동사를 갖춘 주절이 와야 한다. 동사는 의미상 '~을 요청하다'라는 의미를 갖는 plead for가 적당하고 주어는 타동사 injure의 과거분사 injured(상처 입은)가 Haitians를 수식하는 것이어야 하므로 ④가 적절하다.

plead to ~에게 호소[요청]하다 plead for ~을 요청하다 earthquake n. 지진 crush v. 파괴하다, 눌러 부수다, 뭉개다

10 **2020 한국외대** ▶▶▶ MSG p.139 ②

관계대명사 what ▶ 관계대명사 what 다음에는 주어, 목적어, 보어 가운데 하나가 빠져있는 불완전한 절이 와야 하는데, what 이하가 완전한 절이므로, ②는 주어 it을 삭제해서 looked like가 되어야 한다.

hastily ad. 급히, 서둘러서 remains n. (사용하거나 먹고) 남은 것, 나머지 sweep v. 쓸다, 털다 stuff v. 채워[밀어] 넣다

그는 패스트푸드처럼 보이는 음식 중 남은 것을 급히 집어든 다음, 테이블에서 그릇을 치우고, 그것들을 비닐봉지에 넣었다.

11 **2006 성균관대** ▶▶▶ MSG p.100 ④

전치사+(동)명사 ▶ clue to는 '~에 대한 단서'라는 의미로 여기서 to는 전치사이므로 뒤에는 명사가 온다. underlie는 '~밑에 있다, ~의 근저에 있다'라는 뜻의 동사로 ④가 현재분사형의 형용사 underlying으로 되어야 '근원적인'의 뜻으로 뒤의 명사를 수식할 수 있다. ②의 경우 '~를 계속 주시하다'라는 뜻의 keep one's eye on에서 eye는 복수형으로도 많이 쓴다. ③에서 '종류'라는 의미의 manner는 반드시 -s 없이 복수 취급한다.

dermatologist n. 피부과 의사 keep one's eye on ~에서 눈을 떼지 않다, ~을 경계하다 all manner of 모든 종류의 underlie v. ~의 밑에 있다, ~의 기초가 되다

실제로 의사들, 특히 피부과 의사들은 여성의 건강에 영향을 끼치는 근원적인 질병과 그 밖의 이상 상태들에 대한 모든 종류의 단서들을 찾기 위해 피부에서 눈을 떼지 못한다.

12 **2022 홍익대** ▶▶▶ MSG p.109 ②

복합분사의 형태 ▶ 명사, 형용사, 부사가 하이픈을 통해 분사와 결합하여 형용사처럼 쓰이는 것을 복합분사라고 한다. 복합분사에서 어떤 분사를 쓸 것인가는 수식받는 명사와의 관계에 의해 결정되는데, 수식받는 명사가 행위의 주체이면 현재분사 형태를 쓰고 행위의 대상이면 과거분사를 쓴다. ②의 수식을 받는 impulse는 seat하는 행위의 주체가 아닌 대상이므로 과거분사를 사용한 복합분사로 나타내야 한다. ②를 deep-seated로 고친다. ④ possibilities가 사람들을 convince하는(설득하는) 행위의 주체이므로 현재분사가 쓰였다.

mold n. 특성; 원형, 선례; 틀, 주형 bring up (논거·화제 등을) 내놓다 deep-seated a. 뿌리 깊은, 고질적인 impulse n. 충동 flirt with 농탕치다, 가지고 놀다; 무서워하지 않고 덤비다 annihilation n. 전멸, 절멸 pose v. (요구 따위를) 주장하다, (문제 등을) 제기하다

프로이트 유파의 심리학자들은 "죽음에 대한 소망"이라는 개념을 내놓곤 했는데, 그것은 개인의 절멸을 가볍게 다루어 몇 가지 더 설득력 있는 가능성을 제기하고 싶은 뿌리 깊은 충동이었다.

---

13 2015 아주대 ▶▶▶ MSG p.132, p.228 ①

Although와 Despite의 구별 ▶ although는 접속사로 뒤에 절이 와야 하는데, that ~ science가 claims와 동격인 절이어서 although 뒤에는 명사가 왔음을 알 수 있다. 따라서 명사를 목적어로 취하는 전치사 Despite로 ①을 고쳐주어야 한다. ② neither A nor B에서 동사는 B에 수일치 시킨다. ③ 과거분사로 organisms를 수식한다. ④ on은 '~에 영향을 미치다'는 뜻의 have an effect on으로 쓰인 것이다. ⑤ 'the+형용사'는 복수보통명사와 같은 뜻으로 쓰인다.

sound a. 완전한; 견고한 in truth 솔직히 altered a. 변형된, 변경된 organism n. 유기체, 생물 protein n. 단백질 the elderly 노인들

이들 식품이 '완전한 과학'에 기초한 것이라는 주장들에도 불구하고, 솔직히 말해, 제조업체들과 정부는 모두 이들 유전자 변형작물이나 이 유전자 변형 작물에서 나온 새로운 단백질이 사람에게, 특히 유아, 노인, 환자에게 미치는 영향에 대해서는 연구하지 않았다.

---

14 2013 명지대 ▶▶▶ MSG p.138 ③

관계대명사 that과 which의 구분 ▶ classroom 다음의 that은 the classroom을 선행사로 한 관계대명사인데 관계대명사 that 앞에는 전치사가 올 수 없고 which 앞에는 올 수 있다. 따라서 to that을 to which로 고쳐야 한다. ① 주절이 과거진행형이므로 부사절인 when절의 동사도 과거시제가 맞게 왔다. ② every 다음에 단수명사 lecture가 맞게 왔다. ④ 'be going to V'는 가까운 미래를 나타내는데, to 부정사로 to fail이 쓰였으며, fail은 '낙제하다'라는 뜻의 자동사로 올바르게 쓰였다.

terrified a. 무서워하는, 겁이 난 miss v. 놓치다 semester n. 학기 panic n. 공포, 공황, 당황 desperately ad. 필사적으로; 자포자기 하여 hopeless a. 절망적인 fail v. 낙제하다 flunk out of ~에서 성적불량으로 퇴학당하다

책상에 앉아 있다가 오늘이 화학 기말고사 날이라는 것이 생각났다. 나는 화학 기말고사를 위해 하나도 공부하지 않아 두려웠다. 사실, 나는 학기 내내 모든 수업을 빼먹었다. 당황해서 나는 한 번도 간 적이 없었던 교실을 찾아 교정을 가로질러 필사적으로 달리기 시작했다. 절망적이었다. 나는 낙제를 해서 학교에서 성적불량으로 제적당할 것임을 알고 있었다.

---

15 2022 가천대 ▶▶▶ MSG p.81, p.82 ①

'조동사+동사원형'과 '조동사+have+p.p.'의 구분 ▶ 총을 쏴서 코끼리를 죽이는 것은 피할 수 있다면 피해야 한다고 했고, 저자인 I는 코끼리를 죽이고 싶은 마음이 전혀 없었다고 했는데, ①에서는 '코끼리를 죽이지 말았어야 했다'는 과거의 행위에 대한 유감을 나타내는 내용이 나와 전체적인 문맥과 어울리지 않는다. 따라서 ①을 뒤에 나오는 ought

not to do it(총을 쏴서 코끼리를 죽여서는 안 된다)과 같은 맥락으로 should not shoot이나 ought not to shoot으로 고쳐야 한다.

shoot v. (총 등을) 쏘다 A is no more B than C (is D) C(가 D가 아닌 것)와 마찬가지로 A도 B가 아니다 not ~ in the least 전혀 ~이 아니다

코끼리를 보자마자 나는 총을 쏴서 코끼리를 죽여서는 안 된다는 것을 확실히 알았다. 총을 쏴서 일하는 코끼리를 죽이는 것은 심각한 문제이다. 그것은 거대하고 값비싼 기계를 파괴하는 것과 견줄 수 있다. 따라서 코끼리를 죽이는 것을 피할 수 있다면 분명히 피해야 한다. 그리고 먼 거리에서 평화롭게 식사하는 코끼리는 소와 마찬가지로 위험해 보이지 않았다. 게다가 나는 총을 쏴서 코끼리를 죽이고 싶은 마음이 전혀 없었다.

---

16 2013 명지대 ▶▶▶ MSG p.33 ③

make의 목적보어 ▶ 5형식 동사 make는 목적보어 앞에 전치사를 쓰지 않는다. 따라서 ③의 as를 삭제하고 viable parts가 되어야 한다. ① 형용사의 어순은 '한정사(the) + 수사(second) + 최상급(most important)'의 순이다. ② where의 선행사 areas가 적절히 사용됐다. ④ introduce는 타동사이며 목적어 없이 뒤에 by the British가 왔으므로 수동태로 적절하게 쓰였다.

crop n. 농작물 colonial a. 식민지의 viable a. 성장[발전]할 수 있는 empire n. 제국 culinary a. 부엌(용)의; 요리(용)의 heritage n. 유산; 대대로 전해 오는 것; 전통

밀에 이어 구세계에서 미국에 도입된 두 번째로 가장 중요한 농작물이 흔히들 쌀이라고 한다. 식민지 시대에 쌀은 밀이 자라지 못하는 지역에서 중요한 공헌을 하였다. 16세기 후반 파나마에 쌀이 도입됨으로써 이들 지역은 스페인 제국 중에 성장 가능한 지역이 되었다. 카리브해의 많은 지역, 특히 영국인들에 의해 인도 노동력이 유입된 지역에서 쌀은 전통요리의 한 부분이 되었다.

---

17 2022 가천대 ▶▶▶ MSG p.209 ②

other ~ than ▶ other는 than과 함께 쓰여서 '~와는 다른', '~이외의'라는 의미로 쓰인다. ②를 than으로 고쳐야 한다. ③ 관계대명사 which에 이어지는 동사이며 바로 앞의 Master Hugh had predicted는 삽입절이다. ④ 결과의 용법으로 쓰인 to부정사이다.

relieve v. (부담 따위를) 덜다 detest v. 혐오하다 enslaver n. 노예로 삼는 사람 contemplate v. 심사숙고하다 discontentment n. 불평, 불만 torment v. 괴롭히다 unutterable a. 말로 표현할 수 없는 anguish n. 고통, 괴로움

그것(글)들은 나로부터 한 가지 어려움을 덜어주었지만, 나에게 덜어주었던 것보다 훨씬 더 고통스러운 다른 어려움을 안겨주었다. 글을 읽으면 읽을수록, 나는 나를 노예로 만든 사람들을 혐오하게 되었다. 나는 그들을 우리의 집에서 우리들을 훔쳐내는 데 성공한 강도떼로밖에 생각할 수 없었다. 내가 글을 읽고 그 주제를 깊이 생각하게 되자, 나의 주인인 휴(Hugh)가 내가 글을 읽을 줄 알고 나면 뒤따라 올 것이라 예상했던 바로 그 불만이 이미 와서는, 내 영혼을 말로 표현할 수 없는 고통으로 괴롭혔다.

① 내가 오랜 기간 동안 함께 근무했던 강 선생님이 내일 은퇴할 예정이다.
② 학교 다닐 때, 나는 인상적인 급우들을 만났고, 그중 몇몇은 절친한 내 친구가 되었다.
③ 그녀가 내게 많은 질문을 했었는데, 그 질문들 중 대부분에 나는 답변할 수가 없었다.
④ 우리가 여기에서 꼭대기를 볼 수 있는 그 건물은 예전에는 아름다웠다.

18 2020 가천대 ▶▶▶ MSG p.101

with a view to ~ing ▶ 'with a view to~(~할 목적으로, ~하기 위해)' 구문 속의 to는 전치사이므로 그 뒤에는 명사 혹은 동명사가 와야 한다. 따라서 ④는 preserving이 되어야 한다. ① declare와 병치를 이루는 원형동사로 앞에 to는 생략되었다. ② 주어는 A president이다. ③ 복합관계형용사로 쓰였다. 즉 whatever means는 any means which와 같으며 여기서 means는 복수명사로 쓰였다.

emergency n. 비상사태 appropriate v. (의회가) ~의 지출을 승인하다; 횡령하다 assume v. (태도를) 취하다; (책임 따위를) 떠맡다; (성질을) 띠다 dictator n. 독재자 spout v. (화염 등을) 내뿜다; 도도히[막힘없이] 말하다

국가비상사태를 선포하고 자신이 추구하는 목적에 의회가 지출 승인을 거부한 정부 자금을 지출할 수 있는 절대적 권리를 자신이 가지고 있다고 주장하는 대통령은 또한 독재자의 역할도 맡아 하고 있는 셈이다. 실제로는 위기가 전혀 아닌데도 그가 "명백한 위기"라고 칭하는 남부 미국 국경에서의 사태를 놓고 황금시간대의 전국 텔레비전 방송 연설을 하는 동안 막힘없이 거짓말을 하는 대통령은 자신의 권력 기반을 유지하기 위해 자신이 이용할 수 있는 모든 수단을 사용하고 있는 중이다.

19 2021 아주대 ▶▶▶ MSG p.211 ③

주어와 동사의 수일치 ▶ 문장의 주어는 the current patchwork이므로 ③에서 동사를 단수동사 is로 고쳐야 한다. 열거되어 있는 national wildlife refuges, state wildlife areas, and county preserves는 모두 전치사 of의 목적어로서 앞의 명사 patchwork를 수식한다.

resurrect v. 부활시키다 degrade v. 분해되다; 저하시키다 cash-strapped a. 재정난에 처한, 금전적으로 어려운 gun club 야외 사격장 assemble v. 모으다, 집합시키다; 정리하다 backhoe n. 굴착기 patchwork n. (쪽모이처럼) 여러 조각[부분]들로 이뤄진 것 refuge n. 피난(처), 도피(처) primeval a. 태고의, 원시 시대부터 내려온 hemispheric a. (지구) 반구의 waterfowl n. 물새

캘리포니아의 센트럴 밸리(Central Valley) 습지대를 개조하는 것은 20세기의 많은 기간이 소요됐던 복잡한 프로젝트였다. 황폐한 농경지와 재정난에 처한 야외 사격장들을 불도저와 굴착기로 한데 정지(整地)하여 부활시킨, 지금은 국립 야생 동물 보호구역, 주립 야생 동물 구역, 그리고 지자체의 자연자원보호구역이 짜깁기된 이 땅은 농경지로 변하기 전에 센트럴 밸리 전역에 뻗어 있었던 4백만 에이커에 달하는 원시 습지에 비하면 많이 줄어든 것이다. 그럼에도 불구하고, 이 서식지들은 지구 반구 수준에서(북반구에서) 생태적으로 중요한데, 3백만 마리의 오리와 2백만 마리의 거위들을 포함해, 태평양 비행경로를 따라 이동하는 물새들의 60%에게 도움을 주고 있다.

20 2020 한국외대 ▶▶▶ MSG p.136

정비문 ▶ ④는 'The building was beautiful.'과 'We can see the top of it from here.'의 두 문장에서 둘째 문장의 the top of it의 it을 which로 바꾸어 관계절의 첫머리로 보낸 것이므로, the top 앞의 on을 삭제해야 한다.

retire v. 은퇴하다 peer n. 또래, 동료

01 ④	**02** ③	**03** ③	**04** ④	**05** ②	**06** ①	**07** ①	**08** ①	**09** ②	**10** ③
11 ③	**12** ④	**13** ①	**14** ③	**15** ③	**16** ②	**17** ③	**18** ①	**19** ①	**20** ②

01   2015 가천대   ▶▶▶ MSG p.201   ④

원급 관용 표현 ▶ not A so much as B는 not so much A as B와 마찬가지로 'A라기보다 B'라는 뜻의 표현인데, 해리엇에게 자유란 국가가 시민의 권리를 간섭하는 것(정치적 자유)이 아니라, 사회 그 자체에 있어서 관용의 문제(사회적 자유)라고 하였으므로, 그녀에게 자유란 정치적 자유(A)라기보다 사회적 자유(B)라는 말이 되어야 문맥상 적절하다. 따라서 ④ so much as가 빈칸에 들어가야 한다. ① rather는 부사이므로 앞뒤를 연결할 수 없다. not A but rather B나 B rather than A는 'A가 아니라 B'라는 뜻의 표현으로 but과 than이 접속사 기능을 한다. ② less than은 '~이하의'라는 뜻으로 앞의 political liberty와 의미상 호응이 되지 않는다.

draw up ~을 작성하다 State n. 국가 interfere with ~을 간섭하다 tolerance n. 용인, 관용 impinge upon ~을 침해하다

해리엇(Harriet)은 자유라는 주제로 논문을 작성했다. 그녀에게 있어 자유는 국가가 어디까지 시민의 행동을 간섭해야 하는지 혹은 간섭하지 말아야 하는지의 문제가 아니었다. 그것은 사회 자체 안에서의 관용의 문제였고, 어떤 사람들이 다른 사람들에 의해 권리를 침해받는 문제였다. 그녀에게 자유의 문제는 정치적 자유의 문제라기보다 사회적 자유의 문제였다.

02   2017 한국항공대   ▶▶▶ MSG p.131   ③

빈칸에 적절한 접속사 ▶ 빈칸 다음에 절이 이어지므로 접속사가 필요한데, 암컷 초파리가 수컷 초파리를 받아들이는 것은 수컷 초파리의 몸짓에 자극을 받는 경우에 일어나므로, 빈칸에는 조건의 접속사 ③이 들어가야 한다. ④도 접속사이긴 하나, 앞의 절을 뒤의 주절과 연결시킬 수 없고, 의미(~도 또한 아니다)로도 부적절하다.

fruit fly 사과즙파리, 초파리 choreograph v. 안무를 하다 tap v. 가볍게 두드리다, 치다 courtship n. 구애, 연애 vibrate v. 떨다, 진동시키다 execution n. 처형; 실행; 솜씨 arouse v. (흥미 등을) 유발하다, 불러일으키다 advance n. 전진; 접근 copulation n. 교미 ensue v. (어떤 일 · 결과가) 뒤따르다

수컷 초파리의 생각은 오로지 암컷 초파리의 마음을 얻는 것 하나뿐이다. 암컷을 발견하자마자, 그는 신중하게 연출된 춤을 추면서 암컷에게로 다가가 따라다니면서 다리로 암컷을 가볍게 친다. 수컷은 한쪽 날개를 떨면서 구애의 노래를 한다. 만약 그의 공연이 적절하여 암컷이 자극을 받으면, 암컷은 수컷의 접근을 받아들여 교미가 성공적으로 이루어지게 된다.

03   2020 세종대   ▶▶▶ MSG p.229   ③

전치사의 목적어 ▶ 'in addition to~'는 '~에 더하여, ~뿐 아니라'라는 의미의 관용표현이다. 그러므로 to가 없는 ②, ④를 정답에서 먼저 제외할 수 있다. 그런데 이 표현에 쓰인 to는 전치사이므로 그 뒤에는 목적어로 명사 상당어구가 와야 하며, 동사가 목적어로 올 때는 반드시 동명사의 형태로 와야 한다. 따라서 합성명사가 온 ③이 정답으로 적절하다.

poor sleeper 수면이 부족한 사람 illness n. 질병 disease n. 질환

수면이 부족한 사람들은 체중 증가뿐 아니라 다른 심각한 질병과 질환에 걸릴 위험도 훨씬 높다.

04   2020 한국외대   ▶▶▶ MSG p.234   ④

강조구문 ▶ 강조 구문은 'It is ~ that(which)'의 형식을 사용하여 강조하고 싶은 초점 요소를 그 사이에 둔다. 문장에서 that 이하가 완전한 문장의 형식을 취하고 있다. 따라서 강조할 초점 요소가 '부사구'인 ④가 정답이다.

make sense of ~을 이해하다

인간이 더 현명해지고 자신의 삶을 더 잘 관리하게 되는 것은 바로 우리의 경험을 잘 이해함으로써이다.

05   2019 가천대   ▶▶▶ MSG p.137   ②

전치사+관계대명사 to which ▶ '~에 적응하다'라는 의미는 'adapt to'로 하며, 지금까지 적응해온 것이므로 현재완료 시제가 적절하다. 그러므로 ②가 정답이 된다.

due ad. (방위가) 정(正) ~으로 latitude n. 위도 seasonality n. 계절적 변동, 계절성 habitat n. 서식지 crop n. 수확; 농작물 livestock n. 가축

서로 정동·서쪽에 위치한 지역들은 같은 위도를 공유하며, 따라서 낮의 길이와 계절 변화도 서로 같다. 그 지역들은 또한 비슷한 기후, 서식지, 질병을 공유할 가능성이 높으며, 이 모든 것은 작물과 가축과 인간은 그들이 적응해온 환경이 동서로 비슷하기 때문에 동서로 더 쉽게 퍼질 수 있다는 것을 의미한다.

06 **2021 세종대** ▶▶▶ MSG p.183 ①

올바른 어순 ▶ 주어로 쓰일 올바른 순서의 명사가 요구되는데, half가 전치한정사로 먼저 오고, 그다음에 한정사인 소유격 our nation's가 오며, 마지막으로 형용사 elderly가 온 ①이 올바른 순서이다. the elderly는 'the+형용사=복수사람명사'의 예로 '노인들'의 뜻인데 여기서는 our nation's라는 소유격이 정관사 the의 역할을 대신한다.

Social Security 사회보장제도, 사회보장연금

오늘날에도, 만약 사회보장제도가 없다면 우리나라 노인들의 절반이 빈곤에 처할 수밖에 없을 것이다.

07 **2004 동국대** ▶▶▶ MSG p.127 ①

문의 구성 ▶ 현재는 이 사향 황소가 생존해 있으므로 완전히 멸종된 것이 아니다. 한때의 사냥으로 거의 멸종당할 위기에 처해 있었다는 것이 빈칸에 들어갈 의미이므로 수동의 분사 hunted 앞에 부사 수식어 once가 위치하는 것이 적절하다.

woolly a. 털이 많은 musk n. 사향, 사향노루 ox n. 황소 extinction n. 멸종

한때 사냥으로 거의 멸종당할 위기에 처했던 털이 많은 사향 황소는 엘레스미어 섬(Ellesmere Island)에 생존해 있다.

08 **2022 세종대** ▶▶▶ MSG p.222 ①

도치 / 현재분사 ▶ 장소의 부사구가 문두에 왔으므로 주어와 be동사가 도치되어야 하며, 600마리 이상의 동물들이 사자, 원숭이, 홍학 등을 포함하는 것이므로 include는 능동을 나타내는 현재분사 including이 적절하다.

park n. 공원 flamingo n. 플라밍고, 홍학

공원에는 사자, 원숭이, 홍학을 포함한 600마리 이상의 동물들이 있다.

09 **2022 수원대** ▶▶▶ MSG p.132 ②

양보의 부사절을 이끄는 접속사 ▶ despite, in spite of는 전치사로서 뒤에 절이 이어질 수 없으므로 ①과 ④는 답이 될 수 없다. 접속사 although가 양보의 부사절을 이끌고 있는 ②가 정답이다. 한편, for가 절을 이끄는 접속사로 사용되면 '(왜냐하면) ~니까'로 해석되므로, ③은 문맥상 적절치 않다.

get along with ~와 잘 지내다 colleague n. 동료

그 신입사원은 영어를 못하지만 동료들과 잘 지낸다.

10 **2020 한국외대** ▶▶▶ MSG p.134 ③

Just as A, so B 부사절 ▶ Just as A, so B는 '마치 A하듯이 B하다'라는 의미이다. as가 접속사이므로 접속사 that을 또 쓸 수 없다. 따라서 ③에서 so 다음의 that을 삭제해야 한다.

fingerprint n. 지문 imprint n. (표면 위에 누르거나 찍어서 생긴) 자국

세상에 똑같은 두 개의 지문이 없듯이, 동물의 발자국도 이와 유사한 독특한 양상을 보인다.

11 **2012 홍익대** ▶▶▶ MSG p.120 ③

명령문, and S+V ▶ '명령문, and S+V' 구문은 '~해라, 그러면 …할 것이다'라는 의미로, and 이하에는 앞 문장의 행위를 했을 경우의 결과에 해당하는 내용이 온다. 반면, '명령문, or S+V' 구문은 '~해라, 그렇지 않으면 …할 것이다'라는 의미로, or 이하에는 앞 문장의 내용을 실행하지 않았을 경우의 결과가 온다. 주어진 문장은 전자(前者)의 경우에 해당하므로, ③을 and로 고쳐야 옳은 문장이 된다. ②는 'ask+목적어+to부정사' 구문에 쓰인 to부정사이며 ④는 '좀처럼 ~않다'라는 의미의 'be slow to부정사' 구문에 속하는 부분이다.

veteran n. 고참병; 경험이 많은 사람 low-down a. 용렬한, 천한, 타락한

사우스캐롤라이나 정계의 중진에게 그 주(州)의 비열하고 추잡한 정치사에서 가장 추한 장면을 지적하도록 청해보라. 그러면 그는 좀처럼 대답을 못할지도 모른다.

12 **2012 성균관대** ▶▶▶ MSG p.211 ④

주어와 동사의 수일치 ▶ ④ has done의 주어가 복수(White and black)이므로 ④는 have done이 되어야 한다. ③의 both는 대명사로 쓰였으며, they와 동격을 이룬다. ⑤ it이 지칭하는 것은 that secret이다.

efficient a. 능률적인, 효과가 있는, 유효한

적어도 그들의 커다란 비밀의 일부는 그들 둘 다 같은 국가에 살고 있다는 사실이다. 백인과 흑인은 지금까지 오랫동안 그 비밀을 공유해왔고 그 비밀을 서로로부터 지키는 일을 효율적으로 수행해왔다.

13 **2011 성균관대** ▶▶▶ MSG p.167 ①

대명사의 수일치 ▶ ① their는 뒤의 the nation이라는 단수명사를 가리키는 대명사이므로 its로 바꾸어야 한다. ②는 'many of+한정사+복수명사'의 형태이다. ③ which는 목적격 관계대명사로 뒤에 타동사 hazard의 목적어가 없는 불완전한 문장이 왔기 때문에 올바르게 쓰였다. ④는 '~하지 않을 수 없다'라는 뜻의 관용표현 have no choice but to V가 쓰인 것이다. ⑤의 even은 '~도[조차]'라는 뜻의 부사로 강조하는 말 앞에 나온다.

sphere n. 구; 분야 hazard v. 위험을 무릅쓰고 하다 speculative a. 사색적인; 투기적인

공적, 사적 양 분야에서, 국가는 국민이 도로에서, 공장에서, 환경에서, 심지어는 투기적 금융에서 어쩔 수 없이 감수해야 하는 많은 위험을 줄이려고 마땅히 노력하고 있다.

14 2013 중앙대 ▶▶▶ MSG p.59 ③

수동태 ▶ ③의 관계사절의 선행사 approach는 '주목을 받는' 것이므로 수동태가 되어야 옳다. 따라서 that is being noted as로 바로 잡아야 한다. ① 동사 observes의 목적어로 how가 이끄는 의문사절이 온 것으로 의문사절의 어순은 '의문사 + 주어 + 동사'이다. ② 등위접속사 and에 의해 현재시제 동사 observes, describes, discusses가 병치를 이루고 있다.

Globish n. 글로비시(영어 원어민이 아닌 다수가 사용하는 단순화된 영어, 원어민이 아닌 이들도 영어로 소통할 수 있도록 한정된 어휘와 기본 구문을 주로 사용하는 형태의 영어) be in need of ~을 필요로 하다 note v. 주의하다, 주목하다

새로 나온 전자책 『Globish The World Over』는 어떻게 10억에 달하는 사람들이 전 세계적으로 사업을 하기 위해서 일관된 언어를 필요로 하는지를 관찰하고, 이 문제가 수많은 비영어권 사람들에 의해 어떻게 해결되고 있는지를 설명하며, 그리고 아마도 진정한 세계어의 유일한 가능성으로 주목받고 있는 글로비시의 접근법에 대한 상세한 개요를 다루고 있다.

15 2022 가천대 ▶▶▶ MSG p.105 ③

현재분사 ▶ a new barely-imagined world 앞에는 동사 sees가 생략돼 있는데, a new barely-imagined world가 appear하는 행위의 주체이므로 목적격 보어로는 현재분사를 써야 한다. 따라서 ③을 현재분사 appearing으로 고친다.

aka ~으로 또한 알려진(= also known as) expound v. 자세히 설명하다 prevalent a. 널리 퍼진 barely ad. 거의 ~않다

트랜스휴머니스트들로도 알려져 있는 포스트휴머니스트들은 우리가 지금까지 해왔던 방식으로 인간이 진화하지 않을 것이라는 증거로 임플란트 같은 미래의 바이오메디컬 기술을 지적한다. 구글의 엔지니어링 이사인 레이 커즈와일(Ray Kurzweil)은 실리콘밸리에 널리 퍼져있는 이론을 자세히 설명하면서, 급격한 기술 발전으로 그동안 알고 있던 인간의 역사가 끝나는 모습을 보고 있으며, 그 대신 그 역사를 대체하기 위해 거의 상상해보지 못한 신세계가 출현하는 모습을 보고 있다.

16 2020 가천대 ▶▶▶ MSG p.218 ②

과거분사의 병치 ▶ 비교 구문 안에서 비교되는 대상은 그 문법적인 구조나 역할이 같아야 한다. 그러므로 주어진 문장에서 than 이하의 to do는 바로 앞의 said처럼 과거분사여야 하므로 ②를 done으로 고쳐야 한다. 이때 done 앞에는 it is가 생략돼 있다.

conserve v. 보존하다, 보호하다 necessity n. 필요, 필요성; (pl.) 필수품

대부분의 사람들은 지구의 자원을 가능한 한 많이 보존하고 싶어 한다. 그러나 그런 일은 말하기는 쉬워도 행하기는 어렵다. 자동차를 타고 출근하기 위해 휘발유를 소비하는 것이든, 전기 동력 세탁기를 사용하는 것이든, 한때는 사치품이나 편의상품으로 여겨졌던 것들이 이제는 필수품으로 간주되고 있으며, 실제로 기꺼이 그것들을 포기할 사람은 드물다.

17 2022 가천대 ▶▶▶ MSG p.167 ③

대명사의 격 ▶ ③을 동사 gave의 간접목적어로 보는 경우, ③ 이하에 possessors와 a better chance라는 두 개의 직접목적어가 접속사 없이 나열된 형태가 되어 문법적으로도 부적절하고 의미상으로도 부자연스럽다. ③을 소유격 대명사 their로 고쳐서 possessors를 수식하도록 만들면, their possessors가 간접목적어, a better chance가 직접목적어가 되므로 옳은 문장이 된다.

sexual selection 자웅선택(생물의 암·수컷이 상대를 선택할 때 색채·행동·울음소리 등의 상대를 끄는 특징에 의한다는 다윈의 학설) invoke v. (규칙 등을) 들먹이다[적용하다]; (근거로 예 등을) 들다[언급하다] inexplicable a. 설명할 수 없는 in terms of ~의 관점에서 plumage n. 깃털 render v. ~로 만들다, ~이 되게 하다 conspicuous a. 눈에 띄는 predator n. 포식자, 육식동물 confer v. 수여하다, 주다 offspring n. 후손, 자손

자웅(雌雄)선택은 포식자들의 눈에 더 잘 띄도록 만드는 많은 수컷 새들의 밝은 깃털처럼 자연선택의 관점에서는 달리 설명할 수 없을 것 같은 많은 것들을 설명하는 데 이용될 수 있었다. 그러한 신체구조는 생존을 위한 싸움에서는 그 어떤 이점도 주지 못했지만 짝을 찾는 싸움에서는 유리했기 때문에, 그러한 구조의 소유자들에게 덜 빼어난 자질을 갖고 태어난 다른 수컷들보다 더 많은 자손을 남길 수 있는 더 좋은 기회를 주었다.

18 2019 명지대 ▶▶▶ MSG p.46 ②

'(직접) 의문문'의 어순 ▶ 의문문에서 의문사 how가 be동사와 함께 쓰일 경우, "how+be동사+주어", 일반 동사와 함께 쓰일 경우 "how+do[does]+주어+동사원형"의 어순을 각각 취한다. ② 다음에 일반 동사 get과 의문부호(?)가 왔으므로, ②를 (직접) 의문문의 어순에 맞춰서 how do you로 고쳐야 한다.

motivated a. 동기가 부여된 task n. 해야 할 일; 힘든 일 draining a. 진을 빼놓는, 기진맥진하게 하는 time-consuming a. 시간이 많이 걸리는 get moving 진전시키다

당신이 아무리 전반적으로 동기 부여가 된 상태라 하더라도, 우리 모두에게는 하고 싶지 않은 몇 가지 일들이 있다. 아마도 우리는 그런 일들을 따분하고, 무의미하며, 진 빠지게 하고, 시간이 많이 걸리며, 짜증나게 하거나 걱정을 야기하는 것으로 여긴다. 그렇다면, 이런 상황에서 당신은 어떻게 헤쳐나가는가? 가장 먼저 해야 할 일은 동기부여가 되었다고 해서 짜릿함이나 희망과 같은 어떤 특별한 감정을 느껴야 한다는 것을 의미하지는 않음을 인지하는 것이다. 동기부여는 오히려 당신이 특정한 방식으로 행동하는 것에 대해 가지고 있는 한두 가지 이유에 불과하다. 당신은 어떤 일을 해야 하는 개인적으로 의미 있는 "이유"를 찾음으로써 그 일에 짜릿함을 느끼지 않고도 그 일을 하기로 결정할 수 있다.

19 2021 아주대 ▶▶▶ MSG p.105   ①

과거분사와 현재분사의 구별 ▶ 의미상 taxes가 designing의 주체가 될 수 없으므로, ①에 쓰인 designing은 수동을 나타내는 과거분사인 designed가 되어야 한다.

design v. (특정한 용도를 위해) 만들다[고안하다] **revenue** n. (정부·기관의) 수익[수입, 세입] **distort** v. 왜곡하다 **incentive** n. (어떤 행동을 장려하기 위한) 장려[우대]책; 의욕 **formal sector** 제도권 **bracket** n. 괄호; 그룹; 계층

세수(稅收)를 증대하기 위해 고안된 대부분의 세금들은 의욕, 특히 사람들의 노동 의욕을 왜곡하는 효과를 가진다. 담배세가 흡연량을 감소시키듯이, 소득세는 제도권에서 사람들의 노동량을 감소시킨다. 내 이웃집 사람은 일하지 않고 대신 집에 있으면서 자녀들을 돌보기로 했는데, 부인의 소득으로 인해 자신이 고소득층으로 분류되었기 때문이다. 만약 그가 일을 나가고 아기 돌보미를 고용했더라면, 그는 자신의 소득과 돌보미의 소득에 대해 세금을 내야만 했을 것이다. 집에 그냥 있음으로써 그는 세금이 면제된 아기 돌보미 활동을 즐겁게 했다.

20 2015 광운대 ▶▶▶ MSG p.125   ②

정비문 ▶ 의문문에서 의문사가 이끄는 절이 believe, guess, imagine, say, suppose, think 등의 목적어가 될 경우 의문사가 문두로 나간다. ②의 경우 what과 which hotel의 두 의문요소가 서로 충돌하여 의미가 어색한 문장이 되었다. 따라서 what을 삭제하고 which hotel을 문두로 보내 Which hotel do you think we will be staying at?으로 고치거나, What do you think of가 '어떻게 생각하니?'의 뜻이므로 think 다음의 which hotel를 of the hotel which로 고쳐 What do you think of the hotel which we will be staying at?으로 고쳐야 한다. ① which store가 주절인 의문절 did you say 앞으로 나간 형태이며, 문장 끝의 전치사 from이 의문사 앞에 올 수 있다. ③ 동사가 know일 경우에 의문사가 문두로 나가지 않으므로 적절하다. ④ How come은 '도대체 왜(=why)'의 의미로 뒤에 '주어+동사'의 어순으로 온다. ⑤ who가 문두로 나가서 의문사로 시작되는 의문문이 된 것이다.

break up (결혼 생활·우정 등이) 끝나다, 깨지다; (남녀가) 헤어지다

① 어느 가게에서 이 책을 샀다고 하셨죠?
② 우리가 어느 호텔에서 묵을 거라고 생각하세요? / 우리가 묵을 호텔에 대해서 어떻게 생각하세요?
③ 우리가 어느 그룹과 함께 여행할 것인지 아세요?
④ 왜 그들이 곧 헤어질 거라고 생각하세요?
⑤ 다음 주에 누가 누구와 결혼한다고 하셨죠?

TEST 33

| 01 ① | 02 ③ | 03 ④ | 04 ① | 05 ② | 06 ① | 07 ② | 08 ③ | 09 ④ | 10 ③ |
| 11 ② | 12 ② | 13 ④ | 14 ③ | 15 ② | 16 ③ | 17 ③ | 18 ⑤ | 19 ⑤ | 20 ③ |

01 2005 가천대 ▶▶▶ MSG p.138 ①

관계대명사 which ▶ 우선 빈칸 앞뒤로 두 개의 절이 있는데, 접속사가 없으므로 앞부분이 주절이 된다. 뒷부분이 종속절이 되므로 절을 이끌 접속사가 필요하다. 빈칸 뒤, 절의 동사가 are인 점으로 미루어 불완전한 문장이므로, 빈칸에는 보어 역할을 할 수 있는 어구가 쓰여야 한다. 관계대명사의 선행사가 앞문장의 구절 혹은 보어일 경우 또 자신의 절속에서 보어 역할을 할 경우 which 혹은 as를 사용하므로 ①이 적절하다. cf.) He is rich, which I unfortunately am not.(그는 부자이다, 불행히도 나는 부자가 아니다.)

certainly ad. 확실히, 분명 serious a. 진지한

나는 당신이 정직하지 않다고 말하는 것이 아니다. 당신은 분명 그러하다. 단지 나는 당신이 하는 일에 대해 진지하지 않다고 말하고 있을 뿐이다.

02 2020 수원대 ▶▶▶ MSG p.236 ③

양태 접속사 as절의 생략구조 ▶ '~듯이'의 양태 접속사 as 다음에는 '주어+be동사'가 생략될 수 있으므로 접속사 as 다음에 과거분사 evidenced가 바로 이어질 수 있다. 즉, as it is evidenced by ~에서 it is가 생략된 것이다. 따라서 ③이 빈칸에 적절하다. ① such는 형용사나 대명사로 쓰일 뿐, 접속사 기능이 없어서 주절과 연결되지 않는다. ② which는 시제를 가진 동사가 없어서 관계절을 이루지 못한다. ④ 분사구문으로 주어와 동사 사이에 삽입될 수는 있으나, 분사구문의 의미상 주어가 '많은 백인 형제들'이어서 '증명되다'와 어울리지 않는다.

destiny n. 운명 be tied up with ~와 관련이 있다

우리의 많은 백인 형제들은, 오늘 여기 그들이 참석한 것에 의해 증명되듯이, 그들의 운명이 우리의 운명과 한데 묶여 있다는 것을 깨닫게 되었습니다.

03 2020 한국산업기술대 ▶▶▶ MSG p.30, p.59 ④

consider 동사의 목적보어 ▶ consider 동사의 목적어에 해당하는 Any prizes가 주어가 되면서 이루어진 수동태 문장이다. Any prizes는 의미상 forfeit의 대상(객체)이 되므로 forfeit의 과거분사로 써야 한다.

contest n. 대회, 시합 forfeit v. 몰수하다

한 달 이내에 찾아가지 않은 사진 경연대회 상금은 몰수된 것으로 간주될 것이다.

04 2013 서울여대 ▶▶▶ MSG p.205 ①

A is as much B as C ▶ 관용적으로 A is as much B as C는 'C가 B인 만큼 A도 B이다' 즉 A를 C와 비교하여 'A는 C만큼 B이다'라는 표현이다. 즉 '주어가 as 이하만큼 (많이) 연방 의제'라는 것이다. 만일 much가 아니라 federal issue를 수식하는 important같은 형용사이면 일반적인 원급비교 구문의 as important a federal issue as ~로 되어 'as 이하만큼 중요한 연방 의제'라는 뜻의 문장이 된다. 한편 as much ~ as 뒤에 중복되는 표현은 생략될 수 있으므로 다음과 같은 원문이 나온다. Clearly, immigration reform is as much a federal issue as maintaining our military or managing our money supply (is a federal issue). 따라서 정답은 ① as much a federal issue as가 된다. ②, ④ 주어와 비교되는 대상인 빈칸 다음의 maintaining 이하가 뒤의 as 다음에 바로 오지 않아서 곤란하다. ③ much는 원급인 federal을 수식할 수 없고 much를 very로 고친다 해도 원급비교에서 very는 쓰이지 않는다. much를 삭제해도 'as + a + 형용사 + 명사 + as'가 되어 잘못이다. as federal an issue as의 어순이어야 하나 여기서 federal은 issue와 의미상 하나의 명사를 이루고 있어 어색하다.

immigration n. 이민 reform n. 개혁 federal a. 연방의

분명, 이민 개혁 법안은 군사력을 유지하거나 화폐공급을 조절하는 것만큼이나 연방 의제(議題)이다.

05 2021 세종대 ▶▶▶ MSG p.132 ②

양보 구문 ▶ 양보의 부사절을 이끄는 표현이 필요하므로, 'no matter how+형용사[부사]+주어+동사'의 형태가 빈칸에 들어가야 하는데, '주어+동사'인 'it(war) is'가 생략될 수 있으므로 ②가 적절하다.

necessary evil 필요악

전쟁은 때때로 필요악일지도 모른다. 하지만 아무리 필요하더라도, 그것은 항상 악이지 결코 선이 아니다.

06 2022 세종대 ▶▶▶ MSG p.30, p.95

see A as B 구문 / too ~ to … 구문 ▶ 'A를 B로 간주하다'는 'see A as B'의 형태로 나타내며, 뒤에 to부정사(to resist)가 있으므로 'too ~ to …' 구문이 되어야 한다.

potential n. 잠재력 vehicle n. 차량, 탈것 resist v. 저항하다

많은 분석가들과 투자자들은 중국 전기차의 잠재력을 뿌리치기에는 너무나도 매력적인 것으로 여기고 있다.

07 2022 서울여대 ▶▶▶ MSG p.7 ②

문의 구성 ▶ 절에는 하나의 주어와 하나의 정동사가 있어야 한다. 뒤의 which 관계절에서 which가 주어이고 occupies가 정동사이듯이, 앞의 주절에도 주어와 정동사가 있어야 한다. 따라서 빈칸에는 ②가 적절하다. ① How huge가 is의 보어인데, 또 is 다음에 수동태의 '과거분사+by 명사'가 이어지므로 부적절하다. ③ 정동사인 is가 없으므로 주절이 되지 못한다. ④ 보어 so huge가 문두에 오고 주어 the unknown world와 동사 is가 도치된 구문인데, so에 상응하는 that절이 뒤에 없어서 'so ~ that절' 구문을 이루지 못하므로 부적절하다.

unknown a. 미지의 occupy v. 차지하다

거대한 미지의 세계가 지구의 71%를 차지하는 바다로 덮여 있다.

08 2019 가천대 ▶▶▶ MSG p.133 ③

양보구문 ▶ 빈칸 이하의 주절은 '단락은 시각적으로 일관성이 있어야 한다는 규칙이 갖는 중요성'에 대한 내용인데 반해, 보기 속의 they seem simple은 '하찮게 보인다'는 뜻이므로, 주절과 빈칸은 글의 흐름상 양보 관계에 있다. 따라서 양보의 의미를 나타내는 ③이 빈칸에 적절하다. ③에 쓰인 것과 같은 '형용사[무관사 명사, 부사] + as + S + V'의 구문은 양보의 의미를 가진다. ①과 ②에는 양보의 의미가 없으며, ④의 경우 As를 삭제해야 한다.

paragraph n. (문장의) 단락 distract v. (마음·주의 등을) (딴 데로) 돌리다 single-space v. 행간 여백 없이 타이프를 치다 subsequent a. 다음의, 차후의 boost v. 증대시키다

단락은 시각적으로 일관성이 있어서 읽는 동안 눈을 산만하게 하는 일이 없도록 하는 것이 대단히 중요하다. 예를 들어, 첫 번째 단락이 행간 여백 없이 타이핑 돼 있다면, 그다음 이어지는 단락들도 그렇게 돼 있어야 한다. 비록 하찮게 보일지는 모르지만, 그러한 규칙들은 실제로 출판물의 겉모습이 더욱 전문적인 것으로 보이게 한다.

09 2006 세종대 ▶▶▶ MSG p.223 ④

so가 문두에 나와서 도치된 구문 ▶ so는 선행하는 낱말의 대용어로 '그러하여, 그런 것 같이'의 뜻으로 be, become, seem, appear, remain, find 등의 동사의 주격, 목적보어로서 그 앞의 형용사, 명사를 받는다. 선택지의 so도 이런 역할을 한다. 그런데 예문에서 보듯이 so 이하는 간혹 도치되기도 한다. ex.) Just as the lion is the king of beasts, so is the eagle [so the eagle is] the king of birds.(사자가 짐승의 왕인 것처럼 독수리는 모든 새들의 왕이다.) 우선 ②와 ④가 정답이 될 수 있는데, 뒤에 명사구 his arrival on the scene이 이어지고 있으므로 이것을 받을 동사와 연결어구가 있는 선택지를 골라야 한다. ④가 정답이 된다.

prosecutor n. 검찰관, 기소자 epigram n. 경구, 풍자시; 경구적인 표현

검찰관의 역할이 점점 익숙해지고 있듯이 사건 현장에 그가 도착하여 말하는 날카롭고 간결한 말투와 질문도 그러하다[익숙해져 있다].

10 2005 단국대 ▶▶▶ MSG p.11

대동사의 쓰임 ▶ 접속사를 사용하여 앞의 동사를 받을 경우 그 형태에 유의하여 일관성을 지켜주어야 한다. 이 문제의 경우 ③의 as it(=America) was를 그대로 두면 be동사의 보어가 애매해진다. 여기서는 '미국 서부가 정착되기 이전, 미국이 지녔던 것과 같은 모험정신'에서 '지녔던, 가지고 있었던'의 본동사 have의 과거형 had와 대동사의 형태로 일치시켜야 적절하다. 따라서 ③을 as it did로 바꾸어야 한다. 이때 did는 본동사인 have의 had를 받는다. ① never again과 ② as a nation은 의도적인 삽입 형태로 혼동을 유도하는 장치이다.

nation n. 국가 spirit n. 정신 adventure n. 모험; 모험심 settle v. 정착하다

미국은 서부가 정착되기 전 국가적인 차원에서 지녔던 모험정신을 결코 다시 가질 수 없을 것이다.

11 2022 경기대 ▶▶▶ MSG p.212 ②

부분 표시어 + 한정사 + 명사 ▶ most of, some of, all of, 분수 등과 같은 부분 표시어 뒤에 명사가 오는 경우, 그 명사 앞에는 정관사와 같은 한정사가 반드시 있어야 한다. ②를 most of the로 고친다.

executive n. 간부, 경영진, 임원

그 회사의 임원들은 대부분의 직원들에게 부분적인 재택근무를 시작할 수 있는 기회를 제공할 가능성을 논의하기 위해 회의를 열고 있다.

12 2019 홍익대 ▶▶▶ MSG p.139 ②

관계대명사 what과 that의 구분 ▶ 주절에 took과 may have been이라는 두 개의 동사가 연결사 없이 왔으므로 틀렸다. 따라서 may have been이 정동사가 되도록 that Smith ~ execution이 may have been의 주어가 되어야 하는데, ②의 that을 what으로 고칠 경우, took의 목적어가 선행사인 what이 될 수 있고, what이 이끄는 명사절이 주어 역할을 해서 동사 may have been과 이어지게 된다.

take A to be~ A를 ~라고 생각하다 impending a. 임박한 execution n. 처형, 사형 집행 nothing more than ~에 불과한 induct v. ~을 일원으로 가입시키다

포카혼타스(Pocahontas)가 어떤 역할을 맡았든 간에, 스미스(Smith)가 임박한 자신의 사형 집행이라고 생각한 것은 자신을 파우해튼(Powhatan) 족의 일원으로 가입시키기 위한 무해한 입양 의식에 불과한 것이었는지도 모른다.

---

13   2020 중앙대   ▶▶▶ MSG p.178   ④

문의 구성 ▶ 문법적으로 잘못된 곳이 없는 문장이므로 ④가 정답이다. ① 명사 system 앞의 한정사이다. ② '다양한'이라는 표현으로 such 다음에 부정관사 a가 오는 올바른 순서이다. ③ have something at one's disposal(무엇을 자기 마음대로 하다)이라는 관용표현에 쓰인 at 이다.

material a. 물질적인 a range of 다양한 alternative n. 대안 have at one's disposal ~을 마음대로 사용하다

이전 역사상 어떤 체제에서도 현재 체제에서만큼 사람들이 편안한 물질적 삶을 영위한 적이 없고, 다양한 대안적 삶의 경험을 마음대로 한 적도 없다고들 한다.

---

14   2010 한국외대   ▶▶▶ MSG p.163   ③

too/as/so/how+형용사+a(n)+명사 ▶ so/as/too/how/however 다음에는 '형용사+a(n)+명사'의 어순으로 이어진다. 따라서 ③ too a good deal을 too good a deal로 고쳐야 한다.

at issue 논쟁 중인, 문제가 되고 있는 opponent n. 반대자 defender n. 방어자, 옹호자

일반적으로 TIPS라고 알려진 물가연동국채가 투자가들에게 너무나 좋은 거래인지가 논란되고 있다. (물가연동국채) 옹호자들이 회계보고를 문제 삼지만, (물가연동국채) 반대자들은 정부가 물가연동국채로 인해 돈을 잃어왔다고 말한다.

---

15   2020 상명대   ▶▶▶ MSG p.203   ②

비교급 구문 ▶ ② 다음에 than이 있으므로 비교급 구문에 맞게 of much higher quality로 고쳐야 한다. 비교급을 수식하는 부사로는 much가 맞다.

entry n. (경기 따위에의) 참가, 출전; 참가자; 출품물 ad n. 광고 impress v. 감명을 주다, 감동시키다

올해의 가장 혁신적인 광고상(賞)에 출품한 작품들은 작년보다 수준이 훨씬 더 높았으며 우리는 모두 깊은 감명을 받았다. 그러나 마침내 우리는 한 출품작이 다른 모든 출품작보다 더 흥미로울 뿐만 아니라 더 혁신적이라고 결정했다.

---

16   2011 숭실대   ▶▶▶ MSG p.31   ③

5형식 동사 allow ▶ allow가 5형식 동사로 쓰였으므로 ③ put은 allow의 목적보어가 되어야 한다. 따라서 ③ put을 to put으로 고쳐야 한다. ①의 'be likely to+동사원형'은 '~할 것 같다'라는 뜻이고, more는 likely를 수식하는 부사이다. ② more and more는 '갈수록 더'라는 뜻으로 형용사 exotic을 수식하는 부사로 쓰였다.

liberal a. 진보적인 aversion n. 혐오 lethal weapon 살인무기, 흉기 derivative n. 파생 상품; 복합 금융 상품 put ~ at risk는 ~를 위험에 빠뜨리다

진보적인 분석가들은 그린스펀(Greenspan)의 규제혐오가 혁신적인 금융상품을 흉기로 바꾸어놓은 방식에 더 초점을 맞출 것 같다. 이런 관점에서 더욱더 색다른 파생상품을 위한 통제받지 않는 시장의 출현은 부주의한 금융기관들이 전체 금융시스템을 위험에 빠뜨리게 하였다.

---

17   2020 숭실대   ▶▶▶ MSG p.105   ③

현재분사와 과거분사의 구분 ▶ 첫 문장의 주어는 Du Sautoy이고, 동사는 cites이며, 목적어는 the Continuator이다. 그리고 the Continuator와 a musical instrument 이하는 동격을 이루는데, 의미상 a musical instrument가 훈련되는 객체이므로 ③을 과거분사 trained로 고쳐야 한다.

improvise v. (연주·연설 등을) 즉흥적으로 하다 musicianship n. (연주·작곡상의) 음악적 기교 improvise v. 즉흥적으로 작곡[연주, 노래]하다 distinguish v. 구별하다, 분별하다

인공지능(AI)이 인간 창조의 영역을 확장시키고 우리가 새로운 것들을 발견하는 데 도움을 주는 한 예로 드 사토이(Du Sautoy)는 사용자들에게 반응하도록 훈련된 악기인 Continuator를 인용한다. 2012년 프랑스의 재즈 음악가인 베르나르 뤼바(Bernard Lubat)는 자신의 연주 방식으로 훈련받은 Continuator와 즉흥적으로 연주하여 관객들이 기계와 음악가의 차이를 구분할 수 없게 만들었다.

---

18   2021 건국대   ▶▶▶ MSG p.143   ⑤

복합관계대명사의 격 ▶ 복합관계대명사의 격은 관계절 내에서의 역할에 따라 결정된다. ⑤에서 복합관계대명사는 needs의 주어 역할을 하고 있으므로 주격이어야 한다. ⑤를 to whoever로 고친다.

distribute v. 분배하다, 배급하다 give out 나누어주다 liquid n. 액체, 유동체 colony n. 식민지; 군체(群體) store v. 저장하다 stomach n. 위(胃), 복부, 배 run v. 운영하다

사람들과 마찬가지로, 개미도 해야 할 일을 분배한다. 몇몇 일개미들은 먹이를 구해서 어린 개미들에게 먹인다. 그 개미들은 사람들이 먹을 음식을 모으는 농부들과 같다. 어린 개미들이 그 먹이를 먹을 때, 그들은 어른 개미들이 먹을 수 있는 액상의(묽은) 먹이를 나누어준다. 일부 군체(群體)에서는 개미들이 몇몇 특별한 일개미들에게 그 액상의 먹이를 먹인다. 이 일개미들은 그것을 배에 저장하며, 그래서 그들의 배는 매우 커진다. 가게를 운영하는 사람처럼 그들은 필요로 하는 누구에게나 액상의 먹이를 나눠주면서 모든 시간을 개미집에서 보낸다.

19 2017 이화여대 ▶▶▶ MSG p.105 ⑤

현재분사 ▶ 현재분사에는 능동과 진행의 의미가 있고, 과거분사에는 수동과 완료의 의미가 있다. ⑤는 people을 후치수식하고 있는데, people이 flee하는 행위의 주체이므로 능동관계에 있다. 따라서 이것을 현재분사 fleeing으로 고쳐야 한다.

refugee n. 피난자, 난민 protracted a. (질병이나 교섭 따위가) 오래 끈 recruit n. 신병, 신입생, 신입회원 wretched a. 가엾은, 비참한 flee v. ~에서 도망치다 be obliged to ~하지 않을 수 없다 revision n. 개정 protocol n. 의정서 persecution n. 박해

현재 전 세계의 난민 가운데 기록적인 수치인 45%가 5년 이상 지속된 "장기 미해결 상황"에 처해 있다. 시리아인들은 이 비참한 집단에 가장 최근에 들어왔으며, 그들 대부분이 도망해 들어가는 국가들은 점점 더 이들을 달갑지 않게 여기고 있다. 실제로, 터키, 요르단, 레바논의 암울한 전망은 지난해 있었던 유럽으로의 집단 이주를 부분적으로 설명해준다. 점점 더 많은 수의 유럽 정치인들과 관료들이 국경을 넘어서 흘러들어오는 난민들을 도와주도록 법에 의해 정해져 있다는 사실에 충격을 받고 있는데, 이들은 1951년에 제정된 유엔 난민협약과 1967년의 유엔 난민의정서의 수정을 요구하고 있다. 유엔의 난민협약과 난민의정서는 박해를 피해 도망친 사람들을 국제적 차원에서 보호하는 것을 골자로 하고 있으며, 유엔 난민기구의 활동에 대한 근거를 제공하고 있다.

20 2016 한국외대 ▶▶▶ MSG p.121, p.221 ③

정비문 ▶ 'not only A but also B' 구문의 A와 B에 문장이 오는 경우, A에는 not only의 영향으로 도치가 일어나지만, B에는 도치가 일어나지 않는다. 따라서 ③의 but also deeply depressed was he는 but also he was deeply depressed 또는 but he was also deeply depressed 가 되어야 한다.

charm v. 매혹하다, ~의 마음을 사로잡다 depressed a. 우울한

① 그는 더 이상 그의 음악으로 관객들의 마음을 사로잡지 않았다.
② 그들은 두 번 다시 서로 헤어지지 않을 것이다.
③ 그는 슬펐을 뿐 아니라 매우 우울했다.
④ 그는 일요일에만 식료품점에 음식을 사러 갔다.

T E S T **34**

| 01 ④ | 02 ② | 03 ④ | 04 ① | 05 ⑤ | 06 ③ | 07 ② | 08 ④ | 09 ③ | 10 ② |
| 11 ④ | 12 ③ | 13 ② | 14 ④ | 15 ④ | 16 ③ | 17 ② | 18 ④ | 19 ② | 20 ② |

01   2012 홍익대 ▶▶▶ MSG p.89   ④

only+to부정사 ▶ 전체 문장의 동사는 served이다. 그러므로 ③ have 와 같이 시제가 있는 동사가 올 수 없다. 빈칸 앞에 only가 주어져 있으므로 결과를 나타내는 부사적 용법의 부정사로 표현해야 한다. ④가 정답이다.

literary a. 문학적인   paradox n. 역설, 패러독스

시시포스(Sisyphus)가 언덕 위로 돌을 계속해서 밀어 올리지만 결국 아래로 다시 굴러 떨어지고 마는 것은 제노(Zeno)의 세 번째 역설의 문학적 원형이 되었다.

02   2014 아주대 ▶▶▶ MSG p.222   ②

장소를 나타내는 부사가 문두에 올 경우의 도치 ▶ 장소를 나타내는 부사구로 문장이 시작되고 동사가 자동사나 be동사인 경우에는 문장의 주어와 동사가 도치된다. 따라서 the body-wall muscle이 주어진 문장의 주어이며, 빈칸은 동사가 와야 할 자리이므로, 단수형 동사 exists 가 정답이 된다.

beneath prep. ~의 바로 밑에   epidermal a. 상피의, 표피의   epidermal cell 표피세포   body-wall n. 체벽   relatively ad. 비교적으로

표피세포 아래 체벽근육이 존재하는데, 특정 환경에서 살고 있는 몇몇 종(種)들의 경우 이것이 비교적 두껍다.

03   2009 서울여대 ▶▶▶ MSG p.199   ④

동등 비교 ▶ 뒤에 as가 나왔으므로 비교 대상이 되는 as가 먼저 나와야 한다. as much ~ as 구문이 되며 '~와 같은 양으로[정도로]'라는 의미이다. 그리고 depend는 on을 전치사로 취하는 동사이므로 how 앞에 on을 써주는 것이 옳다.

juror n. (한 사람의) 배심원   relevance n. 적절, 타당성; 관련(성)

배심원들에게 있어 목격자의 신뢰성은 종종 그 증거의 내용이나 적절성만큼 이나 어떻게 목격자가 증거를 진술하는지에 달려 있다.

04   2007 경희대 ▶▶▶ MSG p.199, p.203   ①

원급비교 as ~ as & 비교급 better than ▶ 주어진 문장은 원급과 비교급을 동시에 나타낸 문장이다. ②의 구문은 선택을 나타내는 등위접속사 or가 아닌, 원급(as good as)과 비교급(better than)이 and로 병치되어, 즉 같은 정도로 좋고 그리고 더 좋다는 의미가 되어 논리에 맞지 않다. 이 문장에서 any high school sitter는 원급과 비교급의 공통 비교 대상으로 쓰인 것으로 빈칸에 ①의 if not better than을 넣어야 한다. ④는 not을 if 뒤에 위치시켜 if not better than이 되어야 한다. ex.) He is as rich as, if not richer than, the woman.(그는 그 여자보다 부유하진 않아도 그 정도는 된다.)

sitter n. 아기나 집을 봐주는 사람

아이들에 대한 나의 경험은 아기 보는 고등학생보다 더 좋지는 않아도 아마 그만큼은 좋다.

05   2020 아주대 ▶▶▶ MSG p.137   ⑤

the extent to which ▶ extent는 '정도'의 뜻이며 부사어 '큰 정도로' 는 전치사 to를 써서 to a great extent로 쓴다. 그리고 '~가 …하는 정도'는 선행사 the extent를 관계절이 수식하는 'the extent to which 주어 동사'의 형태로 나타낸다. 따라서 빈칸에는 ⑤가 적절하다.

be related to ~와 관련 있다   extent n. 정도

그것은 사람들이 그 프로그램에 참여했던 정도와 관련된 것 같다.

06   2019 가천대 ▶▶▶ MSG p.82   ③

과거추측의 would have p.p. ▶ 사람이 스포트라이트를 받는 것이므로 수동태여야 하고 비주류 아티스트들을 MTV가 처음으로 우리에게 소개해준다고 볼 때 이들은 전에는 스포트라이트를 받은 적이 없었을 것이므로 부정(not)의 과거추측인 would not have p.p.(혹은 would have not p.p.)가 적절하다. 다만 마지막 as절의 대동사 did는 were given the spotlight를 대신한 were로 고치는 것이 더 정확하다.

meteoric a. 유성 같은; 빠른   unplugged a. 언플러그드로 연주하는, 전자 악기를 사용하지 않는   mainstream a. 주류의

MTV는 유성처럼 빠르게 성장해서, 콘서트 실황, MTV 언플러그드, 만화로 된 음악상 시상식 및 그 외의 많은 프로그램들을 통해 단순한 뮤직비디오의 수준을 훨씬 뛰어넘는 확장을 보여주었다. 우리는 또한 MTV로 스포트라이트를 받은 것처럼 스포트라이트를 받은 적은 없었을 비주류 음악과 아티스트들을 우리에게 소개해 준 것에 대해 MTV에 고마워할 수 있다.

07   2022 세종대 ▶▶▶ MSG p.57, p.92   ②

수동태/완료부정사 ▶ 주어인 The Portuguese megalithic structure는 believe하는 행위의 대상이므로 수동태 문장이 되어야 하며, 마찬가지로 use하는 행위의 대상이므로 수동태이고 지금 믿어지고 과거에 사용되었으므로 완료부정사여야 한다.

megalithic a. 거석의 ceremonial a. 의식의 astronomical observatory 천문대

포르투갈의 거석 구조물은 천문대뿐만 아니라 종교나 의식의 목적으로도 사용된 것으로 믿어진다.

08   2010 고려대 ▶▶▶ MSG p.163   ④

too/as/so/how+형용사+a(n)+명사 ▶ 'too/as/so/how+형용사+a(n)+명사'의 어순으로 쓴다. 그리고 'too ~ to부정사' 구문에서 to부정사의 의미상 주어는 to부정사 앞에 'for 목적격'의 형태로 오고 부정문은 to부정사 바로 앞에 부정어를 써서 나타낸다. 따라서 ④가 적절하다.

inevitably ad. 불가피하게, 필연적으로 awkward a. 어색한, 거북한

나는 영어전용의 세계에서 국외자인 어머니와 장을 보러 갈 때마다, 우리의 (장보는) 일은 부득이하게도 너무나 어색한 상황을 초래하여 나는 소리를 질러 어머니를 돕지 않을 수 없었다.

09   2022 세종대 ▶▶▶ MSG p.136   ③

관계사절 / 삽입절 ▶ reflect의 목적어가 되는 명사절을 이끄는 역할과 자신이 이끄는 절에서의 주어의 역할을 동시에 할 수 있는 표현이 필요하므로, 선행사를 자체에 포함하고 있는 what과 whatever가 제시돼 있는 ②와 ③으로 정답의 범위를 좁힐 수 있다. 그런데 predict동사는 '목적어+현재분사'라는 5형식구문이 아니라 절을 목적어로 취하는 3형식구문으로 쓰이는 동사이므로 ③이 정답이다. 이때 climate modellers have predicted는 what will occur에서 what과 will 사이에 삽입된 삽입절이다.

extreme a. 극도의, 심한 drought n. 가뭄 reflect v. 반영하다 atmosphere n. 대기

그 지역은 기후모형 이론가들이 세계 대기 중의 온실가스 증가의 결과로 발생할 것이라 예측한 것을 반영하는 극심한 가뭄을 연이어 기록하고 있다.

10   2019 서울여대 ▶▶▶ MSG p.211   ②

주어와 동사의 수일치 ▶ how a steam engine works는 의문사 how가 이끄는 의문사절인데, 의문사가 이끄는 절이 주어일 경우에 동사는 단수 동사를 쓰므로, ②의 are를 is로 고쳐야 한다.

steam engine 증기 기관 work v. 작동하다

증기 기관이 어떻게 작동하는지는 널리 알려져 있지만, 일부 사람들이 증기 기관에 대해 한 번도 들어본 적이 없다는 것을 우리는 여전히 의심할 수 없다.

11   2018 세종대 ▶▶▶ MSG p.199   ④

as much as ▶ as many as는 '수'를 나타내는 표현과 함께 쓰고, as much as는 '양'을 나타내는 표현과 함께 쓴다. 130 tons는 무게, 즉 양(量)의 개념이므로, as much as와 함께 써야 한다. ④를 much로 고친다.

massive a. 큰, 육중한, 무거운 weigh v. 무게가 ~이다

거대한 대왕고래는 이제껏 지구상에서 산 가장 육중한 동물로, 다 자라면 길이가 100피트를 넘을 수 있고 무게는 130톤이나 나갈 수 있다.

12   2020 세종대 ▶▶▶ MSG p.130   ③

결과를 나타내는 so that 구문 ▶ ③ 이하는 변화된 이후의 모습에 해당하므로, ③을 결과의 부사절을 이끄는 so that으로 고쳐야 한다.

gratitude n. 감사 transform v. 변형시키다; 바꾸다 awe n. 경외, 두려움 appreciation n. 평가; 인식; 감사

우리가 감사하는 마음으로 가득 차게 되면, 우리는 우리를 더 큰 경외감과 감사함을 가지고 살도록 변화시키는 더 높은 수준의 자각을 하게끔 변모하게 된다.

13   2020 중앙대 ▶▶▶ MSG p.123, p.143   ②

복합관계대명사 whatever와 접속사 that의 구분 ▶ 복합관계대명사 whatever는 선행사를 포함하면서 그것을 제외한 나머지 부분은 불완전한 상태의 종속절(명사절)을 이끈다. 그런데 it 이하는 'it happen동사 that절'의 구문으로 완전한 상태이므로, ②whatever를 접속사 that으로 바꾸거나 삭제하는 것이 적절하다.

prose a. 산문적인, 지루한, 평범한 account n. 보고서, 설명 obsessed with ~에 집착하는 circumstantial a. 정황적인 apologetic a. 변명하는; 미안해하는

그 단조로운 보고서는 정황적 세부사항들에 집착할 뿐 아니라, 그 세부사항 또한 어떤 사람이 그 범인에게 걸려드는 일이 일어날 수 있음을 설명하면서, 극단적으로 변명할 뿐이다.

14 2014 한국항공대 ▶▶▶ MSG p.105 ④

문의 구성 ▶ 두 번째 문장에서 Even with one eye closed는 부대상황을 나타내는 분사구문이고 the retinal 이하가 주절이 된다. you're focused on에서 on의 목적어는 growing이 아니라 an object이고, the retinal image of an object you're focused on까지가 주어부가 된다. 문장의 정동사가 주어져 있지 않은 상태이므로 growing은 주절의 동사로 쓰이는 것이 적절하다. image에 동사를 수일치 시켜야 하므로 단수형인 grows로 고쳐야 한다. ① 관계대명사의 선행사는 단수명사 scene이 아니라 복수명사 aspects이므로 that절의 동사인 yield도 복수로 맞게 왔으며, yield는 여기서 타동사로 쓰여 목적어 information을 받았다. ② viewed는 when it(=a scene) is viewed에서 '주어+be동사(it is)'가 생략되고 남은 형태이다. ③ 부대상황을 나타내는 분사구문으로 'with+목적어+과거분사'의 형태가 왔으며, 눈이 감는 것이 아니라 감기는 것이므로 목적보어로 과거분사인 closed가 왔다.

monocular depth cue 단안 깊이 단서(한 눈만으로 지각할 수 있는 깊이 지각 단서로, 그 예로는 중첩, 상대적 크기, 직선 조망, 수평선에서의 높이 등이 있음) aspect n. 모습, 상(相); 각도 scene n. 장소, 현장; 장면 yield v. 산출하다; 가져오다 retinal a. 망막의

단안 깊이 단서란 한쪽 눈으로만 보았을 때 깊이에 관한 정보를 제공하는 현장의 상(相)들이다. 한쪽 눈을 감는다 해도, 당신이 초점을 맞추고 있는 물체의 망막 이미지는 물체가 더 멀리 떨어질수록 작아지며, 물체가 더 가까이 올수록 커진다.

15 2018 숙명여대 ▶▶▶ MSG p.57 ④

능동태와 수동태의 구분 ▶ ④의 주어로 주어져 있는 Some important reforms는 introduce하는 행위의 주체가 아닌 대상이므로, 능동 관계가 아닌 수동 관계에 있다. 그러므로 ④를 수동태로 고쳐 have been introduced로 써야 한다.

vulnerable a. 취약한 subterfuge n. 핑계; 속임수 strait n. 해협; (보통 pl.) 곤란, 궁핍 democratic a. 민주적인

우크라이나는 러시아의 압박과 속임수에 취약하다. 우크라이나의 경제는 매우 궁핍한 상태이며, 러시아산 에너지, 특히 러시아산 천연가스에 크게 의존하고 있다. 중요한 개혁 정책들이 도입돼 왔지만, 우크라이나는 안정적이고 독립적인 민주주의 국가를 수립하기 위한 노력에 있어서 아직 갈 길이 멀다.

16 2019 가천대 ▶▶▶ MSG p.121 ③

either A or B ▶ 접속사 either 뒤에는 or가 쓰여서 either A or B라는 상관접속사 구문을 만든다. 그러므로 ③을 or로 고쳐야 한다. ① 부대상황을 나타내는 'with 분사구문'을 이끌고 있다. ② 현재완료진행 시제이며, fret이 여기서는 자동사이므로 능동태이다. ④ 명령문에 쓰인 동사원형이다.

fret v. ~에 대해 초조해하다 decline v. (인기·물가 등이) 떨어지다 birthrate n. 출산율 divorce v. 이혼하다 workload n. (사람·기계의) 작업 부하(負荷); 표준 작업량 couple v. 연상하다, 결부시켜 생각하다 accompanying a. 수반하는 electronic device 전자기기

선진국에서는 결혼하는 커플의 수가 줄어들고 있는 가운데, 많은 사회학자들이 출산율 저하를 걱정해왔다. 오늘날 우리 사회에서 결혼하지 못하게 하거나 쉽게 이혼하게 만들고 있는 것은 과연 무엇인가? 어떤 이들은 우리의 일상적인 업무량이 현저하게 증가했다고 주장한다. 그것을 그에 동반되는 통신 및 전자 장치의 증가와 결부시켜 생각해보라.

17 2020 가천대 ▶▶▶ MSG p.31 ②

permit + 목적어 + to부정사 ▶ 동사 permit이 5형식 문형에 쓰일 때 목적보어로는 to부정사가 온다. 따라서 ②를 to buy로 고쳐야 하며, 이때 해당 부분은 'which(주어)+permits(동사)+countries that have exceeded their limit of greenhouse gas emissions(목적어)+to buy(목적보어)'의 구조로 파악할 수 있다. ④ They say에 이어지는 두 번째 접속사 that이다.

emission n. 배출; 배기가스 exacerbate v. 악화시키다 emit v. 방출하다 indulge v. 만족시키다, 충족시키다; 제멋대로 하게 두다 meager a. 빈약한; 불충분한

환경 전문가들은 교토 의정서에 의해 2005년부터 부분적으로 규제되어 온 온실가스 배출권 거래 제도가 지구 온난화를 악화시킬 뿐이라고 지적한다. 그들은 자국의 온실가스 배출 한도를 초과한 국가가 한도를 넘지 않은 국가로부터 배출권을 구입하는 것을 허용하는 그 제도는 더 많이 소비하고 더 많이 배출하는 국가가 하고 싶은 대로 하도록 하는 결과를 낳을 뿐이며, 온실가스 감축 효과는 미미하다고 말하고 있다.

18 2014 명지대 ▶▶▶ MSG p.113 ④

능동형 분사구문 ▶ ④의 Caught 뒤에 목적어가 와서 수동형 분사구문이 될 수 없다. 따라서 Caught를 Catching으로 고치거나, 분사구문의 시제가 주절의 시제보다 명백히 앞선다는 것을 강조하기 위해 완료형 분사구문인 Having caught로 고치는 것이 적절하다. ① if는 가정법이 아니라 조건절로 쓰인 접속사이며, if caught with a lover는 원래 if wives in classical Greece were caught with a lover에서 반복되는 주어와 동사가 생략된 형태이다. ② 조동사 would는 과거의 불규칙적인 습관을 나타내는 말로 쓰였다. ③ an incensed Athenian husband who were named에서 who were가 생략된 형태이며, named는 5형식 동사 name의 수동태 과거분사로 그 다음에 Euphiletos가 목적보어로 쓰였다.

classical a. 고전의; 고대 그리스·로마의 segregate v. 격리하다 other than ~이외의, ~을 제외한 notorious a. 악명 높은 instance n. 소송사건; 사례, 경우 incensed a. 분개한, 격노한 court n. 법정 justifiable homicide 정당 살인 adulterous a. 간통에 빠진, 불륜의 on the spot 현장에서; 즉석에서

고대 그리스의 아내들은 그들의 남편 이외의 다른 남자들로부터 격리된 삶을 살았으며, 만약 정부와 함께 있는 것이 발각될 경우 가혹하게 처벌받았다. 가장 약한 (처벌인) 경우, 여인의 남편은 그 여인과 이혼해서 그녀를 원래의 가족으로 돌려보냈다고 한다. 가장 악명 높은 일례로, 에우필레토스(Euphiletos)라 불리는 아테네의 한 분개한 남편이 아내의 정부인 에라토스테네스(Eratosthenes)를 살해한 후에, 법정에서 정당한 살인으로 승소했다고 한다. 불륜관계인 두 사람이 함께 자고 있는 것을 붙잡은 에우필레토스는 아내의 벌거벗은 정부를 현장에서 죽였던 것이다.

19 　2021 아주대 ▶▶▶ MSG p.146 　　　　②

복합관계부사 wherever ▶ 문맥상 '어디를 향하더라도'라는 의미가 되어야 하므로 ②의 whenever를 '어디에[어디로] ~하든지(no matter where)'라는 의미의 wherever로 바꾸어야 한다.

pigment n. 색소 head v. (특정 방향으로) 가다[향하다] like n. 비슷한 사람[것]; 같은 사람[것] presumably ad. 아마, 짐작건대 criminality n. 범죄 관련성, 유죄; 범행들 legacy n. 유산 liberal n. 자유주의자, 진보주의자

인간의 신체는 아직도 논란의 중심에 서 있다. 피부색은 많이 중요하다. 멜라닌 색소를 많이 지닌 피부를 갖고 뉴욕 거리를 걷는다는 것은 당신이 어디를 향하든지 경찰이 당신을 예의주시하리라는 것을 의미한다. 그러나 트럼프 대통령과 오바마 대통령 둘 모두와 같은 사람들은 피부색의 의미를 문화 및 역사적 관점에서 설명할 것이다. 경찰은 생물학적 이유로가 아니라 역사 때문에 당신의 피부색을 의심의 눈초리로 바라볼 것이다. 아마도 트럼프 진영에서는 흑인들의 범죄 관련성을 백인 자유주의자들과 흑인 사회가 저지른 역사적 오류의 불행한 유산이라고 설명할 것이다.

20 　2018 광운대 ▶▶▶ MSG p.27, p.33 　　　　②

정비문 ▶ urge는 5형식 문형으로 쓰기는 하나 want처럼 '가목적어-진목적어' 구문으로는 쓰지 않고 목적어로 사람명사를 취해야 한다. 그런데 ②는 문장의 내용상, 목적어로 Ed가 아닌 관계자들을 취하는 것이 적절하므로 이들을 가리키는 일반인 대명사 them을 사용하여 We urged them to clarify to Ed that he was on probation.으로 고쳐야 한다.

examine v. 검사하다; 진찰하다 probation n. 보호 관찰

① 우리는 에드(Ed)에게 전문의의 진찰을 받을 것을 촉구했다.
② 우리는 에드(Ed)가 보호 관찰 아래 있다는 것을 그에게 분명히 해줄 것을 관계자들에게 촉구했다.
③ 우리는 어른이 있어주길 원했다.
④ 우리는 에드(Ed)에게 그가 보호 관찰 아래 있음이 분명해지기를 원했다.
⑤ 우리는 전문의에게 에드(Ed)를 진찰할 것을 촉구했다.

| 01 ① | 02 ② | 03 ② | 04 ③ | 05 ① | 06 ① | 07 ① | 08 ① | 09 ③ | 10 ② |
| 11 ④ | 12 ② | 13 ⑤ | 14 ⑤ | 15 ② | 16 ③ | 17 ③ | 18 ④ | 19 ① | 20 ① |

01 2014 가천대 ▶▶▶ MSG p.131　

if를 대신하는 접속사 provided ▶ that절 안에서 두 개의 절을 연결하는 접속사가 필요한데, provided는 '만약 ~이면'이라는 뜻의 접속사로 쓰이므로 문맥상 ①이 빈칸에 적절하다. ② unless는 자체에 부정의 뜻이 있으므로 부정어 not과 함께 쓰이지 않는다. ③ whatever는 문법적으로 관계형용사로 볼 수 있으나 '어떤 일이 과하지 않다 하더라도'라는 의미가 되어 어색하다. ④ whereas도 접속사이지만 '일이 과하지 않은 반면에'라는 의미가 되어 어색하다.

excessive a. 과도한 dull a. 단조로운, 지루한 idleness n. 게으름; 나태

나는 업무가 양적으로 과하지 않다면, 가장 단순한 일조차 대부분의 사람들에게는 할 일 없이 노는 것보다 덜 고통스럽다고 생각한다.

02 2020 덕성여대 ▶▶▶ MSG p.156, p.236　②

동격의 어구 ▶ 빈칸에는 commitment와 동격을 이루는 명사가 들어가야 하는데, 과거분사 seen의 후치수식을 받으므로 정관사 the가 필요하고 '종류의 사랑'은 kind of love이므로 ②가 적절하다.

commitment n. 헌신 intimacy n. 친밀감 stagnant a. 침체된

텅 빈 사랑이란 친밀감이나 열정이 없는 헌신, 즉 침체되어버린 30년간의 결혼 생활에서 때때로 발견되는 그런 종류의 사랑이다.

03 2005 한양대 ▶▶▶ MSG p.137　②

올바른 관계사 표현 ▶ 주절의 주어 A number of ~ energy와 동사 show 사이에 들어갈 표현을 고르는 문제이다. 이미 주절이 있으므로 종속절 혹은 구의 형태가 되어야 한다. ①은 등위접속사절이 되는데, 이러한 등위접속사절은 주절 뒤에 이어져야지 주절 내에 삽입될 수 없다. ③은 which의 선행사가 a number of ~ energy인데, 주어 they도 의미상 같은 것을 가리키므로 중복된 표현이다. some of which는 대명사구로서 종속절 내에서 역할이 없으므로 ④ 역시 적절치 못하다. 전체적으로 '많은 무공해성 에너지 자원 속에는 태양력, 풍력, 그리고 수소가 있다'라는 내용과 '그 에너지 자원들이 미래의 큰 전망을 보여준다'라는 내용이 결합된 문장이다.

non-polluting a. 오염시키지 않는, 무공해성의 hydrogen n. 수소

많은 무공해 에너지 자원들 중에는 태양력, 풍력, 그리고 수소가 있는데, 미래의 큰 전망을 보여준다.

04 2010 홍익대 ▶▶▶ MSG p.158, p.163　

too+형용사+a(n)+명사/이중소유격 ▶ so/too/as/how/however 다음에는 '형용사+부정관사+명사'의 어순으로, 그리고 such/quite/rather/what 다음에는 '부정관사+형용사+명사'의 어순으로 써야 한다. 따라서 too good a friend of theirs로 쓰는 것이 맞다. a friend of theirs는 이중소유격(한정사+명사+of+소유대명사)의 형태이다.

administration n. 행정부 supportive a. 받치는, 지탱하는; 부양하는

미국의 신임 행정부는 이스라엘을 지지하는 동시에 솔직하게 대할 기회를 가지게 되었다. 지난 3년 동안 많은 이스라엘 사람들이 내게 조지 부시(George W. Bush) 대통령은 그들의 너무 좋은 친구였다는 말을 해왔다.

05 2017 가천대 ▶▶▶ MSG p.137　①

전치사+관계대명사 ▶ '전치사+관계대명사'의 표현에서 어떤 전치사를 쓸 것인가는 선행사와 관련 있는 전치사 혹은 관계대명사절에 쓰인 동사나 형용사와 관련 있는 전치사를 문맥에 따라 판단하여 결정해야 한다. 첫 번째 빈칸의 경우, pass는 통과 혹은 관통의 의미가 있으므로 첫 빈칸은 전치사 through를 써야 하고, 두 번째 빈칸의 경우에는, 텅 비어 있는 공간 '안에서' 우리 자신을 발견하는 것이므로 장소의 전치사 in을 써야 한다.

little more than ~에 지나지 않은 hollow n. 움푹한 곳, 공동(空洞)

공간. 우리들 대부분은 공간을 생각할 때 공허, 어딘가로 가기 위해서는 반드시 통과해야 하는 미지의 장소, 온전히 먼 곳, 혹은 우주에서 별빛이 닿는 곳을 생각한다. 시간은 곧 돈일지도 모른다. 그러나 공간은 공허 혹은 우리가 존재하고 있는 텅 비어 있는 곳에 지나지 않는다.

06 2010 서울여대 ▶▶▶ MSG p.33, p.140　

관계절의 수식 ▶ 문장의 동사는 will make이고 developed 이하의 수식을 받은 the technology와 빈칸이 and로 연결되어 주어부를 이루므로, 빈칸에는 명사 the science가 관계절 it has made possible의 수식을 받은 ①이 적절하다.

carry out 실행하다 redundant a. 말이 많은, 장황한; 풍부한

인간 게놈 프로젝트를 실행하기 위해 개발된 기술과 그 기술이 가능케 만든 과학은 결국 그 문제 전체를 불필요하게 만들 것이다.

07 **2021 세종대** ▶▶▶ MSG p.103 ①

have a difficult time ~ing ▶ 'have a difficult time (in) ~ing'는 '~하는 데 어려움을 겪다[애를 먹다]'라는 의미의 관용표현이다.

citation n. 인용, 인용문; 소환, 소환장

많은 학생들이 언제 인용문을 사용해야 하는지를 아는 데 어려움을 겪는데, 그 정보가 일반적인 상식이라고 생각하는 경우에 특히 그러하다.

08 **2021 세종대** ▶▶▶ MSG p.73 ①

as if 구문 ▶ 이미 완전한 문장이 완성돼 있으므로, 빈칸 이하에는 부사 상당어구가 올 수 있다. 따라서 '마치 ~처럼'의 의미인 'as if+가정법 구문'이 제시돼 있는 ①이 정답이다. ② like는 전치사이므로 원칙적으로 뒤에 절이 올 수 없다. ④ 전치사 like의 목적어가 없다.

plagiarism n. 표절, 도용

다른 누군가의 생각이나 말을 훔쳐서 그것을 마치 작가의 독창적인 생각인 것처럼 글에 사용하는 것은 표절이라 불린다.

09 **2009 아주대** ▶▶▶ MSG p.113 ③

분사구문 ▶ 주절의 주어인 the wolf 앞부분에는, consider the wolf a dangerous predator라는 5형식 구문에서 the wolf를 의미상 주어로 한 수동의 분사구문인 ③이 적절하다. ①, ②, ④는 능동태여서 부적절하고, ⑤는 부사 once 다음에 술부만 온 형태여서 부적절하다. Because it was once considered a dangerous predator여야 한다.

predator n. 포식동물, 포식자, 육식동물; (약한 사람들을 이용해 먹는) 약탈자 extinction n. 멸종

과거 한때 위험한 포식동물로 간주되었기 때문에 늑대는 계속 사냥 당해 이제는 거의 멸종에 이르렀다.

10 **2011 한국외대** ▶▶▶ MSG p.71 ②

if 생략시 가정법 과거완료의 형태 ▶ 가정법 과거완료의 문장이다. 종속절에서 접속사 if가 생략되고 주어와 동사가 도치되어 had I not clung to the branch로 되었다. 따라서 ②는 주절의 가정법 과거완료 형태에 맞도록 would have knocked로 고쳐야 한다.

shiver n. 떨림, 전율; 오한 knock off 부수다, 때려눕히다 with might and main 전력을 다하여, 힘껏

나무가 떨리고 있었다. 바람이 불었는데, 만약 온힘을 다해 나뭇가지에 매달려 있지 않았다면 내 몸을 날려버렸을 그런 돌풍이었다.

11 **2021 서강대** ▶▶▶ MSG p.147, p.179 ④

적절한 품사 ▶ core는 형용사이고, 그다음에 전치사 of가 제시돼 있으므로 ④는 명사 purpose여야 한다.

surveillance n. 감시 capitalism n. 자본주의 commodification n. (예술 따위의) 상업[상품]화 profit-making n. 이윤 창출

감시 자본주의는 이윤 창출이라는 핵심적인 목적을 가지고 개인 정보를 상품화하는 것을 중심으로 한 경제 체제이다.

12 **2022 홍익대** ▶▶▶ MSG p.139 ②

관계대명사 what ▶ ②에는 is의 주어가 되는 명사절을 이끄는 역할과 그 명사절의 주어의 역할을 동시에 할 수 있는 표현이 필요하다. 그러므로 ②를 선행사를 포함한 관계대명사 what으로 고쳐야 한다.

matter v. 중요하다 reasonably ad. 합리적으로; 상당히, 꽤 loyalty n. 충성심

내게는 지금 대부분의 조직에서 가장 중요한 것이 조직에 대해 자부심과 충성심을 가지고 있는 매우 지적이고 근면한 관리자들을 두는 것으로 보인다.

13 **2017 성균관대** ▶▶▶ MSG p.218 ⑤

문의 구성 ▶ where the coursework ~ how to talk with children은 Santa school을 선행사로 하는 삽입된 관계부사절이다. ⑤ 이하는 A and B의 구조인데, 등위접속사로 연결된 표현은 그 문법적인 구조나 역할이 같아야 하므로, building의 형태에 맞춰 ⑤를 winning으로 고쳐야 한다. 이때, winning over Santa skeptics and building his business는 주절에 이어지는 분사구문이다.

customs broker 관세사 enroll v. 입회[입학, 입대]하다; 등록하다 coursework n. 특정 학습 과정에 필요한 수업 내용 win over 설득하다, 자기편으로 끌어들이다

관세사로서 은퇴한 후에 부수입에 관심이 많던 귀퍼트씨(Mr. Guippert)는 강좌에 아이들과 대화하는 법이 포함돼 있던 산타 스쿨에 등록하여, 산타클로스의 존재를 믿지 않은 사람들을 자신의 편으로 만들고 사업도 키워나갔다.

14 **2022 성균관대** ▶▶▶ MSG p.169 ⑤

재귀대명사 ▶ 대시 이하에 지각동사 watching 다음에 '목적어+원형동사' 형태가 병치돼 있는데, 이때 struggle to cheer의 의미상 주어는 watching의 목적어인 them(자녀들)이고 목적어도 them(자녀들)이다. 주어의 행위가 주어 자신에게 미치는 경우, 재귀대명사를 사용하므로, ⑤는 재귀대명사 themselves가 되어야 한다.

parenting n. 육아 first and foremost 다른 무엇보다도 commitment n. 약속; 전념; (돈·시간·인력의) 투입

팬데믹 상황에서 자녀양육을 그렇게 어렵게 만드는 것은 다른 무엇보다도 증가된 시간 투입이 아니다. 그것은 자녀들이 괴로워하는 모습을 가까이서 보는 것, 즉 그들이 위축되고, 스스로 기운을 내려고 노력하며, 살을 빼는 모습을 지켜보는 것조차도 아니다.

---

15 **2021 홍익대** ▶▶▶ MSG p.211, p.214   ②

주어와 동사의 수일치 ▶ 접속사 but 이하는 강조를 위해 보어인 so narrow가 be동사 앞으로 와서 주어와 동사가 도치된 구문이다. 동사 is의 주어는 the bounds of human understanding, 즉 복수다. 그러므로 ②의 is를 are로 고쳐야 한다.

nouishment n. 영양분 bound n. (pl.) 경계, 한계 acquisition n. 습득, 취득

인간은 이성적인 존재이며 그러한 존재로서 과학으로부터 그의 적절한 양식과 자양분을 얻는다. 그러나 인간이 이해할 수 있는 범위는 너무나도 좁아서, 특히 이런 점에서, 인간의 (과학적 양식) 습득의 정도 면에서든 확실성 면에서든, 만족은 거의 기대할 수 없다.

---

16 **2012 서강대** ▶▶▶ MSG p.64   ③

적절한 전치사의 사용 ▶ 동사 concern은 수동태 구문에서 전치사 for와 함께 '~에 대해 걱정[염려]하다'라는 뜻으로 쓰인다. 주어진 문장에서 concern은 '~와 관계가 있다'라는 의미로 쓰였기 때문에 ③의 for를 with로 고쳐 'is concerned with(~와 관계가 있다)'로 표현해야 한다. ①의 what은 the thing which를 대신해 쓰인 것이다. ②의 be coherent with는 '~와 밀접하게 관련이 있다'라는 뜻이다.

intonation n. 억양 coherent a. 시종일관한, 조리가 서는 rhetorical question 수사 의문문, 반어문 statement n. 서술문, 평서문

의문문은 보통 알지 못하는 것을 나타낸다. 의문문에서 올림조(끝을 올리는 억양)를 사용하는 것은 "모르는 것이 (화제로) 올라 있다"와 밀접하게 관련이 있다. 그러므로 서술문에서 하강조가 사용되는 것은 "아는 것이 (화제에서) 내려가 있다"와 관련이 있다. 사실, 하강조로 끝나는 의문문은 실제 의문문이 아니라 서술문을 나타내는 수사의문문으로 이해되고 있다.

---

17 **2019 한양대 서울** ▶▶▶ MSG p.144   ③

장소의 관계부사 ▶ 관계대명사 이하는 불완전한 문장이어야 하는데, ③ 이하가 완전한 문장을 이루고 있으므로, 여기서 관계대명사 which를 쓴 것은 잘못이다. 선행사가 the countries로 장소이므로 관계대명사 which 앞에 전치사 in을 넣거나 관계부사 where로 대체시켜야 한다.

cradle n. 요람 invest v. 부여하다 postdiluvian a. 노아의 대홍수 이후의 have reference to ~에 관계가 있다 mark v. 주목하다

메소포타미아와 아시리아는 비록 인류의 요람은 아니었다 할지라도, 노아(Noah)의 후손들이 최초로 그들의 두드러진 역할을 수행한 현장이었다. 다양하고 중요한 사건들은 그 사건이 일어난 국가들을 깊은 관심의 대상으로 만들 수밖에 없다. 특히 그 국가들에서 노아의 대홍수 이후의 초기 시대와 관련이 있는 지역은 인류의 도덕적 발전을 주목하며 기뻐하는 이들의 호기심을 반드시 자극하게 된다.

---

18 **2021 가천대** ▶▶▶ MSG p.167   ④

대명사의 수일치 ▶ ④는 앞에 나온 a rate를 받는 대명사이므로 단수로 써야 한다. ④를 that으로 고친다. ① only가 이끄는 부사구가 문두에 와서 도치가 일어났다.

insertion n. 삽입, 끼워 넣기 rivet n. 리벳 reverse v. 거꾸로 하다, 반대로 하다; 뒤집다, 뒤엎다 meteoric rise 급부상; 천문학적인 급상승 planetary a. 행성의; 지구의 dominance n. 우세, 우월, 지배 extinction n. 사멸, 절멸 attrition n. 마찰; 소모; 감소

우리의 우주선은 빠지고 있는 것보다 더 많은 리벳을 끼워 넣음으로써 강화되고 있었다. 약 1만 년 전부터 비로소 그 과정이 다소 영구적으로 뒤바뀔지도 모른다는 징후가 있어 왔다. 그때는 '호모 사피엔스'라는 단 하나의 종(種)이 지구를 지배하는 종으로 급부상하기 시작한 때였다. 그리고 대략 지난 반세기 만에 인류가 종과 개체군을 자연적으로 감소되는 속도를 훨씬 뛰어넘는 속도로 멸종으로 내몰고 있다는 것이 명백해졌다.

---

19 **2022 아주대** ▶▶▶ MSG p.55   ①

수동태와 능동태의 구분 ▶ '남성성을 정의한 영화 장르'라는 의미이므로 ①은 능동태인 the film genre that defined masculinity로 바꾸어야 한다.

masculinity n. 남성성 silhouette n. 검은 윤곽, 실루엣 inscribe v. (이름 등을) 새기다, 쓰다 overworked a. 혹사당하는, 과로한; 남용된 underfed a. 음식을 제대로 먹지 못한, 배를 곯은 confines n. 범위, 영역, 한계 domesticity n. 가정(성) pick oneself up (넘어졌다가) 일어서다, 회복하다 showdown n. 마지막 결전, 최후의 대결, 결판

서부극은 수십 년 동안 남성성을 정의한 영화 장르였다. 바로 서부극에서 John Wayne과 Clint Eastwood의 실루엣이 John Ford와 Sergio Leone 같은 전설적인 감독들에 의해 틀이 잡혀, 문화사에 새겨졌다. 현실에서 카우보이들은 혹사당했고, 배도 곯았으며, 제대로 보수도 받지 못했지만 영화 속에서 그들은 가정의 한계보다는 황야의 자유를 선택한 거칠고 독립적인 방랑자가 될 수 있었다. 그래서 서부극은 여러 번에 걸쳐 사망 선고가 내려졌어도, 언제나 먼지투성이의 땅에서 몸을 일으켜 다시 한 번 결전을 벌일 준비를 하는 것이다. 완전히 미국적인 남성의 궁극적인 영화적 상징인 카우보이를 위협할 수 있는 존재는 아마 지금도 슈퍼히어로뿐일 것이다.

정비문 ▶ ①에서 whatever는 수여동사 tell의 직접목적어이면서도 접속사로서 복합관계대명사 역할을 하고 있다. '믿음(belief, faith)'을 나타낼 때 관련 전치사는 to가 아니라 in이다. 따라서 올바르게 문장을 고치면, I have no faith in whatever he tells me가 된다. ②에서 접속사 before같은 경우 구태여 행위 전후를 나타내려고 시제를 구분하지 않아도 그 자체로 행위 전후가 구분되므로 시제가 같아도 된다. 따라서 올바른 문장이다. ③의 경우 일종의 특수 구문, 즉 변형된 문장으로서 목적어절이 전치된 문장이다. 본래의 문장으로 바꾸면, Do without what you cannot afford to buy이다. 이것은 하나의 표현기법일 뿐 잘못된 문장은 아니다. ④의 복합 관계부사가 이끄는 양보 부사절에서 '(의문부사+ever)+형용사+주어+may+2형식 동사'는 올바른 문장 형식이며, 또한 '의무나 당위'를 나타내는 'ought to+동사원형'의 부정형은 'ought not to+동사원형'이므로 문법적으로 올바른 문장이다.

can afford to do ~할 여유가 있다 do without 없이 지내다

① 나는 그가 말하는 어떤 것에 대해서도 믿음이 없다.
② 6주가 지나서야 나는 그를 다시 보게 되었다.
③ 당신이 구입할 여유가 없는 것은 그냥 없이 지내라.
④ 사람이 제 아무리 부자라 할지라도, 태만해서는 안 된다.

01　2019 가천대　▶▶▶ MSG p.127　②

접속사 once ▶ 접속사 once는 '일단 ~하면, 일단 ~하고 나자'라는 의미를 갖는다. 한편, 접속사 lest는 '~하지 않도록'의 의미를 갖는다.

contemptuously ad. 경멸적으로, 모욕적으로 disparage v. 폄하하다, 비방하다 barbaric a. 야만적인 classical a. 고전적인 preceding a. 바로 전의, 선행하는 ostentatious a. 허세를 부리는, 과시하는 refinement n. 세련됨, 고상함

고딕(Gothic)"이라는 단어는 중세 시대 전성기와 후기에 서유럽에서 번성했던 예술과 건축 양식을 일컫는다. 이 용어는 원래 야만적이라 여겨진 이 시대의 문화 산물들을 경멸적으로 비방하기 위해 사용되었다. 일단 고전적인 건축이 르네상스 시대에 부활하고 나자, 앞선 시대의 고딕 양식은 과시적이고, 세련미가 없는 것으로 여겨지게 되었다.

02　2021 수원대　▶▶▶ MSG p.140　④

목적격 관계대명사의 생략 ▶ 빈칸 다음의 절에 타동사 predict의 목적어가 없어 불완전한 절이므로 완전한 절이 와야 하는 ①(접속사), ②(전치사+관계대명사), ③(관계부사 혹은 접속사)는 빈칸에 부적절하고, 관계절의 수식을 받을 수 있는 명사 ways가 있는 ④(전치사+명사)가 적절하다. no one 앞에는 목적격 관계대명사가 생략되었고 come about에서 about은 전치사가 아닌 부사이므로 그다음에 부사구인 in ways가 올 수 있다.

take form 구체화되다, 나타나다　vaporous a. 수증기 같은, 헛된, 꿈같은 impulse n. 충동

사건은 본질적으로 되풀이할 수 없었다. 그것은 아무도 예측할 수 없는 방식으로 생겨났고, 꿈같은 상상이나 갑작스런 충동으로부터 나타났다.

03　2020 한국외대　▶▶▶ MSG p.139　①

문의 구성 ▶ 문장의 빈칸에 적절한 것으로는 보어가 될 수 있는 명사절이다. ②와 ③의 형용사절은 관계대명사가 수식하는 선행사가 없기 때문에 틀린 표현이다. '함께 공유될 것'이라는 의미에서 선행사 that을 which 관계절이 수식하고 있는 ①이 적절하다.

propaganda n. (주의·주장 등의) 선전

가장 효율적인 선전은 함께 공유될 것이며, 영상물이 문자메시지보다 훨씬 더 공유하기 쉬운 경향이 있다.

04　2020 한국외대　▶▶▶ MSG p.123　③

문의 구성 ▶ that절의 주어는 cuneiform이고, 빈칸 다음에 명사구 form of writing이 있다. 따라서 빈칸에는 동사와 명사구를 수식해주는 형용사가 적절한데, 동사 was 다음에 형용사의 어순은 '한정사(the)+최상급 형용사(earliest)+형용사(known)'이므로 ③이 빈칸에 적절하다.

note v. 주목하다　cuneiform n. 설형문자

설형문자가 지금껏 알려진 가장 오래된 형태의 글자였다는 점에 주목하는 것이 중요하다.

05　2007 단국대　▶▶▶ MSG p.22, p.43　①

일반적 사실을 나타내는 현재시제 ▶ 문장의 본동사를 포함해야 하므로 일단 ③과 ④는 정답에서 제외된다. 이 문장은 일반적 사실을 기술하므로 현재시제인 ①이 적절하다. ②의 경우 involved를 aid를 수식하는 과거분사로 보아도 use는 uses여야 하고 목적어를 취하려면 능동태 to link여야 한다.

suited a. 어울리는, 적합한　mnemonics n. 기억술(단수취급)

외국어는 암기법의 사용에 이상적으로 적합하다. 널리 알려진 한 가지 암기 방법은 모국어의 단어와 외국어의 단어를 연결시키기 위해 이미지를 사용하는 것이다.

06　2021 세종대　▶▶▶ MSG p.120, p.227　④

명령문 / split A into B ▶ 'split A into B(A를 B로 분할하다)'의 split이므로 전치사는 into이며, four이므로 복수 payments이고, 하나의 형용사로 쓰일 때는 두 단어를 하이픈으로 연결하므로 interest-free이다.

split v. 쪼개다, 분할하다 interest-free a. 무이자의 payment n. 지불, 납부

지금 구입하시고, 총 금액을 네 번의 부담 없는 무이자 할부로 내십시오.

07 **2021 아주대** ▶▶▶ MSG p.200 　　　　①

배수비교 ▶ 배수비교는 'twice[three times] as 형용사의 원급 as~'를 써서 표현한다. 따라서 ①이 빈칸에 적절하다. closely는 부사로서 형용사 related를 수식하고 있다.

favouritism n. 편파, 편애

어떤 어머니가 편애를 보인다면 그것은 삶에 대한 기대의 차이에 근거해 있을 것이다. 그 어머니는, 모든 사람과 마찬가지로, 자녀 중의 그 누구보다도 자신과 두 배나 밀접한 관계에 있다.

08 **2013 단국대** ▶▶▶ MSG p.133 　　　　①

형용사 + as + 주어 + 동사 ▶ 빈칸 이후에 완전한 절이 왔으므로 빈칸은 부사구나 부사절이 올 수 있다. ①은 '형용사 + as + 주어 + 동사'의 형태인데 접속사 as가 양보의 의미를 나타낼 경우 형용사는 as 앞으로 온다. 따라서 ①이 부사절의 형태로 양보의 의미를 나타내어 주절과 문맥상 호응하므로 빈칸에 적절하다. ② 절과 절은 접속사 없이 연결이 불가능하므로 주어 He 앞에 although나 though와 같은 양보의 접속사가 필요하다. ③ 종속접속사도 없고 주어와 동사가 의미 없이 도치되었다.

unlettered a. 무교육의; 무지의　unpolished a. 세련되지 않은; 예의 없는

그는 교육을 받지 못하고 세련되지 않았지만 몇몇 가장 중요한 점에서는 여전히 신사였다.

09 **2008 경기대** ▶▶▶ MSG p.111 　　　　④

분사구문 ▶ 분사구문과 주절의 주어 일치를 묻는 문제로, 빈칸은 주절의 주어와 동사의 자리가 된다. 수동 분사구문 Inaugurated a second time ~의 생략된 의미상 주어가 사람이므로, 주절의 주어도 사람이어야 한다. 사람이 주어로 제시된 선택지는 ④뿐이다. focused는 과거분사로 앞의 명사 a new term을 수식한다.

inaugurate v. 취임시키다; 취임식을 거행하다　look forward to ~을 기대하다　domestic a. 국내의

1901년 3월 4일 두 번째 임기에 취임한, 윌리엄 맥킨리(William McKinley)는 외교 정책보다는 국내 정책에 초점을 맞춘 새로운 임기를 기대하고 있었다.

10 **2004 홍익대** ▶▶▶ MSG p.95 　　　　③

so 형용사 ~ as to부정사 ▶ 'so 형용사 ~ as to부정사'는 '~할 만큼 ~하게; ~하게도 ~하다'라는 의미이다. ex.) The house is so designed as to be invisible from the road.(그 집은 도로에서 보이지 않게 설계되어 있다.) 따라서 ③ such를 so로 고쳐야 한다.

mutually ad. 서로, 상호간에　intelligible a. 이해할 수 있는

알래스카 에스키모인들과 캐나다 북부의 이뉴잇족들이 사용하는 언어는 매우 흡사해서 서로 의사소통이 가능하다.

11 **2022 성균관대** ▶▶▶ MSG p.11 　　　　④

동사의 태 ▶ grapple은 '(해결책을 찾아) 고심하다, 씨름하다'라는 의미로 쓰일 때 '자동사+전치사'인 grapple with로 사용된다. ④ 앞의 주어 I가 grapple with questions하는 행위의 주체이므로, 마지막 문장은 능동태가 되어야 한다. ④를 grappling으로 고친다. grappled 다음의 like my predecessors는 삽입된 '전치사+명사' 구임에 유의한다.

assume v. 생각하다　predecessor n. 전임자　implicit a. 암시된, 내포된

그 당시 나는 이 책을 선정하고 서론을 쓸 때는 전임자들처럼 그 프로젝트에 내재된 질문들과 씨름하게 될 것이라고 생각했다.

12 **2019 홍익대** ▶▶▶ MSG p.175 　　　　④

부정대명사 ▶ ① 가주어 it에 대한 진주어로 that절이 쓰였다. ② those who are에서 who are가 생략된 형태이다. ③ as if 다음에는 일반적으로 가정법이 쓰이지만, 직설법이 오기도 한다. ④ 문맥상 '혹 어느 것이라도'보다는 '모든 것을 다'가 적절하므로, everything(모든 것)으로 고쳐야 한다.

employ v. 고용하다　attitude n. 태도

기업들이 마치 모든 것을 다 알고 있는 것처럼 행동하는 다년간의 경력을 가진 사람들보다 경력은 전무하지만 성실한 태도를 갖고 있는 사람들을 채용하려고 하는 것은 전혀 놀라운 일이 아니다.

13 **2022 홍익대** ▶▶▶ MSG p.105 　　　　④

현재분사와 과거분사의 구분 ▶ its informational apparatus는 design하는 행위의 주체가 아닌 대상이므로 수동관계를 나타내는 과거분사로 수식해야 한다. ④를 designed로 고친다.

apparatus n. 장치, 기구, 기관　chancery n. 대법관 기록소　surveillance n. 감시　archives n. 공문서 보관소　and the like 그 밖의 같은 것, ~따위

독자는 이 책에서 탐구된 가장 영향력 있는 사태 진전들 중의 하나가 "정보국가"의 부상(浮上)과 주민들에 대한 정치적 통제를 확고히 하는 데 도움을 주도록 고안된 정보장치 — 대법관 기록소, 비서, 감시 기관, 문서 보관소 등 — 의 부상이라는 것을 알아차릴 수 있을 것이다.

14 **2020 홍익대** ▶▶▶ MSG p.137 　　　　①

전치사 + 관계대명사 ▶ 관계대명사 뒤에는 불완전한 절이 오고 '전치사+관계대명사' 뒤에는 완전한 절이 온다. ①의 뒤에 완전한 절인 one lives가 왔으므로 ①은 '전치사+관계대명사'가 되어야 하는데, 선행사인 web은 살아가는 장소에 해당하므로 관계대명사 앞에 올 전치사로는 in이 적절하다. ①을 in which로 고친다.

flesh n. 살; 육체 web n. 직물; 거미집 tactility n. 만져서 알 수 있음; 촉감 reducible a. (단순하게) 축소[환원]시킬 수 있는 unilateral a. 일방적인, 단독의

육체는 사람이 소유하고 있는 것이 아니라 사람이 그 안에서 살고 있는 그물망이다. 육체는 단지 내가 다른 사람이나 나 자신을 건드릴 때 건드려지는 것이 아니라 건드릴 수 있는 상태, 즉 그 어떤 특정한 건드림도 뛰어넘는 그리고 주체가 수행하는 일방적인 행동으로 환원될 수 없는 촉지성이기도 하다.

15 2020 홍익대 ▶▶▶ MSG p.105   ④

현재분사와 과거분사 구분 ▶ any canonical genres는 dedicate하는 행위의 주체가 아닌 대상이므로 이 둘은 수동관계에 있다. 따라서 수동을 나타내는 과거분사로 수식해야 한다. ④를 dedicated로 고친다.

interaction n. 상호작용 categorization n. 범주화 institutional a. 제도의 setting n. 환경; 장소와 때 canonical a. 교회법에 의거한; 권위 있는, 규범적인 dedicate v. (시간·생애 등을) 바치다; 전념하다 spectacular a. 볼만한, 장관의; 화려한 enunciation n. 발음 (방법); 공표, 선언, 언명 ethnicity n. 민족의식

상호작용 자체가 어떻게 사회적 범주화에 대한 상징적 탐구를 위한 장소와 과정을 제공하는지에 대한 명확한 견해를 갖고서, 이제 우리는 새로운 민족의식을 극적으로 선언하는 것에 전념하는 규범적인 장르가 전혀 없을지도 모르는 공식적인 제도적 환경을 살펴보려 노력할 수 있다.

16 2021 아주대 ▶▶▶ MSG p.31   ④

동사 call의 용법 ▶ 동사 call이 '~을 …라고 부르다(=name); ~을 …라고 생각하다'는 뜻으로 쓰일 때에는, 전치사 as 없이 '목적어+보어'의 5형식 구문을 취한다. 따라서 ④에서 전치사 as를 삭제해야 한다.

volunteer v. (어떤 일을 하겠다고) 자원[자진]하다, 자원 봉사를 하다 ox n. 황소 mule n. 노새 falcon n. 매 parrot n. 앵무새 bribe v. 뇌물을 주다, 매수하다

개는 자원해서 의무를 다하는 유일한 동물이다. 다른 동물들, 즉 말, 소, 노새, 매, 곰, 또는 앵무새가 우리를 도우러 오기를 바란다면 우리는 그들을 강요하거나 매수해야 한다. 우리는 심지어 말을 우리의 노예라고 부를지도 모른다. 그들이 인간을 위해 무엇이든 하기로 동의하려면 먼저 그들의 정신을 실제로 깨뜨려야 한다.

17 2020 홍익대 ▶▶▶ MSG p.137   ④

전치사 + 관계대명사 ▶ ④의 앞에 전치사 against가 이미 있으므로, 뒤에 다시 전치사 in이 올 수 없다. 따라서 ④에서 전치사 in을 삭제하여야 한다.

expose v. 노출시키다 representation n. 표시, 표현; 설명 migration n. 이주 chronotope n. 크로노토프(문학에서 예술적으로 표현된 시간과 공간이 본질적으로 서로 연관되어 있는 특성) reference n. 문의; 참조; 관련 regardless of ~와 상관없이

일상의 대화를 통해, 우리앙가토 사람들은 현대의 크로노토프에 의해 조직된 이주민의 삶이 보여주는 것들에 정기적으로 노출된다. 시간이 지나면서, 노동자 계층의 화자들은 이주 여부와 상관없이 그들 자신의 삶을 측정하는 기준점으로 이주에 관한 이야기를 이용하는 법을 배운다.

18 2022 건국대 ▶▶▶ MSG p.171, p.219   ④

지시대명사의 수일치 ▶ ④가 가리키는 것은 단수명사 ecology이므로 ④를 that으로 고쳐야 한다.

anecdotal a. 입증되지 않은, 일화적인, 이야깃거리가 많은 looming a. 희미하게 나타나는 biodiversity n. 생물의 다양성 comprehensive a. 포괄적인, 종합적인; 이해력이 있는, 이해가 빠른 temperate a. (기후·계절 등이) 온화한; (지역 따위) 온대성의; (행동이) 차분한, 절제된 ecology n. 생태학 microcosm n. 소우주, (더 큰 것의) 축소판

생물 다양성의 위기가 다가오고 있다는 일화적 증거가 현재 과학에 의해 힘을 얻고 있다. 영국에서 지난 20년 내지 40년 동안 이루어진 식물, 나비, 조류에 대한 포괄적인 조사에서 생태학자들은 모든 토착종의 3분의 1에 있어서 상당한 개체 수의 감소를 발견했다. 그 문제가 단지 지역적인 것이라 해도 충분히 나쁜데, 상황은 그렇지가 못하다. 영국의 온대성 생태계는 세계의 다른 많은 지역의 생태계와 비슷하기 때문에 과학자들이 자세히 연구할 수 있었던 가장 좋은 (세계 생태계의) 축소판이다.

19 2022 아주대 ▶▶▶ MSG p.111   ④

분사구문 ▶ ④에서 주절의 주어가 we이므로 접속사 while 이하는 '~로 인해 부담을 지다, ~한 부담에 짓눌리다'는 의미가 되도록 수동태인 'be burdened from'이 사용되어야 한다. while we are still burdened from legacies이었던 절이 분사구문이 되면서 주어 we가 생략되었고 are는 being으로 바뀐 후 생략되었다. 접속사 while은 정확한 의미전달을 위해서 생략되지 않았다. 따라서 ④는 while still burdened from legacies로 바로잡아야 한다.

enhance v. (지위나 가치 등을) 높이다, 고양시키다, 강화하다 ally n. 동맹국 legacy n. 유산 confrontation n. (무력 등의) 대결, 대치; 직면, 조우 armistice n. 정전(停戰), 휴전 bilateral a. 쌍방의, 양쪽의 treaty n. 조약, 협정 transcend v. 초월하다, 능가하다

우리의 방위 공약은 여전히 아시아-태평양 안보 구조의 핵심에 있지만, 우리의 동맹국들과 우방들의 강화된 능력에 기초하여 새로운 상황과 파트너십을 반영하도록 발전할 것이다. 민주적 경향을 지원하고 경제 통합을 위한 틀을 형성하는 것을 돕는 것이 아시아-태평양 지역의 공동체 의식을 고양시키게 될 핵심적인 정책 목표이다. 그러나 우리는 냉전 시대의 유산, 특히 한반도에서의 군사적 대결이라는 유산의 부담에 여전히 짓눌린 채로는 미래로 온전히 나아갈 수 없다. 평화 조약을 가능하게 하기 위해 한국을 정전 상태로부터 안정적인 평화로 이끌고, 소련과 일본의 양국 관계를 발전시키는 것이 그러한 유산을 초월하기 위한 주요 조치가 될 것이다.

20 **2018 광운대** ▶▶▶ MSG p.235   ①

정비문 ▶ ①은 He was unkind, he was unkind even to me.에서 앞
절과 공통된 부분인 he was unkind를 생략한 형태이므로, even 앞에
쓰인 not은 삭제해야 한다. 즉 He was unkind는 긍정문인 것이다. ②
와 ③에 쓰인 so와 neither는 각각 긍정문과 부정문 뒤에서 '~도 (또한)
그러하다'는 의미를 만든다. ④ 긍정문 뒤에는 부정의 부가의문문을 만
든다.

unkind a. 불친절한, 인정[동정심]이 없는

① 그는 불친절했습니다. 심지어 나에게도 불친절했습니다.
② 그는 불친절했고, 제인(Jane)도 그랬어요.
③ 그는 친절하지 않았고, 슈(Sue)도 그랬어요.
④ 그는 불친절했습니다. 그렇지 않습니까?
⑤ 그는 친절하지 않았습니다. 심지어 그녀에게도 친절하지 않았습니다.

| 01 ③ | 02 ④ | 03 ① | 04 ③ | 05 ⑤ | 06 ① | 07 ④ | 08 ⑤ | 09 ③ | 10 ② |
| 11 ③ | 12 ③ | 13 ② | 14 ① | 15 ② | 16 ⑤ | 17 ⑤ | 18 ③ | 19 ⑤ | 20 ⑤ |

01　**2019 가천대**　▶▶▶ MSG p.73　③

as if 가정법 과거완료 ▶ 'It was as if + 가정법 과거완료' 구문은 '마치 ~이었던 것 같았다'는 의미이다.

elude v. 피하다　foreboding a. 예감하는, 전조의, 불길한　dread n. 공포, 불안　guarded a. 보호[감시]받고 있는, 신중한　reserve n. 과묵함, 말이 없음

그녀가 지켜보면서 인내심을 갖고 연구했음에도 불구하고 그의 기분이 그러한 이유를 그녀로서는 포착하기 힘들었고 그것이 그녀를 불길한 두려움으로 가득 차게 한 것은 알려진 사실이었다. 그의 신중한 과묵함이 그녀에게는 부당하고, 사려 깊지 못하며, 놀랍게 여겨졌다. 마치 그가 그녀의 영역 너머로 벗어나, 그녀가 닿을 수 없는 낯설고 담장으로 둘러싸인 어떤 곳으로 들어가 버린 것 같았다.

02　**2021 가톨릭대**　▶▶▶ MSG p.105　④

과거분사 ▶ 문장의 주어는 Gameheaven이고 본동사가 has been praised이므로 빈칸에는 접속사 없이 또 다른 동사가 올 수 없고 business model을 수식하는 표현이 와야 하는데, tailor는 '(용도·목적에) 맞추다'는 의미의 타동사로, 'A를 B에 맞추다'는 tailor A to B의 형태로 쓴다. 주어진 문장은 문맥상 세계적인 성장에 '맞춰진' 비즈니스 모델이 되어야 적절하다. 따라서 빈칸에는 과거분사를 사용한 ④ tailored to가 정답이 된다.

praise v. 칭찬하다, 찬사를 보내다　pay-based a. 유료의

'게임천국'은 모바일 게임의 세계적인 성장에 맞춘 비즈니스 모델로 찬사를 받아왔으며 대부분의 매출을 게임 매출과 부분적인 유료 게임 서비스를 통해 거둔다.

03　**2021 서울여대**　▶▶▶ MSG p.137　①

전치사 + 관계대명사 ▶ 빈칸 뒤에 명사가 주어져 있으므로 소유격 관계대명사 whose가 필요하다. 그리고 '~로부터 제외[배제]되다'는 be excluded from으로 나타내므로 전치사 from이 있어야 한다.

public goods 공공재　commodity n. 일용품, 필수품, 물자; (pl.) 상품　exclude v. 제외하다, 배제하다

공공재는 그 누구도 그것의 즐거움으로부터 배제될 수 없는 상품이다.

04　**2020 아주대**　▶▶▶ MSG p.163　③

형용사 such ▶ such가 형용사로 사용될 때, 수식하는 명사가 단수인 경우에 such는 a, an의 앞에 놓인다. such a great number of가 한 덩어리를 이루고, offer A to B의 전치사 to가 그 앞에 나온 ③이 올바른 형태이다.

offer A to B A에게 B를 제공하다　portion n. 몫, 지분　enterprise n. 사업, 기업경영

크라우드 펀딩을 통해 그렇게도 많은 투자자들에게 벤처의 일정 지분들을 제공하는 것은 거의 당연하다 할 정도의 일반적인 사업방식이다.

05　**2022 아주대**　▶▶▶ MSG p.224　⑤

도치 ▶ that절의 주어 the admiration의 동사가 'might+have+p.p.'인 것으로 보아 과거 사실에 반대되는 가정을 나타내는 가정법 과거완료 구문임을 알 수 있다. 따라서 if절은 'If+주어+had+ p.p.'가 되어야 하는데, 이때 If를 생략하면 주어와 조동사는 도치된다.

bond n. 유대　palatable a. 맛있는, 마음에 드는　retrospect n. 회상, 회고　admiration n. 감탄, 흠모　mutual a. 상호간의, 쌍방의

그 유대감을 어느 정도 내 마음에 들게 만들어 준 것은 당신에 대한 나의 개인적인 높은 존경심이었다. 돌이켜보면, 당신이 나에 대해, 나의 정치적 신념과 활동에 대해 조금 더 알았더라면 존경심이 상호적이지는 못했을지도 모를 것 같다.

06　**2021 세종대**　▶▶▶ MSG p.46　①

문의 구성 ▶ that절 안의 주어 your membership과 호응하는 정동사가 제시돼 있지 않은 ②와 ④를 정답에서 먼저 제외할 수 있다. ③의 경우 '~ 때문에'라는 의미의 due to 뒤에 전치사구가 목적어로 제시된 형태이므로 옳지 않다. 따라서 ①이 정답이 되며, 'be due to 부정사'는 '~할 예정이다'라는 뜻이다.

membership n. 회원 자격[지위]　expire v. 만기가 되다, 종료[만료]되다

당신의 회원 자격이 두 달 후에 만기될 예정이라는 것을 알고 계셨나요?

07 **2021 덕성여대** ▶▶▶ MSG p.35 ④

가목적어 구문 ▶ 5형식 구문에서 to부정사구가 목적보어 뒤로 후치된 경우에는 반드시 가목적어 it을 써야 하므로, 가목적어 it이 쓰인 ④가 정답이다. 주어진 문장은 'make+가목적어(it)+목적보어(difficult)+진목적어(to obtain)'의 구조를 가진 구문이며, for young adults는 to obtain의 의미상 주어이다.

decent a. (사회 기준에) 괜찮은, 남부럽지 않은; (수입 등이) 상당한

경쟁은 젊은이들이 대학 학위 없이 괜찮은 직업을 얻는 것을 어렵게 만든다.

08 **2016 아주대** ▶▶▶ MSG p.44, p.143 ⑤

문의 구성 ▶ 빈칸은 접속사 than 뒤에 위치해 있으므로, 주어 없이 동사만 제시돼 있는 ①, ②, ③은 정답이 될 수 없다. 따라서 정답은 ⑤가 되며, ④의 경우, several years ago와 같이 명확한 과거를 나타내는 표현은 현재완료시제와 함께 쓸 수 없으며 의미적으로도 부정의 none은 부적절하다.

cybernetic a. 인공두뇌학의 revolution n. 혁명 foresee v. 예견하다, 앞일을 내다보다

인공두뇌학의 혁명은 많은 사람들이 몇 년 전에 예상할 수 있었던 것보다 훨씬 빠르게 전개되었다.

09 **2021 아주대** ▶▶▶ MSG p.36, p.222 ③

장소표시 부사어가 문두에 오는 경우의 도치 ▶ 빈칸 앞 전체가 장소 부사어인데, 장소 부사어가 문두에 오면 일종의 강조용법으로 그다음에 주어와 자동사(lies)는 도치된다. 따라서 ③이 빈칸에 적절하다.

extensive a. 아주 넓은, 방대한 cave n. 동굴

플로리다 근처와 쿠바 북쪽의 일단의 섬들에는 블루 홀이라고 알려진 일련의 독특한 동굴들이 방대하게 펼쳐져 있다.

10 **2005 세종대** ▶▶▶ MSG p.130 ②

결과의 부사절 ▶ '~해서 …하다'라는 '결과'의 부사절은 다양한 표현법이 있는데, 가장 대표적인 것을 정리하면 so+형용사[부사]+that, such+(a[an])+형용사+명사+that, so+형용사+a[an]+명사+that(단, 명사가 불가산이거나 복수면 근본적으로 so ~ that 형태는 쓸 수 없다.) 등이 있다. 이 문장은 skills라는 복수명사가 있으므로 ②의 so를 such로 고쳐야 한다.

surgical a. 수술의 speciality n. 전문[전공] (분야)

우리 몸의 다양한 부분들이 워낙 서로 다른 외과적인 수술 기술을 필요로 했기 때문에 많은 외과적인 신기술들이 발달해왔다.

11 **2014 서울여대** ▶▶▶ MSG p.136 ③

관계대명사 who와 whose의 구분 ▶ exploit은 동사와 명사로 모두 쓰일 수 있는데, 동사인 경우 '부당하게 사용하다'라는 뜻의 타동사로 이때는 목적어를 필요로 한다. 주어진 문장에서는 동사의 목적어가 주어져 있지 않으며, 연결사 없이 동사형인 may have been이 바로 이어지고 있으므로 적절하지 않다. 따라서 '위업, 공훈'이라는 의미의 명사로 보아야 하며, 이 경우 who를 소유격 관계대명사 whose고 고쳐, ruler를 선행사로 받아 exploits 이하의 문장이 관계절을 이룰 수 있도록 하는 것이 적절하다. 그러므로 ③을 whose exploits로 고친다. ① 주어진 문장은 원래 A 5,250-year-old tableau of a victorious ruler whose exploits may have been critical to the founding of Egyptian civilization is carved in the limestone of a desert cliff in Egypt.이었는데, 주어인 A 5,250-year-old tableau of a victorious ruler whose exploits may have been critical to the founding of Egyptian civilization이 너무 길어서 보어인 carved를 문두로 보내고 주어와 동사를 도치시킨 형태이며, in the limestone of a desert cliff in Egypt는 부사구로 보어를 수식해 주므로 보어에 딸려 함께 문두로 나갔다. ② '수사+단위명사+형용사'의 표현에서 단위명사는 단수로 쓴다. 따라서 '5,250(수사)+year(단수 단위명사)+old(형용사)'가 형용사구가 되어 명사인 tableau를 올바르게 수식해 주고 있다. ④ may+have+p.p는 '~이었을지도 모른다'는 뜻으로 과거사실에 대한 가능성 있는 추측을 나타내므로 맞게 쓰였다.

carve v. 조각하다, 새기다 limestone n. 석회석[암] desert n. 사막 tableau n. 인상적인 장면 exploit n. 위업, 공적, 공훈 found v. 설립하다, 세우다 civilization n. 문명

이집트 문명을 세우는데 결정적이었을지도 모르는 위업을 가진 전승을 거둔 통치자의 5천2백50년 된 인상적인 장면이 이집트의 한 사막절벽에 있는 석회암에 조각되어 있다.

12 **2020 홍익대** ▶▶▶ MSG p.227 ③

전치사 ▶ '~와 상관없이'라는 의미의 표현에서 independently 뒤에는 관용적으로 전치사 of가 온다. ③을 of로 고친다. ④ 목적격 관계대명사로 쓰였다.

thesis n. 주제 discourse n. 담론; 강연 independently of ~와 관계없이 mechanism n. (목적을 달성하기 위한) 방법, 메커니즘

중심 주제는 언어가 그러한 기능들을 수행하기 위해 사용하는 메커니즘에 관한 특정 이론과 관계없이 담론의 구조와 기능에 대해 이론을 세우는 것이 가능하고 또 유익하다는 것이다.

13 **2021 가천대** ▶▶▶ MSG p.130 ②

문의 구성 ▶ ②는 'so ~ that …' 구문의 that절 속의 주어 역할을 해야 한다. 문장 속에서 주어, 목적어, 보어 등으로 쓰일 수 있는 to부정사가 이러한 역할을 할 수 있으므로, ②를 to have로 고치는 것이 적절하다. ④ 불완전자동사로 쓰인 appeared의 보어로 쓰였다.

enormous a. 거대한, 막대한 moth n. 나방 zest n. 풍미, 맛; 열정, 열의 meagre a. 빈약한; 불충분한 pathetic a. 애처로운

기쁨의 가능성이 그날 아침에는 너무도 크고 너무도 다양해서 인생에서 단지 나방의 몫 만큼만을, 그것도 낮 나방의 몫 만큼만을 산다는 것은 가혹한 운명처럼 보였고, 자신의 보잘 것 없는 기회를 한껏 누리려는 그의 열정은 측은해 보였다.

14 2017 국민대 ▶▶▶ MSG p.145 ①

관계대명사와 관계부사의 구분 ▶ 관계대명사 which의 뒤에는 불완전한 절이 오는데, ①의 뒤에는 완전한 절이 왔으므로 적절치 않다. 따라서 ①을 완전한 절과 함께 쓰이는 관계부사 where로 고쳐야 한다.

pending a. 미결의 active a. 유효한 for the time being 당분간 get back to (회답을 하기 위해) ~에게 나중에 다시 연락하다 reminder n. (약속을) 상기시켜주는 편지[메모]

미결 폴더는 당장 당신이 대응할 필요는 없지만, 당분간 '유효한' 상태로 둘 필요가 있는 메시지를 넣어두는 곳이다. 예를 들어, 누군가가 당신에게 나중에 다시 연락하겠다고 약속을 했고 후속조치를 취할 수 있도록 상기시켜줄 메모가 필요한 경우가 해당된다.

15 2021 건국대 ▶▶▶ MSG p.85 ②

be free to + 동사원형 ▶ 'be free to+동사원형'은 '자유롭게 ~하다', '마음껏 ~하다'의 의미이다. ②를 동사원형 construct로 고친다.

be to do with ~와 관련되다, ~에 관한 것이다 construct v. (기계·이론 등을) 꾸미다, 구성하다 identity n. 동일성; 정체성 constrain v. 강제하다, 강요하다; 속박하다 psyche n. 영혼, 정신 institutionalize v. 제도화하다, 관행화하다

여기서 문제는 사람들이 그들의 정체성을 그들이 원하는 어떤 방법으로든 자유롭게 확립할 수 있는지, 아니면 정체성 구축이 무의식적인 정신에서부터 제도화된 권력 구조에 이르는 다양한 종류의 힘에 의해 제약을 받는지에 관한 것이다.

16 2022 성균관대 ▶▶▶ MSG p.55 ⑤

수동태와 능동태의 구별 ▶ turn A into B는 'A를 B로 바꾸다'의 의미인데, as절에서 A인 the food we eat이 주어가 되어 앞으로 나갔으므로 목적어가 없다. 우리가 먹는 음식이 생명을 주고 신경에 영양을 공급하는 피로 바뀌게 되는 대상이 되므로 ⑤를 수동태 is turned into로 고쳐야 한다.

purse n. 지갑 life-giving a. 생명[생기]을 주는 nerve-nourishing a. 신경에 영양분을 공급하는

공부의 목적은 인간이 동전을 지갑에 지니고 있는 것처럼 지식을 소유하는 것이 아니라, 지식을 우리 자신의 일부분으로 만드는 것이다. 즉, 우리가 먹는 음식이 생명을 주고 신경에 영양분을 공급하는 피로 바뀌듯이, 지식을 사고로 바꾸는 것이다.

17 2020 이화여대 ▶▶▶ MSG p.113 ⑤

수동 분사구문 ▶ ⑤의 앞에 쓰인 대명사 each는 rocket pod를 가리키고 있는데, 이것은 '~에 설비[장비]하다'라는 의미의 타동사 equip의 주체가 아닌 '대상'이므로 수동 관계이다. 따라서 each 이하는 수동의 분사구문이 되어야 하므로, ⑤에서 equipping을 equipped로 고쳐야 한다. ② 수사와 명사가 하이픈으로 연결되어 일종의 형용사와 같은 역할을 할 때, 하이픈 뒤의 명사는 단수로 쓴다. ④ 주어에 부분 표시어가 포함돼 있는 경우, 동사는 부분 표시어 뒤에 온 명사에 수를 일치시킨다. 동사로 were를 쓴 것은 aircraft가 복수로 쓰인 것이기 때문이다. aircraft는 단수와 복수의 형태가 같다.

accidental a. 우연한, 우발적인, 뜻밖의 detonation n. 폭발 aircraft carrier 항공모함 injure v. 상처를 입히다, 다치게 하다 costly a. 희생이 큰; 비용이 많이 드는 deviation n. 벗어남, 탈선, 일탈 in the interest of ~를 도모하기 위하여 pod n. 포드(연료·장비·무기 등을 싣는 비행기 동체 아래의 유선형 공간) equip v. (~에 필요물을) 갖추다

1967년, 통킹(Tonkin) 만(灣)에 있던 미(美) 항공모함 포레스탈(Forrestal)호에서 발생한 우발적인 무기 폭발로 인해, 승무원 134명이 사망하고 161명이 부상을 입었으며, 7개월 동안 많은 비용을 들여 수리를 해야 했다. 그 참사는 융통성을 도모하기 위해 규정에서 벗어난 데 따른 것이었다. 그 항공모함의 많은 항공기에는 주니(Zuni) 로켓 포드가 달려 있었는데, 각각의 로켓 포드에는 4개의 비유도 로켓이 장착돼 있었다.

18 2012 서강대 ▶▶▶ MSG p.40, p.140 ③

적절한 전치사의 사용 ▶ 두 번째 문장에서 the effect와 your words 사이에 목적격 관계대명사가 생략되어 있는데, have the effect on~에서 the effect가 선행사로 쓰였기 때문에 ③을 likely to have on으로 고쳐야 옳은 문장이 된다. ① in large measure는 '상당히, 대체로'라는 의미이다. ②의 worth는 목적어를 취하는 전치사적 형용사로 쓰이며, ④ go는 전치사 through와 함께 쓰여 '~을 거치다, 경험하다'라는 뜻으로, 뒤에 목적어 several drafts를 받을 수 있다.

jotting n. 대강 적어두기 margin n. 가장자리, 여백 draft n. 밑그림, 초고

글 쓰는 법을 배우는 것은 대체로 읽는 법을 배우는 것이다. 다른 사람이 읽을 가치가 있다고 생각할 어떤 글을 쓰기 위해서는 여러분의 글이 독자에게 끼칠 영향을 생각하려고 하면서 여러분 자신이 각각의 초안을 주의 깊게 읽어야 한다. 글은 여러분이 읽고 있는 책의 가장자리에 간단히 몇 글자를 적어두는 것 혹은 잡지에 간단히 메모하는 것부터 시작될 수 있으며, 그것은 몇 번의 초안 과정을 거치고 나서 완성될 것이다.

19 2017 이화여대 ▶▶▶ MSG p.137 ⑤

전치사+관계대명사 ▶ 관계대명사 뒤에는 불완전한 문장이 와야 하는데, ⑤의 경우에는 which 뒤에 완전한 문장이 주어져 있으므로 옳지 않은 표현이다. 관계대명사 앞에 적절한 전치사를 넣어주어야 하겠는데, 문맥상 the process는 우리가 이러한 견해에 도달하도록 한 방법에 해당하므로, 수단이나 매체를 의미하는 전치사 through를 which 앞에

써야 한다. 따라서 ⑤를 by the processes through which we arrived at this view로 고친다. ② How we know는 간접의문절로 주어의 역할을 하고 있다. ③ with는 앞쪽의 faced에 연결된다. ④ 종속접속사 If 다음에 what과 how로 시작하는 두 개의 관계절이 각각 주어와 전치사의 목적어로 쓰였다.

exploration n. 탐험; (문제 등의) 탐구 common sense 상식 vexing a. 까다로운, 성가신 so to speak 말하자면 self-evident a. 자명한 inevitably ad. 필연적으로, 불가피하게

우리가 알고 있다고 믿고 있는 것을 우리는 어떻게 해서 아는 것일까? 우리가 알고 있는 것은 일반적으로 실재 세계, 즉 사물이 실제로 존재하는 방식에 대한 우리의 탐구와 이해의 결과로 간주된다. 결국, 상식적으로 보면 이러한 객관적인 실재는 발견될 수 있다. 우리가 어떻게 아는가는 훨씬 더 까다로운 문제이다. 그것을 해결하기 위해서는, 정신은, 말하자면, 자신 밖으로 나가서 자신이 활동하고 있는 것을 관찰해야 할 필요가 있다. 왜냐하면, 이 시점에서 우리는 외부 세계에서 우리와 별개로 명백히 존재하고 있는 사실들과 더 이상 직면하지 않고, 그 본성이 전혀 자명하지 않은 정신적 과정과 마주하게 되기 때문이다. 우리가 알고 있는 것이 우리가 그것을 알게 된 방법에 좌우된다면, 그러면 우리 눈에 보이는 실재의 모습은 우리 자신 밖에서 사실인 것의 진정한 모습이 더 이상 아니고, 필연적으로, 눈에 보이는 이 모습에 도달하게 된 과정에 의해서도 결정되는 것이다.

20　2018 광운대　▶▶▶ MSG p.214　　⑤

정비문 ▶ 'there be동사' 문장인 There is a mistake.(실수가 있다.)에서 be동사 앞에 조동사가 온 There can be a mistake.(실수가 있을 수 있다.)도 가능하다. 마찬가지로 2형식동사 seem이나 keep도 조동사 대신 쓰일 수 있다. There seems to be a mistake.(실수가 있는 것 같다.)와 There keeps being a mistake.(실수가 계속 있다.) 여기서 seem은 to부정사를, keep은 현재분사를 각각 보어로 취한다. 그리고 be동사 다음의 명사(주어)와 수 일치하는 것은 seem동사와 keep동사이다. 따라서 ④에서는 복수명사 power black-outs에 대해 keep으로 수 일치한다. 그러나 regret은 이러한 2형식동사에 해당되지 않고 사람을 주어로 해야 하는 동사이므로, ⑤는 사람을 주어로 하여, I regret there being power black-outs.로 고쳐야 하고 여기서 being은 동명사이다.

regret v. 후회하다 interrupt v. 가로막다, 방해하다 power black-out (전기의) 정전(停電); 소등

① 폴(Paul)은 나를 방해한 것을 후회하고 있다.
② 스티브(Steve)는 계속 나를 방해하고 있다.
③ 나는 톰(Tom)에게 방해받은 것을 유감스럽게 생각한다.
④ 정전이 계속 되고 있다.
⑤ 나는 정전이 있는 것을 유감스럽게 생각한다.

01 ③	**02** ②	**03** ③	**04** ②	**05** ①	**06** ④	**07** ③	**08** ①	**09** ④	**10** ①
11 ③	**12** ①	**13** ②	**14** ④	**15** ③	**16** ②	**17** ④	**18** ④	**19** ②	**20** ③

---

01 2020 한국산업기술대 ▶▶▶ MSG p.58   ③

동사 grant의 수동태 ▶ '~을 승인하다', '~을 주다'는 의미의 동사 grant
는 'grant (sb) sth' 또는 'grant sth (to sb/sth)' 형태를 취한다. 주어진
문장에서 주어는 복수인 only those이고, 의미상 수동태가 되어야 함
을 고려한다.

senior researcher 선임 연구원 qualified a. 자격 있는

많은 이들이 선임 연구원 자리에 지원했지만, 오직 자격을 갖춘 사람들에게
만 인터뷰가 승인되었다.

---

02 2004 세종대 ▶▶▶ MSG p.223   ②

as와 than 다음의 도치 ▶ 양태, 비교의 접속사 as와 than 뒤에서, 주어
가 명사(구)이고, 동사가 조동사나 be동사인 경우 도치가 가능하다. 이
때 do는 hold를 대신하는 조동사로 썼다.

overall a. 전부의, 전체에 걸친

과학자들은 지난 10년 동안의 전반적인 온난화 경향이 그 어느 해의 1년간
의 기온보다 훨씬 더 많은 의미가 있다고 강조한다.

---

03 2021 아주대 ▶▶▶ MSG p.48   ③

과거완료 시제 ▶ 본동사의 시제는 started로서 과거이지만, '해적들을
사략선의 선원들로 탈바꿈시킨 것'은 그보다 앞선 시점의 경험을 나타
내므로 대과거가 쓰여야 한다. 따라서 빈칸에는 ③이 적절하다. they
had been 뒤에는 necessary가 생략되었다.

monarch n. 군주 pirate n. 해적 privateer n. 사략선(私掠船)(전시에 적의
상선을 나포할 수 있는 허가를 받은 민간 무장선); 사략선 승무원

잉글랜드의 군주들은 과거에 그랬던 것처럼 해적들을 사략선의 선원들로 탈
바꿈시키는 일이 더 이상 필요 없다고 믿기 시작했고 그 대신 해군만이 잉글
랜드의 해상 전쟁을 책임져야 한다고 느끼기 시작했다.

---

04 2020 세종대 ▶▶▶ MSG p.121, p.221   ②

'not only ~ (but) also …' 구문 + 도치 ▶ not only ~ (but) also … 구
문에서 not only가 문두에 오면 도치가 일어나 'not only+do+주어+동

사원형'의 어순이 된다. they 앞에 but이 생략되었는데, but은 접속사
여서 생략하지 않는 것이 원칙이지만 여기서처럼 구어영어에서는 종종
생략되기도 한다.

essential a. 근본적인, 가장 중요한

사람들은 성공하기 위해 열정이 필요할 뿐만 아니라 계속해서 시도하는 것
도 필요하다. 포기하지 않을 수 있는 능력이 필수적인 것이다.

---

05 2021 세종대 ▶▶▶ MSG p.143   ①

talk의 용법 ▶ talk는 '~에 관해 이야기하다'의 의미일 때 자동사로 쓰
여서 뒤에 전치사 of나 about을 동반한다. 따라서 ②와 ④를 정답에서
먼저 제외할 수 있다. ③의 경우, however는 부사이므로 전치사 about
의 목적어 자리에 올 수 없다. 따라서 ①이 정답이 되며, whatever가
이끄는 복합관계대명사절이 명사절로서 전치사 of의 목적어가 되는 구
조이다.

abandon v. 단념하다, 그만두다 hypnosis n. 최면, 최면상태 couch n. 소파,
침상

프로이드는 마침내 최면을 단념하고, 그저 환자들로 하여금 자신의 그늘진
사무실의 소파에 누워 그들의 마음속에 떠오른 것은 무엇이든 이야기하도록
권했다.

---

06 2018 한국외대 ▶▶▶ MSG p.136, p.140   ④

문의 구성 ▶ 빈칸 앞까지 이미 완전한 절이 완성돼 있으므로, 빈칸 이
하는 the things를 수식하는 역할을 해야 한다. 따라서 the things를
선행사로 하는 관계대명사절을 만드는 ④가 정답으로 적절한데, 이때
you think는 삽입절이며, things 뒤에는 do의 목적어가 되는 목적격
관계대명사가 생략된 것이다. ②는 you think를 삭제해야 하며, ①과
③은 완전한 절 뒤에 다시 동사가 이어지게 되므로 정답으로 적절하지
않다.

genuinely ad. 진정으로; 순수하게

진정으로 창조적인 삶을 살기 위해서는, 당신이 할 수 없다고 생각하는 것들
을 해야 한다.

07　2019 가천대　▶▶▶ MSG p.133　　③

양보의 접속사 as ▶ 접속사 as가 양보의 의미를 지닐 때 형용사, 부사, 관사 없는 명사 등이 문두로 나오게 된다. 형용사 hard가 문두에 나와 있으므로 빈칸에는 as가 이끄는 절인 ③이 적절하다.

dialectical a. 변증법적인 thesis n. 명제 antithesis n. 안티테제, 반명제 naive a. 때 묻지 않은 manipulative a. 교묘히 다루는, 속임수의 figure v. 생각하다, 판단하다

나는 모두가 인생을 살아가면서 이와 같은 우정을 적어도 하나는 갖고 있으리라 생각한다. 우리는 그녀가 명제이고 내가 반명제인 변증법적인 관계였다. 그녀는 솔직하고, 신뢰할 수 있고, 친절하고, 순진했다. 나는 속임수를 부리고, 이기적이었으며, 교활했다. 그녀는 나의 최고의 친구였다. 외모로는 알아내기 어려웠겠지만, 그녀는 착한 여자였고, 나는 나쁜 여자였다.

08　2020 이화여대　▶▶▶ MSG p.70　　①

가정법 ▶ 주절의 동사가 '조동사의 과거+have+p.p'인 것으로 미루어 가정법 과거완료의 문장임을 알 수 있다. 가정법 과거완료에서 if절의 형태는 'if+주어+had+p.p'이므로, 첫 번째 빈칸에는 I had known과 I had known beforehand가 가능하다. 한편, had known의 목적절의 동사 자리인 두 번째 빈칸에는 가정법이 아닌 직설법 시제가 쓰여야 한다. 그런데 가정법 과거완료는 과거사실의 반대를 가정하는 것이므로 기준시제는 과거이며, 따라서 두 번째 빈칸에는 'will+동사원형'이 아닌 'would+동사원형'이 쓰여야 한다. 그러므로 ①이 정답이 된다. In hindsight가 쿠알라룸푸르 지사 설립이 이미 지나간 과거지사임을 말해준다.

in hindsight 지나고 나서 보니까 establish v. 설립하다, 창립하다; 제정하다 branch n. 지부, 지점, 지사

지나고 보니, 내가 만약 우리 회사가 쿠알라룸푸르에 지사를 설립할 거라는 것을 알았더라면, 말레이어 수업을 시작했을 텐데.

09　2021 아주대　▶▶▶ MSG p.140　　④

목적격 관계대명사의 생략 ▶ ④가 선행사 the people을 수식하는 관계절로 빈칸에 적절하다. 이때 선행사 the people과 관계사절의 주어인 the communicators 사이에는 타동사 address의 목적어가 되는 목적격 관계대명사 whom이 생략되어 있다.

mass communication 대중[대량] 전달, 매스컴 fracture v. 균열시키다 identify v. 확인하다 address v. ~에게 말을 걸다 post hoc 이 다음에 reference n. 언급; 참조

대중 전달은 일종의 균열된 상호작용이기 때문에, 우리는 전달자가 말을 걸고자 했던 사람들(수신자들)에게 사후에 조회해 봄으로써만 실제 수신자들이 누구인지 확인할 수 있다.

10　2011 명지대　▶▶▶ MSG p.175　　①

every+기수+복수명사 = every+서수+단수명사 ▶ '~마다'라는 의미는 'every+기수+복수명사 = every+서수+단수명사' 형태로 쓴다. four가 기수이므로 year는 복수명사가 되어야 한다. ① year를 years로 고친다. ②는 'consider+목적어+목적보어' 구문에서 목적어 the Olympic Games가 주어로 앞에 나가 수동태가 된 것이다. ④는 competition이 '경기, 시합'의 뜻일 때 가산명사로 쓰이므로 복수명사가 온 것이다.

take place (행사가) 열리다, 개최하다 competition n. (경연) 대회, 시합, 경기

4년마다 개최되는 올림픽 대회는 가장 경쟁적인 운동 경기로 여겨진다.

11　2010 성균관대　▶▶▶ MSG p.135　　③

문의 구성 ▶ 하나의 문장 내에서 새로운 절이 시작되고 있으므로, ③의 those를 접속사의 역할도 함께하는 관계대명사 whom으로 고쳐야 한다.

resident n. 거주자, 살고 있는 사람 as a result of ~의 결과로서

1992년 10월 이집트 지진은 600명의 카이로 주민의 목숨을 앗아갔고 수천 명을 치료받게 하였는데, 그들 중 많은 사람들이 부상 때문에 죽을 것으로 예상되었다.

12　2021 국민대　▶▶▶ MSG p.137　　①

전치사 + 관계대명사 ▶ at ordinary times는 삽입된 부사구이며, 불완전한 절과 함께 쓰이는 관계대명사 which 다음에 완전한 절이 와서 틀렸다. 따라서 완전한 절과 쓰이는 '전치사+관계대명사'의 형태로 ①을 고쳐야 하는데, 수여동사 give가 3형식으로 쓰일 경우 전치사 to와 함께 쓰이므로, ①을 to which로 고쳐야 한다.

sane a. 정신이 온전한 assent n. 동의, 찬성 supposition n. 가정 as good as ~와 마찬가지인

모든 사람들이 동등하다는 것은 평상시에 정신이 온전한 그 누구도 동의하지 않은 주장이다. 위험한 수술을 받아야 하는 사람은 모든 의사가 다 마찬가지라는 가정에 따라 행동하지 않는다.

13　2020 국민대　▶▶▶ MSG p.29　　②

3형식 동사 mention ▶ 동사 mention은 4형식으로 혼동하기 쉬운 3형식 동사이다. 따라서 ② mention 다음에는 두 개의 목적어 me와 that절이 올 수 없다. that절만을 목적어로 취하고 me 앞에는 전치사 to가 필요하다. 따라서 ②를 mentioned to me로 고친다. 참고로 동사 remind, inform, convince의 목적어는 항상 사람이고, 그 뒤에 'of +N'이나 'that절'이 올 수 있다. 사람 목적어 뒤에 명사가 오면 전치사 of가 필요하지만, that절은 전치사 없이 간접목적어 뒤에 바로 와서 4형식 구문이 될 수 있다.

gender n. 성별 memory n. 기억 article n. 논문; 기사

민호는 기억에 영향을 미치는 성별의 차이와 관련한 프레젠테이션에 참석했다고 내게 말했다. 그는 김 박사님이 발표를 했다고 내게 말했고, 그는 또한 김 박사님이 기억에 관한 여러 편의 논문을 썼다고 내게 상기시켜 줬으며 다음 발표를 내게 알려주었다.

14 2022 성균관대 ▶▶▶ MSG p.57   ④

수동태와 능동태의 구별 ▶ 부사절의 주어는 a senior Biden administration cyber official이고 executives가 목적어이다. 이 관리가 경영자들에게 경고를 하는 주체이므로 ④를 능동태 warned로 고쳐야 한다.

vulnerability n. 약점이 있음, 취약성 executive n. 경영[운영]진 take action ~에 대해 조치를 취하다 flaw n. 결점

바이든(Biden) 행정부의 한 사이버 담당 고위 관리가 월요일 미국의 주요 산업 경영진들에게 그녀가 공직 생활을 하며 보아온 "가장 심각한 결함 중 하나"를 해결하기 위해 조치를 취해야 한다고 경고했듯이, 전 세계의 수억 대의 기기가 새롭게 드러난 소프트웨어 취약성에 노출될 수 있을 것이다.

15 2019 가천대 ▶▶▶ MSG p.167   ③

대명사의 수일치 ▶ Although절의 단수 주어 this system을 다시 받는 대명사도 단수여야 하므로 ③을 its로 고쳐야 한다.

hail v. 환호하여 맞이하다 the blind 맹인 godsend n. 하늘의 선물

브라유(Braille) 문자들은 6개의 점자 시스템으로 구축되어 있다. 이 문자들은 야전의 병사들이 불빛 없이도 의사소통할 수 있는 무언의 방법을 찾으라고 요구했던 나폴레옹(Napoleon)을 위해 만들어진 의사소통 방법에서 나온 것이다. 비록 이 체계는 그것의 복잡성으로 인해 처음에는 거부되었지만, 전 세계의 맹인들은 그것을 하늘이 내려준 선물이라며 환호하고 있다.

16 2021 숭실대 ▶▶▶ MSG p.117   ②

분사형 전치사 ▶ 주절의 it이 giving의 의미상 주어가 될 수 없으므로, ②를 그대로 둘 수 없다. 따라서 ②를 '~을 가정하면', '~을 고려할 때(considering)'라는 의미를 가진 분사형 전치사 given으로 고쳐야 한다.

all-time a. 시대를 초월한, 사상 (최고[최저])의 margin call 마진 콜, 추가 증거금 청구(선물계약 기간 중 선물가격 변화에 따른 추가 증거금 납부 요구) steep a. 가파른, 급격한

어제는 아마도 추가 증거금 납부요구가 사상 최고로 많았던 날이었을 것이다. 그러나 시장 상황을 고려할 때 그것은 예상치 못한 것은 아니었다. 시장이 그렇게 급격하게 하락하고 많은 주식이 영향을 받게 되면, 추가 증거금 납부요구를 보게 될 것이다. 그것은 물리학의 중력 법칙과 거의 같은 것이다. 막대한 증권담보대출이 1929년 주식 시장 붕괴의 커다란 요인이라는 말이 있었다.

17 2015 가천대 ▶▶▶ MSG p.211   ④

주어와 동사의 수일치 ▶ what이 이끄는 절이 일반 동사의 주어일 때 동사는 단수로 하고, be동사의 주어일 때에는 보어에 따라 수를 결정한다. ④의 경우, 그 다음에 보어로 하나의 to부정사구가 왔으므로 단수 취급하여야 한다. ④를 is로 고쳐야 한다. ① 접속사 whether는 뒤에 위치한 or와 호응한다. ② Rightly understood는 Being rightly understood라는 분사구문에서 Being이 생략된 형태이다. ③ that은 What science can do for us를 선행사로 하는 목적격 관계대명사이다.

distrust v. 불신하다 overlook v. 간과하다 pragmatic a. 실용적인 point out 지적하다 probability n. 개연성; 확률 otherwise ad. 다른 상황에서는 blind a. 눈이 먼; 되는대로 하는 self-willed a. 자기 뜻대로 하는, 고집이 센

개인적 행동이든 사회적 행동이든, 행동지침으로서의 과학을 불신하는 사람들은 과학의 실용적인 특징을 간과하는 것처럼 보인다. 올바르게 이해된다면, 과학은 다양한 정도로 확실한 확률만을 우리에게 지적해줄 수 있다. 과학이 우리를 위해 해줄 수 있는 것이면서 과학이 아니면 우리가 너무나 눈멀거나 자기 의지에 갇혀 알아볼 수 없을지도 모르는 것은, 개인에게 옳은 것이 사회집단 구성원으로서의 그에게는 틀린 것일 수도 있다는 점을 우리가 이해하도록 도와주는 것이다.

18 2021 건국대 ▶▶▶ MSG p.144   ④

적절한 관계부사 ▶ ④ 관계부사 where 다음에 완전한 절이 와서 이상이 없는 문장처럼 보이지만, 관계부사 where의 선행사로 장소가 아니라 시간을 가리키는 1484년이 나왔으므로 ④는 when이 되어야 한다.

basis n. 기지, 근거지 irregular a. (길이) 울퉁불퉁한 strip n. 좁고 긴 땅 fortification n. 요새화; 방어 시설 edge n. 테두리, 가장자리 gorge n. 골짜기, 협곡

황금소로(Golden Lane)의 기초는 12세기 로마네스크 양식의 오래된 성벽과 스태그 해자(Stag Moat)로 알려진 자연 협곡 가장자리에 프라하 성 북쪽 외곽 요새를 이루는 나중에 세워진 성벽 사이에 있는 폭이 4~8미터로 다양한 울퉁불퉁하고 좁고 긴 땅이다. 프라하 성의 북쪽 요새 건설 작업은 블라디슬라프 야기엘론(Vladislav Jagiellon) 왕이 구도시를 떠나 성에 정착하기로 결정한 1484년 직후 건축가 베네딕트 리드(Benedikt Ried)에 의해 시작되었다.

19 2018 이화여대 ▶▶▶ MSG p.192   ②

문맥상 올바른 부사 ▶ ②는 뒤돌아 앉은 채로 역마차를 타고 있었다는 의미가 되어야 하므로, '뒤를 향해'라는 의미의 부사 backward를 써서 표현해야 한다. backwardly는 '마지못해'라는 의미이다. ②를 riding backward로 고친다. ① 주어인 The Englishman, the gambler and the blond man은 jam하는 행위의 주체가 아닌 대상이므로, 수동관계를 나타내는 과거분사를 썼다. ③ '자동사 lie의 과거형+전치사 below'의 형태이다. ④ cheeks와 unstirred 사이에 being이 생략된 분사구문이다. ⑤ save가 '~을 제외하고'라는 의미의 전치사로 쓰였다.

blond a. 금발의 jam v. 쑤셔 넣다, (꽉) 채워 넣다 stagecoach n. 역마차, 승합마차 drummer n. 고수(鼓手); 출장판매원 cattleman n. 목축업자, 목동 occupy v. (시간·장소를) 차지하다; 점령하다 sill n. 문지방, 문턱 steady v. 견고하게 하다; 흔들리지 않게 하다 nugget n. 금괴(金塊); 귀금속 덩어리; (pl.) 귀중한 것 back and forth 앞뒤로, 이리저리 chunk n. (장작 따위의) 큰 나무 토막; (치즈·빵·고기 따위의) 큰 덩어리 glance n. 흘긋 봄, 일견(一見)

영국인, 도박꾼, 그리고 금발의 남자가 앞자리에 바싹 붙어 나란히 앉아서, 역마차를 거꾸로 타고 가고 있었다. 떠돌이 장사꾼과 목장주인이 불편한 중간 자리를 차지했고, 두 명의 여성이 뒷자리에 함께 앉았다. 목장주인은 앙리에트(Henriette)와 마주 보고 있었는데, 무릎이 그녀와 거의 닿을 정도였다. 그는 한쪽 팔을 창턱 위로 드리운 채 몸을 지탱하고 있었다. 그의 넓은 가슴을 가로질러 메어져 있는 회중시계의 쇠줄을 따라 거대한 금괴가 앞뒤로 부드럽게 미끄러지듯 움직이고 있었으며, 검은 머리카락은 덩어리 진 채 모자 아래로 내려와 있었다. 그의 눈은 앙리에트를 주시하고 있었으며, 그녀 속의 어떤 생각을 알아차리고, 그녀에게 일부러 웃음 지어보였다. 앙리에트는 뺨은 움직이지 않은 채, 시선을 내려뜨려 장갑을 낀 자신의 손가락 끝을 흘긋 보았다. 역마차를 빽빽하게 메운 그들은 모두 모르는 사람들이었으며, 목적지를 제외하면 공통점이 전혀 없었다.

---

20 2021 숭실대 ▶▶▶ MSG p.113   ③

분사구문 ▶ 생략된 분사구문의 주어는 주절의 주어와 일치한다. ③에서 생략된 분사구문의 주어는 주절의 주어 I이고, 음향 상태가 발코니 뒤쪽이 좋다는 것을 듣고서 그쪽으로 가기로 한 것이므로, 분사구문의 태는 수동태가 되어야 한다. 따라서 ③을 Having been told that으로 고쳐야 한다.

having said that 그렇긴 해도 acoustics n. 음향 상태[효과] trial n. 재판, 공판 be acquainted with ~를 알다

① 그렇긴 해도, 나는 여성과 남성이 근본적으로 같다는 것에 동의하지 않는다.
② 이러한 일들을 하고 난 그녀는 체포되어 교도소에 수감될 때까지 그것들을 숨겼다.
③ 발코니 뒤가 음향상태가 가장 좋다는 말을 들은 나는 문이 열리면 곧장 그곳으로 가기로 결심했다.
④ 많은 재판을 취재해왔기 때문에 나는 법정 예절을 잘 알고 있다.

| 01 ③ | 02 ④ | 03 ② | 04 ① | 05 ② | 06 ④ | 07 ② | 08 ① | 09 ④ | 10 ③ |
| 11 ③ | 12 ③ | 13 ② | 14 ② | 15 ② | 16 ② | 17 ③ | 18 ④ | 19 ① | 20 ④ |

01 **2013 가천대** ▶▶▶ MSG p.137   ③

알맞은 전치사 표현 ▶ 관계대명사 whom 앞의 전치사를 찾는 문제인데 whom의 선행사는 사람이므로 앞의 astronomer가 선행사이다. whom이 이끄는 절의 내용이 혜성이 그 천문학자의 이름을 따서 명명되었다는 내용이다. '~이름을 따서 명명되다'라는 표현은 전치사 after와 함께 be named after로 쓴다. 따라서 ③ after가 적절하다.

comet n. 혜성 astronomer n. 천문학자 asteroid n. 소행성

그 혜성은 소행성들을 찾기 위해 하늘을 조사하던 한 천문학자에 의해 지구로부터 3억 7천만 마일 떨어진 곳에서 최초로 발견되었으며, 그 천문학자의 이름을 따서 명명되었다.

02 **2008 경기대** ▶▶▶ MSG p.113, p.114   ④

분사구문 ▶ 완전한 절 뒤에는 접속사 없이 절이나 동사가 이어질 수 없으므로 ①과 ③은 빈칸에 올 수 없다. ④ each with its own cell wall ~은 each (being) with its own cell wall ~에서 being이 생략된 일종의 분사구문으로, 완전한 절 뒤에 올 수 있다. 그리고 each (being) with its own cell wall ~은 and each is with its own cell wall ~을 분사구문으로 고친 것으로, and each has its own cell wall ~과 같은 의미를 표현한다. 전치사 with는 '소유, 소지, 구비' 등의 의미를 나타내어 '~을 가지고, ~이 있는' 등의 의미로, be with는 have와 같은 의미로 해석된다.

split v. 쪼개다, 나누다 protoplasm n. 원형질

박테리아가 너무 커지면 반으로 쪼개져서 두 개의 새로운 박테리아가 생겨나는데, 각각의 박테리아는 자체의 세포벽과 원형질을 가진다.

03 **2008 홍익대** ▶▶▶ MSG p.223   ②

비교급 ~ than+주어+동사 ▶ '비교급 ~ than(접속사) S+V'이므로 ④는 제외된다. higher ~ than its own citizens do(=give the city high marks)에서 비교문은 병치구조이고, than 다음에서 괄호 안 부분을 대신한 대동사 do와 주어는 '동사+주어'의 어순으로 도치되기도 하므로 ②가 정답이다.

mark n. 점수, 평점 resident n. 거주자, 살고 있는 사람

인디애나주 중부지역 주민들에 대한 한 조사에 의하면, 그린캐슬시 밖에 사는 사람들이 그 도시의 시민들 보다 더 높은 점수를 그 도시에 준다고 한다.

04 **2022 아주대** ▶▶▶ MSG p.55   ①

현재완료 수동태 ▶ 'for+기간'이나 'since+시점' 등의 부사구가 나오면 주절의 시제는 주로 완료시제가 된다. for thousands of years가 기간을 나타내는 시간 부사구이므로, 동사시제는 완료의 형태가 되어야 한다. 또한 주어인 it은 engineering으로서 '실행되는' 대상이므로 수동태가 되어야 한다.

engage v. 참여시키다 engineering n. 공학 discipline n. 학과, 학문의 분야

공학은 과학, 기술, 공학 및 수학에 학생들을 참여시키는 것을 목표로 하는 STEM 교육의 일부이지만, 하나의 학문분야로서 수천 년 동안 실행되어 왔다. 기자의 피라미드, 스톤헨지, 파르테논 신전 등에서 공학의 예들을 볼 수 있다.

05 **2021 세종대** ▶▶▶ MSG p.206   ②

문의 구성 ▶ 빈칸 앞에 종속절이 주어져 있으므로 빈칸 이하는 주절을 이루어야 한다. 비교 구문에 쓰인 as 혹은 than 뒤에 주어가 온 형태는 또 다른 종속절을 만들므로 ②를 제외한 나머지는 정답이 될 수 없다. ②의 경우, than이 접속사로 쓰인 것이 아니라, 주어 they 앞의 more often than not 전체가 '종종', '대개', '자주'라는 의미의 부사구이므로 주절을 이룰 수 있다.

verify v. (진실인지) 확인하다; 입증하다 precise a. 정확한 supervision n. 감독, 관리, 지휘 more often than not 자주, 대개, 종종

학생들이 정확한 정의를 입증하거나 결정하기 위해 사전을 찾을 때, 그들에게는 훌륭한 결정을 내리기 위한 지도가 종종 필요하다.

06 **2021 아주대** ▶▶▶ MSG p.205   ④

the+비교급, the+비교급 ▶ 'the 비교급~, the 비교급~'은 한쪽의 정도가 변함에 따라 다른 쪽도 변함을 나타내는 비례 비교 구문으로, '~하면 할수록 그만큼 더 ~하다'라는 뜻이다. 어순은 'the 비교급+주어+동사, the 비교급+주어+동사'의 형태이며, 빈칸에 들어가는 the more는 피수식어 fluid를 수식하는 형용사의 역할을 하므로 the more fluid와 같이 붙여 써야 한다. 따라서 ④가 빈칸에 적절하다. 한편, 빈칸 앞의 sweats는 '땀을 흘리다'는 의미의 3인칭 단수 현재형 동사이다.

sweat n. 땀 v. 땀을 흘리다 tradeoff n. 거래; 균형 fluid n. 유동체; 분비액

신체는 땀을 만들어 체온이 과다하게 상승하는 것을 막는다. 그러나 신체가 더 많이 땀을 흘릴수록, 신체는 더 많은 체액을 상실하게 된다는 점에서 부정적인 절충적 측면이 있다.

07 2022 세종대 ▶▶▶ MSG p.105, p.227   ②

현재분사 / 전치사 ▶ 전체 문장의 동사는 came이므로 동사 ban은 주어를 수식하는 분사가 되어야 하겠는데, A new law가 ban하는 행위의 주체이므로 능동을 나타내는 현재분사를 써야 한다. 그 뒤에 위치할 전치사로는 영향이 미치는 대상 앞에 쓰는 on이 적절하다.

come into effect (새 법률 등이) 실시되다, 발효하다 ban v. 금지하다

대부분의 과일과 야채에 대해 플라스틱 포장을 금지하는 새로운 법이 프랑스에서 새해 첫날부터 시행되었다.

08 2020 한국외대 ▶▶▶ MSG p.113   ①

분사구문 ▶ 빈칸 뒤에 완전한 절이 왔으므로, 빈칸에는 문장을 수식할 수 있는 부사절이나 분사구문이 올 수 있다. 부사절의 주어가 주절의 주어와 같을 경우 부사절의 주어를 삭제하고 분사구문을 만드는데, 부사절 As the politician was unwilling to admit that he was wrong의 주어가 주절의 주어 the politician과 같으므로, the politician을 삭제하고 being을 생략한 ①의 Unwilling to admit that he was wrong이 빈칸에 적절하다.

the opposition 반대당, 야당

그 정치인은 자신이 틀렸다는 것을 인정하길 꺼려서, 자신의 실수에 대해 야당을 비난했다.

09 2018 서울여대 ▶▶▶ MSG p.11, p.138   ④

문의 구성 ▶ 빈칸 앞의 that은 the kind of emotional response를 선행사로 한 목적격 관계대명사 that이다. 따라서 빈칸에는 주어와 동사가 와야 하는데 동사는 주절의 동사 bring about을 대신한 대동사 does를 쓸 수 있으므로 ④가 적절하다. ②의 경우는 '지구온난화의 위협이 북극곰에게 유발하는 감정적 반응'이라는 의미를 만들어 글의 흐름에 어울리지 않는다.

buzzing a. 윙윙거리는, 와글거리는; 웅성대는 response n. 응답, 대답, 답장, 회신; 반응

윙윙거리는 곤충의 소멸은 지구온난화가 북극곰에게 가하는 위협이 일으키는 그런 종류의 감정적 반응을 일으키지는 않는다.

10 2005 경희대 ▶▶▶ MSG p.167   ③

부정대명사 certain ▶ certain은 부정대명사로 쓰일 수 있으며, 이때는 '~중 어떤 사람들, 어떤 것들'이라는 의미를 갖는다. 동사의 수는 certain of 뒤에 오는 표현에 일치시켜야 하므로, ③ is를 are로 고친다. ④에서 learning은 of의 목적어로 쓰인 명사이다.

institution n. 기관

평화연구의 결과로 만들어진 일부 방법들이 지금 전 세계의 고등교육기관에서 연구되고 있다.

11 2016 중앙대 ▶▶▶ MSG p.164   ③

관사의 생략 ▶ 동일인물을 나타내거나 지칭하는 표현이 and를 통해 나열된 경우, 관사는 앞의 명사에 한 번만 붙이는 것이 원칙이다. 그러므로 ③에서 the scientist를 관사 없이 scientist로 써야 한다.

commentary n. 해설; 논평, 비평 incomplete a. 불완전한, 불충분한

1950년대에 그 섬에 왔던 노르웨이 출신 탐험가이자 과학자인 토르 헤위에르달(Thor Heyerdahl)의 이론들에 대한 언급 없이는 이스터 섬에 대한 어떠한 논평도 불완전할 것이다.

12 2022 성균관대 ▶▶▶ MSG p.227   ③

between A and B ▶ between peace on earth 다음에 관계대명사 which절이 삽입되어 있고, or mutual destruction 다음에 관계대명사 which절이 삽입되어 있다. 앞에 between이 있으므로 ③의 or는 and가 되어야 한다.

beyond[within] one's grasp 손이 미치지 않는[미치는] 곳에, 이해할 수 없는[있는] mutual a. 서로의, 상호 관계가 있는 improbable a. 사실[있을 것] 같지 않은

선택은 인간이 이해할 수 없는 지구상의 평화와 이해할 수 있지만 가능성이 매우 낮은 상호파괴 사이에 있는 것이 아니라 폭력의 정도와 빈도가 더 큰 것과 더 낮은 것 사이에 있는 것이다.

13 2021 국민대 ▶▶▶ MSG p.107   ②

감정동사의 분사 ▶ 감정을 나타내는 동사 satisfy가 sense라는 사물을 수식하고 있으므로, '현재분사'로 나타내야 한다. 따라서 ②를 a satisfying sense of direction으로 고쳐야 한다.

humanity n. 인류, 인간 direction n. 방향; 지시, 명령 exclusive a. 배타적인 self-interest n. 사리사욕

인류는 물질세계에서조차 배타적인 사리사욕 추구로는 성공이 얻어지지 않는다는 점을 이해하는 경제학의 도움으로 인류 자신의 업적을 평가할 수 있을 때에야 비로소 만족스러운 방향 감각을 가질 수 있다.

14 **2019 가천대** ▸▸▸ MSG p.219　　　　②

비교대상의 병치 ▶ 비교구문에서는 비교되는 대상이 서로 같은 자격의 것으로 병치구조가 되어야 한다. 따라서 ②를 amateur's conscience를 의미하는 amateur's로 바꾸어야 한다.

conscience n. 양심 interpretation n. 해석 statute n. 법규, 법령 judiciary n. 사법부

중요한 것은 "양심"의 의미에 대해 더 많이 생각해보는 것이다. 판사의 양심은 아마추어의 양심이 아니라 전문가의 양심이어야 한다. 한 판사의 법령 해석이 옳은지, 그리고 또 다른 판사는 어떤 상이한 결론에 도달할지 의문을 가질 필요가 있다. 그렇게도 신중한 고려가 사법부에 대한 사람들의 신뢰가 뿌리내리는 데 도움을 줄 수 있다.

15 **2022 한양대** ▸▸▸ MSG p.157　　　　②

기수+단위명사+형용사+명사 ▶ '기수+단위명사+형용사'가 명사를 수식하는 한정적 용법으로 사용될 때는 하이픈으로 연결하며, 단위로 사용되는 명사를 반드시 단수로 써야 한다. 따라서 ②를 twenty-year-old로 고쳐야 한다.

orbit n. 생활의 궤도; (인생) 행로 celebrated a. 명성이 높은, 유명한 awed a. 경외심 어린 promising a. 유망한 augur v. 점치다, 예언하다

클라라와 요하네스 브람스는 1853년 처음으로 인생의 행로에서 마주쳤는데, 그때 그녀의 사랑하는 남편인 저명한 작곡가 로베르트 슈만은 20세의 브람스에게서 너무나 드물고 촉망되는 재능을 발견한 결과, 즉시 모든 주요 저널들에 열정적인 편지를 써 보내 젊은 음악가의 미래의 명성을 예언하여, 그 재능에 대한 음악계의 경외심 어린 관심을 불러일으키기 시작했다.

16 **2020 아주대** ▸▸▸ MSG p.122, p.124　　　　②

whether A or B ▶ 'the question of 의문사 절(~냐 하는 문제)' 구문인데, 뒤에 or vice versa(아니면 그 반대이냐)가 있으므로 적절한 의문사는 what이 아니라 whether이다. 따라서 ②에서 what을 whether로 바꾸어야 한다.

takeover n. 기업 인수, 경영권 인수; (정권 등의) 탈취, 장악 metaphor n. 은유 reinforce v. 강화하다, 보강하다, 증강하다 vice versa ad. 반대로, 거꾸로 not exactly [전혀] ~가 아닌

우리의 상황에서 중요한 것은 특히 적대적 기업 인수 건수의 증가이다. 지배적인 FIGHT 은유가 공격적인 사업 관행을 강화한 것이냐, 아니면 그 반대이냐 하는 문제는 닭이 먼저냐 달걀이 먼저냐 하는 문제이지만, 위에서 개략적으로 진술한 사회경제적 틀도 또한 공격성의 개념적 모델을 전혀 좌절시키지는 않았다고 말해도 무방하다.

17 **2021 국민대** ▸▸▸ MSG p.55　　　　③

동사의 태 ▶ ③의 주어는 the church authorities인데, 이것은 decide하는 행위의 대상이 아닌 주체이므로 능동태 문장이 되어야 한다. ③을 had decided로 고친다.

parsonage n. (교구) 목사관 take issue with ~을 문제 삼다 feature n. 특징

그들은 같은 집을 유지할 수 있었고, 실제로는 더 이상 그렇지 않았지만 그 집은 여전히 종종 목사관으로 불렸다. 새로 온 목사의 젊은 아내는 그 곳의 몇몇 특징들을 문제 삼았고, 그래서 교회 당국은 그 집을 수리하는 대신 그녀가 더 이상 불평할 수 없도록 새 집을 짓기로 결정했었다. 그러고 나서 그 오래된 목사관은 나이든 목사에게 싼값에 팔렸다.

18 **2018 한국산업기술대** ▸▸▸ MSG p.151, p.200　　　　④

many와 much의 구분 ▶ 비용, 즉 돈이 드는 것은 수가 아닌 양의 개념이며, many는 '수'를 나타내고, much는 '양'을 나타낸다. 따라서 ④의 many를 much로 고쳐야 한다. ① movie는 film하는 행위의 주체가 아닌 대상이므로 수동태로 써야 한다. ② 문두에 부정어구 Not only가 쓰였으므로 주어와 동사가 도치된다. ③ 배수비교는 '배수사 +as+형용사 원급+as'의 형태로 쓰인다.

flop n. (책·연극·영화 등의) 실패작 film v. 촬영하다 the Pacific Ocean 태평양

많은 실패작들은 영화화하기 어려운 비현실적인 이야기들로 되어 있다. 한 예로, 영화 『플루토 내쉬(Pluto Nash)』가 있다. 2002년에 제작된 이 코미디 영화는 미래에 달에서의 생활에 대한 것이었다. 또 다른 유명한 실패작은 1995년에 제작된 액션 영화 『워터월드(Waterworld)』였다. 그 영화의 제작자는 물만 있고 땅은 없는 세계를 구현하기 위해 애썼다. 그 영화는 하와이 부근의 태평양에서 촬영되었다. 하와이는 영화를 제작하기에 비싼 장소일 뿐만 아니라 바다는 보통의 촬영장처럼 통제할 수도 없었다. 『워터월드』는 감독이 계획했던 것보다 제작 시간과 비용이 두 배나 더 들었다.

19 **2020 한국산업기술대** ▸▸▸ MSG p.55　　　　①

올바른 수동태 표현 ▶ ①에서 주어는 it(= Stonehenge)으로서, '설계되고, 건축되는' 대상(객체)이다. 수동태로 표현해야 하므로 been designed로 바꾸어야 한다.

sacred a. 신성한 observatory n. 관측소 monument n. 기념물 sarsen stone 사르센 스톤(스톤헨지에 있는 거대한 돌)

스톤헨지가 정확히 어떻게 그리고 왜 지어졌는지는 여전히 수수께끼이다. 연구에 따르면 그것은 신성한 사원 혹은 천문 연구 관측소라는 두 가지 목적 중의 하나로 그것을 사용했던 고대 종교 집단에 의해 설계되고 건축되었던 것 같다. 과학자들은 영국 남부지역의 솔즈베리 평원에 있는 현재 장소로 전국 각지에서 그 거대한 돌들이 옮겨져 왔다고 생각한다. 그 기념물에 대한 작업은 기원전 2000년경 시작되어 기원전 1500년경까지 계속되었다고 생각된다. 엔지니어들은 원래 장소에서 솔즈베리까지 각각의 사르센 스톤을 옮겨오는 데 대략 600명 정도가 필요했으리라고 추정하고 있다. 무거운 것을 들어 올리는 현대식 건설 중장비가 당시에 없었던 것을 고려할 때, 이는 놀라운 일이라고 과학자들은 생각한다.

20 **2021 숭실대** ▶▶▶ MSG p.114 ④

정비문 ▶ ① people being people은 '사람은 사람이니까(다 같으니까)', ② all other things being equal은 '다른 모든 조건이 같다면', ③ weather permitting은 '날씨가 허락한다면' 등으로 모두 관용적으로 쓰이는 독립분사구문이다. 그런데 ④의 경우, '그렇긴 하지만', '그러나'의 의미로 쓰이는 독립분사구문은 that being spoken이 아니라 that being said이다.

selfishly ad. 이기적으로 run v. (언급된 시간에) 진행되다

① 이제, 사람은 사람이니까, 모든 선수들이 이기적으로 행동했다.
② 다른 모든 조건이 같다면, 가장 간단한 설명이 가장 좋은 경향이 있다.
③ 날씨가 허락한다면, 그 전시회는 매일 밤 열릴 것이다.
④ 그렇긴 하지만, 현재 시스템을 유지하는 것이 시스템이 전혀 없는 것보다는 훨씬 나을 것이다.

01 ④	02 ②	03 ①	04 ③	05 ③	06 ③	07 ④	08 ④	09 ④	10 ⑤
11 ②	12 ③	13 ③	14 ④	15 ③	16 ④	17 ④	18 ④	19 ③	20 ③

01 2017 가천대 ▶▶▶ MSG p.131 ④

적절한 접속사 ▶ 종속절의 "지난 20년간 서양에서 해조류에 대한 관심이 급증했다."라는 내용과 주절의 "서양의 해조류 소비량은 일본에서 소비되는 양에 비하면 극히 적은 수준에 그칠 것으로 보인다."라는 내용은 양보 관계에 있다. 따라서 빈칸에는 양보절을 이끄는 종속접속사 ④ although가 들어가야 한다.

seaweed n. 해초, 해조류 staple n. 주요 산물; 주요[기본] 식품 diet n. (일상의) 식품, 음식물; 규정식; 식이 요법 upsurge n. 급증 fraction n. 파편; 소량; 분수

해조류는 일본과 중국에서 주식으로 오랫동안 이용되어왔다. 서양에서, 해조류는 대체로 건강식품으로 간주되고 있으며, 지난 20년간 식품으로서의 해조류에 대한 관심이 급증하긴 했으나, 서양의 해조류 소비량은 일본에서 소비되는 양에 비하면 극히 적은 수준에 그칠 것이다.

02 2020 덕성여대 ▶▶▶ MSG p.71 ②

가정법 과거완료 구문의 도치 ▶ if절의 동사가 'had+p.p.(과거분사)'의 형태인 가정법 과거완료 문장에서 if를 생략하면 주어와 조동사 had는 도치된다. 가정법 과거완료이므로 주절은 '주어+조동사의 과거형 +have+p.p.(과거분사)'의 형태가 되어야 함을 알 수 있다.

carpenter n. 목수 show up 나타나다

목수가 나타나는 데 사흘이 걸리리라는 것을 알았더라면, 내가 재료를 구해서 직접 그 일을 했을 것이다. 그 일은 지금쯤이면 끝났을 것이다.

03 2015 가톨릭대 ▶▶▶ MSG p.137 ①

부분명사 + of which ▶ 두 개의 절로 구성된 문장이므로 빈칸에는 연결사가 필요하다. 빈칸에 접속사 and를 넣어 두 절을 연결하면 and she speaks both of them very fluently가 되는데 여기서 and를 없애고 them을 which로 바꾸어 관계절을 만들면 both of which she speaks very fluently가 된다. 따라서 빈칸에는 ①이 적절하다.

switch v. 전환하다, 바꾸다 fluently ad. 유창하게

젠슨(Jensen) 박사의 딸은 영어와 중국어를 번갈아 말할 수 있는데 그녀는 두 언어를 모두 매우 유창하게 한다.

04 2020 덕성여대 ▶▶▶ MSG p.236 ③

동격의 어구 ▶ 빈칸에는 앞의 명사(회사 브랜드)와 동격 관계에 있는 명사 상당어구가 들어가야 한다. make of car에서 make는 '제품'이라는 의미를 가진 명사이다. Italian은 모음으로 시작하므로 부정관사는 an이 되어야 한다.

available a. 구할 수 있는, 이용 가능한 make n. (특정 회사에서 만든 기계장비 등의) 제품, ~제

이용 가능한 유일한 차는 이탈리아산 자동차인 빨간색 피아트뿐이었다.

05 2020 세종대 ▶▶▶ MSG p.30 ③

'find + 목적어 + 목적보어' 구문 ▶ 'find+목적어(this dictionary)+목적보어(valuable)'의 5형식 문장을 만드는 ③이 빈칸에 적절하다. ① find가 3형식 동사로 쓰이기도 하지만, dictionary는 가산명사이므로 한정사가 있어야 한다. 한정사인 this가 앞에 있다고 하더라도 '사전을 찾아내다'는 의미상 부적절하다.

electronic a. 전자의 feel free to do (~을) 마음 놓고 해도 괜찮다

만약 이 사전이 유용하다고 생각하고 유사한 전자사전을 원하신다면, 저희 웹사이트를 자유롭게 방문하세요.

06 2022 아주대 ▶▶▶ MSG p.149 ③

of+추상명사 ▶ 'of+추상명사'는 형용사의 의미를 지니는데, 추상명사를 수식하는 형용사가 결합해 'of+형용사+추상명사'의 형태로 쓰이는 경우가 많다. 'of 형용사(less practical) 추상명사(use)'인 ③이 적절하다.

imaginary a. 상상에만 존재하는, 가상의 pious a. 경건한 aspiration n. 열망

상상 속의 독자는 (작가의) 경건한 희망과 열망의 표적이 될 수 있지만, 그들이 현실의 독자와 비평가보다 실제적으로 덜 유용하다.

07   **2021 세종대** ▶▶▶ MSG p.163   ④

감탄문의 어순 ▶ 감탄문은 'What + a(an) + 형용사 +단수 가산명사 + 주어 + 동사', 'What + 형용사 + 불가산명사/복수명사 + 주어 + 동사', 'How + 형용사 + a(an) + 단수 가산명사 +주어 + 동사', 'How+형용사/부사+주어 + 동사'의 형태로 나타낸다. 따라서 'How+형용사+주어 +동사'의 형태인 ④가 정답으로 적절하다.

dynamic a. 역동적인, 활발한

우리가 전국에서 가장 다양하고 역동적이고 아름다운 주(州)에 살아서 실로 얼마나 다행스러운가.

---

08   **2022 한국공학대** ▶▶▶ MSG p.105   ④

문의 구성 ▶ '영수증을 보관하다'라는 표현으로는 keep receipts가 적절하고, 영수증이 경비를 증명하는 것이므로 receipts 다음에는 현재분사 verifying이 적절하다. 따라서 ④가 정답이다.

full-time a. 상근의, 전임의 reimburse v. ~에게 변상하다, 상환하다 verify v. 입증하다 receipt n. 영수증 expense n. 비용, 경비

출장비를 환급받길 원하는 전임강사는 경비를 증명하는 영수증을 보관해야 한다.

---

09   **2015 한국외대** ▶▶▶ MSG p.31   ④

문의 구성 ▶ 주어진 문장에서 line up은 '자동사+부사'의 구조로, '힘을 모으다, 집결하다'의 의미이다. 뒤에는 목적을 나타내는 to부정사가 이어지는 것이 자연스러우므로, ①과 ③을 정답에서 먼저 제외시킬 수 있다. ④의 경우, to make다음에 목적어 it(=space travel)과 목적보어 (a more affordable proposition)인 명사가 이어지는 5형식 문형을 이루므로 문법적으로 올바른 형태이다.

billionaire n. 억만장자 commercial a. 무역의; 민간의 line up 줄을 서다, 준비하다 affordable a. 입수 가능한; (가격이) 알맞은 proposition n. (특히 사업상의) 제안

우주여행은 억만장자들만을 위한 것이 아닐 것이며, 그래서 우주여행을 더 저렴한 사업 제안으로 만들기 위해 민간 기업들이 힘을 모으고 있다.

---

10   **2011 성균관대** ▶▶▶ MSG p.211   ⑤

주어와 동사의 수일치 ▶ 이 문장의 주어는 The point이고 동사는 have not yet been studied이다. 주어가 단수명사이므로 ⑤ have not을 has not으로 고쳐야 한다. ①은 physical decline ~ driver's capability가 완전한 문장으로 관계대명사 which 앞에 전치사가 온 것이다. 선행사가 the point로 '어떤 특정한 때, 시점'을 의미하므로 전치사 at이 쓰였다. ③은 관계대명사절의 동사인데 관계사절의 주어가 physical decline으로 단수이므로 begins가 온 것이다. ④는 뒤에 명사

capability가 있으므로 소유격 형태로 쓰였고 driver가 가산명사이므로 앞에 부정관사 a가 쓰인 것이다.

decline n. 쇠퇴 with age 늙어감에 따라, 나이를 먹어서 adversely ad. 반대로; 불리하게

나이로 인한 신체적 쇠퇴가 운전자의 능력에 불리하게 영향을 미치기 시작하는 시점은 아직 연구되지 않았다.

---

11   **2022 성균관대** ▶▶▶ MSG p.174   ②

부정대명사 ▶ anything that은 '~하는 것은 무엇이든'이라는 무제한적 의미인데, 이 문장에서는 '~하는 어떤 것', 즉 잘 익은 과일처럼 입 안으로 떨어지는 어떤 것이라는 의미로 한정되어 있으므로 ②를 something으로 고쳐야 한다. Happiness is not anything that ~은 Happiness is nothing that ~과 마찬가지로 어색한 문장이다.

drop v. 떨어지다 ripe a. 익은, 숙성한 mere a. 단지 ~만의 fortunate a. 운 좋은

행복은 매우 드문 경우를 제외하고는 단순히 운이 좋은 상황에 의해 잘 익은 과일처럼 입 안으로 뚝 떨어지는 그런 것이 아니다.

---

12   **2020 홍익대** ▶▶▶ MSG p.105   ③

분사의 용법 ▶ 앞의 명사를 수식하면서 진행수동의 의미를 나타내야 하므로, ③은 being이어야 한다.

acceleration n. 가속, 촉진; 가속도 e.g. 예를 들면 concentrate v. 집중하다

갈릴레오(Galileo)는 가속도가 여러 힘의 작용으로부터 비롯된다는 것(예를 들면, 물체의 무게가 가진 힘에 의해 생성되는 낙하의 가속도)을 알고 있었지만, 주제의 이 부분에 대해서는 집중하지 않았다.

---

13   **2021 국민대** ▶▶▶ MSG p.55   ③

동사의 태 ▶ ③ 뒤에 목적어가 주어져 있으므로 which 이하는 능동태 문장이 되어야 한다. ③을 featured로 고친다.

dialectic n. 변증법 originate v. 비롯하다, 생기다 exemplify v. 예시하다 tease out (정보 따위를) 어떻게 해서든 빼내다, (복잡하거나 알기 힘든 정보·의미를) 알아내려고 애쓰다

"변증법"이라는 용어는 고대 그리스에서 유래했는데, 거기서 그것은 플라톤의 소크라테스적 대화에 예시되어 있었으며, 이 대화는 어떤 주제에 관한 진리를 알아내는 것을 목적으로 하는 질의응답 기반의 토론이 특징이었다.

14   **2019 가천대** ▶▶▶ MSG p.113   ④

완료형 분사와 단순형 분사의 구분 ▶ ④는 앞의 the object를 수식하는 분사구인데, 글의 내용상 '경매에서 입찰되고 있는'의 의미가 적절하므로, 완료형이 아닌 단순형의 being bid upon으로 고쳐야 한다. ① '무슨 일이 있어도, 기필코(=by all means)'라는 의미의 관용 표현이다. ③ 복합관계대명사는 앞에 나온 전치사의 영향을 받지 않고 관계절 안에서 주어 역할을 할 때는 주격, 목적어 역할을 할 때는 목적격으로 사용한다.

bidder n. (경매에서) 값을 붙이는 사람, 입찰자 auction n. 경매 sustain v. (피해 등을) 입다[당하다] auction n. 경매 optimistic a. 낙관적인

입찰자가 경매에서 기필코 입찰받기를 원하면, 실수를 저지르게 될 가능성은 더 커진다. 설사 경매에서 이긴다고 하더라도, 손실을 보게 되었다는 것을 생각할 만큼 생각하고 난 후에 깨달을지도 모른다. 경매에서 경매물은 누구든 입찰 중인 물건의 가치에 대해 가장 낙관적인 견해를 가진 사람에게 돌아간다.

15   **2017 한국산업기술대** ▶▶▶ MSG p.35   ③

보어의 품사 ▶ 마지막 문장에서, makes 다음의 it은 가목적어이고 to stumble upon things가 진목적어이며, 이 사이에 목적보어가 들어가서 5형식 문장을 이룬다. 그런데 보어가 될 수 있는 것은 부사가 아니라 형용사이므로, ③의 more easily를 형용사 easy의 비교급인 easier로 고쳐야 옳은 문장이 된다. ① contrast는 '대조시키다'라는 의미의 타동사인데, 주어인 activities가 대조하는 행위의 대상이므로 수동태로 표현하는 것이 맞다. ④ 가정법 과거의 귀결절에 쓰인 조동사 would이며, in everyday life가 if절을 대신한다.

contrast v. 대조[대비]시키다; 대조하여 뚜렷이 드러나게[두드러지게] 하다 anonymity n. 익명, 무명, 작자불명 accountable a. 책임 있는; 설명할 수 있는 stumble upon 마주치다, 우연히 만나다 inadvertently ad. 무심코, 부주의하게, 우연히

인터넷에서의 우리의 활동은, 마치 우리가 온라인으로 하는 것들이 어떻게든 현실성이 덜한 것처럼, 실생활과 종종 대조된다. 온라인상에는 익명성이 존재하기 때문에, 우리는 우리가 하는 행동에 대해 책임감을 덜 느낀다. 또한 인터넷으로 인해, 일상생활에서라면 대개 피할 것들을 무심코 접하게 되기가 훨씬 더 쉬워진다.

16   **2021 가천대** ▶▶▶ MSG p.167   ④

대명사의 수일치 ▶ ④는 These same questions를 가리킨다. 이것은 복수이므로 ④를 복수 대명사 them으로 고쳐야 한다. ① miracles를 받는 대명사다. ③ 주어는 These same questions이다.

perchance ad. 우연히; 아마도 reveal v. 드러내다; 알리다; 누설하다 utter v. 발언하다, 말하다 disturb v. ~의 마음을 어지럽게 하다; 불안하게 하다 confound v. 어리둥절하게 하다 omit v. 생략하다, 빠뜨리다

아마도 우리의 기적을 설명해주고 새로운 기적을 보여줄 책이 우리를 위해 존재한다. 현재로서는 말로 표현할 수 없는 것들이 다른 어떤 곳에서는 말로 표현될지도 모른다. 우리의 마음을 어지럽히고 당혹스럽게 만들고 어리둥절하게 만드는 이 똑같은 질문들이 이번에는 모든 현인(賢人)들에게도 하나도 빠짐없이 떠올랐다. 그리고 각각의 현인들은 그들의 능력에 따라 그들의 말과 삶을 통해 그 질문들에 대답했다.

17   **2021 숙명여대** ▶▶▶ MSG p.24   ④

be packed with ▶ 동사 pack은 pack A with B(A를 B로 채우다)의 형태로 사용되는데, 목적어 the mind가 주어가 되어 수동태가 되었다. 따라서 B에 해당하는 innate structure앞의 전치사는 ④ by가 아니라 with가 되어야 한다.

rationalism n. 합리주의 empiricism n. 경험주의 take a course 강의를 듣다 innate a. 타고난 deduction n. 추론

합리주의와 경험주의 사이의 대논쟁은 철학, 심리학 또는 사상사(思想史)의 강좌를 수강하는 모든 이들에게 친숙하다. 그 논쟁은 마음이 생득적인 구조로 가득 차 있는 것인지 아니면 환경에 의해 작성되는 빈 서판인지, 그리고 지식이 이론을 이용한 추론에서 생겨나는 것인지 아니면 관찰해서 얻는 데이터를 수집하는 것에서 생겨나는 것인지와 같은 문제들을 포함한다.

18   **2022 이화여대** ▶▶▶ MSG p.176   ④

부사 almost의 용법 ▶ almost는 부사이므로 명사 aspects를 직접 수식할 수 없다. 따라서 ④의 almost aspects를 almost all aspects로 고쳐야 한다.

screening n. 심사, 검사 assessment n. 평가 people of color 유색인 pathologist n. 병리학자 incorporate v. 통합하다 constitute v. ~을 구성하다 racism n. 인종차별

일부 사람들은 인종을 기반으로 한 점수 조정을 하는 의료 심사 평가가 유색인들에게 해롭다고 주장한다. 은퇴한 병리학자이자 의학연구실 대표로서 나는 조직적인 인종차별이 의학계에는 미국 사회 거의 모든 측면에 존재하는 것처럼 존재하지는 않는다고 주장하려는 건 분명 아니다. 그러나 나는 이와 반대되는 주장을 들은 적이 있다. 인종 간의 차이를 결정의 알고리즘에 통합하지 못하는 것도 또한 인종차별을 성립시킨다는 주장이었다.

19   **2022 한국항공대** ▶▶▶ MSG p.105   ③

현재분사와 과거분사의 구분 ▶ 팔다리를 뜻하는 limb은 스스로 통제하는 주체가 아니라, 두뇌로부터 '통제되는 객체'이므로, ③의 controlling을 controlled로 고쳐야 한다.

puzzle v. 이해할 수 없게 만들다 stroke n. 뇌졸중 contralateral a. 대측성(對側性)의, (몸의) 반대쪽에 일어나는 ipsilateral a. 동측성(同側性)의, 몸의 같은 쪽에 일어나는 limb n. 사지(四肢), 팔다리 detect v. 발견하다 decode v. (암호를) 해독하다; 이해하다

NeuroLutions라는 기업을 창립한 로이타르트(Leuthardt) 박사는 뇌졸중을 겪은 이후 손을 사용하지 못하게 된 환자에게서 들은 말을 수년 동안 이해할 수가 없었다. "만일 당신이 뇌졸중 환자와 대화를 하면, 그들은 자신의 손을 움직이는 것을 상상할 수 있고, 자신의 손을 움직이려고 시도할 수도 있습니다. 그러나 실제로 그들은 손을 움직일 수가 없습니다."라고 그는 말한다. 그래서 로이타르트 박사는 그런 생각이 어디에서 나오는지를 찾고 있었다. 그리고 그는 그런 생각들이 뜻밖의 장소에 있음을 알게 되었는데, 바로 뇌졸중으로 손상되지 않은 뇌 부위였던 것이다. 보통, 뇌와 신체는 뇌의 오른쪽이 신체의 왼쪽을 제어하는 대측성 모델을 따른다. 그러나 로이타르트 박사가 이끄는 팀은 제어신호가 동측성 쪽에도 존재한다는 것을 발견했다. 즉, 통제되는 팔다리와 뇌의 부위가 같은 쪽에 있다는 것이다. 로이타르트 박사가 이끄는 팀은 이 동측성 신호를 탐지하고 해독하는 시스템을 만들었다. 그다음에 그들은 환자가 손의 움직임을 상상할 때 환자 대신 환자의 불구가 된 손을 쥐었다 폈다 해줄 기기에 그 시스템을 연결했다. 그러나 기계로 작동되는 손이 로이타르트 박사의 궁극적인 목표는 아니었다. 그는 도움 없이도 자신의 손을 움직일 수 있는 능력을 환자들이 회복할 수 있도록 돕기를 원했다.

---

20   2017 한국외대   ▶▶▶ MSG p.43

정비문 ▶ 시간과 조건의 부사절에서는 미래시제 내용을 현재시제로 나타내야 하므로 ③을 If he arrives로 고쳐야 한다. ① When he will arrive와 ② when he will leave는 간접의문절로 부사절이 아닌 명사절이다. 이 경우에는 미래를 미래시제로 나타낸다. ④ 단순 미래가 아닌, 의지를 나타내는 will 조동사의 용례이므로 조건의 부사절에서도 will로 나타낸다.

for sure (의심할 여지없이) 확실히[틀림없이]   over there 저쪽 자리에

① 그가 언제 도착할지 확실하게 아는 사람이 없다.
② 사람들이 그가 언제 떠날지 몹시 알고 싶어 한다.
③ 그가 도착하면, 악단에서 그 음악을 연주할 것이다.
④ 원하신다면, 저쪽 자리에 앉아서 기다려주세요.

01 ①	02 ④	03 ①	04 ②	05 ①	06 ④	07 ③	08 ④	09 ③	10 ③
11 ④	12 ④	13 ②	14 ④	15 ②	16 ③	17 ⑤	18 ④	19 ②	20 ③

01　**2022 한양대**　▶▶▶ MSG p.125　①

의문사절 ▶ 빈칸 이하 King ~ a captial까지가 완전한 절을 이루고 있으므로 의문대명사나 관계대명사인 ②와 ④는 배제된다. 주어와 문장 전체의 동사(is) 간의 수의 일치를 고려하면 ⑤도 배제된다. 문맥상 아서 왕의 수도 부지 선정 '장소'가 아니라 '이유'에 해당하는 말이 들어가야 하므로 빈칸에는 Why가 적절하다.

capital n. 수도, 중심지

아서 왕이 수도를 건설하기 위해 그 특정 장소를 선택한 이유는 수수께끼이다.

02　**2021 단국대**　▶▶▶ MSG p.122, p.124　④

whether A or B ▶ or과 상관적으로 쓰이는 접속사가 필요하므로 빈칸에는 whether가 들어가야 한다.

considerable a. (수량이) 꽤 많은; 상당한　extension n. 확대　potter about 빈둥거리다

기술의 발전은 여가시간의 대폭적인 확대를 허용할 것이며, 이 여가시간에 각각의 개인은 집에서 한가로이 보내는 것이든, 정원을 가꾸는 것이든, 혹은 음악을 감상하는 것이든, 자신이 선호하는 활동을 할 수 있다.

03　**2022 서강대**　▶▶▶ MSG p.224　①

문의 구성 ▶ powerfully 이하가 술부이고 빈칸부터 the 1850's까지가 주어이므로 빈칸에는 명사 The building과 이 명사를 뒤의 명사 railroads와 연결해 주는 전치사 of를 사용한 ①이 적절하다. ④ to부정사도 명사적 용법으로 주어를 이룰 수 있으나 대개 '가주어(it) - 진주어(to부정사)' 구문으로 쓰이고 여기서처럼 일반적 의미가 아니라 과거적 의미의 구체적인 사건을 나타내는 데는 동명사(Building)나 ① 같은 명사 표현이 적절하다.

railroad n. 철도　stimulate v. 자극하다; 활기 띠게 하다

1850년대 미국에서의 철도 건설은 철강 산업에 강력한 자극을 주었다.

04　**2021 단국대**　▶▶▶ MSG p.47, p.55　②

능동태와 수동태의 구분 ▶ suppose가 '~라고 믿다, 생각하다'라는 뜻으로 쓰일 때는 타동사로 쓰여서 'suppose+목적어+to 동사원형'이나 'suppose+that 절'로 쓰이는데, 보기 모두 동사 suppose에 대한 목적어가 없다. 따라서 문제에서는 'suppose+목적어+to 동사원형'에 대한 수동태인 'be supposed to 동사원형'이 쓰였음을 알 수 있으므로, ②가 정답이다.

be supposed to V ~할 것이다　weather forecast 일기예보

내일 비가 올 것이다. 그것은 일기예보에서 예상한 것이다.

05　**2021 단국대**　▶▶▶ MSG p.81　①

준조동사의 부정 ▶ had better는 '~하는 것이 좋을 것이다'라는 의미로, 이를 부정할 때는 had better 다음에 부정어를 쓰고 그다음에 동사원형이 와야 한다. 따라서 ①이 정답이다.

miss v. 놓치다　connecting flight 연결항공편　destination n. 최종 목적지

우리는 늦지 않는 것이 좋을 것이다. 그렇지 않으면 뉴욕 행 연결항공편을 놓치게 될 것이고 최종 목적지에 도착하는 데 세 시간 이상 늦게 될 것이다.

06　**2020 아주대**　▶▶▶ MSG p.222　④

only가 포함된 부사어가 문두에 오는 경우의 도치 ▶ only의 수식을 받은 부사어가 문두에 오면 일종의 강조용법으로 그다음 이어지는 문장에서는 조동사가 주어 앞으로 나오는 도치가 일어난다. 그런데 주어가 단수이므로 does를 사용한 ④가 적절하다.

match v. 와 조화를 이루다, 어울리다　scissors n. 가위　activate v. 작동시키다

그들은 RNA와 DNA가 가까이 조화를 이룰 때에만 Cas9의 3D 구조가 Cas9의 가위를 작동시킨다는 것을 발견했다.

07　2022 아주대 ▶▶▶ MSG p.136　③

소유격 관계대명사 whose ▶ 의미상 the poor를 선행사로 가지면서 명사 devices를 수식할 수 있는 소유격 관계대명사 whose가 사용되어야 하고, whose devices가 관계사절의 주어가 되어 서술부인 do very little과 연결되는 형태가 가장 자연스럽다.

gap n. 격차　by default (달리 손을 쓰지 않아서) 자연스럽게, 자동적으로

자신들의 데이터를 기본적으로 보호해주는 기기를 살 수 있는 부자들의 개인 정보 보호 및 보안과 자신들의 기기가 기본적으로 데이터 보호를 위해 할 수 있는 것이 거의 없는 가난한 사람들의 개인 정보 보호 및 보안 사이에 이제 점점 더 많은 격차가 생기고 있다.

08　2021 세종대 ▶▶▶ MSG p.221　④

도치 구문 ▶ that절을 완성시킬 주어와 동사가 필요하므로 주어가 제시돼 있지 않은 ①과 ③을 정답에서 먼저 제외할 수 있다. 정동사가 주어와 도치되는 것은 문두에 부정의 부사구나 부사절이 오는 경우이므로, at no time이 문두에 온 ④가 정답으로 적절하다.

grand jury 대배심　at no time 결코 ~하지 않다　take action 조치를 취하다

저는 오늘 대배심에 말했고 지금 여러분에게 말합니다. 저는 그 누구에게도 거짓말을 하거나, 증거를 숨기거나 없애거나, 다른 불법적인 행동을 하라고 결코 요구하지 않았습니다.

09　2007 세종대 ▶▶▶ MSG p.121　③

B as well as A 구문 ▶ 형용사 vulnerable은 전치사 to와 함께 쓰이며, 빈칸 앞의 to companies와 뒤에 to companies가 대구를 이루는 구가 필요하므로 B as well as A (A뿐만 아니라 B도 역시)가 적절하다.

budget n. 예산　outsource v. (타사 일을) 하청하다

지난달 예산으로 전에 외주를 주었던 일자리를 스페인으로 도로 옮겨오는 회사들뿐만 아니라 아웃소싱에 취약한 회사들에게도 세금을 줄여주었다.

10　2011 중앙대 ▶▶▶ MSG p.234　③

It ~ that[who] 강조구문 ▶ It ~ that[who]의 강조구문에서 강조되는 요소인 his friend or him이 had requested의 주어이므로 ③ him은 he가 되어야 한다. 가주어-진주어 구문으로 뒤의 명사절 whether it ~ the favor가 진주어이고 앞에 가주어 it이 나온 것이다. It was not clear~와 같이 부정이나 불확실성을 표시할 경우 뒤에 진주어로 whether절이 올 수 있다.

favor n. 호의, 친절; 친절한 행위

부탁을 한 쪽이 그의 친구였는지 혹은 그였는지가 불명확했다.

11　2021 홍익대 ▶▶▶ MSG p.212　④

주어와 동사의 수일치 ▶ 주절의 주어는 단수명사 the number이므로 동사인 ④는 is skyrocketing이어야 한다. ① 신문과 잡지의 이름 앞에는 정관사를 쓴다. ② 선행사가 복수명사 citizens이므로 복수동사 are를 썼다.

survey n. 조사, 검사　skyrocket v. 급상승하다, 급등하다

서울 타임스가 최근 조사한 바에 따르면, 구입하고 싶은 책을 서점에서 찾을 수 없어서 그 책을 온라인 서점에서 주문하는 시민들의 수가 요즘 들어 급증하고 있다.

12　2021 단국대 ▶▶▶ MSG p.167　④

대명사의 수일치 ▶ ④에 쓰인 its는 students를 받는 소유격대명사이므로 이 명사에 수를 일치시켜야 한다. ④를 their own으로 고쳐야 한다.

conduct v. 수행하다, 처리하다　be aware of ~을 알다

EU에서 행해진 관련 연구는 제2외국어를 일찍 배운 학생들이 다른 문화에 대해 더 잘 알고 있고 전반적으로 자신들의 모국어에 더 능하다는 점을 보여준다.

13　2021 단국대 ▶▶▶ MSG p.61, p.105　②

현재분사와 과거분사의 구분 ▶ 주절의 정동사는 continued이고 ②는 앞의 명사 businesses를 수식하는 역할을 하고 있는데, business와 자동사 rely는 능동관계이므로 현재분사를 써야 한다. ②를 relying on으로 고친다. ① continue는 부정사와 동명사 모두를 목적어로 취한다.

slide v. (서서히) 내려가다[떨어지다]; 미끄러지다　by a large margin 큰 차이로　interpersonal a. 개인 간에 일어나는　contact n. 접촉　manufacturing n. 제조업, 제조공업　sink v. (물가·가치 따위가) 내리다, 떨어지다　stagnant a. 불경기의, 부진한　recession n. 경기후퇴

서비스 생산은 대인 접촉에 의존하는 기업이 주도하여 큰 폭으로 하락세를 이어간 반면, 제조업 생산은 글로벌 경기 침체로 주요 수출품목의 생산이 계속 지지부진하면서 크게 감소했다.

14　2021 숙명여대 ▶▶▶ MSG p.135　④

문의 구성 ▶ 두 번째 문장의 that은 the actual battle을 선행사로 하는 주격관계대명사이다. 따라서 that 다음에는 시제를 가진 정동사가 와야 하므로, ④를 과거시제 동사 followed로 고쳐야 한다.

mighty a. 강력한, 힘센　single combat 1대 1의 대결, 결투　embolden v. 대담하게 하다, 용기를 돋우어 주다　preempt v. 선취하다, 선제적으로 조치하다, 미리 기선을 제압하다　spare v. (불쾌한 일을) 모면하게[겪지 않아도 되게] 하다　bloodshed n. 유혈; 유혈의 참사

고대 전쟁에서 군대는 때때로 가장 강한 전사를 1대 1의 결투에서 적군의 전사와 대결하도록 보내곤 했다. 그 결과가 이어진 실제 전투에서 한 쪽 편을 대담하게 하거나(대담하게 하여 전투에서 이기게 하거나) 한 쪽 편의 기선을 미리 제압하여 불필요한 유혈 참사(전투)가 일어나지 않게 했다.

고대 세계의 7대 불가사의는 다양한 목적을 충족시키는 것이었다. 일부 불가사의는 바빌론의 공중정원처럼 장식적인 것이었다. 다른 불가사의들은 에페소스의 아르테미스 신전처럼 영적인 것이었다. 알렉산드리아의 등대는 아름다운 동시에 기능적이었지만 보다 더 실용적인 기능을 수행했다. 밝게 비추는 등대 불빛은 수백 년 동안 배들을 이집트의 그 항구로 안전하게 인도했고, 그로 인해 알렉산드리아라는 항구도시는 고대 세계에서 지중해 무역의 중심지로 자리 잡았다.

15 2020 아주대 ▶▶▶ MSG p.55 ②

수동태와 능동태의 구분 ▶ ②의 contradict는 '~와 모순되다, 어긋나다'는 의미의 타동사인데, 뒤에 목적어인 명사가 있으므로 수동태가 아니라 능동태로 쓰는 것이 적절하다. ②를 과거시제 능동태인 contradicted로 바꾸어야 한다.

pernicious a. 해로운, 치명적인, 악성인 contradict v. 부정하다, 모순되다 hierarchical a. 계층에 따른 by virtue of ~의 힘으로, ~에 의해서 qualified a. 자격을 갖춘

보수주의자들은 평등을 모든 역사적 경험과 모순되는 또 다른 해로운 추상(관념)으로 보았다. 보수주의자들에게 사회는 당연히 계층적이었고, 지능, 교육, 재산, 출생에 의해 일부 사람들은 능력이 부족한 다른 사람들을 지배하고 가르칠 수 있는 가장 좋은 자격이 있다고 그들은 믿었다.

16 2019 가천대 ▶▶▶ MSG p.53 ③

시제의 일치 ▶ ③을 would rid, could not fashion과 같이 과거 시제로 시제 일치시키고, 능력이나 가능성의 의미를 표현하기 위해 could pass로 바꾸어야 한다.

bargain n. 거래, 협상, 흥정 get by 통과시키다 pass v. 백인으로 통하다 for whatever it's worth 그럴만한 일이든 아니든(= whether or not it is of any use/value) compromise n. 타협

내가 나 스스로와 했던 온당한 타협은 조지프(Joseph)처럼 들려서 나를 백인으로 통하게 해주기에 충분한 유수프(Yousuf)라는 이름으로 살기로 한 것이었지만, 나는 백인으로 통할 수 있는 그 어떤 이름으로도 변형시킬 수 없는 무함마드(Mohammad)라는 이름을 아예 없애버리고 싶었다. 그리고 그럴만한 일이든 아니든, 이런 부류의 타협을 하는 사람은 나뿐만이 아니었다.

17 2022 이화여대 ▶▶▶ MSG p.193 ⑤

어순 / 부사의 위치 ▶ 보통 타동사 뒤에 목적어보다 부사구(전명구)가 먼저 오는 경우는 타동사의 목적어가 길 경우이나, ⑤에서는 목적어가 ships로 길지 않으므로 목적어가 먼저 와야 하고, 부사는 동사 앞에 오거나 목적어 뒤에 '짧은 부사 - 긴 부사구'의 순서로 오므로, ⑤를 safely guided ships into the Egyptian harbor for centuries나 guided ships safely into the Egyptian harbor for centuries로 고쳐야 한다.

seven wonders 세계 7대 불가사의 decorative a. 장식적인 temple n. 사원 spiritual a. 영적인 place v. 위치시키다, 자리 잡게 하다 Mediterranean a. 지중해의

18 2022 아주대 ▶▶▶ MSG p.147 ④

불가산명사 ▶ workforce는 불가산명사이므로 단수로 나타내야 한다. 따라서 ④를 the number of people leaving the workforce로 고쳐야 한다. the number는 직역하여 '... 특징은 ... 떠나는 사람들의 수(수가 많다는 것)이다'로 되게 표현했기 때문에 the number이고 만일 a number of people leaving ...이면 is의 보어가 동명사구가 되고 a number of people이 동명사의 의미상 주어가 되는데, 둘 다 의미는 같다. 한편, ①은 앞에 are quitting으로 되어 있어 만일 than they were라면 than they were quitting에서 were quitting을 were로 대신한 것일 테지만, than they did라고 한 것은 than they quit(과거형)에서 quit(과거형)을 대동사 did로 대신한 것이다. 둘 다 가능하다.

be on high alert 높은 경각심을 갖다 disillusioned a. 환멸을 느끼는 grieve v. 상심하다 burn out 에너지를 소진하다 muscle through ~을 헤치고 나아가다 take stock of ~의 품질을 조사하다, 점검하다, ~을 찬찬히 살펴보다 trajectory n. 궤적 attrition n. 소모

오늘날 많은 사람들이 역사적으로 과거와는 다른 이유로 퇴직하고 있으며 조직은 높은 경각심을 갖고 있다. 환멸을 느끼거나, 상심했거나, 에너지를 소진한 많은 직원들에게는, 아무리 보상을 인상 받는다 해도, 끝까지 버텨낼 전망이 지속 가능하게 느껴지지 않는다. 사람들은 자신들의 삶을 점검하고 있으며, 그들의 경력 궤적(직업진로)을 두드러지게 변화시킬 가능성은 그 어느 때보다 높다. 오늘날의 (노동력) 소모의 또 하나의 뚜렷한 특징은 많은 사람들이 노동력을 완전히 떠나서 산업 전반에 걸쳐 노동력 부족을 가속화시킨다는 것이다. (노동의) 수요는 증가하지만 공급은 감소하고 있다.

19 2022 한국항공대 ▶▶▶ MSG p.217 ②

부사의 병치 ▶ ②는 and 앞의 successfully와 함께 performed를 수식하는 역할을 하고 있다. 동사를 수식하는 것은 부사이므로, ②를 reproducibly로 고쳐야 한다.

control n. 대조군 confidence n. 신용; 확신 explosive n. 폭발물 setup n. 장치, 설비 reproducibly ad. 재현 가능한 방식으로, 재현 가능하게 elaborate a. 정교한 institute v. 시작하다; 실시하다; 설립하다 apparatus n. 장치, 기구 lumber n. 목재

생물학 실험에서 대조군의 사용은 현재 보편적으로 받아들여지고 있으나, 이 기법의 더 많은 사용이 바람직할 물리적, 화학적, 의료적, 산업적 연구가 많이 있다. 중요한 모든 변수를 파악해 그것들을 일정하게 유지하는 능력에 대해 잘못된 확신을 가지기는 너무나도 쉬운 일이다. 2차 세계 대전 동안, 이미 수백 번이나 성공적으로 그리고 재현 가능한 방식으로 작동했으며, 그리하여 잘 이해된 것으로 보이는 실험장치 속에서 폭발물에 대한 특정한 절대적인 실험이 시행되었다. 그러나 어느 시점에서, 다소 놀라운 결과가 얻어졌

으며, 오류가 있었음이 대조군을 사용한 추가 실험에서 밝혀졌다. 원인이 되는 변수를 찾기 위해 정교한 조사가 시작되었고, 장치의 틀을 위해 사용할 동일 종류의 목재를 운송한 지 수개월이 지난 후에, 목재상이 이전과는 다른 목재를 실험이 잘못되기 직전에 공급했다는 사실이 마침내 밝혀졌다. 이전의 실험들은 그 틀이 아무런 영향도 끼치지 않는다는 점을 보여 주는 것 같았음에도 불구하고, 이것이 원인이었다. 만약 대조군을 지속적으로 사용했더라면 이 오류를 막았을 것이다.

20   2014 광운대   ▶▶▶ MSG p.125   ③

정비문 ▶ ③은 한 의문문에 있는 두 가지 의문요소가 서로 충돌한다. What do you think of가 '어떻게 생각하니?'의 뜻이므로 think 다음의 which car를 of the car which(관계대명사)로 고치거나, which car(의문형용사+명사)를 '어느 차'라는 의미로 쓰려면 앞의 what은 없애야 하고 which car를 문두로 내어 Which car do you think I finally decided to buy after all?로 고쳐야 한다. Where have you been with whom?(너는 누구와 함께 어디 있었니?)처럼 두 의문요소가 충돌하지 않는 경우도 있다. ① 선행사가 a reason이므로 이유를 나타내는 관계부사 why가 쓰였다. ② 'How often ~?'은 '몇 차례나, 얼마만큼 자주 ~인지'를 묻는 표현이다. 동사 tell의 목적보어로 부정사가 왔는데, 부정사의 부정은 not을 부정사 바로 앞에 써야 하므로 not to do는 적절하다. ④ think 다음에는 접속사 that이 생략되었고 the best way는 그 앞에 전치사 in이 생략된 부사어이다. '최상급명사 one can'은 '최상급명사 possible'과 마찬가지로 '가능한 가장 ~'의 뜻이다. ⑤ 'How come ~?'은 '어째서, 왜'라는 의미로 이유를 물어보는 표현이다. 그 다음은 의문문이어도 주어와 동사가 도치되지 않는다. 또한 'such+a(n)+형용사+명사' 순서로 쓰는 관사의 어순에 따라 such a funny jacket의 어순으로 쓰였다.

extend v. 베풀다, 제공하다   courtesy n. 예의, 친절; 호의   after all 결국, 즉

① 네가 나에게 동일한 호의를 보이지 않는 이유를 말해 주겠니?
② 그걸 그러한 방식으로 하지 말라고 도대체 내가 몇 번이나 말했니?
③ 너는 내가 최종적으로 구매하기로 결정한 차를 어떻게 생각하니?/너는 내가 최종적으로 어느 차를 구매하기로 결정했을 것이라 생각하니?
④ 너는 네가 할 수 있는 최선의 방법으로 그 상황을 다뤘다고 생각하니?
⑤ 어째서 오토바이를 타기 위해 그런 우스꽝스러운 재킷을 입어야 하니?

01 ①	02 ①	03 ②	04 ①	05 ③	06 ①	07 ②	08 ①	09 ④	10 ④
11 ②	12 ①	13 ③	14 ③	15 ③	16 ④	17 ③	18 ②	19 ①	20 ④

01 2015 홍익대 ▶▶▶ MSG p.172 ①

결과의 부사절을 이끄는 such that ▶ 빈칸의 전후에 완전한 절이 위치해 있으므로 이 두 절을 이어줄 접속사가 필요하다. 보기 가운데 접속사의 기능을 하는 것은 ①뿐이다. ②는 '~와 같은'의 의미로 여기서 as는 전치사이다.

warp v. 왜곡시키다 geodesic n. 측지선; 최단 기선(곡면 위 또는 공간 내에서 두 점을 연결하는 선 가운데 길이가 가장 짧은 것) shadow n. 그림자, 그늘 three-dimensional a. 3차원의 as such 그것으로서, 그 자체로는

우리는 태양이 시공간을 크게 왜곡시켜서 그 결과 3차원 공간에서 거의 원의 형태인 그림자를 드리우는 측지선을 따라 지구가 위치하게 된다는 것을 증명하는 데까지는 나아가지 못했다.

02 2020 아주대 ▶▶▶ MSG p.124 ①

양보 부사절 & 가정법 현재 ▶ 'A or B'와 호응하는 것은 Whether이며, 이것은 접속사이므로 뒤에 '주어+동사'의 구조가 와야 한다. 따라서 ①이 정답으로 적절하다. Whether it be A or B는 'A이든 B이든 간에'라는 의미의 가정법 현재 문장으로, 가정법 현재에서 동사는 원형을 쓴다. 참고로, 가정법 현재는 법조문에 주로 나타나지만, 현대영어에서는 직설법 현재로 거의 대체되고 있다. ③ Whether를 생략하고 Be it으로 할 수 있다.

prescription n. 처방전, 처방

베이루트이든 바레인이든, 심지어 디트로이트이든 간에, 당신이 처한 환경이 어떤 조건이든 그 조건에 당신은 음악적 처방을 할 수 있다.

03 2022 서강대 ▶▶▶ MSG p.123 ②

문의 구성 ▶ prove 다음의 that은 접속사이고 photography가 that절의 주어이므로, 빈칸에는 동사로 시작되는 술부인 ②가 적절하다.

photography n. 사진 imitate v. 모방하다 contemporary a. 동시대의

사진이 하나의 예술 형식임을 증명하려고, 초기 사진가들은 처음에는 동시대 화가들의 그림을 모방했다.

04 2021 서울여대 ▶▶▶ MSG p.31, p.222 ①

문의 구성 ▶ 장소의 부사구가 문두에 왔으므로 '자동사+주어'가 와야 하며, 그 뒤에는 수식어구가 이어질 수 있다. 따라서 ①이 정답이 된다. 'is(자동사)+a star(주어)+(which is) called the Sun(수식어구)'이다.

solar system 태양계 star n. 항성

태양계의 중심에는 태양이라 불리는 항성이 있다.

05 2021 서울여대 ▶▶▶ MSG p.31 ③

'make + 목적어 + 목적보어' 구문 ▶ make가 이끄는 5형식 문장을 만드는 게 적절한데, ②가 들어가서 진목적어인 to부정사구를 받는 가목적어 it을 두게 되면 타동사 detect의 목적어가 없게 되어 부적절하다. 따라서 ③이 정답이다. 여기서 them은 viruses를 받고 impossible은 난이형용사로 이것을 수식하는 to부정사 to detect 다음에 목적어가 없는 것이 맞다.

nature n. 속성 detect v. 발견하다, 간파하다

박테리아의 발견과 연구가 이루어진 후에도, 바이러스의 성질은 오랜 세월 동안 그것들(바이러스들)을 발견하기에 불가능한 것으로 만들었다.

06 2021 서울여대 ▶▶▶ MSG p.11, p.55 ①

동사의 태 ▶ account for가 '(부분·비율 등을) 차지하다'라는 의미로 쓰였는데, 빈칸 뒤에 목적어가 주어져 있으므로 능동태여야 하며, 현재의 상태에 대한 내용이므로 시제는 현재가 적절하다.

greenhouse gas 온실가스 emission n. 배출; 배기가스 transportation n. 운송; 교통기관

2019년의 한 연구에 따르면, 미국 전체 온실가스 배출량의 3.3%를 소가 차지하는데 비해, 전기 생산과 운송은 50%를 차지한다.

07 **2021 덕성여대** ▶▶▶ MSG p.58 ②

동사의 형태 ▶ 관계부사 when 앞에 명백한 과거시점의 부사구 in 1926이 있으므로 첫 번째 빈칸에는 과거시제가 쓰여야 하겠는데, 수잔 렝글렌이 돈을 받은 것이므로 수동태 was paid가 적절하다. 한편, 두 번째 빈칸의 경우, 빈칸 다음에 목적어 full recognition이 있고 과거시점 부사구 in 1960이 있으므로, 빈칸에는 received가 적절하다.

player n. 선수 tour n. 관광; 순회공연; (스포츠 팀의) 해외원정

프랑스 선수 수잔 렝글렌(Suzanne Lenglen)이 원정 경기에서 미화 5만 달러를 받았던 1926년에 시작된 프로 테니스 경기는 1960년에서야 완전한 인정을 받았다.

08 **2022 아주대** ▶▶▶ MSG p.11, p.97 ①

올바른 동사의 쓰임 ▶ 동사 benefit은 '~에서 득을 보다'는 의미로 사용될 때 자동사로 사용되고, 전치사 from 또는 by와 함께 사용된다. 그리고 '~와 함께 일하다'는 의미의 work with가 전치사 from의 목적어가 되므로 동명사 형태로 써야 한다.

primary care provider 1차 의료기관 obese a. 비만의 specialize in ~을 전문으로 하다 dietitian n. 영양사

모든 사람이 자신의 1차 의료기관과 좋은 관계를 맺는 것이 중요하지만, 비만인 많은 사람들은 비만 의학을 전문으로 하는 의사와 비만 및 체중 관리를 전문으로 하는 등록된 영양사와 함께 작업함으로써 도움을 받게 될 것이다.

09 **2021 세종대** ▶▶▶ MSG p.227 ④

문의 구성 ▶ 빈칸 뒤에 주절이 완성돼 있으므로 빈칸에는 종속절이나 전치사구 등이 올 수 있다. ③과 ④가 'between A and B' 형태의 전치사구인데, '이용자 주문 방식'라는 의미는 on-demand로 나타내므로 ④가 정답으로 적절하다. 이때 전치사 between은 '~의 사이에'라는 뜻이 아니라 '~이다 ~이다 해서'라는 이유나 원인의 의미로 쓰였다.

enhance v. 향상하다; (능력·매력 따위를) 높이다 on-demand a. 온디맨드[주문]식의(이용자의 요구에 따라 네트워크를 통해 필요한 정보를 제공하는 방식의)

실시간 방송 수업이다 이용자 주문 방식 수업이다 해서, 여러분의 교육을 향상시킬 수 있는 기회는 있다.

10 **2011 서울여대** ▶▶▶ MSG p.211 ④

비교급 뒤의 대동사의 일치 ▶ 비교급 뒤의 대동사는 일반동사일 경우 do동사를, be동사는 be동사로 받아야 한다. taller 앞이 to be로 be동사이므로 ④도 they are로 바뀌어야 한다. ①은 주어가 authors로 복수이므로 복수형 동사 acknowledge가 온 것이며 뒤에 that절이 왔다. ②에 쓰인 'tend to+동사원형'은 '~하는 경향이 있다'라는 뜻이며 주어 women이 복수형이므로 동사 역시 복수형 tend가 쓰였다. ③의 'claim

to+동사원형'은 '~을 (사실이라고) 주장하다'의 뜻이며 men이 복수형이므로 복수형 동사 claim이 쓰였다.

author n. 저자 weigh v. 무게[체중]가 ~이다

작가들은 여자들이 자신의 체중을 실제 체중보다 적게 말하는 경향이 있고 남자들은 실제보다 키가 더 크다고 주장하는 경향이 있다고 인정한다.

11 **2018 세종대** ▶▶▶ MSG p.211 ②

주어와 동사의 수일치 ▶ ② 앞의 의문대명사 which는 'physical activity와 sleep 둘 중 어느 것'의 의미로 단수 취급한다. 따라서 ②를 comes로 고쳐야 한다. ① experts와 we 사이에 목적격 관계대명사 whom이 생략되었고 이것이 전치사 to의 목적어이다. ④ 한정사 다음 형용사들의 순서에서 기수(two)나 서수(second)는 최상급 형용사(most important) 앞에 위치한다.

come first 최우선 고려 사항이다, 가장 먼저다 physical activity 신체활동 component n. 성분, 구성요소

우리가 대화를 해본 전문가들은 어느 것이 먼저인지에 대해서는 의견이 달랐지만, 신체활동과 수면이 건강의 가장 중요한 두 요소라는 데는 모두가 동의했다.

12 **2020 서강대** ▶▶▶ MSG p.147 ①

가산명사의 수 ▶ ①에 쓰인 outlet은 가산명사이므로 앞에 부정관사를 두거나 복수로 써야 한다. 따라서 ①을 were given outlets로 고친다. ② them은 working class voters를 가리킨다.

outlet n. 배출구, 출구 pour v. 쏟아져 나오다, 쇄도하다 concoction n. 혼합, 조합; 날조; 음모, 계획 misanthropy n. 사람을 싫어함, 염세, 인간혐오 nativism n. 선천론, 생득설(生得說); 원주민 보호주의; 토착 문화 부흥[보호]

노동자 계급 유권자들에게 그들의 분노를 표출할 배출구가 주어지자마자, 그들로부터 분노가 쏟아져 나왔다. 포퓰리즘은 인간혐오와 토착주의를 경제 전망에 대한 진심어린 우려와 뒤섞는 복합적인 책략이다.

13 **2012 서강대** ▶▶▶ MSG p.37, p.55 ③

수동태와 능동태의 구분 ▶ raise는 타동사이므로 뒤에는 반드시 목적어가 나와야 한다. 그런데 목적어가 없으므로 수동태가 되어야 하며, '(문제들이) 제기되다'라는 올바른 의미의 문장이 된다. 따라서 ③을 are raised로 고친다.

rely upon ~에 의존하다 intuition n. 직관 regardless of ~에 상관없이

우리들의 실질적인 활동들 중 대부분에 있어서 우리는 우리의 감각에 의존하고 우리가 신뢰할 수 있는 직관들을 개발시킨다. 어떤 중요한 문제들이 제기될 때 다른 사람들이 뭐라 말하든 상관없이 우리의 감각들과 직관들은 행동을 위한 최적의 안내자들이다.

14 **2021 동국대** ▶▶▶ MSG p.105 ③

현재분사와 과거분사의 구분 ▶ 동사 take는 as와 함께 쓰여서 '~을 …로 간주하다'는 뜻으로 쓰이는데, ③ 앞의 관계대명사 who의 선행사는 60세 미만의 일본여성으로, 이들은 하나의 집단으로 간주하는 주체가 아니라 '간주되는 객체'이다. 따라서 ③을 과거분사인 taken으로 고쳐야 하며, 이때 taken 앞에는 being이 생략되었다.

skinny a. 비쩍 마른 lose weight 체중이 줄다

미국과 선진공업국들의 여성들이 점점 뚱뚱해질 때, 대부분의 일본 여성들은 점점 마르고 있다. 더욱 마른 사람들은 60세 미만의 일본 여성인데, 이들은 30년 전에 이미 국제기준으로 말랐고, 하나의 집단으로 볼 때 그 후로도 줄곧 지속적으로 체중이 줄어들고 있다.

15 **2013 한양대** ▶▶▶ MSG p.65 ③

be dedicated to ~ing ▶ be dedicated to의 to는 전치사이므로 그 다음에 동사원형이 올 수 없고 동명사가 와야 한다. 따라서 ③은 creating이 되어야 한다. ① 동네는 경계가 구분이 되는 대상이므로 동사형은 수동태가 되어야 한다. ② '황폐해진 건물'이라는 수동의 뜻이 되어야 하므로 과거분사 dilapidated가 맞다. ④ 현재분사형의 pleasing은 '즐거움을 주는'이라는 능동의 뜻을 나타낸다.

demarcate v. 경계를 표시하다 overlap n. 겹침 dilapidate v. 헐다, 황폐케 하다 graffiti n. (공공장소에서 하는) 낙서 disrepair n. 황폐; 파손 dedicated to ~에 전념하는, 헌신하는 aesthetically ad. 미학적으로, 심미적으로

동네들은 소득 수준에 따라 매우 분명하게 구분되며 겹치는 부분은 많지 않다. 저소득층 사람들은 황폐한 건물, 깨진 유리, 낙서 및 일반적인 파손 상태로 특징지어진 열악한 동네에서 살고 있다. 그곳 사람들은 미적으로 만족스러운 환경을 만드는 데 헌신하지 않는다.

16 **2020 숭실대** ▶▶▶ MSG p.111 ④

문의 구성 ▶ 마지막 문장의 주어는 Hippocrates이고 동사는 believed이다. 그리고 that절이 and에 의해 병치된 문장인데, the humor ~ by the spleen은 "black bile"과 동격을 이루는 삽입구이다. 따라서 too much "black bile"에 연결되는 시제를 가진 동사가 필요하므로 ④를 과거시제 동사 resulted로 고쳐야 한다.

humor n. 기질, 성미, 기분 black bile n. 흑담즙(黑膽汁); 우울 secrete v. 분비하다 spleen n. 비장(脾臟), 지라 melancholia n. 우울증

의사들은 항상 우울증을 일반적인 슬픔과 구별되는 것으로 보아왔지만, 우울증을 일으키는 것과 우울증을 치료하는 최상의 방법은 지난 몇 년 동안 크게 바뀌어왔다. 기원전 5세기에 히포크라테스(Hippocrates)는 육체가 네 개의 기질로 구성되어 있으며, 지라에 의해 분비되는 기질인 "흑담즙"이 너무 많으면 우울증을 초래한다고 생각했다.

17 **2021 숙명여대** ▶▶▶ MSG p.34 ③

지각동사의 목적보어 ▶ 두 번째 문장에서 등위접속사 and 다음에 listen to라는 지각동사가 왔는데, 지각동사의 목적격 보어로는 동사원형이 와야 하므로 ③을 do로 고쳐야 한다.

fashion v. 만들어내다, 변화시키다 hiss n. 쉬[쉿] 하는 소리; 쉭쉭거리는 야유 hum n. 윙윙거리는 소리 squeak n. 끼익[찍] 하는 소리 pop n. 펑[뻥]하는 소리

언어는 우리에게 너무 자연스러운 것이어서 언어가 얼마나 기적적인 선물인지를 쉽게 잊는다. 전 세계에서 우리 종(種)의 구성원들은(사람들은) 그들의 호흡을 쉿 하는 소리(치찰음), 윙윙거리는 소리(공명음), 찍찍거리는 소리(소음음), 펑하는 소리(파열음)로 변화시키며, 다른 사람들이 이와 똑같은 행동을 하는 것을 듣는다. 우리는 그렇게 하는 것은 우리가 그 소리를 좋아해서뿐만 아니라 소리의 세부적인 것들이 소리를 만들어 내는 사람이 가진 의도에 대한 정보를 담고 있기 때문이기도 하다.

18 **2019 건국대** ▶▶▶ MSG p.56 ②

수동태가 불가한 자동사 happen ▶ happen은 수동태로 쓰일 수 없는 자동사이므로, ②는 능동태인 happened가 되어야 한다.

come to an end 끝나다 wonder v. 의아하게 여기다 disastrous a. 재난의

6천5백만 년 전에, 공룡의 시대가 갑자기 끝을 맺게 되었다. 공룡 모두가 지구상에서 사라졌다. 과학자들은 왜 이런 일이 발생했는지 항상 의아하게 여겼다. 멕시코에서의 한 새로운 발견이 그들에게 답을 줄지 모른다. 그 발견은 폭이 180킬로미터에 이르는 하나의 거대한 원이다. 이 원은 아마 지구를 강타한 어떤 매우 큰 물체에 의해 생겨났을지 모른다. 그 물체가 지구를 강타했을 때, 그것은 지구의 기후와 해수면에 변화를 일으켰을지도 모른다. 이러한 변화들이 공룡들에게는 재난이 되었을지도 모른다.

19 **2018 건국대** ▶▶▶ MSG p.137 ①

전치사+관계대명사 ▶ ① which 다음에 완전한 절이 왔으므로 그 앞에 전치사가 필요한데, 선행사로 쓰인 명사 manner는 전치사 in과 함께 주로 쓰이므로, ①을 in which로 고쳐야 한다. ⑤ 앞에 using으로 시작되는 분사구문이 삽입되어 콤마가 생긴 것일 뿐이므로, 관계대명사의 계속적 용법으로 쓰인 that이 아니다.

commercial n. (TV의) 광고 arresting a. 시선을 사로잡는, 아주 매력적인 craft v. 공들여 만들다 signature a. 전형적인; 우수한 restless a. 가만히 못 있는

원격조종장치(리모컨)는 1980년대에 대중화 되었고 그것은 지금까지 사람들이 텔레비전을 보는 방식에 중대한 영향을 미쳤다. 산업 연구원들은 새로운 시청 양태를 빠르게 목격하기 시작했으며, 그들은 이것을 "TV채널 돌리기(grazing)"라고 표현했다. 많은 시청자들은 리모컨을 광고 시청을 피하기 위해 사용한 반면, 다른 시청자들은 전체 프로그램을 다 보지 않고 특정한 채널에 그들을 멈추도록 시선을 사로잡는 이미지나 소리를 찾아가면서 채널을 쉬지 않고 탐색할 줄 알게 되었다. 그 결과, 많은 케이블 방송국은 독특한 로고, 그래픽 디자인 그리고 다른 여러 기술들을 사용하여 독특한 시각적 스타일을 공들여 만들었는데, 이로 인해 그 방송국은 리모컨으로 업그레이드된 텔레비전 시청자들에게 즉시 인지될 수 있게 되었다.

20 2015 한국외대 ▶▶▶ MSG p.74 ④

정비문 ▶ would rather 뒤에 완전한 형태의 절이 오는 경우, 가정법 과거 동사가 와야 하며, 이때 부정 표현은 didn't 혹은 couldn't 등이어야 하므로 ④는 "I would rather you didn't say anything about it at all."로 고쳐야 한다.

productivity n. 생산성 fortunate a. 운 좋은, 다행한

① 그 회사는 생산성을 늘리기 위해 더 많은 것을 해야 하지 않습니까?
② 우리 자신들보다 더 불행한 사람들을 고려하지 않아도 되겠습니까?
③ 나는 잊지 않기 위해 그 전화번호를 적어 두었다.
④ 나는 네가 그것에 대해 아무 것도 말하지 않으면 좋겠다.

01 ②	**02** ④	**03** ④	**04** ①	**05** ④	**06** ①	**07** ③	**08** ①	**09** ②	**10** ①
11 ④	**12** ①	**13** ①	**14** ④	**15** ④	**16** ④	**17** ②	**18** ①	**19** ④	**20** ①

01 **2013 단국대** ▶▶▶ MSG p.124 ②

양보의 부사절을 이끄는 whether ▶ 빈칸 뒤에 절이 왔으므로 빈칸에는 이를 연결해줄 접속사가 필요한데, 문맥상 빈칸 이하가 '보수가 많든 적든 간에'라는 의미의 부사절이 되는 것이 적절하므로 양보의 부사절을 이끄는 ② whether가 정답이다. ① 문법상 빈칸은 선행사를 포함한 관계대명사인 what이 들어가기에 옳지 않은 자리이다. 관계대명사 what은 계속적 용법, 즉 콤마 다음에 쓸 수 없다는 점에서도 정답에서 먼저 제외시킬 수 있다. ③ where를 접속사로 볼 경우 '~의 장소에서, ~곳에서'라는 뜻으로 쓰이므로 그 의미가 적절하지 못하며, 관계부사로 볼 경우에도 앞에 장소를 나타내는 적절한 선행사가 없으므로 부적절하다. ④ how를 접속사로 볼 경우 '~의 방식으로, ~대로(=the way, as)'라는 뜻으로 쓰이므로 그 의미가 적절하지 않다. 관계부사로 볼 경우에도 관계부사 how는 계속적 용법으로 쓰일 수 없으므로 부적절하다.

fairly ad. 상당히 follow v. 뒤를 잇다; (직업에) 종사하다 vocation n. 직업

상당히 많은 소득은 매우 중요한 것이다. 하지만 보수가 많든 적든 간에 사람은 자신에게 가장 적합한 직업에 종사해야 한다는 것이 더욱 중요하다.

02 **2021 서울여대** ▶▶▶ MSG p.221 ④

부정의 부사어구가 문두에 온 도치 ▶ 부정의 부사어구가 문두에 와서 도치가 일어난 문장인데, has는 현재완료에 쓰인 조동사이므로 과거분사 been이 빈칸에 적절하다.

precision n. 정확, 정밀 apparent a. 명백한, 곧 알 수 있는; 겉보기의

수학적 정밀도에 대한 필요성이 컴퓨터 기술 분야에서보다 더 두드러진 곳은 없었다.

03 **2022 서강대** ▶▶▶ MSG p.214 ④

관계사절의 수일치 ▶ 주어는 the East Wing이고 동사는 is characterized이다. 접속사 없이 절이나 술부가 이어질 수 없으므로 ①과 ③은 제외되고, 선행사 shapes가 복수명사이므로 관계절의 동사를 are로 한 ④가 적절하다.

wing n. (건물 본관 한쪽으로 돌출되게 지은) 동(棟)[부속 건물] geometric a. 기하학적인

I. M. 페이(Pei)가 설계한 워싱턴 DC에 있는 국립미술관의 동관건물은 그의 작품을 대표하는 불규칙한 기하학적 형태라는 특징을 가지고 있다.

04 **2021 세종대** ▶▶▶ MSG p.211 ①

주어와 동사의 수일치 ▶ ② stallion은 가산명사이므로 단수로 쓰면 부정관사를 동반해야 한다. ③ 복수명사 앞에 부정관사가 올 수 없다. ④ 주어가 war horses이므로 복수동사가 와야 하며 보어 역시 복수명사여야 한다. 따라서 ①이 정답이 된다.

specialist n. 전문가 insist v. 주장하다; 강조하다 stallion n. 종마(種馬), 씨말

한 전쟁 전문가는 그 전투에 참가한 모든 군마는 종마(種馬)여야 했다고 주장했다.

05 **2020 세종대** ▶▶▶ MSG p.95 ④

'too ~ to …' 구문 ▶ 'too ~ to …' 구문에서 to 뒤에는 동사원형이 온다. 그러므로 ③을 정답에서 먼저 제외할 수 있다. 한편, ①과 ②처럼 to fear이면 to fear의 의미상 주어가 you여서 holding you back을 목적어로 취하기에 부적절해진다. 그러나 ④처럼 to let이면 '공포로 하여금 당신을 억제하게 하다'는 뜻으로 적절해진다. 따라서 ④가 정답이 되며, 사역동사 let 다음은 명사 fear가 목적어로 왔고 원형동사 hold 이하가 목적보어로 온 것이다. 그리고 앞의 to experience는 'too ~ to …' 구문에 쓰인 to부정사가 아니라 amazing things를 수식하는 역할을 하고 있음에 유의한다.

amazing a. 놀랄 정도의, 굉장한 hold ~ back ~을 저지[방해]하다

경험해야 할 놀라운 것들이 너무나 많아서 당신은 결코 공포로 하여금 당신을 억제하게 할(공포에 억제당해 가만히 있을) 수가 없다.

06 **2021 세종대** ▶▶▶ MSG p.212 ①

half의 용법 ▶ half, all, both 등은 'half/all/both+(of)+한정사+명사'의 형태로 쓴다. ①이 이것에 부합하는 형태다. 이때 well over는 half를 수식하는 역할을 한다. ② new job이 수식어구 in the United States에 의해 한정되고 있으므로 그 앞에는 정관사가 와야 하고 복수명사여야 한다.

account for (~의) 비율을 차지하다; ~의 원인이 되다

1980년대 후반, 미국에서 새로 생겨난 일자리들 중 절반 훨씬 이상은 무역이 증가한 데 따른 것이었다.

07 2021 세종대 ▶▶▶ MSG p.140 ③

문의 구성 ▶ 선행사 confidence가 주어져 있으므로 자체에 선행사를 포함하고 있는 관계대명사 what을 쓸 수 없다. 따라서 ①, ②를 정답에서 먼저 제외할 수 있다. 선행사와 주어 they 사이에 목적격 관계대명사가 생략되었고, 동사 need 다음에 목적어 자리가 비어있는 ③이 빈칸에 적절하다. 여기서 excel은 자동사로 쓰였다.

confidence n. 신뢰; 자신감 excel v. 뛰어나다, 출중하다, 탁월하다

함께 사용하도록 기획된 그 책들은 네 가지 기술을 다루면서 학생들이 그들의 교육에서 뛰어나기 위해 필요로 하는 자신감을 키우도록 도와준다.

08 2021 세종대 ▶▶▶ MSG p.113 ①

분사의 용법 ▶ 자동차가 타동사 snatch와 chase의 대상이므로 수동을 나타내는 과거분사 형태가 되어야 하며, 불꽃이 lick하는 행위의 주체이므로 능동을 나타내는 현재분사를 써야 한다. 따라서 ①이 정답이다. 해당 문장은 A car came racing up the hill, and it was snatched and chased by licking flames.에서 and 이하를 분사구문으로 나타낸 문장이다.

surreal a. 초현실적인, 기상천외의 snatch v. 와락 붙잡다, 움켜쥐다, 잡아채다 chase v. 쫓다, 추적하다 lick v. 핥다

어둠이 깔리면서 현장은 점점 더 초현실적으로 되었다. 자동차 한 대가 널름거리는 불꽃에 붙잡힐 듯 쫓기면서 언덕을 질주하여 올라왔다.

09 2009 세종대 ▶▶▶ MSG p.194 ②

명사를 수식하는 형용사 ▶ ①과 ④는 형용사로 쓰인 enough가 수식받는 명사 moisture 앞에 와야 한다. ③에서 take place는 happen과 같은 자동사여서 목적어를 취할 수 없다. ②가 정답이며 for growth는 부정사의 의미상의 주어로 쓰인 것이다.

existence n. 존재, 실제 vegetation n. 초목, 식물 moisture n. 수분 take place 일어나다, 발생하다

연중 대부분의 기간에 물이 아니라 얼음이 존재한다는 것은 초목들이 성장하기에 충분한 수분을 가지지 못한다는 것을 의미한다.

10 2014 한국외대 ▶▶▶ MSG p.139 ①

명사 extent와 함께 쓰는 전치사 ▶ 타동사 reject의 목적어로 their authentic natures가 이미 주어져 있으므로, '의문형용사+명사'의 형태인 What extent의 문법적인 역할이 없는 상태이다. 한편, 명사 extent는 '~의 한도까지', '~까지'의 의미로 쓸 때 전치사 to와 쓰므로, ①을 To what extent로 고치면, what extent 부분이 전치사 To의 목적어가 되어 앞서 언급한 문제가 해결된다. ③ 목적의 의미를 나타내는 부사적 용법으로 쓰인 부정사이다. ④ how이하의 간접의문절이 전치사 for의 목적어가 되는 구조이다.

extent n. 정도; 범위, 한계; 넓이 authentic a. 믿을 만한, 확실한

여성은 어느 정도까지 자신의 본모습을 의식적으로 버리고서 여성이 어떻게 보여야 하는가에 대한 남성 중심의 기대를 따르는 것일까?

11 2018 서강대 ▶▶▶ MSG p.214 ④

관계대명사의 수일치 ▶ 관계대명사의 수는 선행사에 일치시킨다. ④의 앞에 있는 관계대명사 which의 선행사는 electrodes로서 복수명사이다. 그러므로 ④를 stimulate로 고쳐야 한다.

paralyze v. 마비시키다 feat n. 공훈, 위업 electrode n. 전극 implant v. 심다, 이식하다 stimulate v. 자극하다 muscle n. 근육

그 마비 환자는 용케도 자신의 손으로 음식을 먹었다. 이런 놀라운 성과는 부분적으로 그의 오른팔에 이식되어 근육들을 자극하는 전극들 덕분이다.

12 2020 서강대 ▶▶▶ MSG p.227 ①

free of ▶ '~이 없는', '~이 면제된'이라는 의미의 표현을 할 때 free 뒤에 전치사 of를 쓴다. ①을 free of charge로 고친다.

labor of love 사랑의 수고, 봉사 활동 marble n. 대리석 statue n. 상(像)

그 예술가는 "사랑의 수고"로서 그것을 무상으로 설계했다. 1918년에 모델이 발표되었지만, 완성은 그 상(像)을 만드는 데 필요한 이탈리아의 대리석을 구할 수 있게 된 전쟁이 끝난 이후까지 보류됐다.

13 2021 성균관대 ▶▶▶ MSG p.114 ①

분사구문의 주어와 주절의 주어의 일치 ▶ 분사구문의 생략된 주어는 주절의 주어 I이며, 이것은 look back하는 행위의 주체이므로 능동을 나타내는 현재분사를 써야 한다. ①의 Looked를 Looking으로 고친다.

be struck by ~에 깜짝 놀라다 pronounce v. (소리 내어) 말하다 civilization n. 문명

내가 40대 중반에 썼던 글들을 지금 돌이켜보면 대체로 문명의 성격과 문화의 발전 방식과 같은 문제들에 대해 내가 얼마나 많은 확신을 갖고 말했는지 깜짝 놀라게 된다.

14 2012 이화여대 ▶▶▶ MSG p.105 ④

현재분사와 과거분사의 구분 ▶ 현재분사에는 진행과 능동의 의미가, 과거분사에는 수동과 완료의 의미가 있다. 주어진 문장에서 new forms of electronic commerce가 allow하는 주체이므로 양자는 서로 능동 관계이고, 뒤에 목적어와 목적보어가 이어지므로 ④를 현재분사 allowing으로 고쳐 수식해야 한다. ② where는 계속적 용법으로 쓰인 관계부사이며, 뒤에 완전한 형태의 절이 온 것을 통해 옳게 쓰인 것을 확인할 수 있다.

arena n. 활동 무대, (경쟁의) 장(場) gap n. 격차 progressively ad. 계속적으로 order v. 주문하다

광고주들은 인터넷을 상업적 표현을 하는 데 있어 매우 중요하면서도 새로운 장(場)으로 인식해왔는데, 인터넷에서는 화면에서 상품을 직접 주문할 수 있게 해주는 새로운 형태의 전자거래를 사용함으로써 판촉과 구입 사이의 괴리를 점진적으로 없앨 수 있다.

15 2020 숙명여대 ▶▶▶ MSG p.218 ④

동명사의 병치 ▶ 타동사 prohibit은 '~하는 것을 금하다'는 의미로 사용될 때 동명사를 목적어로 취한다. 병치 구조임을 나타내는 접속사 or 다음의 ④는 앞서 나온 prohibit의 목적어 acting, advertising과 병치를 이루어야 하므로 transplanting이 되어야 한다. 한편, ①은 makes의 가목적어, ②는 진목적어이다.

criminal offense 형사 범죄 organ n. (인체 내의) 장기[기관] arrangement n. 주선 transplant v. 이식하다 donor n. 기증자

새로운 영국 법은 살아있는 사람이나 죽은 사람의 장기를 공급하는 대가로 돈을 주거나 받는 것을 형사 범죄로 규정하고 있다. 그 법은 또한 이런 일을 주선하는 브로커 역할을 하는 것이나, 장기를 판다고 광고를 하는 것이나, 환자의 가까운 친척이 아닌 살아있는 기증자의 장기를 환자에게 이식하는 것을 금지한다.

16 2021 홍익대 ▶▶▶ MSG p.212 ④

부분표시어 + 한정사 + 명사 ▶ most of, some of, many of 등의 부분표시어 뒤에 명사가 오는 경우, 그 명사 앞에는 반드시 한정사가 있어야 한다. 따라서 ④ structures를 the structures로 고쳐야 한다.

occupant n. 점유자, 거주자 alteration n. 변경, 개조 prowess n. 훌륭한 솜씨, 기량 aesthetic a. 미학적인 mundane a. 현세의, 세속적인 suburbia n. 교외 거주자

우리는 건축물이 점유자에게 맞춰나가기보다 점유자가 건축물에 맞춰나갈 것을 종종 요구하며, 기존의 계획에 대한 사소한 변경조차도 건축학적인 기량의 발로라고 찬양한다. 비록 최고의 건축가는 표준적인 구성요소를 구조적으로, 미학적으로 최대한 구현할 수 있지만, 우리가 짓고 있는 건축물들 중 대부분은 가장 세속적인 교외지역 거주자들을 위한 것이다.

17 2021 이화여대 ▶▶▶ MSG p.211 ②

의미의 적절성 / 동사의 수일치 ▶ 과거의 과학자들이 체지방을 oily storage compartment라고 여겼다고 했으므로, ②에서 pretty much active는 반대로 pretty much inert이어야 하고, 주어가 body fat and the cells 이므로 동사는 was가 아니라 were여야 한다. ②를 were pretty much inert로 고친다.

oily a. 기름기의 compartment n. 구획, 칸(기차 등의) potent a. 강력한 stuff n. 물건, 물질 secrete v. 분비하다 endocrine organ n. 내분비 기관 compare A to B A를 B에 비유하다, A와 B가 같다고 여기다 gland n. 분비선, 샘 thyroid n. 갑상선 pituitary n. 뇌하수체

과학자들은 과거에는 체지방과 체지방을 이루는 세포가 불활성 상태에 있는, 그저 기름 저장 덩어리라고 생각했다. 그러나 과거 10년이 채 안 되는 기간의 연구가 보여준 바에 따르면, 지방세포는 화학 공장처럼 작동하며, 체지방은 강력한 물질로서, 호르몬과 근본적이고 때로는 해로운 영향을 끼치는 다른 물질들을 분비하는 고도로 능동적인 조직이다. 최근 몇 년 동안 생물학자들은 지방을 "내분비 기관"이라 부르면서, 혈류 속으로 호르몬을 직접 방출하는 갑상선이나 뇌하수체와 비슷하다고 여기기에 이르렀다.

18 2020 한국항공대 ▶▶▶ MSG p.105 ①

과거분사와 현재분사의 비교 ▶ 문장 전체의 주어는 the behaviour of a flock인데, 행동은 고려되는 대상이므로 ①은 수동의 의미를 나타내도록 과거분사 Taken이 되어야 한다.

collectively ad. 집단적으로, 전체적으로 choreograph v. 안무하다 loop n. 고리 whorl n. 나선 assertion n. 주장, 단언

복잡성 이론을 설명하기 위해 종종 제시되는 예는 새떼의 행동이다. 집단적으로 고려하면, 새떼의 행동은 안무가 잘 짜여 있고, 목적이 있는 것처럼 보인다. 새떼는 장애물을 피하고, 먹이 위를 선회하고, 지구를 반 바퀴 도는 이동을 하면서도, 하늘에서 온갖 종류의 고리와 나선형을 만들어 보일 수 있지만, 명백한 중심적 통제자는 없다. 복잡성 이론은 새떼가 펼쳐 보이고 우리가 목격하는 이 세계적 활동이 개별 새들의 단순한 상호작용에서 발생한다는 주장에 근거하여 이러한 행동을 설명한다.

19 2022 명지대 ▶▶▶ MSG p.222 ④

'only+부사어'에 의한 도치 ▶ only가 들어있는 부사어가 문두에 올 경우, 의문문형 도치가 일어난다. 따라서 ④를 will we be able to로 고쳐야 한다.

cognitive a. 인지의 reason v. 판단하다 interconnected a. 상호 연결된 avenue n. 길; 방법 stretch back to ~까지 거슬러 올라가다 symbiosis n. 공생 exploding a. 폭발적으로 증가하는

우리는 인지 컴퓨팅의 시대에 살고 있다. 기계는 데이터를 계산하고 조직하는 것보다 훨씬 더 많은 일을 해낼 수 있다. 즉 기계는 학습하고, 판단하고, 사람들과 새로운 방식으로 교류한다. 이 시대에 인간과 기계는 더욱 상호 연결될 것이다. 어떻게 인간과 컴퓨터가 연결되어 이전에 인간 혹은 컴퓨터가 해왔던 것보다 더 지능적으로 공동 행동을 할 수 있을까? 이런 생각은 『인간

-컴퓨터 공생』이라는 1960년의 논문으로 거슬러 올라가는데, 이 논문은 "인간의 두뇌와 컴퓨팅 머신은 함께 결합되면 오늘날 우리가 알고 있는 컴퓨터가 접근해보지 못한 방식으로 생각하게 될 것이다"라고 예측했다. 오직 스마트 머신의 도움이 있어야 비로소 우리는 폭발적으로 증가하는 오늘날 세계의 복잡성을 적절히 다룰 수 있을 것이다.

---

20   **2018 한국외대** ▶▶▶ MSG p.193   ①

정비문 ▶ 빈도부사 rarely는 본동사의 앞에, be동사의 뒤에, 그리고 조동사와 본동사의 사이에 위치하는데, ①에서 and 다음의 does가 본동사이므로 does앞에 rarely가 위치해야 한다. 따라서 rarely does cleaning으로 고쳐야 옳은 문장이 된다. 부정부사 rarely를 강조할 경우 문두에 오는 것이 가능한데, 이 경우 도치가 일어나므로 ②는 올바른 문장이다.

wash the dishes 설거지를 하다   speak one's mind 속마음을 털어놓다
ridicule v. 조롱하다   national holiday 국경일

① 그는 설거지를 거의 하지 않으며 청소도 거의 하지 않는다.
② 십대들이 그들의 부모에게 완전히 솔직한 경우는 거의 없다.
③ 그 학생은 조롱을 당할까봐 두려워 속마음을 털어놓고 이야기하지 않았다.
④ 그 학교는 주말이나 국경일에는 거의 문을 열지 않는다.

01 ②	02 ③	03 ③	04 ①	05 ④	06 ③	07 ③	08 ②	09 ④	10 ②
11 ②	12 ⑤	13 ①	14 ④	15 ②	16 ③	17 ①	18 ⑤	19 ④	20 ④

01 2008 성신여대 ▶▶▶ MSG p.128 ②

이유의 부사절을 이끄는 접속사 as ▶ 뒤에 완전한 형태의 문장이 이어지고 있으므로, 빈칸에는 접속사가 쓰여야 한다. '보어+as+주어+be동사'는 양보나 이유를 나타내는 절인데, 여기서는 이유를 나타낸다. 따라서 ② as가 적절하다.

breathe v. (숨을) 내쉬다, 호흡하다 polite a. 예의 바른, 정중한

미국인들은, 사람의 얼굴에 대고 숨을 내뿜지 않도록 교육받기 때문에, 예의를 차리려는(상대방의 얼굴에 숨을 내쉬지 않으려는) 행동에서 자동적으로 부끄러움(미안한 감정)을 전하게 된다.

02 2021 단국대 ▶▶▶ MSG p.53 ③

시제 일치 ▶ 빈칸에 들어갈 동사는 관계대명사절의 삽입절에 쓰인 것인데, 많은 사람들이 부모가 자신들로부터 가족을 빼앗아갔다고 '생각하는' 시점은 부모를 향한 분노를 '설명하는' 시점과 동일해야 하므로, 주절과 같은 과거시제여야 한다. 따라서 ③이 정답으로 적절하다.

grip v. 꽉 쥐다; (마음 따위를) 끌다, 사로잡다 unforgiving a. 용서하지 않는, 용서 없는 fury n. 격노, 격분 deprive v. ~에게서 빼앗다

많은 사람들이 자신들로부터 가정과 가족을 빼앗아갔다고 생각되는 부모를 향해 용서할 수 없는 분노에 사로잡혀 있다고 설명했다.

03 2009 세종대 ▶▶▶ MSG p.93 ③

타동사의 목적어 역할을 하는 대부정사 ▶ want는 타동사이므로 목적어 역할을 하는 대부정사가 필요하며, 이때 to 뒤에 stop in and read the books가 생략되어 있는 것이다.

set up 설립하다 stop in ~에 잠시 들르다, 방문하다

프랭클린(Franklin)의 훌륭한 생각들 중 하나는 사람들이 책을 공유할 수 있는 클럽을 설립하는 것이었다. 원하는 사람은 누구든지 잠시 들러서 책을 읽을 수 있었다.

04 2020 세종대 ▶▶▶ MSG p.219 ①

비교 구문에서의 병치 구조 ▶ as common을 통해 as ~ as 동급 비교 구문이 되어야 함을 알 수 있다. 그런데 비교 구문에서 비교되는 대상들은 그 문법적인 구조나 역할이 같아야 한다. 주어진 문장의 as 뒤에 '전치사 + 명사' 형태의 in newspapers가 있으므로, as 뒤에 동일한 형태가 제시돼 있는 ①이 빈칸에 적절하다.

frequent a. 자주 일어나는, 빈번한 genre n. 양식, 장르

다음 표들은 나머지 4개 장르보다 신문에서 적어도 3배나 흔하게 나오는 가장 빈도가 높은 단어들을 보여준다.

05 2021 한국산업기술대 ▶▶▶ MSG p.212, p.137 ④

관계대명사 ▶ 완결된 절 다음에 빈칸부터 또 절이 이어지는데 ①, ②, ③은 모두 절과 절을 연결해주는 접속사가 없어 부적절하다. 따라서 접속사의 역할을 하는 관계대명사 which가 있는 ④가 정답으로 적절하다.

Food and Drug Administration 식품의약청 liver n. 간 kidney n. 신장 pancreas n. 췌장

식품의약청에 의하면, 건강한 사람은 하루에 오직 2그램의 크레아틴이 필요한데, 그 중 절반은 몸 안에서 간, 신장, 췌장에 의해 만들어진다.

06 2021 한국산업기술대 ▶▶▶ MSG p.221 ③

도치, 시제 ▶ 'not only ~ but (also) …' 구문에서 부정 부사구인 not only가 해당 절의 맨 앞에 위치하면, 뒤따르는 주어와 동사가 도치되어야 한다. 또한 but 이하에서 과거완료 시제가 쓰였으므로, 빈칸에 들어갈 동사도 과거완료 시제여야 한다. 따라서 ③ not only had I written 이 정답으로 적절하다.

at one time 한꺼번에, 동시에

다음날 아침에 나는 잠에서 깨어나 그 낱말들에 대해 생각해보았는데, 내가 한 번에 그토록 많은 글을 썼을 뿐 아니라 세상에 있는지도 몰랐던 낱말들을 썼다는 것을 깨닫고는 대단히 자랑스러웠다.

07 **2021 세종대** ▶▶▶ MSG p.73 ③

올바른 종속절의 형태 ▶ '마치 ~처럼'의 의미를 가진 as if 뒤에 가정법 동사 were를 쓴 ③이 정답이다. 나머지는 모두 관계대명사의 격이나 수가 바르지 않으며 의미상으로도 어색하다.

take care of ~을 돌보다 parent n. 부모

이제 그녀는 마치 자신이 아버지의 부모이기라도 한 것처럼 아버지를 돌봐 드려야 한다.

08 **2021 세종대** ▶▶▶ MSG p.135 ②

수식어구 ▶ 문장의 주어는 document이고 동사는 is이므로 빈칸부터 Geoffrey Chaucer까지는 주어를 수식하는 역할을 해야 한다. 따라서 주격 관계대명사절을 만드는 ②가 정답으로 적절하다. ① 이미 정동사 is가 있으므로 정동사 bears가 다시 올 수 없다. ③ 주어를 수식하는 현재분사 bearing을 쓴 것은 옳으나, 정관사 the와 지시형용사 that을 나란히 쓸 수 없다. ④ bear가 '(이름·칭호 등을) 지니다'라는 의미의 타동사로 쓰였으므로 목적어 앞에 전치사가 필요하지 않다.

fragmentary a. 파편의; 조각조각난 household account book 가계부 date v. ~의 연대를 추정하다 bear v. (이름·칭호 등을) 지니다

제프리 초서(Geoffrey Chaucer)의 이름이 들어 있는 알려진 최초의 문서는 1356년에서 1359년 사이의 것으로 추정되는 조각난 가계부다.

09 **2006 세종대** ▶▶▶ MSG p.33, p.123 ④

사역동사 make의 쓰임 & 접속사 that ▶ 사역동사 make는 목적보어로 동사원형을 취하므로 우선 ②는 제외된다. 그리고 ①과 ③의 경우 관계대명사 which 뒤에 완전한 절이 오게 되므로 which의 문법적인 역할을 설명할 수 없게 된다. 따라서 ④가 적절하다.

identical a. 동일한 blanket n. 담요 uproot v. 뿌리째 뽑다, 몰아내다

우리의 집이 없어지고 우리의 삶이 뿌리째 뽑혔을지라도, 아주 똑같은 담요를 보자 나는 그 담요가 쉽게 우리 가족이 될 수도 있었을 거라는 것을 깨달았다.

10 **2015 한국외대** ▶▶▶ MSG p.139 ②

선행사를 포함한 관계대명사 ▶ 전치사(from) 다음에 접속사 that절이 올 수 없고, ② that 이하는 ③ 다음에 목적어 자리가 비어 있고 the worst hangover가 목적보어인 구조이며, ② that 앞에 선행사가 없으므로, ②를 선행사를 포함한 목적격의 관계대명사인 what으로 고쳐야 한다.

hangover n. 잔존물, 유물; 숙취(宿醉); (약의) 부작용

그 남자는 의학계가 최근 역사에서 가장 고약한 숙취로 여길지 모르는 것(숙취)으로 고생하고 있었던 것으로 드러났다.

11 **2021 단국대** ▶▶▶ MSG p.178, p.198 ②

nothing과 anything의 용법 구분 ▶ nothing은 자체에 부정의 뜻이 담겨 있으므로 다른 부정어와 함께 쓰지 않는다. ②의 앞에 부정어 not이 있으므로 nothing이 아닌 anything을 써야 한다. ②를 doing anything으로 고친다.

support oneself 자립하다, 자활하다 full time 전업으로, 전 시간 근무하여

자립하기 위해, 예술가들은 종종 가르치는 것과 단지 전업으로 예술작품을 만들어 돈을 버는 일만 하는 것 사이에서 선택을 해야 한다.

12 **2021 숙명여대** ▶▶▶ MSG p.105 ⑤

현재분사와 과거분사의 구분 ▶ which 관계절 안의 images는 찍는 행위의 주체가 아닌 대상이므로, ⑤는 수동을 나타내는 과거분사 taken이 되어야 한다.

observatory n. 관측소, 천문대 elevated a. (주변이나 지면보다) 높은, 고가(高架)의 light pollution 광공해(가로등 같은 인공조명이 너무 많아 별빛을 볼 수 없는 것과 같은 상황) contend with (곤란한 문제나 상황과) 씨름하다 atmospheric turbulence 대기 난류(大氣亂流) vantage point (무엇을 지켜보기에) 좋은 위치

지상 천문대는 일반적으로 광공해가 거의 없는 높은 지역에 위치하지만, 대기 난류와 씨름해야 하며, 이는 이런 좋은 위치에서 찍힌 이미지들의 선명도를 제한한다(떨어뜨린다).

13 **2021 중앙대** ▶▶▶ MSG p.37 ①

자동사와 타동사의 구분 ▶ ①의 arose는 자동사 arise의 과거형인데 fear라는 목적어가 뒤에 있으므로 타동사 raised로 바꾸어야 한다.

disruption n. 혼돈, 혼란 panic buying 패닉 바잉(공황으로 인한 사재기 열풍), rattle v. 덜컹거리게 하다 run out of ~가 부족해지다

팬데믹의 갑작스러운 혼란이 영국 슈퍼마켓에서 사재기에 대한 두려움을 증가시켰는데, 알 수 없는 신종 바이러스에 의해 이미 뒤흔들린 이 나라가 이제는 크리스마스 전에 신선한 식품이 부족해질까를 걱정해야 했다.

14 **2022 단국대** ▶▶▶ MSG p.135 ④

문의 구성 ▶ 한 문장에 접속사 없이 두 개의 동사(supported, required)가 올 수 없으므로, required 앞에 development schemes를 선행사로 하는 주격 관계대명사가 필요하다. 따라서 ④ required를 that required로 고쳐야 한다.

allocate v. 할당하다 tropical rain forest 열대 우림 deforestation n. 삼림 벌채 finance v. ~에 자금을 공급하다 clear v. (토지 등을) 개간하다, 개척하다

열대 우림에 속하는 지구 표면의 양은 이미 그 원래 면적의 절반 이하로 줄어들었는데, 왜냐하면 최근까지 세계은행은 삼림 개간을 필요로 하는 개발 계획을 위한 자금 대출로 삼림 벌채를 지원했기 때문이다.

15 2021 홍익대 ▶▶▶ MSG p.55 ②

수동태 ▶ a government policy는 실행의 주체가 아니라 실행의 대상이므로 ② puts into는 능동태가 아니라 수동태로 되어야 한다. 따라서 puts into가 is put into로 되어야 하겠지만, 앞 절에서 should be가 쓰였으므로 should be put into로 고치거나 should be를 생략하고 put into로 고쳐야 한다.

representative n. 대표자; 하원의원 put into practice 실행하다 civil disobedience 시민 불복종

민주적으로 선출된 대표자들 중 대다수가 특별한 법이 제정되어야 한다거나 어떤 정부의 정책이 실행되어야 한다고 표결로 정하면, 그러면 이에 대한 항의로 법을 위반하는 것은 민주주의 정신에 위배되는 것 같으며, 특히 극소수의 시민들이 시민 불복종 행동에 참여하고 있는 경우는 더욱 그러하다.

16 2021 숙명여대 ▶▶▶ MSG p.47 ③

현재완료시제 ▶ 두 번째 문장의 시제는 현재완료시제인데, 현재완료는 'have+과거분사(pp)'의 형태를 가진다. has 다음에 not only가 삽입돼 있는 것이며, 따라서 그 뒤에는 become의 과거시제 동사인 became이 아니라 과거분사인 become이 와야 한다. ③을 과거분사 become으로 고친다.

e-commerce n. 전자상거래 retailer n. 소매업자, 소매상

제프 베조스(Jeff Bezos)가 1994년 Amazon을 설립했을 때, 아마존은 온라인 서점으로 시작했다. 그러나 지난 26년 동안, 이 회사는 북미에서 가장 큰 전자상거래 소매업체가 되었을 뿐만 아니라 또한 다른 시장으로도 사업을 확대했다. 그리고 그 다양성이 아마존의 가장 큰 강점 중 하나였다.

17 2021 숙명여대 ▶▶▶ MSG p.191 ①

동사를 수식하는 부사 ▶ 동사를 수식할 수 있는 것은 부사이므로 ①을 mistakenly로 고쳐야 한다.

generalize v. 일반화하다 downright ad. 철저하게, 아주, 완전히 nasty a. 끔찍한, 형편없는 fallacious a. 잘못된, 틀린 leap n. 뜀, 도약; (논리 따위의) 비약

우리는 단 한 번의 경험으로 특정 회사에 대해 잘못되게 일반화를 한 사람들을 알고 있다. 특정 문화권 출신의 사람들에 대한 고정관념은 널리 만연해있고 일반적으로 잘못된 것이다. 외국 문화에 대한 성급한 일반화는 완전히 고약한 것일 수 있으며, 미미한 증거를 근거로 하여 포괄적인 일반화로 잘못 비약하는 것을 보여주는 좋은 예이다.

18 2020 이화여대 ▶▶▶ MSG p.217 ⑤

병치구조 ▶ rather than 전후에 오는 표현은 그 문법적인 구조나 역할이 같아야 한다. ⑤와 관련하여 쓰인 rather than 앞에 '동사+목적어'의 구조인 trade resource가 주어져 있으므로, rather than 이하도 동일한 형태여야 한다. 따라서 ⑤에서 that they를 삭제하여 build trust만 남겨야 한다.

civilian a. 일반인의, 민간의 executive n. 간부, 경영진, 임원 resort to ~에 의지하다 collaboration n. 협력, 제휴 compromise n. 타협, 화해, 양보 minimize v. 최소화하다

민간 지도자들과 군사 지도자들 모두 저자들이 "위험한 협상"이라 부르는 것에 직면해 있는데, 이 협상에는 곳곳에 함정이 도사리고 있으면서도 훌륭한 조언은 부족하다. 중역마다 그리고 장교마다 위험의 근원은 상당히 다르지만, 그들은 같은 종류의 행동에 의존한다. 양자(兩者) 모두 빠른 진전을 이뤄내야 한다는 압박을 느끼고, 힘과 통제력을 발휘하고, 협조보다는 힘에 의존하며, 신뢰를 쌓기보다는 협력을 얻기 위해 자원을 거래하고, 잠재적 피해를 최소화하기 위해 원치 않는 타협을 한다.

19 2017 이화여대 ▶▶▶ MSG p.116 ④

with 분사구문 ▶ 'with+명사+분사'는 이른바 'with 분사구문'으로, 부대상황을 나타내는 표현이다. 이때 명사와 능동 관계일 때에는 현재분사를 쓰고 수동관계를 나타낼 때에는 과거분사를 쓴다. 주어진 문장에서, 'with the figures of the town sheriff, his posse of honest men, and US marshals featured prominently' 부분은 with 분사구문인데, 이때 목적어인 the figures of the town sheriff, his posse of honest men, and US marshals가 feature하는 행위의 주체이므로 능동관계이다. 따라서 목적어 뒤에 현재분사를 써야 한다. ④를 featuring으로 고친다.

sparsely ad. 드문드문하게; (인구 따위가) 희박하게 inhospitable a. 대접이 나쁜; 무뚝뚝한, 황량한 tribe n. 부족, 종족 settlement n. 정착, 개척지 deprive v. ~에게서 빼앗다, 박탈하다 western n. 서부극, 서부음악 sheriff n. 군(郡) 보안관 marshal n. 연방 보안관 feature v. 중요한 역할을 하다; (영화에) 주연하다 prominently ad. 두드러지게

대평원은 수십 년 동안 인구가 희박한 상태로 있었으며, 물이 거의 없고 호전적인 인디언 부족들이 있어서 사람이 살기 힘든 사막 지대로 간주됐다. 대체로, 대평원은 1861~1865년의 남북전쟁이 끝난 후에야 백인들이 정착하게 되었는데, 이 시기에 대평원에 살던 인디언들은 점차 정복당해, 마침내는 그들의 땅 대부분을 정착민들에게 빼앗겼다. 축산업과 광산에 종사하는 사회가 발전함에 따라 도시도 성장하게 되었다. 그 같은 여러 장소에서 법·질서 체계를 부과하는 것은 주된 관심사가 되었고, 여러 서부극에서 또 다른 주된 테마가 되어, 마을의 보안관, 정직한 남자들로 구성돼 있던 그의 추적대, 연방 보안관 등과 같은 인물들이 두드러지게 중요한 역할을 맡았다. 1870년경에는, 대평원의 일부 지역만이 정착되지 않은 상태라고 설명될 수 있었다.

20 2022 한국외대 ▶▶▶ MSG p.61 ④

정비문 ▶ ④에서 looking at의 목적어 it은 주어인 Her new book을 가리키므로 삭제해야 한다. ① 'be ready to부정사' 구문에서 to부정사의 목적어가 문장의 주어와 같을 때 to부정사의 목적어는 쓰지 않는다. inspect 다음에 it이 있으면 틀린다. ② an argument which is rather difficult to refute와 같으므로 난이 형용사 difficult 다음 to 부정사의 목적어가 없는 것이 맞다. rather는 'rather+a+형용사+명사'의 형태가 일반적이지만, 'a+rather+형용사+명사'의 형태도 가능하다. ③ 형용사 long 다음 to부정사의 목적어가 주어인 The report와 같으므로 to read 다음에 목적어가 없는 것이 맞다.

inspect v. 조사하다, 검사하다 refute v. 논박하다, 반박하다 definitely ad. 명확히, 확실히

① 그 집은 며칠 내로 당신이 검사하도록 준비되어 있을 것이다.
② 그 논문은 반박하기 다소 어려운 주장을 포함하고 있다.
③ 그 보고서는 하루 저녁에 읽기에는 너무 길었다.
④ 그녀의 새 책은 확실히 볼 만한 가치가 있다.

| 01 ③ | 02 ④ | 03 ② | 04 ② | 05 ① | 06 ③ | 07 ① | 08 ① | 09 ② | 10 ③ |
| 11 ④ | 12 ③ | 13 ⑤ | 14 ① | 15 ② | 16 ④ | 17 ② | 18 ③ | 19 ② | 20 ④ |

01　**2018 서울여대**　▶▶▶ MSG p.114　③

분사구문 ▶ breeding까지 완전한 절이 주어져 있으므로, the only 이하가 앞 절에 연결되어야 하는데 접속사가 없으므로 빈칸에 현재분사 ③ being을 넣어야 the only부터 aristocratic까지가 의미상 주어인 독립분사구문이 되어 연결될 수 있다.

celebrity n. 유명인, 명사(名士)　breeding n. 혈통　aristocratic a. 귀족의

오늘날의 영국에서 계급은 혈통보다는 명성에 관한 것인데, 유명인과 귀족 사이의 유일한 연관성은 둘 다 상대적으로 부유하다는 점이다.

02　**2021 한국산업기술대**　▶▶▶ MSG p.144　④

복합관계형용사 ▶ 동사가 will go여서 간접의문절을 만드는 의문형용사 Which나 Whose는 빈칸에 부적절하고, 복합관계대명사 Whoever는 명사 team을 수식할 수 없어 부적절하다. 따라서 team을 수식할 수 있고 Any team which wins … 의 의미를 만드는 ④ 복합관계형용사 Whichever가 정답으로 적절하다.

championship game 챔피언 결정전, 결승전　hold v. (모임 등을) 열다, 개최하다

오늘 밤에 이기는 팀이면 어느 팀이든 캘리포니아에서 개최될 결승전에 진출하게 될 것이다.

03　**2022 단국대**　▶▶▶ MSG p.113　②

문의 구성 ▶ 콤마 뒤에 완전한 절이 왔으므로 그 앞에는 분사구문이 적절한데, 'consider+목적어+목적보어'의 5형식 구문에서 목적어인 surfing 이 주어로 앞에 나가 수동태의 형태가 된 것이다. 따라서 빈칸에는 수동의 의미를 나타내는 과거분사인 ② considered가 적절하다.

intense a. 격렬한, 치열한　athleticism n. 운동 경기[스포츠]열

오랫동안 아웃사이더의 스포츠로 여겨졌던 서핑은 격렬한 운동성과 고도의 기술력을 필요로 하는데, 이는 도쿄 올림픽에서 첫 선을 보일 때 전 세계에 드러나게 될 것이다.

04　**2020 세종대**　▶▶▶ MSG p.224　②

'so + be[do]동사 + 주어' 구문 ▶ 앞에 있는 긍정문의 내용을 받아 '~도 역시 그러하다'라는 의미를 갖게 하는 표현은 'so+be[do]동사+주어'이다.

oyster n. 굴　mollusk n. 연체동물　slug n. 민달팽이　snail n. 달팽이

굴은 뼈대가 전혀 없고 부드러운 몸을 가진 동물인 연체동물이다. 민달팽이와 달팽이는 연체동물이다. 대합조개와 오징어도 마찬가지이다.

05　**2018 세종대**　▶▶▶ MSG p.130　①

such ~ that 구문의 어순 ▶ 결과를 나타내는 'such ~ that …' 구문의 어순은 'such +a +형용사 +명사+that'이므로, ①이 올바른 어순의 표현이다.

get lost 길을 잃다

그 도시는 너무나 넓은 곳이라서 길을 잃어버리기 쉽다.

06　**2020 세종대**　▶▶▶ MSG p.132　③

no matter how 구문 ▶ '당신이 아무리 힘이 세더라도'라는 의미의 양보절을 완성해야 하겠는데, 형용사 strong은 부사의 수식을 받아야 하므로, no matter what strong이 아닌 no matter how strong이 정답이다. 참고로 what은 의문형용사, how는 의문부사이다.

measure n. 치수; 분량, 크기　out-muscle v. 힘으로 압도하다

당신이 아무리 힘이 세더라도 말(馬)을 힘으로 압도할 수는 없기 때문에, 힘은 신체적으로 측정되는 것이 아니다.

07　**2018 단국대**　▶▶▶ MSG p.71　①

가정법 과거완료의 주절 ▶ 조건절은 if가 생략되어 조동사 had가 문두에 오고 주어와 동사가 도치된 형태이다. 조건절인 if절의 시제가 과거완료(had completed)이므로, 가정법 과거완료 형식에 맞춰 주절의 동사는 '조동사의 과거형+have+pp'가 되어야 하겠는데, '실험실이 마감 시한까지 안전 연구를 마치지 못해서, 생산을 지연시켜야 했던 것'이므로 문맥상 ①이 빈칸에 적절하다.

laboratory n. 실험실; 연구소 deadline n. 마감시한

실험실이 그들의 안전 연구를 예정된 마감시한까지 마쳤더라면, 그 회사는 새로운 종류의 아기 장난감의 생산을 지연시키지 않아도 되었을 것이다.

---

08 2021 가톨릭대 ▶▶▶ MSG p.147, p.176

불가산 명사와 부정형용사 ▶ life가 집합적으로 '생명체'라는 의미일 때에는 불가산명사로 관사 없이 쓰이며, '지구 이외의 다른 행성'을 단수로 another planet로 표현해도 좋고 복수로 other planets로 표현해도 좋다. 따라서 ①이 빈칸에 적절하다. the other planet은 두 행성 중 다른 한 행성을 의미하고, the other planets는 하나 혹은 일부 행성들을 제외한 다른 행성들을 모두를 나타낸다.

space exploration 우주 탐험 unmanned a. 무인의 steppingstone n. 디딤돌; 수단

우주 탐사를 위한 주요 목적 중 하나는 다른 행성에서 생명체를 찾는 것이었고, 초기의 무인 우주 프로그램은 인간이 우주로 가는 디딤돌 역할을 했다.

---

09 2009 세종대 ▶▶▶ MSG p.123, p.214

동격의 명사절을 이끄는 접속사 that ▶ ②가 정답이다. There로 시작되는 존재구문의 형식이며 proof 이하는 proof와 동격인 내용이므로 동격의 명사절을 이끌 수 있는 that이 쓰여야 한다. ①의 경우 It ~ that 강조구문의 형식을 띠고 있는데, 이 강조구문이 성립하려면 It is와 which를 삭제한 후 완전한 문장이 되어야 한다. It is와 which를 삭제하면 성격이 다른 명사 2개가 접속사 없이 주어 자리에 위치하므로 문장이 성립되지 않는다.

inhabitant n. 주민, 거주자

최소한 1만 5천 년 동안 아메리카대륙에 사람들이 살아왔다는 상당한 양의 증거가 존재한다.

---

10 2007 한국외대 ▶▶▶ MSG p.152 ③

a great deal = much ▶ much와 같은 의미의 다른 표현은 great deal이 아니라 a great deal이다. ③을 a great deal로 고친다.

bilingual education 2개 국어 병용 교육 miss v. 놓치다, 빗맞히다, 못 맞히다

오늘날 2개 국어 병용 교육의 지지자들은 나와 같은 학생들이 가족이 쓰는 언어로 교육을 받지 못해서 많은 것을 놓치고 있다는 것을 암시해준다.

---

11 2020 성균관대 ▶▶▶ MSG p.123 ④

명사절을 이끄는 종속접속사 that ▶ 문장에서 보어를 이루는 ②의 접속사 that이 이끄는 절과 ④의 관계대명사 what이 이끄는 절이 등위접속사 and로 병치되어 있다. 그러나 관계대명사 what은 그 자체에 선행

사를 가지고 있기 때문에 불완전한 절을 취해야 하는데, what 다음에 완전한 절이 왔으므로 옳지 않다. ④ what을 접속사 that으로 고친다.

in any case 어쨌든 have an impact on ~에 영향을 주다 intelligibility n. 이해할 수 있음, 명료함

내가 깨닫지 못했던 것은 희귀한 단어들은 종종 문맥을 통해서 그 의미를 추측할 수 있다는 것과, 그 희귀한 단어들은 읽고 있는 것을 전반적으로 이해하는 데에 거의 영향을 주지 못한다는 것이었다.

---

12 2022 단국대 ▶▶▶ MSG p.191

분사를 수식하는 부사 ▶ ③은 과거분사 inhabited를 수식하고 있는데, 형용사는 분사를 수식할 수 없고 이러한 역할은 부사가 하므로, ③을 부사 sparsely로 고쳐야 한다.

bush n. 관목; 미개간지 continent n. 대륙 expanse n. (바다·대지 등의) 광활한 공간, 넓디넓은 장소 sparse a. (인구 따위가) 희박한 inhabit v. ~에 살다[거주하다] vegetation n. 식물, 초목 be prone to ~하기 쉽다

러시아의 산불과 기후 변화 사이의 연관성에 대해서는 의심의 여지가 없다. 그 나라의 유명한 미개간지 — 사람이 드물게 살고 있지만 초목들로 가득 차 있는 그 대륙의 광대하고 종종 건조한 지역 — 은 항상 산불에 취약했다.

---

13 2021 숙명여대 ▶▶▶ MSG p.105 ⑤

현재분사와 과거분사의 구분 ▶ ⑤ using 이하는 batteries를 수식하고 있는데, batteries는 사용하는 행위의 주체가 아니라 대상이므로 ⑤를 수동을 나타내는 과거분사 used로 고쳐야 한다.

cell n. 전지(cell이 모인 것이 battery) basis n. 토대, 기반 capacity n. 용량, 수용력 lifespan n. 수명

배터리의 기반이 되는 전지는 차량 내부의 한정된 공간에서 최대의 성능을 발휘하기 위해 단위 부피당 높은 용량을 가지고 있어야 하며, 전지는 일반적인 모바일 장치에서 사용되는 배터리와 비교하여 훨씬 더 긴 수명을 가지고 있어야 할 필요가 있다.

---

14 2022 단국대 ▶▶▶ MSG p.211

주어와 동사의 수일치 ▶ that절의 주어 the curriculum이 단수이므로 동사의 수도 단수여야 한다. ①을 is already overloaded로 고친다.

schoolmaster n. 교사 curriculum n. 교육[교과] 과정 overload v. 과부하가 걸리게 하다 lighten v. 가볍게 하다 physique n. 체격

교사들은 교육 과정이 이미 과부하 상태여서 줄일 필요가 있으며, 학교가 한 소년이 커서 훌륭한 군인이 될 수 있도록 해줄 수 있는 최선의 준비는 학교생활의 여건이 허용하는 한 그의 지능과 체격을 기르는 것이라는 데 동의했다.

15 2022 가천대 ▶▶▶ MSG p.167 ②

대명사의 수일치 ▶ ②의 대명사 their가 가리키는 대상이 a successful news outlet이므로, ②는 단수형 대명사인 its가 되어야 한다.

news outlet 언론매체 timely a. 시기적절한 shelf n. 선반

사람들이 정보에 대한 욕구를 참지 못하기 때문에, 성공한 언론매체는 기사를 최초로 발행한다는 명성에 의존한다. 출판물이 시기적절한 인쇄를 필요로 하던 인터넷 이전 시기에, 신문이 선반에 놓일 가장 빠른 방법은 사건이 일어나기 전에 사건에 관해 기사를 쓰는 것이었다.

16 2022 건국대 ▶▶▶ MSG p.214 ④

관계사절의 수일치 ▶ 관계대명사의 수는 선행사에 일치시킨다. 마지막 문장의 주격 관계대명사 that의 선행사는 the light라는 단수명사이므로, that절의 동사도 단수가 되어야 한다. ④를 enters로 고친다.

gemstone n. 보석의 원석 bring out (빛깔·성질을) 드러나게 하다 angled a. 모난, 각이 있는 facet n. (보석의 깎인) 면 sparkle v. 반짝이다

원석은 자연적으로 생기는 광물이다. 원석의 가치는 다양한 방법으로 측정된다. 원석의 가치는 보석의 색, 투명도, 크기, 그리고 보석이 얼마나 잘 깎였는지에 의해 측정된다. 보석 세공인은 보석의 아름다움을 드러내 보이기 위해 원석을 깎아낸다(세공한다). 원석은 각진 면을 갖도록 깎이기 때문에 반짝인다. 그 면은 보석에 들어오는 빛을 반사하여 보석이 빛나게 한다.

17 2021 한국산업기술대 ▶▶▶ MSG p.105 ②

현재분사와 과거분사의 구분 ▶ expose는 '노출시키다'라는 뜻의 타동사이고 시민들이 위험에 '노출되는' 수동의 의미이므로 ② 현재분사 exposing은 수동태의 과거분사인 exposed로 고쳐야 한다. ①의 it은 가목적어이고 to control이하가 진목적어이다.

legislation n. 법률제정; 법령 workplace n. 직장

몇몇 나라 정부는 시민이 노출되는 위험의 양과 종류에 대한 통제를 자신들의 책임으로 여긴다. 그들은 법을 이용하여 개인 건강을 보호하고, 직장에서의 부상을 예방하며, 재정 문제를 잘 다루도록 시민들을 돕는다. 또 다른 국가들에서는 시민들이 자신을 보살피고 자신의 안전과 다른 사람의 안전에 대해 책임을 져야 한다.

18 2018 건국대 ▶▶▶ MSG p.139 ③

보어로 쓰인 관계대명사 what ▶ 관계대명사 that은 앞에 선행사가 와야 하는데, ③ that 앞에는 선행사가 주어져 있지 않다. 따라서 이것을 선행사를 자체에 포함하고 있으면서 문장의 보어 역할을 할 수 있는 관계대명사 what으로 고쳐야 한다. ①은 of the size에서 of가 생략된 것이므로 of가 있을 때와 마찬가지로 앞의 명사 a celestial body를 수식할 수 있다. 비슷한 예로 '내 나이(또래)의 여자'는 a woman of my age이지만 이것을 a woman my age라고도 한다.

improbable a. 일어날 듯[있음직]하지 않은; 사실 같지 않은 celestial body 천체 block out (빛·소리를) 차단하다 tremendously ad. 엄청나게 immense a. 엄청난, 어마어마한 total eclipse 개기식(皆旣蝕) last v. (특정한 시간 동안) 계속되다 shadow n. 그림자

개기식 동안 실제로 일어나는 것처럼, 달 크기의 천체가 엄청나게 거대한 태양을 완전히 가릴 수 있다는 것은 다소 있을법하지 않은 것처럼 여겨지지만, 이런 일은 확실히 일어나는 것이다. 비록 달의 크기는 태양보다 상당히 작지만, 지구로부터의 이들의(달과 태양의) 상대적인 거리 때문에 달은 태양을 가릴 수 있다. 개기식은 7분 정도 계속되는데, 이 시간 동안 달의 그림자는 초속 약 0.6킬로미터의 속도로 지구를 가로질러 지나간다.

19 2018 건국대 ▶▶▶ MSG p.97 ②

동명사의 용법 ▶ 두 번째 문장의 but 이하에서 주어는 'A or B'의 형태를 취하고 있으며, too much knowledge가 A에 해당한다. B에 해당하는 표현으로는 pursued ~ determination이 주어져 있는데, pursued는 목적어를 취할 수 있긴 하지만 문장의 주어로 쓰일 수는 없다. 따라서 이 자리에는 목적어를 취하는 역할과 주어가 될 수 있는 역할을 동시에 할 수 있는 품사인 동명사를 써야 한다. ②를 pursuing으로 고친다.

reflect v. 심사숙고하다 miserable a. 불쌍한, 비참한 fool's errand 헛고, 헛고생 conceal v. 숨기다, 비밀로 하다 guarantee n. 보장 fraction n. 부분

우리는 우리가 무엇을 원하는지 그리고 왜 그것을 원하는지 항상 스스로에게 물어보고 또 그것에 대해 매우 주의 깊게 생각해볼 필요가 있다. 지식은 도움이 되는 것처럼 보이지만, 너무 많은 지식 또는 어쩌면 너무 많은 결의로 그 지식을 추구하는 것은 아마 우리의 삶을 상당히 비참하게 만들지도 모른다. 이에 대한 한 가지 이유는, 그 어떤 한계 이상으로 지식을 추구하는 것은 단지 헛수고일 뿐이라는 것이다. 우리는 모든 것을 알 수 있고 우리의 지성이 충분히 강하다고 어떻게 해서든 가정하고 있다. 하지만 왜 그렇다고 가정해야 하는가? 우리 자신이 자연의 작품이며, 만약 자연이 그것의 모든 섭리를 이해할 수 있는 무언가를 창조해 낼 만큼 강력하다면, 자연은 또한 우리로부터 무언가를 감출 수 있을 만큼 강력할 것임에 틀림없다. 우리가 우주의 작은 부분보다 더 많은 것을 이해할 수 있는 능력이 실제로 있다는 보장은 없으며, 사실 그럴 가능성도 거의 없다.

20 2022 한국외대 ▶▶▶ MSG p.212 ④

정비문 ▶ 'the number of+복수명사'는 단수동사로 받는다. 그러므로 ④에서 be동사 are을 is로 고쳐야 한다. 이때 the infected는 'the+과거분사'의 형태로, '감염된 사람들'이라는 복수보통명사로 취급한다. ① 학문명(linguistics)은 형태가 복수더라도 단수동사로 받는다. ② 기간, 거리, 금액, 무게 등의 복수명사(ten years)가 하나의 단위를 나타낼 때는 단수로 취급한다. ③ not only A but also B 구문이 주어로 쓰인 경우 동사는 B에 일치시킨다. the students여서 are이다.

linguistics n. 언어학 the humanities 인문학 faculty n. 능력; 교수진 vital a. 절대로 필요한 infect v. 감염시키다

① 언어학은 인문학의 핵심 분야 중 하나이다.
② 10년은 혼자 집에 머물러있기에 결코 짧은 시간이 아니다.
③ 대학에서는 교수진뿐만 아니라 학생들도 필수적이다.
④ 불행하게도, 감염자의 수가 상당히 크게 늘어나고 있다.

| 01 ① | 02 ② | 03 ① | 04 ① | 05 ② | 06 ② | 07 ③ | 08 ② | 09 ① | 10 ④ |
| 11 ⑤ | 12 ④ | 13 ④ | 14 ② | 15 ④ | 16 ③ | 17 ④ | 18 ② | 19 ④ | 20 ② |

01　2013 가천대　▶▶▶ MSG p.121　①

not A but B 구문 ▶ '아이들은 사물의 이름을 부르는 것에 열중한다' 라는 말을 통해 마지막 문장 역시 '아이들이 이름을 배우는 것은 기계적 이거나 마지못해서가 아니라 열정적으로 행해진다'라고 해야 논리상 자연스럽다. 빈칸은 'A가 아니라 B이다'를 뜻하는 구문이 와야 하는데 일반적으로 not A but B의 형태를 사용하지만, not 대신에 A 앞에 동시부정을 나타내는 neither ~ nor …표현이 와도 강조하는 대상이 B에 해당하므로 무방하다. 따라서 ①의 but이 빈칸에 적절하다.

infant n. (주로 1세 미만의) 유아, 아기　eagerness n. 열의; 열망　mania n. 광적인 열중[열심], 열광　reluctance n. 꺼림, 주저함　enthusiasm n. 열정; 열광

유아가 말을 하고 이름을 배우는 열의는 언어 발달의 주요한 특징이다. 아이들은 사물의 이름을 부르는 것에 열중한다. 이것은 '이름 사냥꾼'으로 불릴 가치가 있는데, 왜냐하면 그들이 이름을 배우는 것은 기계적이거나 마지못해서가 아니라 열렬히 행해지기 때문이다.

02　2021 수원대　▶▶▶ MSG p.169　②

재귀대명사 ▶ busy가 동사로 사용되어 '(~을 하느라) 바쁘다, ~에 매달리다'는 의미로 사용될 때 'busy oneself with[in] ~'의 구문을 취하는데, busying의 의미상 주어가 I이므로 ② myself가 적절하다.

go about 계속 ~을 (바삐) 하다　in private 사사로이　busy oneself with ~로 바삐 움직이다[종사하다]　venture to V 감히 ~하다　come forward (도움 등을 주겠다고) 나서다　in public 공개적으로　state n. (한 나라의) 국사(國事), 국정

내가 왜 사적으로는 여기저기 다니면서 조언을 하고 다른 사람들의 관심사로 바쁘지만, 공적으로는 감히 나서서 국정에 관한 조언을 하지 않는지 누군가는 궁금하게 여길지도 모르겠다.

03　2012 동덕여대　▶▶▶ MSG p.139　①

관계형용사절 ▶ 주어진 문장을 두 문장으로 분리하면 'The lawyer ~ his clients'와 'In that(앞 문장 전체) case, he will face ~'이다. 하지만 이 두 개의 문장을 주절과 종속절로 이루어진 한 문장으로 다시 표현하기 위해서는 지시형용사 that이 관계형용사 which로 바뀌어 콤마(,) 뒤에 사용되는 계속적용법의 관계절로 되어야 한다. ①이 정답이며, 'The lawyer ~, in which case he will ~'의 문장에서 which는 앞 문장 전체를 선행사로 하며 case를 수식하는 관계형용사의 역할을 한다.

find a person guilty ~에게 유죄판결을 내리다　defraud v. 사취하다, 갈취하다, 돈을 속여 빼앗다　sentence n. 형벌, 형; (형의) 선고

그 변호사는 그의 고객들을 사취한 혐의로 유죄판결을 받을 수도 있고, 그럴 경우 그는 장기 징역형에 직면할 것이다.

04　2022 서울여대　▶▶▶ MSG p.125, p.184　①

의문사절 / 가주어 it ▶ 빈칸 이하는 전치사 of의 목적어가 되는 의문사 절이 되어야 하므로, to be fully vaccinated를 받는 it을 가주어로 하고 '주어+동사' 어순인 ①이 정답이다.

shade n. 그늘; (색조·뜻의) 미묘한 차이, 사소한 차이　vaccinate v. ~에게 백신접종을 하다

올 겨울, 백신접종을 완전히 다 받았다는 것에는 미묘하게 차이 나는 많은 의미가 있다.

05　2022 세종대　▶▶▶ MSG p.123　②

가주어 it / 형용사 보어 ▶ how가 이끄는 명사절이 진주어이므로 가주어 it이 필요하고, be동사의 보어로는 형용사가 와야 한다. 따라서 ②가 빈칸에 들어가기에 적절하다.

respond v. 응답하다; 응하다, 반응[감응]하다　customer n. 고객, 단골

고객들이 그 돈을 이미 써버렸을 경우 은행들이 어떻게 대응할지는 명확하지 않았다.

06　2022 덕성여대　▶▶▶ MSG p.82　②

ought to have p.p. ▶ 자물쇠 수리공을 부르지 않고 직접 문을 열려다 문을 부순 데 대한 유감을 표현해야 하므로, 과거의 일에 대한 후회나 유감을 나타내는 ②가 정답으로 적절하다.

locksmith n. 자물쇠 수리공

어젯밤에 직접 문을 부수기 전에 너는 자물쇠 수리공을 불러서 문을 열도록 했어야 했어.

07 **2022 한국외대** ▶▶▶ MSG p.236 ③

생략 구문 ▶ ① even이 impossible 앞에 오면 '심지어 불가능하기까지 한'의 뜻으로 difficult와 'B, not A(A가 아니라 B)'구문을 이루기에 부적절하고 even 없이 not impossible이면 '불가능한 것이 아니라 어렵다'가 되어 적절해진다. 즉 even은 'difficult, sometimes even impossible(어렵고, 때로는 불가능하기까지 하다)'처럼 긍정구문에 더 적절하다. ② though 다음에 it is가 생략된 것으로 보아도 '심지어 불가능하기까지 하지만 어렵다'는 부적절한 의미가 된다. ④ 형용사 뒤에 접속사 even though가 온 구조이므로 부적절하다. ③ if 다음에 it is가 생략되었고 if는 though의 의미로 쓰여 '불가능하지는 않더라도'가 되어 빈칸에 적절하다.

calculate v. 계산하다 impact n. 충격; 영향 ecosystem n. 생태계

많은 과학자들은 지구온난화가 생태계에 어떤 영향을 미치는지를 계산하는 것이, 불가능하지는 않더라도, 어려운 일이라고 말하고 있다.

08 **2012 경희대** ▶▶▶ MSG p.221 ②

도치 구문 ▶ 주어가 너무 길어서 To many men이라는 부사구가 문두에 오고 주어와 동사가 도치된 문장이다. 빈칸 뒤에 동격의 that절이 이어지므로 동격을 이루는 명사이자 주어인 the realization을 that 앞에 위치시킨다. 주어가 단수이므로 동사는 has가 된다.

make a decision 결정을 내리다 cool head 냉정한 두뇌(의 소유자)

많은 경우에 옳은 결정을 내리기가 어렵다는 것을 여러 사람들이 깨닫게 되었지만, 가장 좋은 결정들은 이성적인 생각과 따뜻한 마음 둘 다로부터 내려진다.

09 **2005 광운대** ▶▶▶ MSG p.168, p.219 ①

비교대상 ▶ rather than을 매개로 전후의 비교 대상이 되는 부분은 문법적 형식이 같아야 한다. 주어진 문장에서는 의미상 to부정사의 동사원형 부분이 서로 비교되는 부분이다. 따라서 ①이 정답이다.

deserve praise 칭찬을 받을 만하다 enticing a. 마음을 끄는, 유혹적인

『해리 포터(Harry Potter)』시리즈의 작가인 롤링(J. K. Rowling)은 아이들로 하여금 하루 종일 비디오 게임이나 텔레비전 시청을 하게 하기보다는 책을 읽도록 유도했다는 점에서 칭찬받을 만하다.

10 **2010 성균관대** ▶▶▶ MSG p.35 ④

5형식 동사 keep의 목적보어 ▶ keep은 5형식 동사로 쓸 때 목적보어로 형용사나 분사 형태를 취한다. 따라서 ④의 명사 awe는 형용사 awful이 되어야 한다.

amazing a. 놀라운, 대단한 awe n. 두려움, 경외심 awful a. 경외심을 일으키는

아시아에는 방문객들로 하여금 계속해서 경외심을 가지고 황홀경에 빠지게 만드는 놀라운 볼거리, 소리, 그리고 진기한 경험들이 매우 많이 있다.

11 **2020 성균관대** ▶▶▶ MSG p.211 ⑤

대동사의 수일치 ▶ ⑤의 주어인 even higher percentages of those less than eighty years old에서 those가 복수여서 percentage이든 percentages이든 복수 취급하기 때문에 does를 do로 고쳐야 한다.

the elderly n. 노인층

일부 아프리카 도시의 조사에 따르면, 현재 80세 이상의 노인 중 절반이 병원에서 사망하고 있고, 80세 미만의 노인 가운데는 더 높은 비율이 그렇다고(병원에서 사망한다고) 한다.

12 **2022 경기대** ▶▶▶ MSG p.211 ④

not only ~ but also … 구문 ▶ ④ 뒤의 but also와 호응해야 하므로, ④는 could face not only가 되어야 한다. ① 가정법 미래의 조건절에 쓰인 조동사이며, if가 생략되면서 주어와 조동사가 도치되었다. ② 전치사 of의 목적어로 쓰인 동명사이며, 바로 앞의 the company가 의미상의 주어이다. ③ should prove to be에서 should가 문두로 가서 도치되었으므로 뒤에 남게 된 원형동사 prove이다.

dump v. (쓰레기를) 버리다 toxic a. 유독한 fine n. 벌금 criminal a. 범죄의

그 회사가 유독성 폐기물을 강에 버렸다는 보도가 사실로 드러나면, 그 회사는 막대한 과징금은 물론 범죄 수사까지 받을 수 있을 것이다.

13 **2020 성균관대** ▶▶▶ MSG p.211 ④

주어와 동사의 수일치 ▶ 명사절로 쓰인 that절 안에서 주어 all the hotels there가 복수이므로 동사도 복수여야 한다. ④ there was를 there were로 고쳐야 한다.

book v. 기록하다; 예약하다 exception n. 예외; 반대

지난 1996년에 미국 애틀랜타에서 하계 올림픽이 개최되었을 때, 한 지역 TV 방송국은 그곳의 모든 호텔들이 한 군데를 제외하고는 전부 예약됐다고 보도했다.

14 **2021 단국대** ▶▶▶ MSG p.182 ②

문의 구성 ▶ as 부사절의 본동사는 are leading이다. 그런데 주어인 this year's three supplementary budgets 다음에 또 다른 동사 are가 와서 적절하지 않은 문장이 되었다. 'be worth+N(금액)'은 '~의 가치가 있다'는 뜻으로 쓰이며, worth 앞에 which is가 생략되어 있다고 보면 'worth+금액'이 그 앞의 명사 budgets를 수식해 줄 수 있으므로, ②는 worth가 되어야 한다.

fiscal a. 국가 재정의 soundness n. 건실, 건전 supplementary budget 추가
예산 trillion n. 1조

올해 세 차례에 걸친 총 60조원 상당의 추경예산이 불과 6개월 만에 111조
원이나 되는 정부 부채의 증가를 초래하고 있어서, 대한민국의 재정 건전성
에 대한 우려가 증가하고 있다.

15 2017 서강대 ▶▶▶ MSG p.111, p.134 ④

분사구문 ▶ 전체 문장은 Just as S V, so S V의 형태로 '종속절 - 주절'
의 형태가 적절히 제시되었으며, ④의 lead 동사에 목적어가 없으므로
여기서는 자동사로서 lead to~의 형태가 되어 있음을 알 수 있다. 그런
데, 접속사와 주어가 생략되어 있는 점으로 보아 분사구문이 되어야 할
것이므로, led는 leading으로 바로잡아야 한다.

inconclusive a. 결론에 이르지 못하는, 언제 끝날지 모르는 penetration n.
침투, 진입, 관통 manipulation n. 조종, 교묘한 조작

비잔틴과 페르시아의 끝 모를 전쟁이 두 나라 모두를 약화시키고 아랍의 침
공과 정복에 노출시켰듯이, 16세기에서 18세기까지의 오스만과 페르시아
의 끝 모를 전쟁도 두 나라 모두를 약화시키고 유럽의 상업적 침투에 노출시
켰으며 결국 두 나라는 19세기 유럽 강대국들에 의해 속수무책으로 조종당
하기에 이르렀다.

16 2021 한양대 ▶▶▶ MSG p.167 ③

대명사의 수일치 ▶ ③이 가리키는 대상은 '수백 명의 군중'이므로 이들
을 지칭하는 대명사는 복수가 되어야 한다. 따라서 ③을 their로 고쳐야
한다.

viral a. (소셜 미디어로 인해 신속히) 확산되거나 대중화되는 plot n. 음모
dialectic n. 변증법 contradictory a. 모순된

그 후 널리 유포되어온 한 비디오에서 독일 코미디언 플로리안 슈뢰더
(Florian Schroeder)는 Covid-19의 존재에 의문을 제기하고 마스크는 그
들의 비판적 의견을 침묵시키려는 음모의 일부라고 의심하는 수백 명의 군
중을 마주해, 서로 반대되는 입장 간의 모순적 과정에 의존하는 논증 방법인
변증법에 관한 헤겔(Hegel)의 사상에 관해 얘기하고 싶었다고 말한다.

17 2008 서강대 ▶▶▶ MSG p.55 ④

수동태와 능동태의 구분 ▶ Tucking into the agenda was an
excursion to Diverlanhose ~는 원래 An excursion to Diverlanhose
was tucking into the agenda에서 보여진 tucking into가 앞으로 오
면서 주어와 동사가 도치된 구문이다. was tucking into의 의미상의 주
어가 an excursion to Diverlanhose이므로, ④는 의미상 tucking into
가 아니라 수동의 tucked into가 되어야 한다.

itinerary n. 여행일정, 방문지 리스트; 여행일기 kayak n. 카약, (에스키모인들이
사용했다는) 가죽배 tuck A into B A를 B에 접어[쑤셔]넣다 excursion n. 소풍,
유람, 여행

지난 11월에 몇 명의 사람들과 포르투갈 북부로 여행할 기회가 생겼다. 우
리 할아버지 코스타(Costa) 씨가 그곳에서 태어나 성장하셨기 때문에 나는
항상 그곳을 방문하기를 꿈꾸었다. 여행일정에는 카약 타기, 승마, 산행 등
내가 즐겨하는 것들이 모두 포함되어 있었다. (게다가) 유럽에서 가장 큰 어
드벤처 공원인 디베란호제(Diverlanhose)로의 소풍도 여행일정에 끼워져
있었다. 내가 가고 싶어 했느냐고? 물론이다!

18 2020 아주대 ▶▶▶ MSG p.227 ②

적절한 전치사의 사용 ▶ ②에서 antithesis는 '~의 정반대되는 것'이라
는 의미로서, 전치사 of가 뒤따라 와서 antithesis of ~의 형태를 취해
야 한다.

epistemological a. 인식론의 appropriation n. 도용, 전용; 충당, 유용
inter-subjectivity n. 공통주관성 defense n. 옹호

사람을 이용하는 것, 즉 다른 사람을 자신의 목적을 달성하기 위한 수단으로
변형시키는 것은 일반적으로 윤리적 행동과는 정반대되는 것으로 여겨진다.
식민지적, 성적, 심지어 인식론적 도용의 폭력에 직면한 윤리 이론가들은 지
배를 존중으로, 지식을 책임성으로 대체하려고 노력해왔다. 그러나 공통주
관성에서 시작되는 한 사상이 결국에는 '주체'의 폭력에 맞선 단순한 '타자
(他者)'의 옹호로 들리는 것처럼 종종 여겨진다.

19 2018 명지대 ▶▶▶ MSG p.145

완전한 절과 함께 쓰일 수 없는 관계대명사 ▶ which는 불완전한 절과
함께 쓰이는데, ④의 which 다음에 완전한 절이 와서 틀렸다. which의
선행사는 others이므로 관계절은 원래 there are hundreds of
others(수백 개의 다른 것들이 있다)에서 others가 which로 되고 of와
함께 앞으로 나간 것이다. 따라서 ④를 of which로 고쳐야 한다.

home n. 원산지 paella n. 파에야(쌀·고기·어패류·야채 등을 스페인 방식으로
찐밥) rice-growing n. 벼농사 paddy field 논 freshwater a. 담수의, 민물의
lagoon n. 석호, 초호; (호수 인근의) 작은 늪 brackish a. 소금기 있는, 염분이
포함된 orange grove 밀감 밭 interpretation n. 해석 dish n. 접시; (식사의
일부로 만든) 요리

발렌시아(Valencia)가 파에야의 원산지인 주요 이유들 중 하나는 발렌시아
가 스페인의 최대 벼농사 지역들 중 한 곳의 중심부에 위치해 있기 때문이
다. 그 벼 중에 많은 양이 발렌시아 남쪽에 있는 담수 석호인 알부페라(La
Albufera) 주변의 논에서 재배된다. 17세기까지만 해도, 알부페라 호수에는
소금물이 들어와있었지만, 점차 소금기가 빠졌다. 알부페라 일대의 논과 이 논
주변의 밀감 밭에서 일하는 노동자들은 18세기에 이미 닭, 토끼, 그 외 이용
가능한 모든 것 등의 현지 재료들을 이용하거나 아니면 그 대신 그들이 갖고
있던 해산물로 파에야를 만들기 시작했다. 이 두 가지 파에야, 즉 고기 파에
야와 해산물 파에야는 오늘날 원조 발렌시아 파에야로 여겨지는 반면, 수백
개에 이르는 다른 파에야들은 이 원조 파에야라는 고전 요리를 현대적으로
해석한(요리한) 것이다.

20 **2021 한국외대** ▶▶▶ MSG p.28, p.98　　　　②

정비문 ▶ do someone a favor는 4형식 문장으로 '~에게 호의를 베풀다, 유익[도움]이 되다'의 의미이다. ②에서 do동사의 주어는 동명사이고 목적어는 myself로, 주어와 목적어가 달라 재귀대명사가 아닌 대명사를 써야 한다. 따라서 myself를 me로 고쳐야 한다.

do somebody a favor ~에게 호의를 베풀다 drive somebody crazy ~를 미치게 하다

① 그는 방으로 들어가 소파에 앉아서 그녀가 귀가하기를 기다렸다.
② 당신이 내 숙제를 도와주는 것은 나에게 아무런 도움도 되지 않을 것이다.
③ 할 일이 남아있지 않았기 때문에, 그는 부엌으로 들어가 얼마간의 저녁식사를 준비했다.
④ 이전의 실수를 계속해서 생각한다면 당신은 미쳐버릴 것이다.

| **01** ④ | **02** ④ | **03** ④ | **04** ② | **05** ② | **06** ② | **07** ④ | **08** ④ | **09** ① | **10** ④ |
| **11** ③ | **12** ② | **13** ③ | **14** ② | **15** ④ | **16** ③ | **17** ① | **18** ③ | **19** ④ | **20** ④ |

01   2020 서울여대 ▶▶▶ MSG p.137   ④

전치사 + 목적격 관계대명사 ▶ 빈칸 다음에 '주어+동사'로 이루어진 완전한 절이 왔는데, 관계대명사 앞에 전치사가 있으면 관계대명사 뒤에 완전한 절이 올 수 있다. 원래 빈칸 이하는 "denial of asylum has potentially deadly consequences for people"인데, people이 관계대명사 whom이 되고 for와 함께 첫머리로 나가 for whom으로 시작되는 관계절이 되는 것이다. 따라서 ④ for whom이 빈칸에 적절하다.

refugee n. 피난자, 난민 flee v. 도망치다 armed conflict 무력 충돌 persecution n. 박해 asylum n. (보호) 시설, 수용소; 망명

난민들은 무력 충돌이나 박해를 피해 도망치는 사람들이며, 망명 거부는 이들에게 잠재적으로 치명적인 결과를 초래한다.

02   2022 서울여대 ▶▶▶ MSG p.35   ④

'가목적어-진목적어' 구문 ▶ 동사 make는 to 부정사를 목적어로 바로 취할 수 없어 가목적어(it)를 쓰고 진목적어(to 부정사)는 문장 끝에 둔다. that절의 동사 make 다음에 '가목적어(it)+목적보어(difficult)+진목적어(for immigrants to succeed in the United States)'의 형태가 이어져야 하므로 빈칸에는 ④ it이 적절하다.

immigrant n. 이민자 language barrier 언어 장벽

이민자들이 미국에서 성공하는 것을 어렵게 만드는 문제들 중 하나는 언어 장벽이다.

03   2022 수원대 ▶▶▶ MSG p.137   ④

관계대명사 앞의 적절한 전치사 ▶ 빈칸부터 help까지가 관계절로 선행사인 authority를 수식하는 구조인데, turn to authority for help이므로 빈칸에는 관계대명사 whom 앞에 전치사 to가 있는 ④가 적절하다.

paleontology n. 고생물학 authority n. 당국; 권위; 권위자 turn to somebody (도움·조언 등을 위해) ~에 의지하다 fossil n. 화석 vertebrate n. 척추동물 namely ad. 즉, 다시 말해서 Baron n. (귀족의 최하위 계급) 남작

그 고생물학 연구 시대에, 또 다른 척추동물 화석 연구자들이 도움을 얻기 위해 의지할 수 있는 위대한 권위자가 한 명 있었는데, 그가 바로 파리의 조르주 퀴비에(Georges Cuvier)에 남작이었다.

04   2022 서울여대 ▶▶▶ MSG p.73   ②

가정법에서 if 생략 ▶ 빈칸 앞에 'would 동사원형'으로 가정법 과거의 귀결절이 왔으므로, 빈칸에는 가정법 과거의 조건절이 적절한데, if it were not for~(~이 없다면)에서 if를 생략하면 were가 문두에 놓이므로 ② were it not이 빈칸에 적절하다.

weep v. 울다, 눈물을 흘리다 conspiracy n. 음모, 모의

나는 소셜미디어의 음모론이 없다면 현재 살아있을 사랑하는 사람을 기억하며 가족식구들이 우는 것을 들었다.

05   2022 수원대 ▶▶▶ MSG p.120   ②

nor와 neither의 구별 ▶ nor는 접속사, 부사로 사용되지만 neither는 부사로만 사용된다. 주어진 문장에서는 접속사 and가 있으므로 접속사에 해당하는 nor를 또 쓸 수는 없다. 또한, nor와 neither 모두 부정어구에 해당하므로 문두에 사용되면 주어와 동사의 도치가 일어난다. 이 두 조건을 충족한 정답은 ②이다. 간편하게 nor=and neither라고 이해해도 좋을 것이다.

in the first place 우선, 먼저 photography n. 사진(술)

우선 사진은 현대의 발견이 아니며, 한 사람의 아이디어도 아니었다.

06   2022 수원대 ▶▶▶ MSG p.81, p.82   ②

would rather의 부정 ▶ would rather는 조동사의 역할을 하므로 부정은 바로 뒤에 부정어가 위치해야 하고, 그 뒤에 동사원형이 뒤따른다. 한편, 과거에 비판했던 것을 현시점에서 후회하고 있으므로, would rather 다음 형태는 완료형을 사용하는 것이 적절하다. 따라서 ②가 정답이 된다.

would rather 차라리 ~하겠다[하고 싶다]

"그의 실수에 대해 그를 비난했습니까?" "예, 하지만 내가 차라리 그렇게 하지 않았더라면 좋았을 텐데요."

07 2021 한양대 ▶▶▶ MSG p.31, p.135 ④

목적격 관계대명사 ▶ 빈칸 앞까지 완결된 절이므로 ①은 접속사 없이 두 술부가 이어져 부적절하고, ③은 빈칸 앞의 명사를 수식할 수 없을 뿐 아니라 그 자체로도 수동태 동사 다음에 목적어와 보어가 모두 와서 부적절하다. ②와 ⑤는 목적격의 관계절에서 목적어 자리가 her로 차 있으므로 부적절하다. 따라서 ④가 빈칸에 적절하다.

critic n. 비평가, 평론가 motion picture 영화 actress n. 여배우

엘리자베스 테일러(Elizabeth Taylor)는 비평가들이 오래된 할리우드 스튜디오 시스템에서 배출된 마지막 대스타라 칭했던 미국의 여자 영화배우였다.

08 2022 한국외대 ▶▶▶ MSG p.128 ④

now that ▶ now that 뒤에는 평서문 형태의 완전한 절이 온다. ①은 조동사와 주어가 도치된 형태이므로 적절하지 않고, ②, ③은 주어가 3인칭 단수이므로 조동사 has가 쓰여야 한다. 따라서 ④가 정답이 된다.

province n. 지방, 지역 loosen v. 느슨하게[헐겁게] 하다[되다], 늦추다, 늦춰지다

여행 규정이 완화되었기 때문에, 그 지방에서는 사람들에게 여행 전에 백신 접종을 완전히 받으라고 조언하고 있다.

09 2021 세종대 ▶▶▶ MSG p.53 ①

시제의 일치 ▶ 주절의 시제가 과거인 경우 종속절의 시제는 과거 혹은 과거완료여야 하며, Mother Nature(대자연)는 여성 대명사로 받는다. 그러므로 ①이 정답으로 적절하다.

behave v. 행동하다 nature n. 본성 never fail to do 기필코[어김없이] ~하다

대자연은 모든 사람들이 언젠가는 대자연이 그렇게 행동할 것이라고 경고한 그대로 행동했지만, 인간의 본성은 어김없이 (우리를) 놀라게 한다.

10 2001 동국대 ▶▶▶ MSG p.207 ④

of all (the) 복수명사 – 최상급 ▶ '모든 ~중에서'라는 표현 'of all ~'로 문장이 시작되므로 최상급을 사용해야 한다. ④를 the most로 고쳐야 한다.

reconstruct v. 재건하다, 재구성하다 undoubtedly ad. 의심할 여지없이, 확실히

역사를 재구성해낼 수 있는 모든 사료들 중에서 일기가 분명 가장 재미있다.

11 2020 서강대 ▶▶▶ MSG p.211 ③

주어와 동사의 수일치 ▶ ③에 쓰인 makes의 주어는 바로 앞에 있는 links이며, 이것은 복수명사이므로 복수동사를 써야 한다. ③을 make the likes로 고친다.

stall v. 오도 가도 못하다 dire a. 무서운; 비참한; 긴박한 like n. (보통 the ~s) 같은 종류의 것[사람]

인접 도시들은 성공을 거두고 있는데도 북부의 도시들이 정체 상태에 있는데, 이는 몹시 나쁜 교통망으로 인해 맨체스터와 같은 도시들이 위건(Wigan)이나 하틀풀(Hartlepool)에서 멀리 떨어져 있는 세상처럼 보이는데도 일부 원인이 있다.

12 2022 숭실대 ▶▶▶ MSG p.137 ②

관계대명사 ▶ Because of부터 crunch까지의 '전치사+명사'구와 주어 many retailers 사이에 what관계절이 삽입되어있는데, what관계절은 선행사를 포함한 관계절이므로 삽입될 수 없다. ②를 the supply-chain crunch를 선행사로 한 주격관계대명사 which로 고쳐야 한다.

supply-chain n. 공급망 crunch n. 불황, 부족 ramp up ~을 증가시키다 discounting n. 할인 wean somebody off ~가 …을 끊게 만들다

구하기 어려운 상품들에 대한 수요를 증가시킨 공급망 부족사태 때문에 많은 소매상들은 할인을 줄이고 있고, 따라서 높은 폭의 이윤을 보고 있다. 이것이 업계가 쇼핑객들로 하여금 그들의 "싸게 싸게 싸게"식 사고방식을 끊게 만들 수 있는 기회일까?

13 2022 아주대 ▶▶▶ MSG p.105 ③

분사의 한정용법 ▶ 감수성은 heighten하는 행위의 대상이므로, ③은 수동의 뜻을 나타내는 과거분사형인 heightened가 되어야 한다.

gorgeous a. 아주 멋진 intricate a. 복잡한 register v. 기록하다

만약 개성이 성공적인 몸짓의 부단한 연속이라면, 그에게는 아주 멋진 점이 있었는데, 그것은 마치 그가 1만 마일 떨어진 곳의 지진을 감지하는 복잡한 기계 중 하나의 친척(동류)이기라도 한 것 같은 삶의 약속들에 대한 고조된 감수성이었다.

14 2022 가천대 ▶▶▶ MSG p.34 ②

let+목적어+동사원형 ▶ let의 목적보어 자리에는 원형 부정사가 와야 하므로 ②를 acquire로 고쳐야 한다. ① that절의 동사이며 주어는 the only fault이다. ③ the tongue을 받고 있는 대명사이다. ④ the habit of lying을 받고 있는 대명사이다.

vigorously ad. 단호하게 astonishing a. 놀랄 만한, 놀라운 decent a. (복장·집 등이) 버젓한, 남부끄럽지 않은; (태도 등이) 예의 바른 abject a. 절망적인, 비참한

내가 보기에 생겨나서 발달하기 시작하자마자 우리가 단호히 공격해야 할 유일한 잘못은 거짓말하는 것인 것 같다. 그러한 잘못들은 아이들과 함께 자란다. 혀로 하여금 거짓말하는 습관을 한 번 갖게 하면, 혀로 하여금 그 습관을 포기하게 하는 것이 얼마나 불가능한지 놀랍다. 거짓말하는 것만 아니라면 점잖다고 할 몇몇 남자들이 그것의 비참한 노예가 돼 있는 것도 바로 그런 이유 때문이다.

15 2021 한양대 ▶▶▶ MSG p.215 ④

문의 구성 ▶ but 이하의 주어 the ways와 짝을 이루는 정동사가 없다. 분사 단독으로는 정동사의 역할을 할 수 없으므로, ④의 resembling을 resemble로 고쳐야 한다.

component n. 요소 live out ~를 실현하며 살다 push back on (변화에) 반대하거나 저항하다 millennium n. 천년 (pl. millennia)

많은 미국인들에게 주택 소유는 여전히 아메리칸 드림을 실현하는 삶의 핵심 요소로 간주되지만, 오늘날 많은 미국인들이 현대적 주거 형태에 저항하는 모습은 수백 년 전, 심지어 수천 년 전 세계의 다른 지역들에서의 모습과 아주 유사하다.

16 2022 아주대 ▶▶▶ MSG p.105 ③

과거분사와 현재분사의 구분 ▶ ③은 '관련된' 세포들이라는 의미가 되도록 과거분사 involved여야 한다.

underlying a. 근본적인[근원적인] rat n. 쥐 neuroscience n. 신경 과학 anterior cingulate cortex 전대상피질

이전의 연구들에서는 근본적인 메커니즘이나 관련된 세포들을 명확히 하지 않았다. 이제 암스테르담에 있는 네덜란드 신경과학 연구소(NIN)의 연구원들은 쥐를 연구함으로써 다른 사람의 고통을 느끼는 능력이 전대상피질(ACC)의 "거울 뉴런"과 관련이 있음을 확인했다.

17 2018 건국대 ▶▶▶ MSG p.179 ①

문맥상 적절한 형용사 relative ▶ 하늘에 있는 별들의 위치가 육안으로 봐서는 변화가 없는 것처럼 보이는 이유로 마지막 문장에서 별들 사이와 별에서 지구까지의 엄청난 거리를 들고 있는데, 이것은 별들의 상대적인 위치를 뜻한다. 따라서 ① relating을 relative로 고쳐야 한다. ① relating to는 '~에 관하여'라는 뜻이므로, '별들에 관한 하늘에 있는 별들의 위치'가 되어 의미적으로 부적절하다.

naked eye 육안 stargazer n. 별을 쳐다보는 사람; 점성가; 천문학자

하늘에 있는 별들의 상대적인 위치는 육안으로 봐서는 변화가 없는 것처럼 보인다. 그 결과 별들은 종종 고정된 위치에 있는 것으로 여겨진다. 별에 대해 잘 모르는 별을 바라보는 많은 사람들은 각각의 별이 밤하늘에 자신만의 영구한(위치가 변하지 않는) 집이 있다고 잘못 생각한다. 그러나 실제로 별은 항상 움직이지만, 별들 사이의 그리고 별에서 지구까지의 엄청난 거리 때문에 그 변화를 여기서는 거의 인지할 수 없다.

18 2020 이화여대 ▶▶▶ MSG p.167 ③

대명사의 수일치 ▶ ③의 주어가 가리키는 대상은 앞에 나온 예측 내용인 트랜지스터 수의 증가를 가리키므로 이것은 대명사 it으로 받아야 한다. ③을 it was accompanied로 고친다. ① in은 전치사가 아니라 부사로 쓰인 것이다.

stream v. 흘러나오다 simulation n. 모의실험, 시뮬레이션 overwhelm v. 압도하다; 당황하게 하다 capacity n. 수용량; 능력, 재능 store v. 저장하다 integrated circuit 집적회로 parallelism n. 평행; <컴퓨터> 병렬처리

디지털 정보는 온갖 종류의 센서, 기기, 시뮬레이션으로부터 흘러 들어와서, 그 정보를 정리, 분석, 저장하는 우리의 능력을 압도하고 있다. 무어(Moore)의 법칙은 집적 회로에 들어갈 수 있는 트랜지스터의 수가 2년마다 두 배가 될 거라고 수십 년 동안 정확하게 예측해 왔으며, 최근까지 그것은 마이크로프로세서의 성능 향상을 동반했다. 오늘날 성능을 향상시키기 위해서는, 멀티코어 칩에 멀티프로세서를 프로그래밍하고 병렬 처리를 이용해야 한다.

19 2020 명지대 ▶▶▶ MSG p.11, p.91 ④

자동사 succumb의 용법 ▶ succumb은 자동사로만 쓰이는 동사로, 뒤에 목적어를 받기 위해서는 전치사 to와 함께 쓰여야 한다. 따라서 ④를 succumbing only to massive army operations로 고쳐야 하며, 이때 only는 '오직'이라는 뜻의 초점부사로 피수식어인 '전치사+명사'구 앞에 온다.

sole a. 유일한 disparity n. (한쪽에 불공평한) 차이 conjure up ~을 떠올리게 하다 mounted a. 말을 탄 brandish v. (무기를) 휘두르다 rifle n. 소총 succumb v. 무릎을 꿇다

수세기 동안 유럽인들의 정복에 저항할 수 있었던 유일한 아메리카 인디언들은 말과 총을 능숙하게 다룸으로써 군사적 열세를 극복했던 부족이었다. 평범한 백인 미국인들에게 '인디언'이라는 단어는 말을 탄 채 총을 현란하게 사용하는 '평원 인디언'의 이미지를 떠올리게 한다. 원래 말과 총은 아메리카 인디언들에게 생소했던 것임을 우리는 쉽게 잊어버린다. 말과 총은 유럽인들이 들어온 것으로, 말과 총을 습득한 인디언 부족 사회는 완전히 변모하였다. 말과 총을 숙달한 덕분에, 평원 인디언들은 침략한 백인들을 상대로 다른 아메리카 인디언들보다 더 오랫동안 싸워서 물리쳤으나, 1870년대 백인 정부들의 대규모 군사 작전에 무릎을 꿇고 말았다.

20 2022 한국외대 ▶▶▶ MSG p.59 ④

정비문 ▶ 지각(감각)을 나타내는 동사는 목적보어로 원형동사, 현재분사, 과거분사 모두 가능하다. ① 그가 건물 안으로 뛰어 들어가는 주체이므로 목적격보어로 원형부정사 run은 적절하다. 지각동사가 수동태가 되면, 목적보어인 원형부정사가 to부정사가 되므로 ②의 to explode는 맞고, ④의 climb은 to climb으로 고쳐야 한다. ③ 그가 거리에서 춤을 추는 주체이므로 원형부정사 dance는 적절하다.

explode v. 폭파하다 brick fence 벽돌담 in broad daylight 백주 대낮에

① 나는 그가 건물 안으로 뛰어 들어가는 것을 창문을 통해 보았다.
② 3마일 떨어진 곳에서도 폭탄이 폭파되는 소리가 들렸다.
③ 나는 그가 거리에서 춤추는 것을 거실 창문에서 볼 수 있었다.
④ 그가 백주대낮에 높은 벽돌담을 넘는 것이 목격되었다.

TEST 48

01 ④	02 ③	03 ④	04 ⑤	05 ④	06 ①	07 ④	08 ①	09 ⑤	10 ③
11 ④	12 ①	13 ①	14 ①	15 ④	16 ④	17 ④	18 ②	19 ③	20 ①

---

01 2016 홍익대 ▶▶▶ MSG p.73   ④

if절의 대용어구 but for ▶ 주절의 동사 형태가 '조동사의 과거+have p.p.'이므로, 가정법 과거완료의 문장임을 알 수 있다. 주어진 문장은 "최근 들어 입수할 수 있게 된 여러 기록들이 없었더라면, 이 연구는 불가능했을 것이다."가 되어야 하고, '만약 ~이 없었더라면'은 'if it had not been for ~'로 할 수 있는데, 이때 이 표현 대신 쓸 수 있는 표현이 'but for ~'이므로, 빈칸에는 but이 들어가야 한다.

wartime a. 전시(戰時)의 postwar a. 전후(戰後)의

최근 들어서 전시(戰時)의 독일 기록과 전후(戰後)의 조사 기록을 이용할 수 있게 되지 않았더라면, 이 연구는 불가능했을 것이다.

---

02 2022 서울여대 ▶▶▶ MSG p.95   ③

문의 구성 ▶ 절과 절은 접속사에 의해 연결되므로 빈칸에는 접속사인 ③이 적절하다. ① 부사이고 ② 전치사이며 ④ 부사이다.

wind instrument 관악기 arrange v. 정리하다, 배열하다 blow v. (입으로) 불다

관악기는 실제로 한쪽 끝에서 공기가 불어넣어질 수 있도록 정렬된 파이프일 뿐이다.

---

03 2020 가천대 ▶▶▶ MSG p.184   ④

for+명사+to 부정사 ▶ 빈칸 앞에 부정사의 의미상 주어를 나타내는 'for+명사'가 주어져 있으므로, 빈칸에는 to 부정사인 ④가 들어가야 한다.

foundation n. 창설, 창립; 기초, 토대 weather v. (재난·역경 따위를) 이겨내다, 뚫고 나아가다 inevitable a. 피할 수 없는, 부득이한 fertile a. 비옥한, 기름진

시간이 지나면서 우리가 서로를 알게 되고 우리가 가장 좋아하는 활동에 함께 시간을 보냄에 따라, 우리는 사랑과 행복이 꽃을 피울 수 있는 비옥한 땅을 마련해 줄 뿐만 아니라 피할 수 없는 폭풍우를 이겨낼 수 있게도 해주는 토대를 쌓아가게 된다.

---

04 2022 숙명여대 ▶▶▶ MSG p.33, p.227   ⑤

make의 목적격 보어 / 대상의 전치사 ▶ make의 목적격 보어로 쓰일 수 있는 표현과 함께 빈칸 뒤의 명사구를 목적어로 삼는 단어가 동시에 필요하다. make의 목적격 보어로 to부정사와 현재분사는 쓰일 수 없고 원형동사, 과거분사, 형용사 등은 쓰일 수 있으며, 대상의 전치사는 for이므로 ⑤가 문법적, 의미적으로 가장 적절하다. ④ than 다음의 십대 여학생과 인스타그램이 비교되어 부적절하다.

body image 신체 이미지(한 개인이 자신의 신체에 대하여 갖는 주관적인 이미지)

2019년의 한 연구에 따르면, 인스타그램은 3명 중 1명꼴로 십대 여학생들에게 신체 이미지 문제를 더 악화시킨다고 한다.

---

05 2022 덕성여대 ▶▶▶ MSG p.69, p.71   ④

가정법 미래의 if 생략 ▶ 주절에 'would+동사원형' 형태가 쓰이는 가정법은 가정법 과거와 가정법 혼합형과 가정법 미래이다. 모든 보기에 조동사 should와 동사원형 be가 있으므로 가정법 미래이며, if절은 'if+주어+should+동사원형'이므로, If he should be given another chance가 되는데, if를 생략해 도치할 경우 ④ Should he be given another chance가 된다.

do one's best 최선을 다하다

혹시라도 그에게 또 한 번 기회가 주어진다면, 그는 최선을 다할 것이다.

---

06 2022 한국공학대 ▶▶▶ MSG p.58   ①

동사의 형태 ▶ '배우다'는 learn의 능동태나 teach의 수동태로 나타내므로 ①의 are taught와 ③의 are learning이 적절하고, 우리가 '받아들이는' 것이므로 능동태의 to부정사 to accept가 적절하다. 따라서 ①이 빈칸에 적절하다.

envision v. 마음속에 그리다, 상상하다 aging n. 노화

당신의 할머니가 십대처럼 보이며, 축구를 하고, 밤새 클럽에서 파티를 즐긴다고 상상해보라. 아니면 당신의 할아버지가 시끄러운 헤비메탈 음악을 들으면서 최신 첨단 컴퓨터 소프트웨어를 당신에게 가르친다고 상상해보라. 그러한 시나리오는 상상하기 어려운데, 우리는 나이가 드는 것과 이에 따르는 고통과 죽음을 불가피한 인생의 사실로 받아들이도록 배우기 때문이다.

07 2021 한국외대 ▶▶▶ MSG p.19 ④

타동사 need의 목적어 ▶ 타동사 need의 목적어로 to 부정사가 와야 한다. 따라서 ④가 정답이다. 이때 claim의 목적어는 every cent(모든 보험금)이며, 이를 관계절 we can이 수식하는데 we can 다음은 claim 이 생략되었다. 그리고 My guess is 다음은 that절인데 접속사 that이 생략되었다. ②와 ③의 'need+동명사'는 '~될 필요가 있다'는 수동의 뜻을 가진 능동의 동명사 구문이어서 의미가 부적절하다.

health insurance policy n. 건강 보험 afford v. 금전으로 형편[여유]이 되다; 제공하다

내가 추측하기로는, 이런 병원들 가운데 어떤 병원이든 그 비용을 감당할 수 있으려면 우리가 가입한 건강 보험에서 가능한 모든 보험금 지급을 청구해야 할 필요가 있을 것이다.

08 2021 세종대 ▶▶▶ MSG p.136, p.227 ①

문의 구성 ▶ 관계사절 속의 정동사가 이어져야 하는데, 주어인 meaning이 단수이므로 단수동사가 필요하다. 따라서 ①이 정답이 된다. ④의 경우, 동사의 시제가 과거인 것도 부적절하고 'A부터 B까지'에 해당하는 관용표현은 from A to B이므로 정답이 될 수 없다.

literacy n. 읽고 쓰는 능력; 교양 fluctuate v. 변동[동요]하다 context n. 문맥

Literacy(문자이해능력)는 문맥에 따라서 의미가 변하는 용어다.

09 2022 숙명여대 ▶▶▶ MSG p.57 ⑤

수동태 ▶ early soap operas는 air하는 행위의 주체가 아닌 대상이므로 수동태 문장이 되어야 한다. 그리고 주절이 이어져야 하는데, 주어인 they는 early soap operas를 받는 대명사이며 초기 연속극이 낮 시간대로 옮겨진 것이므로, 수동태가 되어야 한다. 그러므로 빈칸에는 ⑤가 적절하다.

soap opera (텔레비전·라디오) 연속극[드라마] become crowded with ~로 붐비게 되다

초기 연속극은 1920년대에 처음으로 저녁에 라디오로 방송되었으나, 1930년대에는 저녁 일정이 코미디언이 진행하는 버라이어티 쇼로 붐비게 되자 낮 시간대로 옮겨졌다.

10 2018 성균관대 ▶▶▶ MSG p.136 ③

관계대명사 ▶ 관계부사 where 다음에는 완전한 절이 와야 하는데, 삽입되어 있는 I thought를 제외하고 보면, 주어가 없음을 확인할 수 있다. 따라서 ③을 주어의 역할을 하면서 앞 절 전체를 선행사로 받을 수 있는 계속적 용법의 관계대명사 which로 고쳐야 한다.

stairway n. 계단 closet n. 벽장 lead up to ~로 나 있다, ~로 향하게 하다 attic n. 다락(방) classy a. 훌륭한; 세련된, 멋진

내가 성장기를 보내고 있었을 때, 내 친구 밥(Bob)은 옷장 안에 다락방까지 이어지는 비밀 계단이 있었는데, 내 생각에 그것은 지금까지 본 것 중 가장 멋진 것이었다.

11 2021 한국외대 ▶▶▶ MSG p.209 ④

부정의 원급비교 not so ~ as ▶ '부정어 주어(Nothing)+원급비교 (as/so ~ as)' 구문은 최상급의 의미를 나타낸다. ④의 for를 as로 고쳐야 한다.

crochet n. 코바늘 뜨개질

최근에 뜨개질의 현재 인기만큼 전 세계 여성들의 관심과 주의를 널리 끌었던 것은 없다.

12 2012 중앙대 ▶▶▶ MSG p.105 ①

부사+과거분사 ▶ ① rehearsal은 '예행연습, 리허설'이라는 뜻의 명사이므로 well의 수식을 받을 수 없고 의미적으로도 부적절하다. '예행연습을 하다'라는 뜻의 동사가 와서 뒤의 is와 결합하여 수동태 is rehearsed가 되도록 하는 것이 맞다. 따라서 ①을 rehearsed로 고친다. 한편 '(시시때때로 변하는) 기분'이라는 뜻으로 사용할 때는 spirits 가 일반적이지만, '태도, 자세'라는 뜻으로 사용할 때는 단수인 spirit을 사용하는 것이 옳다.

play n. 연극 variation n. 변화, 차이 audience n. 관객

연극이 아무리 예행연습이 잘 된다하더라도, 모든 공연은 조건상의 차이, 배우들의 자세, 관객들의 반응의 차이 등으로 인해 매회 조금씩 다를 것이다.

13 2022 중앙대 ▶▶▶ MSG p.53 ①

시제일치 ▶ 주절의 시제가 현재인데 disruption을 수식하는 형용사절의 시제가 과거 진행인 것은 문맥상 어색하므로 ①을 is being caused by로 고쳐야 한다.

disruption n. 붕괴, 혼란 pandemic n. 팬데믹, 전 세계적 유행병 meet the timeline 기한을 맞추다 peer review 동료 심사

코로나 팬데믹에 의해 초래되고 있는 상당한 혼란의 결과로, 우리는 많은 연구자들이 평상시 동료 심사 과정과 관련된 기한을 맞추는 데 어려움이 있으리라는 점을 매우 잘 알고 있다.

14 2012 서강대 ▶▶▶ MSG p.11 ①

적절한 전치사의 사용 ▶ '~로 구성되다'라는 표현은 be made up of 로 쓴다. 따라서 ①을 made up of로 고쳐야 올바른 문장이 된다.

property n. 재산; (사물의) 속성[특성] independent of ~와 관계없이

세상은 물체들로 구성되어 있다. 그것들은 그것들을 경험하는 어떤 사람들이나 다른 존재들과는 관계없이 (고유의) 성질들을 가지고 있다. 돌을 예로 들면 돌은 별개의 물체이며 딱딱하다. 비록 사람들이나 다른 존재들이 우주에 존재하지 않는다 하더라도 돌은 여전히 별개의 물체이고 여전히 딱딱할 것이다.

15 2022 이화여대 ▶▶▶ MSG p.226 ④

문장구조/동사의 태 ▶ suffocate는 타동사로 '숨 막히게 하다'는 뜻이거나 혹은 자동사로 '숨 막히다'는 뜻인데, 문맥상 무거운 요구 아래에서 숨이 막힌다는 뜻이 되어야 한다. 따라서 ④를 자동사 능동태인 you are suffocating under the weight of demands나 타동사의 수동태인 you are suffocated under the weight of demands로 바꾸어야 한다.

revere v. 숭배하다 strive for ~을 위해 애쓰다 internalize v. 내면화하다 suffocate v. 숨 막히다, 숨 막히게 하다 lag behind 뒤처지다 venerate v. 공경하다, 숭배하다

사회적으로 우리는 근면을 숭앙하고 근면을 위해 애써야 한다고 배운다. 우리가 그다지 그렇게 하지 못하고 있다는 것을 마음속으로 받아들이면서도 말이다. 당신은 과도한 시간 일하고 있을 수도 있고, 아니면 마치 당신의 시간과 몸에 대한 과도한 요구의 무게 아래 숨 막히고 있는 것처럼 느낄 수도 있다. 그러나 그 노동은 다른 누군가의 숭앙 받는 근면에 늘 뒤처지게 될 것이다.

16 2019 가천대 ▶▶▶ MSG p.191 ④

부사의 역할 ▶ ④는 바로 뒤에 있는 동사 guarantee를 수식하고 있는데, 동사는 부사로 수식해야 하므로 이것을 absolutely로 고쳐야 한다. ② 앞의 명사를 수식하고 있는 과거분사이며, procedures와 followed 사이에 which were가 생략되어 있는 것으로 파악하는 것도 가능하다.

finding n. 연구결과 skeptic n. 회의론자 validity n. 정당성, 타당성

미(美) 항공우주국 울프-사이먼(Wolfe-Simon)의 연구결과는 우주에서 생명체를 발견할 가능성을 높이고 있다. 그럼에도 불구하고, 그녀는 그녀가 따른 실험 절차가 모든 의심을 해소하기에 충분히 적절했는지 궁금히 여기는 일부 회의론자들에 직면해 있다. 이들 과학자들은 도출된 결론의 타당성을 확실하게 보장하는 적절한 통제가 이루어지지 않았다고 주장한다.

17 2014 서강대 ▶▶▶ MSG p.137 ④

전치사+관계대명사 ▶ 관계대명사가 전치사와 함께 쓰이지 않는 경우 뒤의 절은 주어나 목적어가 없는 불완전한 형태여야 하는데, they are members는 완전하다. they are members of the clauses이므로 ④를 of which로 고쳐야 한다. ① to a great degree처럼 degree 앞에 전치사 to를 쓰므로 to which가 맞다. ② 분사구문이 주절의 주어 adjuncts를 수식하는데, adjuncts(부가어)가 구두점이 찍히지 않는 대상이 되므로 수동의 의미관계이다. 따라서 과거분사 unpunctuated가 맞다. ③ they occur in the clauses이므로 in which가 맞다.

adverbial n. 부사어구 integrate v. 통합시키다 clause n. 절(주어 동사가 갖춰진 문장 구성 성분) punctuation n. 구두점 initial a. 처음의 adjunct n. 부가어(동사수식 부사어) disjunct n. 이접사(離接詞)(문장수식 부사어) conjunct n. 연결사(접속부사어)

부사어구가 절 구조 속에 통합되어 들어간 정도가 문두와 문미 두 위치에서의 부사어구의 구두점에 영향을 끼쳤다. 흔히 구두점이 찍히지 않는 부가어(동사수식 부사어)는 그들이 위치해 있는 절과 긴밀히 연관되어 있다. 반면, 이접사(문장수식 부사어)와 연결사(접속부사어)는 문장 부사들이고, 그것들에 비교적 자주 찍히는 구두점은 그것들이 속한 절과의 느슨한 연관성을 보여준다.

18 2020 아주대 ▶▶▶ MSG p.218 ②

상관접속사에 의한 병치 ▶ 상관접속사 'not only A but (also) B'에서 A와 B에는 문법적으로 같은 품사 또는 같은 구조의 어구가 쓰여 병치를 이루어야 한다. 따라서 ②에서는 앞에 쓰인 어구와 같이 but 뒤에 전치사 through가 와야 한다.

traumatic a. 정신적 외상을 초래할 정도의, 대단히 충격적인 intensity n. 강렬함 straightforward a. 솔직한 acquisition n. 습득

정신적으로 충격적인 사건은 그 공포와 강렬함 면에서 견딜 수 없기 때문에, 그것은 종종 즉시 진실로 인식될 수 없는 기억으로 존재한다. 그러한 경험은 사실을 있는 그대로 파악하는 것을 통해서 뿐 아니라, 어디서 왜 의식적인 이해와 기억이 실패하는지를 알아가는 과정을 통해서도 가장 잘 이해될 수 있다. 문학은 독자들에게 오직 간접적이고 또한 놀라운 방법으로만 말할 수 있는 것들에 귀 기울이도록 가르치기 때문에 정신적으로 충격적인 경험에 대해 창문을 연다(이해할 수 있게 한다).

19 2021 한국항공대 ▶▶▶ MSG p.100 ③

be accustomed to 동명사 ▶ be accustomed to에서 to는 전치사이므로 그 뒤에는 목적어로 '명사 또는 동명사'가 와야 한다. 따라서 ③을 receiving으로 고쳐야 한다.

tinnitus n. 이명(耳鳴) vibration n. (가는) 떨림, 진동 counteract v. ~에 반대하다; (반작용으로) 중화하다 impervious a. ~에 영향 받지[휘둘리지] 않는 phantom limb pain 환지통(이미 절단해서 상실한 팔다리가 아직 있는 것처럼 느끼는 통증) limb n. 사지(四肢), 팔다리 amputate v. (손·발 등을) (수술로) 절단하다 itching n. 가려움

이명(耳鳴)은 소음이 아니다. 그것은 뇌에서 일어나고 있는 것이다. 그것을 없앨 물리적인 진동은 없다. 그것은 음파가 아니다. 바로 이 전기적인 활동은 소음 억제 기술에 영향을 받지 않는다. 이명에 관한 현재의 이론은 그것이 환지통(幻肢痛)과 비슷하다는 것이다. 당신은 누군가가 사지(四肢) 잃었을 때, 즉 팔이 절단되었을 때에 대한 이야기를 들어본 적이 있다. 그들은 그 팔이 여전히 있다고 느끼거나 그 팔이 있었지만 이제는 더 이상 없는 곳에서 고통을 느끼며 심지어 가려움도 느낀다는 것이다. 당신은 이제는 더 이상 없는 한쪽 손에서 손가락들에 가려움을 느낄 수도 있다. 요점은, 뇌가 이 신체 부위에서 신경 신호를 받는 데 익숙해져있는데 뇌는 더 이상 그 신호를 받지 못하고, 그래서 뇌는 그 부위로부터 들어오고 있어야 하는 것에 대해 사실상 최상의 추측을 하게 되고, 이어서 뇌는 그 부위에서 마지막으로 느낀 것 혹은 그와 비슷한 것을 공급한다는 것이다. 그리고 요점은 이명이 종종 이와

대단히 비슷하다는 것이다. 당신은 어떤 주파수의 청력을 잃게 된다. 뇌는 그 주파수의 청각 신호를 받는 데 익숙해져 있는데, 더 이상은 받지 못하고 있다. 그래서 뇌는 소리 같지만 실제로는 뇌의 청각계통에서 일어나는 전기적인 활동에 불과한 것으로 그 격차를 메우게 된다.

---

20 **2021 한국외대** ▶▶▶ MSG p.185 ①

정비문 ▶ '간절히 바라는, 열렬한'의 의미인 형용사 'eager'는 주어에 사람을 사용한다. 따라서 ①을 'Tom is eager to please Jerry.'로 고쳐야 한다.

please v. 기쁘게 하다 exit n. (공공건물의) 출구 dreadful a. 끔찍한

① Tom은 Jerry를 기쁘게 하고 싶어 한다.
② Tom이 그 책을 읽기는 어렵다
③ Tom이 출구를 찾는 것은 중요하다
④ Tom이 그곳에 가는 것은 끔찍하다.

01 ③	**02** ①	**03** ①	**04** ④	**05** ④	**06** ②	**07** ③	**08** ③	**09** ②	**10** ②
11 ②	**12** ⑤	**13** ③	**14** ④	**15** ④	**16** ②	**17** ③	**18** ⑤	**19** ②	**20** ④

01   2007 가톨릭대 ▶▶▶ MSG p.137, p.214   ③

문의 구성 ▶ by which부터는 형용사절로 앞의 명사 name을 꾸며준다. which는 전치사의 목적어로 왔기 때문에 뒤에는 완전한 절이 와야 한다. 그리고 that부터 society까지는 또 형용사절로 앞의 shift를 꾸며준다. 그러므로 by which절의 주어는 shift이고 빈칸에는 동사가 들어가야 한다. ①과 ②는 목적어가 없어서 맞지 않고 ④는 주어가 shift로 단수이기 때문에 정답이 될 수 없다.

transform v. 변형시키다, 변모시키다; 전환하다 agrarian a. 농지의, 토지의

유럽을 농업 사회에서 산업 사회로 바꾼 거대한 사회, 경제, 기술적 변화는 산업혁명이라는 이름으로 알려져 있다.

02   2018 단국대 ▶▶▶ MSG p.224   ①

neither와 nor의 구분 ▶ 부사인 neither와 접속사 nor를 구분할 수 있는지를 묻고 있다. 보기 모두가 절로 구성되어 있으므로, 절과 절을 연결하는 접속사 nor는 빈칸에 바로 쓰여 앞의 절과 연결할 수 있지만, 부사인 neither를 쓰려면 접속사 and가 추가로 필요하다. 따라서 ②와 ④를 먼저 정답에서 제외할 수 있다. 한편, 부정의 뜻을 가진 접속사 nor 뒤에 절이 올 경우 그 절에는 도치가 일어나므로, ①의 nor is it이 정답이 된다.

burnout n. 번아웃, (심신) 소모 exhaustion n. (심신의) 극도의 피로

번아웃(심신 소모)이 발생하는 가장 잘 알려진 이유는 충분한 휴식 없이 과도하게 일을 한 것에서 비롯된 극도의 피로이다. 그러나 그런 건강상태만으로 번아웃이 일어나지는 않으며, 또한 그것이 번아웃을 일으키는 유일한 길도 아니다.

03   2019 덕성여대 ▶▶▶ MSG p.139   ①

관계형용사 what ▶ 빈칸에는 명사 money를 수식하면서 자체에 선행사를 포함하고 있는 관계형용사 what이 와야 한다. 'what+명사'는 'all the+명사+that'의 의미로 사용된다. 주어진 문장의 경우 불가산명사 money가 있으므로 양을 수식하는 little이 money 앞에 와야 적절하며 what little은 '(양적으로) 그 얼마 안 되는 모든'의 의미이다. 참고로 what few는 '(수적으로) 그 얼마 안 되는 모든'의 의미로 가산명사 앞에 쓰인다.

hand over 넘겨주다, 양도하다 leave v. 남겨두다

나는 내가 남겨두었던 그 얼마 안 되는 모든 돈을 건네주었다.

04   2021 한국외대 ▶▶▶ MSG p.224   ④

가정법 과거완료 ▶ 가정법 과거완료의 문장이다. '~이 없었다면'에 해당하는 표현은 If it had not been for 혹은 if를 생략하여 조동사 had와 주어 it이 도치된 Had it not been for이다. 따라서 ④가 정답이다.

make a mistake 실수를 하다

만약 당신의 조언이 없었더라면, 나는 중대한 실수를 했을 것이다.

05   2019 서울여대 ▶▶▶ MSG p.199, p.227   ④

by as early as+시간 ▶ '~때면 이미', '늦어도 ~까지는'라는 뜻의 'by+시간'과 '일찍이 ~에'라는 뜻의 'as early as+시간'이 합쳐진 'by as early as+시간(일찍이 ~때면 이미)'이라는 관용구문을 묻고 있으므로, ④가 정답이다. 전치사가 in이면 보통 in을 생략하고 as early as 2050라고 쓴다.

be expected to do ~할 것으로 예상되다

카카오나무는 기온 상승과 이전보다 건조한 기상 상태로 인해 일찍이 2050년이면 사라질 것으로 예상된다.

06   2019 세종대 ▶▶▶ MSG p.105   ②

분사+정동사 ▶ 파생상품은 거래하는 행위의 주체가 아닌 대상이므로, derivatives와 동사 trade는 수동관계에 있다. 그러므로 derivatives는 수동을 나타내는 과거분사 traded로 수식해야 한다. 한편, 분사는 단독으로 문장의 정동사로 쓰일 수 없으므로 과거동사 grew가 와야 한다.

derivative n. 파생물; (주식이나 채권 등에서 파생한) 복합금융상품, 파생상품 whopping a. 엄청나게 큰 trillion n. 1조

전 세계에서 거래된 신용파생상품의 가치는 지난해보다 129% 증가하여 무려 12조 7900억 달러에 달했다.

07 **2019 세종대** ▶▶▶ MSG p.113 ③

분사구문의 태+명사 ▶ 분사구문의 주어는 주절의 주어와 같을 때 생략한다. 따라서 주어진 문장의 분사구문에 생략돼 있는 주어는 the region이다. the region은 beset하는 행위의 주체가 아닌 대상이므로 수동관계이며, 따라서 과거분사를 쓴 수동분사구문이 되어야 한다. 한편, 형용사는 명사를 수식하는 역할을 하므로, ethnic 뒤에는 동사 strive가 아닌 명사 strife가 와야 한다.

fertile a. 비옥한, 기름진; 다산(多産)의 extremism n. 극단론, 과격주의 beset v. 포위하다; (위험·유혹 등이) 괴롭히다 ethnic a. 인종의, 민족의 strife n. 분쟁, 다툼, 갈등

인종분쟁과 빈곤에 시달리고 있는 그 지역은 오랫동안 종교적 극단주의의 온상이 되어 왔다.

08 **2020 한국산업기술대** ▶▶▶ MSG p.33, p.97 ③

사역동사 have의 목적보어 ▶ have가 사역동사로 쓰이는 경우, 목적어와 목적보어의 관계가 능동인 경우에는 동사원형이, 수동인 경우에는 과거분사가 목적보어로 온다. 주어진 문장에서 목적어인 our photos는 의미상 타동사 take의 객체(대상)이다. 따라서 수동관계에 있으므로, 과거분사로 써야 한다.

postcard n. 엽서 benefit from ~로부터 이익을 얻다

엽서와 책에서 우리와 우리 자녀들을 본다. 우리의 모습이 사진으로 찍혀서 우리가 이익을 얻지는 않는다. 외국인들이 이익을 볼 뿐이다.

09 **2022 숙명여대** ▶▶▶ MSG p.227 ②

문의 구성 ▶ 빈칸 앞에 between이 왔으므로 A and B의 구조가 되어야 한다. 따라서 ③, ④, ⑤는 빈칸에 적절하지 않고, within 다음의 대명사는 a language를 받으므로 단수가 되어야 한다. 따라서 it이 적절하며, 그리고 partly because of ~ within it까지가 삽입된 전치사구이므로, 뒤에 문장이 오기 위해서는 접속사가 필요하고 뒤에 목적어 about five thousand가 이어졌으므로 동사가 필요하다. 이를 만족하는 보기는 ②이다.

distinguish v. 구별하다 sublanguage n. (어떤 그룹에서만 통용하는) 특수 언어, 2차 언어 dialect n. 방언, 사투리

세계에 정확하게 몇 개의 언어가 있는지 아는 사람은 아무도 없는데, 이는 부분적으로 언어와 그 언어 안에 있는 하위 언어 또는 방언을 구별하기 어렵기 때문이다. 그러나 그 수를 세어보려고 한 사람들은 일반적으로 약 5천개의 언어를 발견했다.

10 **2017 한국외대** ▶▶▶ MSG p.214 ②

관계대명사절에서 선행사와 동사의 수일치 ▶ 관계대명사의 수는 선행사에 일치시킨다. ②에 쓰인 관계대명사 that의 선행사는 two other bodies인데, 이것은 복수이므로, that절의 동사도 복수가 되어야 한다. 따라서 ②를 that are로 고쳐야 한다. ① 두 개의 다른 천체가 지구 가까이에서 궤도를 도는 주체이므로 현재분사 orbiting은 맞는 표현이다. ② refer to A as B의 수동구문은 A is referred to as B이므로 referred to as는 바르게 쓰였다.

orbit v. (다른 천체의) 궤도를 돌다 title n. 명칭, 칭호

지구 가까이에서 궤도를 도는 또 다른 두 개의 천체가 있는데 이들은 엄격히 말하면 위성(달)이라는 명칭을 가질 자격이 없지만, 때때로 위성(달)이라 불린다.

11 **2021 한국외대** ▶▶▶ MSG p.167 ②

대명사의 수일치 ▶ ②의 its는 복수명사 children을 가리키므로 its를 their로 고쳐야 한다.

marked a. 뚜렷한 preference n. 선호(도) Oedipal a. 오이디푸스 콤플렉스의

아이들을 종종 관찰해보면 일찍이 2살 초입에 이성(異性) 부모에 대한 두드러진 선호도와 또 다른 초기 오이디푸스 성향의 징후들이 드러난다.

12 **2008 성균관대** ▶▶▶ MSG p.126 ⑤

의문대명사 what ▶ ⑤ that 뒤의 절은 앞의 전치사 of의 목적어 역할을 하는 명사절로, be동사의 보어가 없어 문장이 불완전하므로 뒤에 완전한 절의 형태가 나오는 명사절의 접속사 that은 부적절하다. be동사의 보어역할을 할 수 있는 의문대명사 what으로 고쳐야 한다.

drastsic a. 철저한 transformation n. 변형, 변모, 변질

이런 새로운 회화 양식은 오래 지속되지 못했고 곧 그림이 어떠한 것이어야 하는가에 대한 피카소(Picasso)의 이해와 그 외 다른 나머지 화가들의 이해에 있어서의 훨씬 더 철저한 변화가 뒤따르게 되었다.

13 **2007 한국외대** ▶▶▶ MSG p.218 ③

등위접속사에 의한 병치 ▶ 등위접속사 and는 병치구조를 이루므로 앞뒤로 같은 형태의 표현이 와야 한다. 따라서 force도 permitting과 마찬가지로 현재분사의 형태가 되어야 한다. ③을 not forcing으로 고친다.

asylum n. 보호 장소 native country 본국 imprison v. 감금하다; 감옥에 넣다

미국은 외국에서 온 정치적 반체제 인사들에게 보호 장소를 제공하여 미국에 남을 수 있도록 허용했고, 틀림없이 투옥되었을 그들을 본국으로 강제 송환하지 않았다.

14 2012 서강대 ▶▶▶ MSG p.149 ④

전치사+추상명사 ▶ '전치사+추상명사'의 형태로서 with great success는 very successfully라는 부사 기능을 한다. 따라서 ④의 부정관사 a는 삭제해야 한다. ① as follows는 관용적인 표현으로 '다음과 같이'라는 의미이다.

gist n. 요점, 골자, 요지 Relativistic dynamics 상대론적 역학

이러한 반대의 요지는 다음과 같이 전개될 수 있다. 상대론적 역학은 뉴턴 역학이 틀렸다는 것을 보여주었을 리 없다. 왜냐하면 뉴턴 역학은 여전히 대부분의 기술자들과 선별된 응용분야에서의 많은 물리학자들에 의해 아주 성공적으로 사용되고 있기 때문이다.

15 2015 한양대학교 에리카 ▶▶▶ MSG p.211 ④

동사의 수일치 ▶ ④의 경우, 바로 앞의 many 뒤에는 bacteria가 생략돼 있으므로, 복수동사 benefit으로 써야 한다. ① bacteria가 주어이므로 복수동사로 써야 하며, outnumber는 타동사이다. ② this 때문에 bacteria를 단수 취급하여 weighs이다. ③ most 다음은 가산 복수명사나 불가산명사가 다 올 수 있는데 여기서는 bacteria를 가산 복수명사로 보아 are이다.

outnumber v. ~보다 수가 많다; 수적(數的)으로 우세하다 digest v. 소화하다; 숙고하다

우리의 몸속에서, 박테리아가 인간 세포보다 그 수가 10배 더 많다. 이 박테리아를 전부 합하면 뇌의 무게와 비슷한 3파운드에 이른다. 우리의 몸속에 있는 대부분의 박테리아는 해롭지 않다. 사실, 많은 박테리아가 중요한 여러 가지 방식으로 우리를 이롭게 해준다. 그것들은 우리가 음식을 소화하는 데 도움을 주며, 중요한 비타민을 만들고, 세균감염에 맞서 싸우는 것을 도와준다.

16 2012 서강대 ▶▶▶ MSG p.219 ②

비교대상 ▶ not A but B가 변형된 B and not A 구문에서 A와 B는 병치구조를 이루므로 비교대상이 서로 같아야 한다. 우리 자신의 감정과 다른 사람의 감정이 비교되는 것이므로 ②를 not to anybody else's로 바꿔야 한다. 여기서 anybody else's는 anybody else's feelings and ideas를 의미한다. ①은 than 앞에서 to부정사를 썼으므로, than 뒤에도 to부정사를 쓴 것이다. ③은 불완전자동사 seem에 대한 보어로 형용사 prior가 쓰였고, 일반적으로 prior는 전치사 to와 함께 쓰인다.

common sense 상식 self-understanding n. 자기이해 mutual a. 상호 간의

상식적으로 타인보다 우리 자신을 이해하는 것이 더 쉽다고 말한다. 결국 우리는 우리가 곧바로 접하게(이해하게) 되는 것은 다른 사람의 감정과 생각이 아니라 우리 자신의 감정과 생각이라고 생각하는 경향이 있다. 자기애해가 상호 간의 이해보다 우선인 것 같고 어떤 면에서는 그러하다. 그러나 왜 우리가 행하는 바를 행하고, 느끼는 바를 느끼고, 변화하는 대로 변화하고, 심지어 믿는 바를 믿는지 조금이라도 진정으로 깊이 이해하려면 우리는 우리 자신을 초월해야 한다. (먼저 우리 자신을 초월하여 타인을 이해하고 나야 진정으로 우리 자신을 이해하게 된다는 뜻)

17 2012 서강대 ▶▶▶ MSG p.15 ③

자동사와 타동사의 구분 ▶ ③의 share는 타동사이므로 전치사 with를 삭제해야 한다. ①의 give는 4형식으로 쓰이기 때문에 간접목적어가 주어가 되는 수동태가 되어도 직접목적어가 남아 있으므로, are given 다음에 직접목적어 priority가 온 것은 맞는 표현이다.

subculture n. 하위문화, 소문화 mainstream n. (활동·영향의) 주류 priority n. 우선권

일반적으로 어느 가치에 우선권을 부여하느냐 하는 것은 부분적으로는 우리가 사는 하위문화의 문제이며 또한 부분적으로는 개인의 가치관에 관한 문제이다. 어떤 주류문화속의 여러 다양한 하위문화들은 기본적 가치들을 공유하고 있지만 그 가치들에 각자 다른 우선권을 부여하기도 한다. 예를 들면 미래의 월급까지도 다 써버릴 정도로 엄청난 액수의 할부로 해서 당장 큰 차를 사느냐 또는 더 작고 값싼 차를 사느냐 하는 문제에 관한 한, "더 큰 것이 더 낫다"는 말은 "미래에 더 많은 것이 있을 것이다''라는 말과 모순이 될 수도 있을 것이다.

18 2021 아주대 ▶▶▶ MSG p.44 ⑤

과거시제 ▶ 과거의 일에 대해 말하고 있으므로 ⑤는 과거시제인 rated가 되어야 한다. 한편, ①의 are 다음에는 quick studies가 생략된 것이며, 일반적인 사실을 기술한 것이므로 현재시제가 맞다.

nasality n. 비음, (소리가) 코를 통하여 나옴 cranky a. 짜증을 내는 wail n. 울음 ham n. (특히 과잉 연기를 하는) 서투른 배우 mimic n. 흉내쟁이 crack up 마구 웃기 시작하다 ape n. 유인원; v. (무엇을 제대로 하지 못하고) 겨우 흉내만 내다 make light of ~을 경시하다, ~에 대해 농담하다 roundhouse n. (권투에서) 옆으로 크게 휘둘러 치는 펀치 smack n. (특히 아이들에 대한 벌로 손바닥으로) 때리기[후려치기] rate v. 운임[임금]을 정하다; ~만한 가치가 있다

나는 그 언어를 그냥 혼자 터득하고 있었지만, 아이들이 새 언어를 빨리 배우듯이 나도 빨리 배웠다. 유치원에 다닐 때 나는 거의 침묵하며 지냈다. 들리는 것이라고는 오로지 선생님의 높은 콧소리뿐이었고, 이해하는 것이라고는 같은 반 친구들의 짜증 섞인 울음소리와 비명소리 이외에는 거의 없었다. 그러나 단 몇 개월 같은 시간이 지나 곧 나는 이미 형편없는 삼류배우이자 흉내쟁이가 되어 선생님들과 아버지의 친구들 흉내로 아버지를 크게 웃기곤 했다. 우리 어머니는 아버지의 말을 흉내 낸다고 나를 꾸짖었다. 그리고 한 번은 어머니의 말에 농담을 하려다가, 불기짝을 세게 맞아 마땅했다.

19 2021 한국항공대 ▶▶▶ MSG p.123 ②

올바른 접속사 ▶ ②의 if 절을 가정법 과거의 if절로 보아도 주절의 동사 형태와 시제적인 의미가 가정법에 맞지 않고, 직설법 과거시제 조건의 부사절로 보아도 if절의 내용이 사실인 것이 분명하므로 의미적으로 부적절하다. 여기서는 '식민지 공무원들이 종종 주변적인 사람들이었다는 그녀의 말은 옳았다.'라는 의미여서 'She was correct in saying that 절'에서 in saying이 생략된 것이므로 ②를 접속사 that으로 고쳐야 한다. Although he was correct that the planets orbit the sun, he was wrong in saying that they follow circular paths.(행성들이 태양 주위를 궤도를 그리며 돈다는 그의 말은 옳았지만, 행성들이 원형

의 길을 따라간다는 그의 말은 틀린 말이었다.)라는 문장에서 앞 절에서도 he was correct in saying ~이라고 할 수 있는데 in saying을 생략한 것이라고 볼 수 있다.

empire n. 제국(帝國) colony n. 식민지 campaign n. 군사행동 dismissively ad. 오만하게, 경멸적으로 imperialism n. 제국주의 superfluous a. 잉여의 functionary n. 공무원, (공공기관의) 직원 marginalize v. 사회에서 소외하다, 사회의 주류에서 몰아내다

19세기에 일반 대중이 분쟁에 참여한 것은 제국의 역할을 살펴보지 않으면 이해될 수 없다. 사람들은 항상 이익을 얻거나 정착을 하기 위해 식민지로 향했다. 그러나 사람들은 또한 새로운 이유로 19세기의 제국주의 군사행동에 참여했다. 후에 한나 아렌트(Hannah Arendt)는 제국주의를 '잉여 인간과 잉여 자본의 수출'이라고 경멸적으로 특징 지웠다. 식민지 공무원들이 종종 주변적인 사람들이었다는 그녀의 말은 옳았으며, 세실 로즈(Cecil Rhodes)는 결국 '잉여 인구를 정착시키고' 그래서 '내전을 피하기 위해' 제국주의를 옹호하곤 했지만, 이 주변으로 소외된 사람들은 점점 더 식민지 분쟁에의 참여를 이용하여 본국 국민으로서의 권리를 주장했다. 예를 들면, 스코틀랜드 사람들은 '잉글랜드' 공동체의 구성원 자격으로부터 제외되었지만, 프랑스와의 전쟁과 인도 제국 통치에 참여함으로써 그들은 '영국' 국민의 일부가 되었고 후자(영국)의 전쟁수행능력을 증가시켰다. 제국은 19세기의 이러한 교환을 구축하는 데 있어 결정적으로 중요한 메커니즘이었다.

---

20 **2021 한국외대** ▶▶▶ MSG p.55 ④

정비문 ▶ 수동태 'be동사+과거분사' 다음에는 일반적으로 목적어가 올 수 없다. prioritize는 '~을 우선적으로 처리하다'는 뜻의 3형식 타동사로, the distribution of vaccines를 목적어로 받을 수 있도록 수동태인 is prioritized를 능동태인 prioritizes로 고쳐야 한다. 진행시제인 is prioritizing으로 고쳐도 좋다.

ascend v. 오르다 zenith n. 정상 prioritize v. 우선적으로 처리하다 distribution n. 분배, 배분

① BTS는 콘서트와 팬 미팅을 위해 노력한 1년 만에 스타덤의 정상에 올랐다.
② 그 기금은 이미 위탁됐기 때문에, 개발도상국에서 연구용으로 이용할 수가 없다.
③ 아이들은 마땅히 기본적인 욕구를 충족시켜주고, 주변에 어른들이 있어서 보살펴주어야 한다.
④ 다코타(Dakota) 족은 다코타어를 말하는 사람들에게 우선적으로 백신을 분배하고 있다.

01 ③	**02** ②	**03** ①	**04** ②	**05** ④	**06** ②	**07** ①	**08** ①	**09** ④	**10** ③
11 ③	**12** ①	**13** ④	**14** ③	**15** ②	**16** ③	**17** ①	**18** ④	**19** ③	**20** ④

---

01 **2018 가천대** ▶▶▶ MSG p.125 ③

의문사가 쓰인 간접의문문 ▶ 전치사 to의 목적어로 빈칸에 적절한 것을 고르는 문제이다. ① as는 의문사나 what관계대명사처럼 명사절을 이끄는 접속사 역할을 하는 것이 아니므로 부적절하며, ② what은 전치사 다음에 올 수 있지만, 그 다음이 불완전한 절이어야 하는데, 빈칸 다음에 완전한 절이 왔으므로 역시 부적절하다. ④ though가 이끄는 절은 전치사 다음에 올 수 없어 부적절하다. 반면 의문사 how가 쓰인 의문사절은 전치사의 목적어로 쓰일 수 있으므로, 빈칸에는 ③이 적절하다.

innate a. 선천적인 index n. 지표 tentatively ad. 잠정적으로 feminist a. 페미니스트의, 남녀 동권론자의 embrace v. 기꺼이 받아들이다, 수용하다 male-dominated a. 남성이 우세한 diaper n. 기저귀

성별에 따른 행동의 차이가 선천적이라는 것을 '증명하기' 위해 아이들을 살펴보는 대신, 우리는 아이를 키우는 방식을 페미니스트 혁명이 어른들에게도 얼마나 잠정적으로 받아들여지는지에 대한 지표로 볼 수 있는데, 이들은 딸들이 예전에는 남성이 우세했던 직장에 들어갈 것으로, 아들들이 기저귀를 갈 것으로, 충분히 예상하는 어른들이다.

---

02 **2013 단국대** ▶▶▶ MSG p.147 ②

문의 구성 ▶ 문장의 주어 역할을 할 수 있는 어구가 와야 한다. '조금, 소량, 약간'이라는 의미의 명사로 쓰일 수 있는 ② Little이 정답이 되며, little은 주어로 쓰일 때 단수 취급하므로 수일치도 올바르게 되었다. ① There 구문의 경우, be동사 다음에 명사가 와야 하므로 주어진 문장에 There는 쓰일 수 없다. ③ be known of가 '~에 대해서 알려지다'라는 의미이므로 사람에게만 쓰는 '아무도 ~않다'라는 의미의 No one은 의미상 적절하지 않다. ④ 부사 ever는 단독으로 주어로 쓸 수 없으므로 이 또한 정답에서 제외된다.

assume v. 생각하다 well-educated a. 잘 교육된; 교양 있는

작가 티오필러스(Theophilus)에 대해서 거의 알려진 것이 없지만, 그의 작품으로 볼 때 우리는 그가 교육수준이 높은 사람이었다고 추측할 수 있다.

---

03 **2021 수원대** ▶▶▶ MSG p.113 ①

being이 생략된 분사구문 ▶ 분사구문의 주어가 생략된 것으로 보아 주절의 주어와 같다고 볼 수 있다. 주어 he와 ask의 관계는 '질문을 받는다'는 의미의 수동 관계이므로 수동태 분사구문인 Being asked가 적절한데, Being은 생략될 수 있으므로 빈칸에는 Asked가 들어가야 한다.

interfere with ~을 방해하다 incident n. 사건

그 비판에 관한 질문을 받자, 그는 대통령이 해당 사건에 대한 수사를 방해하지 않으려고 침묵을 유지했다고 말했다.

---

04 **2018 단국대** ▶▶▶ MSG p.71 ②

혼합가정법 ▶ if절에 과거완료시제가 쓰였으며 주절 중의 than이하에 현재시제를 나타내는 actually are가 와서 주절이 현재의 가정의 상태를 실제 상태와 비교하는 내용이므로, 가정의 상태도 현재인 혼합가정법이어야 한다. 혼합가정법의 주절에는 가정법 과거시제가 오므로, ②의 would be가 적절하다.

fatalities n. 사망자, 사망자수

만일 플레밍(Fleming)이 페니실린을 발견하지 않았더라면, 지금 매년 실제보다 훨씬 더 많은 사망자수가 있을 것이다.

---

05 **2011 경희대** ▶▶▶ MSG p.59 ④

수동태와 능동태의 구분 ▶ 주절의 시제가 과거(emerged)이므로 that 이하의 종속절의 시제는 과거나 과거완료가 되어야 한다. 따라서 ①이 먼저 정답에서 제외된다. ②와 ③은 능동형으로 목적어가 나와 있지 않으므로 정답이 될 수 없고, '발견된' 것이므로 수동태인 ④가 적절하다.

blackbird n. 지빠귀 starling n. 찌르레기 corpse n. 시체, 송장, 유해 litter v. 흩뜨리다, 어지르다

대략 500마리의 붉은 색 날개를 가진 지빠귀와 찌르레기들이 루이지애나에서 죽은 채로 발견되었다고 오늘 밝혀졌다. 그 조그마한 새들의 시체들은 분명 하늘에서 죽은 채로 떨어져, 라바르(Labarre) 시 근처 고속도로의 일부 구간을 뒤덮었다.

06 2022 단국대 ▶▶▶ MSG p.31 ②

trust + 목적어+to부정사 ▶ trust의 목적격 보어로 to부정사가 와서 '안심하고 ~시켜 두다', '능히 ~하리라고 생각하다'의 의미를 갖는데, 빈칸 뒤에 목적어가 주어져 있으므로 능동의 to부정사가 와야 한다. 따라서 ②가 정답이 된다.

democratic a. 민주적인 safeguard v. 보호하다

대만이 1월 11일의 선거를 앞두고 있는 가운데, 대만 국민들에게 문제는 차이(Tsai) 총통이 그들의 민주주의적 생활방식을 능히 지켜줄 것이라고 그들이 여전히 생각하는가 하는 것이다.

07 2022 단국대 ▶▶▶ MSG p.51 ①

현재진행 시제 ▶ 현재 시점에서의 사실에 관한 진술이므로 현재와 관련된 시제가 쓰여야 한다.

striking a. 인상적인 speaker n. 연설자; (영·미 국회의) 하원의장 peak n. 절정

하원의장의 경력에서 지금 이 순간 가장 인상적인 것은 권력의 정점에 있는 그녀가 자신의 지위를 보호하고 있지 않고 오히려 그 지위를 적극적이고 심지어 모험적인 방법으로 이용하고 있다는 것이다.

08 2021 한국외대 ▶▶▶ MSG p.29 ①

4형식 동사로 착각하기 쉬운 3형식 동사 donate ▶ donate는 수여동사가 아니라 'donate + 목적어 + to 명사'의 형태를 취하는 3형식 동사이다. 따라서 ①이 빈칸에 적절하다.

donate v. 기부하다, 기증하다 charity n. 자선, 자선 단체 the disabled 장애인

폴(Paul)은 정신 장애를 가진 여동생이 있었기 때문에 기계를 팔아서 그 돈을 장애인 자선단체에 기부했다.

09 2022 숙명여대 ▶▶▶ MSG p.111, p.137 ④

문의 구성 ▶ 주어 앞뒤로 분사구문이나 계속적 용법의 관계절이 올 수는 있지만 전부 주어 앞에 온다거나 전부 주어 뒤에 오는 것보다는 주어 앞뒤로 하나씩 나뉘어 오는 것이 자연스런 영어 표현이다. 이 점에 비추어 ④가 주어 a technique called proton-induced X-ray emission 앞에 과거분사의 분사구문이 오고 주어 뒤에 which 관계절이 와서 적절하다. which 관계절은 삽입된 절이므로 빈칸 뒤에 콤마가 있는 것도 적합해진다. ① 두 개의 분사구문이 모두 주어 앞에 왔으며, 마지막에 온 주어와 빈칸 다음의 동사 is finding 사이에 콤마가 있어 부적절하다. ②와 ③과 ⑤ called로 시작되는 분사구문과 which 관계절이 모두 주어 뒤에 와서 부적절하다. 그리고 보기들 중에 has the ability to analyze, that was originally developed, without having to destroy는 모두 장황한 표현이므로 can analyze, originally developed, without destroying으로 각각 고쳐야 한다.

proton-induced a. 양성자 유도의 criminology n. 범죄학, 형사학

원래 대기오염물질을 탐지하기 위해 개발된, 양성자 유도 X선 배출이라 불리는 기술은, 거의 모든 물질의 화학 원소를 그 물질을 파괴하지 않고 빠르게 분석할 수 있는데, 의학, 고고학 및 범죄학에서 사용되고 있다.

10 2011 성균관대 ▶▶▶ MSG p.228 ③

적절한 전치사의 사용 ▶ '~한 능력을 가지고 태어나다'라는 의미는 be born of가 아니라 be born with로 쓴다. ①의 more than은 '~이상의'라는 뜻이다. ④ born은 뒤의 명사 cells를 수식하는 형용사이다. ⑤는 that절의 주어가 동명사구 growing new born cells이므로 단수동사가 쓰인 것이다.

textbook n. 교과서 decade n. 10년

10년 이상 된 교과서에서는 사람은 타고난 두뇌 그대로 삶을 마치며 새로운 뇌세포를 만들어갈 수는 없다고 말할 것이다.

11 2016 서강대 ▶▶▶ MSG p.36 ③

명사 open과 opening의 구분 ▶ ③에서 open은 형용사일 때 '열려 있는', 동사일 때 '열다', 명사일 때는 '옥외, 야외' 정도의 의미이므로 모두 적절치 않고, 문맥상 '레스토랑의 개점식'에 해당하는 말이 와야 하므로 open을 opening으로 바로잡아야 한다.

jump-start v. 활기를 불어넣다 make a splash 요란하게 이목을 끌다

모든 레스토랑들이 화려한 개점식을 통해 브랜드 인지도를 창출하고 사업에 활기를 불어넣기를 원하지만, 당신은 레스토랑 주인들이 요란하게 이목을 끌려고 노력하는 아주 다양한 방법들을 알게 될 것이다.

12 2015 서강대 ▶▶▶ MSG p.124 ①

if와 whether의 용법 구별 ▶ ①에서 over는 '~에 관하여'를 의미하는 전치사이다. if와 whether는 모두 명사절을 이끌 수 있긴 하지만, if가 이끄는 명사절은 전치사의 목적어로 사용할 수 없다. 따라서 ①을 debate over whether language로 고쳐야 옳은 문장이 된다. ② call이 5형식 동사로 쓰였다. 앞의 a table은 call의 목적어이고 뒤의 a table은 목적보어이다. ③ 형용사 very가 명사를 수식하는 경우엔 정관사 the를 반드시 붙여준다. ④ opens는 the very question을 선행사로 하는 관계대명사 that의 동사이며, everyone agrees는 삽입절이다.

i.e. 즉, 다시 말하면 conventional a. 관습적인 tie together 연계시키다

플라톤(Plato)의 저서 『크라티루스(Cratylus)』에 나오는 언어는 자연적인 것인가 — 다시 말하면 우리는 책상이라는 말이 책상이라는 사물의 본래 모습이기 때문에(본래부터 책상을 책상이라 부르게 되어있기 때문에) 책상을 책상이라고 부르는 것인가? — 아니면 관습적인 것인가 — 다시 말하면 우리가 그렇게 부르기로 했기 때문에 책상을 책상이라고 부르는 것인가? — 에 대한 논쟁은 소쉬르(Saussure)의 가르침들을 시작하고 그것들을 연계시킨다고 우리 모두가 동의하는 바로 그 문제이다.

13 **2018 숙명여대** ▶▶▶ MSG p.227 ④

올바른 관용표현 ▶ '(돈·목숨·운명이) 걸려 있는', '문제가 되는', '위태로운' 등의 의미를 가진 표현에서 stake 앞에는 전치사 at을 쓴다. 그러므로 ④를 at stake로 고친다. ⑤ as best (as) one can은 '될 수 있는 대로 잘', '힘이 닿는 데까지'라는 의미의 관용표현이다.

reliable a. 의지할 만한, 신뢰할 수 있는 nonrational a. 이성적이지 않은, 비합리적인 hunch n. 군살, 혹; 예감, 육감 and the like 그밖의 같은 것, ~따위 employ v. 고용하다; 사용하다 gravely ad. 진지하게; 중대하게, 예사롭지 않게 at stake (돈·목숨·운명이) 걸리어; 문제가 되어; 위태로워져 reason out 논리적으로 생각해내다

이성은 신뢰할 수 있는 판단이 필요할 때 우리가 적절히 의지하는 도구다. 우리는 비합리적인 도구 — 습관과 육감 따위 — 가 흔히 사용된다는 것을 알고 있다. 그러나 상황이 복잡할 때, 우리의 결정이 사랑하는 사람과 우리 자신에게 중대한 영향을 미칠 때, 판단을 내리는 것에 매우 많은 것이 걸려 있을 때에는, 우리는 할 수 있는 한 최선을 다해 그 문제를 '논리적으로 생각한다.' 왜냐하면 그렇게 하는 것이 성공 가능성이 가장 높기 때문이다.

14 **2021 숙명여대** ▶▶▶ MSG p.128 ③

이유를 나타내는 전치사(because of)와 접속사(because)의 구분 ▶ ③ because of는 전치사로 뒤에 명사나 동명사구 밖에 올 수 없다. 그런데 두 번째 문장의 because of이하에 절이 왔으므로 ③을 접속사 because로 고쳐야 한다.

whisper v. 속삭이다, 소곤거리다 phrase n. 구절, 관용구 distortion n. 왜곡, 곡해 culminate v. (~으로) 끝이 나다[막을 내리다] mumble n. 중얼거림 reanalyze v. 재분석하다 preceding a. 이전의, 앞선, 선행하는

Broken Telephone으로 알려진 게임에서는 한 아이가 두 번째 아이의 귀에 한 구절을 속삭인다. 그리고 그 두 번째 아이는 세 번째 아이의 귀에 그 구절을 속삭이고, 이것이 반복된다. (구절을) 왜곡하는 것이 누적되어 마지막 아이가 그 구절을 말하면, 그것은 원래 구절과 다르게 익살스럽다. 이 게임은 각각의 아이들이 단순히 가장 심하게는 웅얼거릴 정도로 그 구절을 형편없이 발음해서가 아니라, 그 구절을 '재분석하여' 앞의 아이가 염두에 둔 단어에 대해 최선의 추측을 해서 말하기 때문에 효과가 있다.

15 **2018 숙명여대** ▶▶▶ MSG p.36, p.197 ②

lie와 lay의 용법 구분 ▶ ②에 쓰인 '눕다'라는 의미의 lie down은 '자동사+부사'의 구조이므로, 뒤에 주어져 있는 a set of rules를 목적어로 취할 수 없다. 그러므로 ②를 '타동사+부사'인 lay down으로 고쳐야 한다. lay down은 주어진 문장에서 '(원칙 따위를) 규정하다', '(규정을) 정하다'라는 의미이다.

hypothesis n. 가설, 가정 enterprise n. 기획, 계획; 진취적인 정신, 기업심; 모험심 mechanical a. 기계적인, 자동적인 formula n. 공식; (일정한) 방식

가설의 발명이나 발견에 대한 일련의 규칙을 정하는 척이라도 해본 사람은 아무도 없다. 어떤 규칙도 정해질 수 없었던 것 같은데, 그것은 그렇게 하는 것이 과학적 모험심의 창조적 측면이기 때문이다. 창조 능력은 상상력과 재능의 함수이기 때문에 기계적인 과정으로 환원될 수 없다. 뉴턴의 가설이나 아인슈타인의 가설처럼 폭넓은 설명력을 가진 위대한 과학 가설은 위대한 예술작품만큼이나 천재의 산물이다. 새로운 가설을 발견할 수 있는 공식이란 전혀 없다.

16 **2018 숙명여대** ▶▶▶ MSG p.19 ③

부정사를 목적어로 취하는 타동사 ▶ seek는 to부정사를 목적어로 취하는 타동사이므로, ③을 seeks to discover로 고쳐야 한다. ① the problem을 후치수식하고 있으며, 앞에 '관계대명사+be동사', 즉 which is가 생략돼 있는 것으로 파악하는 것도 가능하다. ④ 전치사의 목적어로 쓰인 동명사이다.

at hand (가까이에 있는 elimination n. 배제, 제거 physician n. 내과의사, 의사 germ n. 세균, 병원균 prescribe v. 규정하다, 지시하다; 처방하다

"원인"라는 단어는 당면한 문제가 어떤 바람직하지 않은 현상을 제거하는 것일 때의 필요조건이라는 의미로 가장 자주 사용된다. 원인을 제거하기 위해서는, 그것이 존재하는 데 있어 반드시 필요한 조건을 찾아 그 조건을 제거해주기만 하면 된다. 따라서 의사가 어떤 종류의 병균들이 특정 질병의 "원인"인지를 발견하려고 노력하는 것은 그 병균들을 파괴시킬 약을 처방함으로써 그 질병을 치료하기 위함이다. 그 병균들이 없는 곳에서는 그 질병이 발생할 수 없기 때문에, 그 병균들은 그 질병의 필요조건이라는 의미에서 질병의 원인이라고 말한다.

17 **2017 이화여대** ▶▶▶ MSG p.229 ③

regardless of ▶ ③에 쓰인 regardless는 형용사이므로 목적어를 취할 수 없다. '~와 상관없이', '~을 개의치 않고'의 의미를 가진 관용 표현은 regardless of이므로, ③을 across the board regardless of로 고쳐야 한다.

reveal v. 폭로하다, 드러내다 juggle v. (일 등을) 잘 조절[처리]하다 across the board 전면적으로, 전부에 걸쳐 marital status 결혼 여부

미국에서 실시한 한 조사에 따르면, 여성은 지난 40년 동안 점점 더 불행해져 왔다. 그와 동시에, 행복한 남성의 수는 증가해왔다. 놀랍게도, 살아오면서 감정적으로 고조된 기분을 느꼈던 여성들은 다른 역할, 목표, 계획을 동시에 감당하는 것에 대해 별로 이야기하지 않았다. 대신에, 그들은 자신들의 삶에 힘을 불어넣어 주는 순간들에 대해 이야기했다. 여성의 행복이 줄어든 것은 직업이나 결혼 여부와 상관없이 모든 여성에게 일괄적으로 적용된다. 특히, 근무시간이 유연하고 가정친화적인 여성들이 매일매일 훨씬 덜 행복한 것은 불가사의한 일이다. 어떤 사람들은 너무 많은 선택권을 가지고 있고, 일은 더 많이 하고 있지만 감정은 더 빈약해지는 것은 가능한 일이다.

18 **2021 한국항공대** ▶▶▶ MSG p.106 ④

'the + 형용사'의 용법 ▶ ④ 앞의 of는 전치사이므로 형용사 deceased가 단독으로 그 뒤에 쓰일 수 없다. 문맥상 고인의 사체라는 말이 되어야 하므로 형용사 deceased 앞에 정관사 the를 넣어 보통명사화해야 한다. 따라서 ④를 the deceased로 고친다.

mummification n. 미라화(化) burial n. 매장 preference n. 선호(도), 애호 artificial a. 인공[인조]의 practise v. (일상적으로) 행하다 dig v. 파다, 파헤치다 dehydrate v. 건조시키다 lifelike a. 실물과 똑같은, 살아있는 듯한 corpse n. 시체, 송장 afterlife n. 내세, 사후 세계 elaborate a. 정교한, 정성[공]을 들인

고대 이집트에서 미라화(化)는 고인(故人)의 매장 선호도에 있어서의 점진적인 변화에 대응하여 발달되었다. 이집트에서 인간과 동물의 사체에 대한 인공적인 보존은 기원전 2686년경부터 서기(西紀)가 시작될 때까지 행하여졌다. 초기의 이집트인들은 파야 할 무덤구덩이의 크기를 줄이기 위해 일반적으로 태아형 자세(옆으로 쪼그리고 누운 자세)로 모래 속에 매장되었고, 뜨겁고 건조한 기후가 사체를 건조시켰다. 사체의 신체적인 특징은 그대로 유지되었고, 사체가 살아있는 듯한 모습은 사후세계의 믿음을 뒷받침해 주었을지도 모른다. 정교한 무덤과 고인에 대한 기념비를 만드는 것과 함께 매장 풍습이 더욱 세련되면서, 고인의 사체는 이제 더 이상 사막의 모래 속에 매장되지 않았다. 그러나 사후 세계와 환생에 대한 믿음이 이집트 매장 관행에 근본적인 것이었으므로, 저승으로의 여행을 준비하고 오시리스(저승을 지배하는 신)에게 심판받도록 사체를 인공적으로 보존하기 위해서 미라화가 발달되었다.

19 **2018 이화여대** ▶▶▶ MSG p.111 ③

분사구문 ▶ ③은 접속사 and 뒤에 주절에 이어지는 분사구문이 주어져 있는 형태이므로 옳지 않다. 연속동작의 분사구문을 만드는 경우, 접속사 and를 생략한 후에 주절의 뒤에 분사구문을 만들어야 하므로, ③은 evoking이 되어야 한다. 이때 이 문장은 The very phrase "Christmas story" had unpleasant associations for me, and it evoked dreadful outpourings ~를 연속동작의 분사구문으로 만든 형태로 파악할 수 있다.

impulse n. 충격, 자극; 충동 persistent a. 끊임없는; 끈덕진 on commission 위탁을 받고; 수수료를 받고서 despair n. 절망, 자포자기 Yuletide n. 크리스마스 계절 association n. 연합; 관련; 연상 evoke v. (기억·감정을) 불러일으키다 outpouring n. 흘러나옴; (감정 등의) 발로, 토로 mush and treacle 달콤하면서도 값싼 감상 hypocritical a. 위선적인 I'll be damned if ~ 결코 ~아니다 propose to V ~하기를 꾀하다, ~할 생각이다 contradiction n. 모순 out-and-out a. 순전한, 철저한 conundrum n. 수수께끼 sparrow n. 참새

같은 주 초에, 『뉴욕타임스』에 있는 사람이 내게 전화를 걸어와서 크리스마스 아침 신문에 실릴 단편소설을 하나 써줄 생각이 있는지 물어왔다. 거절하고 싶은 마음이 곧바로 들었지만, 그는 매우 호감이 가는 사람인데다 또한 집요하기도 했다. 그래서 나는 통화가 끝날 무렵에 한번 해보겠다고 말했다. 그러나 전화를 끊자마자, 나는 깊은 낭패감에 빠져들었다. 크리스마스에 대해 내가 뭘 안단 말인가? 의뢰를 받고 단편소설을 쓰는 것에 대해 내가 아는 게 있지 않은가? 하고 나는 속으로 물었다. 나는 디킨스, 오 헨리, 그리고 크리스마스의 참뜻을 살린 또 다른 대가들의 망령들과 싸우면서 자포자기의 상태로 며칠을 보냈다. "크리스마스 이야기"라는 말 자체가 나에게는 즐겁지 않은 연상 작용을 일으켰고, 위선적인 값싼 감상과 입에 발린 달콤한 말의 홍수를 떠올리게 해서 심히 불쾌했다. 크리스마스 이야기는 기껏해야 소원을 성취하는 이야기나 어른들을 위한 동화에 불과했으며, 나는 그런 것을 쓰도록 스스로에게 허용한 적이 결코 없었다. 그러나 누구든 어떻게 감상적이지 않은 크리스마스 이야기를 쓸 생각을 할 수 있겠는가? 그건 모순된 말이었고, 불가능한 일이었고, 철저한 수수께끼였다. 차라리 다리 없는 경주마나 날개 없는 참새를 상상해보는 것이 나을 것이다.

20 **2021 한국외대** ▶▶▶ MSG p.71 ④

정비문 ▶ I wish 다음에는 가정법 과거와 가정법 과거완료만 올 수 있는데, ④에서 I wished 다음에 know가 와서 틀렸다. 부사절의 시제와 주절의 시제가 동일하므로, I wished 다음에는 '가정법 과거'가 적절하다. 따라서 know를 knew로 고쳐야 한다.

ridiculous a. 말도 안 되는 privilege n. 특권 budget n. 예산

① 나는 네가 오늘이 아니라 내일 여기에 왔으면 좋겠다.
② 말도 안 되는 너만의 특권을 없애버릴 때이다.
③ 내가 예산만 더 많다면, 이것은 문제가 되지 않을 것이다.
④ 시험이 시작되었을 때, 내가 정답을 알면 좋을 텐데라는 생각이 들었다.

MEMO

MEMO

MEMO

MEMO

MEMO